THE FRONTIER
GANDHI

OTHER LOTUS TITLES

FORTHCOMING TITLE

MY LIFE AND STRUGGLE
THE AUTOBIOGRAPHY OF ABDUL GHAFFAR KHAN

THE FRONTIER
GANDHI

TRANSLATED FROM PUKHTO
BY IMTIAZ AHMAD SAHIBZADA

FOREWORD RAJMOHAN GANDHI

LOTUS COLLECTION
ROLI BOOKS

Lotus Collection

© This translation, Imtiaz Ahmad Sahibzada, 2021
Foreword © Rajmohan Gandhi

First published in 2021

The Lotus Collection
An imprint of
Roli Books Pvt. Ltd
M-75, Greater Kailash II Market, New Delhi 110 048
Phone: ++91 (011) 40682000
E-mail: info@rolibooks.com
Website: www.rolibooks.com
Also at Bengaluru, Chennai, & Mumbai

Cover design: Sneha Pamneja
Layout: Bhagirath Kumar
Production: Lavinia Rao

ISBN: 978-81-949691-4-3

Typeset in ITC Galliard Std by Roli Books Pvt. Ltd.
Printed at Saurabh Printers Pvt. Ltd., Greater Noida, India

Dedication

The normal practice is that when one authors a book, it is dedicated to someone. The verses of this poem of Makhfi Sahib, have proved to be my life long companion in my thoughts, actions and the struggle of my political life. That is why I want to dedicate this book to them and wish to bring it before the public with them:

'Khawenda wudana klray Zamoong de yawalai Hujra;
Yaw zai pe kshay de zanaklray, De Pukhto dalla khwara;
Yaw zlre, yaw saa yawshanay klray,
Day beyal aw beyal Pukhtun sara.'

'Oh God for us Pukhtuns create,
Of brotherhood a structure,
Where we Pukhtuns may congregate
Our numerous dispersed groups;
One heart, one breath create for them,
These individual beings.'

'Kashmir na ter Herat horay, Baluchistan na ter dooray;
Da tol Pukhtun dae har cheray,
Tse rangay prot zaray zaray;
De yaw wajud pa shanay klray,
Ya khudaya da zara zara.'

'From Kashmir to Herat all spread out, Baluchistan, beyond,
They're all Pukhtuns, no matter where,
Disorganised, dismayed;
And of them make a whole that's strong,
Oh God of strength, compassion.'

Dedicated to my niece,
Shandana Humayun Khan,
at whose special request this
translation was undertaken.

– Imtiaz Ahmad Sahibzada

Contents

Foreword

In earlier generations, Indians called him 'Khan Sahib' or 'Badshah Khan'. Many spoke or wrote of him as 'the Frontier Gandhi'. Hindi-speakers called him 'Seemaant Gandhi'. However, 'Bacha Khan' is how Pakistanis referred to him and still do.

If many could not remember Khan Abdul Ghaffar Khan's full name, no one who saw him, whether directly or in a photograph, could forget his towering appearance. In my biography of him, first published in 2004,[1] I recalled Badshah Khan's 'immensely tall figure, absolutely straight back, great nose, kindly eyes, and permanent air of nonviolent defiance'.

He died in 1988. It would have been an amazing privilege to present my biography to him. Instead of that, I am being asked to write a foreword to his autobiography! The honour humbles me. It makes me want to hide.

I hope nonetheless that many Indians, Pakistanis and Bangladeshis – and others too – will pore over this indispensable piece of our subcontinent's history.

Collaboration across the India-Pakistan-Afghanistan border has produced this book, with a leading Indian publisher bringing out a text created in Pakistan about our joint recent history. How wonderful.

Here is my understanding of how the Pashto original of this text was born. Badshah Khan seems to have dictated his story, from birth to the 1947 creation of Pakistan, in 1965, when he was living in exile in Kabul. He was 75 then.

Since he lived until 1988 (reaching the age of 98), missing from this autobiography are forty-one years (from 1947 onwards) of Badshah Khan's life. That was a substantial chunk of time, during which interesting things continued to happen to, through and around Badshah Khan. Readers should be aware of this absence.

Badshah Khan dictated the story in his language Pashto (also spelt Pakhto or Pukhto). This translation into English is the painstaking work of a distinguished Pakistani civil servant, Imtiaz Ahmad Sahibzada, now in his eighties, who has also translated some of the brilliant poetry of Badshah Khan's eldest son, Ghani Khan.

In 2003, when I was working on my biography of Badshah Khan, I had the good fortune to find, in a library, a previous English version[2] (published in 1969) of an autobiography by him. Therein it was stated that Badshah Khan had *dictated* the story of his life – in Pashto, in Kabul – to Kanwar Bhan Narang, a former Frontier Province legislator who was living in Kabul at the same time, and that a woman named Helen H. Bouman had translated the text into English.

Though I do not know it for a fact, it seems likely that the Pashto text from which Imtiaz Ahmad Sahibzada has produced this English translation is connected to the text that led to the 1969 book. However, the story emerging in this translation, while remaining confined to the pre-1947 period, seems fuller than what the 1969 book presented, and I note that Badshah Khan appears to have given a 1981 date to this text.

I do not know how many days Badshah Khan took to dictate his story. Whether, while dictating it, he had papers and books to consult is also not known, although towards the end he refers to Maulana Abul Kalam Azad's account of the acceptance of Partition, which we know was offered in Azad's *India Wins Freedom*, first published (a year after the Maulana's death) in 1959.

****

I was only ten when, in 1945 or 1946, I first met Badshah Khan. Visiting Delhi, he stayed for a few days in our family's Connaught Circus flat above the offices of the *Hindustan Times*, which my father, Devadas Gandhi, the Mahatma's youngest son, was editing. Ten years younger than Badshah Khan, my father had been a co-prisoner with him in 1930–31 in Gujarat Jail, in western Punjab. Also in that jail at the time were Dr. M.A. Ansari of Delhi, Dr. Saifuddin Kitchlew of Amritsar and Kashmir, and Maulana Zafar Ali Khan of Lahore, all of them significant figures in the subcontinent's modern history.

When, following the release of prisoners in early 1931, my father visited the Frontier Province for a few days, he was hosted by Badshah Khan, who continued thereafter to regard my father as a friend. According to this autobiography, when it became clear that India would get its independence, Badshah Khan urged the Mahatma to become Prime Minister and be 'fully in control', adding that if he were to put anyone else there – 'even your son Devadas' – power would change him and 'even Devadas would not accept your guidance'!

Had Gandhi followed the advice, claims Badshah Khan, 'Hindustan' would have 'been spared the destruction' it saw in 1947. Was there any chance of Gandhi wanting to act on the advice? Students of Gandhi's life know of his 1931 statement, made in response to a journalist's question after the Gandhi–Irwin Pact was signed, that he would not take the Premiership of independent India. That position, said Gandhi, 'would be reserved for younger minds'.[3]

Twenty-three years after meeting him in Delhi as a ten-year-old, I saw Badshah Khan again in 1969, when he visited India (from his exile in Afghanistan) for the Gandhi centenary. My last encounter was in 1987, when an ailing Badshah Khan visited India again and was given the Bharat Ratna.

I managed to call on him at Mumbai's Raj Bhavan. He was reclining on a bed when I showed up in his room. Beckoning me to sit beside him, he drew me close and pressed a kiss on the forehead.

This Pakhtun lion possessed an affectionate heart.

In our Covid-19 times, readers of this autobiography will be struck by Badshah Khan's recollection of the influenza pandemic of over a century ago, around the time of the First World War. The pandemic struck Badshah Khan, his wife Mehr Qandh and their son Ghani. Telling us tersely that Mehr Qandh did not survive, he turns to other things.

His reticence over this death, and over the death a decade later of his second wife Nambata, is more than a matter of cultural restraint. It suggests emotions that were too deep for words. Nambata died from falling off a stairway in Jerusalem shortly after arriving there, with Badshah Khan and his older sister Shama, as part of a trek that had also included Mecca and Medina.

Badshah Khan's simple khaddar clothes; his famed life-long habit of not letting others carry his bundle of travel necessaries;

his disdain for eminent positions; his blunt speech; his burning passion for the Pakhtun people and fierce loyalty to Pakhtun self-respect (a loyalty that invited a total of 27 years in prison before and after independence); his undying passion for Muslim-Hindu unity – these and other aspects of his life come across from these pages.

His hold over his Pakhtuns seems utterly exceptional. He commands, and he is followed. Wherever necessary or possible, whether in prison or outside, he also cleans, and cooks, and grows flowers and fruits, and trains his *Khudai Khidmatgars*. These are tasks for which he wins more admirers than followers.

What is less known, and what this autobiography's careful reader will discern, is Badshah Khan's astuteness. Quickly reading people and events, he knows who might become his allies and who would wish to obstruct him. Inevitably missing from this written account, however, is the power of Badshah Khan's earthy, frank, and direct oratory.

Good portions of the autobiography cover his times in prison, which consumed large chunks of his life before 1947 and would consume additional chunks after British rule ended. His tours across undivided India elicit unexpected glimpses of times and places, glimpses that future scholars are likely to cite.

Of natural interest are the accounts of Badshah Khan's conversations with Gandhi, first in the latter's Sabarmati ashram in Ahmedabad, later in Sevagram in the centre of India, and thereafter in Bihar in early 1947, when the two jointly confronted the fires of communal hate that would shame the subcontinent later that year.

The Pakhtuns played an astonishing role in the fight for the subcontinent's independence. In practical as well as psychological terms, nonviolent defiance by Badshah Khan's *Khudai Khidmatgars* was easily one of the most dramatic components of the national struggle.

And yet when Partition was accepted, Badshah Khan and his followers were quickly and quietly abandoned.

This autobiography will remind India of how a staggered Badshah Khan responded to that betrayal. Elsewhere, too, Badshah Khan had provided his recollections of the negotiations that culminated in the decisions of the 1947 summer. Some of these additional recollections may be seen in D.G. Tendulkar's 1967 book, *Faith is a Battle*,[4] in the record of Haridev Sharma's 1968 interview with Badshah Khan in Kabul,[5] and in my 2004 book.

Gandhi accepted with sadness a partition he had failed to prevent. An unhappy Badshah Khan also accepted it. The two were saddened afresh when, despite Gandhi's urging, Nehru, Patel, Azad, Rajagopalachari and Rajendra Prasad were unwilling to demand from Mountbatten an autonomous Frontier Province within Pakistan as part of 1947's subcontinental settlement.

Just as failure did not stop Gandhi from fighting for a pro-poor, secular India where minorities would feel secure, betrayal did not stop Badshah Khan from fighting within Pakistan for Pakhtun dignity and minority rights.

If our world wants to picture non-violent defiance, or inter-faith partnership, or a refutation of the clash-of-cultures theory, or a commitment to the rights of the vulnerable, it cannot do much better than study these two men together: Ghaffar Khan and, older by 21 years, Mohandas Gandhi, brothers in spirit, each armed with the swords of conscience and courage.

His foes in Pakistan repeatedly called Badshah Khan 'a Hindu' even as, in India, Gandhi's enemies, accusing him of appeasing Muslims and weakening Hindus, finally killed him. But 'the brothers' refused to be cowed down, were ready to walk alone if need be, and unafraid of prison or bullets.

Their stories haven't ended. The dream isn't dead: the dream of India and Pakistan living in peace and friendship, enabling their wonderful people to fulfil their hopes, live in equality and mutual respect, and find their destiny.

May this autobiography of a noble Muslim soldier who continued, after being let down, to march fearlessly and faithfully, help in preserving that dream, and, where needed, in reigniting it.

Rajmohan Gandhi
Urbana, Illinois
January 2021

Notes

1. Rajmohan Gandhi, *Ghaffar Khan: Non-violent Badshah of the Pakhtuns* (New Delhi: Second Edition, Penguin, 2008)

2. Abdul Ghaffar Khan, *My Life and Struggle* (Delhi: Hind Pocket Books, 1969)

3. Pattabhi Sitaramayya, *History of the Indian National Congress* (Bombay: Padma, 1947), pp. 755–63.

4. Tendulkar, *Abdul Ghaffar Khan: Faith is a Battle* (Bombay: Popular Prakashan, 1967)

5. Haridev Sharma, 'Interview with Badshah Khan in Kabul, July 10, 1968,' (Oral History Transcript, Nehru Museum and Memorial Library, New Delhi)

Note on this Translation

My Life and Struggle is an English translation of the Pukhto autobiography of the renowned Pukhtun social reformer and political leader, Abdul Ghaffar Khan. Prior to this translation, an account of his life, with the same title, was published in English in 1969 in New Delhi, which was the work of K.B. Narang and Helen Bouman. The 1969 account of Bacha Khan's life was the result of him narrating his life story to K.B. Narang, in Urdu, while Bacha Khan was in exile in Jalalabad, Afghanistan. The narration was recorded and then translated into English, for the book. However, Bacha Khan felt that this 1969 account of his life and struggle was not complete and began to write his own autobiography thereafter, with the help of numerous associates. Bacha Khan's autobiography was thus first published in Pukhto in 1983, in Kabul. Subsequently the book was also published by the Baacha Khan Trust in Peshawar, Pakistan. This book is a translation of Bacha Khan's only written, Pukhto autobiography.

The Pukhtuns are an ethnic group that number about fifty million. Pukhtun tribes form a large part of the population of Afghanistan and a minority in Pakistan. They also form a large diaspora community in many other countries, having been displaced by war and conflict in their troubled region. Abdul Ghaffar Khan belonged to the Khyber-Pakhtunkhwa (earlier the North-West Frontier Province) province of Pakistan. His life spanned the period 1890–1988. He is buried in Jalalabad, Afghanistan.

Affectionately known as 'Bacha' Khan or 'King' Khan amongst his people, Ghaffar Khan's life was dedicated to the social reform of the Pukhtuns, who traditionally adhere to a strict code of life called 'Pukhtunwali', which is governed by rather rigid tribal norms. Bacha Khan is an acknowledged leader in the hearts of the Pukhtuns across the world, due to his lifelong struggle to modernize Pukhtun society and his teachings of non-violence, adopted by his *Khudai*

Khidmatgar (Servants of God) movement, especially during the struggle for independence against British colonists in British India. He stands tall in the pantheon of leaders of the movement for independence. His success in mobilizing the Pukhtuns of the then North-West Frontier Province and the Tribal Areas through a non-violent struggle, had significant bearing on this movement, in which the *Khudai Khidmatgar* allied with the Indian National Congress party. Few are aware that, during the struggle for independence, the *Khudai Khidmatgar* lost the most number of workers, compared to any other party struggling for independence.

Today the principles of the *Khudai Khidmatgar* bear even greater relevance to the Pukhtuns and to others who reside in this troubled part of the world. Since the start of the conflict in Afghanistan, the social fabric of Pukhtun society, in both Pakistan and Afghanistan, has been rent asunder by war and destruction, their homes and villages have been decimated and they form one of the largest refugee communities globally. An increasing consciousness amongst the Pukhtuns against oppression and war, in both countries, has led to a resurgence of the teachings of Bacha Khan. His powerful political weapon of non-violence, his emphasis on including women in all walks of life, his belief in religious tolerance and pluralism are, today, values that bear increasing relevance to the people of a much troubled region.

Preface

As a child and young adolescent, I was aware of Abdul Ghaffar Khan and his struggle but had neither seen nor spoken to him. I first saw him when, as Secretary to the Government of N.W.F.P Information Department, I, along with many other civil servants and party activists went to receive him at Torkham on a cold winter day in 1972. This was the period of the Awami National Party (ANP) – Jamiat Ulema-e-Islam (JUI) government of Maulana Mufti Mahmood in which Arbab Sikandar Khan Khalil was the governor and Afzal Khan Lala of Swat was the most important ANP minister. I saw him brave the extreme cold, clad in his traditional grey *khaddar* shalwar kameez with a *saadar* around him. Standing on a platform in an open truck, along with Shad Muhammad Megay, his life-long companion, carrying two pairs of his clothes, he crossed the barrier while his fans among the students in Afghanistan, with red flags and banners, covered the hill on the Afghanistan side, among slogans of *Pukhtunkhwa* and *Bacha Khan Zindabad*. The crowd that threw bouquets of marigold flowers at him, which he occasionally got hold of and threw back, was so thick that our return journey to Peshawar from the border took well over five hours – a distance of forty miles, normally covered in two. Realizing the historical significance of the event, I had taken my young nephew, Nadir Zeb, who much later as General Nadir Zeb, often remarked that it was an unforgettable experience for him.

I next saw and met him at Dar-ul-Aman, the residence of Ghani Khan in Charsadda, when in February 1974, accompanied by my wife, I went to invite him to the wedding of my youngest brother, Dr. Waheed Ahmad Sahibzada. Waheed was getting married to the daughter of Abdul Ali Khan, Bacha Khan's youngest son. It was evening and father and son were sitting just outside the veranda of the house. My wife entered the house while I shook hands with him and Ghani. I was introduced to him as my father's son and he was informed that I was the older brother of Dr. Waheed to whom Ali Khan's daughter was engaged in the summer. He acknowledged the fact and told me that he and my father, the late Colonel Ahmad Khan Sahibzada, were contemporaries in the Mission School, Peshawar.

Father and son were discussing the role of oil as a weapon in Middle Eastern and world politics. Not knowing enough about the subject, I chose to quietly take my seat. Soon tea was sent out by Roshan, Ghani's wife. There were three cups with three saucers-full of *halwa*. Ghani passed one to me, took one himself and placed the third before his father. Ghani and I tucked in and soon finished the portions. He did not eat but seeing that I had finished my share, gently pushed his saucer in front of me and observed, 'Here! Take my share as well!' Although satisfied, I did as I was asked since I did not wish to give offence to the old man, by then frail with a very prominent nose which seemed to occupy most of his face.

I next saw him in the summer of 1987 when, after being hospitalized in India following a stroke, he was flown into Peshawar in a paralyzed condition by a special plane. He was accompanied by his daughter Meher Taj and other family members. I was at the airport because Arbab Jehangir, then the chief minister of the Province, had decided that, Bacha Khan should be given an official reception on account of his iconic status for the Pukhtuns. I was then the Chief Secretary of the Province and Fida Muhammad Khan was the governor. He was taken to the Bolton Block of the Lady Reading Hospital in a specially equipped ambulance of the Capital Development Authority, specifically requisitioned for the purpose, while we went to the Governor's House for high tea arranged for the visiting dignitaries.

I finally saw him lying-in-state in his coffin in Jinnah Park, Peshawar, while we filed past his body just before the *Namaz-e-Janaza*. Rajiv Gandhi, then the prime minister of India, Mohammad Yunus and one or two other Indian ministers flew from Delhi to Peshawar to attend the funeral prayer. I was then Secretary to the Federal Government in the Ministry of Local Government and Rural Development, Islamabad, and had been specially directed to accompany the contingent from the Federal Government by the Chief of Staff to General Zia-ul-Haq, then the President of Pakistan, in a specially chartered C-130 aircraft of the Pakistan Air Force.

This translation of Bacha Khan's autobiography has been undertaken, as mentioned in the dedication, at the special request of Shandana Humayun Khan. She made the request when I visited her in her office in Islamabad on 24 November 2016 in connection with the book *A Breath of Fresh Air,* containing Ghani Khan's speeches in the Central Legislative Assembly of India, 1946–47, which I had researched and compiled, and Shandana had, in a major way, assisted in printing. This translation was started on the 25 November 2016 and completed on 5 January 2018.

I am indeed very grateful to my son, Aimal Khan Sahibzada, who bore the brunt of typing the text of this book, despite the fact that he would do so after a full day's work in office and at the sacrifice of his weekends. I am also grateful to Sher Hamza, a graduate student at the National University of Science and Technology, Islamabad, who would drive over each day after classes and spend an hour or two typing. I am grateful to the young man from Mardan, Mohammad Jan, who assisted Shandana Khan in the proofreading of this book. My data entry operator at the office of the Wafaqi Mohtasib (Ombudsman) of Pakistan, Muhammad Amjad, was extremely helpful in typing four chapters of the book during his leisure time at home. And of course, my grandson Akbar Khan, who, despite the best of intentions, managed to come for only two sessions to type the remaining part of the text. I am also grateful to my granddaughter, Malalai Zarnigar, for taking copies of the photographs reproduced in this book.

I am also extremely grateful to two other persons – namely Malala Yousafzai and Mukulika Banerjee – for very kindly agreeing to endorse the book. I am also, needless to say, very grateful to Roli Books for doing such a thorough job of the editing of the manuscript.

Finally, were it not for Shandana Humayun Khan and the persons listed at the end of the book, this publication would not have been possible.

Imtiaz Ahmad Sahibzada

1

Introduction

I WAS BORN IN HASHTNAGAR IN THE VILLAGE OF UTHMANZAI IN 1890. At that time, it was not customary to record a child's date of birth and neither did anyone know how to read and write. When I claim that I was born in 1890, I do so based on my mother's – may God bless her soul – following statement: 'When your brother, Dr. Khan Sahib, was getting married, you were eleven years old.' Dr. Khan Sahib got married in December 1901 which means that I was born in 1890. I was the youngest child of my parents. The eldest in the family was our sister,[1] followed by Dr. Khan Sahib and another sister[2], and then me. The love of parents for their youngest is always more than that for the others and the youngest is always the apple of their eyes. I, too, was very dear to my parents. It so happened that the first to die was my eldest sister. After that, Dr. Khan Sahib passed away and then my other sister died. I was the last and remained to be so.

The village of Uthmanzai is twenty miles northeast of Paikhawar (Peshawar) in the middle of Hashtnagar, on the banks of the Swat–Bajawar river. Hashtnagar covers the area from Abazai to Naukhar, where the Muhammadzais are settled. I am from the Muhammadzai tribe. This is a beautiful, fertile and well-inhabited tract which was allotted to us by Pukhtun kinsmen according to the distribution of territories. My grandmother was a Yousafzai from Swabi's Marghuz village and my grandfather was a Muhammadzai from Uthmanzai. He was the renowned khan of the village. It is quite natural for the children of a Muhammadzai and a Yousafzai to be very talented and clever. Our girls are more talented than the boys. My only daughter has a bachelor's degree with a diploma in teaching. Of my granddaughters, three are doctors, while others have either a master's or a bachelor's degree. I had sent my eldest son, Abdul Ghani, to the US for a degree in chemical engineering. But when I was imprisoned by the British in 1931 and my land was confiscated, he could not complete his education due to lack of funds and returned home. My second son, Abdul Wali, though very intelligent and capable, could not go to Europe for higher education for the same reason. It is strange that though I was a prisoner of state, like Dr. Khan Sahib and Qazi sahib,[3] their children were provided with a stipend for their education and expenses, while I was not. The provision of this expense was actually not a concession to state prisoners but a legal right. Inspite of that, my two sons were deprived of it. My youngest son, Abdul Ali, whom I call *Lalee*, is a postgraduate from the University of Oxford. One of my sons has married a Yousafzai, the other a Moomand, and the third a Parsi. My daughter is married to a Kashmiri. Four of my granddaughters are married into the Yousafzais, two among the Khattaks, and one is married to a Punjabi. We do not marry our children to wealth as we consider decency, capability and dignity more important in a marriage. Nor do we marry them without their consent.

Hashtnagar is a beautiful and a fertile region. Across Razar and Uthmanzai, near Sheikhano Derai on the other bank of the river, when the remains of an ancient city were unearthed, it was discovered that these predate the Gandhara civilization.[4] This city was called Pushkalavati,[5] meaning the 'lotus city' and was a big trading and cultural centre. The present river, which now flows between Razar and Sheikhano Derai, flowed close to the west of Sheikhano Derai then, and the entire ancient city stretched up to the limits of Razar. The inhabitants of this place were Pukhtuns who were Buddhist. Buddhism by religion travelled from here via Swat and Gilgit to Tibet and China and spread there.

From the artefacts of the excavated remains found in the region, we know that industry, trade, agriculture and learning had progressed a great deal. This city was not only the political capital of Gandhara but also the commercial, manufacturing and industrial hub of most of Asia and was its centre of learning. It had contacts with Hindustan via Attock and Margalla; with Kashmir, Tibet and China via Swat and Gilgit; with Central Asia via Dir, Chitral and Badakhshan and, from there, with Europe. It also maintained contacts with Iran, Iraq, Turkey and Syria via Kabul, Kandahar and

Sistan and was the central clearing house of all manner of commercial goods and the cradle of learning.

The Family

My father, Bahram Khan, was the Khan of the village and, as a well-respected elder, was known as the Mesher Khan. He was not like the other Khans. In our village, no other Khan had a bigger landholding than his but he never gloated over this fact. He was a fair and true Pukhtun who never oppressed anyone, nor allowed the weak to be subject to anyone's cruelty. If anybody treated him harshly, he would bear it with equanimity without harbouring any revenge. His brothers and cousins often subjected him to great excesses and iniquity, and though he usually had the chance to take revenge, he would forgive them. In fact, he would be good to them and also do them favours. A pious and peace-loving man, he observed the five daily prayers. He was tolerant and bore hardship with perseverance. Whenever unknown travellers would come to our *hujra*, my father would serve them a meal himself. Even though there were servants, he would serve them himself saying, 'These are guests of God. I must serve them myself.' Invariably, it would happen that such guests would arrive at night in the winters and when the servant would take breakfast for them in the morning, he would return with the message that the guests had left with the blankets! He was not like the other khans who cultivated the company of rulers, maintaining contacts with them, or served them.

My grandfather, Saifullah Khan, was also like that. When the British, aiming to occupy Buner, attacked it, leading to the jihad of Surkawi, the other khans assisted them but my grandfather rallied to the help of his nation. Similarly, my great grandfather, Abeedullah Khan Baba, was liberal minded, brave and a highly recognized leader, who helped his people and was hanged at the instance of the then ruler of Peshawar, the Durrani Sardar, Sultan Muhammad Khan Tillaee. The government of the Durranis came to an end due to its debauchery, cruelty, and internal conflict and struggle for power. After them came the rule of the Sikhs. When the Durranis learnt that the Sikhs were coming, they quickly retreated to Kabul, leaving the fate of the Pukhtuns at the hands of the Sikhs.

My mother was a very empathetic, knowledgeable and pious woman with a happy temperament. We had a big farm house where we had many cows and buffaloes. Every day, the poor people from the neighbourhood would flock to our house for curd and buttermilk and my mother, with a smiling face, would greet them and give them skimmed milk and curd.

Historical Background

Babur defeated Ibrahim Lodhi, took the throne and crown of Hindustan due to the simplicity, foolishness and selfishness of the Pukhtuns, along with the instigation and assistance of the Iranians.[6] It was in 1540 that Sher Shah Suri rose and recaptured the Pukhtun kingdom from Babur's son, Humayun. Later, when Sher Shah captured Delhi, Humayun fled and sought refuge in the court of Iran, where the Iranians gave him shelter, waiting for the opportunity to weaken the Pukhtuns.

Sher Shah raised the flag of Pukhtun rule over Calcutta, developing programmes in the fields of industry, commerce and agriculture for the upliftment of the people. Later on, these became the reason behind the fame of the Mughal emperor, Akbar. It was not Akbar's brains but that of Sher Shah which was behind these programmes. There was also a time when the Iranians ruled the Pukhtuns. They insulted and looked down upon them. It was in Kandahar that Mirwais Khan's grandfather rose and freed the Pukhtuns from the slavery of the Iranians, raising the Pukhtun flag over Isphahan.[7] There was also a time when Nadir Afshar ground the Pukhtuns into dust but when he was murdered in 1747, the *Loya Jirga*[8] of the Pukhtuns assembled in Kandahar and, after a great deal of thought, agreed on the leadership of Ahmad Shah Baba (Ahmad Shah Abdali).

Ahmad Shah defeated the Iranians and laid the foundations of Pukhtun rule. Not only did he free Pukhtunkhwa, but all of Hindustan, from the clutches and oppression of Mughal rule.[9] The British had come to Hindustan at this time. Ahmad Shah learnt of their efforts when he conquered Delhi and decided to expel them. When the British came to know of this, they sent an emissary to the Iranian court, instigating them to attack Afghanistan. Ahmad Shah learnt of this plot and gave up his efforts to control the British, and immediately left for Afghanistan. When he reached the Jhelum river, he stood on its banks and addressing all the tribes and subtribes of the Pukhtuns, told them that, from this place to the Amu Darya, lay their territory of Pukhtunkhwa. There was also a time when, on account of their profligacy, extravagance, the oppression of the Durranis, their internal differences and internecine warfare, the Pukhtuns degenerated to such an extent that they were no match for the Sikhs on their own land. Not only did the Sikhs conquer the lands of their forefathers but also the lands held by the Pukhtuns, and no one was prepared to take up cudgels in defence of their honour and their name.[10] The rule of the Sikhs was extremely oppressive. My maternal grandfather, Muhammad Din Khan, used to tell us how one day, he was returning from Sholgara and was crossing the river when a Sikh motioned him to come back and take him across the river on his back. Grandfather told him that he had not been broken-in to carry loads! But the Sikh forced him. He allowed the Sikh to mount on his back but as they reached the middle of the river, he started prancing about and unseated the Sikh in deep water and deserted him.

From the other end of Hindustan, *Syed* Ahmad Barelvi[11] and Shah Ismail also came to defend the honour and name of the Pukhtuns but they did not have the support of the then government of Afghanistan. In fact, there was a conflict with Yar Muhammad Khan, as evident from this old *charbaita* of the Pukhtuns:

Laro Yar Muhammad, Syed wubasi de Panjtara,
Sayed la baray warklray Ilahi parwardigara!

Yar Muhammad for Panjtara has left, to drive Syed away;
The Syed make victorious, Almighty God today!

The sympathy of the Pukhtuns of these areas was with *Syed*. He wanted to enforce the Shariat law and in accordance with the law, wanted to give a share of inheritance to sisters, daughters and wives. He also wanted to get rid of certain unjustified customs and social practices. This did not have the desired effect on the khans and maulanas and they raised a hue and cry that one Sikh has left and another has come to take his place. These well-wishers of the Muslims and the Pukhtuns were branded as Wahabis. The Pukhtuns lacked national and political consciousness and rose in opposition to Barelvi sahib and his companions, slaughtered some of them and drove the others across the Abaseend to Hazara. Some Muslims of

Hazara, instead of assisting Barelvi sahib, passed on information about him to the Sikhs, who came and put the remainder of them to the sword. *Syed* sahib and Ismail sahib were martyred in the Battle of Balakot in 1831. When *Syed* sahib drove the Sikhs away from the Pukhtun land, the rulers of Afghanistan told him to leave the land to them. It is a pity that *Syed* sahib stood up for the women of the Pukhtuns, and these Pukhtuns, devoid of any honour, did not stand by them.

The story goes that Arbab Bahram Khan of Tehkal, a disciple of *Syed* sahib, used to travel annually in the month of *ramzan* to Bareli, where he used to complete the reading of the *Quran* and the *taraveeh* with *Syed* sahib. At that time, there were no easy means of communication. Once, while travelling on horseback near Gujranwala, he felt thirsty. There was a well near the road where some women had come to fetch water. When he approached the well, he signalled them, asking for water. All but two left after filling their pitchers. These two women gave water to him and began to cry, telling him that they were Pukhtun women who had been abducted by the Sikhs and had also given birth to two children each. When Arbab reached Bareli, he was very distressed. *Syed* asked him the reason whereupon he recounted the entire tale of the Gujranwala incident. On Friday, at the congregation prayer, *Syed* sahib mounted the mimbar, recounted this story and declared Jihad. I am not recounting history here. I am only trying to elucidate the point that the Pukhtuns were able to establish large kingdoms but were never able to retain them because collective life, nationalism and unity were absent amongst them. Although the Pukhtuns did not lack capable politicians and statesmen – who established great sultanates in the past – the successors of these great men lacked national consciousness, unity and capability when the founders died. To acquire wealth and power, they would go for each other's throats. There was no nationalist feeling even among the masses to prevent their leaders from taking the wrong path, or not to provide opportunities to selfish and misguided leaders. Nor could the people select capable, unselfish, well-meaning, public-spirited leaders to retain their kingdoms. Since the masses had no nationalist feeling, they were easily influenced by self-serving leaders. Disunity and internecine warfare were common and the strength of Pukhtuns frittered away. Their enemies waited patiently for an opportunity to strike. They would get their opportunity and take over the kingship from the Pukhtuns, and drive them to the hills. They would enjoy the spoils of the lands taken over, while the Pukhtuns were compelled to roam the mountains aimlessly. Whenever their repentance was accepted by God and competent men were born amongst them, they would, once again, expel their enemies from their homeland and begin the task of reconstructing their homes and hearths all over again.

After the Sikhs came the rule of the British. They had come over the seas, but they knew very well that, historically, all the invasions of Hindustan had begun from the north-west. To safeguard their conquests in British-Hindustan, they crossed over into the Pukhtun lands so they could occupy the passes, routes and rivers from which the invasions had taken place.

Apart from their military strategy, they paid attention to the political situation of these areas and saw that here, too, the same policy was in action that many rulers before them had adopted and tested. The truth is that Akbar built his fort in Attock, across the Abaseen and the Pukhtun lands, after the Mughals fought the Pukhtuns in the Khyber Pass, in Krappa and finally at the Karakar Pass of Buner, where Birbal was killed with his army in 1586. He, along with his ministers, assembled in Attock and told them that since the Pukhtuns had not been defeated in war, they should deliberate over what strategy could be adopted to vanquish them. Consequently, they arrived at the conclusion that the Pukhtuns have two prominent character traits. One, that, as a nation, they were extremely devout Muslims and had a firm belief in Islam. Second, the human frailty of their great love of wealth. In this light, they formulated a policy to find learned men, such as the maulana and pirs, who would, under the cover of Islam, not only attain their political objectives but also buy the loyalties of political leaders, maliks and khans. That is why, at the instigation of the Mughals, we have seen that Akhund Darweza and many other religious leaders like him, issued fatwas of hereticism against a religious luminary, a practicing Muslim and a scholar such as Pir Rokhan, in order to arrest the development of Pukhtun consciousness and nationalism.

The British saw that the very same policy, after the Mughals, had been adopted by the Durranis and, after them, was inherited by the Sikhs. The British, because they were the product of twentieth century development in education and science, adopted the prescription of Emperor Akbar's methods: on the one hand, their efforts were to use the religious leaders of the Pukhtuns for their political purposes and, on the other, to buy their political leaders with wealth and titles. Ironically, the very Islam that the Mughals used to enslave their Muslim brethren is now being used by the maulana, pirs and the learned, who have sold their faith to further the objectives of the infidel West.

The Temperament and Customs of the Pukhtuns

Even though the British had arrived, I remember that the Pukhtuns still held on to many good customs and attributes. They felt degraded while telling lies. They maintained the bond of brotherhood and kinsmanship. Reposing confidence in one another, they came to the each other's assistance on issues of honour. They had good relationships with each other and maintained love and affection. And even if they had differences, they never spoke of each other with disrespect. It was not like it is today – claiming one thing and intending another. Life was simple and without ostentation, with no big fuss over anything. Clothes were simple and made of locally-spun cotton and woven cloth. They would not exchange their coarse cotton cloth for the finest of satins. They wore large, baggy trousers and long shirts of *khaamta*, locally made *chapalay* and caps and turbans of cotton cloth as headgear. The women wore coloured clothes and trousers, known as *mashruba*. The food was simple, because of which the people were in good health. Spices were unheard of; tea was yet unknown. Usury, alcohol and adultery were considered a sin. When it was known that a family indulged in such practices, children would never be married into such families, nor would they marry their children. Morally, they were not so degraded and depraved as they are today. When a special guest came, they would quickly slaughter a chicken and make a rich gravy of yellow, calrified butter of cow and buffalo milk. The bread was of a rare variety of leavened wheat-flour, baked in an open oven – soft and tasty. In the evening, corn was roasted on the *butt* and people ate it with *gura*. As for the food, there was no difference between the rich and the poor. They ate together and from the same dish. Just as food and clothing were simple, so were the dwellings. A house consisted of a big room and all the inhabitants collectively used it to sleep in; and when a male guest came, he used the *hujra*. Most people had such houses. People who were better-off, or were khans, had a veranda and *deodai* along with the room. Even here, there would be a separate *hujra* for the guests. The mansions and bungalows of today were not there. But the happiness and well-being of that simple life is not to be found in these beautiful bungalows, rich food and fashionable clothes. Men and women were healthy and strong and diseases were not rampant. Boys and girls played together late into the night and, although they were adults, they looked upon each other as brothers and sisters. Morals were very strict. Games played an important part in life and there were several of them. They included those involving running, weightlifting, and hide and seek at night. This was the reason for their being so healthy. Although there was no third party (as referee) in the games, the players never cheated each other.

The Effects of the British Occupation

Before the arrival of the British, there was no worthwhile system of education for the Pukhtuns. Whatever existed was not accessible to everyone. Only the children of the maulana would undergo an education related to prayer, ablution, fasting, alms, Haj, sacrifice, zakat and similar religious practices. They could read well enough to lead the religious prayers, but could not write. The method for such an education was that the maulana would be seated in the mosque and, along with acting as the Imam, would also teach boys to read the *Quran*. Whenever parents wanted to teach their children, they would send them to the maulana in the mosque. The maulana would begin to teach them a *siparah* and the parents, based on what they could afford, would distribute sweets on the occasion. When one *siparah* was completed, they would give the maulana a *shukrana* and, on the commencement of the next *siparah*, sweets would again be distributed. The maulana was not given any pay in return for imparting education. Teachers were very fond of their pupils and considered them like their own children, and the pupils too did not consider their teachers as anything less than their fathers. The teachers never explained the meaning of what was taught to the students. The poor souls were not aware of it themselves and, therefore, were not to be blamed. Once the maulana of our mosque, when teaching the boys, got annoyed with one of the pupils. In anger he proclaimed, '*Innal lazeena kafaroo, kharbishaweeya!*' at which the pupil too repeated, '*Innal lazeena kafaroo, kharbishaweeya!*' When we heard this, we laughed heartily. He got angry with his student. But, we told him 'What is the fault of this boy, because he repeats whatever you say?'

To educate the people of Hindustan, the British opened schools on more modern lines, but the schools established for the Pukhtuns were in name only and of low quality. There were primary schools in a few big villages, but, even in those, only a handfull of boys would enrol. In the rest of Hindustan, initial schooling was imparted in the mother tongue and only the unfortunate Pukhtun was taught in an alien tongue. On top of this, they instigated the maulanas and told them that if the people got educated, the respect for them in the community would diminish, affecting their livelihood. They told them to wake up to this danger and ensure that they did not allow the children of the Pukhtuns to be educated. The maulanas carried out the propaganda that Pukhto was the language of hell and would be spoken in hell. No one ever asked the maulana when he had come back from hell or which inhabitant of hell had informed him of this! The maulanas also used to say that whoever got educated in the *madrassah* (reference here to primary school built by the British), seven generations of his would be condemned to hell. They used to sing:

Sabaq de madrassay waee,
De para de paisay waee,
Pe Jannat kshay ba ay zae ne wee,
Pe dozakh kshay ba gasay waee!

He goes to the *madrassah,*
For earning some rupees,
No place in Heaven will he find,
But be condemned to hell!

The maulana prevented the people from attending the *madrassah* but made no effort to make any alternate arrangements. The strange thing was that, on the pretext of their faith, the maulanas deprived the people from acquiring knowledge, although Islam is a faith in which the acquisition of knowledge has been made mandatory for both men and women. But we are such an unfortunate people that in the name of Islam, we have been deprived of acquiring knowledge. These were the reasons why the Pukhtuns lagged behind all the nations of the world – not only in gaining knowledge but in everything else. How unfortunate that this fate should befall the land of the Pukhtuns, which was once the centre of learning for the people of the world. When Europe was passing through the Dark Ages, there stood large centres of learning and universities in this land of the Pukhtuns, illuminating the surrounding countries with the light of learning. People would come from far off places to this land of ours to acquire knowledge. But now, in the name of Islam, we have been pushed behind all the other nations of the world.

My being Spoilt

The children of my parents were still-born. They, therefore, went to many shrines and maulana. They told them that God will give you a son, and when you do have one, you must pierce his ear and put a golden ring in it. They also said that till he attains the age of seven, you will have to annually put a silver necklace around his neck. And when he completes his seventh year, you will remove the ring and necklace and give them in charity.

I was the youngest son of my parents. The youngest offspring is always very dear to the parents. I, too, was the apple of my parents' eyes and this, sadly, affected me badly and was also the cause of grief to my mother. Whenever I asked for something, and if she granted my wish, it would be fine. But if she were to refuse, because it was not in my interest, I would roll on the ground and wail. I would continue doing so until mother accepted and complied with my wish. Thus, every day, I would be running around in the afternoon sun and no one could dare tell me not to do so. And even if they did tell me, I was not the kind to comply. Invariably, while roaming around in the afternoon sun, my eyes would start hurting and I would be restless day and night. My mother would also have no rest on my account. Night and day, she would be rocking my cradle and when she would get exhausted, she would ask the maid to take her place. I would immediately begin to yell, and she would attend to me again. Night and day, I tired her out, attending to me and rocking my cradle. She would say to me, 'Oh son! Why do you put me to such trouble, that when I leave you even for a little while, you begin to yell again and prevent me from resting?' I would respond, 'What can I do? I am going blind.'

We used to harvest a lot of wheat. The storage bins would invariably be full. When the new crop of wheat came, we would sell what remained of the old crop. Next to our house was the little shop of two brothers, Ram and Kev Singh. All day long, I would be running away with wheat from our storage bins to this small shop to get things in exchange. In those days, shops did not have the things we see today. At most they stocked *amlook*, walnuts, chickpeas and vermicelli. In the late afternoon and evenings, they would fry eggplant pakoras. My mother would, two or three times a day, give me some wheat which I would carry in the hem of my shirt, but I would never be satisfied with that. Frequently, I would steal the grain behind her back, from the storage bins, and would be on the look out for her to get busy somewhere before I ran out to the small shop. Sometimes, if my mother happened to see me doing this, she would yell out to me, 'Stop! You will not leave!' But I would press on and run off. More than this, she did not do. I was the darling of her heart and did not know what was good and what was bad for me. This attitude on the part of my mother was not good for me because it encouraged me to steal. My mother should have stopped me from doing this and explained to me that this was a bad thing to do, that it was wrong and I should not do it again, considering that what I demanded was always given to me by her. She should have made me understand and got me out of this bad habit. After all, the bosom of the mother is the first and most important *madrassah*.

My son, Wali, told me that once, in London, he was about to leave his apartment when he saw a lovely apple which had fallen from a tree. A child was standing there, and he motioned him to pick it up, but the child wagged a finger at him to indicate that it did not belong to him. He was just a child. Who had taught him this? His mother! Habits inculcated in childhood persist in grown-ups, and it is with great difficulty that they can rid themselves of them. When I would sleep beside my mother and wake up crying, refusing to stop, my mother would say to me 'there comes the monster, there comes the goblin'. Till today, I have the fear of the monster and the goblin, even though I understand full well that monsters and goblins do not exist. We had one big room in the house in which all of us slept. I was fairly grown up but could not sleep alone. I used to sleep with my mother because, when alone, I had nightmares. When I left for Peshawar for education, and my father visited Peshawar, I would be overjoyed because I would get to sleep beside him.

I was very fond of listening to stories and I had such a good memory that no matter how short or long a tale was, I would remember it. I still remember the tales from my childhood. In a room of our house there used to be a *dunkacha*. In the middle of this platform, there used to be cooking stoves on which meals would be cooked. This would simultaneously heat the room. To one side of these stoves would be spread out a *puzakai*, which had cotton-wool filled mattresses on top of it. The women sat on one side, the men on the other. When it was time for meals, the women would serve us, and when we had finished our meals, only then would they eat. At that time, men never had their meals with the women as they did not consider this proper. Nor did the women eat with the men, for the same reason. In winter we usually ate *ghatay wrujay*. There was no tea at that time. When we woke up early in the morning, rice would be ready. Along with the rice we had clarified butter, pickle and sometimes *qruth*. In summer, when we woke up, we generally sprinkled *gura* over the *qruth* and ate it with maise bread. We would break the bread into the curd and eat it. Whenever I went to the mosque to study, my mother would spread clarified butter over wheat bread and sprinkle *shakkar* over it. But this was not the food of the Pukhtun masses; it was the diet of the khans. The poor would eat stale bread with butter milk.

My mother was very fond of keeping buffaloes, and looked after and fed them herself with grass and *butawa*. In the afternoon she would feed me cream and milk. Women generally used to be very fond of cream and would not give it to anyone because it would affect the production of butter but she loved me so much that I would get it. Whenever she tasted anything and liked it, she would give it to me and, if I was not there, she would keep it for me. Whenever I ate with my father, and chicken had been cooked, everyone would get one piece each, but my father would give me his share too. In front of a room of our house, there was a beautiful *mandao* and a *deodai*. In this room, there were large *kandwaan*, in which maize would be stored in one and wheat in the other. This room also had *khumaan*, in one of which rice was stored, in the other lentils, and in the third, *shakkar* and *gura*. Garlic and chillies would lie next to the *khumaan* and tins of clarified butter. Because of the cattle, we used to get a lot of milk, and when Ramzan came, my mother would cook *kheer*. It used to be delicious and when time came for *paishmanay*, it would have on it a thick layer of cream. I loved that cream and it used to be delicious. I was still a child and it was not mandatory for me to fast but, on account of this cream, I would, each evening, insist that I should be woken up for *paishmanay*. But, being sleepy, I would not be able to get up and my mother would tell me that she had done her best to wake me up, but I would go back to sleep. When I would wake up in the morning, I would create a hue and cry about not being woken up.

2

Enrolment in School and
Conditions of the Time

Initial Education

Fortunately for me, my father, though a devout Muslim, was otherwise liberal-minded. He was not taken in by the propaganda of the maulanas and admitted both my brother and I into school. He entrusted me and my cousin, Mahabat Khan, the son of my deceased youngest paternal uncle, to Ismail *Ustaz* in the village mosque. My mother and father were extremely pleased at the commencement of my education and distributed sweets on the occasion. I finished my reading of the *Quran* with Ismail *Ustaz* but never understood it. In our village there was one primary school but, at this time, my older brother, Dr. Khan Sahib, was studying in a school in Peshawar. He took me along to Peshawar and admitted me to the same school in which he was studying because, at the time, the conditions in the villages were far from good. Factionalism, enmities and *tarboorwali* were rampant. Fights and murders were common and false cases abundant.

The School at Peshawar

These were the days when under the *jirga* system, the British were interfering in the domestic affairs of the Pukhtuns and had, for the purpose, put in a special arrangement which was not compatible with the traditional, tribal customs of the Pukhtuns. Most often the innocent were imprisoned and the guilty went free. Let alone the men, they also dragged our women to the courts. For a law abiding citizen, life was difficult. Had I stayed in such an environment I, too, would have been affected. However, though I gained by going to Peshawar, I lost out on the education front. Although I did my primary education from this school but, frankly speaking, the village school would have been better. The medium of instruction in both the schools was Urdu, but in Uthmanzai the teacher was a Pukhtun, and would explain things to us in Pukhto. The other thing was that in Peshawar I was with Dr. Khan Sahib, who was not only interested in games himself but would also motivate me to participate in them. Like most children my age I, too, was not overly interested in my studies. Dr. Khan Sahib was the captain of the school cricket team. I was better than the others in games. I was also fond of swimming. When I was in the village, my mother kept me under constant watch lest I should go to the river for a swim and drown. I kept a watch on my mother and would run down to the river at every opportunity. My mother's fears were not misplaced. On two occasions, I was swept away by the river but was rescued. When I was in the Municipal Board School, I mingled with the children of the sanitary staff and used to play with them. People would address this staff as *bangian* and *churian*. But this did not stop me from playing with them and resulted in everyone looking down upon me. But I paid no attention to this. Dr. Khan Sahib was fully engrossed in his social life and did not pay much attention to me. When a month or two were left for the examination, only then would he begin to study seriously and forced me to do so as well. Due to the efforts put in only during this month or two, I would only just manage to pass the examination.

Dr. Khan Sahib was friends with Ghulam Sarwar Khan of Dosarro, Arbab Juma Khan of Tehkal, Purdil Khan of Charsada and *Mian* Muhamad Zaman of Qazikhel. They were very kind and affectionate towards me and I, too, gave them great respect. Similarly, he had a great relationship with Sheikh sahib of Peshawar and Hafiz jee and Bashir, goldsmiths. It was in school that I made friends with Sameen Jan Khan, who was senior to me by a year. He was under the care of Ghulam Sarwar Khan. My relationship with him was one of love and affection, from childhood until his death. When my brother, Dr. Khan Sahib passed his matriculation, we returned to the village, where, during the vacation, I was enrolled in the village *madrassah*.

The Environment of the Village

One day, coming out of the *madrassah*, what do I see but a huge procession, preceded by one man and followed by the khans and maliks. The common people of the surrounding area were also following it. From the middle of the procession, one of my cousins signalled to me, touching his forehead. I was busy watching the procession go by and did not understand what the signal meant. I came home after the procession passed. My cousin also came after a while and scolded me, saying that, though educated, I was so stupid that I could not understand what he was trying to convey, i.e. to salute 'the sahib.' I asked him who the man was, and was informed that he was a *thanedar* sahib. I asked him how I was to know this. In response, he said, 'Well, you know now, and in future, be careful.' Such was the might and glory of the British rule at the time that the masses considered even the *thanedar* a great dignitary.

One day, the malik sahib came and said that he was to accompany the assistant commissioner for a spot inspection and that I should also go with him, which I did. We both mounted our horses. When we arrived at the *tehsil* in Charsada, the assistant commissioner also arrived, mounted on a horse. We went and carried out the spot inspection. When we returned and were about to part ways, I mounted my horse and shook hands with the assistant commissioner. On our return, my cousin was infuriated with me and told me that I should have dismounted and only then shaken hands.

The officer in-charge of the agricultural research farm near Tarnab was an Englishman called Mr. Brown. I had completed my education at the time and had a great interest in agriculture. I would occasionally visit the farm, and we became great friends. One evening, he was my guest. We had finished our meal, and were having a chat. It was late when he decided to leave, and I suggested sending an escort of men with him as the irrigation inspection bungalow was about a mile from Uthmanzai. He said that he had no need for the men to come. Just one man would suffice, who should accompany him with a lantern so that when the people saw his hat, they would dare not say anything to him.

There was a widow who lived in our village whose son had been arrested by the police. The superintendent of the police had come to the village and people were calling on him. This woman too learnt of the visit and went along with the others. At that time, people from far off places used to assemble when they heard that an Englishman was visiting a place. This woman petitioned him about the imprisonment of her son. He summoned the *thanedar*, questioned him and then told the old woman that her son would be released. The woman was so relieved that she lifted her hands in prayer and said, 'May God make you a *thanedar*.' At that time, a *thanedar* was considered a very big officer. The superintendent was wearing a suit. When the old woman saw that he had no *saadar* over his shoulder, she told him, 'Son! You don't even have a *saadar*. I have some very good woven cotton at home and, if you so desire, I will bring you a *saadar*!'

The police had wide-ranging powers: they could arrest, release or torture one and nobody could question them. The guilty would be released and the innocent detained. Nobody could question them as to the number of eyes in their heads. Even the khans and maliks would pride themselves on their friendship with the *thanedar*, and based on this, would ride rough-shod over the common people.

Ajab Khan lived in Sudham. Once, he fell out with the *thanedar* over some issue. The *thanedar* got him involved in a false criminal case and had him hanged. The oppression of the British occasionally led to opposition from the more honourable Pukhtuns, who would pounce on them. There was a khan from our village called Abdul Hameed Khan. His older brother, Umer Khan, was in the good books of the police and had brought the *thanedar* to insult his younger brother. May God not grant any Pukhtun the power to inflict harm on anyone; and if he does this, then like the child of a scorpion, he will devour his own mother. The *thanedar*, Ramdas (servant of God) was a Hindu from Punjab, and was a tyrannical and corrupt man. He did not get along with Abdul Hameed Khan and nor did Abdul Hameed Khan like to associate with the police. Abdul Hameed Khan and his brother, Umer Khan, had a common *hujra*. One night, when Abdul Hameed Khan was asleep, his brother assisted the *thanedar* to attack his house. The *thanedar* knocked on the door; Abdul Hameed Khan woke up and asked, 'Who is it?' Ramdas replied that it was him. Abdul Hameed Khan opened the door for him. On entering, the *thanedar* ordered the inmates not to move. The Khan raised his head and requested the *thanedar* to forgive them and not bother them. The *thanedar* considered this an insult and was enraged. He took hold of his rifle, pointed it at him and shot him. Shots were exchanged between him and the police. He was hit and so was Ramdas. Ramdas held his breath lest people said he was alive and kill him. The fact is that the cruel are never brave. The brave never oppress anyone. At night, the matter was reported and the Magistrate came. We learnt of it in the morning and went to where the incident had occurred. The encounter with the *thanedar* was a big event and many people had gathered. The Khan was jailed but the *thanedars* had learnt their lesson. Other events similarly to this would take place. Ajun Khan of Tangi, when he was humiliated by the *tehsildar*, abducted him. These encounters, even though individual in nature, were the ones which kept the nation alive.

But success cannot be attained by such tactics. A collective movement and sacrifice is needed for success. Those who have such feelings and emotions need to find like-minded people and collectively oppose oppression, high-handedness and humiliation. When such a group is formed in a nation, and the nation is organized, only then can success be achieved, and nobody can keep the nation enslaved. One difference between individual and collective action is that the government can silence and eliminate individual protests. This is the reason that in individualism, there is a lot of fear and pity. However, a government cannot kill a collective movement because there is no fear in it. Many individual movements led by the Pukhtuns have been silenced and eliminated by the Mughals, the British and by Pakistan, but the *Khudai Khidmatgar* movement, which was a collective movement, was neither affected by the oppression, killings, beatings, imprisonment, humiliation and guile of the British, nor eliminated. And neither have the thirty-two years of repression by Pakistan, the confiscation of property, permits and inducement finished it. Amongst the Pukhtuns, many great kings and chiefs have been born, but no one has engendered a collective existence or consciousness. The first movement to do so is the *Khudai Khidmatgar* movement, which has created a collective consciousness for the collective good among them.

Mission School

When I took the exam for the fifth grade and passed into the sixth, Dr. Khan Sahib passed his tenth grade. There was no college in our entire province. That year the eleventh grade was added to the Mission School, and so Dr. Khan Sahib took admission in the eleventh grade and had me admitted into the sixth grade. We lived in Peshawar city as long as we were in the Municipal Board School, and when we joined the Mission School, we lived in its boarding house in the cantonment. The atmosphere of the cantonment was clean and fresh, and good for ones health. The premises had football and cricket grounds and tennis courts. It had two boarding houses, one for the Muslims and the other for the Hindus, but they accommodated us in a place separate from these two. My paternal uncle's son, Mahabat Khan, who was the same age as I, had also passed the fifth grade in the village and had come here for education. There were many boys, some old and some young, in the boarding who were not Pukhtuns and were from Sawabai *tehsil*. All of them were very well-behaved. We lived with them like brothers. The instruction in this school was better than that of the Board school. The teachers were also very good and took great pains with the pupils.

My Teacher
In front of our boarding was the principal, Mr. Hoare's bungalow. Mr. Wigram, our headmaster also lived in that bungalow along with his brother, also called Dr. Wigram, a physician in the Mission Hospital. The Wigram brothers were from a well-to-do family in England. They had both been offered to the Mission. I do not have words to express the love and affection with which they served the people. Though I was very young, I was still aware and somewhat understood things. Even from the meagre salary that Mr. Wigram received, he would give stipends to some of the Pukhtuns. One day, I developed an infection and pus in my foot. When Dr. Wigram heard about it, he took me to his bungalow, heated some water, washed my foot in it and then bandaged it. The truth is that they acted according to a Hadith of our Prophet – *Khair-un-nas man-yanfa-un-nas* which means that the best among you is the one who serves people. But look at us! Let alone the whole of mankind, we are not even prepared to serve our own nation, our brothers, our near and dear ones. Forget about service, we allow our people to live in hell; and that is why God has reduced us to helplessness and humiliation. Mr Wigram played a big role in igniting a passion in my heart for the service of God's creation: humanity, nationalism and brotherhood. I used to think and say to myself, 'Look at him,

he has come from a far land; they are not of us or of our faith and yet they have come to serve our children and also assist the poor from their very limited earnings. And we do nothing for our children and our land.' Then my thoughts would wander to our land and people and I would ponder over the fact and say to myself, 'Our khan, nawab, maulanas and educated people, despite the fact that we are one people, of one faith, we do not have the passion to help the children of our own poor nation.' In the Mission School, half an hour was set aside to study the Bible. There was an Englishman, named Valdegrew, who taught us the Bible and preached. I was young and did not understand these things but Sameen Jan Khan, who was a class senior to me, would tell me not to pay attention to the preaching and lectures of Valdegrew. He would block his ears with his fingers, because they had a telling effect on him, and he was afraid that he might be swayed away.

Village Games

I was frugal since my childhood and would save from my maintenance money. It is for this reason that, during my entire life, I have never asked anyone for a loan, and nor have I been in debt. People have borrowed from me, and many have not repaid their loans. My brother, Khan Sahib, was more generous. In the summer vacation the teachers gave us a lot of homework, but when we arrived in the village, we were immersed in playing games. We were not inclined to study, and nor did anyone insist that we should not play. People, too, were fond of playing games. There were many kinds of games and pastimes. The *hujras* were full of people and they played *tathee* and *patta kunjaka* (village games) at night. The unmarried young men slept in the *hujras* and the married ones in their homes. In the *hujras,* the youth would chat and play games till late at night. There was not much to do and people were generally not as busy as they are nowadays. Life was not very complicated; selfishness was absent; it was a straight forward and easy life. There was much happiness at *Akhtar* (Eid) and people sent a variety of dishes to each other's houses. Many swings and *banreecheghs* would be put up. The women would also put up swings in the homes, or *banreecheghs*. When the *gura*-making season ended and people were free of this task, the games of *ainda* and *kabaddi* would start. *Kabaddi* was played in many places and the youth would display their strength. There would be a fierce *kabaddi* competition in our village every year and youth from far away would participate in this. Thousands of spectators would attend. The khans of our village would be divided into two groups and select a referee, who sided with neither group. The people would be seated all around with an open space in the centre for the game. From one side a young man would emerge and walk around the open space. Anyone from the opponent's side who thought that he had the strength and ability to compete with him would get up and come out into the arena. The wrestling would start with the permission of the referee. The youngsters of the winning party would come, carry the wrestler who had won, on their shoulders and stride around the open space in a victory parade. The khan would give him a prize and his supporters would shout, 'Ala! Ala!' at the other party. In this connection, I remember an event, when once at such a *kabaddi* match, a young man from Uthmanzai rose and another one from Doaba got up to challenge him. As was the practice of those days, each contestant would call upon his pir or shrine for assistance. When they turned to their saints for blessings, the on lookers accosted the wrestler from Doaba and said, 'By the time your baba (saint) crosses the river, the wrestler from Uthmanzai would have finished off with you because his saints are buried near the *kabaddi* ground.' And it so happened that the wrestler from Doaba was defeated. Sometimes nobody would win, and both wrestlers would tire themselves out and the referee would go and separate them. Sometimes, though rarely, a quarrel would also take place in a game.

There were other games too like *angai, shrangae, landee marae, patpatonay, bangreewatae, gaitkai, patta kunjaka, cheendro* and others. Cards were also played in the *hujras*. Games with walnuts were also played. I was fond of all these games and used to beat the others at them. I would excel at everything that interested me and that is why I excelled at games. In the *hujras,* the game of *pooch* was also played and bets were placed on winning. Whichever side lost used to bring tea, meals, fruit or sugarcane, whatever the bet was for. Most commonly, the bet was for tea, as tea was a novelty and liked by everyone. My father used to tell me a very interesting tale about tea. Once an officer visited a *madrassah*. Shahbaz Khan, who was a well-known khan of our village, brought tea, and gave him a cup. At that time, green tea was the custom and was drunk in special small teacups without handles, known as *balghamai*. Mir

Afzal Khan, his distant cousin, was also with him. My father gave his cup to him, telling him that the tea was hot. He did not understand and gulped it down. His entire mouth was scalded because at that time tea was unknown to many and was not generally drunk.

Since I was not interested in my studies, I was not good at them. However, being interested in mathematics, geometry and history, I was good at these subjects. The reason for this lack of interest in other subjects was that my initial education was at the hands of a Punjabi teacher, in an alien tongue. Since I did not really understand these subjects, I would avoid them.

Akhtar (Eid) and other Festivities

During the festivals of Eid, big fairs would be held which were attended by thousands of people. Tent pegging and *atarn* took place, professional dancers would perform, people would gamble and ride on swings and there would be musicians. There would be wooden horses for rides; some people would be mounted on camels and others on horses. The khans, who were considered powerful, would be accompanied by many attendants. Most khans would take their neighbours with them and treat them to kebabs, *katlamas* and sweets. This was a kind of *qalang* of the poor on the khans. Occasionally a quarrel would take place at the fair, which sometimes assumed the form of a collective fight in which one could not differentiate between the guilty and the innocent. It so happened that once, when I was young and had gone to the fair at Nasro, a quarrel took place between the khans of our village and those of Prang village. After the quarrel, they quickly left the fair. We were not informed. On such occasions, people always inform their fellow villagers and take them out from the fair. The village of Prang was very close to where the fair was and, on one call for help, the villagers of Prang arrived and attacked us. Our servants stood up to them, but we were few and hopelessly outnumbered. I was very young and mounted on a mare when these people came at us. Ibadat Kaka of Razar took hold of me and lifted me off the mare, and as soon as he did so, a man from Prang hit the mare, with a big staff. The blow fell on the saddle. If it had not been for Ibadat Kaka's courage and quick thinking in lifting me off the mare, God knows whether I would have survived that blow or not. Many people were wounded in this fight and, amongst our servants, hardly anyone escaped unhurt. This fair was held on the third day of Eid, near the *tehsil* of Charsada and was called the Nasro Mela. In this fair, excellent tent pegging took place. From far and near, well-kept horses and fine riders would congregate. The game would start with great enthusiasm, the riders competing in the prowess of riding and tent pegging. The audience was also very enthusiastic. From games such as these, feelings of manliness, courage and rivalry were generated among the onlookers. When the moon of the lunar month of *Shawqadar* i.e *Shaban-al-muazzam*, was sighted, people would make merry, especially the girls and boys who would run around in the streets and enjoy themselves. On the fifteenth of this month would be *Shawqadar*. On the night of *Shawqadar*, too, there would be a big fair. The women and girls would, in their homes, indulge in fireworks and light *totkay, churchurai, mahtabai* and *patakhay* (various types of fire-crackers and lanterns). The men and boys would form two groups outside, fill bamboos and horns with gunpowder, and would fire them at each other. Sometimes one group would be in retreat and sometimes the other. At times, they would throw *shatai* and *ordandai* up at the sky. Those who fired the horns wore leather clothes so that the fire would not affect them. There used to be laughter, happiness and exuberance. The religiously-inclined would not consider these activities on this night as appropriate. They spent the night in prayer and believed that prayer during this time lead to many blessings. In those days, these cultural activities were the strength of Pukhtun life. As the effects of colonial rule increased, these cultural manifestations and enthusiasms of the time began to fade away.

The Month of the Imams

Just as we had festivals of joy and happiness, we also had days of grief and sorrow. The month of the Imams, i.e., Muharram is, a collective memorial of the Muslims – and there is an important message in it for us Muslims. The Prophet of Islam, may the peace and blessings of Allah be upon him (PBUH), had lit a brilliant light of democracy in Madina. I do admit that this democracy was limited to the city of Madina and to the Muslims i.e. the leader of the Muslims and the successors of the Prophet (PBUH) were appointed on the advice of the companions of the Prophet. There was darkness in the rest of the world. And this lamp remained lit till the life of Hazrat Umer, may Allah's pleasure be upon him. After his death, the desire for wealth and power took hold of the Muslims and this light was extinguished and remains so till today. Europe, which was in darkness, lit this lamp there. They were enlightened by it. And the Muslims, who extinguished this lamp, have not been able to light it again. Today, all the Muslim countries of the world do not have democracy. When power was transferred to the hands of the *Bani Umayya* family, Mawyia rose and changed the status of the Muslims. Mawyia, during his life time, based on his wealth and power, obtained the loyalty of the people for his son, Yazeed, as the Ameer of the Muslims, after his death. For the foundation of the Islamic caliphate, democracy and national government, the messenger of Allah (PBUH) and his companions made colossal efforts, waged a relentless struggle, and gave many sacrifices and bore many hardships. *Bani Umayya*, with guile and subterfuge, reaped the fruit. That is why, though everyone else remained silent, Hazrat Hussain could not. He gave us Muslims the lesson of opposition to a tyrant.

Muharram is known amongst the Pukhtuns as the month of the Imams. This is the month of grief and sorrow, particularly in the first ten days when nobody would indulge in any festivity, laughter or jokes. For the souls of the *Hassanian* (the Prophet's grandsons), and in the name of God, people would distribute sweet drinks and give alms. The women in their homes and the men in the *hujra* would read accounts of the battle (of Karbala) and the people, afflicted by grief, would cry. This would be considered a pious act. At night, the women would wail. Boys and girls would, in these first ten days, collect grain for charity and give a charitable feast on the tenth day. Men and women would visit the graveyard and, in memory of the thirst of Imam Hussain, pour water over the graves. In the evening everyone would, according to their means, give alms called the charity of the *Hassanian*. At night, they would wail and sing:

Hassana, sok ba de jari wai, wai
Hassana, de zlre laalee

Oh Hassan! Who will wail for thee!
wai, wai!
Oh Hassan, so dear to me heart!

And then they would beat their chests and wail loudly.

We Pukhtuns hold Hussain in great respect in our hearts. He is very dear to us because he was the grandson of the Prophet (PBUH), and was very dear to him. Furthermore, he rose in support of the truth and democracy and we, too, have risen for our right and for democracy. He too was oppressed, and so are we. He rose in opposition to tyranny, and so have we. He fought to win the right to democracy for the Muslims, and so have we. He, too, was striving for peace, and so are we.

Village Customs

Our ways of enquiring after the health of the sick, taking part in the joys of others and condoling with the relatives of those who passed away were full of sincerity but immersed in custom. When someone fell ill, their relatives and friends would call and enquire about their health. Not only relatives and friends but the common folk of the village would also do so. And if a patient was seriously ill, people would be at their bedside night and day, and pray for their health and give alms to the poor. There was no worthwhile arrangement for treatment. For every ailment, there was a different curative saint and a different procedure at the grave of each saint, to the point that even the dust of the graves was considered holy with curative qualities. Apart from the saints, the prayers of the maulanas, *mians* and *sayids* and their talismans were a method of treatment. There were also physicians practicing Greek medicine. Grey-haired old women would avert the evil eye; old men would, by means of local herbs, offer treatment. The barbers would treat boils and wounds, but the trend was generally towards the shrines. And the people of the neighbourhood would not attend to their work on the day someone died; and if the deceased was a man of means and standing, the whole village would leave its work and attend to the burial rites. They would assemble for the burial, the menfolk in the *hujra* or mosque and the women in the house. The women who came to the house participated in the wailing and crying. Amongst the men, only the close relatives and friends of the deceased would cry. When it was time to wash the body, the men would go and pick up the cot on which the corpse was lying. The wailing of the women would rise in tempo. They would beat their faces and bosoms and name the deceased in their lamentation. Relatives and friends would place money on the plank where the deceased was laid for bathing, which would be given to the maulana. The body would be shrouded, placed on the cot, and friends and relatives be given the opportunity to see his face. The funeral procession would start and the people would follow it, with four pall-bearers carrying the cot on their shoulders. They would reach the graveyard and the cot would be placed on the ground. People would be informed that the *janaza* prayer was going to be held. Those who had done their ablutions would take part in the funeral prayer. Neat rows would be formed and the *janaza* prayer would be held. The maulana would form rows, seated on the ground for the *skhat*.

Skhat and Khairat

The amount of *skhat*, or funeral alms, was always in accordance with the status and financial standing of the deceased. If he was a well-to-do khan and was well known, the alms would be substantial and there would be much ado about it. If he was poor, the alms were insubstantial and the maulanas were fewer. And if there were no alms, there would be no maulanas. *Gura*, soap, cloth for turbans, copies of the *Quran* and money would be placed in the middle, with the maulanas seated around. The chief maulana would then proceed to accept the *skhat* from the next of kin of the deceased for the expiation of his sins. A maulana would first accept everything and then offer it to the next. When the full circle of the seated maulanas was completed, they would then proceed to distribute the alms amongst themselves.

To me, this game of the acceptance of the alms was like the *shahdola*. That which belonged to others was being offered and accepted, and both God and the people were being deceived. I have visited all the Arab lands. I have never, even in Mecca, Madina, Najaf and Karbala, seen this procedure of distribution of alms. When someone dies there, the people are informed and the corpse is brought to the mosque in a funeral procession. After the prayer, the next of kin of the deceased takes the corpse to the graveyard for burial and the other Muslims disperse. Islam has come to us from Arabia, but the fact is that such customs have been created for us by self-serving people. These customs are not a part of Islam. How can wealth be offered to another, and that also when the deceased is indigent and in need? Moreover, the record of a man's deeds is complete on earth at his death. How can the dispensation of the funeral alms be made a part of his good deeds? Once a man came to the Prophet (PBUH) and stated, 'Oh Prophet of Allah! My father is dead, leaving behind him two rooms full of dates. I wish to give these dates away as alms for the benefit of his soul.' The Prophet (PBUH) tells him, 'If your father had, during his life time, given away but two of these dates in the name of God, the blessings of these would be more than these two rooms full.' The people have not understood the actuality and truth of sin and virtue at the hands of the maulanas, who do not practice the tenets of the faith. The maulanas have made them believe that even God is like the kings of the world and needs taxes and gifts. They do not even give a thought to the fact that God is not in need of anything, whether alms or charity, or sacrifice, prayers, fasting or Haj. These are all things meant for our welfare. If one does good, it is for oneself, and if one commits evil, it is also for oneself. If you do good, you will fare well in this world and it would be of use to you in the next. And if you do ill, you would be disgraced and degraded in this world and be punished in the next.

I used to engage with the maulanas. I honour and respect them a lot. But I always argue and exchange views with them on such issues and tell them that this system of funeral charity and alms is not considered good in Islam. There is a reason where Islam has made alms and charity compulsory. When our dear Prophet (PBUH) said that, 'Sacrifice deters evil,' do you know what this evil is? This is the evil that is created between the rich and the poor through hatred. When the affluent help the indigent in times of need, love is created in their hearts for the rich and impending doom is prevented. But when the rich never ask about the welfare of the poor, and the poor are in difficulty and the rich enjoy their opulence, the poor feel in their hearts that although land is a collective gift from God to them, they still have to spend their lives in such misery. They ask why these others, who are their kith and kin – should they be so comfortable? Thus, they begin to bear a grudge in their hearts against the rich, which slowly begins to grow until it becomes evil incarnate. At the time of meeting the Prophet (PBUH), before everything else, the issue of the repayment of debt would be a primary concern. The Prophet (PBUH) never led the *janaza* prayer of anyone until the debt of the deceased was paid off. If the next of kin of the deceased were unable to pay, the Prophet (PBUH) would make sure that the other Muslims collect donations and repay his debt. It was only when debts were repaid, that the *janaza* would be held. Today, everything is the opposite. The successors of the deceased, who are unable to meet their obligation, either mortgage their property or borrow money on interest, but they always arrange for the customary funeral charity. It is not only this (what they arrange) but also the dues of the *Pirano-Pir* sahib (the saint of all saints, Abdul Qadir Jilani), which amounts to a one-eleventh share; the thanksgiving to *Kaka* sahib (another saint), the shares of the *syeds, mians* and the *sahibzadas*. If all these offerings were to be spent on the collective good of the community, we too would now be amongst the developed nations of the world. For funeral alms we are willing to borrow money after mortgaging our property or borrow on interest, so that this custom can be observed.

Once, I went to the Murree hills in the summer where I met several maulanas who were known to me and happened to be there. In the evening, while taking a stroll we stopped before a bungalow. I turned towards them and asked, 'What do you think of this bungalow?' They responded that it was very beautiful. I asked, 'What about its green lawns and orchards?' They replied that the lawn and the flowers were beautiful and so was the orchard. I then asked them about the children playing on the lawns. In response, they said that the children were very fair and rosy-cheeked. I said to them, 'Can you see that car that the driver is cleaning?' They said that yes, it was a very fine car. I then said, 'Look at that man sitting on that chair, look at his clothes, what are they like?' They said that he was wearing very fashionable clothes. I asked whether they knew who the man was. They asked, 'Who is he?' I told them that he was the maulana of the Englishmen, who not only live in bungalows themselves, but also provide their maulanas with bungalows. When the nation has enough to eat, its maulanas also have enough to eat. When the nation is well-clothed, its maulanas are also well-clothed. When the nation moves around in cars, its maulanas also roam around in cars. And we, when our people do not even have mud houses to live in, you still live in mosques. And when we ourselves are hungry, you move from door to door saying, 'Give us alms, may God bless you.'

When *skhat* would be distributed, the maulanas would raise issues that would be discussed through moralistic tales. A man had died in our village. A maulana stood up for the funeral oration and said that there was a man who lived in sin. He indulged in usury, gambling, murder, adultery, theft, dacoity and had not performed a virtuous deed in his life, except that each Thursday night, he would give away seven loaves of bread in charity, in the name of God, to the mosque. The man died. His sons, wives and successors wailed his death and wondered what his condition would now be in his grave. Finally, one night, he appeared in a dream to one of his sons and told him not to worry about him, as he was very comfortable and was having a good time. The son said to him that 'During your lifetime you were not a virtuous man.' He replied that it was true, but that their mother knew that each Thursday evening he would give seven loaves of bread as charity. Those loaves had stood him in good stead here. When they had buried him and left, the angels, *Nakeer* and *Munkeer*, had come to him and had begun to question him, '*Man rabbuka wa ma deenaka?*' (Who is your God and what is your religion?). He could not answer and so they raised their maces to beat him. When they were about to do so, two loaves of bread appeared before them and saved him. And when *Nakeer* and *Munkeer* left, holes were created in the four sides of his grave, and from each hole a flame of hell entered. But the four loaves of bread came and stood as shields in front of each hole and prevented the flames from entering. He said that this loaf is serving me. Then the maulana said that, in charity, there was much blessing and that he had dedicated the benefit of this parable to the soul of the deceased. This parable appeared very strange to me. I said to him that, 'This means that one may indulge in every wrongdoing, oppression and cruelty, but give seven loaves of bread as charity, and (then) one can have a good time.'

After the funeral alms, other acts of charity would begin. Every evening, for the benefit of the soul of the deceased, there would be a meal distributed until the Friday. Following this a meal would be distributed on each Friday, and this would be repeated for forty days. On the fortieth day, there would be a big feast, which was then followed by the annual feast. In this fashion, during the year, hundreds of thousands of rupees of our national wealth would be spent. If this amount was deposited in the *bait-ul-mal* (national treasury) and spent on national needs and the poor, how much would the nation have benefitted?

A Humorous Tale

One day I was sitting in the *hujra* when the son of our Imam sahib came and told me that he was getting married and asked me to help him out. I told him that I noticed that during the funeral rites of a deceased person, he always came into possession of large amounts of wealth. If he was really in need of it, then why did he pass it on to others? He replied that nobody really wishes to part with such wealth. It is out of fear that they pass it on to each other and secondly, he believed that nobody would give him a share in it and that he would get a beating if he did not do so. I asked him what he thought of this: if there were to be no question of being beaten and if he could also get the wealth. He replied, that in that case, he would not pass it on to anyone. I asked him whether he was telling the truth and was prepared to act on this. He replied that yes, indeed, he was telling the truth and was quite prepared to act accordingly. So, I then informed him that my uncle's daughter had died that day. There was a lot of *skhat* to be distributed and he could easily get married with the proceeds. I said, 'Sit in the circle and when your turn comes, and you accept the *skhat* for yourself, do not pass it on and say that you are in need of it and cannot part with it in favour of another.' He said that he would do this, but who would leave it to him? The father of the deceased was the khan of Shamozai, and he feared that he might be humiliated at his hands. I told him that I would be standing behind him and nobody could humiliate him. He replied that if my help was available, then he did not care about anyone else. So, we decided on this. When he was leaving, I told him to be aware, that nothing of this should be disclosed to anyone. When the *janaza* was held and the maulanas sat in a circle for the distribution of the *skhat*, he looked around for me and went and sat in the circle after spotting me. When the process of acceptance of the *skhat* and its passage from one maulana to the other started, I slowly came forward and stood behind him. When the *skhat* was passed on to him, and he took possession of it, he became pale and looked back at me and said that he needed this *skhat* and that he would not part with it in favour of someone else. The maulanas intended to make some mischief, but I moved forward and asked them what the Shariat had to say in the matter. They responded that Shariat did give him the right to either pass it on to someone else or retain it. So, I then motioned to him to go and pick up the *skhat*. On top of sacks full of *gura* lay a lot of cash, which I picked up and handed over to him, asking him to pick up the *gura* as well. He picked up the *gura*. Only the copies of the *Quran* and cloth for the turbans were left. There was a mad scramble for these by the maulanas who stood amazed at this. Later, they informed the deceased's family that justice had not been done to the corpse. When the maulana took the *gura* to the *mandi* the next day and sold it, Shamroz Khan went and recovered it by force. In the light of the Shariat, this was the wealth of someone else. They had no right over it. But then, they were not unduly concerned about the observance of Shariat.

There was a man in our village who used to say that there was no Islam left but only its mockery. What could be expected of the followers if such was the character of the maulanas. Later, they decided that if they left this practice, which they have observed for so long, the attention of the masses would be diverted from them, and it would be said that these maulanas did not understand things and only Abdul Ghaffar did. So, they started with the practice of *skhat* all over again. And if they suspected any maulana, he would not be allowed to sit in the circle. The poor maulanas are not to blame for this. We ourselves as a nation are to blame if we delegate the responsibility and authority of our faith to a few and do not care about their education and upbringing, and they are compelled to beg for alms from door to door. This is our own fault. The truth is that, on conversion to Islam, we retained some of the customs and practices of Hinduism. This is because when Islam came, it did not come to us as a result of preaching; it came and spread through the sword. So, we were not apprised of the true meaning of religion by anyone and remain ignorant till date. These are the effects of the caste system: that one caste would be exclusively reserved for the service of the faith, one for purposes of governing, one for trade and commerce, and one for other common services. This is not a part of Islam. In fact, the acquisition of knowledge in Islam has been made mandatory for every Muslim.

Our maulanas pay no attention to worldly knowledge and political life and the rich amongst us are not inclined towards religious knowledge. Whenever a capable man, who is willing to serve the people, has been born among us, he has either been branded a Wahabi or a Hindu or a Kafir, and with this branding, has been deprived of serving the people. Neither have they served the masses themselves, and nor have they allowed others to do so. Islam has been reduced only to observing prayer and eating food.

Weddings and Happy Occasions

Our weddings are very joyous occasions. With the coming of age of a boy in the family, a search for a fiancée for him would begin. No one asks for the consent of the girl or the boy. The mothers and sisters of the boy would be in search (of a girl). When a girl was chosen, they would discuss the matter with her mother. The father would get to know the response through the mother. When both the sides agreed, some women from the boy's household would go to the girl's house for the *goot* and fix a date for the engagement ceremony. In those days, whether khans or the common people, *walwar* was taken from the boy's family according to their standing. The marriage of girls who had not attained puberty was also the custom, to the extent that even young children were engaged. Sometimes it would also happen that neither the boy nor the girl would be born, yet the parents would make a promise for them to get married. A boy and girl betrothed in childhood could not break the engagement, even if they did not like each other when they grew up.

For the preparations, a few days before the wedding, the relatives of the boy and the girls of the neighbourhood would collect in the boy's home for *tang-takor*. At night, when the girls were done with their daily chores, they would collect and sing lovely *meesray* to the musical sound of the pitcher and the *tambal*. I loved this music and celebration of the girls. In the weddings of the khans, celebrations were on a more lavish scale. There was feasting over many days, for which people would come and stay in various homes in the village. The homes would be full of women and the *hujras* full of men. There would be wedding processions. Shotguns and *gharbeenoona* were fired. Dancing girls would also perform, and people would shower money on them. Usually tent-pegging would also take place. For tent-pegging, people kept good horses and practiced the sport. Money would be placed on the peg while pegging the tent and whoever managed to carry the peg, the money would be his. The date of the wedding would be fixed. After dawn and the afternoon meal, if the house of the bride was far away, the wedding processions would leave immediately. The women would have separate music arranged for themselves. The musicians would play the dhol and *surna* for them in the streets and the women would dance inside the house. In the evening, the day before they were to bring the bride back, the women would assemble and leave with platters of henna on their heads and huge *mashaloona* in their hands. The path would be lit and they would go along singing. For their protection, these marriage processions would be preceded and followed by a few armed men. When they arrived at the house of the bride, they would first dance with the henna and then apply it on the hands and feet of the bride, who would have been sitting in a corner of her house for a few days before her wedding, surrounded by friends. The women would then return to their village. The next day, both women and men would proceed to the bride's house in the marriage procession. The women would enter the house and the men would sit outside in the *hujra*. The maulana would come and perform the nikah. The minstrel would sound his dhol and would collect money for it. Some would offer flowers and also collect money. On the other side the *bhat* would put his fingers in his ears and loudly sing *madhay*. Some would burn *spalanee* and collect money. Whether someone liked it or not, he would not resist out of fear of being shamed, and therefore, would reluctantly part with his money. In short, there was plunder. The maulana, too, would not perform the nikah without money. When the nikah was performed, the bridegroom would enter the house of his father-in-law, stand up on a bed and wear a new pair of clothes over the ones he was wearing. His relatives and friends would shower sweets, peeled walnuts and coins over him, which the children would collect. Usually, for the wedding day, an extremely expensive pair of clothes would be made for the bride. These would be worn by the bride on the night of the wedding after which she never wore them again, because they were so expensive. When she died this pair was usually given to the maulana.

The bride would be seated in a *dolai, or* palanquin, which was carried by four professional *batyaaran*. The *dolai* would be followed by the bridegroom and the rest of the procession. Outside too, the bridegroom would be showered with coins and sweets by his relatives and friends. Shotguns would be fired. Both the young and the old, to express their joy, would yell 'Ala! ala!' It was a big spectacle. When the *dolai* entered the house of the bridegroom, and the guests and other people from the village would leave, the women of the house would perform certain rituals. For several days people would visit and lift the veil of the bride to see her face and give her money. The next day, the bridegroom, along with his friends, would visit his father-in-law's house. This was called the *salami*. A good feast would be served. After the meal the bridegroom would enter the father-in-law's house and touch his mother-in-law's feet and she would give him some money. The boy's family would then leave for their house. After a few days, the relatives of the bride would come to the boy's house. This occasion was called the *uwama* (the seventh). The women relatives of the bridegroom would collect themselves and clothes brought from the bride's father's house would be distributed among them. The bride would then go to her father's house and spend a few days there.

Today, the wedding ceremonies of those times appear strange to people. Ideally, the boy and the girl should have liked each other and only then got married. But, to be fair, the marriages of that time, when compared to those of today, were much more successful because of the high moral standards prevalent. They had true love and affection for each other. In Europe and America, when a boy and a girl get to know each other, only then do they marry. But they do not have as much love and affection for each other as do the men and women of our country.

We need to reform some of our customs and traditions. Many people give away their daughters for the sake of wealth. Marriages should be arranged based on compatibility. It should not be that for the sake of wealth a young girl is handed over to an old man.

Commission in the Army

When my brother, Khan Sahib, left for Bombay to study medicine, I was left alone with my cousin, Mahabat, in the boarding house. After a few days we shifted from our boarding house to Peshawar city and rented a *balakhana* in a big bazaar. We went to school from there but were not very enthusiastic about our studies. We had an old servant, whom we called Barani Kaka. He had, for some time, served the khans of Momin Khan Derai. Several khans from Derai were serving in the army. He too had been with them in the army and so he would often tell me stories of life in the army. As it was, I was not too inclined towards my studies. I enjoyed Barani Kaka's tales and slowly they influenced me and I mentally got ready for service in the army. I was in eighth grade at the time. I was still young and did not understand things. I believed whatever Barani Kaka said and would follow him. He told me that those who were educated and were from a good family could get a direct commission in the army as a sardar, or junior commissioned officer (JCO). There was no difference, he said, in the status of the sardar and the British. For this, an application to the viceroy of India was required. On his approval, a direct commission was granted. And so, he advised me to apply to the viceroy through the post. Dr. Khan Sahib had a friend named Fazl-e-Mahmud. We both went to him and had him write out the application and sent it to the address of the commander-in-chief. Barani Kaka and I kept this secret to ourselves. I neither divulged it to my father, nor did I consult with him. A long time passed. I was in tenth grade and had forgotten about the application when an order came to our deputy commissioner from the capital to enquire about me and the status of my family. The deputy commissioner directed a *tehsildar* accordingly and he passed the order on to the *patwari* to find out about our land holdings.

When the *patwari* went to the village, a strange thing happened. In those days, a man from the village had been murdered. The *jirga* had, in this case, without any justification, condemned my paternal uncle's son, Shamroz Khan, along with six or seven of our servants to fourteen years' imprisonment. The British had not established a *jirga* system for the sake of justice and maintaining law and order, but for the sake of making sure that justice did not take place. There was factionalism and often the guilty would, on intercession of the influential and payment of money, manage to save themselves. So, the opposing side would always try to take revenge, and in this way, enmities would last over generations. This situation will persist; the Pukhtuns continue to fight among themselves and not against the British. I had personally discussed the issue of the *jirga* system with an assistant commissioner. In the *jirga*, members would be nominated from the party of the accused. No matter how guilty he was, he was acquitted. And if the *jirga* did not have membership from the party of the accused, and no influential person intervened on his behalf, no matter how innocent he is, he still gets to be convicted. Not only the assistant commissioner but every Englishman understood this, but they had created the system for this purpose and had stuck to it. All our earnings were spent on all this. Whatever we earned, the police, lawyers, *jirga* members and then the jail officials would extract it from us and leave our children penniless. If you study the Frontier Crimes Regulation Act, you will find that nobody else has enacted such a shameless law as this, which the British enforced on us. In those days, the rumour had also spread that we were to be deprived of our property for this murder. This was a minor matter in the law. So, when the *patwaris* came to determine the extent of our landholdings, it was our firm belief that the rumour was well-founded. Our family was struck by extreme grief that not only were our menfolk unjustifiably convicted, but our landholding was also being confiscated. We tried our best not to disclose the true extent of our landholding to the *patwaris*. We did manage to keep some of our land from scrutiny but they mentioned in their report that we owned a lot of property but had not revealed all that we owned. The *patwaris* did not keep our secret because the elders of our family, like the other khans, did not maintain a good relationship with the officials of the administration. Those individuals who kept up with the police and civil officials treated them to meals, so that they could have them exploit the people. Often, they would be touts for the police and the civil officials. We were content with our own landholding and did not indulge in this.

My father came to Peshawar city and recounted this whole affair to us. He was very depressed and we also got worried. The next morning my father went to the deputy commissioner and requested that he should investigate and find out whether they were involved in the murder, and if so, whatever punishment he would inflict on them would be acceptable. And if they were not found guilty, then this was no justice, that not only were their menfolk arrested, but their land would also be confiscated. The deputy commissioner replied, 'Who says that your land is being confiscated?' My father informed him that *patwaris* had visited the village and recorded all their holdings. He laughed heartily at this and told my father that this was because his son had applied to the viceroy for a direct commission and the viceroy had directed them to ascertain his landholding and status and inform him. When we came from school, my father was sitting in the *balakhana*. He was happy and laughed when he saw us and accosted me, 'Oh unbridled one' – he would, out of love, call me this – 'this is all the outcome of your shenanigans!' Then he revealed to me the entire story.

After that I had my medical examination. As I was in good health and had a sound physique, orders came for my enrolment. In those days, Dr. Khan Sahib had come home to the village from Bombay after three years, and was going to London for the remaining part of his education. He too accompanied me to the recruiting officer. He gave Dr. Khan Sahib a lot of useful information about London. He gave him advice and apprised him of his experiences. At the time, Dr. Khan Sahib also felt that I should be recruited into the army. He left for London a few days later. Our matriculation examination was on and two papers were still left. I was happy to leave the examination unfinished when the recruiting officer asked me to report to him. My request for a direct commission had been accepted. I was very happy and deep in thought whether the infantry or the cavalry would be preferable. My friends were of the view that, for me, the infantry would be better. For one, my health was sound, and for another, my physique was good and my height too was six feet and three inches. At the time, the cavalry regiment, in which our khans of Deri Zardad were employed, was transferred from Jacobabad to Peshawar. Those khans were our friends. Barani Kaka and I left to call on them. I had never seen soldiers before. Whenever an officer came, and soldiers saluted him, I saw that they wore impressive uniforms. In front of each company of men there stood only one Englishman and a desi sardar, with girdled swords. Barani Kaka had told me that there was no difference between an English and a local officer; but when I saw the quarters of the desi officers, I found that there was a vast difference between the two. We were standing when a lieutenant appeared. I was standing with the khan who was a *risaldar*. His hairstyle was like that of an Englishman. The Englishman could not tolerate this and accosted him in a humiliating tone, saying, 'Khan Sahib, you too wish to be an Englishman?' This poor man did not dare to reply. When I witnessed this incident, a revulsion arose in my heart for such a service and I said to myself that I would never be able to tolerate such language and behaviour from an Englishman. After a while, orders came that I should present myself on a date at Mardan. They were commissioning me into the Guides Infantry. The Guides consisted of one infantry battalion and one cavalry regiment.The Guides unit was always in Mardan and was not transferred from place to place like the other units. In the Indian Army, this was a very famous unit. In this unit, sons of the big khans of the Frontier and *jagirdars* were recruited as naiks, *lance-naiks* and *daffedars* and, here I was, being taken in as a sardar. But I was no longer interested in joining the army. My father was keen that I should take up this appointment because, at the time, it was considered a very respectable job. But I did not agree. My father was annoyed with me, but my mother agreed with me. She was not enamoured by the service of the British.

After Education Again

Being overjoyed at the offer of recruitment into the army, I had left my education during the matriculation examination. That whole year was wasted in this quandary. The next year I again decided to continue my studies. I conferred with Maulvi Abdul Aziz's younger brother, Maulvi Abdul Halccm, who was also a class mate of mine. We had learnt that the school in Campbellpur had good arrangements for education. Teachers took a lot of interest in their pupils and went to a lot of trouble in teaching them. Arabic was fluently spoken there. It was one of my compulsory subjects. Both of us enrolled ourselves in the school in Campbellpur. There were a few boys from Peshawar enrolled here. We attended classes for a few days, but they did not come up to our expectations. Someone praised Qadian to us, so we decided to go there, and left. At the time when we left for Qadian, Hakim Nur-ud-din sahib was the *khalifa* of the *Jamat*. We went to see him. His discourse of love and affection had a profound effect on us. We were sitting with him when Mirza Ghulam Ahmad's son, who is now the *Amir* of the *Jamat* and was studying in college, arrived, and we took our leave. We came to the boarding house of the school where all the boys had but this to say, 'Forget about Ibn-e-Maryam. Ghulam Ahmad (Qadian) is better than him'. In other words, do not think of Ibn-e-Maryam (Hazrat Issa/Jesus Christ) as Ghulam Ahmad is better than him. We had never heard this before. Then the boys took us to a heavenly graveyard. The more we learnt about this place, the more amazed we were. We were in a quandary whether to leave or stay. The next night I dreamt that there was a big, deep well and I was standing on its brink. A white-bearded man extended a helping hand to me and saved me from falling into the well, and warned me, 'Beware!' When the morning came and Abdul Haleem and I got up for the morning prayer, I told him about my dream. He too had dreamt. Offering our prayers, we left for our village. Abdul Haleem went and got himself re-admitted to his old school while I left for Aligarh. I did not find a place in the boarding house in Aligarh and so took up lodgings in a hotel in the city. In Aligarh, there were quite a few Pukhtun boys from our part of the world who lived in the boarding house. In those days, Nawab Viqar-ul-Mulk was the Secretary of the Aligarh College. One day, after prayers, as we were coming out of the mosque, I arranged his slippers for him to wear. He quickly did the same for me and thanked me and told me not to do so again. Amongst us Pukhtuns the custom was that, as a sign of respect for elders, we would always arrange their footwear before their feet. Sometimes we would call on Nawab sahib at his bungalow and discuss things with him. In his bungalow there was a small mosque in which we prayed together. He was a very pleasant man, totally devoid of pride and arrogance. Amongst the leaders of the Muslims there was no one who lived so simply. He was devoted to the nation and the Muslim cause. He treated us like friends, and this carved a path in our hearts, because the sentiments he expressed were sincere.

In those days in Aligarh, enthusiastic meetings of the Muslims took place wherein a demand was made to the government for Aligarh College to be upgraded and named the Aligarh Muslim University. Similar meetings were taking place in the rest of Hindustan and donations were also being collected. These meetings gave me a lot of pleasure and I made every effort to attend as many of them as I could and listen with great attention to the speeches of the leaders. When the summer vacations started, I was told that I would get a place in the boarding house, but this did not happen. There was a big difference between Aligarh boarding life and that of Aligarh city. The society in the boarding house was cultured and learned while in the city this was not so. The other thing was that the monsoon had set in and made movement between the city and the college difficult.

At the time my brother, Khan Sahib, who had seen conditions in London, wrote to me and asked me to join him for an engineering degree. I left Aligarh for the village during summer vacations and showed the letter to my father. But he did not agree to this proposal. Finally he came around and agreed, and gave me three thousand rupees for expenses. He reserved a place for me on the PNO ship. But my mother was opposed to my leaving. Someone had put into her head that once someone sees England, he forgets his own land. That one son of hers had already left and if the other also leaves and does not return, she would be left childless. No matter how hard I tried, I was not able change her mind. In those days our land was going through very difficult times. There was factionalism, *tarboorwali* and lawlessness. At night, everyone was on guard for the safety of their lives and property in the hands of fellow Pukhtuns. During the day, they would fear lest they be unjustifiably implicated in false criminal cases. This was so because generally people were implicated based on factionalism and old enmities. And it also happened that one would himself create a situation to implicate his enemies. I apprised my mother of all this and told her, 'Look mother, either I would be killed by someone or, like my cousin, Shamroz Khan, I would be falsely implicated and imprisoned.' It was better that she should give permission for me to go abroad for education. She would not give me an answer but cry silently to herself. So, I abandoned the idea of going to London and decided that I would not study any further but dedicate the rest of my life to the service of my land and my people.

Efforts to restart my studies, going to different cities and schools, and exchanging views with different people benefitted me greatly and gave me a lot of experience. My father was an influential khan of his village and I was his son, however, my interactions were generally not with the other khans but with the poor. I used to mingle with the tanners, carpenters, masons, blacksmiths, weavers and the tenants. I had very little of the attributes and habits of the khans and the maliks. The characteristic of a khan of that period was that he was considered a very influential khan when he did not know the extent and boundaries of his landholding. The management of one's own land and working the land oneself was not considered befitting to the status of a khan. However, I worked the land my father had given me with my own hands. I had one servant, Qadeer, who belonged to the tanners' caste. Both of us would carry manure for the sugarcane crop on bullocks, and used to fill the sacks with manure with our own hands. Qadeer was with me since childhood. He was very faithful but smoked hashish and would sing its praise to me.

But I understood that he wanted to convert me to the use of hashish so that I could then procure it for him and spare him the expense. I forbade him from singing the praises of hashish to me. My other friends and relatives either smoked tobacco in a *cheelam*, took snuff or smoked cigarettes, but God safeguarded me from all these addictions. When I stayed behind in the village, I got involved with very bad company. My companions were upto all kinds of antics and I too got involved. They were quarrelsome and always looking for a fight, and got me into quarrels with people. But it was God's grace that very soon I changed my company and began to associate with people who were good.

3

A New Field and Fresh Thoughts

Association with Scholars

I ESTABLISHED AN ASSOCIATION WITH FAZL-E-MAHMUD SAHIB, MAULVI Abdul Aziz sahib of Pakli, Fazl-e-Rabbi sahib and Maulvi Taj Muhammad sahib, manager of the Dar-ul-uloom at Gadar. Maulvi Taj Muhammad sahib was from Baghdad. He had a bachelor's degree in arts in addition to his religious education. He was a second master in the Islamia High School in Peshawar. Maulvi Fazl-e-Rabbi was from Pakli and was a graduate of Deoband. He was, in the true sense of the term, a real scholar and a nationalist. Maulvi Abdul Aziz sahib was the brother of my classmate, Maulvi Abdul Hameed. He had studied in Bhopal, and was from the family of the chief maulana of Uthmanzai. Fazl-e-Mahmood Makhfi was from Charsadda. He was a matriculate and a revolutionary poet. At that time, the British had established a free port in the Persian Gulf where they sold arms and ammunition to the Arabs to revolt against the Turks. The Pukhtun tribesmen had found out about this availability of weapons. They would go and smuggle weapons from there and sell them to the tribesmen. When the British saw these weapons with the tribesmen, they were surprised as to where they had got them from. When they investigated the matter, they found out these were brought from the Persian Gulf, via Iran and the Baloch to Afghanistan and the Pukhtun tribes. So the British, to prevent this arms trade, established a post in the Persian Gulf headed by Gergson. This post needed a man who was familiar with English, Pukhto, Arabic and Persian. Makhfi sahib knew all four languages and was taken in as an interpreter. This service kindled in his heart the fire of patriotism and public service. He brought about a revolution in Pukhto poetry. In place of the traditional tresses and curls and black moles on the cheeks of the beloved, flowers and nightingales, he sang the praises of the nation, the wretched condition and distress of the poor and helpless. For me, he was the Shakespeare of Pukhto. The Pukhtuns owe a great deal to him but, unfortunately, they have not given him the honour he deserved.

In those days, Haji sahib of Torangzai's fame was spreading. All members of this group undertook to serve the cause of the faith under his guidance. Haji sahib was not like the other saintly figures amongst the Pukhtuns. He was not just a reformer by the pen but was also a man of action, who desired reform of all those customs and traditions in which the Pukhtuns were entangled and which harmed them both in this world and the next. I also developed a relationship with Haji sahib through Makhfi sahib. Haji sahib, at first, lived in his own village but when the father of Abdul Akbar Khan gave him a piece of land between Umerzai and Uthmanzai, he built a place for himself and shifted there. Every Friday afternoon a large congregation would gather there and I, too, would be part of it.

The Making of *Madrassahs*

When I studied at the Mission School, Peshawar, I was highly impressed by our headmaster, Mr. Wigram, and his brother, Dr Wigram. Their sacrifices had affected me deeply, to the extent that I also started to think about serving my people and my country. In those days, because of ignorance and lack of education, our people were in very bad shape. There were no arrangements in place, either by the government or the people, to provide education, and even in villages which had a primary school, the maulana would not allow anyone to study. So, I wanted to establish some Islamic *madrassahs* to educate the children of the Pukhtuns and spend my life in this service. In 1910, Maulvi Abdul Aziz sahib and I established a *madrassah* in Uthmanzai and I started to tour the province to open *madrassahs* in other places. I began to sensitize the Pukhtuns towards the need for education and established many *madrassahs* within a short span of time.

From Muftiabad, which is near our village, some people came and requested me for a visit, as they wanted a *madrassah* in their village. I went and gathered the people and talked to them about the benefits of learning. At this point, Chitrali maulana (Chitral is a hamlet of our village, Uthmanzai) came with a gun in his hand. We were having a discussion when he stood up, declaring that he did not recognize or accept this education that was introduced by Abdul Ghaffar Khan, and that this could not be considered education. He went on to state that one of the books taught in these *madrassahs* contained the text 'A dog is barking' and another book contained 'What is a big fish?' He asked, 'What is this question mark? Is this learning?' He said that he had come with the intention to have this matter decided, whether by the book or the gun. I told him that he knew very well that I was not a man of the gun and that, on the way to Uthmanzai, he should mention the matter of the gun to a cousin of mine, Muhammad Khan, and he would soon find out how much of a man he was. I also said, 'Maulana sahib, the acquisition of knowledge has been made compulsory for us Muslims by both God and his Prophet (PBUH); and if the maulanas were preventing people from studying in the schools established by the English, then it was necessary that they should make alternate arrangements for their education. If they too did not make such arrangements, and prevented us from serving the people, then may God take care of this nation!'

The Pukhtuns are a vibrant nation. They also have the qualities of patriotism and sacrifice, but they need to be woken up from their slumber. Nations are not woken up merely through prayer. To awaken a nation, leaders are needed who are selfless, honest and are ready to serve their people. When such leaders are born in a nation, their efforts generate love, compassion, brotherhood and kinsmanship, and help the nation progress. The selfish and lazy khans, maulanas and those who follow saints have condemned us to our present state of helplessness. If progress and prosperity could be attained merely through prayers and giving alms, why would our dear Prophet (PBUH) have struggled so much and undergone so much hardship for what he believed in? He would much rather have occupied a corner of the mosque and prayed. And who could have prayed like he did? Things would happen and the people would prosper. But the fact is that prayer without action is unacceptable to God. How are the Pukhtuns to blame for this? Whoever has established so-called piety in themselves, the people have always rallied around them by giving them alms, run around for them, served them by giving them substantive holdings of land; even wed their sisters and daughters to them, but those pious people have not truly educated this unfortunate lot in the tenets of their religion. The Pukhtuns believed that these pious people were their deliverers, both in matters of faith and in worldy matters. But such people have neither been concerned about the faith nor the welfare of the masses. They were merely concerned about themselves and did everything for themselves. They have done nothing for the people, the land, or the faith.

The maulanas began to oppose our schools by saying that Urdu was spoken in them. However, this was just a ploy, because the religious education imparted in our schools was better both in content and method than that imparted in the mosques. The maulanas have never explained the meaning of the *ayats* in the prayers, while we have done so to countless children. The fact is that our opponents were not concerned with Islam at all. Islam has, in fact, made the acquisition of knowledge mandatory on both Muslim men and women and stressed that, for the attainment of knowledge, they should even go to China if they have to. Although, in China, there was no knowledge in Arabic, this meant that Islam is about the acquisition of knowledge. If these maulanas were truly fond of knowledge, they would enrol themselves as our helpers. They knew that they would go out of business if the Pukhtuns got educated. It never occurred to them that if the Pukhtuns got educated, the people would prosper. And when the people prospered, they would as well. They did not have an existence separate from the people. The khans were better than them. Despite the fact that if the people were to become knowledgeable and the institution of the khan would be affected, let alone opposing our schools, they helped us a lot. We used to reassure the maulanas that when the nation prospered, so would they, but they could never imagine that the entire Pukhtun nation and they could prosper together. They were so used to an easy life and feeding off others, that they had no attributes of hard work left in them.

When the maulanas began voicing opposition to our *madrassahs*, we turned to the Haji sahib of Torangzai and nominated him as the patron of our *madrassahs*. In this way, we saved ourselves to some extent from the mischief of the maulanas and managed to achieve a lot. Haji sahib was a reformist saint and not like the other saints. A great attribute of his was that, unlike the other saints, nobody could buy him in any way, an art in which the English were the past masters. To trap the maulanas, the Englishman had, in this way, 'engaged' the Muslims. It was only Haji sahib who had been saved from this. Similarly, in the opposition to our *madrassahs* the British also had a hand, even though the maulanas had their own axe to grind with us.

I remember, one day, in Sevagram (Mahatma Gandhi's ashram in Wardha), many people had gathered around Gandhiji. After the prayer, he told the people they were slaves and lived a life of abject humiliation today because they were collectively guilty of a great ingratitude, and ingratitude is a great sin in God's eyes. He told them that they were confronted with hardships in life because though God had given them hands and feet, they did not put them to use. Also, their caste of the Brahmans had become useless and lived off society. On account of this ingratitude, they had been afflicted by this curse. In the *Bhagwad Geeta* it said that those who did not work but ate, were equivalent to thieves.

Relationship with Deoband

With the establishment of these *madrassahs*, my association with Haji sahib of Torangzai and his companions i.e. Makhfi sahib, Maulvi Fazl-e-Rabbi and Maulvi Taj Muhammad became stronger and more intimate. Sometimes I would call on them for an exchange of views at Gadar, and whenever they came to call on Haji sahib, they would also come to see me in Uthmanzai. Maulvi Taj Muhamad was the manager of the *madrassah* at Gadar and also delivered lectures there. Our relationship with Deoband was slowly initiated through Makhfi sahib and Maulvi Fazl-e-Rabbi sahib. At that time Hazrat Maulana, Mahmood-ul-Hassan, was the principal of the Dar-ul-uloom, Deoband. He was a pious devotee of God and a great scholar who advocated action in addition to the acquisition of religious knowledge. He was always thinking about how Hindustan could be freed from the slavery of British rule. The freedom of the land was our common objective. When we used to visit Deoband, we would stay with the maulana. At the time, Deoband was full of Pukhtun students. We used to go to Deoband on the pretext of meeting these students. One student of the maulana, Aziz Gul, would make arrangements for our meals and lodgings. Through Maulana sahib, we gradually got to know Maulvi Ubaidullah Sindhi and Muhammad *Mian*. Unfortunately, I have forgotten the names of the other maulanas whom I had befriended there. The maulana sahib of Khurja was a good friend of mine. A loving person who would come to Deoband and bring many delicious things for us to eat whenever he learned of my presence. The pickles and kulchas of Khurja are very famous. Unfortunately, I have forgotten his name, which is probably in my lost notebooks. The truth is that there was love and camaraderie amongst us. There is always love between those who have the same objectives. They will have differences of opinion amongst themselves, but this is always a blessing for the group. If one is to investigate the factionalism that one sees amongst groups nowadays, one would find that it is so because their objectives are not the same. This is why a difference of opinion, instead of being a blessing, becomes a curse for them, because they do not serve God and benefit their people but create differences for their own, selfish motives. The ways of the flesh are many and the path of God is one. Service for the sake of God, and factionalism within the group are two contradictory phenomena.

Most of our consultations used to be with Maulana Mehmood-ul-Hassan and Maulana Ubaidullah Sindhi. In those days, the British were at the prime of their power and had instilled fear in the hearts of the people. They also had an excellent intelligence system. So whenever we used to travel to Deoband, out of fear, we would never buy a direct ticket to Deoband. We would always get off the train either at a station before or after Deoband and cover the rest of the way either on foot or through some other means so that the British did not find out. Maulana Ubaidullah Sindhi had taken a place near a big mosque at Fatehpur where he taught boys the *Quran*. Those boys who had passed their bachelor's exam would receive a stipend of fifty rupees each from him, in addition to being taught free. In those days fifty rupees was a lot of money. He was of the view that, among the educated Muslim youth, he would, through the teaching of the *Quran*, kindle passion for freedom and public service in their hearts. But Sindhi sahib failed in the attainment of his objective. He was no doubt a great scholar. No one understood the *Quran* as well as he did, and nor could anyone teach like him. But the Muslims no longer had the attribute of struggle left in them. In these very schools of the British, the Hindus had also been educated. This had one kind of effect on the Hindus, and another on the Muslims. In the Hindus, it had generated a love for their nation and a desire to serve the people, and in the Muslims, let alone love and service, they were not even aware of nationhood and the land. One of Sindhi sahib's students was a graduate, who had studied the *Quran* and its translation with the maulana. Although Sindhi sahib reposed the fullest confidence in him, he was found to be an informer for the British. He would send a daily diary on the activities of the maulana and his students to the government. When this was the condition of Sindhi sahib's favourite and rightly-guided student, what could be expected of others? Love of the nation and its service is not solely dependent on education. When we were starting our movement for the freedom and service of our people, I earnestly sought out many amongst the educated in the towns and cities, but I could not find such people amongst them who were prepared to serve their people in the name of God. I have always maintained a lot of respect for the saints and the learned and served them too, in the hope that they had thousands of acolytes and followers, and if they were to side with us, lots of people would assist and join our ranks. I have also fawned a great deal on the maulanas and run after them but only a few joined me; like a pinch of salt in flour. When I was disappointed with them, I came away from the cities and spread out to the villages, hamlets and the masses. In four months, so many people had joined me that the British were perturbed. I had courted the educated for twelve years but, disappointed, returned to the villages and gathered thousands who joined me.

The Sheikh-al-Hind and Sindhi Sahib

Whenever we travelled to Deoband, Sheikh-al-Hind sahib would inform Sindhi sahib of our visit. Often he would come to Deoband and sometimes I would travel to Delhi, to call on him and also to hold discussions with him. Sindhi sahib's place was next to the Fatehpuri Masjid. Fatehpuri was a Masjid of Delhi where the Friday afternoon congregational used to be held. It had a *madrassah* for teaching Arabic and Maulvi Saif-ur-Rahman was the head teacher there. But I never went directly to Sindhi sahib's place because there was always a man from Criminal Investigation Department (CID) present there. This was a time when the police would be after those who received a copy of Maulana Azad's *Al Hilal* and the government would blacklist them. Only God could help those whom government suspected of having love and affection for his country's freedom and service. That is why I never went directly to his place, but went to the Fatehpuri Masjid to meet him. When the prayer was over and we did not have much to discuss we would meet in the Masjid. Sindhi Sahib would then leave for his house and I would go to attend to my other work. If we did not conclude our discussion, Sindhi sahib would take me out with him for a cup of tea. We used to have tea and discuss matters in hand. After seeing Sindhi sahib, I would not stay in Delhi but leave for the village by the night train. But sometimes, if I had other work, I would stay with Maulvi Saif-ur-Rahman, who was from Doaba. He was a very learned and competent man with political insights. Unlike the other maulanas, he was not a man of limited vision and was also not bigoted. He was a man of lofty thought and vision, and was not easily irritated. He was an interesting conversationalist with a good sense of humour.

Nationalism

The feeling of nationalism awoke in me when I began to associate with nationalists. I had, long ago as a student, experienced this feeling but it developed in the sessions I had with Makhfi sahib, Maulvi Abdul Aziz and the *Mohtamim* sahib, who had a strong impact on me. In those days, I was fond of two things: one was farming and the other, study. For farming, my father had transferred to me sixty *jareebs* of land in Muhammad Narai. I cultivated this land myself; and for study I would diligently read Maulana Abul Kalam Azad's newspaper, *Al Hilal*. This was a paper in which subjects were covered with great knowledge. It was the standard bearer of freedom that put across to the people the true meaning of Islam. The other paper I subscribed to was the *Zamindar*. This was brought out by Maulana Zafar Ali Khan and was nationalist in orientation. It was not like this when it came into the ownership of his son, Akhtar Ali Khan. I also read the *Madina* from Bijnor, which was also a very nationalistic paper. Also available to me was the English paper the *Civil and Military Gazette*. Along with these, I would read many religious and other books. When I was a student, I was not fond of studying. However, when I started working on the *madrassahs*, I developed a taste for reading. In those days, whoever subscribed to *Al Hilal* and *Zamindar* was a thorn in the side of the British and was blacklisted. This was because both these papers were nationalistic in outlook and were considered to be fuelling the feelings of nationalism and freedom. Foreign governments are based on creating fear in the hearts of the citizens, and when fear is removed from the hearts of the people, the foundations of foreign governments are shaken. An alien government is like a thief; when the owner of the house wakes up, the thief takes flight. That is why the British Government did not like such newspapers. A number of times the police came for me and advised me not to subscribe to these newspapers. I replied very curtly that if the government did not like these newspapers, it should shut them down. They would reply that the government was not inclined to do so, to which I would reply that I, too, was not inclined to stop subscribing to them.

Whenever Makhfi sahib managed to get hold of a good book he would lend it to me. One day he brought me Abdul Haleem Sharar's novel, *Ziad* and *Halawa*, and told me to study it seriously. My temperament was such that, unlike others, I could not read extensively, but would try to understand thoroughly whatever I read to digest its meaning. This novel was about Spain and the way in which the Christians of Spain overthrew the eight-hundred-year old Muslim rule. I benefitted a great deal in my work from reading this book. Whenever Makhfi sahib himself wrote a piece of poetry, he would bring it and read it out to me. I used to enjoy his poetry a lot. It not only gave me a lot of pleasure, but also had a profound effect on me. I still remember quite a few of his verses. Makhfi sahib and I read the *Al Hilal* together and discussed its articles in depth, reading them many times over and, whenever possible, would read them out to others. The truth is that *Al Hilal* taught us the reality of Islam and re-oriented our outlook.

This was a time when, on account of the fear of the British, no one could dare, even in the sanctity of his own *hujra*, speak out against the British. When we wanted to discuss such things, we would go to a remote and secure place. Our village is thickly populated, we could not talk privately there, and rarely tried to do so. Sometimes we went to Hajiabad, Haji Sahib's place, or elsewhere. Once, Maulvi Fazl-e-Rabbi sahib, Makhfi sahib and I went to Muhammad Narai, which is a hamlet in a beautiful rural setting of ours in the *maira*, watered by a fine canal. The evening meal was prepared for us. After the evening prayer, we were strolling on the road and chatting when, looking behind us, we realized that a man was following us. We were agitated. We thought this man was spying on us. We beat a hasty retreat and left a cooked meal uneaten and did not so much as inform the owner of the house and our host. In great haste, we reached another of our hamlets, Marwandai, in the late evening. Tenants have their dinner early and had eaten theirs. They cooked another meal for us, which we ate and then spent the night there. It was in such difficult circumstances that we started our work. Despite this, our work prospered from day to day because it was meant for God's humanity, and not for our personal gain; in fact, we stood to lose by it.

The First Marriage

At the end of 1912, my father arranged a marriage for me. I was still young and was studying in school. He got me engaged into a family of the Kinankhel khans of Razar, a village adjacent to ours. I do believe that my father-in-law, Yar Muhammad Khan, was the first khan who took no *walwar* for his daughter. At that time, whether a khan or a commoner, *walwar* was always taken for a daughter or sister. People did not consider this custom as evil. Although the Pukhtuns still take *walwar* for daughters or sisters, it is now considered evil. This is a grievous sin in Islam. In fact, Islam gives a share to sisters and daughters in the inheritance of their fathers, brothers and sisters. My father-in-law was a very hospitable man, who had many friends and acquaintances. He was particularly gracious and generous to the poor of his village. When he died, I saw how the women, men, other relatives and friends grieved for him. Though not literate himself, he was extremely interested in education. He would tell my father that he had sent one son to London to study and he would send the other one too. When he fell seriously ill, I heard that he had wanted to record his will and give his women relatives their due share, in accordance with Shariat, but his relatives did not allow him to do so. He had many khans as friends, but after his death, no one cared to look after his little children. In the story of the *Char Darwesh,* there is a tale of a rich merchant's son, who had inherited immense wealth from his father, but he squandered all of it on his friends. When he was penniless and in a pitiable condition, a wayfarer recognized him and asked him whether he was not the son of the rich merchant. He told him that he was, whereupon the wayfarer asked how was it that he was in such difficulty when he had so many friends who used to fawn on him? How was it that they had not extended any help to him? Where were they now? He replied that they were not his friends but the flies of the feast table. When the table was laid out, they would hover around, and when the table was cleared, the flies flew away. I had a lot of respect and sympathy for the honour of our womenfolk because, unlike other nations of the West, we had no respect for our women. They were considered inferior to men, although inferiority and superiority are solely dependent on one's deeds. Those whose deeds were bad should be considered as inferior, irrespective of their gender. If a woman performed good deeds, then it was only right that she should be considered superior. God has created men and women to populate the earth, as equal companions. They are like the two wheels of a carriage, which cannot move with one wheel. Pukhtun women are very pious, loving and bashful, and anxious to serve their menfolk. Whenever we visited the homes of our relatives, even though they had domestic help, they would insist that the women of their family serve us. They would place before us whichever delicious dish they had cooked and would eat what was left over. The men never ate with the women and the women also considered this unacceptable. I was the first to take umbrage at this and ate with the women when there were no guests. Gradually, this custom was abandoned by everyone. When I got married, my wife found it very strange to eat with me and would not easily do so as she was so self conscious. The women would eat whatever was left after the men had eaten, and even if this was not enough, they would be content with it. The older women would invariably backbite about the younger lot and say 'Sister! just look at the women of today, how brazen eyed and unabashed they are with their husbands. God has condemned them to this time.' But after some time, they also got used to the idea of eating with their husbands and this was no longer considered odd. Guests, too, had no set time (to arrive). Whatever time the guests came, the women, poor souls, were compelled to arrange their meals. Whether it was midnight, the blazing afternoon or a summer's day in the monsoon, when a guest came, he would expect a good meal and the host would be compelled to oblige. In our movement this tradition was also reformed. We exhorted the people that, from now on, they would not impose themselves on anyone at an awkward time; and if they happened to do so, they should eat whatever was ready and available. In this way, we eased the hardship of the women to some extent.

At that time, boys were not allowed to study and the education of girls was considered equivalent to heresy. The maulana did not allow anyone to study. I remember clearly that when I admitted my daughter into school, let alone the others, even the household of my father-in-law was annoyed with me, even though this school was only for girls and in a khan's house. It was a sort of private and special *madrassah*. The wife of the khan herself taught there. Even today many khans do not admit their daughters into school. The maulanas never considered the fact that Islam had made education compulsory for both men and women. They not only opposed the *madrassahs* but were also vehemently opposed to the reading of newspapers. At first, they declared that the newspapers were full of lies and meant to make money from the subscribers. Then, gradually, when the people began to understand things better and realized that newspapers also contained discussions about God and his Prophet, the maulanas started a propaganda that, by being quoted in the newspapers, disrespect was shown to the *ayats* of the *Quran* and the Hadiths, because after being read, the newspapers were trashed and thrown onto dungheaps.

I would read out the newspapers to the people in the *hujra*, but no one really paid any attention. They only showed a little interest in *Al Hilal* because, firstly, it contained discussions on God and his Prophet and, secondly, it was the paper of Maulana Abul Kalam Azad. Even today, the Pukhtuns are not interested in newspapers. They will spend thousands of rupees on meaningless practices and worthless customs but would not spend a paisa on newspapers. This is the reason that such a brave and large nation does not have even one national newspaper in its mother tongue. There was an influential khan who once saw a young boy in Peshawar with a number of newspapers in his hand, calling out to people to buy them. The khan thought they were being distributed free, so he took one from him. But when the boy asked him for the money, he returned the newspaper. As the Pukhtuns had no love for newspapers, they also had no love for their own language. When I would talk about it to the educated, they would retort that Pukhto was no language, as there was no knowledge in Pukhto! I would tell them, 'The other languages have not come down from the sky. The speakers of each language have developed it themselves.' If the Pukhtuns have not paid any attention to their mother tongue, the Pukhto language is not to blamed, this was their fault as well as mine.

When I got married, my wife would also ask me why I read the newspapers as they were full of lies. I would say that this was just propaganda carried out against them and that reading newspapers was essential. She would then say 'How am I to know, this is what people say?' She would then ask me what they contained. I would explain to her that they had information about the current conditions in all the countries of the world. The women of the Pukhtuns are more intelligent than the men. Gradually, she developed an interest in education. I would give her information on the *Quran* and the faith and other essential matters. She was very dear to her father and exercised a lot of influence in his household. Because of her, a lot of changes took place in my father-in-law's household and for the better. I would always try to remove the sense of inferiority from the minds of the women, which had been inculcated in them by ignorant and selfish men. I would argue with my wife that men and women are equal in the eyes of God, and that honour and dishonour depend on one's deeds. I would also tell her that women themselves were responsible for their inferiority complex because they viewed their sons and daughters differently and instilled in their daughters' minds that God had created men superior to women and that sons were more important than daughters. Then I would also tell them that of all the creations of God, human beings were the most honoured and, therefore, bore greater responsibility, compared to the rest of his creation. But when I look at this nation of mine, I find no difference between them and the animals. They are concerned with the satisfaction of their hunger, just like the animals. They are also concerned about their homes and so are the animals. They procreate and are worried about their children, and animals, too, give birth to the young and nurture them. Why should they then be considered the most honoured of all creations? Like the animals they, too, kill one another. They would only be justifiably considered the most honoured of creations, when a collective consciousness, brotherhood, love and affection are generated amongst them. Just because animals have four feet and human beings have only two, human beings cannot be considered superior to them. One day, while talking to her, I told her that when a husband dies, the wife spends the rest of her life as a widow, but when a wife dies, the husband immediately gets married again. In all fairness, it should be that when the husband dies, the woman too should immediately remarry. I asked her whether she understood what I was talking about. She replied that, yes, she did. I said to her that it is not known who will die first, but if I were to die and she was still young, she should have no hesitation or shame in taking another husband. She retorted that I should not indulge in such shameful talk!

The Muslim League Session in Agra

In 1913, the annual session of the All-India Muslim League was held. In those days the annual sessions were held in December, during the Christmas vacations. When I read that the Muslim League session was to be held in the city of Agra, I decided that I would definitely participate because this was a political meeting. We had no such meetings in our own land and nor were the people accustomed to them, and even if some understood what all this was about, no one could even consider participating out of fear of the British. The maulanas would debate issues which neither benefitted Islam nor the country. For example, some would pronounce an Arabic word appearing in the *Quran* in one way and others would do so totally differently. Some would say that repenting verbally was acceptable to God, while others disputed this. Similarly, some would consider raising the index finger during prayers as compulsory; others would consider it wrong. The maulanas would debate such matters and carry piles of books on donkeys and camels from place to place, discussing these issues extensively but not coming to any conclusions. Hence, they would divert the attention of the people from more important matters of immediate concern to them. I could detect the hand of the British in all this, because occasionally the issue would also be raised that if it came to a war between Russia and Britain, whom would it be better for us to extend our support to? In response to this question there would be no difference of opinion. Everyone would be of the view that the British were followers of the book and the Russians were stark atheists and that it was consequently incumbent on us to help the British. The fact was that the British are Christians and so were the Russians.

One day, in Muhammad Narai, we had gathered after the Friday prayers, when a debate started whether verbal repentance was acceptable to God or not. Maulana sahib of Dara said that if someone says it was acceptable, he would prove to him that it was not. And if someone said that it was unacceptable, he would prove to him that it was. His intentions were clearly to show to the people that he was such a learned maulana that he could prove an illegal matter to be legal. He had such a hold over the congregation that the people sitting there looked at one another and exclaimed that he was, indeed, a very learned religious scholar. But in matters of faith, there was only one approach. So, I said to him that if God and the Prophet were of the view that it was acceptable, then how could he demonstrate that it was not; and if they were of the view that it was not acceptable, then how could he prove that it was? The maulana sahib did not like what I said and diverted the discussion in another direction. They would show off their '*maulanaism*' to the people and do incalculable harm to the nation. They had created such hatred amongst people that most people had stopped social interactions amongst each other. The main leader of one of the factions was the maulana sahib of Mankee Sharif and, of the other, the maulana sahib of Hadda. They would declare each other infidels. The fact is that both believed in one God and one Prophet and were followers of the same *Hanafi* school of jurisprudence, to the extent that they were the disciples of the same pir.

I left for Agra with my classmate, Abdul Haleem, to participate in the Muslim League session. We got to Naukhar for the night. The *thanedar* there was Ghulam Sarwar Khan of Dwosaro. The area around the thana was still an open space. Ghulam Sarwar Khan used to live in Khat village. We spent the night with him. The mail train left Peshawar at 11 p.m. and arrived in Naukhar at 1 a.m. We were to travel by this train to Agra. So, after we had our dinner in Khat village, we left at 12 midnight and walked the rail track to the station. On the way we heard growling beasts, gradually getting closer to us. While we were wondering what this sound could possibly be, suddenly the animals attacked us. Panic overtook us and we raised a hue and cry. It was by the grace of God that they did not maul us. We found that they were wolves. Ghulam Sarwar Khan even fired at them with his revolver. Finally we reached the station and after taking leave of Ghulam Sarwar Khan, we boarded the train. In Agra, we rented some lodgings in a sera*i*. The session was to start the next morning. A huge pandal had been erected for the session; stairs were placed on and below the stage. We bought tickets and took our seats. Sir Ibrahim Rahimtoola was to preside over the proceedings. Maulana Abul Kalam Azad, Sir Aga Khan and a number of other prominent personalities of Hindustan were seated on the stage. After the presidential address, different resolutions were tabled and various people spoke on them. Sir Aga Khan also spoke, and very eloquently in Persian. After the session, we visited the Taj Mahal, the Shahi Mosque and roamed around the city. From Agra we travelled to Delhi, where we were guests of Maulvi Saif-ur-Rehman. In Delhi, too, we did some sightseeing of all the worthwhile monuments. One day, while sitting in the Shahi Masjid, an old man with a white beard accosted me and said that Delhi was never faithful to anyone and it appeared that the downfall of the British was now their fate, as they had changed their capital from Calcutta to Delhi. In those days the imperial capital was transferred to Delhi. Thirty-four years later, the prophecy of that old man came true.

In those days both parties, the Congress and the Muslim League, would seek posts and privileges from the British and pass resolutions, making demands. Most of the intelligentsia of Hindustan was part of the Congress. When Gandhiji came from South Africa and became a member of the Congress, the stance of the Congress changed. In place of mere resolutions and demands, the struggle for achieving the rights of the people started in earnest. The truth is that no one confers rights on anyone; rights are always snatched. When the policy of the Congress changed from requests and entreaties to action based on struggle, people like Jinnah sahib, Jeeka Rao Sapru and others like them, who were unable to face hardship, left the Congress. Jinnah sahib joined the Muslim League and the others formed the Labour Party. The fact was that when the issue of the Rowlatt Act arose, Jinnah sahib, Sapru and some others were against it. So the question arose, that if the government did not accept our demands, what would we do? These people stated that they would mount a protest. After this the question arose that if the government still did not accede to their demands, then what would they do? These people replied that they would still protest. Gandhiji stated that if their demands were not accepted by the government, a protest would be started by the masses. It was this difference of opinion over which they parted ways.

Education and Sermonizing in our Village and Land

After a few days in Delhi we returned to our village where I found out that my son, Ghani, was born while we were away. My wife had no brother so she was overjoyed at the birth of a son. On Fridays, many people would gather at the home of the Haji sahib of Torangzai. They would come from far and near for the Friday prayer. And if I was not on tour I too would go there. The *mohtamim* of the *madrassah* and Maulvi Fazl-e-Rahim Rabbi sahib would also occasionally come for consultations. After the prayer I would also address the gathering and give people advice, but the maulanas were not in favour of this, because our maulanas, like the Brahmins, considered themselves the sole guardians of the faith. I wanted to reform my nation for the sake of God and did not care for them. They finally secretly started their propaganda against me, accusing me that although I had shaved my beard and yet I sermonized; that I should first live my own life in conformity with the Shariat and only then preach to others. They were not at all concerned about the beard and Islam; they only intended to give me a bad name. The nation was ignorant. When the maulana would tell the nation that this was the faith, it would accept it. The maulanas gave so much importance to the beard that they equated Islam with it. In all honesty, faith is about doing good deeds. Faith is concerned with one's character and the doing of good deeds. The growing of beards and the shaving of moustaches was part of the culture of the Arabs. Not only did the companions of the Prophet (PBUH), but even the enemies of Islam amongst the Arabs, like Abu Jahal, Abu Lahab and others, had beards. Despite this, and to absolve myself from this objection of the maulanas, I allowed my beard to grow. But even then, I could not get away from the maulanas. They would then say that my beard was less than a fist in length. The history of the world is witness to the fact that whenever such persons have risen for the reformation of their people, they are opposed by those in power and authority as they are seen as a threat. Look at the *Khudai Khidmatgar*. As the nation became more aware, the strength of those in power diminished. Study the life of your own Prophet (PBUH). His own uncles and cousins opposed him. And for what reason? For the sake of power. The inhabitants of Madina came to his assistance because they neither had religious nor political authority. When the Jews opposed him, it was also for the sake of power.

Our *madrassahs* were doing well. The Pukhtuns are a vibrant nation, only if there is someone born amongst them to awaken them. Till such time that such persons are not born, the nation cannot be awakened. In a short period, people established *madrassahs* in many places and with great enthusiasm, enrolled their children in them. But this also meant we needed more resources. Without money, no task can be accomplished. The Pukhtuns were not misers. They were fond of guests, were generous and liberally distributed alms. But the way in which the maulanas prescribed them to give charity was of no use to us at the time. The nation was accustomed to donating cooked food as charity. In fact, the times had changed. There was no longer a need for 'cooked charity', there was a need for charity in cash and kind. If the nation could only change itself to suit the needs of the times, it would prosper; if not, it would lag behind. In the matter of *zakat* too the maulanas would prescribe that the *madrassahs* were not entitled to *zakat*. Many debates had been held with the maulanas on these issues but they were not prepared, even for the sake of the progress and education of the nation, to part with a grain of rice. The nation was fed up with customs and rituals but lacked the courage to give them up. To abandon custom and tradition is not an easy thing; it is extremely difficult and requires moral courage. When we went on a tour of the nation, in every place people would gather for us. When we talked to them, some people would gather around us. Some would say that I should pat them on their backs. Some would bring *gura* and salt for me to bless. Some would say that I should bless them directly. I would tell the people that I was not the man for such things and that I had merely come to serve them and that they should make a distinction between me and those who were in the business of dispensing blessings and amulets. Through such means, they were intent on extracting charity from them in the form of *shukrana, nazrana* and *malikana*, and I was not asking them for anything. Muhammad Akbar Khan sahib would ask me why I said this to the people, because, in this manner, people would collect a lot of donations for their *madrassahs*, and here you are, repelling them from yourself. I used to tell Khadim sahib that I wanted to reform them and free them from the shackles of evil customs and traditions. Once, when leaving on a tour of the Sudham area, the Maulana of Shahbaz Garhai, Shah Rasool sahib, joined the group. The khans of Sudham provided me with horses for the journey and we would ride them turn by turn.

The Haji sahib of Torangzai was extremely interested in education. He would constantly be in search of ways to help the *madrassahs*. One day I told him, 'Haji sahib, in your langar, there are many disciples and students who sit idle. If you were to instruct them to devote one day a month to help the *madrassahs*, they would benefit greatly.' The Haji sahib laughed heartily and said, 'If they were willing to work, then what would they be doing here? These are free-loaders who consider manual labour beneath their dignity. The Prophet (PBUH) has said, "Al Qasib Habeeb Ullah", which means, he who works is a friend of Allah.'

4

With the Sheikh-al-Hind Sahib

The Sheikh-al-Hind's Letter

WE WOULD VISIT DEOBAND ONCE OR TWICE IN A YEAR AND CALL ON Maulana Mahmud-ul-Hassan and Maulana Ubaidullah Sindhi to discuss ways and means of freeing ourselves from the yoke of British slavery. In the beginning of January 1914, a letter arrived from Hazrat Maulana Mahmud-ul-Hassan, the Sheikh-al-Hind, asking us to come to Deoband. So I, Makhfi sahib and Maulana Fazl-e-Rabbi left for Deoband. When we arrived at the station, we went directly to the *madrassah*, from where Maulana Uzair Gul took us to the house of Maulana sahib. We did not venture outside the house because of our fear of the CID. The Sheikh-al-Hind sahib also summoned Maulana Ubaidullah Sindhi from Delhi. After a great deal of debate and discussion, we concluded that we needed to establish two *marakiz*: one in Hindustan and the other in the free Tribal Areas, where the inhabitants were not on the British pay and were also revolutionary in nature, so that an army for the liberation of Hindustan could be raised and trained there. We were of the view that this *markaz* could be established in Buner, where the party of the Hindustani mujahideen lived. This was the group which, after the martyrdom of Saeed Ahmad Barelvi and Shah Ismail Shaheed, left Hazara for Buner and established themselves in Sitana and, till date, received replenishments in the shape of men and money from Hindustan. But the old spirit and passion, which had energized Saeed Ahmad Shaheed and Shah Ismail Shaheed, were now lacking in them. They were such a useless lot that they had neither made people around them aware of their mission, nor had they created amongst them a like-minded group. One day, Maulana Abul Kalam Azad and I talked about this group. The Maulana was also favourably inclined towards them, but I informed him they were no longer of any use. They were dependent on the resources of Hindustan and exploited it. They were of the belief that war should be fought with the sword and spear and with the bow and arrow because the companions of the Prophet (PBUH) fought with these and were victorious, and this was *sunnat*. They did not consider the fact that, at that time when the companions of the Prophet (PBUH) fought with these weapons, their opponents, too, were not better equipped. Today the world had moved on and was more developed. It was the time of the cannon and the gun. The sword and spear and the bow and arrow were no match for these. But the people of Hindustan were not aware of this and nor were they aware of the aims of this group. The pity was that even the prominent leaders and ulema of the Muslims were unaware of this fact. We knew about the realities of this group. Makhfi sahib had personally visited Buner to assess the situation and had spent many nights with these fanatics in their caves. We now made our friends in Deoband understand that neither were these mujahideen of any use and nor was this place appropriate for a *markaz*.

Search for a Place for a *Markaz* in the Free Area

We decided that a delegation from amongst us should visit the free Tribal Area in search of a suitable place for a *markaz*. Makhfi sahib and I were selected for this. First, we were to travel through the Tribal Areas, select a place and inform them. Then Sindhi sahib would come and see the place for himself. If he also agreed to this, we could then start the work. Before the decision, I was very enthusiastic about this work, but when the decision was taken and the responsibility was assigned to me, I felt heavy with the weight of responsibility, as if a mountain had fallen on me. When the *jirga* was over, we returned to our rooms. I cried copiously in my solitude, my heart became a little lighter and I went to sleep. When I woke up the next morning, I reassured my heart. When we returned to the village, it was peak winter. It was bitterly cold and the ganrai was running. Makhfi sahib and I fixed a date to meet at the Takht-e-Bahi railway station. Takht-e-Bahi is about twelve miles from our village. I kept the matter very secret; firstly out of fear of the government and secondly from the fear that my mother would not give me permission to go on this mission. I made the excuse of visiting the Dargah at Ajmer Sharif.

She was very pleased with this because my in-laws were acolytes of Ajmer Sharif and my father-in-law visited it annually on pilgrimage. He held the belief that it was Ajmer Sharif that had bestowed him with children. Faqirs from Ajmer Sharif came annually and took a lot of money from him. When my son Ghani was born, the faqirs of Ajmer had come to Razar. They found out that the khan had had a grandson and came to Uthmanzai in the hope of milking this cow! But their spells did not work on me. They told me tales implying that Ghani was born because of the intercession of Ajmer Sharif. I told them that Ghani was my son and Ajmer Sharif had nothing to do with his birth. They were surprised to hear this and wondered what kind of a person I was. Disappointed, they went away.

From my village I went to Muhammad Narai for the night. The next morning, mounted on a horse, I left for Takht-e-Bahi. I reached the station in the afternoon. Makhfi sahib had arrived earlier. Handing over the horse to the servant, we left for Dargai in a train and arrived there in the evening. There were tongas for hire outside the station and we left for Batkhela by tonga. There was a police post located on the crest of the Malakand Pass. The police surrounded our tonga and searched it. They questioned us. I was scared in case I was recognized. This was because, at the time, there was a lot of surveillance in the tribal agencies. If they suspected anyone, he would be arrested and put in the stocks. It was a long, solid plank of wood with holes in it, in which the legs of the suspect would be placed and then riveted with bolts. They would then mete out such treatment to the suspect that even Halagu Khan would not have subjected anyone to. And the British political agent of Malakand was even worse than a pharaoh. People were not scared of God so much as of him. It was dark, no one was suspicious of us, and when they gave permission to our tonga to proceed, only then did we heave a sigh of relief. We arrived in Batkhela in the late evening. We did not know anyone in Batkhela nor was there any serai or hotel there. But the *hujra* and mosques of the Pukhtuns are always open to guests and wayfarers. We did not go to a *hujra* in case we were recognized and the government found out. We went to a mosque instead. It was bitterly cold, and we had no warm clothes with us, but the mosque was warm, and a fire was burning inside it. Covered by a *saadar*, we spent a nice, comfortable night and left early in the morning. We crossed the concrete bridge across the river in Chakdarra, and walked the rest of the distance as, in those days, there was no other means of transport on these roads. It was at a mosque in Amluk Darra that we spent the next night. Early in the morning, at prayer time, we left. We travelled all day and by night reached the banks of a river. The water was no more than a trickle and was very cold. We crossed over the rapids and by the late evening, with great difficulty, arrived at Makhfi sahib's village. We were extremely exhausted, had crossed the icy water and were shivering from the cold. We were really famished, but since the dwellings of Makhfi sahib's kith and kin were close by, they quickly lit fires for us. When we warmed up, they brought out food. We tucked into it and had a good meal. They then set out beds for us and we lay down. In the mosques, one slept on the floor, and in the *hujra*, on beds.

This area is called Seend because a *seend* (river) flows through it. In Makhfi sahib's village it is a delight to sit on top of the mountain and look down upon the river, which meanders below like a snake. It is a beautiful village with rice being the main crop. Makhfi sahib's father was born in this village but Makhfi sahib himself was born in Charsadda, in the Hashtnagar area. His father was a great scholar and had married and settled in Charsadda. At that time, there were no *madrassahs* in the region. Every maulana, when he tied the turban of learning and became a maulana, either of his own village or that of another, would teach for the pleasure of God. Generally, the people of the mountains would come down to the plains for education. Makhfi sahib's father had also come down in this connection, and then stayed on. If he were not an enlightened scholar, how could his son, Makhfi sahib, have acquired temporal knowledge at that time, in addition to religious learning? I was not accustomed to walking and was very tired. We rested here for a few days. Makhfi sahib left me and set out for Hindustan in order to bring Maulana Ubaidullah Sindhi. With a paternal cousin of Makhfi sahib's, whose name I have forgotten, I left in search of a place for the proposed *markaz*. Makhfi sahib left for Peshawar and I for Chamarkand. When we parted ways, I really felt the absence of Makhfi sahib. Chamarkand is a small place located on a mountain top on the border with Afghanistan. When the maulana sahib of Hadda was in Afghanistan and had attained a saintly status, Amir Abdur Rahman had expelled him. He had then come to Chamarkand, which attained great fame on his account.

From Makhfi sahib's place we walked to Jar, a small hamlet located inside a fortress. When we arrived, the gate of the fortress was closed. There being no village nearby, we were wondering what to do. Finally, I told my companion to bang on the gates. A voice from the inside asked us who we were. We replied that we were guests. After a while the gate opened, and they looked us up and down. When they realized that we were not dangerous people, they allowed us in. Once inside the fortress, we went directly to the mosque. Food was brought out for us and we spent the night in the mosque. We left early in the morning and reached the house of Babaray maulana sahib by night. On our way, when someone from the area would join us, I would ask them about Babaray maulana sahib and they would tell me that he was a very great saint. For each group of guests, he would himself take out a cooking pan of clarified butter to have with bread. Babaray maulana sahib was a white-bearded, pious man. As always, when the tribesmen fought the British, Babaray maulana sahib came out in support of the tribesmen for the *ghaza*. He was a great antagonist of the British and was a true *ghazi*. Though he did not know us, we were warmly welcomed. For breakfast, he took us to his *khilwatkhana* and treated us to his special tea. After tea, we took leave of him and left for Chamarkand, which was not far from there. When we reached the base of the mountain and were about to start climbing it, suddenly some herdsmen, who were grazing their cattle, started to target us with stones from their slings. When we realized that they were only a few boys throwing stones at us, we bagan to shout and raised a big hue and cry. They were amused and laughed. This was a big joke for them, but if we had been hit by a stone, we would have been finished. We were to climb the mountain on a narrow, winding, long path. I was not one to climb a mountain. I would get tired quickly and take frequent breaks. Resting frequently, we finally made it to the top. I had heard that, just as the inhabitants of the plains were not good at travelling in the mountains, so were the inhabitants of the mountains not good at travelling in the plains.

Chamarkand

Chamarkand is a very captivating place. Perched on top of a mountain is a spring of clear water, warm in winters and cool in summers. On top of the spring, stands a magnificent maple tree.

Next to it is the mosque of the maulana sahib of Hadda and next to the mosque are the *langarkhana* and a few empty shacks. At the end, there were a few fruit trees near a house. There was a wheat field. In front of the house there were a few flower beds. When he heard our voices, the owner of the house came out. He was a sheikh of the maulana sahib of Hadda, who lived here all alone. He came and greeted us. The sheikh told us tales from the time of the maulana sahib of Hadda and of how he had lived in this place and what enthusiasm there was in everyone during his lifetime. People from far off places would assemble there for the Friday prayer. The maulana sahib was a true *ghazi*. The sheikhs recount strange miracles of their pirs. In my own area, I had heard of the miracles of Manki sahib and of Swat sahib. My father, a *mureed* of Swat sahib, once told me a story that he had heard from a sheikh of Swat sahib's. The story was that Swat sahib was obsessed with the issue of meeting the expenses of the langar, and when one morning, he was getting ready for ablutions for the prayer, he told the sheikh to pick up a *loota* (to clean himself with). When he picked up the *loota*, it miraculously turned out to be a precious stone (*sang-e-paras*). He picked up another. That, too, was a *sang-e-paras;* another one also turned out to be a *sang-e-paras.* At last, he understood that this was an answer to his concern of the night before. So, he fell at the feet of the sahib in respect and sought his forgiveness. His father, too, was convinced of the veracity of this tale, and would tell me that the miracles attributed to the *auliya* were true. Similarly, I had also heard tales of such miracles being performed by the pir – of how a boat, sunk in the river for over twelve years, was retrieved. This was neither in accordance with the word of God, nor the hadith of the Prophet. The maulanas lacked the courage to educate the people; this was all talk with no substance. I did not agree with such tales and told my father that if Swat sahib could work such miracles, why did he collect *shukrana* from the people? The sheikhs of Haji sahib of Torangzai also had similar tales about him and, through these means, deceived the poor Pukhtun nation and exploited it and impressed them with their own greatness. People would also ascribe such tales to me and some would even say that I had long arms and was, therefore, a saint! Some would say that a certain well had become brackish and when I poured a pitcher of water into it, it became sweet miraculously and people from faraway places came to it. They would say that the water of the well had healing powers; that the illnesses of those who drank from it were cured; and those who washed their clothes with it needed no soap. Others would say that, even though food in my house was only cooked for ten people, it would suffice even for a hundred guests, with some left over. In this way, equally strange stories were attributed to me. This is what the common people would say. I would tell my companions that they were *Khudai Khidmatgar,* not sheikhs. That I neither recruited sheikhs nor *mureeds.* We had but one objective towards which we collectively strove.

Sheikh sahib recounted to us many miracles of the maulana sahib of Hadda, but the respect in which we held the maulana was not because of his miraculous powers but because of his unrelenting struggle against the British. The maulana sahib of Hadda was a disciple of Swat sahib's and, as I have mentioned earlier, he was expelled from Afghanistan, from Hadda to Chamarkand, by *Amir* Abdur Rahman. But here, he assisted him secretly in his struggle against the British. This sheikh told us that, in each battle, *Amir* Abdur Rahman would assist him by sending rifles and bullets. Sheikh sahib was a knowledgeable and competent man. To supplement his income, he had kept honey bees and said that all the expense of his house was earned from the honey of the bees. When he brought out food for us, along with bread, he brought out some of the honey. I have never enjoyed the most sumptuous meal of my life, to the extent to which I enjoyed this simple meal. For one, we were hungry, and this village was located way up in the mountain, where the hope of finding food seemed very remote. We liked this place very much because on one side was the Moomand area and it was also close to Bajawar and, on the other side, it was close to Sarkanro and Kunar. In addition, from a strategic point of view, it was very secure, because, at that time, there were no fighter planes. But the place was very small, and our plan could not be implemented there.

Salarzai and Mamoond

We stayed with the sheikh sahib for a night and then went to Salarzai, where we also visited many villages. From Salarzai we proceeded to the Mamoonds. The Salarzai and Mamoond are the two main tribes of Bajawar. They are totally autonomous. In the remaining area of Bajawar there are several small *khanates* and *nawabi* fiefdoms. The land of the Mamoond is very fertile and productive. I liked this area a lot. Its villages are also big. Kitkot and Kabari, when compared to others, are big villages with large, well-built mosques. People have used old tree trunks in their construction but, unlike our villages, they do not have many mosques. Each village has one mosque and the whole village gathers there for prayers. In each mosque, arrangements of running water for ablution have been made and the people are meticulous in offering prayers. The water is very cold and, for people like us, ablutions with it are tough to do. But the mosques are warm.

It was winter, and we spent the night covered only by a *saadar*. We tried not to be recognized because quite a number of students from these areas come to our area for education. In Kitkot and Kabarai, we were suspicious of one or two persons, but we paid no attention to them. But they must have thought why a khan from Paneerak (in Charsadda) came here. Once, someone asked me whether I was the khan of Paneerak and I told him that I was not. We spent the nights in the mosques without engaging in conversation with anyone. We would eat whatever was brought to us. One night, in Kitkot, a white bearded malik invited us to be his guests. He took us inside his living quarters where the women waited upon us and placed a basket of bread before us. It was a very nice house and they were very good hosts. We saw other villages of the Mamoond as well. Finally, we agreed on Zaygai. I preferred this village for a *markaz*. For one, its inhabitants were good and honourable; for another, this area, unlike other areas of the Pukhtuns, was not influenced by the British. It was not in receipt of their *mawajib* and nor had the British got them accustomed to being bribed. They were strong opponents of the British. The British did not give money to the inhabitants of Bajawar, like they did to the other tribes. Here they gave *mawajib* to the khans. So, the common folk were free of the influence of the British. We stayed here for the return of Makhfi sahib and Sindhi sahib. Here, like the past custom of our area, the practice was that, every twenty years, the tribes would gather to redistribute the lands among themselves. They would then have to go and occupy the village which fell to their lot. This was the common practice of the Pukhtuns in the past. But in those areas which came under the direct administration of the British, this practice of *Wesh* was abandoned in favour of a permanent settlement. Those Pukhtun tribes which are free, continue to redistribute their lands amongst themselves every twenty years.

I thought to myself that if we stayed on doing nothing, people would get suspicious. I decided to weave a tale so that I could pass the time until the return of Makhfi sahib. So, I sat in a small room of the mosque for *chehla*. I only left the room for congregational prayers and to answer the call of nature, and that too with my face covered with a *saadar*. The rest of the time I stayed in the small room, repeating to myself selected verses from the Holy *Quran*. I had also formally become a *mureed* of the Sheikh-al-Hind, Mahmud-ul-Hasan sahib. My *chehla* had a profound effect on those people. They thought that I was a saint. They would come to me for blessings and amulets. One day a woman came with her son in her arms. She told me to offer a prayer for her son so that he was weaned from breastfeeding. He was three years old and still breastfed. If she refused to feed him, he would cry and make a nuisance of himself. I told her to finely grind red chilli and sprinkle it on her nipples. Hopefully her son would not insist on breastfeeding again. The woman left and did as I had suggested. The next day she came feeling very happy with a big bowl of honey in her hand. She told me that my prayer had been granted by God and that her son no longer demanded to be breastfed, and although she forced him to do so, he would not suckle. How could he want to do so? She had rubbed finely ground red chillies on her nipples and they burnt his mouth. They considered this a miracle worked by me! The Pukhtuns are, as a race, quick to believe in miracles and people have instilled these things in their minds. Whenever someone has put on the heavy robes and turban of a cleric and assumed an air of piety, people have collected around them, giving them *shukranas*, and served them. But these so-called saints have always made them serve their own purposes.

Even after the *chehla* we waited for Makhfi sahib and Maulana Ubaidullah Sindhi but they did not show up. I was obsessed with worry about them. However, when we learnt that the war had broken out in Europe, we decided to return. Makhfi sahib's cousin accompanied us till Malakand, where he took his leave and I took the train from Dargai to Takht-e-Bahi and then proceeded to my village. After a few days, I met Makhfi sahib. He told me that Sindhi sahib had still not arrived at the place and time that he had fixed with him. He was expecting that either the maulana would come or would send someone to whom we could show the proposed place for the *markaz*, and then leave for Hindustan to collect resources for our work. Meanwhile the World War started and we had to abandon our project. We did not get the opportunity to get together again.

The First World War (1914–1918)

The interest of the Muslims of Hindustan in the war increased when Turkey entered the war on Germany's side. For one, Turkey was a Muslim country and its ruler was considered a *khalifa* of all Muslims and, for another, they thought that our land would also be left to us if Turkey and Germany defeated England. They did not consider the possibility that if the British were defeated at the hands of the Turks and the Germans, then Hindustan would also become a colony of either the Germans or the Turks. How is it possible that the Germans and Turks would be the ones who would be killed in the war, and would leave the land to the Hindustanis? But a nation which is no longer imbued with the spirit of sacrifice will forever look towards another: sometimes to the Germans, sometimes to the Turks and sometimes to the imam. The other weakness of the Muslims of Hindustan was that they were not interested in their internal affairs but were preoccupied with those of foreign lands. They were always immersed in the thought that they should come to the assistance of Turkey. When one cannot free oneself from the yoke of slavery, of what help can one be to any other country? If we really want to help the other Muslims of the world, then it is necessary to free Hindustan from the British because it is on account of Hindustan that they are powerful, and it is because of the power of Hindustan that they conquer other Muslim states. In the war against Afghanistan, all the foot soldiers were Hindustanis, only the officers were British. And the Turks too were defeated by the platoons of Hindustan.

On the advice of Hazrat Maulana Mahmud-ul-Hassan sahib, Sheikh-al-Hind, Hazrat Maulana Ubaidullah Sindhi sahib, Maulvi Saif-ur-Rahman sahib and the Principal of the Arab Fatehpuri *madrassah* of Delhi, were sent to Haji sahib of Torangzai, advising him that he should migrate to the free Tribal Areas, raise the tribesmen against the British and light the fire of insurrection on all the frontiers of British Hindustan, and also prepare Afghanistan to enter the war on the side of the Turks and the Germans and start a *ghaza* against the British. Their objective was that if the British were to take their forces to oppose the Turks and Germans, they would be left weak by opposing them and would be defeated and expelled from Hindustan. And if the British were to leave their forces in Hindustan to cope with them, they would then be left weak in opposition to the Turks and Germans, who would defeat them, and we would be released from our subjugation. Even before the start of the war, we were thinking of establishing a *markaz* either in the free Tribal Areas, to oppose the British, or to create an alliance with Afghanistan. When the war began and the British suffered reverses in different places, we began to think that we too should do something. We should either emigrate to the free Tribal Areas or to Afghanistan. We had not yet come to a decision when Maulvi Saif-ur-Rahman sahib arrived and brought the message of the Sheikh-al-Hind and his companions. So, we all got ready to emigrate. Haji Sahib left for Buner in the dead of night. Makhfi sahib, Mohtamim sahib, Maulvi Abdul Aziz sahib and Maulvi Fazl-e-Rabbi sahib also accompanied him. I stayed behind to maintain a link between them and their accomplices in Hindustan and ensure that they got assistance when needed.

The *Hijrat* of Haji Sahib

The government created chaos in the country when it heard of Haji sahib's departure, because his departure at this point was fraught with danger. The government appointed senior officers to investigate why Haji sahib had left. I spread the rumour that Haji sahib had been warned by a senior government officer that he was to be arrested on account of the *khilafat*, which is why Haji sahib left in the dead of night. The government was intending to do exactly this. The Criminal Investigation Department (CID) also came for me, to inquire about who this officer was, who had informed Haji sahib of his impending arrest. What could I tell them? When this rumour died down, I went to Buner to find out how Haji sahib and his companions were managing. I went secretly but did not know whether my departure remained unknown to the government or not, because it was quite difficult for people like me to conceal their movements from the British government. When I arrived in Buner, I found that Haji sahib had gone on a tour with his companions. The place which the Pukhtuns of Buner had given to Haji sahib as a serai was a beautiful place. There was a big hillock beside which was an irrigated stretch of land. The hillock was not suited for habitation, but it was well suited for Haji sahib. The people of Buner had gathered a lot of wood and other materials to build houses. I was of the view that the house for Haji sahib should be built here.

My Travel to Buner

Haji sahib was in Pacha Kilay, where the shrine of Pir Baba was. We joined the people who were going to the shrine. Once in Pacha Kilay, we called on Haji sahib. A lot of people had gathered to see him. They were our companions and Haji sahib's eldest son was also with them. The people were talking about *ghaza* and jihad. Bacha Gul was talking in whispers when the time for the afternoon meal approached. Haji sahib was caught up in the crowd. Bacha Gul and I disengaged ourselves from the crowd, hoping that we would have our meal and discuss matters. In the entire area, the local people had cooked food for their guests according to their means. We crossed the stream to the houses across it, where arrangements for our meal had been made. There we sat down in a *hujra*, alone. Our hosts brought us freshly baked loaves of leavened bread and chicken cooked in *ghwaree* in *kalukhani* soup plates. It was a lovely meal. I have had many sumptuous meals in my own area but this was delicious. The water and climate of Buner were also very good for the health. No matter how much we ate, it would be digested quickly. I used to have three meals a day and even then I would be hungry. After lunch we got away from the crowd and began to discuss the events. During these discussions I learnt that the religious elders of this area, the *syeds*, the maulanas, the *mians* and the saints were not too happy with the coming of Haji sahib to Buner because they had lost some of their importance in the eyes of the people. So, they wanted to create conditions that would make him leave. To do so, they started a campaign amongst the people for *ghaza* and jihad on the one hand, and on the other, a silent propaganda campaign amongst the people, that if these people had actually come to wage a jihad, then they should be doing so. But if they had come for trade, hoping that, in addition to their property in the plains, they would also acquire some in the hills, then this was a totally different matter. So, Bacha Gul said that, in this manner, they had compromised their standing and Haji sahib was also of the view that it had now become necessary to start a jihad, because the nation was ignorant and the propaganda against them had been done in such a fashion that jihad had now been instilled in their hearts. If we do not wage jihad, these people would no longer have faith in us and they would not cooperate with us to achieve the objective for which we had come. I, however, did not agree with this assessment and felt that, in the present circumstances, the declaration of jihad would do incalculable damage to our cause. So, I made a plea to Haji sahib and our other companions not to pay attention to what people were saying. This was nothing but the talk of selfish people who had no concern with jihad. They thought that under the shade of a big tree, freshly planted saplings do not prosper. And so, for this reason, they were bent on removing him from the scene, one way or the other, in order to leave the field open to themselves. It had become necessary to face them and to make them understand in clear terms that they alone were no match for the British and nor did they have the necessary wherewithal for the purpose. Therefore, it was important to carry out a reconnaissance of the free tribesmen, get them to join us, organize them to stand against the British, and arrange quality arms for them and prepare them for war. This would help us gather strength and once this was done, we could then face the British in jihad. Like the rest of the free tribesmen, the Pukhtuns of Buner did not possess either the required arms, nor did they have any training. So, if we were to start the operations only with them, we would not succeed in our objectives. But the adverse propaganda had had such an impact on Haji sahib that he was not prepared to listen to my advice.

The Scheming of the British in Buner

The British had a big hand in this adverse propaganda. Firstly, they wanted Haji Sahib to return to Torangzai, and for this, they dispatched a big *jirga* of the khans and the elders of the area to him. On the other hand, they waged a propaganda campaign against him, compelling him to return; and if he did not return before the other tribesmen joined him, operations would begin. I spent two or three days with him and then returned to my village. After a few days I heard of the declaration of the jihad by Haji sahib. There was no one to compete with the power of the British. For a day or two, he put up a slight resistance but lacked the ability to continue. The British had distributed a lot of money amongst the tribesmen to catch him alive. For this, they had even found volunteers and when they were close to getting hold of him, Haji sahib learnt of this and escaped to Swat overnight, and from there crossed over to Bajawar and finally to the Moomand territory of Srakamar, where he took up residence. Haji sahib agreed with my view, but the propaganda against him had spread to such an extent that public opinion did not permit him to act on my advice. It is very difficult to combat public opinion. Combating adverse propoganda can only happen when there is a group of strong, selfless, like-minded people who have the confidence of the masses; of people that rise to tour the area and explain to the masses the reality of the situation at hand. But here, there was neither such a dedicated group and nor had anyone worked in this manner before; and nor had any opportunity to do so arisen. Such a group can only be formed after an earnest effort. Haji sahib fled with the same haste with which he had gone to Buner. The maulanas, the *mians* and the British were successful in their strategy.

The *Madrassahs* Were Proscribed

Instead of being harmed, the British benefitted from this turmoil. For one, they captured Buner, and they also got an opportunity to ban all the *Islami madrassahs* that we had established. The teachers and organizers were imprisoned. They also imprisoned those who used to collect donations for the *madrassahs* and looked after their management. The truth was that these *madrassahs* did not belong to Haji sahib but to the nation and were run with the resources and management of the people. However, to counter the adverse propaganda of the *maulanas*, we had appointed Haji sahib as the patron of these *madrassahs*.

The government meted out extremely harsh and cruel treatment to the teachers and organizers. They were sent to the jail in Dera Ismail Khan. From the point of view of climate and the treatment of prisoners, the Dera Ismail Khan jail was considered the worst in the province. Prisoners were bound in heavy fetters and were used like bullocks for hard labour to grind wheat, extract oil and tied to Persian wheels to draw water from wells. They had their beards shaved, were beaten up and shamed. In those days, the food given to prisoners was such that, let alone human beings, even animals would not eat it. It was not more that six or seven years later that I myself was jailed there in connection with the *khilafat* movement. The trousers I was given to wear were so short that they were only up to my knees; and the shirt was so short that when I would prostrate myself in prayer, my back would be revealed. They would tailor all the clothes to one size, and God help the prisoner who was tall and fat! The food was such that, even though there were no dogs in jail, a cat before which I placed it, along with the curry, refused to eat it.

Apart from this, the sheikhs and acquaintances of Haji sahib were also arrested. The police were authorized to arrest any of Haji sahib's relatives, friends and acquaintances as they deemed fit. They created such fear in the hearts of the people and terrorized them so much that whoever was addressed as 'Sheikh sahib' would reply, 'Your father must be a sheikh!' Prominent sheikhs of Haji sahib refused to acknowledge themselves as such and turned their backs on him; and some amongst them were such cowards that they began to speak ill of him and disgrace him. All this was so that the British would find out and they would be spared the rigours of imprisonment. It was a shame that the tyranny and injustice of British rule should increase the fear in their hearts and not awaken the desire and enthusiasm to put up a resistance to it. These were all religious people, and for them, the beard was an essential pillar of faith. Even the shaving of their beards did not ignite their honour to retaliate. In jail, neither the azan nor collective prayers were allowed. All this was rectified when we, the *Khudai Khidmatgar*, entered the jails. Then nobody would shave off anyone's beard and the azan and the congregational prayers would be observed five times a day. The quality of food improved, the use of prisoners to grind wheat, draw water or extract oil from oil-seeds, all came to an end. Not a lump of *gura* or an ounce of *ghwaree* was allowed in jail. For one lump of sugar, a prisoner could be condemned to solitary confinement. We managed to reform all this. I understood that the more the religious lot were oppressed, the more scared and gutless they became; and, in political prisoners, the more they were tyrannized, the more their political courage and guts increased. All these benefits for the nation's prisoners were obtained due to the sacrifices of the *Khudai Khidmatgar.* These reforms were brought about when the government of the *Khudai Khidmatgar* came to power.

In those days, orders for my arrest were also issued. However, I was fortunate as a few days before this, the DSP of the Charsadda police, Hafiz Zain-ul-Abidin, who was from Amritsar, had visited our village. Coincidentally, he and I had exchanged notes about the functioning of our *madrassah.* He told me that they, too, like us, had established a national *madrassah* in Amritsar, the expenses of which were met from the sale of the hides of sacrificial animals and if we also made a request to our people to gift us the hides, we would be spared the trouble of collecting donations. I asked him, 'What are your intentions? You want me to get killed by the maulanas? Here the maulanas are the sole beneficiaries of the hides of sacrificial animals; they would rather be prepared to get skinned than to give somebody the hides of these animals'. He assured me that he would assist us in this matter. I told him that it might be possible with his help. If he were to tell the khans and maliks that, instead of giving the hides to the maulanas, they should give the hides to these national *madrassahs* because they would be blessed for this, they may agree. This was because the word of an officer had a great effect on our khans, maliks and maulanas. During this discussion, he came to know that all these *madrassahs* belong to the nation and Haji sahib had nothing to do with them. Haji sahib's name had been associated with them only to keep the maulanas quiet and to counter the propaganda against us. It is for this reason that I was not arrested, but the *madrassah* was shut down and proscribed and, except for Maulvi Abdul Aziz sahib, who had accompanied Haji sahib, all the other teachers were arrested. They were freed almost a year later but the poor souls had been so frightened by then that if anyone mentioned the words sheikh, *madrassah* or the *haji* to them, they were ready to fight. After some time, when the battle between Haji sahib and the British took place in a Moomand territory, these people were arrested once again and remained imprisoned for about nine months. Thus, they would be arrested whenever battles between the Haji and the British took place. The British were under the impression that Haji sahib, with the backing of the sheikhs, wanted this land to be freed from the clutches of their slavery. Little did they know that these ignorant people neither knew of the blessings of freedom and nor were they aware that they were the slaves of the British. They were just clerics with a sole aim in life: to earn a place in heaven for themselves by merely turning their rosary; and the kind of heaven that was sought was one full of *hoors*, *ghilman* and rivers of honey, milk and wine flowing in it, with many kinds of fruit which did not even need to be plucked as it would itself fall into open mouths. They had been told by many religious luminaries preaching from the pulpit that this world belonged to the kafirs. The Muslims here would be in a pitiable condition: hungry, thirsty, naked, humiliated and degraded. They would, however, live it up in the next world. The other world belonged to the Muslims. And they accepted this. No one gave any thought to the question as to whether religion was meant for this world, or for the next, or for both. In our daily prayers, we first ask God for welfare in this world. Moreover, no one has ever returned from the other world to tell us about it. But the history of this world is before us. Those to whom a religion has been given, and they have accepted it and acted upon its injunctions, have prospered in this world with respect and governed themselves, and have been blessed with a life of peace and prosperity. Can't you see by looking at the Arabs and what their condition was before Islam? And when Islam came and they acted on its injunctions, all aspects of their lives were transformed. On account of Islam they became the owners of government, wealth and standing. Just cast a glance on each aspect of the lives of the Muslims of that time and think about it, and take note of what these self-proclaimed contractors of the faith have to say, and judge for yourselves whether the Islam that they propagate is the Islam of Allah, His Prophet (PBUH), or that of the rich of today? As for what they proclaim, do they do so for the sake of God or for the sake of the rich?

The Emigration of the Haji Sahib to the Moomand Territory
The departure of Haji sahib from Buner to the Moomand territory benefitted us greatly in one way, in that he was now more easily accessible and we could ask about his welfare more frequently. This is because most of the people of the Moomand tribe have two homes – one up in the hills and the other in the plains with us, in Hashtnagar. There is daily movement of people going to and fro, who inform us of the goings-on up there, and them of the

happenings here. Buner was distant, and, for another, not many of our people travelled there.

On account of the start of the First World War and of Haji sahib's *hijrat* to the Moomand territory, our travels to Hindustan came to an end. All my companions had left with Haji sahib. The British too had created such conditions in the land that I could not gather enough courage to visit Hindustan. Secondly, the Sheikh-al-Hind and Maulana Mahmud-ul-Hassan sahib had emigrated to Saudi Arabia and gone to Mecca for Haj. There, the Sharif of Mecca, on the advice of the British, and in opposition to the Turks, had signed a fatwa against the maulanas. He had also put pressure on the Sheikh-al-Hind to sign this, but he had refused to do so. Hence, the Sharif of Mecca had the Sheikh-al-Hind arrested and handed over to the British and he, along with his companions, was then detained on the island of Malta. Maulana Ubaidullah Sindhi had also emigrated from Hindustan and arrived in Afghanistan. Along with him some nationalist Muslims and Hindus had also emigrated and had established an independent government of Hindustan in Kabul under Raja Mahinder Pratap. Those who were left behind could not establish contact with us, again, because of the fear of the British. Only once did they send me twenty-three pounds by mail, which amounted to four hundred and fifty rupees, which I then sent to Haji sahib. They did not come to the assistance of Haji sahib in any manner. The truth is that they had promised Haji sahib complete assistance, and he was in real need of it. My father had given me sixty *jareebs* of land in Muhammad Narai for my subsistence, which I used to farm myself. Whatever the income from that land was, I would send it to Haji sahib. But this would be sent via Bacha Gul, Haji sahib's eldest son, who would not hand it over to him. Haji sahib and his companions were left penniless. They had no means of income and, like the other sheikhs, were dependent on whatever was cooked in the langar. It would have been appropriate for Haji sahib to have made some arrangements to establish a *madrassah* for them. They would have taught in it and the children of the area would have acquired some religious knowledge. Plus, the people would be trained in preaching and could have spread out across the area. They could have gathered like-minded people around them, binding and organizing all the tribesmen with a common thread. At last, Mohtamim Taj Muhammad sahib rose to his feet in a gathering of the sheikhs and, standing on the *mimbar,* told them that they were occupied night and day with thoughts of their langar and that there was a need for them to show a little concern for the welfare, education and the reform of their people as well. The poor man had hardly said this when the sheikhs did not allow him to continue and pulled him down from the *mimbar.* This group of companions consisted of capable men who had left their hearths and homes, rendered countless sacrifices and gone to the Moomand territory to accomplish a mission. For them, unlike the sheikhs, the food from the langar was not their sole concern and neither were they waiting for the joys of heaven. Between their heaven and that of the sheikhs, and the path to their heaven and that of the sheikhs, there was a vast difference. It seemed as if Bacha Gul had conspired with the British and was creating misunderstandings between Haji sahib and his companions. Our companions could not spend their lives in idleness, and they lost hope. The British, too, were making efforts to uproot them from this place. Makhfi sahib consequently left for Afghanistan and Maulvi Fazl-e-Rabbi sahib followed him. Maulvi Abdul Aziz sahib left for Swat, while Maulvi Taj Muhammad sahib went to Kamangara and stayed there alone. From there he joined the *lakhkar,* formed by *Amir* Amanullah Khan, consisting of the Mangal tribe of Paktia, to fight against the *lakhkar* of the *gud* maulana of Shorosh, which was in opposition to the *Amir* of Afghanistan. He was subsequently killed in the battle in Khost. Maulvi Abdul Aziz sahib then came to Swat.

The Problem of the Ruler of Swat

In those days, the Kohistan maulana sahib had come to Swat to save the Swatis from the oppression and tyranny of the Nawab of Dir, who had occupied a large part of Swat and had proclaimed Abdul Jabbar Shah, a *syed* from Sitana, the ruler of Swat. The Kohistan maulana sahib was the disciple of Haji sahib of Torangzai. He should have selected a local Swati as the ruler of Swat. In fact, the appropriate course of action for the Kohistan maulana sahib would have been to have established, in the footsteps of the inhabitants of Madina, a democratic government, in accordance with the wishes of the people. But it appears that because of the internal feuds of the Pukhtuns, their factionalism, enmities and lack of unity in their ranks, he could not do so.

The history of the Pukhtuns is replete with such events, that whenever such an opportunity has presented itself, they have, instead of one of them, imposed a *mian* or a maulana to rule them. And those whom they have imposed on themselves have, in time, exploited and been harsh to them. This is the reason why in a heaven-like territory they have not been able to satisfy their hunger with the output of maize, but continue to be hungry, thirsty, deprived and illiterate. Until such time as they come to regard the honour of their nation as their own and its dishonour as their dishonour, they will not be able to change their condition. The position and standing that the developed nations have attained cannot be achieved by mystic exercises. In those nations, honest, dedicated and selfless leadership has been born, that has felt the destruction of their nation. They have shunned the luxuries of life and exhorted their people, united and awakened them, and thus put them on the path of prosperity.

Syed Abdul Jabbar Shah ruled for a while but then got caught up in the controversy of being a *Qadiani*. I do not wish to argue the point of whether he was in fact a *Qadiani* or not. If he was one, he must have been one even before he was appointed as the ruler. When they were making him the ruler, why did they not investigate this aspect? The truth was that no one believed that the state of Swat would remain intact. But when it became apparent that it would stay as such, they started this propaganda against *Syed* Abdul Jabbar Shah. The other thing was that the administration of *Syed* Abdul Jabbar Shah was a weak one in which power and authority was exercised by the Kohistan maulana, who was against the British, and so they conspired to replace him with someone who could take this away from him, so that no one in the area could make a move without their consent.

On account of the growing opposition to Abdul Jabbar Shah amongst the common people, the Kohistan maulana was compelled to remove him from the scene and put someone else in his place. It was the ambition of the eldest son of Haji sahib of Torangzai, Bacha Gul sahib, that in place of *Syed* Jabbar Shah, he should become the ruler of Swat, for which he had a good chance. The Kohistan maulana was a devotee of his father and so he arrived on the scene and obtained a promise from him to act accordingly. He returned to the Moomand territory with the intention of raising a *lakhkar* of four or five thousand men. Maulvi Abdul Aziz, who was greatly annoyed with Bacha Gul and knew him intimately, was, at the time, a companion of the Kohistan maulana sahib, over whom he exercised great influence. In fact, he was sort of a personal secretary to him and the Kohistan maulana would consult with him in all matters. So, before Bacha Gul could return from the Moomand territory, Maulvi Abdul Aziz convinced the Kohistan maulana sahib and made him proclaim *Mian* Gul Abdul Wadood as ruler of Swat. When Bacha Gul arrived, everything was settled and *Mian* Gul Abdul Wadood was firmly in the saddle. At that time, the policy of the British with respect to the free Tribal Areas had undergone a change: they now desired to create small fiefdoms and *khanates* in each tribe, and through them, control the tribesmen against rebellions and insurrections. This was the reason that gaining control over a few nawabs and *khans* was a relatively easy task for the British. Each one would, out of fear of the British, be their sycophant. For this purpose, the British gave the khan of Khar a lot of money and means to attack Nawagai and capture it. If he were to be successful in this venture, the British would accept him as the nawab of the area and give him a large *jagir*. The British understood that Nawagai was the gateway to this area and whoever was in possession of it would also be the arbiter of the faith of the people. The tribesmen, too, were aware of this and that is why many battles took place between them and the khan of Khar. But the khan of Khar failed to capture Nawagai. Similarly, the British spent a lot of money among the Afridis, the Wazirs, the Mahsuds, and the Bhittanis, but remained unsuccessful in the creation of the *nawabis* and the *khanates*.

Mian Gul Abdul Wadood strengthened his position and chased the Kohistan maulana away. Maulvi Abdul Aziz sahib had played a major role in his becoming the ruler and was still ready to assist him further, so he remained loyal to him. In those days, I went to Saidu to see Maulvi Abdul Aziz sahib and spent one or two nights with him. I also attended some sessions with *Mian* Gul sahib. A *jirga* from Swat had also called on *Mian* Gul sahib at the time. I also took part in their discussions. During the discussions, I came to know that these people feared the British more than they feared God. The buildings that can be seen in Saidu today did not exist at the time. There was just a small fortress of mud in which *Mian* Gul,

Maulvi sahib and all their other companions lived. Special guests were also put up there. I had also visited Saidu in my youth and spent a night there. At that time, I knew very little and did not fully comprehend the essence of Islam. I used to believe that shrines and saints interceded with God for the granting of our wishes and demands. The people believed that Pir Baba (a saint) granted one's wishes. I, too, along with some companions, had gone to the shrine of Pir Baba with this in mind, and then from there, over the Jawari Pass, had crossed over to Swat. We visited the shrine of Swat Babaji and spent the night in Saidu.

The Atrocities of the British

This was the situation prevailing in the upper parts of the land. The situation in the lower parts was that the British had terrorized the people to such an extent that they could not breathe a word of truth. As for the government, if it suspected that anyone had love for his land, people, or Islam, they would pressurize them, and if this did not succeed, they offered them appointments, titles and money. If this, too, did not work, then they would be jailed. They would be made to grind corn, provide labour to run oil-expellers and subjected to torture which even an uncivilized nation would be ashamed to inflict on animals. There has been propaganda that the British were a just people. I acknowledge that they were just but only in those matters in which their own self-interest was not involved. The question of justice did not arise when their political interests were involved. The spies and informers of the British were spread out all over the land. Whatever was discussed in the streets, *hujras* and mosques, was relayed to the police. The police had full authority to identify a so-called culprit, and when this was done, no one would question the veracity of the fact. The police was also dishonest, particularly that of the Punjab, which, in its efforts to please the Englishmen, carried out such atrocities that no one before them had ever done.

The khans, maliks and maulanas would convene different *jirgas*, some out of fear, some in expectation of rewards, some for government appointments. Ever ready to serve, they were recruited, and used to say that God has directed, 'to obey God and His Prophet; and obey those in authority' and that the British are those placed in authority over us, and to obey them is a religious obligation. This was so even though in the *ayat* of the Holy *Quran*: along with the words 'those in authority,' the words 'from you' have been clearly mentioned. In other words, 'those in authority' must be from amongst you, one of us.

It was through such means that the maulanas would find *Quranic* justifications to obey the British. In the *Quran*, God speaks about the religious scholars of the Jews who, for the sake of a little money and satisfaction of their personal desires, would interpret the *ayats* of the *Torah* and the *Zaboor* to suit themselves. Every religion, when it falls into the hands of self-seeking people, is no longer imbued with the initial spirit of revelation. It then becomes the religion of the moneyed class and exists in mere form.

Saadullah Khan of Umerzai played a major role in this work in our area. For one, he was a khan, and for another, was also an employee of the British. He would occasionally host a lunch and gather the khans, maulanas and the poets, and organize *jalsas* to please the British, sing their praises and persuade the people to cooperate with them. One day, I was sitting in my *hujra* and reading maulana Abul Kalam's *Al-Balag*, when I heard that there was to be another *jalsa* in Umerzai. Maulana Abul Kalam had written a very illuminating and learned lead-article, so, I thought I must go and read this out to the people attending the *jalsa*. But I could not muster enough courage to do so. The strange thing was that the maulanas of the free tribesmen would assert that jihad against the British was mandatory for Muslims, while those of the settled areas would, with equal force, say obedience and cooperation with the British was necessary. Like the maulanas of Palestine and those of Madina, one group would give a fatwa of one kind, and another of another kind. In one religion, there could not possibly be place for two different interpretations of the same subject. But the truth is that today the moneyed classes, on account of their wealth, have taken over control of the faith, and the faith is no longer the true, unadulterated, pristine faith revealed by God. The true faith of God is service to mankind, love, justice, tolerance and honesty. In this lies the benefit of humanity. What passes off today as religion is no more than a game that the rich have created for themselves, to attain their selfish objectives. The truth is that all heavenly religions are truthful, and the *Quran* proclaims that 'all God-conscious people shall repose belief in this *Quran*, too.' And, if there have been other books revealed by God, they would have faith in them too. So, I do not understand why there are so many quarrels and wars in the name of religion.

5

The Rowlatt Act and Us

The War in Europe

WHEN THE FIRST WORLD WAR REACHED AN IMPASSE IN EUROPE, I thought of going to Kabul to ask for assistance from the Afghan government. It was the time of *Amir* Habibullah Khan's rule and I was convinced that his was a free and powerful government and would help us in our struggle against the British. So, I decided to make the excuse that I was going to Afghanistan for business. Although my father agreed to the idea, my mother opposed it. Finally, I managed to persuade her. My father promised me some money for the trip. I decided to take Jumadar Ajabullah Khan as a companion, a worldly and clever man from our village. He had also served in the intelligence department of the British and had visited these countries. I applied for a business permit but was not given the permission and so this visit could not take place. During the war years, there were often skirmishes between the British and the free Tribal Areas. But the tribesmen never agreed on a common strategy and were never united. For this reason, the British were never at a disadvantage. When the Moomand would attack the British, the Wazir, Masood and Afridis would sit tight. And when the Afridis and British fought each other, the Moomand, Wazir and Masood would be unaware of this. Even when the Wazir fought the British, the Masood, who inhabited the same area, would not be prepared to fight, let alone the Moomand and the Afridis. Each one saw this as the other's war and was not bothered. It would have been ideal if all the tribesmen had joined hands as one movement, been trained as such and revolted together. If the British had then gathered their forces to counter them, they would have had trouble fighting the Turks and the Germans in the

War, and the tribesmen would have met with great success. But the World War ended with a British victory and the defeat of the Turks and the Germans.

The Epidemic and the Death of My First Wife

On account of the war in Europe, the world was struck by a widespread epidemic of influenza. In Hindustan, too, the epidemic took a heavy toll. This was such a strange epidemic that it would invariably affect the young, both men and women, and not a single member would be spared once it entered a household. In smaller villages, the dead would be left unattended, as there would be no one left to bury them. I was the first to be affected by the disease, but somehow God cured me. After me, Ghani, my five year old son, was afflicted. Ghani was a lovely child; his mother was very fond of him and she cried inconsolably. One day, Ghani's condition became critical; his mother was seated at his bedside with his head in her hands. I had offered the evening prayers and was sitting on the prayer mat. I was praying and gazing upon Ghani who was lying unconscious, when suddenly his mother got up and placed his head upon the pillow and walked around the bed and stood behind his head and raised her hands in prayer, crying, 'Oh God! Place his illness on my head and cure this child.' It was a strange miracle of God. The next day she fell ill, and the intensity of her illness increased everyday, while Ghani got better by the day. Ghani was cured, and his mother died. Her children were left to me. At the time my other son, Wali, was three years old and their sister was a year old.

So many people died in the villages that people could not attend all the burials. From early morning till late evening, we were busy digging graves. With great difficulty, we would sometimes complete the task, but often some bodies remained to be buried. Many of the dead were buried without a shroud. For the care of the dead, we set up a fund with which we bought cloth used for burials. Even in these circumstances, some people would approach us and fraudulently take away cloth for shrouds. Some crafty people would cry and deceive us. Finally, we arranged to send the shrouds through our own people. We also decided for the provision of medicines. In the initial days of the outbreak, no one had any idea of the cure, but later, when the disease was prolonged, the doctors and the *hakeems* found a cure for it, and we would make the medicine and dispense it to the patients. In the war, too, our people suffered greater casualties than the others. Whose war was it and who suffered the casualties? The benefit and loss was someone else's and it was we who fought. I am of the view that we were little more than paid assassins. For the sake of money, we had left our homes to kill others. We were not conscious of the need for freedom of our own land and honour to have fought the British, or at least to have remained aloof in our homes and left the British to face the Turks and the Germans on their own. Let alone the Germans, we fought the Muslim Turks on the side of the British and won the war for them. In compensation for the victory, the British gave us the Rowlatt Bill, which was a cruel and tyrannical law, and this calamity befell us as a punishment from God.

The Rowlatt Act[12]
Gandhi, in response to the promise of the British, that they would grant Hindustan self-government when they won the war, had extended assistance to them. However, after the victory in war, let alone fulfilling their promise, they enacted the Rowlatt Act in 1919. Mahatma Gandhi was disappointed and raised his voice against the Act. Even some Englishmen were loud in their condemnation of this. All over Hindustan, a movement and agitation against this black law was initiated. Various *jalsas* and *jaloos* were held. Many railway stations and official installations were burnt. The British too exercised little restraint and killed innumerable demonstrators by resorting to firing. They imprisoned them, degraded and humiliated them. Till this time, in our area, political *jalsas* were unknown and nobody knew how to organize them. Although, a movement did exist for education and the building of *madrassah*, that too had been banned during the war years.

One evening, I was eating my dinner when I heard a dhol. When I listened carefully, the drummer was proclaiming that the next day a *jalsa* against the Rowlatt Act would be held at the *Eidgah* of Haji sahib of Torangzai, adjacent to his mosque near Umerzai. I did not find out who had planned the *jalsa*. The next morning, we had our breakfast and we left for Haji sahib's mosque. The inhabitants of my village had never heard the word '*jalsa*' before. It seemed a strange thing to them. So, many people went to attend it. On investigating

I learnt that the call for this *jalsa* was made by Muhammad Akram Khan, a khan of our village. I also found out that, at the time of the announcement, a police official had come to the village and had a heated discussion with the khan. The khan made the announcement out of spite for the police. There could not have been a greater contradiction between the khan and the announcement. We saw that Akram Khan did not attend the *jalsa* and learnt later that he was with Ralph Griffith sahib, the assistant commissioner of Mardan. Most of the popular khans and prominent maulanas had come to attend the *jalsa*. I got up and told the crowd that it was necessary to appoint an elderly person to preside and regulate matters in such meetings. The people replied that I should be president. Although I repeatedly requested that an elderly person should be appointed, the people persisted and made me the president. The common people did not understand the meaning of the term 'president'. When they returned from the *jalsa,* they spread the word that I had become the *Bacha* of the Pukhtuns. At the time, we did not understand what speeches were all about and so, whatever little we had learnt from the newspapers, we conveyed to the people. At the end, another khan proposed that this was a *jalsa* of the inhabitants of our village Uthmanzai only and there would be a *jalsa* of the whole area on the same day, the following week. From the point of view of speeches, this could hardly be called a *jalsa*, but from the point of view of the impact it had, it can be said that it aroused a lot of enthusiasm and love in the people.

Our *Jalsa*

To plan for the forthcoming *jalsa,* many people offered their services. I too mounted my pony and toured the villages of Doaba and Hashtnagar. To arrange the *jalsa*, I went to Daulatpura, a famous village of Doaba. There I met with the main khan who promised that he would attend the *jalsa*. He told me a very interesting but strange tale. He said that a *samsara* had got into the habit of visiting the house of a man in a village and drinking milk. His wife told him that the *samsara* was being a nuisance and asked what should she do about it. He himself had been frightened by the *samsara* but replied that it was a saint and to do nothing to it. One day, the *samsara* was drinking milk from the pot when the woman picked up her *sobarlai* and beat it to death, although she was worried that the *samsara* was her husband's saint and wondered what he would do to her. She told her husband that she had committed a grave sin and wanted his forgiveness. The husband asked her to go on. She told him that the saintly *samsara* had been killed by her. He asked her where it was. She showed it to him; at which point he fell upon it and tore the dead *samsara* to pieces and told the wife that there was nothing saintly about it, only that he was afraid of it.

Everyone was enthused with national fervour. The khan was an official, *jirga-nasheen* khan, but had developed revulsion for the British. I invited both the khans and the common people to attend the *jalsa*. On the day of the *jalsa*, more than a hundred thousand people assembled. Women in the thousands fetched water in their pitchers from the river for the participants. During the proceedings of the *jalsa*, *Mian* Akbar Shah Kakakhel was sent to me by the government. He gave me the message of the chief commissioner, to the effect that the law, which was in force in the Sarhad province, was like the father of the Rowlatt Act and crueller than it, and that it would be more appropriate for us to raise our voice against this rather than the Rowlatt Act so that the government could take note for remedial action. In this way the rigour of the Rowlatt Act would not be felt by us. But, what assistance had been given to us by Hindustan in the repeal of this law that we are now assisting it against the Rowlatt Act? He added that the chief commissioner promised to reconsider this law and would do whatever was recommended. I replied, '*Mian* sahib, Hindustan did not come to our assistance in any way and did not discharge its moral duty. It is also our moral duty to join our voice with its call against the Rowlatt Act. Everyone is obliged to act according to his own conscience.' *Mian* sahib realized that I was not falling for his bait, and so he said that if I were to permit him, he too would like to speak at the *jalsa*. I told him to go ahead. In his speech, he inadvertently said that the government occupied the position of respect as one respects their parents. This did not go down well with the people and they booed him to sit down. When I looked at the crowd it was really enthused and was furious with *Mian* sahib. If I were not present and if I had not obtained a promise of non-violence from the people earlier, God knows what would have become of poor *Mian* sahib. On the one hand, I was amazed at the enthusiasm of the people and, on the other, at the worship of the British by the *mians*. The people also entrusted the presidentship of this *jalsa* to me. We did not know how to deliver speeches. Often, we wrote a speech down and then read it out to the people. Abbas Khan, may God bless him, was a good friend to whom I had given a written speech. But when his turn came, he was shaking. He kept on repeating 'This black law.' I whispered to him to proceed but he was shaking and replied that darkness had clouded his eyes and he was unable to see. Finally, he sat down. This was the state of our speech making. But despite this, the *jalsa* was a big success. Resolutions were passed and dispatched to the government and the newspapers.

There was an unusual enthusiasm and love amongst the people. Hundreds of women of our village turned up. It was summer and they would go to the river and fetch drinking water for the participants. Two people from our village did not attend the *jalsa* – Khan Bahadur Muhammad Umer Khan and Muhammad Akram Khan, who was responsible for the publicity of the first *jalsa*. Instead of attending the *jalsa*, Khan Bahadur Muhammad Umer Khan had gone to Mardan to call on the assistant commissioner, Griffith sahib, thinking he would gain face with the British. But neither did he gain face with the British and nor did he save face amongst his own people. Griffith was of no assistance to them and they too were arrested along with us. Till the very end we did not understand why Akram Khan had publicized the *jalsa* against the Rowlatt Act. But the people used to say that he wanted his *tarboors* and the khan to oppose the British so that they could be destroyed. However, he himself got caught up in his scheming. This *jalsa* at Uthmanzai ignited a fire among the Pukhtuns and created a great deal of enthusiasm in their hearts. Another *jalsa* was arranged in Tehkal, organized by Arbab Raza Khan. He had informed the entire area and invited us as well. We left early in the morning on the day of the *jalsa*. When we crossed the bridge at Sardaryab, Ashiq, a fruit merchant from Peshawar city, seated in a tonga, met us. He motioned to us; we reined in the horses of the tonga and got down. He took Abbas Khan, Bhaijan, Ahmad Shah *Ustaz* and me aside and told us that the war between the Afghans and the British had started in Afghansitan, and that martial law had been imposed in the entire province the previous night. The *jalsa* at Tehkal was banned and he had brought some communication from the government of Afghanistan. We were to take these and distribute them on this side of the border. He handed over the papers to our companions and returned to the city, while we returned to the village. During these days, Qazi Shahkirullah had been commissioned by the British to tour our area and find out who was against and who was for the British. So, he would tour the villages and deliver hard hitting speeches against the British in the *hujras* and the mosques. One day, seated in our *hujra,* he told us that he had been sent by the British on intelligence work during the First World War and had been appointed with a general on a warship in the Gulf. There was a village of the Arabs on the shore. An Englishman was sent to it through the auspices of the British ambassador. The inhabitants of the village killed the Englishman. When the news of the murder came, the ship was ordered to bombard the village. When that village was razed to the ground, the troops were ordered to go and find out whether any men or women were still alive, and if so, they were to be killed. He also accompanied them. When he arrived in the village, he saw that a woman had been martyred while breast feeding her child. The condition of the woman and the child affected him such that when they returned to the ship, though he wanted to talk to his officer, he also did not want to see his face because he was so angry. He told him to get out of his sight. He felt they had destroyed so many Muslims just for the sake of one Englishman. That is when he decided that he would not serve them any longer. He was a kafir, but after this, he became a Muslim.

Similarly, Qazi Shahkirullah sahib toured all the villages of Hashtnagar. The khans, maulanas and the people of Hashtnagar were all opposed to the British. Qazi sahib ascertained everyone's position. He had written to the government only about the position of one of our khans i.e. Muhammad Umer Khan, that no one in the entire area could rival him in his loyalty to the British. On account of this report, Muhammad Umer Khan got a big promotion in his standing with the British. Substantial powers were conferred on him along with the title of 'Khan Bahadur'.

On account of the martial law, our people were frightened because they used to hear of the atrocities of the British in Punjab and Hindustan through the newspapers. We were particularly distressed. Every day, there would be a rumour that the army was coming to surround the village. On hearing these rumours, both the men and women of our village would be very disturbed and great commotion would ensue. To evade arrest, I also could not occupy my house or *hujra*, but would roam around in the village to cheer people up. One night, there was a strong rumour that troops were about to come to the village. Someone informed me that malik Sultan Muhammad Khan, with a few of his armed servants, had set up a post along the road. He had said that since they could not rid themselves of the British and as death only came but once, he was going to confront the troops. I quickly went to him. I saw malik sahib standing, wearing a sword and applauding his servants, who were manning a trench. I called out to him and asked him what he was up to. He replied that this day was the day of reckoning. I then asked him whether he had any guns. He replied that he had five guns. I asked him how many bullets they had and he replied that they had twenty to twenty-five bullets. I then told him that a single gun of the British had that many bullets. How would five guns and twenty bullets face the British? When he heard this, he first became quiet and then instructed the servants that since they were no match for the British, they should saddle his horse! He mounted the horse and fled by night to the free Tribal Areas. Similarly, several khans of our village drew themselves to a side.

My Arrest

I went to the *maira* wasteland on the outskirts of a village, from where, along with Abeedullah Kaka, a former tenant, I proceeded to Kachee-Kopar (located in Malakand Tribal Agency). An outlaw from our village, Murtaza Khan, had also taken refuge there and he also joined us. We left for the village of Speenkhero. There was a post of the border police adjacent to the *banda* of Harichand. As we approached, we were ordered to halt and prove our identity. Fear overtook me as we were also in possession of unlicensed weapons, but Murtaza Khan seemed to know them well. He advanced and informed them that we were friends and we could proceed. When we neared Speenkhero, they separated Murtaza Khan from us and we went ahead. The elder Babaji learnt of our presence and came out to greet and honour us. We spent a night at Speenkhero and left early morning with the intention of going to Afghanistan. The people advised us that it was best for us to take the route through Prang-ghar (Prang mountain). We would be able to cross the river by a *zango* and, via Jalalabad, would proceed straight on to Kabul.

But I was afraid of crossing the river by the *zango* because I was big built and heavy, and was afraid that the ropes of the *zango* would break. I had no intention of travelling this way, but my friends forced me to do so, and so we left for Prang-ghar. When we began climbing the mountain I realized that we, the inhabitants of the plains, were ill suited to mountain travel and I was even worse than my companions. We had hardly covered some distance, when I got exhausted and could not proceed further. Somebody had even showed us the way through Boocho. This was a little longer but was even and the crossing over the river was also across a fjord. So, I proposed that we take this route. We turned back and took the path to Boocho and arrived there late in the day. We went to the *hujra* of Akram Khan, who turned out to be a very good and hospitable man. The next morning, after breakfast, we were about to leave when we were surprised to see my father arrive. He said to me that I should not go and that the deputy commissioner had sent him to inform me that I was not guilty of anything except holding a *jalsa* and that this did not constitute a crime. No action would, therefore, be taken against me. I told my father that martial law had been proclaimed and that the British, not known for their justice even in the most trivial of matters, could not be expected to not act against me when I was accused of organizing a *jalsa* against them. But my father did not give me permission to leave. He was a man of honour and so he trusted the promise of the British. He could not understand their deceit. He told me that the Englishman would not retract from what he had promised him. He forced me to come back with him to the village. When we arrived in Muhammad Narai, he left me there, and himself proceeded to Uthmanzai. I was afraid and did not believe that the British would leave me a free man. So, I would hide all day in the graveyard, a large one near Muhammad Narai, and come home for the night. My whereabouts were not unknown to the British and nor were they unaware of my movements. My father himself had informed them of my return. One day, in the afternoon, when I had come home for lunch and was sitting in the *hujra*, the *thanedar* along with a heavy contingent of policemen arrived and arrested me. The news of my arrest spread like lightning across the area. Whoever heard of it came to Muhammad Narai where my relatives had all assembled in our house. They were wailing and raising a hue and cry. My mother's condition was very bad. The *thanedar* was a good man and allowed me to visit my house. My mother was cursing my father, that if only he had not forced me to return, I would not have been arrested. I tried to console her but she continued to cry. Some people were of the view that I should escape, and that they would engage the police for long enough to allow me to get out of the area. But little did they know that it was martial law and I, to save myself, was not inclined to endanger the safety of other people. My mother embraced me, kissed me, and told me that she had entrusted me in the care of God. I was taken to the thana at Khanmahi, and from there, to Mardan, where I was immediately taken before the superintendent of the police. One *thanedar* and one *komedan* accompanied me; both were in uniform. However, when they entered with me into the Englishman's office, they took off their shoes. In doing this, I thought they degraded themselves. After that they took me to jail. When I was being fettered, they found that the fetters were tight on my feet because I was very big built. No matter how many pairs of fetters they tried, they found that they would not fit my feet. Finally, with great effort and force, they riveted a pair on my feet. They were very tight and clung tightly to the skin. After a short while they took me out of jail and manacled my hands. They seated me in a car. Two Englishmen, one a police officer and the other a civil officer, accompanied me and took me from Mardan to Peshawar. At that time, I realized that during martial law, when the government summons anyone, it was not right for him to give himself up. Giving oneself up is a mistake. I regretted my return but to what avail.

When we arrived in Peshawar, I was taken to the bungalow of the superintendent of police, and made to wait with the police surrounding me. A little later, a boy from our village, who had cut a telephone wire and had been sentenced to two years' imprisonment, was taken inside the superintendent's house and then brought out and taken away. Then I was taken inside. There were ten or twelve Englishmen in the room. As I entered, one asked me whether I had revolted against the government. I responded that I had not revolted against the government. Another one inquired if I had organized *jalsas* against the government. I told them that we had not said anything about revolting against the government in the *jalsa*. Rather, we had voiced a request to the government for this law not to be enforced on us. Another asked that was it not so that I had toured the area and encouraged the people to rise against the government? I replied that I had mostly contacted the khans and that they were all well-wishers of the government. Another asked me whether I had not proclaimed myself '*bacha*.' I replied that no, I had not. He said, 'Is it not a fact that the people addressed you as *Bacha*?' I replied that those who called me *bacha* were unaware and ignorant people. These poor, rustic souls could not differentiate between a president and a *bacha*. I was the president of the *jalsa*, so they suspected that president and *bacha* was the same thing. I was then brought outside where the police escort was waiting for me. Surrounded by the police escort I walked to the police station of the cantonment, where I was locked up in a cell. On account of the tight fetters, my ankles got wounded and began to bleed. I saw *thanedar* Zeerad who would not come near me out of fear, and would always avoid me. He had studied with me in the Mission School at Peshawar and we had lived together in the boarding house, where we had a brotherly relationship.

The next morning, I was taken again to the police station. There was an inspector, called Said Akbar, who was an Afridi and was the officer in-charge of the police station. He told me that I had to present myself at the courts and should, therefore, proceed. I told him that my feet were wounded and that I could not go to the court on foot. He said that I could hold *jalsas* and yet I could not walk, and that he could not arrange transport for me. I told him that he should judge for himself whether I could proceed on foot. He told me that he had no desire to have a look at my feet and that I should get up and walk. I retorted sharply that I would not walk and that if he could make me do so, he was welcome to try. The inspector gave in when I stood my ground. The government had a strange way of governing, and strange servants. When I was polite with them, they were rude, and when I was firm and curt, they were polite. He called for a policeman to fetch a tonga and took me for the court hearing. I stood outside for a while but was not presented before the court. From there I was taken back to the jail. They took me to a barrack in the jail and gave me an old blanket and a mat. I put the mat over an unused weaving frame. I had never seen a jail and stood in great fear of it. Not only me but all Pukhtuns feared the jail. For those who have not experienced being in jail, it becomes a big bogey for them. But on account of our *Khudai Khidmatgar* movement, no one fears it any longer. Our tribal brothers, even today, are very scared of being put in jail. All the other prisoners with me in the barrack were well-clad and appeared to be educated. But I was depressed and concerned for myself. In Hindustan, the British had hanged many people and put many before the firing squad. I thought that I, too, would meet the same fate. Day and night, I prayed and chanted prayers and would prostrate myself before God and beseech him. If I were to be jailed for life, that would be alright, if only I could be spared the gallows. In a few days I got to know my fellow prisoners and learnt that they were all from Afghanistan and that the British had jailed them on account of the war.

It must have been after ten or twelve days when a sepoy came and informed me that I had a visitor waiting outside, and wanted to know if I had any message to send to the village. At first it occurred to me to send a message to my father, that some of my papers lying in the house of Fazlu, the blacksmith, should be retrieved and burnt since they were about my tours of the free Tribal Areas and the establishment of a *markaz* there. If these papers were to fall into the hands of the government, they would provide a lot of evidence against me. But after a little pondering, I thought that what relationship and sympathy could this sepoy possibly have with me, to have sleepless nights on my account, and that, in this way, they were intending to get to my secrets. The jail employees are invariably informers of the CID and often deal with political prisoners in this manner, as they are inexperienced, and they speak to them very gently and in confidence and get them to divulge their secrets. In this way, many of my letters have been handed over by them to the CID.

The boy who had been convicted to two years' imprisonment for cutting a telephone wire used to serve prisoners in the *langar* of the jail. I asked him why he had been brought to the police officer's house. He replied that both the jail and the police officers had pressured him that, if he were to be asked on whose instigation he had cut the telephone wire, he should reply that it was on the instigation of Abdul Ghaffar Khan. If he did so, he would be spared two years imprisonment. (He said) that they questioned him, that the wire must have been cut by him (or was it) at someone else's instigation? But he had told them that he had not cut it at any one's instigation. Finally, they asked him in clear terms if the act was done upon Abdul Ghaffar Khan's instructions. He said to them that he had acted on his own volition and that he would not lie.

The Arrest of my Father and Fellow Villagers

Sixteen or seventeen days had passed after my arrest and it was early evening when an employee of the jail came and told me that 160 to 180 detainees had been brought in from Uthmanzai. I was still wondering who they might be, when they were brought into our barrack. As I looked closer, there was my father, Attaullah Dada, Shamroz Dada, Haider Khan Kaka, Abbas Khan, Faiz Muhammad Khan, Abdul Ghaffar Khan Barni, the Masher maulana sahib of Shamozai and Burhan Dada. In short, the detainees consisted of about 150 people from our village alone. Our entire family was there with all the khans of Uthmanzai and most of the prominent maulanas, pirs and prominent people. There were a few khans from Razar who were related to us – Burhan Khan, Qalandar Khan, Pacha sahib of Babara and some persons from Charsada. All had been caught based on the names contained in the report of Qazi Shahkirullah. My father was happy to see me and said that he was grateful to God for reuniting him with me. A rumour had spread about me that I had been hanged. That is why my father felt so relieved on seeing me alive. I, too, was happy, as I had begun to feel lonely of late. They informed me of their arrest and told me that the maulana had not yet given the call for the morning prayer and it was still dark, when the troops surrounded our village and, in the spacious ground adjacent to the mosque, positioned their cannons. British soldiers were seated on them. Whenever someone emerged from his home, he would be arrested and brought to the open ground. When light dawned, the policemen spread themselves out in the streets and brought out people from their homes and asked them to bring out weapons and surrender them to the government. Those who did not bring out the weapons on their own, and if they were later recovered from their homes, would be put before the firing squad. Out of fear, the people brought out their weapons and piled them up in the open ground and then they were assembled in front of the cannons. When the ground was filled with weapons, and people and weapons were collected from the homes, the women climbed onto the rooftops and began to wail loudly. The whole village was in fear and awe when the British mounted their guns and loaded them. Everyone thought that they were about to be killed and so they began to recite verses from the Holy *Quran*. The women on the rooftops began to wail even louder. At this juncture, the deputy commissioner and a few other army officers arrived and stood before the assembled men and said, 'Oh inhabitants of Uthmanzai! Understand that the government's arms are stretched far and wide. One arm is stretched over into Afghanistan and the other is here, over you. I have fined your village 30,000 rupees and arrested 150 of you. Fifty of you because they have held *jalsas* against the government, and the rest of you all will remain jailed until the fine of 30,000 rupees is paid.' Then, the villagers said, 'We were taken to the jail in Charsadda.' The next day, even Muhammad Akram Khan, who used to spy on them, was brought to the jail with his hands tied. The British had played a strange trick on him. He neither gained their pleasure, nor were they pleased with him. Akram Khan was placed in the same barrack as us. I thought that he would have regretted his conduct and would be ashamed of himself, but he was so shameless that we had to face any number of difficulties on his account. He would spin tales about some of us, get into arguments with others and would come to physical blows with some. He would curse the British and would say that God has ordained that they will never be friendly to the Muslims. But one day his son wrote to him that the assistant commissioner, Mr. Wylie, had visited Khanmai (his village) on tour and had gazed for a long time at his photograph hanging in the *hujra*. Just because of this piece of news, he forgot about all the evils he had associated with the British. He wrote to his son that they were obliged now to send a gift to the assistant commissioner. This conduct was the outcome of the effects of slavery in which human beings forget basic humanity and are deprived of all human virtues.

A man from Kabul was imprisoned along with us. Whenever the roar of cannon fire reached us, and it used to seem as if it was the outcome of an ongoing battle between the forces of the British and the Afghans, he would rise with great enthusiasm and begin to jump up and down. He would shake his arm as if holding a sword and, in a loud voice, would proclaim, 'Strike! Strike!' The government suspected that all the people who had been caught for participating in the *jalsa* were in secret communication with the Afghan government, and that the newspapers that had come from Afghanistan had been distributed by us, and that we also corresponded with Afghanistan. The government was busy investigating this. My father informed me that Saadullah Khan of Umerzai had tried to tactfully extract information from him about whether he or I had any secret understanding with the Afghans, and whether Afghan newspapers were dispatched to us. My father further added that Saadullah Khan had pressurized him to let him know whether he had any copies of such newspapers with him and, if so, he should send them to him so that he could read them. He wanted that he should uncover this secret and convey it to the British, to gain face with them. But the truth was that we had no understanding with the Afghans, nor were we in correspondence with them and neither had we distributed any papers. I had not taken a single paper which Ashiq, the fruit vendor, had brought with him. They were taken by Bhaijan, Akbar and Ahmad *Ustaz*. When I was released, my mother told me about the newspapers of Bhaijan and how, on their account, they had almost got into serious trouble, but God had saved them. She said that it so happened that Bhaijan took the papers from Ashiq, putting them in his box, which he then left for safe custody in our house, and fled to the free Tribal Areas along with Akbar and others. He had not informed us that his box contained the newspapers from Afghanistan. When the police came to search our house, this box was lying in the room. When the police entered this room, my mother said that she was quick to think and told them that this room was that of her son who was a doctor, that he was a Captain in the army, and asked why they were conducting a search of that room; that her other son's room was the other one. So luckily, the police did not search this room. And when they (the family) later opened Bhaijan maulana's box, the newspapers came out. If the police had found these newspapers, they would be considered enough evidence for the corroboration of the allegations against us. Who could then prove, and who would believe, that this box belonged to Bhaijan?

In those days we would receive information about violence in Hindustan, but we had repeatedly instructed our people in the *jalsa* not to resort to violence. As a result, our people remained peaceful. The British had no other evidence against us besides the fact that we had held a *jalsa*. But that did not constitute a crime. They tried for three months but could not find a reason to take any action against us. Then they started to work on our companions. They prepared Ahmad *Ustaz* to become an approver, and (told him) that they would promise to grant him a pardon. A Jamadar would come to Ahmad *Ustaz* and take him to the office. We got suspicious and started to investigate him and found all this out. As he was a good friend of Faiz Muhammad Khan, we requested him to convey that this was not appropriate conduct, that for the sake of saving himself, he was prepared to throw all his companions into the fire. Consequently, he pleaded with him, and so did we, but he had lost heart and was fed up in jail, and did not listen to us. The police had already recorded his statement and had forwarded it. The man in-charge of the martial law was Sir George Roos-Keppel himself. He was also our chief commissioner. He had great affection for the Pukhtuns and was their well-wisher. He said that he would not institute proceedings against us and so refused to give his permission in this regard. This was because a lot of time had passed since the events, and circumstances had changed. A khan recounted to me that they had gone as a *jirga* to him, to release the elderly prisoners. He told them to leave, as he was releasing their *Bacha* along with all the others.

Conditions in the Jail

The conditions in the jail at the time were very tough and people were terrified of being arrested. The food was not like food, the clothes could hardly be called as such, and jail life was far from human. Without any reason, prisoners would be subjected to corporal punishment and disgrace and they could not dare to ask why. They were made to work like animals, grind corn and draw water through Persian wheels. We were political prisoners. We were given 'red spinach' to eat. One day, I jokingly said to the jamadar sahib that it was delicious, and would he be kind enough to find me its seed, so that when I was free, I could grow some for myself. He replied that there was no doubt about the good qualities of this spinach and that we had not yet realized its real taste! First, he said, it is laid before the bullocks of the jail and when some is left over, it is given to us. That this spinach cannot be grown in the fertile lands of Peshawar Valley. It came from the wastelands of Dera Ismail Khan, where every wild weed was called a spinach. One would have refused to eat it if one had seen the pots in which it was cooked, despite being starved. The loaves of bread were such that even cattle would not feed on them. Let alone cleaning the grain, the prisoner who grinds the wheat eats raw, uncooked flour, and to make up for the weight, he mixes mud with it. The other thing is that the jail employees do not issue the full amounts of the authorized ration, and so, in order to maintain the required weight of the loaves, they are undercooked. We ate the food of the jail for a few days, but could later arrange for our meals from our homes. But we ate our food in the jail. We were not allowed to do so in the barrack because, at the gate (to the barrack), they could accept bribes from us. The jail employees subjected us to the humiliation of body searches each time we had our meal at the gate of the jail. This was meant only to humiliate us and to extract bribes from us. Our *darogha* Amirchand, was not a corrupt man. The deputy *darogha* was Ganga Ram. He was corrupt to the core, and we were entrusted to him. I, personally, was against offering bribes, but my other companions were not against the practice, particularly Haji Akram Khan and those people who ate *pan* or took *naswar* or *gazaaray*. Finally, on account of a scuffle between Haji Akram and the jail staff, the arrangements of getting our food from our homes came to an end. It was only he who was involved in the scuffle, but the punishment was given to all of us and our food supply from our homes was stopped.

We were allowed a visitor only once a week. This meeting was also strange and involved a lot of hullabaloo. All the prisoners would be collected, brought to the gate and lined up in rows behind it. Those who had come to meet us would be made to stand in rows outside the gate. We would then talk by shouting out to each other through the open gate because otherwise we were not audible to each other. They would bring us news of the outside world and would inform us that the people were being subjected to a lot of cruelty. Life in jail, they would say, was infinitely better than life outside. They said that the widows and orphans had been exempted from the payment of the fine imposed on the village. But Umer Khan and the police had joined forces and had left no one's honour intact. They would recover the fine from the widows and the children and, let alone this, the *lambardars* recovered fines from the people three times over, and would beat and humiliate them if anyone objected. The people would pay the fine out of concern for their self-respect. When, instead of 30,000 rupees 100,000 rupees had been recovered as a fine, those 100 prisoners who were taken in as hostages, and those of us who remained, were taken to the jail in Charsada. We were not aware of our being taken to Charsada. The jail staff had stopped our own food and would feed us the same red spinach and the hard and bitter maize bread. We were elated to hear that the *lat* (colloquial for Lord) sahib had sent a message that he had freed all the prisoners, along with their *Bacha*. The next day, orders came for us to get ready as we were to leave for Charsada. We were chained in pairs and entrusted to the custody of one policeman each. One end of the chain would be in the hands of the policemen. We were seated in *tum-tums*. Each policeman would occupy the front seat and we would be seated at the back. We were taken to Charsada and locked in the jail. During this period of arrest, the hardship that troubled me the most was the condition of my feet. My feet were wounded because of the tight fetters, and I changed my clothes, bathed, walked and slept with great difficulty. Lying down, turning over in bed and offering my prayers – everything was a real torture for me. The fetters would get very hot in the summer and equally cold in the winter. Despite all this, these fetters were not removed from my feet. Our doctor was an Englishman, a good man, but he could not defy the government because he did not have the courage to order the removal of the fetters. Except for me, no other prisoner that was imprisoned in connection with the agitation against the Rowlatt Act, was fettered. The treatment meted out to the other political prisoners was not given to us, and we were treated like other, common criminals.

The people who were taken in with me were set free after three and a half months. I was the only exception. My father was very upset and did not want that we should be separated. On parting, he embraced me, and I could see tears well up in his eyes. But he was helpless as the power lay with someone else. When my mother found out (that I had not been released), she was extremely grieved. But this grief was very different from the earlier one. Earlier there was fear of being shot and hanged. And this time, although imprisoned, there was hope of my being set free. My mother used to send me food which used to be enough for me, the other prisoners and the warden. But when I learnt that this food arrived in jail through bribery, I told the jailors and the policemen that I was not stealing this food and that I have a right to it. That I am a political prisoner, jailed for serving the nation and the country. I was officially entitled to this food, which was also given to me in Peshawar jail. But they were not bothered about the nation or the country and I was forced to send a message to my mother to stop sending me food, and she acquiesced. For me, eating food by bribing someone is a sin. A few days later, I was again transferred to Peshawar jail. Other prisoners of conscience were also part of the group. The group was to go on foot to Peshawar. I told the policeman that, if he agreed, we could go in *tum-tums* and that I would pay the fare for the other prisoners too. But he refused. The police wanted a bribe in addition to the rent money. I agreed that we would travel on foot. My friends and family asked why I did this. What will the people say? We pay too much attention to what people have to say. I responded that I do not listen to what people have to say, I focus on the task at hand. If the nature of the task is illegal or immoral, no matter what people say, I would not do it. When the police realized that I was prepared to travel on foot, they regretted their offer to me to do so, but by then, it was too late. My mother, sisters and other relatives who had learnt of my release, had come to Qazikhel and lived in a house on the road side to meet me. During our meeting, I realized that they had bribed the policemen accompanying me. If I had known this earlier, I would have refused this meeting.

We took the shorter route through *Mian* Gujaro to Peshawar. When we reached Agra, Mir Qadir Khan, who later came to be known as Nawab sahib, and his father, arrived and took us to his *hujra* and arranged for our meal. Though I objected, they insisted and gave us a sumptuous meal and only then did they allow us to proceed further. It was early evening when we arrived in Peshawar. Sadullah Khan and others were studying in Peshawar at the time and had learnt of our coming, and had come out to meet us and brought us a meal. We had the meal near Shahibagh. It was late, and the jail did not accept prisoners at that hour. So, I was taken to the kotwali. I spent the night in an extremely dirty place. The next morning, I was taken to the jail. The jail wardens locked me up in a barrack along with the other prisoners. I was given the jail food.

At the time, Inson sahib was the deputy commissioner. He knew my father well. My father went to call on him and made a request, as a result of which I was given permission to get my food from home. When this happened, I was transferred from the barrack in which I was lodged to the lock-up adjacent to the main gate of the jail. My food would be brought to the gate of the lock-up and I would be summoned. I would go and eat it there. Although I was alone in the barrack, I was not given my food there. At the time, Redi Khan of Lund Khwar was also imprisoned here. He was jailed by Bruce sahib, an Englishman who was against the khans and the police and knew of their shenanigans. The *darogha* of the jail was also an enemy of the corrupt khans. He did not take bribes and pursued those who gave or took them. Redi Khan, too, was in an unenviable position. He was put to hard labour and was made to do mud plaster on the jail walls. He would be full of mud and had no personal arrangements for food. He had fallen on very bad days indeed. Till the time I was there, I would cautiously share my meals with him. After six months, I was released on a bail of 30,000 rupees.

Release from Imprisonment

When I returned to the village, people came to see me and welcome me home with great love and affection. The agitation against the Rowlatt Act imposed a lot of hardship on the people in the form of monetary loss and freedom, but it created an awareness among them, which was the beginning of political consciousness among the Pukhtuns. When I learnt of the conditions prevailing in the village, I realized the extent of the suffering they had borne. I was not subjected to such hardship in jail as they had been put through in the village. My mother told me that when I was arrested, the brightness of the day assumed the darkness of the night for her, and she became listless. She said that someone told her that whatever happens is the will of God and, after him, that of the police *kaptan* sahib. She said that there was no cash at home but there was plenty of jewellery belonging to me, to Dr. Khan Sahib and to her. She collected all this and, taking a maidservant along, went to the house of the *kaptan* sahib and personally handed over all the jewellery to him. She restrained herself but failed, and finally burst into tears before him. The police *kaptan* was a good man and consoled her greatly. Addressing her as 'mother', he told her not to worry, as God would have her son released soon.

Preparation for the Second Marriage and Re-arrest

I was engaged to a girl from the same family as that of my first wife. My first wife was the niece of the *Masher* khan and my fiancée was his daughter. My mother and father were both busy in preparations for the engagement and had fixed the date of the wedding. The task of buying the wedding dress was assigned to Abbas Khan and me. Abbas Khan was my friend since childhood and was very close to me. We first went to Naukhar, where some boys from our village were studying, and we called on Babu Sultan Muhammad, a Punjabi. He was a very good man and a nationalist. My friendship with him was because he was educating the children of the Pukhtuns. I too had a firm belief in this. He had resigned from various government positions with the British and had established an orphanage and a school in Naukhar. I and Babu sahib were sitting and talking, when a man came and stood for prayer next to us. I got suspicious and asked Babu sahib who this man was. He was a very trusting soul and replied that he was a very good man who said his prayers, and that he was one of 'them'. I replied that there were two vacant rooms here, and why did he not offer his prayer in the other room? Later, I was in jail when I learnt that Babu sahib was arrested. The man was an inspector of the CID and was sent from Punjab after him. The government suspected that Babu sahib was making counterfeit notes. When the matter was investigated, Babu sahib was arrested along with the equipment.

We went from Naukhar to Peshawar and bought the wedding dress and then left for the village. When we came to Sardaryab and were crossing the bridge and were about to climb into the *tum-tum*, we saw the police *thanedar* along with a contingent of policemen sitting in a *tum-tum* approaching the bridge. When we crossed them, they turned around and started following us. We became suspicious. When we arrived at the *thana*, they motioned us to stop. When they saw us, they huddled to a side and started whispering amongst themselves. They then came back and informed us that orders from above had come for our arrest, and that we were being taken back to Peshawar. We asked them what the orders were about, to know the situation. However, they themselves did not know. The luggage that we had was handed over to them and we set off again for Peshawar with the police escort. We arrived there late in the evening and were taken directly to the bungalow of Short sahib. He was the police *kaptan* in charge of Peshawar district. His bungalow was opposite the Mission College. We were made to stand by the road side. It was the month of *poh-mah* and it was bitterly cold. It became late evening and we got tired. There were no arrangements for us, nor for the police, to sit. We repeatedly asked the police as to how long we were to wait in this cold, and that they should go and hurry up the process a bit so that we could have our hearing. But the police officers did not have the courage to do so. We were engaged in conversation when an officer emerged from the bungalow and whispered something to them. Abbas Khan and I were then separated from each other. On being separated, Abbas Khan asked me what were we going to say. I told him we would tell the truth. He was taken towards the Mission College and I was taken in the direction of the railway station. I was tired and was feeling cold as well. There was a little bridge on which I sat. I did not find out anything about Abbas Khan, but it was very late in the evening when I was taken before Short sahib. He was sitting in front of a fire in one of the rooms. The room was nice and warm. I warmed up and felt comfortable. There was an empty chair next to the fireplace. Short sahib motioned me towards it, so I sat down. Short was a very hot-tempered man. He began to interrogate me. I told him the truth. When I started to speak, he told me to speak softly. When I spoke softly, he told me to speak loudly. So, I said to him, 'When I speak softly, you ask me to speak louder. And when I spoke loudly, you ask me to speak softly! You should decide and tell me one way in which I should speak, and I will do accordingly.' On this he got very angry but restrained himself and remained silent. When my statement was complete, I was taken again to my own familiar haunt and friend – the kotwali of the cantonment and the *thanedar,* and I was locked up. There were a few old, torn and lice-infested blankets lying on the floor which I wore and went to sleep on the cold, bare, cement floor. The next evening, Said Akbar Khan, my friend and *thanedar,* took me to the office of the deputy commissioner and produced me before him. The deputy commissioner was Inson sahib, a very good man. I pleaded innocence. He extended a lot of assurance and directed Said Akbar Khan to treat me well and give me good food. It was the order of the sahib and so, when we returned, the lice-infested blankets were changed, and I also began to be fed well. I was here for eight or nine days when, one day, the police came and produced me before their senior officer. I was to be produced before Short sahib again. There was a small space next to his office in which I was made to wait. I was deep in thought when my sight fell on a man who walked over quickly and lifted the blind of the office door and entered in great haste. I did not see him clearly but suspected that it was Qazi Shahkirullah. I asked the orderly who the man was. He told me that he did not know him. Even though people were known to him, he would not easily disclose their identity. I asked him directly whether he was not Qazi Shahkirullah. It was, in fact, him. I stopped myself from thinking about other matters and concentrated on the door of the office, waiting for Qazi (Shahkirullah) sahib to emerge, so that I could greet him to ensure that he would not deny the incident the next day. Mr. Short was the head of all the spies of the province and they all had direct links to him. I was afraid lest Qazi sahib might go out of the office by another door, because spies are also careful in such matters and do not use the same route twice. I was pleading to God to bring him out through the same door so that we could see each other. Let alone the common people, he used to deceive the *maulanas* as well. I wanted to reveal his identity and position to the people. Qazi sahib emerged after a long while. When he came close to me, I rose to my feet and greeted him. He turned pale. I said to him 'Qazi sahib, you had become a Muslim (after the incident in the Persian Gulf). When was it that you became a kafir again?' He lowered his gaze, said nothing, and left quickly in embarrassment.

Release and the Second Marriage

A while later the police produced me before the deputy of the chief of intelligence of the province. He was from the village of Jehangira. He told me that I was free. I asked him why they had arrested me, and why I was now being released. I was told that they were merely subordinates and had no say in the matter, and that their officers were sitting inside, and that I could ask them this question. During this time, the British were at the peak of their power and no one could broach a subject with Short sahib. But for those who have seen jails as political prisoners and not as common criminals, fear is eliminated from their hearts. I went straight to Short sahib, and asked him why I had been arrested, and why I was now being set free. He told me that someone had thrown a bomb in Naukhar and they suspected that I was responsible for this. But that, it was found after investigation that I was innocent. I told him that the investigation could have been undertaken before my arrest; that I was a citizen of this country and that it was not difficult to arrest me. Look at how I had been put to such trouble for the past ten to twelve days. He retorted, 'What standing and status could you people have?' He added that it was their pleasure to arrest or release us when they liked. To this I replied 'fine, if this was the order of the day, then fare thee well!' And with this, I left. They called after me repeatedly to return, but I did not do so. From there I walked to the city. No one knew of my release. I went to the shop of *Hakeem* sahib of Cheena and was surprised to see Qazi Shahkirullah talking animatedly and quoting *ayats* of the Holy *Quran* and the Hadith of the Holy Prophet (PBUH). When he saw me, he immediately left the shop, embarrassed. I went to the village from there. When I enquired about Abbas Khan, I found that he had been released and had arrived in the village before me.

I admit that foreign governments cannot establish themselves without resorting to violence and instilling fear in the hearts of the people. But this also creates hatred between the rulers and the ruled. If, at the time, the British had treated us kindly instead of using force and tyranny, so many movements against them would not have started and neither would their authority have eroded so quickly.

As I have mentioned, my first wife, who was the mother of Ghani and Wali, had died during the influenza epidemic, which had raged during the First World War. In these days, I was ready to enter into my second marriage. In 1919, I got married again. The weddings of the Pukhtuns are full of customs. I wanted to bring about reforms in them. That is why I started with myself and married according to the simple requirements of Shariat. The next day, I held a *waleema* reception and served a good lunch to the people of my village, my friends and relatives. Each one of them gave me two rupees each as *naindra*, but I refused to accept it, even though it was owed to us for what we had contributed to them on their weddings. At the lunch, I exchanged views on social reforms with the guests. At the time, it was the custom for the *kasabgars* to serve the guests. Some would burn *spalanee* some would play the *dhol*, and some would have brought flowers to hand out. Some would sing *charbaitas* accompanied by the *rabab*. The guests would be exploited to the extent possible, and whether they liked it or not, they would, for fear of their self-respect, make the desired payments to the *kasabgars*. At my wedding, for the first time ever, I put a stop to these practices and instructed the *kasabgars* not to trouble the guests, and that I would pay them myself because they were my *kasabgars*. Similarly, dancing girls would be hired (to perform before the men in the *hujras*) and the guests, whether they wanted to or not, would have to throw money at them. There would be musicians and marriage processions. The festive firing of guns and *gharbeens* would also take place. In short, there would be a lot of extravagance all around. I put a stop to all this in my wedding. And I did all this because these customs were harmful for the people and the nation, and the people were fed up with these but no one had the courage to come out against them. I began to put a stop to all these bad practices and said to the people that they should abandon these useless customs.

6

The *Khilafat* Movement and *Hijrat*

IN THOSE DAYS, THE ALLIED POWERS HAD OCCUPIED ALL OF TURKEY. Mustafa Kamal and his associates had begun to oppose them. In Hindustan, the Muslims had started a large movement in support of the *Khilafat* and had organized committees in many places for the purpose. Many *jalsa* took place. The Muslims of Hindustan were a strange lot. In the war, their assistance to the British had been more than anyone else's. Their leaders arranged for the people to join the army. The maulanas, saints and religious leaders had issued fatwas in their favour and against the Turks. The *Khilafat* had done them incalculable harm. If they had thought on these lines before, it would have benefitted them greatly; but even this was better than nothing.

Jalsa of the *Khilafat* Committee in Delhi
In the middle of 1920, the *Khilafat* Committee called for a big *jalsa* in Delhi. It was announced that only those who were prepared for the worst should come. I too participated in this *jalsa*. It was a big affair and Muslims from every corner of Hindustan had come to attend.

Aziz Hindi was a young emotional boy. He wanted to put forward a proposal in the *jalsa* of *Hijrat*[13] from Hindustan. Most of the leaders did not think on these lines. They tried to make him understand that this was not the occasion to move this resolution, but he was not deterred. The Muslims, as such, are emotional people. They did not think of the consequences of this resolution and the course of action and adopted it straight away. When the news of the *Hijrat* spread, small convoys of people gradually began to leave for Peshawar. For their assistance and comfort, a *Hijrat* committee was formed in Peshawar. These convoys would be received very enthusiastically by the people at the railway stations, and processions would be held in Peshawar. Initially, the British had strongly opposed the *Hijrat* movement, considering it a danger to their government, but when they realized that the people could not be deterred, they tried to induce as many as possible to join the *Hijrat*. The Pukhtuns, unlike the others, observed the spectacle, which had a galvanizing effect on them. The maulanas, too, in their sermons, would proclaim that *Hijrat* was an obligation now and those who did not emigrate, should consider their wives divorced from them. Such conditions were created in the country that, except for '*Hijrat*', nobody was prepared to listen to anything else. On behalf of the government, too, conflicting reports were spread. Both men and women were ready for the *Hijrat*.

Hijrat

The people would look down upon those who did not go on the *Hijrat*. I called for a big *jalsa* in our village. Many people came for it. It was in this gathering that I urged that we should exercise a little patience in such matters. I suggested that I would send a few people to Kabul to bring back information to us and we could then analyse the situation better, and then decide on whether to migrate or not. When I put forward this proposal, Adil Shah, a pir from our village strongly opposed it. He said that we were not prepared to leave our wives behind to the British soldiers and that if I was not prepared for *Hijrat*, then I should not go, but that I should not dissuade others from going; that they would, God willing, leave early the next morning. Hindustan was set ablaze and Pukhtunkhwa was being burnt! Whether upper or lower Pukhtunkhwa, it was all desolate and suffered huge losses. Particularly when the caravan from Sindh, under the leadership of Junejo sahib, arrived in Peshawar, the Pukhtuns were ablaze with passion to join the *Hijrat*. Men and women left the land on *Hijrat*. Amongst these, the British sent many spies so that they could carry out propaganda among the *muhajareen* so that they would not stay in Afghanistan but return to their own country. It was no *Hijrat at* all; it was a big commotion full of emotional vigour. There was no thought or planning involved; no one understood the real meaning of *Hijrat*. Muhammad Ali and his brother Shaukat Ali, leaders of the *Khilafat* Movement, had sent the message to *Amir* Amanullah Khan that he should proclaim his acceptance of the *Hijrat* so that this would affect the British, and thereby, be of benefit to our *Khilafat* movement.

I too, was obliged to join a small caravan, consisting mostly of youngsters, to leave for Afghanistan via Shabqadar and the Moomand territory. Our first night was spent in Krappa. Many people accompanied us when we began the journey to the sound of dhols. But when we took the road from Shabqadar to Krappa and left the music behind, very few remained with us; and when night descended in the wilderness at Krappa, only a handful remained. Anyway, we spent the night in the rocks and boulders of Krappa. The next morning I, along with a few companions, left to call on the Haji sahib of Torangzai. The rest of the convoy left for Masal Khan's village. After seeing Haji sahib we also proceeded to Kudakhel, Masal Khan's village, and the next day we left from there and arrived at Gardau in Kama. Sardar Khan was the khan of the Moomand. He had come out with his tribe to welcome us. He received us with open arms and took us to his village and looked after us very well. The next day, when leaving for Jalalabad, Sardar Khan insisted that we should stay with him; that we were the *mohajirs* and they were the *ansars*, and that they would share their landholding with us equally. He said that the inhabitants of Kabul would not assist us as much, and that their proposal would turn out to be the best for us. We thanked him profusely and told him that we had not come in search of lands and property, and took leave of him.

We arrived in Jalalabad where Sardar Hashim Khan was the governor. We called on him and discussed matters. He put me up with himself while the remaining members of the convoy left. Hashim Khan was very worried about these large convoys of the *muhajareen* coming to Afghanistan. He was very distressed and was making efforts that some steps should be taken to put an end to this, because Afghanistan would not be able to accommodate so many people. The British were encouraging large outflows of people for the reason that the migrants would face difficulties themselves and would also create difficulties for Afghanistan. A few days later, Hashim Khan arranged for me to go to Kabul. We left Jalalabad and at Gandamak we came across Pir Adil Shah, along with his family and companions, who were all returning home. I said, 'Pir sahib, it appears that you are taking your womenfolk back to the British soldiers.' He responded, 'What can we do? There we were harassed by our women to join the *Hijrat* and here the women have harassed us that it is difficult for them to manage in this country. So, they have made us return.'

In Kabul

When we arrived in Kabul, we saw that the *muhajareen* had settled themselves under the trees near the Lahori Gate. We did the same. The government had made separate arrangements for us, but I did not wish to separate myself from the *muhajareen*. In Kabul, a committee of *muhajareen* from all over Hindustan was constituted of which both Arbab Raza Khan and I were members. Through this committee, the *muhajareen* coordinated their affairs with the government of Afghanistan. When the number of *muhajareen* reached twenty or thirty thousand, the government of Afghanistan informed that theirs was a small country, and thus, could not absorb so many people. So, we sent Abbas Khan to inform Peshawar accordingly.

Amanullah Khan told us that he did not have the power to take on the British in a war, and that he would be ready to support us, no matter how we chose to fight the British to free our country. He proposed two options to us. If we were prepared to serve, he would enrol our youth and constitute them into separate battalions and train them. Then, if we could engage the British in a war, we could do so. If we wanted land, then land would be made available in Kunduz and Mazar-e-Sharif and this could be given to us. We could create our own colonies and make our own arrangements. Also, we could have full political and administrative autonomy to regulate our affairs. And if we wanted to have relationships with foreign powers, we could do so. He told the *muhajareen* in clear terms that, whether they wanted employment, lands or commerce, he was prepared to assist them in all three. We unanimously decided that we should be given military training and employment. We decided to organize ourselves into battalions that would stand up amongst the *muhajareen* to discuss and arrive at a decision to convey to the (Afghan) government so that it could plan for us. Each time, however, the informers of the British would take this opportunity and one of them would get up and voice his opposition, saying that he had come neither to get land nor for employment, but to wage jihad. That if the government of Afghanistan considered itself weak and was unable to take on the British in the war, he should be allowed to return (to India) as the objective of his *Hijrat* could not be fulfilled. After him, another informer would rise to his feet and endorse what the other had said, and say that he would also leave. And when they would get up to leave, a group (of *muhajareen*) would follow them. In this way, the entire group would disintegrate. One person would hastily approach me and ask me not to speak to the government and to return to their group to discuss the matter. And when I would go to them, they would all have left the venue. Then I suggested to them to take up the offer of the land and that I would join them. But they were not prepared to accept this either.

Just as the Pukhtuns were in a hurry to go to Afghanistan, they were now equally hasty to return. The *muhajareen* left in groups and very few stayed behind in Afghanistan. Some took up employment, others preferred taking land. Thus, the *Hijrat* was a failure and the Muslims of Hindustan, particularly the Pukhtuns, suffered on account of it. Afghanistan, too, was badly affected. The British also set their aim on removing Amanullah Khan from his throne. It was only the British who benefitted from all this. Some of my friends went to Tashkent in the hope that Russia would assist them in the liberation of Hindustan. I stayed behind in Kabul along with a few companions.

One day, I went to Amanullah Khan and discussed many matters with him. Amongst other things, I told him that he knew how to speak Turkish, Persian and a few other languages, but that he did not know how to speak his own language (Pukhto). My comment had a profound effect on him. He promised that he would learn it. When he was removed from Afghanistan, I went to Bombay to call on him. There, true to his word, he spoke to me in Pukhto.

In Kabul we had a good relationship with Nadir Khan and his family. He was the defence minister and his brother, Sardar Abdul Aziz Khan, was the minister of education. One day he asked me to go and have a look at Habibi College. I asked the *taliban* of a mosque in Persian who they were. They also replied in Persian and said that they were Afghan. I then asked them which country they belonged to and they responded 'Afghanistan'. I then asked them that if they were Afghans, did they understand 'Afghani'. At this they kept quiet. I asked them what kind of Afghans were they when they did not know how to speak their mother tongue? Similarly, I exchanged views with Mahmud Tarzai, who was the foreign minister and a brilliant man, at a banquet which he had hosted for Afghan *muhajareen*. Someone asked him what kind of Afghanistan this was where 'Afghani' was not spoken. Tarzai sahib replied that Persian, too, was a language of Afghanistan. As a response to this I told him, 'Tarzai sahib, Pukhto is the national language of Afghanistan and is also the language spoken by the majority. In all the countries of the world, the language of the majority is not only the official language, but also the medium of instruction.'

Return to Bajawar

After the return of the *muhajareen*, we hired a room in a serai of Kabul and lived there. A few days later, I went to Nadir Khan and told him that since the *Hijrat* was a failure and as there was nothing else for us to do here to further our objectives, I intended to go to Bajawar and begin my efforts in education, to nurture the children of the Pukhtuns. I asked for his advice and he agreed with me on this. I left Kabul for Jalalabad with a few remaining companions. In Jalalabad, I conferred with Sardar Hashim Khan as well. He also agreed with my proposal and planned for our journey to Bajawar and gifted me with a horse. We travelled the first night from Jalalabad to Salampur, from where we proceeded to Kagapanr in the Moomand territory for the second night, which we spent in the house of the maulana sahib of Kagapanr, an old acquaintance of ours. From there, we proceeded to Chamarkand. In Chamarkand there was a group of mujahideen who had earlier accompanied *Syed* Ahmad Barelvi sahib and Ismail Shaheed sahib and, after their martyrdom at the hands of the Sikhs, had settled in Buner. They had already established a *markaz* in Chamarkand. They realized in Buner that their *Amir*, Naimatullah, was working for the British, so they murdered him. They were now divided into two groups, one consisting the Punjabis and the other Bengalis. The Punjabi group had come to Chamarkand. In Chamarkand they were staying on without any purpose and looked towards Hindustan for assistance. Food was cooked by them in turns and they called this *musavat*. The assistance from Hindustan proved to be their undoing. The details shall be unfolded later in this narrative. I told them that they owned two mules and there was no fruit available in this part of the Moomand territory. On the other side of this pass was Kunar, where there was plenty of fruit. If they were to buy fruit in Kunar and sell it here, they would be able to live on the returns and would no longer be dependent on assistance from Hindustan. From Chamarkand we went to Kotki, where Zigrawar Khan and Zlrawar Khan were. They were very good men and good Pukhtuns. Wherever there was a *ghaza* against the British, they would join it. We discussed various matters with them. From here, we went to Shingarlgul. The maulana of Shingarlgul, Amir-ud-Din, was our patron and a nationalist. We met with people there and then toured the Salarzai and Mamoond tribes.

The *Madrassah* of Khaloona in Dir

From there we crossed over into the territory of Dir and arrived in a village by the name of Khaloona, inhabited by the Akhundzadgan and the Parachgan. Both these families are enlightened and good people. Both were nationalistic in outlook and were wealthy. With their assistance, we established a *madrassah* and told them to seek the services of Makhfi sahib for its management. This *madrassah* progressed well in a very short time and the number of its students went upto four hundred. The political agent of Malakand was bitterly opposed to the awakening of the Pukhtuns. He summoned the nawab of Dir and told him of the difficulties these *madrassahs* and education had created for them, and that he should not create such difficulties for himself and, therefore, should demolish it. The nawab of Dir demolished the *madrassah* in Khaloona and set it on fire.

When we arrived in Dir, we stayed with the son of Shahu baba who was a *mureed* of Haji sahib of Torangzai. We got to know him in Torangzai, when we stayed with him for a few nights. One night, Safdar Khan, a messenger, arrived with a message from Nawab sahib, summoning us to Dir. I told him that we would go to him the next morning. But Nawab sahib wanted to see us the same night and so I left with him. When we arrived, Nawab sahib was waiting for us by himself. During discussions he told me that, in his heart of hearts, he really hated the British and that whatever I wanted was also his desire – but what could he do, as they had installed Miangul sahib in Swat to oppose him. And if he were to make the slightest movement, sahib would be instigated to attack. Therefore, if tomorrow he were to oppose my actions in public, I should not mind, and that his actual sympathy and love were with me. When people gathered the next day and talks were held near Nawab sahib's house, up in the *balakhana* were Abdul Mateen Khan and the khan of Tor, whom I saw from a distance and exchanged greetings with. They had been detained by the nawab. From the nawab's house we went to Barawal Banda at night. At that time, the heir apparent of the nawab of Dir lived here. We wanted to meet him but were unable to do so. From there we went to Barwa. There we met the khan of Thana. He used to frequently visit the banda of Ghulam Haider Khan of our village and was a friend of his. I had struck up an acquaintanceship with him. We told him that we wanted to see the younger son of the nawab. He told us that he was still asleep because he stays awake at night, to guard himself. We could not meet him either and then went on to Tor. From there we came to Jar. The khan of Jar was a very good man. The khan of Jar had a very good relationship with one of my *tarboors*, Sarbiland Khan. He frequently visited him in Muhammad Narai and spent many days at a time with him. The next morning, we went to Khar. The khan of Khar was an intelligent, brave and a good Pukhtun. We spent a few days with him. One day I said to him, 'Khan! You are still better off than us and take some benefit from the Holy *Quran*.' He asked me how. I replied that even if they did not act on its injunctions, they at least guarded their hay stacks with it. On every hay stack a Holy *Quran* would be placed, so that no one would dare steal hay from it. I told him that they guarded their things with it, but that we neither acted on it, nor used it to safeguard our belongings. From Khar we went to Nawagai. The khan of Nawagai was a simple, kind-hearted man. From there we proceeded to Ghaziabad and met the Haji sahib of Torangzai. Here, only one of my companions, who was a carpenter named Faqir and whom I had left in Ghaziabad, accompanied me. The rest of my companions had left me one by one for their homes leaving the two of us.

I returned from Afghanistan with the intention of establishing *madrassahs* in the free Tribal Areas, to educate the children of the nation. This could not be done by one man alone but by a group, and unfortunately, our group had dispersed.

7

Intellectual Revolution

Educational and Reform Effort

WHEN I SAW THE CONDITIONS PREVAILING IN AFGHANISTAN AND THE Tribal Areas, and after I spent fifteen years grappling with the ups and downs of the tribesmen and Afghanistan, I came to the conclusion that a revolution could not be brought about in a hurry and was not an easy task. Revolution is the outcome of patient work. It requires education and knowledge. Revolution needs people who can convince the nation of the need for revolution. When I reflected over this, I concluded that our nation was neither inclined towards commerce, nor industry, nor agriculture, or education. On the other hand, it was immersed in harmful customs and traditions and was involved in enmities. This nation needs to be rid of these traits so that it becomes politically aware. This requires an atmosphere of peace. Till that time, I was of the belief that all this requires a revolution. Violence seemed to me the only path to this, then. But after this experience, I realized that one cannot train horses during war. I decided to go back to my village and to start work along the principles of non-violence. I would first set up national *madrassahs* to educate revolutionaries. So, I returned to Uthmanzai and made sustained efforts to reopen all those *madrassahs* which the British had shut down during the war.

It was the end of 1920, when a function was scheduled in the Aligarh Muslim University. My friend, Qazi Attaullah Khan, was invited and we both went to Aligarh. During this period, the Congress and the *Khilafat* held a joint *jalsa*. We intended to participate in the *Khilafat jalsa* after the function at Aligarh. But on account of our engagements, we could not attend the *Khilafat jalsa* and returned to Uthmanzai. Many students from our province were studying at Aligarh. We exchanged views with them. There were several students amongst them who had left college on account of the non-cooperation movement with the government and their support for Turkey. My older brother, Dr. Khan Sahib, after an absence of about fifteen years, had returned home. When he completed his medical education, the First World War had began, and he was recruited into the Army Medical Corps and was now a captain and posted to the Corps of Guides at Mardan.

The Azad School at Uthmanzai (1921) and the *Anjuman*

In 1921, with the assistance of our friends, we laid the foundations of the Azad School in Uthmanzai. In this effort, Qazi Attaullah Khan, *Mian* Ahmad Shah, Haji Abdul Ghaffar Khan, Muhammad Abbas Khan, Abdul Akbar Khan Akbar, Taj Muhammad Khan, Abdullah Shah and Khadim Muhammad Akbar were my companions. Next to the *madrassah*, we established the *Anjuman-e-Islah-Ul-Afaghina* for the purpose of combating social evils and customs among the Pukhtuns, to encourage them to shun violence and to inculcate in them a sense of nationalism and brotherhood. This *Anjuman* had the following members: Muhammad Abbas Khan, the President Abdul Ghaffar Khan (both were from Uthmanzai), Haji Muhammad Akram Khan of Khan Mahi, Jamadar Noor Muhammad Khan of Torangzai, Muhammad Zareen Khan of Torangzai, Abdul Akbar Khan of Umerzai, Ghulam Mohiuddin of Tungi, Fakhr-e-Qaum *Mian* Sahib, *Mian* Jafar Shah of Ziarat, Fazl-e-Akram of Narai Qala, Fazl-e-Rabbi of Badraga, *Mian* Ahmad Shah of Qazi Khel, *Mian* Abdullah Shah, Khadim Muhammad Akbar of Charsadda, Taj Muhammad Khan of Charsadda, Maulana Shah Rasool of Amazogarhai, Shad Muhammad Khan Mirzai, Sher Bahadur Khan of Kotarparn, Jalil Khan of Jalil, Khushhal Khan of Barikab, Shah Pasand Khan of Charghullai, *Amir* Mumtaz Khan, Barrister Muhammad Jan of Bannu, Muhammad Ramzan Khan of Dera Ismail Khan, *Hakeem* Abdus Salam of Haripur, *Mian* Sahib of Pakhlai, Qazi Attaullah of Mardan, Samin Jan Khan of Mohib Banda, Ali Asghar Khan, lawyer from Hazara, Effandi Sahib of Malakand and Hamza Khan, a friend from Gadar.

Our school had a shortage of teachers. So, I too would teach the boys. The other thing was that we were desperately short of money to pay the teachers. In Lahore, a *Khilafat* conference was scheduled which we went to attend. We met *Amir* Mukhtar Khan of Mirakhel (Bannu) who had also come for the conference with his two sons. His sons had left their studies at bachelor's level in Islamia College, Peshawar, in solidarity with Turkey. He placed them at our disposal, to teach in our school. The older boy was *Amir* Mumtaz Khan and the younger was Maqsood Jan. Infact, Maqsood Jan was the first headmaster of our school. When he left to complete his education at Islamia College, *Amir* Mumtaz took over from him. The British were not in favour of our *madrassah*. Whenever a new teacher would join the school, they would first try to frighten him. If he did not get scared, then they would tempt him with a good salary in some other school. Even Maqsood Jan, when he was coming to Uthmanzai, was harassed by the police.

Those days we started touring from village to village and door to door, to generate love and affection, brotherhood and national feeling amongst the people, and also for education, for the reform of evil social customs and practices, and assistance for education among the masses. My tours alarmed the British. Sir Hamilton Grant was the chief commissioner of our province. He called for my father and asked him what his son was up to. Whereas all the people were quietly sitting at home, his son was busy setting up *madrassahs*, touring the villages and inciting people against them. He asked him to stop me from doing so. His secretary was a man named Saadaullah Khan of Umerzai. He once said to my father, 'Look how much respect the chief commissioner has for you; he does not listen to anyone else to the extent that he listens to you. And you are not even able to stop your son's activity in order to please him.' My father came to me, sat me down and said, 'My son, you should stop these activities. You have got yourself into a lot of trouble. The government is unhappy about this and if nobody else is doing this, why do you have to do so?' I replied, 'All right Baba, if you say so, I will not do it. Many people have also stopped praying and I, too, will stop. But then do not ask me why I do not pray.' He said, 'Prayer is compulsory.' To which I replied, 'Baba, so is knowledge.' So, my father said, 'All right, well, go ahead and continue what you are doing.' Then he went to the chief commissioner and told him that we could not leave our faith, just to please them.

The Presidency of the *Khilafat* Committee
In Peshawar, differences had grown amongst the workers of the

Khilafat movement. They had split into two factions. One day, the followers of Haji Jan Muhammad convened a public *jalsa* in Shahibagh where proposals were put up that Haji Jan Muhammad was the most suitable person for the presidency of the *Khilafat* Committee as he had rendered many services to the nation and had also undergone several terms of imprisonment. There was a *Syed* from Peshawar, and the next day, his supporters convened a similar *jalsa* and put forth the proposal that he was of the progeny of the Prophet, had served the nation well, and that there was no other person as deserving of the presidency as he was. The people would then be asked whether he was acceptable to them and they would shout out that he was. This continued and one would be declared the president one day and, the next day, the other. There appeared to be no reconciliation in sight and the movement suffered a setback. The people of Peshawar were very good at political work, but this difference of opinion had reduced them to chaos and confusion. Whenever I visited the office of the *Khilafat* movement in Peshawar, both factions would separately tell me their version of the story, asking me to become the president of the Committee. I had no personal interest in doing so as I was not fond of public office and would always shy away from it. Finally, they compelled me to accept. I, however, laid down the condition that I would only accept if the donations, which were collected in Sarhad for the movement, would be spent in the province on the education of the people and not sent to Punjab. This was because, at the time, thousands of rupees would be collected here and sent to Punjab, where the leaders would enjoy themselves at our cost. They agreed to my condition, and thus, I became the president and Abdul Qayyum Khan Swati was chosen as its secretary. When we finished the work related to the school, I and *mian* Ahmad Shah began to tour the villages.

The Pukhtuns considered agriculture and trade as lowly occupations and would say that this was the work of the *baniya*. And the definition of a khan to them was that of one who did not even know the boundaries of the land which he owned! I would say to them to think about it – was such a person a khan or an ass? On one hand, we were touring the countryside trying to reform the Pukhtuns, and on the other, we were busy working in our fields ourselves. My schoolmate, Abdul Haleem had, at the time, been employed in the department of agriculture. With his help, I planted an orchard. Till then fruit and vegetables used to come to the villages from towns. When I created an orchard, I would also cultivate vegetables in it and would ask people to come and see what a blessing the outcome of one's own labour was. I would encourage them and say that if they could only focus their attention on agriculture, how productive the land of the Pukhtuns could become. It produced every kind of fruit, vegetables and grain. When the people's attention was attracted to agriculture, I established a market place to sell *gura* in Uthmanzai. My cousins and other khans would make fun of me and say, 'Look at him, indulging in the profession of the *baniyas*.' All our commerce and trade was, at the time, in the hands of the Hindus and *Parachas*. The Muslims would feel ashamed to trade. All the profit from our agricultural labour was taken by the Hindus and *parachas*. I did not bother about these taunts. Every month, I would gather the khans over a cup of tea and would ask them the current price of their lands and then inform them that, from just 10 per cent of the capital cost of their land, and whatever they earned from their lands in a year, I managed to earn an equivalent amount in a month. I would then show them the accounts of the *gura* market. I would also tell them that we employed *munshis, darwais* and *pandis* with us in this market, and they all earned a good wage for themselves. I would also remind them that commerce was an easy task and had a sizeable margin of profit. I would compare it to the hardship of farming and how this was dependent on the *patwari* and the *tehsildar*. All our lives were spent in looking at the sky, sometimes beseeching God for rain and sometimes for sunshine. In this way, I would make them understand the benefits of commerce. In a short time, the attention of the Pukhtuns was drawn towards trade and commerce, which gradually came into our hands. In this way, prosperity through agriculture and commerce came to our area. As a result, and due to its practical demonstration, people began to take an interest in agriculture and commerce, and such a revolution overtook them that, today, the ordinary, struggling people of that time are well off with big agricultural farms, commercial establishments and industrial units.

8

Jail and the Tale of the Jail

Pukhtano Juno dey zulfay baad ta neesee, Chay shamal ay
booen ralree ter Ranthambor!
(Khushal Khan Khattak)

Let the Pukhtun damsels, their stresses
To the northern breeze unfold;
So their scent is gently wafted,
Till (the Jail) in Ranthambor!
(Poem added by translator)

Arrest under Section 40 FCR

ON 17 DECEMBER 1921, WE WERE BUSY MAKING A FOOTBALL FIELD FOR the *madrassah*, when the police came and arrested me under Section 40 of the Frontier Crimes Regulation (FCR) and took me to Peshawar jail. Instead of the lock-up, I was put in jail. After me, my other associates were also arrested. I was locked up in the cell where criminals are normally kept. When I entered the cell, a nauseating smell invaded my nostrils. Looking around, I saw a pan full of human excreta. I came out immediately and told the warden that it was repulsively filthy and that it should be cleaned. He replied curtly that this was a jail and that I should move into the cell at once. Night and day, I was alone in this cell. My meals would be passed to me through the iron bars. Only when the addict sweeper of the jail would come to the cell to clean it, would its gate be opened, and when the cleaning was done, the gate would be locked again. At the time of cleaning too, a warden of the jail would stand over the head of the sweeper. The next day I found out that our other associates were also locked up in similar cells. In these cells there were ten of us, Abdul Akbar Khan Akbar, Abdul Qaiyum Khan Swati, myself and seven other prisoners who were all from Peshawar. Abdul Akbar Khan Akbar was arrested on charges of being a Bolshevik, and the rest of us for being *Khilafatists*. Because of the inhuman behaviour of the jail staff, our other associates were agreeable to being released on bail and were consequently set free. I permitted Abdul Akbar Khan Akbar to do so and told him that he was not a *Khilafati* and should get bail. Only Abdul Qaiyum Khan Swati and I were refused bail. When they realized that we were not prepared to pay bail, they removed us from these cells and took us before the deputy commissioner. The deputy commissioner was a strange man, and so was the case against me. When the deputy commissioner asked as to what offence I had committed, he was told by the police that, for one, I had participated in the *Hijrat* movement and, for another, was now establishing free *madrassahs*. The deputy commissioner told him that if I had done the *Hijrat* once, then why was I allowed to return? I told him that, regretfully, they had not only taken over our land, but now they were not even prepared to allow us to live in it. On this, sahib bahadur (the deputy commissioner) got angrier and directed his men to put me back in jail, sentencing me to three years rigorous imprisonment. Abdul Qaiyum Swati, too, like me, was sentenced to three years rigorous imprisonment.

I have already told you the story of the quality of the food in jail. The *darogha* of the jail, *Amir* Chand, was an honest man, and had a soft spot for the nationalists. He put me in the cell, no doubt, but did not put me to the task of grinding corn, and nor did he put fetters on my feet. He did give me the food of the jail, but it was somewhat more hygienic. Our cell was facing north and did not get either the morning or the afternoon sun and was consequently very cold. They had provided me with three old blankets and one floor mat on which it was very difficult to get any comfort from the extreme cold. It was the months of *poh-mah* and rain. We were exposed to the cold wind and were locked up night and day in the cell. But I was fortunate that there was a raised platform in my cell on which rice straw was piled. I would spread the floor mat over it and lie down. Whenever a good sweeper was on duty, we would be taken out for an hour or so in the sunshine. We could not sleep well at night because every three hours the guard would be changed, and the guard commander would clang the lock of the cell and cry out to us to say something. He would not leave until we responded, and if the response was late, the next morning a punishment would await us. I have also told you of the quality of clothes in the jail. Among the clothes provided to me, the shirt was not even up to my waist, and while praying, when I prostrated myself, the shirt would recede to my rib-cage; and the trousers were barely up to my knees. The attitude of the jail wardens was no less than that of the angels of punishment. It is only occasionally that a reasonable person is found amongst them.

In those days the possession of anything edible was considered an offence in the jail. There was a *lambardar* from our village who once offered me a piece of *gura* in my cell, which I declined to accept. He then placed it in my cell and left. A while later, the warden on duty informed me that the jailer sahib was coming on his rounds. On hearing this I was concerned about the piece of *gura* and did not know what to do with it. I concealed that piece of *gura* with considerable effort and anxiety. The *darogha* sahib came on his rounds but left without conducting a search. In those days, the prisoners and their cells were searched everyday. When the *darogha* left, I threw that piece of *gura* outside and resolved that, while in jail, I would abide by its rules and principles. I have seen my fellow political prisoners who indulged themselves in this and would, therefore, flatter the jail staff inordinately and would also bribe them.

The *Mujahideen* of Chamarkand

My elder brother, Dr. Khan Sahib, and a few others had come for the weekly meeting to see me in jail. They had brought a message from the government that I could run the *madrassah* but should not tour the villages. If I were to agree not to do the tours, they would set me free. But I did not agree to this. There were other prisoners in the cells, including the mujahideen of Chamarkand. When I was returning from Kabul, I had adviced them and also warned them against going to the Punjab and Sarhad provinces. They did not listen to me, and so had come to this pass. Before my imprisonment, they had been severely beaten up. When I was imprisoned with them, they finally got rid of this treatment. When these mujahideen were in Buner, they consisted mainly of Bengalis. The Bengalis were very affectionate people. The Punjabis amongst them were big intriguers and factionalists. When the Bengalis intermingled with them, they created factions amongst them. Finally, they murdered their own *Amir*, Naimatullah. The people of Buner expelled them from their area and so they finally went to Chamarkand. One of their leaders, Maulvi Fazal Elahi, was a factionalist and a dangerous man. I had met him in Kabul and advised him but could not change his nature, and on account of this factionalism, he had killed a very good worker, Maulvi Bashir. Later, after independence and the creation of Pakistan, Fazal Elahi went to Punjab. At that time, I was in jail. Maulvi Fazal Elahi, at the instance of the government and to please it, carried out a propaganda campaign against me and spread rumours. The police had befriended him and would ask him to bring to them any man of worth amongst the mujahideen. One of their companions, who was also a hafiz, was taken in hand by the police and made an informer. Whoever the police wanted to arrest, they would identify him to this man. He would go after him and, on the pretext of soliciting donations, would make him come down to the Sarhad province and then hand him over to the police. These prisoners from the mujahideen informed me that this man had been dispatched after another of their prominent leaders, and whether I could arrange for him to be alerted. They also told me that there was a Moomand in jail, who was being released in a day or two. His home was near Chamarkand. If I agreed to give him a letter, it could be delivered to him, and all their other companions would be freed of this menace. At first, I was not prepared to do so, because this was considered an offence in jail, but when I thought about it and found that he was a big menace for the people, I wrote the letter and handed it over to the Moomand. When he was freed, out of fear, he threw the letter near the main gate of the jail. That letter, by a strange coincidence, was picked up by the *lambardar* of our village who returned it to me. I asked him where he had found the letter. He told me that he was on guard duty and found it outside the main gate. If the government had got hold of this letter, it would have meant ten years imprisonment for me. I was still in jail when a few people from Kohat were brought in – a man with his nephews. They were all handsome young men. They, too, were thrown into the cell with us. The practice in jail is that the prisoners are taken outside early in the morning and given brooms to sweep the premises. They would be taken out from their cells early morning during the months of *poh-mah*. When they would bend over to sweep, there was a Punjabi warden who would kick them in their arses and knock them over and curse them. So, one day I asked them what they had been jailed for. They told me that they had fought over someone telling them not to eat excrement! It was the instigation of the devil and the code of honour of 'Pukhto' which made them react (to this). I asked them, 'Have you brought that devil and the Pukhto code with you to the jail, or left them both behind for the benefit of your relatives? See how this black-faced sepoy is treating you? Is that same devil and "Pukhto" not instigating you against him? Would it not have been better to have borne the insult of your relatives, rather than have to undergo this humiliation here in jail?'

Other political prisoners were brought here from Dera Ismail Khan jail to attend their hearing in the courts. One was Malik Khuda Bakhsh and the other Ramzan Khan, and a few friends of theirs. All the other political prisoners were in the barracks. Only I was confined to the cell and could meet the prisoners from Dera. Common criminals, too, are confined to cells for a week and then taken to the barracks. But I was confined to the cell for two months.

Transfer to Dera Ismail Khan Jail

Two months later, I was transferred to the jail in Dera Ismail Khan, meant for habitual criminals and die-hard political prisoners. At the time of departure, I was manacled and these were not removed even when I reached Dera jail. They locked me up in a cell and brought me twenty *seer* of grain to grind the next day. But I was fortunate that the grain was weevilled and not difficult to grind.

The Tale of the Jail

You will recall that an article used to be published monthly on life in jail in the *Pukhtun* magazine under the title, 'The Twentieth Century and I'. But due to my repeated arrests and due to my busy schedule, that subject was left incomplete. Since I was now confined in the jail at Hazaribagh and had no books to read, I thought that I should take advantage of this forced inactivity and make an effort to complete that article under the new title of 'The Tale of the Jail' (15 October 1931).

The condition of this jail was deplorable. The poor prisoners had to face many hardships. The staff was corrupt to the core and took bribes. Prisoners who had some money led a reasonably good life, while those who did not were miserable. The strange thing was that, in this jail, the *darogha* was not the one in sole authority; each employee had full powers, and each one ensured that his orders were obeyed. No one had any respect for the *darogha*; he had no authority, and no one obeyed him either. The reason for this was that he was an old man and was about to go on pension. The other reason was that he did not understand English. He had been promoted from a sepoy to a *darogha*, and the superintendent did not understand anything but English. So, the affairs of the jail were managed by the deputy *darogha*, Ganga Ram. The awe in which he was held was infinitely greater than that of the *darogha*. On account of this, the management of the jail was badly affected. When I was confined in the cell, a few prisoners from Peshawar came and said that they would bribe the *darogha* to take me out of the cell. But I told them that on moral grounds, I opposed the idea of giving bribes. That I was not a prisoner as such, but one who refused to provide surety for release on bail.

The food in this jail was inedible. The *darogha* used to pilfer, and the deputy *darogha* too had his share. I would grind grain in my cell. The chickpea that was given to me to grind was all weevilled and did not contain one grain that was whole. Its flour could not be sifted either, because then all that would remain would be the chaff. They would not bake bread from this kind of flour because its weight would decrease. Here, too, the poor prisoners were cheated. Bread baked from this flour could not even be held because it would break into small pieces and fall apart; so, it was held with both hands. I had never eaten chickpea flour bread and that too which contained more than 50 per cent impurities, on which one could not chew. With great effort I would eat only one piece.. What can I say of the quality of its dal and spinach? When someone falls sick in jail, he is taken to the hospital. But I was a political prisoner, there was no going to hospital for me. Only this badly lit, small room had fallen to my lot, in which I stayed all alone, day and night. The doctor would bring medicines for me here, and the superintendent would check on me once a month. After a few days I got better. I lost forty pounds in the one and a half months I stayed here. On account of a bad diet and lack of vegetables, I got pyorrhoea. My teeth got infected, my gums receded, and blood would ooze from them. Because of a poor diet, a disease had struck all the prisoners and four or five of them died almost each day. No one bothered to ask, because in the government of the British, a prisoner is not considered to be a human being and is treated like an animal.Nobody feels sympathy for the poor prisoners. When the disease spread, the superintendent got worried and, for its prevention, would occasionally summon two or three other Englishmen for consultations. But the disease could not be controlled by consultations alone, and nor is this possible. The disease was the outcome of bad food and vitamin deficiencies and nobody bothered to investigate that aspect. Who was there to do so? The problem arose because of the corruption of the jail employees. Even the ration that the government had authorized for the prisoners was stolen from them. The superintendent was strange and totally unaware of what was going on. He was led in whatever direction his subordinates chose, because his eyes were shut to the realities of the situation. One day a strange thing happened. Those who had been in jail know fully well, and those who have not been will find out that, every Tuesday, very early in the morning, all the prisoners are made to sit in rows in their barracks. The superintendent and other jail staff inspect their health, clothes, and cleanliness, and hear complaints, if any. On one such occasion, a prisoner got up and complained against the behaviour of a member of the jail staff, that he was beating him and was humiliated by him; he was cursed, and money was extorted from him; that he was a poor man, so from where could he arrange for money to be brought so that the staff member could be bribed? The superintendent asked the staff what they had to say in their defense. They told him that, 'Sahib, he wants wheat bread and *gura*.' So, the superintendent addressed the prisoner and said, "No! No!" The poor prisoner again recounted his tale to him. The superintendent again asked his staff, and was told that the prisoner wanted *gura* and *ghwaree*. So, the superintendent, raising his swagger stick and waving it at the prisoner, repeated, 'No! No!' The prisoner tried hard to make him understand what he wanted to say but failed. Finally, he ordered that the prisoner was a rogue and that he should be taken and confined to a cell – the deer desired to avenge its horn but lost its ear!

On the day of the superintendent's visit, he always made it a point to visit the latrines. That day would be a particularly trying one for the prisoners. Those who had loose stomach were greatly inconvenienced and humiliated, because once the latrines were cleaned, no one was allowed to use them until the inspection was over. If a prisoner had the urge to relieve himself, and had the courage to seek permission, he would run hurriedly to relieve himself. He would hardly have squatted, when the *lambardar* would be upon him. Sometimes he would ask for permission once or twice but instead of being given permission, would be humiliated. I have personally seen many poor prisoners who have relieved themselves in their trousers. Curses apart, this is that moment of humiliation which God may save everyone from. The British have enacted laws for us, but they are only meant to deceive the world. They are meant neither for them nor for their employees.

When I was unwell, I would be given milk and rice. After a week, when I got better, I was discharged from the hospital and was then back to my own jail food. But when the doctor saw the condition I was in, and the state of my health, he instructed the *lambardar* of the hospital that I was to be given a little milk from the supply of the hospital every evening. After the evening prayer, I usually meditated a little. I was absorbed in my meditation when someone called out to me. When I looked back, I saw the *lambardar* standing next to the railing of my room. He told me to put forward my bucket as he had brought milk for me. I got up and asked him where he had brought it from. He replied that Babu sahib had issued instructions that every evening he was to give me some milk because I was weak. I asked him whether this had been authorized by the government or whether the doctor had done so in his kindness. He replied that it was on account of the kindness of Babu sahib. I asked whether the doctor had sent it from his home or from the hospital. He replied that it was from the hospital. I said to him that he should not be offended, and that he should also convey my good wishes to the doctor and tell him I was grateful for his love and kindness, but that I cannot accept this milk. The *lambardar* was surprised to hear this and asked me why. I replied, 'Because this is not my right, it is somebody else's right, and to usurp that was haram in my view.' He asked me how this was somebody else's right. I told him that this milk has been authorized in the hospital for those who were sick and weak. Each sick person is authorized a certain quantity. I had no share in it. That either he would have to dilute the milk by adding water or would have to reduce the authorized quantity of each sick prisoner by a gulp to provide for me. Both these were immoral. One day, the *darogha* sahib came and told me that I was getting weaker by the day, and that from now on, he would personally look after my food; that my food would be brought from his home. I thanked him profusely but did not agree to his suggestion. I told him that I considered food from his home as my own, but if tomorrow he was either transferred from this jail or I was sent to another jail, then who would arrange good food for me? Then it would be me and the jail food. Now, at least, I had got somewhat used to it. The other reason was that anything which one could not do openly but had to resort to clandestine means, weakened one morally and made them abandon their principles, and created fear in their heart. I told him that though I had great respect for his offer, these things were harmful to my real purpose, and so I begged to be forgiven. In jail, by doing such acts, one became weak and vulnerable. The extent to which one could eliminate one's desires and needs, one would be happy and content to the same extent and avoid dependence on anyone. Similarly one day, the *darogha* sahib came while I was grinding grain. He said to me, 'Stop grinding this grain. There are two thousand two hundred prisoners in this jail, and what answer will I give to God? That this political prisoner was entrusted to my care, and was following His (God's) path and that I had subjected him to the arduous task of grinding corn?' I told him to look at the prisoner in the opposite cell – who was a convict of dacoity and murder and was in jail for this – grinding corn. Then why should I, who was a prisoner of conscience and was here for a pious purpose, not do so? When the *darogha* sahib realized that I would continue to grind grain, he sent me some flour with a few grains in it and said that when the superintendent came around, I should grind this. I told him that I will not do so. If he asks me what you give me to grind, I will not tell lies and tell him it is flour. In reply to this, the jamadar told me that then he would be demoted. So, I said, 'This is why I am insisting that you should not give me this, as this creates fear in one's heart.'

The Offences of the Jail

The moral standards of this jail had fallen greatly. The honour, neither of the young nor the old, was safe. If a prisoner pleased

Ganga Ram and the jamadar, he could do whatever he liked with anyone. For two rupees, some prisoners had their enemy humiliated and had been allowed to take boys to their rooms to satisfy their lust, although the rules of jail prohibit men and boys to be confined in one room. One day I told the *darogha* sahib that he was a Muslim, a pious man and also led the prayers, but that the honour of Pukhtun boys was not safe in his jail. That in the Peshawar jail where the *darogha* was a Hindu, the honour of the Pukhtun boys was safe. One day, a man from Bannu (Bannusai) came and asked me to write a letter for him, to send to his father. I asked why he wanted to write home. Tears welled up in his eyes and he replied that his father was poor and did not own anything. But that he had a wife whom his father should sell and send him the money. I got angry and said to him, 'Are you not ashamed to talk like this?' He said to me 'Khan, little do you know. When I came to this jail, I was given twenty *seers* of grain to grind, which I did well. But when the jamadar came, he said that the grain had not been ground properly. He caught hold of me and beat me until he was exhausted. Every day he tells me to give him money, otherwise I would be in this condition for the rest of my life. I am not such a weakling that I cannot do physical labour. But they make some excuse or another. By continuously beating me on the head, they have made me bald. All the arduous tasks of the jail have fallen to my share. Despite this, I am beaten every day. They are now telling me that they will produce me before the sahib and have me beaten with rods. This, I consider a big insult, which is why I have come to you to write the letter, so that I could get some money and am freed of this monster.' Many people have been killed by the jail employees for money. Those who escape from jail or who can enjoy themselves in it is because they are either hardened criminals or have money. I have already told you about the quality of food in jail and how the prisoners are worked like bulls; made to work oil-extracting presses; draw water with Persian wheels; grind grain and perform other tasks unbecoming of human dignity and beyond physical endurance. Such treatment could not have been meted out to human beings by the harshest and tyrannical of governments. Whatever is the whim and fancy of each Englishman and person in authority, is the law. Other countries have one law for everyone. In our country, there is one law for the British and another for the local; one law for the government servants and another for the common citizens; one law for the rich and another for the poor. Like a nose of wax, British law adjusts in the direction it is turned in. Restricted to spending my days in a small cell in solitary confinement, my weight slowly went down, and my health deteriorated. Finally, the jail officials were compelled to take remedial action by taking me out of this life of seclusion. One day, the superintendent sahib came and told me that, in future, I was to work in the jail workshop during the day, and at night, I was to sleep in my small cell. Then, hopefully, he would soon plan for my early release.

My Labour

When I came out of solitary confinement, they took me to the jail workshop. This was a large workshop where hundreds of prisoners worked and various articles were made. My work was to make envelopes, but along with it, I also worked as a weaver because I liked the work and was of the view that one should master a trade so that one could earn a livelihood from it and not be dependent on others. My instructor was a malik from Bannu, a good man with a wonderful temperament. He was also a master of his chosen craft and took great pains in teaching me. In a short while, I learnt how to weave *khaamta* and towels. If I had not been transferred from this jail and had stayed on, I would soon have mastered this craft. When I was transferred, just this one longing remained, that I had to leave this craft midway and could not take it to its logical conclusion.

Another instructor in the workshop was a maulana from Bahadur Killi, another good soul who taught me the art of making envelopes. Sometimes, he would cook cauliflower in the workshop. One day, while he was cooking, the superintendent arrived and smelled it. He looked in every direction but could not locate the cooking pot. When he left, the cauliflower had, regretfully, all been burnt. My instructor was very upset, but what could he do? Gradually the interaction of the jail inmates with me increased and, in a few days, many of them got to know me. All sorts of people can be found in jail. I also found out the reason for my solitary confinement. The jail staff generally keep the political prisoners away from the common criminals because they are afraid that if the political prisoners find out about their activities, they would also incite the common criminals, and if this happens, the money-making of the jail staff would suffer. In this jail, corruption was rampant, and anything could be achieved through bribery. These corrupt jail employees had devised numerous ways of collecting bribes from the inmates. The most reprehensible of these methods was to humiliate a man of status and honour. When one gave ten rupees to Ganga Ram and told him that he desired to humiliate a prisoner, he would pocket the money and go away in the company of a few *lambardars*. He would make some excuse and direct the prisoner to take off his trousers. In this fashion he would have the poor wretch humiliated publicly. This was the most successful way of earning money – because, today, you would have me humiliated by Ganga Ram, and tomorrow, I would write home and ask for money, or would ask to meet a relative for this. I would then give Ganga Ram a bribe and, to take revenge, would have you humiliated at his hands. Sometimes, brawls amongst the Pukhtuns would also erupt due to this.

Factionalism in Jail

Unfortunately, factionalism in this jail was rife amongst the Pukhtuns. They were divided into two camps – prisoners from Peshawar and those from Kohat, Bannu and Dera Ismail Khan. The jail staff would take advantage of this factionalism and would provoke the prisoners to violence over trivial matters. After the violence, a strange spectacle would be enacted. Those prisoners from whom the jail staff could extract money would be locked-up in guarded cells so that they could not send messages out. Touts would be let loose who would visit them once or twice daily and convey conflicting information to them, and scare them that criminal cases were being prepared against them. They were told that they would either be hanged or sentenced to life imprisonment because many other inmates were prepared to testify against them. The touts would tell them that such and such a prisoner (whom they had fought with) had died and another was on the verge of death, and this was the time to do something about it; this was the time, or else they would be doomed. The poor prisoner would panic and send home a telegram asking for money. Those whose relatives came quickly with the money would be let off, no matter how guilty they were; and those who could not do so, would suffer and be punished.

The more I learnt about conditions in jail, the more disheartened I got about the fate of the poor Pukhtuns. Finally, I decided that it was essential that I see the leaders of both parties, talk to them and warn them against the consequences of their actions. I have always believed that the Pukhtuns, as a race, are very good people. They can be reformed with very little effort, on the condition that someone could explain matters to them. They are in such a bad situation today because no one is prepared to explain things to them, or are bothered about them. In this jail, there was an old prisoner, Naseer, from *Ranlrezai*. Once he invited me to have tea with him. Normally I am against such entertainment in principle, but on this occasion, and on account of his being elderly, I accepted the invitation. He, too, used to work with me in the workshop. He was well versed in *darai* and *nawar* weaving. He took me around the workshop and showed me specimens of his skill and art, which surprised me. I told him, '*Kaka*, it is a pity that we Pukhtuns work so well for others but do nothing for ourselves. If you continue the skill and craft that you have mastered in jail, when you are free, it can benefit you and the nation greatly.' He promised that he would do so when free. But when, I went on a tour of *Ranlrezai* in 1929, I met the old man and saw that he had not yet started this work. Soon tea was brought out and we drank it. I was amazed at his boldness and quietly asked Naseer Kaka whether they were not afraid of the jail staff. He laughed, and said, 'Kaka! You are still new, and yet unaware of the condition of the jail. In jail, if you bribe the staff, you can do whatever you wish. I am a poor man and cannot bribe anyone. Whatever you see is on account of the kindness of the jail staff, that this year they have awarded me the contract to supply *naswar* and tobacco. I can live well off the proceeds. I give them a share and my brothers too benefit from the operations.' On hearing this I was surprised and asked him, 'Kaka! The jail and contract?' He told me that everything in jail was awarded based on a contract, and these contracts were given out annually through competitive bidding. Here contracts were awarded for the supply of *gu*ra, *ghwaree*, rice, tobacco, *naswar*, milk, meat and other things. There was a separate contract for each item. After tea, I discussed the problem of disunity in the ranks of the Pukhtuns and explained the damage caused by factionalism and family feuds. I told them that if they weren't evil, then they should make their Pukhtun brothers understand the implications of these practices and forbid their brothers from falling into them. When I was leaving, they showed me their store house of tobacco and *naswar*. They took me aside to a place in the room and asked whether there was anything there or not. Apparently, there was nothing there, just plain ground. They dug up the place a little and a lid appeared. Beneath it was a big pot and in it were packets of different kinds of *naswar,* ready to be sold at prices ranging from two to eight annas each.

Gradually, I started to work in the workshop and met with every Pukhtun there and would try to make him understand the implications of factionalism. They all gradually began to realize the truth, which began to spread amongst them. One day, a khan from Bannu who worked with me in the workshop, invited me to a meal and cooked a huge platter of *sheera* for me. The *sheera* from Bannu was very popular in the jail and was always prepared for an honoured guest. Besides me, some other guests had also been invited. They appeared to me to be men of status, standing and influence, and chiefs of their own factions. After the meal, I said that I wanted to discuss an important matter with them. I told them that since the time that I had come to this jail, and whatever conditions I had come to know about, had led me to the conclusion that the Pukhtuns were in a very bad shape. Apart from the different kinds of cruelty and bribery, the honour of the Pukhtuns was not safe here. That I had heard that one Pukhtun often bribed the jail staff in order to humiliate his Pukhtun brother. To avenge himself, the other Pukhtun also does the same. They should observe this closely, and see how harmful this is for their earthly existence and for their life in the world to come. The jail staff was involved in these practices for their own monetary benefit, whereas we had nothing but loss to suffer. Our money was gone, our honour was gone. Today you spend money for my humiliation, and tomorrow I, for your humiliation. In this way, no Pukhtun was left with honour. The other thing which I told them was the divison of the Pukhtuns into two parties – one belonging to Peshawar and Mardan, and the other belonging to Kohat, Bannu, and Dera Ismail Khan, and that generally, they quarrelled over trivial matters. I said to them that I wanted to bring one matter to their notice and, if they thought over it and it pleased them, they would be freed of this degradation. All Pukhtuns belong to the same nation, are brothers and are descended from the same ancestor. We share a common honour and humiliation. If we were to act on the Hadith of the Prophet (PBUH) of 'What you do not consider to be good for yourself, do not inflict on another,' we would achieve success very soon. Whatever we intend to do with our fellow Pukhtun, it is necessary that we give this a good thought and look within ourselves and consider, that if someone were to do the same to us, whether it would please or grieve us. If it were to please us, then it should be done; and if it were not to please us, then we should refrain from doing so. The other thing to remember is that if, amongst us Pukhtuns, anyone does something wrong or immoral, we must not assist him. Because, if we do so, both the nation and society are harmed, and it is such individuals who are responsible for the destruction of their nations.

It is necessary that we always befriend people who are virtuous. If, amongst us, one person does something bad, it is incumbent upon us to expel him from our brotherhood and social interaction. Today, when the Pukhtuns are on the wrong track, the reason for this is that we cannot differentiate between good and evil, and nor is there anyone amongst us to make us understand. I suggested to them that we need to differentiate between good and evil, and after each night's prayer, promise God that we would shun the company of those who disobeyed His injunctions, and boycott them. If we are to honour and keep this promise, the condition of the Pukhtuns will change at once. It was necessary for each one of us to make as much effort as we could, to make each Pukhtun understand this. On this, we offered a prayer for peace, happiness and tranquillity, and took leave of each other.

When Ganga Ram learnt that I was guiding the prisoners towards the right path, which would put a stop to his bribery and corruption, he immediately complained to the superintendent, and spun a web of lies and falsehood against me, and made him confine me, once again, to my former dark and dingy cell. I could get no sleep at night due to the mosquitoes and had nothing to cover myself from them. I had a blanket, no doubt, but to wear it at night is an impossible proposition in the heat of the summer. I would usually sit up at night and was concerned about the possibility of being bitten by a scorpion. I would get hold of my *panlra* and, like a blind man, hit the floor randomly around me. In the morning, when I would look around, I would see two or three dead scorpions on the floor. The poor prisoners are kept safe from these deadly creatures only by the grace of God.

My Sin in Jail

Early one morning the superintendent and the *darogha*, Ganga Ram, entered my cell. The superintendent's look and attitude towards me had undergone a change, and from his appearance it was clear that he was angry. In his hand he had a sheet of paper. He read it out to me, pointing out that under the jail rules, these constituted serious offences, and that he wanted to institute a criminal case against me. He had accused me of the following crimes:

'You are a dangerous revolutionary and inciting others to revolution in the jail. You preach to the jail employees that service of the government is a sin. On account of your preaching, the sweeper of these cells has resigned from service. You carry out propaganda amongst the prisoners and make efforts to incite them to rebellion.'

I replied that I would say nothing about the institution of a case against me, and that he should proceed as he considered just and appropriate; that whoever had informed him of all this, had not reported the truth but spun a tale based on a web of lies and falsehood. I did acknowledge that one sweeper had resigned on my instigation, but the truth about this was not as reported to him. The fact of the matter is that, one night, the *darogha* had posted the sweeper over me as a guard. During a conversation, he informed me that he had many children to support, and could not make ends meet on his meagre salary. Sometimes the prisoners, of their own accord, and without him asking for it, gave him something. He did not force them to do so, and asked what the position is in Islam if he accepts this money. I told him that taking this money was unjustified because they were beholden to him. They would be willing to do so of their own accord, only if they were not bound to him; and that it would be proper if he would manage within his own salary. He told me that living just on his meagre salary was not possible for him. So, I then told him that, instead of his service with the government, he should start a business of his own and that, perhaps, he would then earn enough from it to support himself and his large family.

If anyone were to ask me such a question even now, I would give him the same answer. As to the other allegations, they were baseless. No doubt, I had preached but not for them to violate the rules of the jail, or to incite them to revolt. On the contrary, I had persuaded them not to fight amongst themselves and to peacefully serve their sentences – performing the labour assigned to them, and not to bribe anyone. Whenever this preaching brings about a diminution in the income of Ganga Ram and his employees, I am declared a rebel and an evil person. Then I told him that this jail was passing through a very bad time, and he was blissfully unaware of it all, and nor could he be informed about it. Even if he was informed, he could not bring about any reforms. That, the other night, he had come on his rounds. There was noise coming from a barrack; that he had gone and seen for himself what the quarrel and noise was about. Did he understand what this noise was about? I did not know what his staff had told him, but the fact is that the quarrel was over alcohol. I have not seen such corrupt and bad-charactered officials that I see in this jail. On my saying this, the man cooled down somewhat as his eyes were opened to the truth. He told me that it would be best if I could give him a written response to the allegations levelled against Ganga Ram. I sent in my written reply, and later found out that he had summoned Ganga Ram and other officials to his bungalow and reprimanded them. But despite knowledge of all this, I was not taken out of the cell because they had warned him that if I were taken out, the prestige and honour of the government in general, and his, would suffer and the administration of this jail would be adversely affected.

When the news of my solitary confinement in the cell reached the other prisoners, they were provoked. I was put under strict security. I would send messages to the prisoners to be careful, as I knew full well the tyranny to which innocent prisoners could be subjected. In this jail a few Hindustani officers and sepoys were also serving their sentences. They had been sentenced for their political views. One of them somehow got to me and told me that they had decided to go on a collective hunger strike, and sought my permission for it. I thanked them and forbade them from doing so, because I was against agitation by the prisoners in jail. In those days, Babu Sultan Muhammad of Naukhar had come to Peshawar to see me and had applied for permission to meet me but that was denied. To meet him was my legal right, but the jail authorities, to keep the circumstances of my solitary confinement in a cell secret, had refused to give the required permission. If the condition of a political prisoner and the circumstances in which he is detained in jail cannot be made known outside, who can get to know the conditions in which the other criminals are held! Anything can be done with them, even if they are to be burnt in a fire. I myself know full well, that if anyone wants to see the justice and civilization of the British, they should visit the jails.

Since my health was failing, the next day the superintendent came to see me. He wrote on my ticket that in the early evening I should be taken out of the cell for an hour each day and be made to walk in the fresh air. From solitary confinement in a cell, day in and day out, I occasionally got really fed up. And when I would think about my own innocence, I would get very angry. But then, I would reassure myself because, in the service of the people and the nation, people have undergone all kinds of hardships. This was a test and a training from God. These trials and difficulties will not be for a lifetime. In the end, the outcome is bound to be favourable.

Dera Ghazi Khan Jail

One day, early in the morning, the superintendent entered my cell in a hurry and informed me that he had transferred me from this jail; the police was waiting outside to escort me and I should get ready to leave. What did I have to prepare to leave? I just had a *Quran Sharif*, and this I slung across my neck, and left. When I arrived at the main gate of the jail, the police manacled me. My feet were already fettered and around my neck was an iron collar. A car was parked outside around which were bayonet-wielding policemen. The superintendent handed me over to a Pukhtun *thanedar* who seated me in a tonga. All the policemen who could be fitted into this tonga were made to sit in it, and those who could not find a place were made to stand on the road side. And so, we left. When we arrived in Darya Khan, the train had already left. This made the *thanedar* anxious but nothing could be done. The reason for our not being on time was that there was a flood in the Abaseend river, and this had dismantled the boat bridge, and its repair took a long time. We had to spend the night at the railway station as there was just one train that passed by daily.

The *thanedar* sahib locked me up in the waiting room and stationed a double guard on me. Anyone who has seen the Darya

Khan railway station would know that it is situated in a waste land. Where were the people, if any were to come and see me? The other thing was – who knew me here? But the police was bent on taking its precautions. At some distance from this place, there lived a pir sahib who had come to know of my presence and came to see me. It was quite possible that he might not have been able to do so, except that he did a clever thing. He had brought with him a basket full of a variety of the choicest sweets of the area. These, difficult to resist, made the policemen allow him to see me! We talked for quite some time. When he was leaving, the pir sahib invited me to a meal. But I thanked him and said that this was not an appropriate occasion for me to accept his invitation because I happened to be the guest of the government. The pir sahib broke into laughter and left quite pleased with himself. Soon it was night, but the police did not take me out of the waiting room, nor did they remove my handcuffs. I was more comfortable in jail because there, at least my hands were free. The *thanedar* sahib was a talkative man, but he was not one for action. In his conversation he would try to give one the impression of being a nationalist, but would always exclaim that what could he do, as the superintendent of the police had sent his *munshi* with him so that he did not show any kindness or consideration towards me. But even after the *munshi* had left, I could not detect any change in his behaviour.

I, very diplomatically, tried to make the *thanedar* sahib understand, that now, since it was dark and there was no one round, we should take a little stroll outside on the platform and breathe a little fresh air, as I was tired from sitting all day. But he turned a deaf ear to all this. I was, therefore, obliged to make him understand that in jail my health had deteriorated significantly and the doctor's instructions had been that I should be made to take a walk in the fresh air for an hour in the morning and an hour in the early evening, every day. If my health was harmed, he would be held responsible for it. This statement had some effect on him and he ordered the policemen to take me outside and allow me to stroll on the platform.

The British and their employees have one trait in common: until one speaks to them very bluntly, they are not likely to listen. The police did not take the manacles off my hands even when I slept but did me the favour of putting both handcuffs on one hand, and tied the chain to the bed. I could not sleep. When the train arrived at the station, some policemen went ahead and had one compartment vacated for our use. I was not aware of the jail to which I was being taken. This had been kept a secret from me When our train stopped at different stations, they would shut the doors and windows of our compartment, and two armed men would stand guard at the door and not allow anyone to come close to us. But this method of concealing my identity did not work as people would see the bayonets and the rifles of the policemen and would gather outside my compartment in large groups. The government, in its stupidity, provided me the publicity that I got! Finally, our train came to a stop at the Ghazighat railway station. A jamadar and two accompanying policemen were waiting for us on the platform, who directed the policemen to remove the manacles from my hands. Nadir Khan, the Pukhtun *thanedar*, was known in the police force as 'the dacoit'. He had, for some reason, separated from us and had stayed behind. When he came and saw my hands were free of manacles, he got flustered and asked who had removed them. The jamadar, who was a Hindu, told him that, on behalf of the authorities of Dera Ghazi Khan, he had been appointed for me, and that from now on, I was his responsibility. That it was his belief that such people never attempted to escape; that I had come to jail of my own accord and had courted arrest. That I was not a dacoit, and asked what the need was for so many policemen, rifles and bayonets. I informed him that the government of North-West Frontier Province (N.W.F.P) had dispatched them to demonstrate its own authority. The *thanedar* sahib was a little embarrassed, but the employees of the government are strange people indeed, and they are not prepared to pay attention to such matters. We were still discussing this, when a Hindu arrived with a glass of milk. I had no intention of drinking the milk, but the sincerity of that man compelled me to have it. The truth is that the issue of 'Hindu and Muslim' has been created by the British and the selfish people associated with them. If the Hindu was actually concerned about the fate of the Hindu, and the Muslim of the Muslim, the condition of our land and its people would not have been what it is. As far as I can remember, and based on my personal experience, I find that the Hindu employees of the government have always treated me much better than my fellow Muslims.

At this point, I realized that I had been transferred to the jail in Dera Ghazi Khan. We left the station for the town of Dera Ghazi Khan, which is twelve miles from the Abaseend river. Here, *yakkas* are plied for hire; the kind that, until recently, were common all over the country. We hired a *yakka*, and with great effort reached the Dera Ghazi Khan jail in three hours. When the gate of the jail appeared, the jamadar told me that, if I did not mind, he would now put manacles on my hands because we were approaching the jail. I told him that I would never forget his kindness and decency and put my hands out to him. He manacled me.

The gate was crowded with visitors. They all stood as spectators to see me, perhaps because I appeared strange to them. They were not to blame as my condition was laughable. When I myself looked at my tall build and short trousers, a cap with ears, an iron ring around my neck, fetters on my feet and manacles on my hands, I could not but appear as a sight to my own self. The food and the clothes of the jail, its rules and regulations are made in such a manner that no prisoner can maintain his dignity and honour.

During those days, the political prisoners were having their meetings and their relatives had come to see them. For this reason, the main gate was crowded. The policemen took me to the office and handed me over to the jail wardens. When the jail staff inspected my jail ticket and warrant, and learnt that I was a political prisoner, they became sympathetic and gave me a lot of assurance. They wrote my name in the jail register. The *darogha* sahib directed that I should be taken to a barrack, and that my manacles, fetters and iron collar were to be removed. When I was being brought to the jail, the political prisoners had heard of my arrival. Most of them came to see me and showed me a lot of affection and helped me to break off my fetters. When this was done, I felt like a different person – at first, I was a prisoner, and now I was free!

At the time of transfer to this jail, I was upset about leaving my own province and the Pukhtuns, because I have such a lot of love for both, that I cannot adequately express in words. I prefer living in poverty in my own land and amongst my own people, rather than living a life of affluence and comfort in a foreign land. But the removal of the fetters did me some good because it was impossible for me to walk, bathe and turn on my side when asleep. In summer, they were hot, and in winter, they were cold. Amongst the visitors gathered in the *deodai* of the jail was Lala Doochand and Ummat-ul-Islam's brother, who was a barrister-at-law. They later told me that when they saw me with manacled hands and fettered feet with the police, they shivered, and thought that I must be a most notorious dacoit. Let alone the political prisoners, here even the common criminals were neither manacled nor fettered, and did not have planks of wood placed with their fetters. Political prisoners were not given the treatment that was extended to them in the jails of our province. I then had a bath and, since food was ready, I ate it and thanked God for extricating me from the jail in Peshawar. If I had continued to remain there, it would have been difficult, if not impossible, to have come out alive. There was a vast difference between the food here and that in the jails of Sarhad. I was provided with a mat and one blanket. I went to my assigned barrack, spread out my bedding and lay down to sleep.

Life in Jail

This was a small, pleasant and a clean jail. It had a total of just three barracks, in the centre of which was a small hospital. One barrack was assigned to those political prisoners who were placed in category 'A'. The next was the hospital; and then there was our barrack. Here, those of us who were placed in category 'C' were housed; and in the third barrack were the common criminals who were also made to work outside, both in the garden of the jail and inside, because the political prisoners there were not allowed to go outside. For the political prisoners there was only one kind of labour, to spin cotton yarn and to make ropes out of *munj*. The spinning-wheel was meant for the special class of political prisoners, and the making of ropes was restricted to 'C' class prisoners. The next day, when the superintendent sahib came and I was produced before him, since I was a 'C' class prisoner, my name too was listed amongst those assigned to the making of ropes. I had never done this work before. All my other companions were good at it and helped me and inducted me into the art of rope making. The next day I told the superintendent that since I could not do this work, it would be better if I were to be assigned to work at a grindstone, because I did not think it was right that I am not be able to complete the task assigned to me. Both the *darogha* and the superintendent were good people, treated me well, and never asked me about not being able to finish my work. So, they then assigned me to the spinning wheel.

The jail authorities had given us 'C' category prisoners a separate kitchen, and its management was totally in our hands. All the provisions and the utensils were clean and according to our requirements. The cooking was also done by our fellow political prisoners, and so our food was edible. Occasionally, the 'A' category prisoners would also treat us to the food of their kitchen. But despite this, relations between the 'A' and 'C' categories of political prisoners were strained. The reason for this was the differentiation that the British had created. I was an outsider and was not aware of the internal differences between them, but I was distressed by the lack of unity in their ranks. Finally, it reached a point that the 'C' category political prisoners refused to accept anything sent by the 'special-class' prisoners. I was opposed to this as there should be no distinction between the political prisoners, and all of them should be treated equally. At the time when I informed the superintendent that I could not handle the rope-making work from *munj*, and that he should kindly put me on to something else which I could do, he assigned me work on the spinning wheel, which was done by the 'special-class' prisoners. He also had clothes tailored for me, which were my size, and transferred me to the 'special-class'. The distinctions which the British had made were with the intention of creating disunity and disarray within our ranks. But I am not in favour of giving trivial matters such importance that they cause harm to our relationships and to the freedom movement. Because whatever we were doing was not for our personal benefit but the well-being of the nation and the country, and no one else. Furthermore, you all know very well that the battle which we are waging against the government today is because we want to remove class differences, and in their place, establish equality. This distinction cannot be removed until such time as we succeed in our mission and assume responsibility for running the affairs of the country. When we gained control of political authority in our own province, we enacted a law that all political prisoners should be treated equally and well. We did away with distinctions. But when the Muslim League government took over from us, that equality of treatment was also done away with, and they meted out such ill treatment to us, which even the British had not done. And this, despite the fact that when the Muslim Leaguers were imprisoned during the time of our government, we had treated them equally and well and in accordance with the law that we had enacted.

We were about twenty prisoners in this 'C' class barrack. Apart from me, there were two Hindus and the rest were Sikhs. We all shared a good relationship. Whatever quarrel or difference of opinion arose between them, I would be called upon to mediate and resolve it. But I had one difficulty – I could not sleep at a stretch at night. Our Sikh brothers would get up at midnight for a bath inside the barrack and start their *pooja-path* (worship ritual). The ritual was not only confined to bathing, but along with that, loud recitations from the *Granth* Sahib, which would wake all of us up. What a pity, that we do not think of the comfort of others. This recitation could also be done quietly. Unfortunately, this practice is also common amongst us Muslims and Hindus. We always follow our own inclination and have very little or no regard for others. This is a great shortcoming amongst us. We should always consider the comfort and well-being of our fellow human beings; and whatever we do, we should first experiment with it ourselves. If we are comfortable with it, only then should we choose it for others.

The jail authorities agreed that I should be transferred from my present barrack, but were afraid, in case this gave rise to an objection by my fellow prisoners. It was the considered opinion of Lala Doonichand Ambalvi and some other friends that I should be transferred to their barrack, so that I could join them there. It was due to their efforts that the superintendent transferred me. We were sixty-six prisoners in all in this barrack – six Muslims, and the rest were Hindus and Sikhs, in equal numbers. This barrack was large and was divided into three compartments. In one compartment almost all the prisoners were Hindus and Muslims, and in the second, they were all Sikhs; and in the third compartment was our kitchen and the store. We all had a common dining room where we all would sit together for our meals, on the same *dastarkhwan*, because we were all educated and tolerant of each other's religion. Here I could sleep well and had no complaints because our companions would show great concern for the comfort of others. The only problem that I faced was that the sleeping platform was small for me, and so two had to be joined to make me comfortable. The other good thing was that, here, I was spared the embarrassment of having to make ropes out of *munj* and was only concerned with spinning, and that I could do well. The jail authorities informed me that they wanted to make me a *lambardar*. I would then not have to weave, I would get significant remissions in my jail sentence and would also be allowed to sleep out in the open. I informed them that I was not prepared to accept this. On finishing my daily work, I would sit down to my studies. In addition to books, three Urdu and three English newspapers were received here daily, from which we learnt of the political conditions and developments in the country. But what gave me most satisfaction and was a source of a lot of comfort, happiness and joy was that I had found good company here, which consisted of people of all faiths. I benefitted greatly from an exchange of views with them. Another advantage was that God provided me with an opportunity to make efforts to dispel, to the extent that I could, all those wrong impressions and misunderstandings about the Pukhtuns, which the British, through their false propaganda campaigns, had created and spread.

False Propaganda against the Pukhtuns

Selfish people had spread such propaganda and disinformation against us, that it cannot be imagined. The people of Hindustan did not have any know-how about the Pukhtuns. These poor people were completely in the dark about the affairs of the Pukhtuns. And, perhaps, I was sent to the Dera Ghazi Khan jail by Providence for this task, because a number of prominent and responsible Hindu and Sikh leaders were interned here, so that I could make them aware of the truth, and thereby, remove the fear and suspicion from their hearts, to make them aware of the reality of the Pukhtuns, and substitute disunity and hate in their hearts with love and amity. When Lala Doonichand became friendly with me, he told me that when he had, for the first time, set eyes on me in the main gate of the jail, and had realized from my appearance that I was a Pukhtun, he was convinced that I had been jailed either for committing a murder or for having been involved in a dacoity. It is possible that the other prisoners might have formed this impression as well. This was despite the fact that Lala Doonichand was a very important leader of Punjab, a prominent lawyer and a well-versed and well-informed man. They just could not imagine how a Pukhtun could be involved in social work, in service to God and the land and that too in God's cause. After knowing and living with me, they became aware of my thinking and actions, and they all developed a lot of love and affection for me. As our relationship grew, these thoughts, which we had suppressed in our hearts, came to light. In the beginning, the conversation between us was always about the Pukhtuns. In the early evenings, we would emerge from our barracks for a stroll. Since we were not allowed to go anywhere else, we would walk around our barracks in the jail compound. During these walks, it often happened that one or another of our companions would emit air from their stomachs. Since in Pukhtun society, this was considered a grave social misdemeanour, I would laugh at them. On some excuse or the other, I would separate myself from them and laugh to my heart's content. Then I would re-join them in the walk. Since my companions were not aware of the fact that I laughed at them behind their backs, one or two of them would again emit air, and I would again be engulfed in a fit of laughter. Finally, this happened so frequently, that I had to force myself to get used to it, and it would no longer make me laugh. Later, when I gave this matter some thought, I no longer considered it such a stigma. In fact, if one thinks about it seriously, controlling the emission of air is bad for the health.

Whenever someone joined me anywhere, the conversation invariably turned to Sarhad and the Pukhtuns, and such questions were asked which would really amaze me. Our arguments would be very bizarre. I would always try to make them understand the reality and remove suspicion and hatred from their hearts. One day, a leader said to me that they had heard the Pukhtuns drank human blood. I replied that, yes, they did so indeed. He then asked me the reason behind it, to which I replied that it was delicious. The man was dumbfounded. I in turn asked him whether he had, up till now, not drunk any human blood. He replied, 'Oh dear!' After a while I asked him whether he had seen Sarhad or the Pukhtuns and whether he was aware of the conditions in which they live or had dealings with them. On hearing this, the man was quiet for a while, and then slowly replied that he knew nothing about Sarhad. I then told him that, perhaps, he had knowledge of the unseen, or had some revelation about the Pukhtuns. He answered that, no, he had heard all this from others, and that most people talked in such terms about them. I told him that, 'All this talk is incorrect. The Pukhtuns, too, are people just like you. Just as there are good and bad people amongst you, similarly, there are amongst the Pukhtuns. All this talk has been invented by the enemies of the Pukhtuns, and it is their propaganda which has spread this misinformation. The objective of all this is to deceive you and to give us a bad name. Because if they do not frighten you and do not give us a bad name, then how could they rule this land?' In the early days, new tales would be told each day in our barrack about the Pukhtuns. This was good for us because it would give me an opportunity to explain matters and rebut them. One day, a Hindu and a Sikh from our barrack, along with some jail officials, got together. I also became part of their gathering. When I arrived, the atmosphere in the group changed, and an argument about the Pukhtuns began. I informed them that the people of Hindustan knew nothing about the Pukhtuns. The truth was that the Pukhtuns were not like what they imagined them to be. On this, Sardar Kharak Singh, who was a prominent leader of the Sikhs, said that there was no doubt about the fact that the Pukhtuns were very easily provoked. I replied that, 'Sardar sahib, this might be so, but our Sikh brothers are no less than them.' Amongst our people there is this great deficiency that we are always concerned about highlighting the shortcomings of others, but are not mindful of our own. Because of this, we are a weak and deprived people. Instead of pointing a finger at someone else, we should point it at ourselves, and before attempting to reform others, it is necessary to reform ourselves. Of all my companions I was closest to Lala Doonichand, but unfortunately, he harboured the most suspicions in his heart about the Pukhtuns. He always discussed matters related to the Pukhtuns with me and had the strangest ideas and thoughts about them. I would do my best to remove these apprehensions from his heart. One day, when I was finally sick and tired of this, I said to him – 'How many of you are there in Hindustan?' He replied that they were about twenty-two crore. I said, 'And we Pukhtuns are only twenty-two lakhs. Despite the fact that you are many more in number and if, even then, you fear the Pukhtuns, then may God have mercy on you and remove this fear from your hearts. But you should always remember that no nation which is engrossed in fear is entitled to exist. This world is not for the faint-hearted. Mark my word, that until you do not acknowledge the Pukhtuns as your brothers, and repose your trust in them, and make them stand shoulder-to-shoulder with you, this country can neither be freed and nor can it be put on the path of development and prosperity. No faint-hearted nation can exist in this world.' When he heard this, Lalaji was satisfied to some extent, and I was spared having to answer many questions.

The Disease of My Teeth

In this new jail I began to get some exercise because I was freed from the chains of my fetters. I was able to exercise, and I thought that, with exercise, my health would improve. I would get stronger and put on some weight. In the jails of Sarhad, both my weight and health had deteriorated. There, I was in continuous solitary confinement and the food was worse than that fed to animals; and there was no political company either to suit my temperament. Here, I spent my days and nights in the pleasant company of learned political companions. National leaders had been gathered here from everywhere. I considered this environment a great blessing from God and wanted to take full advantage of it. I expanded the horizons of my vision, gained much experience, and also studied a great deal. Despite all this, my health deteriorated by the day, and the exercise which I did was of no benefit to my health. My weight maintained its downward trend even though I was quite comfortable here and faced no great difficulty at all. The superintendent of the jail, *Mian* sahib, was a good and pious man and thinking that the food of the jail was not enough for me he authorized a ration of half a *seer* of milk a day for me as a supplement, but even that was of no help, and my weight continued to go down. One reason for this, in my view, was also that I was very much in love with my wife, and I would dream of her every night. The other reason could be that, due to the bad diet in the jails of Sarhad, I had developed pus in my gums. When the doctor examined me, he told me that this was the cause of my bad health and pyorrhoea. On the day of the parade, my companions and I mentioned this to the superintendent. He wasted no time in examining my gums and agreed with our assessment – that the reason for my deteriorating health was, indeed, this. However, he said that for an accurate diagnosis and treatment, the services of a good dental surgeon would be required and that such a dentist was not available in this town. The superintendent sahib addressed a letter to the inspector general of prisons to have me transferred to Lahore, because my gums and teeth were infected, and my health had been damaged. This letter was the result of the goodness and kindness of the superintendent's heart, because in the British government, nobody considered the suffering of prisoners as anything better than that of a stray dog. I have, in my time, seen many prisoners who go through their illness patiently waiting, until finally, one day, they put down their heads and die. To have a recommendation letter written for a prisoner in jail requires a lot of luck. Similarly, such good fortune is also required for the request to be accepted. This deceitful government, which the British had established to humiliate and degrade humanity, can at best be described as a paper government. In other words, it was a government whose primary concern is to send letters from one office to another endlessly, and vice versa. So much time is wasted sending replies that the real purpose of the entire exercise is defeated. This problem is not restricted to the jails, it is endemic in the remaining departments of government as well.

One year, the floods in our rivers in Hashtnagar hit the village of Dadniro. The poor, unfortunate inhabitants of the village wrote many applications for assistance. In response to this, the deputy commissioner, and many other officers came to inspect the site. But by the time the official paperwork was completed, the village had been swept away along with very productive agricultural land, which was enough for twenty *galrain* of *gura*. But remember that all such difficulties are faced only by the unfortunate inhabitants of this land; if the British themselves are in such need, then decisions are made over the telephone. Why should this be so? Because this government has not been established by them for the benefit of the people, but for their own benefit.

The political prisoners were treated well in Dera Ghazi Khan jail, and the 'C' class prisoners also managed to pass their time well. The *darogha* was a good man and, besides other things, he provided us daily with both Urdu and English newspapers. If anyone arranged for any fruit or other essential commodities for himself, he could do so. After some time, a certain Maulvi Ismail sahib, who was from the Ghaznavi family, came to the jail, and after a few days, without any justification, exchanged heated words with the *darogha*, the outcome of which was disastrous. All our companions thought ill of the maulana sahib's conduct, and the *darogha* sahib also took it to heart, because he never treated us the way other prisoners were dealt with in the other jails. From that day on, he stopped coming to visit us, and withdrew all the other concessions that he had granted us. He arranged for four Pukhtun *lambardars* to supervise us. The leaders would secretly arrange for their daily newspapers and would also read them secretly. One day, a Pukhtun *lambardar* saw this and he went and snatched the newspaper from their hands. They pleaded with him to return it, but their request was not accepted. The *lambardar* proceeded towards the door of the barrack to show the paper to the *darogha*. One man hurriedly came to me and told me to go after him as the *lambardar* had snatched the newspaper from his hands and was taking it to the *darogha*; and that I should prevent him from doing so and retrieve it. I went and called out to him. He came, and I asked him for the newspaper. He told me that if the *darogha* found out, he would be relieved of his duty. I told him to take a look at these people, and to tell me what crime they had been brought to this jail for. He returned the paper to me and I gave it back to them. News was received that the inspector general of jails was coming on tour to the Dera Ghazi Khan jail. He was a very bad-tempered man and was bitterly opposed to the Congress and other nationalist prisoners. He had ordered that nobody in the jails should be allowed to wear either the Gandhi cap or the black turban of the Sikhs. All the Sikhs of this jail wore black turbans; and those who were Muslims or Hindus, wore Gandhi caps. It was the goodness of the present superintendent that he had neither told the Sikhs not to wear black turbans nor the Muslims or the Hindus not to wear Gandhi caps. When the inspector general was coming, the superintendent told us that the black turban and Gandhi cap were prohibited in the jail and that, if for a short while, we were not to wear them, it would be good of us. We did not agree to this proposal of the superintendent. When the inspector general came and saw my companions in black turbans and with Gandhi caps on their heads, he lost his temper and asked the *darogha* why he had not taken the turbans and caps away from us. The superintendent informed the inspector general that the *darogha* had informed him of this, but he had permitted them to wear this headgear. The inspector general ordered that the turbans and caps should be taken away from them. The political prisoners then sat down and discussed the issue amongst themselves and decided that this was their legal right; that whenever they wanted to wear them, they would do so. And if these were to be taken away from them, then they would be obliged to take off their other clothes as well! Here, I intervened and told them that I myself wore a turban, and that I had put on a cap out of deference to them, but now, in these circumstances, what was I to do? Sardar Kharak Singh told me that I should not join their agitation. The next day the superintendent sahib summoned each one of us, individually. Whoever was wearing a cap was told to take it off. The Sikh inmates were also told to take their black turbans off. Thus, he removed their caps and turbans, and they, in accordance with the decision already taken, took off their other clothes as well. After a few days, the deputy commissioner arrived to inquire into this. He was accompanied by the superintendent and the *darogha*. They came to our barrack. The political prisoners gathered for them. Sardar Kharak Singh told the English deputy commissioner that they had rendered many services to the government. That they thought that since their faces were white, their hearts would be white as well. During this exchange, a Sikh cried out '*Jo Bole, So Nihal* (Whoever cries out).' so Nihal.' All the other Sikhs present responded with the cry of '*Sat Sri Akal!*' The Englishman was alarmed and left our barrack in a hurry. He got very angry with the superintendent and said that *Mian* sahib had kept 'horses' in the jail, and that they got out of control because they were too well-fed. He ordered him to institute criminal proceedings against them. The next day, the *darogha* informed us that it was the rule of their jail and that whoever violated it was sentenced to one year's imprisonment. So now, he was ordering them to wear their clothes. And if they did not do so, then tomorrow, criminal proceedings would be instituted against them. When these political prisoners heard this announcement, from amongst the Muslims, Maulvi Muhammad Ismail, and from the Hindus, a man who was my friend but whose name I have since forgotten, refused to wear their clothes. The remaining Muslims and Hindus all complied and wore their clothes. Among the Sikhs, not even one agreed to wear his clothes. The following day the magistrate came. One by one, all the offenders were brought before him and he would sentence each one of them to nine months' additional imprisonment. And the superintendent of our jail, *Mian* sahib, who was a very good man, was suspended and demoted to the next, lower rank i.e., he was given the rank of an assistant surgeon and transferred from this jail. Captain Hayes was posted in his place. The only fault of *Mian* sahib was that he was a pious and good man who did not treat the political prisoners harshly. Our new superintendent was an Englishman who was also a reasonable man and did not misbehave with prisoners. He had earlier been transferred from the army to the civilian government. He was not as bad as the other civilians usually are, and nor was he as cunning and perfidious. The poor soul did not know anything. Whatever the *darogha* told him, he would carry out. His attitude towards us was that of an English gentleman. But being an army man, he was a little too upright and, therefore, a misfit in the system. The first day when he visited our barrack, he saw that some of us were inside, others outside, some bathing and some walking. He did not say anything then but when he visited the second time, he could not tolerate this any more. He stood in the middle of our barrack and stamped his foot and said that he did not wish to see this any further; that he came to the barrack only for a few minutes and wanted to see a better standard of discipline. In future, during these visits, all the prisoners should be seated in their respective places. On his departure they would then be at liberty to do what they wanted. Our political brethren were, perhaps, of the view that he, too, like the *Mian* sahib, would wish not to see things as they were. In the early evening, the *darogha* came and read out the orders of the superintendent to us and we came to know what his thinking was. On the day of the parade, when the superintendent visited our barrack, all the prisoners were seated in their appointed places. When I saw this, I was very surprised. When the superintendent left, I said to my fellow prisoners that it appeared as if they too had become sycophants like me, because during the time of the previous superintendent, they would not be seated, and if I pointed this out to them, they would say that they were not sycophants like me. But today, they too were all seated inside. How was it that what appeared as something bad to them yesterday, had become good and acceptable today? When the superintendent came for the other parades, some of the prisoners held books in front of themselves. These too were then prohibited. He ordered that whenever he came, books were not to be read. After this, at the time of the parade, the reading of books was banned. One wonders what our brothers would have done if our former superintendent had done this. Since he was an Englishman and had authority behind him, no one had the courage to take any steps against him. The pity is that we confront those who treat us well and bow down before those who beat our heads with a cane. This is a bad trait indeed and we should shun such habits. After a few days the *darogha* was also transferred, but his substitute was also a good person, who treated us well.

During this commotion the order for my transfer to Lahore jail, for dental treatment, had come, but the jail authorities did not disclose it to us. I was sitting in the barrack when, early one morning, a *lambardar* came and told me that the *darogha* sahib had summoned me to his office. When we arrived in the office, the police was waiting. I got suspicious that perhaps orders for my transfer had come and I was being taken to Lahore for dental treatment. Upon arrival, the *darogha* sahib said to me that orders for my transfer had arrived and that I was to go the next day to Lahore, with the policemen. I told him that at least he should have allowed me to inform my companions and take leave of them. But the *darogha* turned down my request and told me that he did not consider my taking formal leave of them as essential, and if I had any luggage there, he would send someone to fetch it for me. I told him that I was a 'C' class prisoner and what baggage could I possibly have? I told him that I intended to go back to the barrack only to bid farewell. But he refused. When my political-prisoner friends heard of my transfer and the manner of my going, they too tried their best that we should see each other. But, unfortunately, we could not meet. The jail authorities, no doubt, did me the favour of not putting fetters on my feet. Or maybe the practice of fettering political prisoners was not ordered in Punjab the way it was in Sarhad. In Punjab, there is a 'special class' of prisoners as well, and there is a vast difference in the diet, clothes and treatment of 'C' class and special class prisoners. The police manacled both my hands. There was a tonga waiting outside near the main gate. They made me sit in it and we were taken to the railway station. When we arrived on the bank of the Abaseend river, the ferry was ready. We crossed the river safely. The railway station is adjacent to the river bank. The police had a seat vacated for me, which I was asked to occupy.

Bacha Khan (sitting on right) with elder brother Dr Khan Sahib (Abdul Jabbar Khan). Dr Khan Sahib was twice Chief Minister of the NWFP in 1937 and 1946 (Congress–*Khudai Khidmatgar* government) and then also Chief Minister of West Pakistan in 1955. Standing left to right: Mariam, daughter of Dr Khan Sahib; Mehr Taj, Bacha Khan's daughter; and Safia Sadullah, daughter-in-law of Dr Khan Sahib.
Courtesy Mohammad Saleem Jan, grandson of Bacha Khan, Peshawar, Pakistan.

Left to right: Abdus Samad Khan Achakzai, Bacha Khan and Dr Khan Sahib. Abdul Samad Khan Achakzai was a Pukhtun leader from Balochistan and founder of the first political party in the Province, Anjuman-i Watan. Dr Khan Sahib was Chief Minister of NWFP in the 1937 and 1946 Congress–*Khudai Khidmatgar* governments and Chief Minister of West Pakistan in 1955 under the One Unit scheme.
Courtesy Mohammad Khan Achakzai, Balochistan.

Bacha Khan with
Red Shirt Movement
volunteers.
Photo credit: Alamy.

Bacha Khan and Sons (left to right); Wali Khan, Bacha Khan, Ghani Khan and
Ali Khan, at Burj Hari Singh, a staff residence of Islamia College, Peshawar.
*Courtesy Mohammad Saleem Jan, grandson of Bacha Khan and son of Yahya Jan,
Peshawar, Pakistan.*

Bacha Khan with Mahatma Gandhi. *Courtesy Nasir Ali Khan, Grandson of Bacha Khan, Uthmanzai, Charsada, Pakistan.*

Bacha Khan with Mahatma Gandhi, Sushila Nayyar (far right) and another associate, Amtus Salam (far left), during their visit to the North West Frontier Province in 1938.
Photo credit: Alamy.

Khudai Khidmatgar–Congress Cabinet of 1946 in NWFP. Left to right:
Mohammad Yahya Jan (Education Minister and Bacha Khan's son-in-law),
Dr Khan Sahib (Chief Minister and Bacha Khan's brother), Qazi Ataullah
(Revenue Minister), and Mehr Chand Khanna (Finance Minister).
Courtesy Mohammad Saleem Jan, son of Yahya Jan, Peshawar, Pakistan.

The NWFP Cabinet of 1946. Second row from the bottom sitting on chairs –
(second from left) Mohammad Yahya Jan (Minister of Education and Bacha Khan's
son-in-law); (third from left) Dr Khan Sahib (Chief Minister); (fifth from left)
Qazi Ataullah (Revenue Minister); (sixth from left) Mehr Chand Khanna (Finance
Minister). *Courtesy Mohammad Saleem Jan, son of Yahya Jan, Peshawar, Pakistan.*

Bacha Khan and Mahatma Gandhi surrounded by their supporters in Uthmanzai.
Courtesy Nasir Ali Khan, grandson of Bacha Khan.

Bacha Khan with social
reformer and freedom
fighter Vinoba Bhave.
Courtesy Mohd Saleem Jan.

Sahibzada Muhammad Khurshid.
Courtesy Muhammad Salim Sahibzada, son of Sahibzada Muhammad Khurshid.

Nawab Sir Sahibzada Abdul Qaiyum (1863–1937) founder of Islamia College, Peshawar, (1913), and was first Chief Minister of NWFP in 1937.
Courtesy Imtiaz Ahmad Sahibzada family.

Bacha Khan sitting in the Constituent Assembly after Independence, 1947.
Photo credit: Getty Images.

Bacha Khan being received by Prime Minister Mrs Indira Gandhi on his visit to India, October 1969. *Courtesy Nasir Ali Khan, grandson of Bacha Khan, Uthmanzai Charsada, Pakistan.*

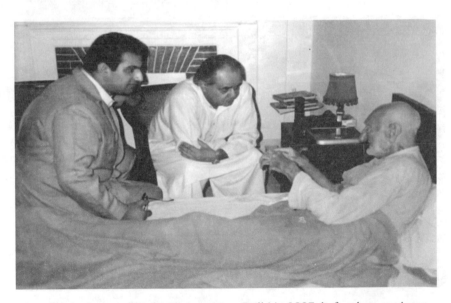

Last living picture of Bacha Khan in New Delhi in 1987, before he went into a coma and passed away, at the residence of Mohammad Yunus (brother of Yahya Jan) who opted to stay in India. Adil Shahryar, son of Mohammad Younas (left) with Dr Humayun Khan, Pakistan's High Commissioner to India can be seen talking to Bacha Khan. *Courtesy Dr Humayun Khan, Peshawar.*

Outside view of Bacha Khan's Mausoleum in Jalalabad, Afghanistan.
Photo by Mohammad Anwar Danishyar, Afghanistan.
Courtesy Ajmal Maiwandi, Kabul, Afghanistan.

Bacha Khan's house in Uthmanzai, Charsada. Left to right: Imtiaz Ahmad
Sahibzada (author); Nasir Ali Khan, grandson of Bacha Khan (at the back),
Shandana Khan (great grand-daughter of Qazi Ataullah) and Azizullah Khan of
Zaminabad Mardan, grandson of Qazi Ataullah. 2017.
Courtesy Shandana Khan.

During this time, people lacked the enthusiasm which they had in the beginning for our movement. It seemed as if the political movement had died down completely. Due to this we were able to complete our journey in comfort and ease, and arrived in Lahore the next morning. I was taken from the station to the Lahore jail on foot. Here, too, there were no signs of enthusiasm in the people for the political movement. We arrived at the jail and the police handed me over to the jail authorities and left. These policemen treated me very well. The jail authorities handed me over to the *lambardar*. Before anything else he took me to the godown and replaced the pair of clothes, which were tailored for me in the Dera Ghazi Khan jail in accordance with my height, with clothes which, like those of the Sarhad jails, were ridiculous; and when I put these on, I was a spectacle to behold. There was no difference between these clothes and those in the jails of Sarhad. I wondered what I looked like to other people. Like a common prisoner, I was put in a solitary confinement. These cells were from a previous era and were made from adobe, and were cracked in numerous places, and there were some apertures in them for light and fresh air. I had been sent to this jail for the treatment of my teeth. This jail also contained many political prisoners, and they had a separate compound. Instead of me being imprisoned with them, I was confined in a cell. I used to tell myself that I had been sent here for treatment, and to be confined in this heat of the summer, and in such a small cell, with ordinary criminals, would really prove beneficial to my health! In the early evening, the gate of my cell was opened, and I was brought out only for as long as it took the sweeper to take out the pan of night soil from my cell and clean it, and to fill a water pitcher for the night and leave. Some curry and roti were brought for me in a black bucket and then, hurriedly, he locked me up in my cell again and left. That food! Who could possibly want to eat it? I forced myself to swallow it and finally, when night fell, I lay down to get some sleep. From those cracks in the walls, flies, mosquitoes, insects and ants emerged and began to bite me. The heat was so intense, that no one could sleep because of it. Even if I occasionally dosed off, the changed guard would come and wake me up. In the jails, the guards are changed every three hours. When the new guard arrives, he calls out to you and continues to do so until you have answered him, and he is satisfied that you are present in the cell and have not disappeared. In this way, the night went by and the morning dawned. Early in the morning, a *lambardar* came and took me out of the cell for a stroll. There, other prisoners were seated in pairs. I, too, was made to sit amongst them. I was paired up with another prisoner. We were not allowed to move or to get up. This place was very nice. Huge trees stood all around and shaded it. To every tree, a dummy prisoner was tied, and a man with a cane in his hand was standing beside each and struck the dummy with great force. I was surprised to see this spectacle, because I had not seen any prisoner being lashed before in any jail. I found out from my fellow prisoners that these were dummies and the prisoners were being taught the gruesome art of how to flog. As we were observing this, a prisoner was brought out. It was not apparent from his clothes that he was a convict. He was wearing a fine pair of trousers, a coat, and had a fancy hat on. He was neither paired up like the rest of us and nor was he made to sit. He was having his walk when the *darogha* arrived. But this Englishman paid no attention to him. This *darogha* sahib, before doing anything else, signed his ticket. After his departure it became apparent to all that he was an Englishman who was convicted for having raped someone. But despite committing such a grave and cruel crime, he was clad in decent clothes, fed a good diet and treated well. And here we were, for the sake of our land, people and Islam, jailed without any cause and suffering imprisonment without having committed any offence. When the *darogha* saw my ticket and signed it, and realized that I was a political prisoner who had come for medical treatment, he, despite this, sent me back to my cell and had me locked up. This *darogha* was a Muslim whose name was Khair-ud-Din sahib. I have observed that in all jails the Muslims were very loyal to the British, and to please them, would treat all political prisoners very harshly. When the political prisoners heard about my arrival and my confinement in a cell, they went to the *darogha* and questioned him as to why he had confined a political prisoner with ordinary criminals. Amongst these political leaders were the leading politicians of the Muslims and the Hindus. The *darogha* feared these politicians, and so he transferred me to the compound of the political prisoners. This was a fine place. For one, it was large, and for another, it had many large and shady trees. Its cells and barracks were made of burnt brick and mortar, and they were large and airy. Whichever political leader learnt of my arrival would come to see me. Here, there were inmates belonging to all schools of thought and persuasions, and their love and affection was a great gift and source of strength for me. I would exchange views with everyone. Their knowledge and experience benefitted me a great deal. My example was that of a *talib* of a *madrassah*, and my time with them was spent usefully. In their company, I learnt a great deal and my experience grew. In this jail there were four of us detained for being *Khilafatists* – one was Agha Safdar, the other Malik Lal Khan, the third was Raza Khan, a *razakar*, and I was the fourth. From the Congress, there were many. I have forgotten all names except that of Lala Lajpat Rai. All the jailed Congressmen were Hindus. After four days, I was called to the office and produced before the superintendent who examined my teeth and gums. He was also a doctor by profession and said that he could not diagnose the disease, only a dental surgeon would be able to do so. He told me that I could call for a dental surgeon at my own expense and gave me permission to get myself treated. When I got back to my barrack, I informed the other political prisoners of this. They arranged for the surgeon, Dr. Prem Nath, who came the next day. He took me for a walk and, in the presence of the *darogha*, examined my teeth and gums. He expressed great sorrow for the condition I was in and voiced his resentment at the fact that my health had deteriorated because of the bad diet that I was given in the jail. He cleaned my teeth and gums with great skill and care, and extracted those which were rotten. For future, he prescribed medicines and instructed me how to use these. He told the *darogha* sahib that medicines were not as effective for this disease as was the required diet. The sympathy, love and affection which the doctor displayed in examining me had a profound effect on me, which, to this day, I have not forgotten. As he was leaving, I told him that I was not poor and that my money was lying in the jail and I could afford his fee; that I would be grateful if he would take his fee. He refused to do so. And when I said this to him again, he replied, 'Would it not be a matter of shame for me to accept a fee from those who, for the sake of the freedom of the nation and the prosperity and welfare of its people, were voluntarily undergoing hardships and imprisonment, on our account? And who undergoes such hardships for us, like going to jail? If we cannot make the sacrifice of going to jail, then we can at least serve them, in the name of God.' When I heard this, I too became silent. Khair-ud-Din Khan, the *darogha* of this jail, was a very clever, cunning and a corrupt man. The superintendent was totally dependent on him and would follow him blindly. Yogurt, milk, bread and meat were meant for those who were sick but he would have the superintendent authorize them for the healthy. He was, however, scared of all those political prisoners who were influential and could have their voices heard in the newspapers. He would please all of them in some way or the other. In addition to this, he would give them special concession in receiving visitors, newspapers, books and journals, and had befriended them. But there were no supplementary food items for those political prisoners who were helpless, and whose voice could not be heard, despite their ailments. To me, this was extremely degrading and shameful conduct for the political prisoners. The superintendent was a total non-entity who would not do anything without a nod from the *darogha*. Most superintendents are like this. I have concluded that there is absolutely no need for superintendents. They are a burden on the jails because only that takes place in the jail what the *darogha* desires. The higher posts have been created by the British to accommodate themselves. These superintendents of the jails were mostly civil surgeons. A civil surgeon should never be appointed as a superintendent. The doctor should be a separate person who has nothing to do with the prisoners or the administration of the jail. In England, the British have adopted this approach for themselves. A doctor cannot do justice to the requirements of the sick and weak prisoners, and therefore, the prisoners do not look upon him as a doctor. In our compound, whenever the *darogha* entered, it was everyone's effort to try and be the first to get to him and offer respect. Because I did not consider this appropriate conduct, I would be compelled by my conscience not to be a part of this. This is not because I was annoyed with the *darogha* sahib, or that I did not wish to greet him. Whenever he came near me, I would greet him, but would never try specifically for this purpose. Perhaps because of this, the *darogha* was annoyed with me. And despite my illness and weakness, and what was prescribed on my ticket, even the milk that I had been authorized in Dera Ghazi Khan jail was stopped, as was the diet which the dental surgeon had authorized for me. My friends felt this, but on account of the concessions he had allowed them, they did nothing about it. Finally, one day my companions mustered up enough courage to tell the *darogha* sahib to kindly authorize the diet which the doctor sahib had prescribed for me. He replied that I should approach the superintendent sahib in this regard. I understood that he was not favourably inclined towards this. I knew full well that the superintendent sahib was completely in his hands and would do nothing without his advice. But I was obliged by my companions to approach the superintendent. The next day, when the superintendent sahib summoned me to his office, I told him that he probably knew that the dental surgeon had proposed a particular diet for me on my ticket as treatment for my teeth, and had told me that this was like a cure for my disease and I should eat it. That I would be grateful to him if he were to authorize this diet for me, or else, that I should be permitted to bear the cost of this diet myself. He refused on both counts and told me that he did not consider it appropriate to sanction it. I thought to myself there was no justice here, and nor was there any law or procedure, and the law consisted of the pleasure and wishes of one man. Arguing with him was pointless. So, I kept quiet and left his office and went to my barrack.

There were many Pukhtuns detained in this jail, but they were not allowed to visit our compound. Sometimes, however, they would perform night-guard duty over us. I hardly ever got an opportunity to talk to them. There was a Pukhtun on the jail staff too, from the village of Sukalr in Doaba, who was fond of me. Even though I would forbid him, he would still occasionally bring me things to eat. I am strictly against receiving food items in jail, because this makes one morally weak and creates fear in one's heart. I would do my best to make him understand and forbade him, but he did not comply. I would enjoy his company. He had recently come from home and would give me news of our area. It was the months of *har-pashakaal* (June–July) and the heat was at its most intense. During the day it was bearable because of the shady trees, but the nights were spent in difficulty because we were confined to the barrack and usually till twelve midnight, nobody could sleep. When the night wore on, the mosquitoes would torture us, because our hands and feet were exposed to their bites. We had nothing to cover ourselves with because, summer and winter, there is only a blanket for a prisoner to cover oneself, and in the summer one does not want to go near a blanket.

I was in this jail for a month and was happy in the company of the people here when, without any notice, I was transferred back to Dera Ghazi Khan jail. When I arrived in Dera Ghazi Khan jail, I realized that peace between the jail authorities and the political prisoners had been re-established. They sent me back to my old barrack. My former companions were very happy to see me and embraced me and greeted me with a lot of affection. There were only a few days left for my benefactor, Lala Doonichand's release from jail. He told me that he was thankful to God that I had returned, and he had met with me. The next morning when the superintendent came on his rounds, the first thing that Lala Doonichand spoke to him about was the sorry state of my clothes, and told him that I should at least be given clothes appropriate to my height and built, and then he showed him my ticket and the recommended orders about my diet. He at once gave directions to the *darogha* that I should immediately be supplied with clothes which fitted me, and if they could not be found in the store, they should be tailored for me. He also authorized half a *seer* of milk and one *chatak* of butter daily, as part of my supplementary diet.

A few days after my arrival, the month of *Ramzan* started. When the fasts approached, our Hindu companions met with the superintendent and requested him for all kinds of facilities for the Muslims. The next day, when the superintendent came, he asked who amongst us would be fasting. He directed that those who were fasting would get, in addition to their normal food, one *seer* of milk and one *chatak* of *ghwaree* as a supplement and, for the *paishmanay*, arrangements would also be made for fresh food to be provided. We all thanked him for his kindness. We were only six Muslims in all. Of these, two expressed their inability to fast, of whom one was a barrister and the other was a student. The remaining four of us started to fast. The heat of *har-pashakaal* in Dera Ghazi Khan is not easy to bear. But with the grace of God, we didn't experience any difficulty in fasting and the month passed in comfort, and Eid arrived. What possible Eid can there be for the unfortunate prisoners? After Eid, Lala Doonichand Ambalvi and Abdur Rashid Khan were to be released. All of the political prisoners decided for a party, which we would give in their honour in our barrack, and a farewell address. In the party, both of them also delivered speeches eulogizing our services to the cause of freedom and the welfare of the people.

Dera Ghazi Khan is a terrible place in terms of its climate. The heat is intense and it rains about once a year, and sometimes once every two years. Instead of raining water, it would rain dust! Sometimes, such a dust storm would come, that it rained dust for two or three days at a time. Such a fine layer of dust would descend from the sky that it could not be seen. But when one looked around, everything was covered in a mantle of dust. When the dust storm came, the sun would be hidden by dark clouds and the bright day would become night. It was impossible to protect oneself from the onslaught of these dust storms. Whatever one ate had dust in it; when one spat it was full of dust; when one blew one's nose, there was dust in it. One could neither save one's clothes from it and nor could the bedding be kept safe. When we got up from sleep in the morning, the bedding contained the outline of our bodies. Everyone wore dusty faces and ears. Everyone was a sight to be seen. When we looked at each other, we would want to laugh. Unlike the others, I suffered more because of my one pair of specially tailored clothes. This was because 'C' class prisoners are authorized only one pair of clothes every six months, and it was impossible to wash them, dry them and save them from the dust. Besides this, winds full of dust would come occasionally. Beyond everything else was the searing wind, which would blow incessantly all of summer. It would begin to blow from seven o'clock in the morning and last till four in the afternoon. It was so hot that when it struck your face you would feel as if it was a fire burning every uncovered part of the body. Ordinary criminals suffered greatly at its hands, particularly those who worked in the sun or in the orchard. Every day four or five of them would fall unconscious from heatstroke. Sometimes on account of the heat, one or two would die. So, I would submit myself to it by reposing trust in God. There is no worse jail than this in the whole of Punjab; that is why it was selected as the jail of choice for political prisoners, and they used to call it the Andaman Islands. Jail employees would be sent here as a punishment posting. In 1922, it was the month of August. It was early evening and I was seated in my barrack when I was handed an envelope carrying a letter from my mother. I was very happy to receive this as I really loved my mother and she loved me too. In the letter, after expressing her love and well wishes for me, she stated that God Almighty has been very gracious and kind to me. He had granted me a son. That she was writing to me first to congratulate me, and for my advice on what he should be named. This was because they had decided that it was I who should name him. When I read this, it made me even happier, and I praised God and made this supplication to Him that this newborn son of mine, along with his other siblings, should grow up a good and pious person. That my children should be good-charactered and knowledgeable and be the servants of their people. May God be their helper and preserver and that they be saved from the cruelties of the oppressors. I proposed the name of Abdul Ali for him and wrote to my mother the next day.

The government of the British is an unaccountable government. Every Englishman is autonomous, like the pharoahs. No matter what its functionaries do to the citizens, there is nobody to question their actions. There were quite a few of our companions who, despite not having the required education or standing, had been given 'special class' (in jail) by the convicting magistrates, while I was imprisoned as a 'C' class prisoner; and, despite the passing of a year, was still treated as such and no one was at all concerned about this. But even though several government functionaries would come to see us and inquire about our health and general conditions and make appropriate arrangements, nobody ever thought of me, or were intentionally displaying a lack of concern. In the summer, all the prisoners except me could sleep out in the open. I was the only prisoner locked up in the barrack. One day the jail authorities summoned me to the office and informed me that they proposed to make me a black-uniformed *lambardar* and that, with this, I would benefit on two counts – one, the remissions for good conduct in my jail sentence would be doubled, and for another, I would be allowed to sleep out in the open. I would have no work other than acting as a messenger for the political prisoners. I, however, refused to accept the appointment, because this was against our principles. Our principles were non-cooperation with the government, whereas this would be considered a kind of cooperation. This, for a political prisoner, was a major weakness: that when free, I did not cooperate, but when jailed, I became a sycophant and a collaborator. This was a big sin and an immoral act.

After the release of Lala Doonichand, elections were held, and he was elected as a member of the Punjab provincial assembly. He raised a big hue and cry about me in the assembly and put the government to shame, saying that, to date, I was being treated as a 'C' class prisoner. The government replied that I was a prisoner of the government of Sarhad, and that the government of Punjab had nothing to do with me. He replied that, as of now, I was in Punjab and that I should be treated at par with the political prisoners of Punjab. He finally convinced Punjab government to issue an order and write to our superintendent to correspond with the Sarhad government on my behalf. The superintendent sahib was a fine man who had a lot of sympathy for me. He immediately wrote to the Sarhad government, but it did not reply. When he insisted and reminded it, the government would give some meaningless response because its aim was to torture me, so that my health would deteriorate further. In the exchange of this purposeless correspondence, a lot of time went by. But Lala Doonichand was a very determined man who did not leave them in peace, and continued to remind them until I was finally placed in the 'special class'. At about this time, I learnt in jail that, after my arrest, the students of our Azad *madrassah* in Uthmanzai had started a big movement all over the area. They held *milad* functions from village to village, which were well-attended. My son, Abdul Wali, would begin the function with a recitation from the Holy *Quran*, then he and Master Abdul Karim would recite nationalist poems, followed by my eldest son, Abdul Ghani, who would deliver very moving and emotional speeches. He would then ask the audience to ponder for a while over why the British had detained his father; what was the offence that he had committed? That I had neither committed a murder, nor a dacoity; and nor was I guilty of any other moral crime. That his father's only crime was that he was imparting education to their children, and was inculcating in them unity, brotherhood and kinsmanship; that he was bent on removing those customs and practices from amongst the Pukhtuns, which were destroying them; that he was determined to make them stand at par with the civilized nations of the world. This was the offence for which the British have jailed him and put him in 'C' class rigorous imprisonment. He would say that it was now necessary for them to continue the good work which I had started and to take it further. The British would then realize that the Pukhtuns had woken up and become aware and that they could no longer be used for their purpose and nor could they be suppressed.

Their efforts had a lot of impact on the people, and everyone started to assist the *madrassah,* which prospered greatly. When I heard all this, I was elated and thanked God that my sacrifices had not gone to waste, and that the nation had realized that Bacha Khan was undergoing imprisonment for its sake. Everyone gave this matter a lot of thought, and our reform and education movements received a great boost from it.

Religious Prejudice

We were five Muslims in this jail. We had not, out of deference for our Hindu and Sikh brothers, eaten meat for a long time, and nor did we long for it. But a *hakeem* sahib from Sialkot was brought as a prisoner of the movement. He was fond of eating meat and the desire to do so also arose within us. So, we took the decision to eat meat like him. We sent *hakeem* sahib to the jail authority and he explained the matter to them. It was the view of the jail authorities that meat could also be cooked in the same kitchen, even though the *darogha* was a Hindu. But we did not like this option because some of our companions strictly avoided meat. Out of deference to them we would cook our meals in the hospital and would not eat in our barrack, but in the hospital. We did this to please our companions. Someone else can only be pleased if one is prepared to undergo a little inconvenience. But, unfortunately, some of our brethren had no consideration for the inconvenience we underwent on their behalf. When we, went to the hospital for the first time, they began a propaganda campaign against us and instigated all our political companions against us, even though most of them were also meat-eaters. When we returned from the hospital, we came to know from their behaviour that they were upset and annoyed with us. I thought of this reaction as totally unjustified and unreasonable. This is one thing lacking in the citizens of Hindustan: we have no tolerance for whatever is considered evil according to our beliefs. The people of Asia claim that we are a religious people, and that in the entire world, religion is only practiced here. But from whatever little experience I have had, I have found that, undoubtedly, Asians are religious, but that is only in name, and is not the true religion of Allah and His Prophet (PBUH). Every religion has prescribed freedom, caring for others and tolerance, but they are not aware of this, and nor has anyone made them wise to it. The truth is that all revealed religions are from God and have been sent to the world to promote love, affection and for the service, benefit, and comfort of humankind. It is incumbent upon the followers of every faith to remove hatred from the hearts of humankind and instil in them love and affection – so that they can be of assistance to each other. But we have not been made aware of this by anyone.

I have read in a book of short stories by Tolstoy that there is a spring from which different neighbourhoods get their supply of piped drinking water, but the inhabitants of each neighbourhood contend that the water from their pipe is pure and sweet and that of the remaining neighbourhood is brackish and impure. Nobody bothered to reflect that if the source of all this water is the same spring, how is it possible that the water of one pipe is pure and sweet, while that of the others is impure and brackish? And Islam advocates that Muslims have belief in the *Quran*, but also in all the religions, 'And those who believe in that which has been revealed to you, and in what has been revealed before you.' (*Sura-e- Baqra: the Quran*).

I slowly approached the place where all our other political companions were gathered and told them that this swaraj of theirs had turned out to be a very difficult proposition for me. And how could swaraj ever be swaraj if everyone did not have the freedom of thought and freedom to follow, whichever religion they prefer; and that I was ashamed of their narrow-mindedness. If the eating of meat was prohibited in one's religion, he should refrain from eating meat; and if it was not prohibited, then it was not appropriate to be annoyed with him for doing so. That we had paid so much deference to their beliefs, that despite the authorities allowing us to cook our meals in the joint kitchen, we would cook somewhere else. So, their objection and annoyance with our cooking meat was unjustified. That this attitude of theirs was not conducive to the swaraj and unity of Hindustan, because the inhabitants of Hindustan followed many religions and beliefs, and so, if the followers of any faith attempted to impose their beliefs on the others, it would become very difficult indeed, and its outcome would be harmful for all. On hearing this, their annoyance and anger cooled down somewhat and they no longer harboured the same anger and annoyance against us.

There were many among our political companions who were accustomed to eating meat and desired greatly to do so. But they were under compulsion of others. I had a Hindu friend from Sialkot named Bhandari. He was a good man who was very fond of meat. He would quietly give me his small pot to bring him a little meat. I would always fill the pot for him, which he secretly ate from. Sometimes, when he would lose his temper, he would curse the Hindus and say what a shame that they advanced religious arguments to them with respect to food. All the political prisoners shared a kitchen, which was a very good thing because we Muslims, Hindus and Sikhs ate together. The freedom movement had made us all brothers. This was the blessing of the Congress and *Khilafat*, that we did not shun each other. One day, by chance, the issue of the *khidmatgar* arose. Maulana Muhammad Ismail Ghaznavi put forth the proposal that there should be a Muslim too in the kitchen. But the Hindus and Sikhs did not agree with this and would say that he was creating a problem in their ranks. I told them that this would lead to greater unity and love, because the Muslim too would get involved in the work of the kitchen and all the work would then be done collectively. No one paid much attention to what I said, and so no one benefitted from my efforts. Just as the Hindus and Sikhs stood firmly in support of their views, so also the maulana sahib was adamant and not conceding anything. This difference of opinion was exacerbated by the day. We had a master sahib, a Hindu who would say that the Hindus were clean and the Muslims dirty. Those Hindus who were more aware would say that this was a matter of cleanliness, and because the Muslims did not give cleanliness much consideration, they did not want them to work in the kitchen. This quarrel went on and became more intense by the day, and attitudes were hardening on both sides. This was a kind of excuse. Actually, the Hindus were not prepared to have a Muslim *khidmatgar* in the kitchen. One day I presented two labourers from our barrack, one of whom was a Hindu and the other a Muslim, before my doctor, for examination, asking him to see which one of them was clean. The Hindu worked in the kitchen and the Muslim used to sweep our barrack. The doctor had a close look at both and then decided in favour of the Muslim; that the Muslim was neat and clean compared to the Hindu. The Hindu was infested with lice on account of his filth. So, I asked my Hindu brothers what they had to say considering the doctor's decision; that their excuse about cleanliness was also no longer valid. In short, after a great struggle, a decision was taken that one Muslim should also work in the kitchen, and that his only job would be to wash our plates. In this manner this tussle was amicably resolved.

These views of the Hindus and their attitude influenced me as well and my heart, in which there was equal love and affection for all God's creation, underwent a little change. One day, I jokingly remarked to my fellow (prisoner) that, 'I had come here with a clean heart, which was devoid of any kind of hatred and prejudice, but now, after being in your company, it has blemished.' Religion is not in this world to create differences and hatred between the followers of different faiths. On the contrary, it is the flag-bearer of love and amity. Another strange thing which I had experienced here was that, in the summer almost all the Hindus would drink cold water from my pitcher and had no qualms about it either. But in the winter, they would abstain from doing so, and would not even come near my pitcher. The truth was that, in the summer, I would cover my pitcher with a piece of cloth which I would moisten at intervals, and the breeze would cool the water. I would go to this trouble, but they could not.

When we were in jail, a Hindu somewhere outside had been irreverent to the memory of the Holy Prophet of Islam (PBUH). So, an enraged Muslim had killed him. The Hindus sided with the blaspheming Hindu and the Muslims with the accused killer. The people's attention was diverted from the freedom movement towards sectarianism. Untill now, all the efforts that had gone into the unity of the nationalist movement were swept away. It was necessary that anyone who committed a wrong act should be condemned. Neither religion nor humanity, nor decency, nor morals permit us to side with or support the perpetrator of the act. Everyone has own religion and belief. Why should anyone do something which upsets or angers the followers of another religion, as no religion permits this? Today, when Hindustan and Pakistan are caught up in this Hindu-Muslim hatred, the reason for this is precisely this. You should also give some thought to the fact that, in Hindustan, sectarian conflict takes place over the issue of the cow and the mosque, and our common enemy uses this against our united, nationalist struggle. If one thinks about this, one is amazed that someone who is conscious and aware is annoyed at the butchering of a cow, and can even kill a man for it. In other words, the value of a human being is even less than that of a cow, or an animal. On the other hand, near the house of God, the sound of the dhol and *surna* of a parting *jaloos* is considered such a big crime that, in the name of God, his creatures are brutally murdered. From such incidents law and order problems are created, entire families are slaughtered, children are set on fire; and all this takes place in the name of a divinely revealed religion. In this regard, I remember a story. In our family, an elder was murdered in the village mosque while prostrating himself before the Almighty in prayer at the hands of his nephew. The police came to investigate. The police *kaptan* was an Englishman. He entered the mosque and stood there with his shoes on. A man in the mosque told him, 'Sahib! Take off your shoes. This is a mosque.' The Englishman retorted, 'In your hearts, you only have respect for the house of God, to the extent that you do not wear shoes in it. And yet, you murder the creation of that very God while he prostrates before God in prayer. This is indeed a strange religion and education!'

The inhabitants of Hindustan are indeed strange. The British have estranged them on account of their pride and arrogance and made them enemies. I say this because whenever an Englishman came to our barrack for inspection, there would always be a strange spectacle. Each one of them (prisoners) would try to attract his attention. Once he paid some attention to us and exchanged a word or two with us, and then, whenever he happened to come again, he would hardly have entered and we would be standing in attention for him with folded hands, and salute him and break out into smiles. This habit was particularly common in our intelligentsia and our educated people. One of my benefactors, who was from Lyallpur and was my instructor in jail, and a very prominent lawyer, whose name was Master Guru Dutt Mal, and would be reading political books all the time, was a very learned and knowledgeable man. But whenever an Englishman spoke to him politely, he would dote on him. He had been handed a two-year sentence by the deputy commissioner, and yet he was happy with him and harboured no grudge against him in his heart. In fact, he would always praise him and say that he was such a good man. The reason for this was, after he had passed a sentence on Master Guru, he had come to the jail once and had enquired about his welfare, and, in his presence, had asked why they had not white-washed the cell of the vakeel sahib. Just for this he was grateful and forgot all about the cruelty and ill-treatment meted out to him. He would, from time to time, tell me this story, 'The deputy commissioner had come to the jail and inquired about me and had asked the jail staff why my cell had not been white-washed.' I would tell him that, 'Master Sahib, you were jailed unjustifiably for two years and sent to such a notorious jail as Dera Ghazi Khan. Moreover, you do not think about the fact that you have incurred a financial loss. All you can think about is the white-washing of your cell.'

I would always laugh at my brethren political prisoners, that their objective was not swaraj. On the contrary, their objective was that the British should make them partners in the governance of the land and give them a small share in it.

Re-transfer to the Lahore Jail

My gum disease had recurred. One day, the *darogha* sahib accosted me in front of the superintendent and told me that the inspector general of prisons would be coming to the jail on tour again and that I should inform him about my disease and request him to send me to Lahore jail again for treatment. But I told him that I was not prepared to make any kind of request to the inspector general sahib because the person actually responsible for my health was the superintendent sahib, and if I had to request anyone, it would be him. The superintendent sahib, too, endorsed what I said, and in response told me that he would send me to Lahore when the inspector general's tour concluded. He wrote recommending my case. Soon orders came, and I left for Lahore. This time my travel was not kept a secret. I met all my fellow political prisoners and took my leave of them happily and arrived safely in Lahore. On arrival, I was immediately taken to my old friend, *Darogha* Khair-ud-Din sahib; because on my first visit for treatment, I was made to appear before him. He asked me whether I had come from the Dera Ghazi Khan jail for treatment, and after that he retained my box and bedding and sent his orderly with me to take me to the compound reserved for political prisoners. When we went ahead a little, I got the impression that I would be taken to the place where we were before. When we proceeded, I saw a tiny little door next to which stood a prisoner *lambardar*. When we approached the small door, the *darogha's* orderly signalled to him and he immediately opened the door, and I entered the place. It was a very small and narrow place. I was still in thought when, inside the room, I was extremely happy to see Agha Safdar and Malik Lal Khan. Lala Lajpat Rai and with him another Hindu leader were also sitting in this barrack. As I entered, they rose and met me very warmly. I was happy to meet them. This place was so narrow that we could not even walk in it or do any kind of exercise. During the day it was tolerable, but at night we were very uncomfortable as there was no breeze, and we could not sleep well because of the oppressive heat. The whole day went by and evening came, but my bedding and box had not been brought to me; and when they brought my food at night, it was not the kind authorized for 'special class' prisoners. In fact, it was a diet meant for those in 'C' class. I mentioned this to my companions, but they took no interest in what I said, and just let it pass. I too kept quiet but took it to heart, that the jail authorities, without any justification or provocation, were treating me in this manner. I could do nothing about it, and nor would my companions allow me to do so. They too were not prepared to do anything on my behalf. My bedding and box arrived, but whatever edible items were in my box were taken out. I was informed that they would be kept in the office and given to me as and when I needed them. This meant that more than half would be eaten by the jail staff. What the superintendent and the *darogha* desire is the law; and whatever they desire to do with the unfortunate prisoner, is what happens. In Dera Ghazi Khan jail, it was not unlawful to keep edible things with oneself; and here it became illegal. Khair-ud-Din Khan came to our barrack the next day. I told him that regretfully he had, without any provocation on my part, subjected me to great hardship for no reason. He replied that my warrant did not have with it a letter from the magistrate regarding 'special class'. So how could they believe that I was really a 'special class' prisoner? After some argument, I realized that it would be of no use and I dropped the subject. The jail staff has extremely strange habits. It is always on the look-out for ways and means to inflict hardship on people. This entire conversation took place in the presence of my companions, but they kept quiet.

Since it was our policy not to cooperate with the government, then it is appropriate that, in jail, we do not cooperate with that very government. Cooperation and amity with the government for a movement like ours was not suitable on any count. The same dental surgeon came again and felt pleased on inspecting my teeth and gums and congratulated me on having saved them. He extracted one of my molars and cleaned all the others thoroughly. He prescribed a new medicine for me to apply to the gums. When leaving, he told the *darogha* sahib that he would come again in four days' time to examine my teeth again.

Study
We began to study the Holy *Quran* in jail, and after the early morning prayer, would be absorbed in its recitation for two to three hours. We were four people and we had four different commentaries on the *Quran*. We listened to all four translations with full concentration, and would then think over these intently. Sometimes we would also voice our own opinions on the meanings. When we started the morning session we resolved to take out of our minds and hearts all those tales which we have heard in our childhood and which had become a part and parcel of our psyche, and to start thinking on the injunctions of the *Quran* with an open mind, to be able to understand its real meaning and context. Until we did so, we would not be able to get to the truth and inner meaning of the *Quran*, because we would have preconceptions in our minds about it. This resolve benefitted us greatly, and in this way, we familiarized ourselves with the true meaning of Islam, but poor Malik Lal Khan, who had not been able to rid his heart of various suspicions, could not keep up with us and left our study sessions. We completed our reading of the *Quran* once and then started again. The knowledge, understanding and pleasure which I got from these study sessions, I cannot express in words. I really got to understand the inner virtues of the *Quran* and the teachings of Islam, and got to the truth of the religion. In addition to the *Dars* (sessions of explanation and translation of the *Quran*), Agha Safdar was taking notes on various topics. I used to read notes as well and then copy them in my own notebook. The most important activity, however, was our nightly exchange of views and thoughts. The day would pass somehow, but the night was a real torture. The exchange of views would make it less intolerable. After a few days, Wali and Mehmood came to see me. During the meeting they told me that they were taking Abdul Wali to Mogata for an eye operation. When I had a look at his eye,

I noticed that the mark in the pupil had increased since I last saw it. I was very upset at this and expressed great sorrow at the condition in which I saw this child. But apart for expressing my concern, what else could I do? At the time that I was jailed, I wrote frequently to the village to take care of Wali's eye and to send him to Mogata. But nobody bothered with poor Wali's condition. During this, a year-and-a-half went by, and when his disease spread, only then was he sent to Mogata, but this did not prove of any use to him. Due to negligence, he lost sight in one eye. Till now, I have not been able to get this out of my heart. Whenever I am reminded of Wali's eye, my heart grieves.

When my meeting with Wali concluded, the deputy *darogha* took me to a man whose relatives had also come to meet him. The *darogha* told me that he too was from our party and was a brother in the non-cooperation movement, and had been jailed for a year for trying to break the statue of Sir John Lawrence – in which he is seen holding a pen in one hand and a sword in the other – but had failed in his mission and was arrested. He did this because he considered the statue a disgrace for the Hindustanis and believed it was incumbent on every Hindustani to destroy it. I told him that he was a very honourable man, and the action taken by him was indeed very courageous and honourable. He replied that, no doubt, it was an honourable act but unfortunately, he had since then been guilty of dishonourable conduct. He had hardly spent a week in jail but had reached the stage where he cried day and night, and pleaded that, no matter how, he should be set free. Today his relatives had been called to come and meet with him. This unfortunate prisoner had beseeched them with folded hands that they should arrange for him to be released on bail. The *darogha* intervened that now he could not be set free only through bail, but that he would have to seek forgiveness with it as well. The prisoner agreed to ask for forgiveness. At this, the *darogha* retorted that he would have to rub his nose in the dirt as well. To this he replied that he was willing to do that as well. The *darogha* further retorted that he would, in addition, be required to make the imprint of the camel's foot in the sand. The prisoner asked how this was to be done, at which I intervened and told him how to do it. Lastly, he was made to make an imprint of his behind in the mud. The poor wretch said that he would do that too, but if only he could be set free. On hearing this I had a good laugh and left him. I thought to myself that if we had such emotional youngsters, with such courage, it would be an impossible proposition to liberate Hindustan, or get a small share in the government from the British. I told Lala Lajpat Rai and Agha Safdar about this and laughed with Lalaji, that if there were such young men in Punjab, then it was hoped that they would very soon succeed in attaining swaraj. We regretted the behaviour of this young man and observed that when one was not up to doing something, he should not attempt it. It was better not to take any action at all than to do this. It is important for our youth that, before acting on anything, they should give the matter some serious thought and consider its likely consequences. Although at this time I had not yet joined the Congress Party, and had been jailed during the *Khilafat*, only Lalaji and I were in 'special class'. However, he could exercise anywhere in the jail compound, morning and evening, whereas I could not. He had a bed to sleep on, whereas I had to sleep on the floor. He enjoyed other concessions as well. The jail staff would try to please him in any way they could. He would meet relatives once a week and he would be sent all kinds of fruits. We were confined in such a small and narrow space that we did not know anything about the outside world. Neither would they allow anyone to come near us and nor were we allowed to leave the place. Because of this, we were not aware of the conditions of the other prisoners. However, in the door leading to our compound there was an aperture through which we could get a glimpse of the prisoners' latrines. In the morning there would be hundreds of prisoners around this. This was a very strange spectacle, which greatly saddened and surprised everyone, the fact that these unfortunate prisoners were being treated in such a humiliating manner. But we could do nothing to help them. I would occasionally tell Lalaji that whenever they regained their freedom, they should do something about these unfortunate prisoners by going to the press and agitating in the assembly. There was only one latrine in which there were maybe five or six places to squat. In the queue would be three or four prisoners standing, wondering to themselves when the others would get up, so that they could take their places and relieve themselves. We had a Pukhtun servant who was a very strange man. He had served about seven years' imprisonment and had earned very little remission of his sentence. Most of his sentence was spent in much hardship, but he had not learnt any lesson from it. All his suffering had been due to his uncontrollable tongue. No matter what pains I took to try and make him understand, it had no impact on him whatsoever. He came to me one day and told me that he wanted to write home and that I should write the letter for him. With great pleasure I got hold of a pen, paper and inkpot. After the usual introductory lines, I asked him to tell me what to write. He told me to write this 'Inform my enemies not to be so happy. There are only a few days left and when I am released, tell them that I will fix you. You will no longer be able to live in the village.' When I heard this, I was amazed – that all my efforts and advice had but led to this outcome! We were quiet for a while. Then I said to him that he had forgotten all the advice that I had given him, and had not even acted upon one! He told me that he had acted upon it but these so-and-sos (his enemies) were expressing joy at his imprisonment. I again sang my usual tune to him and told him that now the world has changed and that we should change too. Can you not see that the Hindus, Sikhs and Muslims are all brothers now and so many of them are imprisoned here? The Hindus and Muslims can live as brothers in this home and we Pukhtuns, who are the progeny of the same ancestor and are one nation, one people and one blood – why should our conduct be such? I gradually calmed the man down and he said, 'OK, I will not write this.' I do not blame the poor man because he was born and grew up in this environment and it is difficult to change one's way of life.

To bring about reform in these matters requires a lot of effort and time. Amongst the unfortunate Pukhtuns, neither have such persons been born, and nor has anyone worked on these lines with them. Nor have they been made aware of all this, so that we can be in a position to criticize and blame them for not being different. I spent the month of Ramzan here and after that I was sent back to the Dera Ghazi Khan jail.

Back to Dera Ghazi Khan

Despite all the trouble and anxiety which I experienced here, I was upset at being transferred because I had the company of people like Lala Lajpat Rai, Agha Safdar and Lal Khan here. I had benefitted greatly from the exchange of views with them. I had a daily *Dars* of the *Quran* with such a scholar of Islam and a liberal-minded politician like Agha Safdar. My companions were upset at my leaving but nothing could be done about it. We were at the disposal of others, and finally the time came for us to be separated from each other. When I reached the *deodai*, the jail staff handed me over to the police and they took me to Dera Ghazi Khan. They took me on foot first to the police lines, and then to the railway station. The *darogha* of the Dera Ghazi Khan jail told the police that there was an order for me to be handcuffed, when actually the instructions of Khair-ud-Din Khan were to manacle me. He was a Muslim and the *darogha* was a Hindu. When we arrived at the Lahore railway station on the return journey to Dera Ghazi Khan, it was evening. The train was ready, so we entered our compartment, and the next day in the mid-afternoon, our train arrived at the Sher Shah railway station where we got down. The police picked up my baggage and we left for the waiting room. There was an armchair there. They set that right for me and I sat down in it. What can I tell you about the service and kindness with which I was treated by these policemen? I slept comfortably the whole night in the train and they did not allow anyone to come near me. When we were about to enter the waiting room, I learnt that the pir sahib and his companions were asleep in it. When we entered, we saw a sheikh pulling a *pakai* for the pir sahib. Beneath the *pakai* were two beds – one was occupied by the pir sahib and the other by his young son. Both were fast asleep. Some followers were occupying the chairs and others were lying on the floor. So I quietly sat in the armchair. I too caught the breeze of the *pakai*. For a little while I dozed off. Soon it was afternoon and we all woke up to pray. The pir sahib saw that the policemen were waiting on me hand and foot. He suspected that I must be some senior officer of the police, and for this reason, was trying to get close to me and show me amity, and gradually began to talk to me as well. His young son became very fond of me and would not leave my side. During their conversation, the pir sahib asked me whether I happen to be an employee of the government. I told him that I was a prisoner and for that reason the policemen were with me. He said that their treatment with me was not that of a prisoner. I replied that I was not a normal prisoner but a political one and had been jailed in the *Khilafat* movement. On hearing this, the stance of the pir sahib changed immediately and he became less friendly towards me. On inquiry I learnt that he was a greatly revered pir of Taunsa Sharif and had hundreds of followers all over Hindustan, and had earned thousands of rupees as *shukrana*. When we offered our prayers and came out onto the platform, the pir sahib's young son, who was just a child but had grown very fond of me, also emerged along with us. When the people of the station learnt that we were leaders of the *Khilafat*, they all gathered around us and broke out into loud cheers of zindabad for us. When the pir sahib saw that his child was also with us, he sent one of his disciples for him who pleaded with the child to come with him. But the child refused and drew himself close to me. The disciple left and informed the pir sahib. He then instructed him to return and fetch the child by force. The disciple now forcibly took him from my lap. There was still some time before the scheduled departure of their train. However, the pir sahib, along with his son, got up and went and sat in their train. Finally, when it was early evening, our train also arrived and we boarded it. We arrived at Ghazi Ghat in the late evening where we spent the night on the river bank. The next day was Sunday, and on Sunday the ferry does not function. So nobody could get across. But the motorboat that ferried the urgent mail took us across. My heart quakes with fear even now when I now recall those surging waves of the Abaseend. But with the grace of God we crossed over safely. The police of Dera Ghazi Khan had come for me. They took me in a *yakka* to the Dera Ghazi Khan jail. We arrived there at around 10 a.m. The main gate of the jail opened and I entered to the acclaim of the clerks, warders and prisoners. They all crowded around me and welcomed me. The inner gate of the jail was opened and I proceeded towards my former barrack. My political companions had also learnt of my arrival. Some of them were waiting for me on the way. They were all very happy to see me; cries of welcome were heard and they all crowded around me. Some embraced me and asked about my welfare. I told them all the stories of the Lahore jail. Soon it was lunch time and we proceeded to the dining area. I felt very sorry at the sight of nude Sardar Kharak Singh in his old age who, along with his other protesting companions, was still without clothes, and no further decision about it had yet been taken.

The Death of My Mother

In the Dera Ghazi Khan jail I received a letter from my mother. She said she missed me terribly and wanted to come and visit me, and that I should give her permission. The more I read and thought about the letter, I wanted to meet her. But when I thought of the arduous journey involved and her old age, I thought the better of it, and did not allow her to undertake the trip. The government had intentionally detained us in such a far-off jail that it was difficult for anyone to come and meet us. So, I did not think it wise to put them through the pains of coming to visit me here. So I wrote back to her that, if all goes well, there was not much time left in my jail term, and I was hopeful that very soon I would be reunited with her in our own home. That this place was very far away, one had to change trains and cross the Abaseend. So I wrote that it was best for her not to take the trouble of coming. But little did I know what God had in store for me; that my mother and I would be separated from each other in such a way, that we would not meet till the day of reckoning. If I had known this, I would have met my mother. Man is so unaware of his fate!

After some time, early in the evening, I was sitting at my weaving frame, when one of my companions hurriedly came to me with a newspaper with the news that my mother had passed away. I recited the *Quranic* verse that, 'Surely we are from Allah and to Him shall we return.' On reading this, a strange feeling overtook me and I greatly regretted my decision of not allowing her to visit me in Dera Ghazi Khan. Perhaps, we were fated not to have our last meeting. I would make every effort to console myself, but my heart would be inconsolable because I had a lot of love and affection for my mother. I would be depressed most of the time and saddened by the fact that I was prevented from being able to be of any service to her in her time of illness and in her last days. However, death is a reality, which must overtake everyone, and it is unwarranted to cry and wail over anybody's death. But love is such a state of mind that nobody can hold back the onrush of his tears. When I was finally set free, my sister would tell me that our mother remembered me even while gasping for her last breaths, and would whisper, 'Has Ghafaray come or not?'

The Squabbles of the Political Prisoners
Our political prisoners would continuously be squabbling amongst themselves over inconsequential matters. And sometimes this would

reach the stage of abuse. Sometimes, we would even go to the extent of picking up sticks to beat each other with. But other companions would intervene to prevent a squabble from breaking out and would bring about a reconciliation. The jail is such a place that it makes one highly irritable. *Mian* Shakirullah Bacha of Gujargarai, Mardan District, would often say, 'If you are critical of each other, it is not appropriate. We are all brothers. This is not your fault; it is all the fault of this fort in which we are imprisoned. At home, the relationship between a mother and father is one of love and affection; but when they are confined with a wall around them, they too quarrel with each other incessantly.' I, too, was human. To the extent of my knowledge and experience, I can confidently say that the basis of all our bickering was our arguments. I often observed that whenever we started discussing some trivial matter, the objective was never to benefit from the knowledge and experience of others. Instead, each one of us thought that he knew better than the other. The result of such discussion is always tangential arguments, followed by harsh words, quarrels and fights. So, if anyone is to escape this fate, whether they are free or in jail, they should stay away from such discussions and exercise control over themselves, their tongues and their authority. But if it is necessary to have a discussion over an important issue, he should express his opinion, but not press the point any further. There is another major shortcoming that our political brothers have. In trivial matters, issues would arise amongst us for being Sikhs, Muslims and Hindus. I have already mentioned that the quarrel erupted in the city of Multan, and it embittered the relationships between Hindus and Muslims in the jail here! And if it has an impact on us, then what is the difference between us and those people who act on the instigation of our enemies and harm their people and their country? We claim that our aim is to bring about unity and brotherhood amongst all the people of Hindustan and liberate our land from the yoke of foreign slavery. Till such time as the country is ruled by the British, it is impossible to conceive of amity between the Hindus and the Muslims. This may be as it is, but if we, the followers of the Congress and the *Khilafat*, also take part in this Hindu-Muslim conflict, then may God take care of Hindustan! Let alone the masses, there is still no brotherhood even amongst the followers of Congress and the *Khilafat*, and their hearts are prejudiced against each other. One day it so happened that one of our attendants, who was a Hindu with long hair and who used to wash our plates, had let his hair down. The Sikhs spread the rumour that he had been converted by them to the Sikh faith. On hearing this, the Hindus were infuriated. They told him to shave his head. The Sikhs, on the other hand, warned him not to shave his head. This tug of war gradually increased and the relations between the Hindus and the Sikhs reached a breaking point. Finally, the matter came to the notice of the jail authorities and they transferred the man from our barrack, but even then the hearts of our brothers were not cleansed of prejudice. 'No compulsion in religion' is what Allah proclaims in His Book, because religion is a matter of the heart. It is the right of each follower of any faith to spread it peacefully through preaching and bring its benefits to the attention of the people. But no religion supports the forcible conversion of anyone, because religion is essentially a personal affair, and its acceptance, or otherwise, concerns the heart and the mind. The next day we were all sitting in the barrack and were discussing various things. During the discussion mention was made of Lala Lajpat Rai. A certain Mohan Lal, an advocate who was a Hindu, merely said that Lalaji was the 'lion of Punjab'. A Sikh took objection to this and responded that the title of 'Lion of Punjab' was that of Sardar (Maharaja) Ranjeet Singh. Gradually this controversy gathered momentum and reached such proportions that the Sikhs and Hindus almost came to blows and picked up sticks to beat each other with. With great difficulty we dispersed this argument and prevented it from escalating into a real fight.

In this jail we would all worship according to our respective beliefs. Amongst the Muslims, there were many who did not pray. Two of us, Maulana Ismail Ghazanavi and I, used to pray. This was also the case amongst the Hindus, many did not pray, and whoever did so, used to on their own. One of my friends, Master Guru Dutt Mal, used to say 'Shanti, Shanti' at the end of his prayer – but he was not at peace himself. I used to laugh and say to him, 'Master sahib, you say Shanti, Shanti but are not at peace.' Only the Sikhs used to worship collectively and the religious fervour and passion that existed in them was neither in Hindus nor in us Muslims. Compared to us, there was much more love, unity and brotherhood amongst the Sikhs. The more I thought about this, the more I concluded that this was because their religious books were in their mother tongue. The religious books of the Hindus are in Sanskrit, which the Hindus do not understand; and of our faith in Arabic, which we do not comprehend. When the Sikhs would sit down for their prayers, they would recite a phrase that has stuck in my memory, that is: 'If we lose our lives, nothing is lost, and so be it; but let not my cherished faith be lost!' Such thoughts which boost enthusiasm also exist in the Hindu faith, and in our religion, but we do not understand their meanings. This is the main reason why the religious enthusiasm displayed by the Sikhs was lacking in both us and the Hindus.

By this time most of our companions were set free because most had been jailed for either six months or a year. The others too would have been set free, had they not been guilty of the agitation. The five of us remained and were company enough for each other. For reading, too, several different kinds of books were available to us. We were living happily and in comfort, spending the remaining period of our term in jail and, except for me, they only had a short time left in jail. Amongst these five persons, two of us were Muslims, two Sikhs, and one Hindu. Maulana Mohammad Ismail Ghaznavi was the other Muslim with me. Amongst the Sikhs, there was Sardar Kharak Singh, Jaswant Singh and another friend of theirs. We were all treated very well by the jail staff. Captain Heares was our superintendent. He was a doctor, and a sympathetic and good man. But a major shortcoming in this place was that no English superintendent would spend more than six months in the jail. It would take six months for us to understand and get accustomed to him, and when we got used to him, he would be transferred. The reason for this was that the climate of Dera Ghazi Khan was extremely hot and the British superintendents could not stay here for too long. Due to this, we would have an English superintendent in winter and a Hindustani one in summer. It was then rumoured that the inspector general of prisons was again coming on an inspection tour. Everyone was anxious as this inspector general was a bad-intentioned and a corrupt man, who always bore a grudge and was particularly nasty with prisoners. The inspector general sahib arrived after a few days and upon arrival, came to see Sardar Kharak Singh. With a certain haughtiness and arrogance, he said to him, 'Well, Kharak Singh, how are you doing?' Kharak Singh responded, 'Yes Ward! I am well!' On hearing this it appeared as if the inspector general (Ward) had been set on fire. He did not see anything further, and forthwith left the barrack in great haste, and told the jail authorities that Kharak Singh had not yet been deflated and called for his ticket. He cancelled the extra milk which the doctor had authorized for him. He also ordered that he should be given the food of the 'C' class prisoners, and that another criminal case be instituted against him. He, too, was a doctor by training. When his tour ended and he returned to Lahore, the *darogha* sahib came and told us what had happened and expressed his sympathy with us. He said that he was just a subordinate official and could not do anything more than to request them to confer amongst themselves, and to give him an appropriate response the next day. On hearing this, our companions were extremely disturbed and worried because they only had four or five months left till their release. The Maulana had just one and a half months left, but to abandon Sardar Kharak Singh was a difficult proposition for them. After all what would people say outside, that they had left the old Sardar alone, while they, the youngsters, ran away? They were consequently in a great quandary. Finally, after a great deal of thought and discussion, it was decided that it was necessary to inform the Congress for it to pass a resolution in their favour to either continue the agitation or abandon it. We would accept whatever the Congress decided. At the time when they were starting their agitation, several companions in our midst had reminded them that the Congress had forbidden such protests in jails, and the Congress officials had also sent them similar messages, that Congress did not permit agitation in jails. For this reason, they ordered them not to start the agitation. But at the time they were full of exuberance and felt that the Congress did not understand the reason for the agitation; that it had to do with their self-respect, their dignity and rights. They were the same people who now anxiously awaited the response of the Congress because they were reluctant to undergo any further hardships. It is necessary to draw a lesson from all this: that whatever we intend to do should not be embarked upon due to emotions and impulse. All the pros and cons of a situation should be carefully taken into consideration, and if we are not prepared to face hardships for it, then we should not undertake it in the first place. The Congress passed its resolution which was shown to Sardar Kharak Singh, who was of the view that it was nothing new, and that whatever step he had taken, he was now not prepared to abandon. That until such time as the government accepted his demands, no matter what hardships he had to face, he would not desist from it. Instead of acclaiming his resolve and admitting their weakness, they started a propaganda campaign against him, implying that he considered himself above the Congress and was not prepared to accept its orders. What a great pity this was and what a terrible thing, that to hide our own weaknesses and to bring down others, we undertake such propaganda and thereby create differences in the ranks of our own party and country! In selfless service there cannot be any difference of opinion. Difference of opinion always arises due to personal reasons. If every man honestly keeps this in mind and looks within his own heart, he will realize that this difference has been created due to his personal considerations. We can hide our own weaknesses from people but cannot hide these from God. What answer will we give Him? So, if we cannot hide our weaknesses from God, we should not hide them from people either. And if we can do something, we should say so openly and if we cannot, then we should say so openly too. We should also help any brother of ours who is undertaking a worthy task instead of opposing him. We must not create division within our party and our nation and must not create difficulties for someone by making accusations against them, instead of giving them courage.

Maulana Ismail sahib and Sardar Jaswant Singh and their companions put on their clothes and began to work and abstained from every kind of agitation. The unfortunate Sardar Kharak Singh remained in the field, alone. The jail authorities lodged a criminal case against him, and he was sentenced to a further period of six months' rigorous imprisonment. But this had no effect on his courage and jovial attitude. He stood resolute like a mountain in opposition to the government and bore their hardships with great patience and equanimity, not retracting from the stance that he had taken. A brave man, he was steadfast and stood strong till the end. The life of our other companions became very tough. They could not face themselves or each other, and started making efforts to be transferred from this jail. The jail officials were also very sympathetic to them. They also did their best to arrange for their transfer and wrote to the authorities about it. The maulana had only a few days left. They went by and he was released. The orders of the others came, and they were transferred. Only Sardar Kharak Singh and I remained as the sole occupants of such a spacious barrack. He was also separated from me later and taken to the solitary cell in the hospital and confined there. I was then the only occupant of the barrack. In this barrack, there was a small door leading into the hospital, which was always locked. It was opened only when the doctor was scheduled to visit. There was a crack in this door and morning and evening, Sardar sahib and I spoke to each other through it. The Sardar sahib was subjected to several hardships by the government. He was considerably weak, and his face was drained of colour, but his talk and joviality remained undiminished. When I would look at Sardar sahib, I would feel great remorse at his condition. I, too, was a prisoner like him and could not do anything for him, except to occasionally share with him whatever little fruits I had. He would not accept it, and it was only after a lot of effort, argument and pleading that he would be persuaded to accept. He used to say that if I were transferred from here, then where would he be able to get fruits from? And for this reason, he felt that he should not get accustomed to eating fruits. It was quite possible that on my departure, God would open some other avenue. The jail authorities were in dire need of my barrack because, of the three barracks, mine was the most spacious and could accommodate more prisoners. There was no other place in the jail in which I could be separately lodged, so they were trying their best to get me transferred elsewhere and after a while I was transferred to Mianwali jail.

Transfer to Mianwali Jail

Before I start my account of Mianwali jail, I consider it necessary to dwell on the rights and privileges which the government has given to 'special class' prisoners. These rights have been so deceitfully drafted that their enforcement is dependent entirely on the discretion of the jail superintendent. If he is a good man and not bent on torture and punishment of prisoners, then they enjoy all manner of rights and privileges. And, if he happened to be ill-intentioned and without integrity and wants to make the prisoners suffer, then the prisoners have no rights whatsoever and they undergo all sorts of suffering. We had experienced and put up with all kinds of superintendents in the Dera Ghazi Khan jail. Our first superintendent was a Muslim; the second was an Englishman; the third was a Hindu; and the fourth was again an Englishman. We enjoyed all our rights during the tenure of the first superintendent. In the time of the second, despite all the squabbling and commotion, we enjoyed several rights. But when Rai sahib took over, our rights were reduced. Whenever someone said that he wanted to order some fruit for himself, he would say that this was a luxury; and if anyone desired to have tea or sugar, this was also considered a luxury by him and he would refuse to give them permission. In short, we were not even allowed to get sweetened chickpeas. In his mind, this was also a luxury. Every day we would be subjected to body search. And even if a small quantity of any edible item was found on one, he would be taken before the superintendent and be invariably punished. Because of the treatment prescribed for my teeth, I was the only one who was allowed to ask for a mango. But even for this, the orders of the superintendent were that it would be stopped if it was found that I had shared it with anyone else. This was the condition of those who were in 'special class'. So you can imagine for yourselves what the condition was of the common prisoners, and those who were in 'C' class. The truth is that the British are bad-intentioned towards their subjects, and the laws which they make for them are not made with good intentions. Although they are busy in the promulgation of new laws every day that are intended to reduce crime in the country, preserve peace and put the people at rest, you can see that crime is on the increase by the day, there is insecurity and the people are unhappy. If there is a good law and the intentions are bad, it will be used wrongly. The British do not wish to establish peace in the country, and nor do they wish to reduce crime, disputes or strife. Is it believable that if a government genuinely wants reform and peace in a country, they will not be able to bring it about? Just think, Hindustan is also ruled by the British and so is Britain. In Britain, peace, law and order are well-established, then why can't they be established here too? Once I happened to discuss the issue of rampant corruption in police ranks with the inspector general of police of my own province. I told him that I fail to understand why they could set up a police force in Britain which was honest, and could not do the same here? They had no intention of doing so!

When I was a boy, I would constantly be in search of the company of maulanas and saints. I would offer the five daily compulsory prayers and the optional ones, and would also be continuously absorbed in spiritual and devotional exercises. But when I looked at myself, I could not detect any change in my behaviour. I would also ask then, that I practice much spirituality, but I am as I was. They would try to explain things to me, but I would not be satisfied. Finally, when I arrived in the jail at Dera Ghazi Khan, I established a relationship Master Guru Dutt Mal. He had a book which was written by a padri. The book was called *Your Forces and How to Use Them*. When I studied this book, I understood the real meaning and use of meditation. It was written that when we meditate and repeat the hundred attributes of Allah, it is necessary for us to develop some of those attributes in ourselves. For example, one of the attributes of Allah is that He is compassionate and merciful. In other words, He is forgiving and kind; so, one should also develop these attributes in oneself.

When I learnt that I had been transferred from this jail, I went to the crack in the door and Sardar Kharak Singh also came to it. We took leave of each other with great laughter and joviality. Policemen were ready at the door to take me away. The jail officials also bade me farewell and I left with the escort for Mianwali. This time we had no difficulty in crossing the Abaseend river because it was winter and there was not much water in it, and there was a boat bridge over it. When we arrived at the railway station of Darya Khan, our train was ready to leave. We boarded it and arrived at Mianwali early next morning. The jail was near the station. I was taken to the jail and handed over to the jail authorities. The darogha met me warmly and, with great affection, led me inside. There were quite a few political prisoners in this jail. Most of them were Sikhs and only a few were either Muslims or Hindus. Amongst the Sikhs a few were also from Sarhad. Two of them were from Peshawar city. I was very happy to see them. There were only three Muslims here – Maulana Akhtar Ali Khan, the son of Maulana Zaffar Ali Khan, and the others were two maulanas from Panipat. One of them was called Sufi Iqbal sahib, who was a very pleasant man and a great conversationalist. Arrangements for supervising the cooking of our food were entrusted to him. He himself was a good cook and invariably cooked food for himself. The darogha handed me over to them. It appeared that the darogha had a special relationship with them. When he was leaving, he showed me a lot of sincerity and told me that he was ready to be at my service at any time, and that whatever problems I faced or whatever I needed, all that I had to do was to give him an indication of it. Later, however, I found from experience that this darogha sahib was not such a good man at all. He would say one thing and do exactly the opposite. He would talk a great deal but would not act on what he said. His other fault was that he was a great sycophant but, at the same time, would quickly become antagonistic to one and humiliate him. In this jail there were two kitchens for cooking – one meant for the Hindus and Sikhs, and the other for the Muslims. The Hindus and Sikhs were mainly responsible for this differentiation because they would normally be averse to the Muslims in such matters and would not allow them to enter their kitchen. Apart from this, some of them were even of the view that if the Muslims entered the kitchen, the utensils would get polluted. So, the Muslims had separated their kitchen from them. I had heard many anecdotes about this, which I do not consider proper to recount here. I also do not hold anyone responsible for this because the prejudices of generations cannot be changed overnight. I am, however, hopeful that gradually understanding and knowledge will dawn, the mutual revulsion between Muslims and Hindus would cease, but only gradually, and for this, time and efforts were needed. Even then I consider this a great achievement that most of the Sikhs and Hindus here did not subscribe to this view. Most ate and drank with the Muslims. Anything that was cooked in our kitchen, they had no qualms about eating it either. The adherents to the old ideas were few, but even then, their influence was not good and was extremely harmful to the love, affection and unity between Hindus and Muslims.

However, the Muslims refused to eat food cooked by those who considered them impure and refused to eat food cooked by them. I met Sardar Sardol Singh here for the first time. He was also a prominent leader of the Sikhs. He was a very knowledgeable and learned man, from whose affection I benefitted greatly. We had fixed a specific time to exchange ideas and thoughts. We always exchanged views on political and religious matters and tried to find out each other's viewpoints. Sardar sahib was a very liberal-minded person and not like the other Sikhs. Of all the Sikh companions with whom I had the opportunity to exchange views, his view point on all matters was the most rational. He was very affectionate towards me. There were many Sikhs here, including Sardar Raja Singh of Peshawar. When the political reforms were implemented, he became the first Advocate General of our province. With him there was another Sikh from our province. He was a tea merchant who imported tea from China and used to keep for me the expensive green tea leaves with a distinctive flavour. Sufi sahib was a great chef. He cooked everything very well, but he used to eat a lot of chillies, and I was not used to eating chillies. Because of this I was in great difficulty. One day, Sufi sahib cooked mince meat and had put so much chilli in it that, on taking the first morsel, it burnt my mouth. I left the mince and started eating the *dodai*. Sufi sahib informed me that because of me he had used comparatively less chillies; otherwise the recipe for this was that for every *seer* of mince, a *seer* of chilli is added. But for my sake he had put in only one hundred chillies. I told him that may God bless him for his consideration, but that I was not used to eating chillies at all, and so it would be better if he could kindly cook separately for me, because, as things stand, they were also inconvenienced and so was I. In this way, it would be easy for both. Sufi sahib was a great religious scholar, a good and well-meaning man, but he ate a great deal. He himself ate a lot of meat and would feed Akhtar Ali Khan the same quantity, and for this reason, Akhtar Ali Khan fawned on him greatly. I never took notice of such things because I used to think that he went to such pains cooking for us, if he ate a little extra, how did it matter? But my other companion, the maulana sahib, would always quarrel with him about this – that he himself ate a lot and fed those whom he liked.

Mianwali jail was no better than Dera Ghazi Khan in so far as climate and searing winds were concerned. If Dera Ghazi Khan was in the wilderness, this was in the desert. And if there were dust laden winds which blew there, here the wind was sand laden. There we had the advantage of living in a spacious barrack. Here there was no barrack, only tiny cells. Compared to this our barrack was much better and was cooler, and it was also quite breezy. The other advantage was that there, outside the barrack, was a platform for each one of us on which we used to sleep in summer, and here, prisoners slept on the floor. Among us political prisoners, another shortcoming was that they can, with just a little effort from the jail staff, be made to side with them and, for the sake of a little personal gain, allow themselves to be used against their companions. And then, may God help them. Let God not subject anyone to such a test. We befriend them right away and start bowing down to the jail staff and think that they have become our great friends. But we don't understand that they have used us and deprived us of our rights. By this I do not mean to say that anyone should have a revulsion for government employees. We should not hate anyone. We should treat everyone well. But we should not become accomplices against members of our own party. We should assist our party members under all circumstances. Such people, to please the jail authorities, are willing to go to great lengths to oppose their own friends and they try to ensure that no one agitates against them. Whenever the issue of agitation comes up, they always oppose it and create dissention within their own party. It is because of these collaborators that the government has harmed us. If we were united in our voice and actions, the government would not have been able to commit such excesses against us and deprive us of our rights. Such action does not suit our status that, just for petty, selfish benefits in jail, we should collaborate with the instruments of the government, against which we have declared a campaign of non-cooperation. If someone was to cooperate with the government, this should only be on reasonable and permissible counts; to do so otherwise would be a sin and a crime.

This practice of befriending jail officials was more rampant in the Mianwali jail than Dera Ghazi Khan. Our Muslim companions were like moths around the *darogha* sahib. They were not prepared to hear even a word against him. And the extent of sycophancy and service that they were prepared to offer the *darogha* sahib, I do not consider it proper to talk about here. He would give them more than their entitlement of milk, yoghurt, envelopes and letters. And when the inspector general would come on tour, the *darogha* would obtain for them a two-month remission in their jail sentences. They could go and visit the office at will, and in the evening, they were allowed to walk outside. Yet, the *darogha* humiliated these collaborators of his more than he humiliated anyone else.

The biggest collaborator of the *darogha* sahib in this jail was Zafar Ali Khan's son, Akhtar Ali Khan. When the *darogha* sahib would come in the evening to take the final count of prisoners, they would go and sit on the chairs with him. One day the doctor sahib came from the hospital on a round. There were no other chairs for him to sit on, except the two that the *darogha* sahib and Akhtar Ali Khan were sitting on. Akhtar Ali Khan, either because of his friendship with the *darogha* sahib, or because of his being the leader of his own party, did not vacate his chair for him. The *darogha* sahib did not consider this behaviour of Akhtar Ali Khan as appropriate, and so he got angry with him, humiliated him, and made him vacate his chair. Addressing him in a very humiliating manner, he told khan to realize who he was and what his status was; that he was no more than a prisoner. That, perhaps, he had lost sight of this and did not realize that the doctor sahib was a high-ranking officer of the jail, and that how dare he occupy a chair while he stood. He expelled him from doing the rounds in the garden with him in a very humiliating manner and forbade him from coming again in future. But when the evening would come, and the *darogha* sahib would come for his round, he would go and tell the *lambardar* to inform him that Akhtar Ali Khan wanted permission to do the rounds. He would refuse permission. One day, I told Akhtar Ali Khan that he was a political prisoner and was Zafar Ali Khan's son at that, and that what he was doing amounted to an insult to all us political prisoners. What is a tour or a round, after all? And why did he so demean himself before the *darogha*? Did he not see that the *darogha* pleaded with me every day to accompany him on his round, but I did not oblige? The garden of the jail was a nice place and full of flowers. Akhtar Ali Khan was forbidden to do the rounds until he had formally apologized to the *darogha* for his misdemeanour and placated him. From this you can draw your own conclusion – can anyone call this a friendship? These people would pride themselves on such a friendship.

In the Mianwali jail, sand is always blown about by the wind, which is very hot and searing in the summer. Everything is full of sand and the sand enters every place. There is nothing that is not full of sand. Despite all precautions, even then there is a little sand in everything, and it appears that such jails are always selected by the British for the political prisoners to torture them and ruin their health. My health, compared to Dera Ghazi Khan, deteriorated further. My weight declined. I reported this to the superintendent several times and requested him to have me transferred to some other jail. He would tell me that he was not able to do anything because the government had selected this jail for the political prisoners. No one gives any thought to what a prisoner says. Under the rule of the British, a prisoner is not considered human. They would take mercy on a dog, but not a prisoner. When the heat of the summer became intense, a well was dug inside the jail, the water of which was cool, and those prisoners who had a special relationship with the *darogha* sahib, were permitted to go to the well. They would always go there for their evening bath. They would always sing praises about the coolness of the water, so that all prisoners would want to go and have a bath there. But, unfortunately, everyone was not allowed to do so. This concession was extended only to the collaborators of the *darogha* sahib. And sometimes, without any good cause, the *darogha* sahib would disallow everyone and would order the *lambardar* to close the door and not allow anyone inside. At such a time the condition of the *darogha's* collaborators was worth seeing, because they were accustomed to bathing with the cool water of the well. When evening came, and it was time to bathe, they would be on tenterhooks and would bang on the door and yell at the *lambardars*, and plead with them to let them in. But they would not oblige. The evening would come, the gates of the jail would be locked, and finally, these miserable people would accept their fate. The *darogha* would also occasionally praise the coolness of the water of this well to me and say, 'If you don't go every day, come at least once and experience the pleasure of bathing there.' But I was not going to allow myself to get used to such things, because I saw the restlessness and humiliation of the prisoners every day. The *darogha* would remind me that I neither went for a stroll in the garden, and nor did I go to bathe, and that I never left my own compound. I would say to myself, that now the *darogha* sahib was requesting me, but once, like the others, he gave me a taste of this, then I, too, would be treated like them. Why would I give anyone such an opportunity? Everyone's dignity and self-respect is in their own hands; and if everyone was to control their own desires and needs, their would always be at peace, content and honourable.

Release

Here too our labour consisted of spinning cotton at a spinning-wheel. I would usually be finished with my assigned labour within two hours and then would devote myself to study.

Finally, my three-year sentence was about to come to an end, and my release from jail was imminent. The date of the release was entered on the ticket. I do not know how our party, the *Anjuman-e-Isla-ul-Afaghina* came to know of this, because I had not indicated it to anyone; and I would certainly not have thought of putting anyone to trouble on this account. However, letters began to arrive from Uthmanzai, asking me about the date of release. But I did not consider this appropriate as I did not wish to bother anyone with taking the trouble of coming here. For this reason, I did not inform any of my friends about it. I did not even know that the *Anjuman* was eager to arrange a reception for me. Though the *Anjuman* desired to do so, the government was against it. They thought that the people would learn of my release and this would be a cause of propaganda in my favour. I still had some days to go, when the jamadar came and informed me that the *darogha* sahib had summoned me to his office. I would not visit the offices, so I asked him the reason of my being called. He informed me that I had been released. I told him that, as I understood, I still had a few days left and that I did not wish to be released before the scheduled date. He went to the superintendent and then returned to tell me that I was not being set free but had been transferred to Peshawar jail. The truth is that I had refused to ask for pardon because the jail officials would humiliate our political companions until they asked for pardon and, for the sake of these four days, I would be obliged to them. I collected my baggage and took leave of all my companions in a joyful manner and embraced them all. They all exhibited great affection for me. When I arrived at the office and saw the policemen, I was reassured. We took leave of the jail officials and proceeded in the direction of the railway station. Since it was not yet time for the train to arrive, when we got to the station, the police made me wait outside. They did not take me into the station for fear that the people might see me. The people of Mianwali are all Pukhtuns. The elders all speak Pukhto, but the younger lot have forgotten it. The doctor at the Mianwali jail did not know how to speak Pukhto. But one day his father had come to meet me, and he spoke to me in Pukhto. The Pukhtuns have this great weakness, that wherever they settle and marry, they turn their backs on their mother tongue. Thousands of Hindus live with us in Sarhad, but they have not forgotten their mother tongue. They know how to speak Punjabi as well as our Pukhto. It is only us Pukhtuns who have this weakness.

The train for Peshawar arrived in the darkness of the night and we got into it. There were not many passengers; most of the compartments were empty and we found enough space and took our seats in comfort. All night long I could not sleep due to happiness. I would wake up frequently and would ask the policemen whether we had crossed the Attock bridge or not. Finally, when I opened my eyes, it was morning and our train had come to a stop at the Khairabad railway station. I love my native land and my people very much. When I entered my own land and saw my own people, I was overjoyed. I was lying on my bunk unconcerned and was in deep thought about the probable hour of our arrival in Peshawar. When the train was not making a move, I got up and opened the door to find out the cause for the delay, and I saw policemen running on the platform, randomly opening the doors of the compartments. When they saw me, they were very relieved.

The *thanedar* came and informed me that they had been searching the compartments for me and asked where on earth I was. I told them that I had been here all along, in this compartment, but they had not seen me because I was lying down. I asked them what business they had with me. He told me to accompany him as tea was ready. They unloaded my baggage from the compartment and I accompanied them. The tea was ready and the inspector sahib was also waiting there. We were still drinking our tea when we saw the train depart. I told them that the train had left. They laughed and told me that they would take me home in a motor car. People complain a lot about the treatment at the hands of the Punjab police. But the treatment I was given, and the way that they catered to my comfort, I shall not forget and remain indebted to them. When we came out of the station, a car was ready. One *thanedar* and two police constables sat with me. The inspector sahib stayed behind. When we approached Naukhar, I was taken on the Mardan road, to Charsadda. At this point I realized that, instead of Peshawar, I was being taken to Charsadda. The car got punctured twice on the way, in sparsely populated areas. Finally, we arrived in Sardherai. On arrival we had another puncture. The *thanedar* sahib was extremely flustered. He got down right away and sat on a tonga that was standing there, and we left for Charsadda in it. When we arrived there, Dilawar Khan, our assistant commissioner, was holding court on the river bank where many people were standing.

When they saw me, they ran towards me and surrounded me. They brought me before Dilawar Khan. He greeted me very warmly and made me sit beside him under the fan. He discussed many things with me, and then gave instructions to the *thanedar* to take me to Uthmanzai. Dilawar Khan also accompanied me. When we left the veranda, I told him that this was enough, and that he was not to put himself to any further inconvenience in accompanying me on the traditional *jeelab* any further. He replied in jest that people pride themselves on this and consider it a great honour if an assistant commissioner should take a few steps in *jeelab* with them. In answer to this, I told him that this was a bother for him and that I did not like such practices. Hundreds of people had assembled outside. I met each one individually and really felt their love and enthusiasm for me. After this, I, along with the *thanedar* and the police, left in a *tum-tum* for Uthmanzai.

9

Political Developments and the Monthly Pukhtun Magazine

In and Around the Village

IT WAS THE HEIGHT OF THE AFTERNOON HEAT WHEN WE ARRIVED IN THE village. When I approached the Azad School, one of the students recognized me. He ran back and cried out loudly that, 'Bacha Khan has arrived!' When they heard this, all the boys, along with the teachers, ran out to the roadside. They got together and the boys started shouting, and a big commotion took place. They all gathered around me and took me with them to the *madrassah*. They would call out in unison, '*Fakhr-e-Afghan*! Welcome back from the jail! *Marhaba! Marhaba!*' The teachers also arrived and we embraced each other in great joy. The students presented me with a welcome address on their behalf. When the villagers got the news, they also hurried to the *madrassah*. It was a moment of great happiness and rejoicing. It was lunch time and time for an afternoon nap so I took leave of them. When I went home, many women from the village, some related, others not, had gathered, and there was no space for me even to enter the house. They were full of admiration and love for me, a lot of feeling and enthusiasm. After seeing and greeting me, most of them dispersed and only a few of our close relatives stayed behind. The first thing I did was to have a bath and change my clothes. I had a little lunch and, being very tired, lay down and fell asleep immediately. I woke up late in the afternoon and went to the mosque. There, too, many people had gathered. We offered our prayers, and then came to the *hujra* and began to chat with those gathered there. Those who learnt of my arrival came to see me. I was really amazed at their enthusiasm.

I found out that, on the one hand, my imprisonment, and on the other, the activities of the *Anjuman* had greatly affected the people. After a few days of rest, I undertook a tour of Peshawar, Mardan, Kohat, Bannu and Dera Ismail Khan. All my companions came to greet me. Finally, after a few days, all this came to an end. When I returned to the village, I was told that all that we had, had been looted. When I was taken to jail, we had plenty of *gura*, maize and wheat, which was stored in our house. This must have been worth a hundred thousand rupees at my time. I was in jail for three years. I had cultivated in my hamlet of Paneerko sugarcane, enough to make five *ganrai* of *gura*. When I returned, my nephew, Sultan Khan, informed me that we had to pay arrears of land revenue to the government amounting to 3,000 rupees. Similarly, I found out that my wife had mortgaged all her gold jewellery. The practice amongst us Pukhtuns is that, on occasions of bereavement and joy, relatives and friends invite, friends and relatives to lunch and waste a lot of money on it. I too was invited by many friends and relatives. I suggested to them that instead of a cooked meal, they should give me the value of its ingredients in kind, and further told them that whatever they were prepared to spend on a meal, they should agree to give me half its cost in cash because our people have been left behind due to wasteful expenditure. We are such a large nation and yet we do not even have one newspaper in our mother tongue, nor do we have *madrassahs* for the education of our children. The Pukhtuns have nothing written in their own language from which their children can benefit. 'Make a *madrassah*,' I urged them, 'and make the Pukhtuns aware, to some extent, of developments in the world.' But all this talk of mine had no effect on them. Every Pukhtun is ever ready to provide a meal but is averse to giving cash. There were only three people who agreed with me and gave me a substantial amount of money. One was my paternal aunt, another was Abbas Khan and the third was Abdullah Shah *Mian*. The others did not agree to my proposal and I, on my part, did not accept their invitation to a cooked meal. The other advanced nations provide for a share in their personal incomes for national activities. There was a Hindu woman who lived in our village. She was old, and people said that whenever she kneaded flour, she would set aside a handful in a separate pot. Someone asked her what she was doing. She replied that this was for the national fund. And our Pukhtun brothers are prepared to waste thousands of rupees on customary meals, but do not contribute a penny to the national fund. This is the reason for our lagging behind all the other nations of the world.

The Award of the Title *Fakhr-e-Afghan*

The *Anjuman-e-Islah-ul-Afaghina* arranged a big *jalsa* in my honour and sent out invitations to members all over the province. On the day of the *jalsa*, thousands of people attended with great love and enthusiasm. A grand assembly of the nation was held in Uthmanzai, in which a welcome address was presented to me. A medal and robes of honour were also given to me on behalf of the people. The title of *Fakhr-e-Afghan* was also conferred on me on behalf of the entire nation. When the time for my speech came, after expressing my gratitude to the organizers of the function and the nation as a whole, I delivered a brief speech and, to uphold the resolve of the nation, recounted a tale which I had read in a book in a *madrassah*. I said to my Pukhtun brothers, 'We have been subjected to that joke of the lion who had grown up in the company of sheep and had acquired their habits. In the tale, the lion cub was in its mother's womb when she attacked a flock of sheep. While attacking the sheep, the cub was born, and its mother died. This cub grew up amongst the sheep. And when it grew up, it had most of the habits of the sheep and would graze along with them, and bleat like them. One day a lion chanced upon this flock of sheep and when the sheep saw him, they ran helter skelter, together with the lion cub. The lion of the jungle saw this lion cub, running here and there with the sheep and bleating like them. This seemed very strange to him. He left the sheep and caught up with this cub and seized him and brought him to a nearby pool of water. He made him stand on the edge of this pool so that he could see his reflection in the water and realize that he, too, like him, was a lion, and that he should not bleat, but roar like a lion! When the lion cub saw his reflection, he realized that he was a lion after all, and immediately began to roar instead of bleating! Oh, my Pukhtun brethren! You, too, are lions. Do not bleat anymore, but roar. Break these chains of slavery. Rise! Gird up your loins! Free your country and yourselves from the slavery of aliens!' This speech had an electrifying effect on the people. The meeting concluded on a very positive and successful note.

My health had deteriorated a lot in jail and I had lost fifty-five pounds. On the advice of Qazi Attaullah Khan, I went to Murree for a few days for a change of environment. Qazi sahib also went with me. It did me tremendous good. Then, from Murree we went via the Galliat to Abbottabad where we spent a few days with my brother-in-law, *Amir* Rahman Khan. With this change in environment my health improved greatly. When I returned, I met Dilawar Khan[14] by coincidence. He was our assistant commissioner at the time. He discussed many things with me at great length. Finally, he took me aside and informed me that Griffith sahib had also really liked my speech in Uthmanzai but did not like one part in it – the part about the lion roaring, because the people were illiterate and ignorant and might draw the wrong conclusions from it. Griffith sahib was our deputy commissioner. I told him that I did not deliver the speech to make Griffith sahib happy and nor did I care about his pleasure, or displeasure, at hearing it. I had delivered it for the benefit of the country and the people, and to make them rise. Dilawar Khan had been appointed as the assistant commissioner by the deputy commissioner for the sole purpose of harming our *Anjuman* and our Azad *madrassah*. And when he took over as the assistant commissioner, the first thing he did was to try and sow the seeds of discord among the members of the *Anjuman*. But he was not successful in this and nor could he harm the *madrassah* in any way. Then he had the government establish an English medium school in Uthmanzai, in competition with our Azad *madrassah*, and used to spread propaganda against our *madrassah*.

In Bannu, the *Khilafat* movement had a profound effect on the people, to the extent that all the *maulanas* of the district had joined it. In fact, all the *lambardars* of the villages had tendered their resignations from their duties and had joined the movement. The British became very apprehensive and panic overtook them. Akbar Khan of Charsadda was then a judge posted in Bannu. The deputy commissioner summoned him and told him that it was imperative to prevent the spread of this movement. He replied that this was not his job. His work related to trying those whom the government arrested for committing offences. That he could not try such a case. Disappointed with this response, the deputy commissioner called for Dilawar Khan who was then a magistrate posted in Bannu. There was also a case of corruption pending against him. When he was told what needed to be done, he readily agreed to do so. The maulanas were very skilfully deceived and so were the *lambardars*, and he was remarkably successful in the failure of the *Khilafat* movement there. Because of this success in Bannu, he was sent to disrupt our educational and social reform movements and was appointed as the assistant commissioner of Charsadda. Charsadda is a very important place. The assistant commissioner here has always been an Englishman. Dilawar Khan was educated at the Mission School, Peshawar, and was for a long time my boarding housemate there. We had brotherly love and affection for each other, and he was only a year or two junior to me. He would often tell the Pukhtuns that if they educated their children in the Azad School at Uthmanzai, where would they get them the required certificates from, and how would they find employment for them? And he would follow us whenever we moved about in our area to attend marriages and deaths. Mostly he would start arguing over matters related to education but it was by the grace of God that he met with failure wherever he went. Despite his adverse propaganda, instead of creating misunderstanding among the people, their sympathy and love for our *Anjuman* and *madrassah* increased even more. His adverse propaganda proved of great benefit for us. Until the very end, God dashed all his hopes of success and all his scheming failed. He went away from Charsadda, a disappointed and heartbroken man, and could not harm our *Anjuman* and *madrassah*. Dilawar Khan was a strange man indeed. He was ready to offer any kind of sacrifice for the British. One day, he came to our *hujra* where many other guests were also present. He turned towards Doctor sahib and said to him, 'Look at this Afghanistan and the ill-treatment meted out to their prisoners. And if the British were to invade Afghanistan, I will be in the forefront with my sword drawn, chopping off the heads of Pukhtuns.' In response Doctor sahib told him that, 'Perhaps I would be in the forefront of the opposing group, because I am a Pukhtun. How could I kill the Pukhtuns for the British?' On hearing this, the poor man was embarrassed in the gathering and started off on another topic.

The *Anjuman* and *Madrassahs*

Many branches of our *madrassah* had been opened in our area due to the efforts of the *Anjuman*. Great enthusiasm amongst the

Pukhtuns had been generated for the education of their children. Khadim sahib and I proceeded on an inspection tour of these branches with the boys of the Azad School. Wali and Saadat Khan of Torangzai would recite poems in our *jalsa*. They had very good voices. Wali could also recite very well from the Holy *Quran*, and this would have a very good effect on the people and would generate enthusiasm amongst them for the cause of educating their children.

Our *madrassahs* in the Yousafzai area were in very good shape. The reason for this was the efforts and sacrifices put in by Sahibzada Khurshid sahib and Nasrullah Jan of Adina. After Hashtnaghar and Doaba, we started on a tour of the Yousafzai area and inspected all the *madrassahs* of *tehsil* Mardan and Sawabai. Khadim Muhammad Akbar sahib would test the students, while I would spend most of my time meeting people and exchanging views with them. We started from the *madrassah* of Maulana Shah Rasul of Bala Garhai. Then we inspected the *madrassahs* at Sawaldher, Katlang and Rustam, and held large *jalsa* at these places. Here I spoke of the benefits of unity, brotherhood, nationalism and knowledge to the people. Both Sahibzada Khurshid and Nasrullah Jan accompanied us on these tours. When we were about to leave Sawaldher for Rustam, we dispatched Khadim sahib and Maulana Shah Rasul ahead of us, straight to Rustam. Nasrullah Jan and I decided that we would spend some time in each village in the Sudham area on the road to Rustam and would apprise the people of our aims and objectives. We left on foot. The only horse which we had, we placed at the disposal of maulana sahib, because he was very old and frail. This was my first tour of Sudham. In this tour, I met Sher Bahadur Khan of Kotarpan and Shahpasand Khan of Chargullai. I talked a great deal with them and met with some other khans of the area. I felt very pleased at meeting the khans of Sudham and greatly appreciated their simple lifestyles. We arrived at Rustam in the evening. We thought that we might manage a *jalsa* here at night, but the patron khan of our *madrassah* was not present in his village and no one else was ready to inform the inhabitants. When Nasrullah Jan and I had had our meal, he started from one end of the village, and I from the other. We visited every *hujra* and mosque in the village and informed everyone that, after the night prayer, a *jalsa* would be held in the mosque. When the people assembled in the mosque, we explained the purpose of our coming and the aims and objectives of the *Khudai Khidmatgar* movement. The next morning, we examined the students of the *madrassah* located there, and for the night went to Galyara. We had a fine *madrassah* here. From Galyara we went to Nawikilli, and from there to Ismailia. We inspected the *madrassahs* located there as well. In Ismailia, Sahibzada sahib and Nasrullah Jan had arranged a large *jalsa* and had collected all the people of the area. The *jalsa* was a big success. Nasrullah Jan was a very capable worker and companion of ours. Because of him, our movement was doing very well. The British did not like this and would make every effort to deprive us of such selfless and dedicated workers. His maternal uncle, an employee of the government, was forced to send Nasrullah Jan to London to become a barrister-at-law, and so he left for London. This place was the focal point of the movement in the Yousafzai area. After this we started a tour of the Peshawar area. We followed this up with a tour of Kohat and Bannu. In Kohat we had established two *madrassahs*, both of which were doing very well because of the sincere efforts of the local workers. In Hangu, the *madrassah* had been established by a *thekadar*, Ali Badshah. Here we held a big *jalsa*, to which people from every part of Kohat came to participate. In Hangu, there is a very large Shia population. Some selfish individuals and government employees have seriously damaged Shia-Sunni relations and have manaed to create hatred between them, instead of love and affection. In the *jalsa* I gave a long speech on the fact that we are all Pukhtuns; if one is a Shia, he is a Pukhtun, and if one is a Sunni, he also is a Pukhtun. We belonged to the same race and were citizens of the same country. We believed in and were guided by the principles of the same *Quran*; they also believed in Hazrat Ali, and so did we. Then, where and what was the difference over? Everyone follows a different path, but we have a common country. Service to it is our joint responsibility; and it is incumbent on us to serve it to the best of our ability. We should realize that this country is ours, and that we should serve it jointly. Only the selfish amongst us have created this hatred between Shias and Sunnis. This speech of mine had a very good effect on the people and the hatred spread by the selfish people decreased somewhat. The Khans of Hangu were very annoyed with me for having delivered this speech. They told me that their efforts of twenty years had been swept away by this speech. I replied that this disunity in their ranks was neither beneficial for them, nor for the nation, and the country as a whole was greatly harmed by it. If there was any gain in it at all, it was for the British, who looked for such an opportunity to fan the flames of disunity.

From Hangu, we went to Thall. There we had some excellent workers. We also inspected the *madrassah* and returned to Kohat. In the entire district of Kohat, nobody else had undertaken for any other *madrassah*, the efforts and sacrifice that the people gave for this *madrassah*. They were also been in the forefront of educational and political activities and assisted me greatly in my mission. From Kohat, I then proceeded to Bannu, where with the cooperation of *Amir* Mukhtar, who is one of my companions of the freedom movement, I undertook a tour of the district and inaugurated two *maktabs* with the assistance of the maulanas. I met with many people and exchanged views with them. Malik Khuda Baksh, an advocate of Bannu city, was quarantined with me for a few days in Peshawar Central Jail and we had got to know each other well. Through him, I met *Hakeem* Abdur Rahim sahib, Barrister Muhammad Jan, and Advocate Muhammad Nawaz Khan, and got to know them as well. When I was in jail in Lahore, I had met a few prisoners from the village of Kakki and had promised them that, whenever I was released and went to Bannu, I would visit their village. With that intention the headmaster, his father and I, went to Kakki. We offered our prayers in a mosque, and then tried to collect the people. An *ainda* match had been arranged and they were all proceeding towards it. I spoke briefly to them, saying:

'Oh, Pukhtun brothers! A kafir does not kill his fellow kafir. Then why do you, who call yourselves Muslims, kill each other? And never does an Englishman betray his nation, and nor will he ever befriend you. Then why do you serve as spies and informers against your brothers and befriend the English? And nor does a Hindu ever give false evidence against another Hindu, and nor do they try to humiliate each other. But oh, Pukhtun brothers! Then why do you unjustifiably give false evidence against each other and seek to humiliate and dishonour each other? Have some fear of your God and be ashamed of yourselves!'

I told them to pray that God bless us with wisdom and knowledge, and fill our hearts with love, affection, brotherhood, national consciousness and unity.

When we were leaving the mosque, a few people gathered around us and one of them held me firmly by the hand and asked me to spend the night with him. I told him that we had to attend to many tasks and that we could not possibly spend the night with him. He insisted that their entire life had passed, their beards had turned grey, but that they had not heard such words from any *mian* or maulanas. That we Pukhtuns are also brothers in our own homes, and that if one kafir does not kill another, then they too should not kill another Muslim brother. People say that the Pukhtuns have not progressed, that they are treading the wrong paths, but the fact is – has anyone ever guided the Pukhtun on the right path? Who has tried to stop him from doing the wrong thing that they can be accused of not paying heed to their warnings? What a pity! They do not have a benefactor like other nations do. They do not have a shepherd, but there are plenty of wolves ready to devour them. When I concluded my tour, and returned to the village, Abbas Khan took me aside and confided in me that *Mian* Maroof Kakakhel was a very dangerous man who was out these days to create differences between Abbas Khan and me. He told me a few things about his activities which were terrible and which I do not want to reveal. Many other people had also told me stories about *Mian* Maroof, which confirmed what Abbas Khan had just said. The differences that had arisen between Abbas Khan and Maqsood Jan, the headmaster of our high school, were also the outcome of his work. I also learnt that he was trying to create factions in the members of our *Anjuman*, and the love and unity once shown by the members of the *Anjuman* was no longer there today. In fact, the members had begun to complain against each other. *Mian* sahib was an active member of our *Anjuman* and was entrusted with the task of looking after the sheep. This news slowly spread and reached the ears of *Mian* Maroof. A few days later, he resigned from the post of inspector of the *Anjuman*. Muhammad Abbas Khan was the president of our *Anjuman*. He was of the view that he should immediately accept Main Maroof's resignation, but I told him not to do so for a few days, and that it would be better to present his resignation before the management for a decision. The next day I met Maulana Muhammad Israil sahib. He mentioned *Mian* Maroof's resignation to me. He also had been affected by the scheming of *Mian* sahib. He told me that, *Mian* sahib's had no control over what he said, and that the other day too, he was holding forth to the people against the *Anjuman*. No matter how, he should be pacified because his resignation would harm the interests of the *Anjuman* greatly and he would start a propaganda campaign against us. I replied that he admitted the fact that he had no control over his tongue. If such a person continued to remain associated with our *Anjuman*, it would be a greater risk to have him remain as a member and for him to carry out propaganda against us, rather than expelling him and having him criticize us. In the former case, the effect on the people would be minimal and people will say that he is not a part of the *Anjuman*. So people will not believe what he says, and he will not be able to harm us as much. The next day we heard that Abbas Khan had accepted his resignation. But the seed which *Mian* sahib had sown in our *Anjuman* and the evil that had taken root in it could not be removed. The members of our *Anjuman* had developed the bad habit of talking behind each other's backs. Gradually, Khadim sahib and Abdul Akbar Khan reached the stage where they would criticize others in the presence of the students, and would talk such nonsense that it was difficult to believe. One day the headmaster sahib told me that the nazim sahib and secretary sahib indulged in such loose talk in the presence of the students, which is most unbecoming of them because they are responsible members of the *Anjuman*, and such loose talk has a bad effect on everybody. It inflicts great harm on both the *Anjuman* and the *madrassah*. I asked him what they had said. He replied that, 'let alone everything else, the other day they were saying in front of the students that your friend, Qazi Attaullah Khan, serves as an informer of the British and had been commissioned by them to spy on you, and that the prevarication that I resorted to in my task, was the result his effect on me.' I was very upset to hear this, that they had begun to suspect Qazi sahib and me. But I could do nothing as they had lost all control over their tongues. I tried to make them understand many times the result of their attitude and actions. But they refused to understand.

This was the period 1925–1926, when a *jalsa* of the *Jamiat-e-Ulema-e-Islam, Hind*, was held in Peshawar. They had also invited us. Maqsood Jan, the headmaster of our *Azad* School, myself, and two or three students of the school participated in it. Ghani, who was thirteen years old at the time, delivered a speech which had a great effect on the audience and the leaders of the *Jamiat*. Maulana

Kifayatullah, who was the president, got up, embraced and kissed Ghani. Sir Sahibzada Abdul Qaiyum sahib was also present and told me that the Islamia College, Peshawar, was holding a *jalsa*, and if I could participate in this, it would be greatly appreciated. I told him that we had an educational poem, and not a political one, and that if he permitted the students of our *madrassah* to recite it on the occasion, only then would I come. We sent that poem to Sahibzada sahib and he allowed us to recite it at the *jalsa*. Two students of our *madrassah* recited the poem. Its contents had such an effect on the audience that tears welled up in the eyes of the students of Islamia College and of most of the Pukhtuns gathered there. And the Englishmen present sat upright in their chairs and asked who these boys were. I told them that they were the students of the *Azad* High School of Uthmanzai. They were astonished and exclaimed in disbelief: 'Really, of the Azad school?'

Hajj and my Travels
I left for Hajj in 1926. I was accompanied by my sister, my brother-in-law, my paternal uncle's son, Attaullah Khan, and my wife. We went to Peshawar and Dr. Khan Sahib reserved a second-class compartment for us. We boarded the train and arrived in Karachi where we stayed at the camp set up for the hajis. However, the wife of Abdullah Haroon sahib[15] arrived and took us all to their spacious home. The ship meant to take the hajis to Jeddah arrived at the Karachi port. Abdullah Haroon tried his very best to get second and first-class tickets for us, but they had all been taken. At the time of boarding, he accompanied us and asked the captain of the ship that we had been unable to get first and second-class tickets for ourselves and requested him to look after us. In the third-class compartment, the passengers were herded together, tightly packed like sheep and goats. When the ship set off, the sea was rough and turbulent. After we sailed for a while, some of the passengers began to throw up. We were all affected by seasickness, but the condition of my sister was bad. We descended from the upper to the lower deck, but there was no appreciable improvement; in fact, if anything, it got worse. So, I then went to the captain and told him that we were really suffering and that he should kindly allot a separate room for us where we could be more comfortable, and that we were willing to pay whatever he demanded. There was a room in the ship in which

baggage was stored. He had that emptied and we shifted in there. It was good that we were separated from the rest, but there was no let-up in our seasickness. The three of them stayed here, while I left and occupied a large veranda outside the first-class compartment. I had paid the captain the extra fare required, so no one bothered me. After seven or eight days, we arrived at the port of Aden where ships dock for twenty four hours. The night was cold. I caught a chill and got influenza. I was lying down in the veranda outside the first-class compartment when an Arab saw me. He came and took me inside with him to a first-class compartment. He really looked after me and I will always remember this. When we arrived at the port of Jeddah, I got a little better. We disembarked from the ship, but to my dismay, I found that all our baggage was left behind on the ship. Attaullah Khan was a simpleton who did not understand anything. He wasn't even able to take his luggage down from the ship. All my baggage and that of my wife, which contained some gold buttons as well, was also left behind. I immediately informed our *muallim* about what had happened. He went in search of the luggage but could not locate it. When we arrived in Mecca *Muazzamah*, we reported the matter to the *shurta* (police). At that time, the government of the Saudi family had been recently established. They had expelled the *Sharif* of Mecca during whose rule, when anyone deprived the hajis of anything, the *muallim* was also considered a partner in the theft. The *Sharif* of Mecca was a debauch, but the Saudis were not like this. They held the *muallim* responsible for any loss the hajis would incur and he would be made to compensate them. In their time, the law and order situation was such that I do not have words enough to express this. The government summoned our *muallim* on our complaint and ordered him to retrieve the baggage or pay the compensation. The *muallim* went to Haji Jan Muhammad of Peshawar and requested him to ask us to forgive him. And when the haji and the *muallim* came to us as a *jirga,* we had no other option but to pardon him.

We observed all the rituals of Hajj as they were prescribed, I will not go into details. I only want to recount one incident. At the time of Hajj, at the behest of the Saudi government, a big *jirga* was scheduled by the '*Motammar-e-Alam-al-Islami.*' For this, invitations were sent to the prominent leaders of every Muslim country from amongst the hajis. From Hindustan, Maulana Muhammad Ali Johar,

Maulana Shoukat Ali, Maulana Zafar Ali Khan, and Maulana Ismail Ghaznavi, participated in the conference, and so did I. Maulana Muhammad Ali and Maulana Shoukat Ali asked the session why the Saudi government had removed the headstones and domes from the tombs, as they were relics from the history of Islam. To this, the Saudi government replied that these were innovations which were prohibited by the edicts of Islamic Shariat, and that we should consider whether they had in the past been beneficial or harmful to Islam and the Muslims.

The two maulana brothers also put forward another proposal that for the office of the *mutawalli* (custodian) of Mecca *Muazzamah*, someone should be selected through consensus from the Muslims of the world. The Saudi government responded that if the Muslims of the world selected a Muslim from India for this task, would he be able to protect Mecca *Muazzamah*? Because they had recently witnessed that when the kafir British invaded Mecca, the Muslim soldiers of Hindustan also came with the British Army and they did not refuse to fire at our sacred places. The outcome of this was that, instead of benefitting the *Motammar* (World Muslim Congress), the proceedings of the conference harmed it, and it came to an inglorious end.

When we got free from the Hajj, I was unwell. My wife and I went to Ta'if. My sister and her husband were in a hurry and so they proceeded to Madina *Munawarrah*. When we were going to Ta'if, a Pukhtun joined us on the way who took us to his house. He had a very beautiful home in Ta'if, which is a well-populated town. It has nice weather and we spent a few days there. One day, during our stay there, a man beckoned to us in Arabic, 'Come! Come!' When we went, he said to us, 'This is the hair of the Messenger (PBUH), and this is his footprint, engraved in stone. Have a look at them.' I told him that we had come all this way to Ta'if because the Prophet had come here to preach Islam, but the people had stoned, injured and heaped indignities on him. But despite that, he stood strong by his commitment and prayed to God to guide them on a righteous path. Our health improved in Ta'if and so we came back to Mecca. There were no cars in Saudi Arabia at the time. We travelled on camels. In Mecca, I met Maulvi Muhammad Ismail Ghaznavi. He was my companion in jail. Jail companions are always very dear to one. During the conversation, I told him that we were going to Madina *Munawarrah*. He asked me to accompany him to Jeddah and told me that there was a route leading from Jeddah to Madina as well. I told him that I did not wish to go to Madina by another route, but he compelled me, and so we accompanied him to Jeddah. When we arrived in Jeddah, he had a rich and influential acquaintance and we stayed with him. In those days, the Saudi king was on a visit to Jeddah and stayed with our host in this very house, with us. King Saud was a very good man. He would join us at our meals and would also be in our company. I did not detect in him the arrogance of our maliks and khans. In fact, he had the temperament of a dervish, even though he was the king. After a few days we left for Madina *Munawarrah*. The secretary to the Saudi king gave us a letter of recommendation for the *marakiz* on the way to look after us. Our caravan consisted of five camels, four or five women, and three or four men. The camel allotted for my use had one saddle for my wife and one for me. The saddle was short. I was uncomfortable in it. At night, we would usually get down from the camel and would walk on the soft sands of Saudi Arabia. This journey was a very pleasant experience. The Arab companions that we had on the journey were those who, in the rule of the *Sharif* of Mecca, had immigrated to Turkey on the coming of the British and were now returning to Madina. When we arrived in Madina, we stayed with one of them. I cloistered myself for ten days in the Masjid-e-Nabawi. There was a pillar in it that I would sit next to. One day I saw Haji Muhammad Amin of Umerzai in that mosque. We greeted each other. On my asking, he informed me that here in the Masjid-e-Nabawi, he had located a small room in which he intended to cloister himself for a year. I asked him what for? He replied, 'For the pleasure of the messenger of Allah, may His peace and blessings be upon him.' I told him that the Prophet would not be pleased by this at all. So, I advised him that what he should do was to recite from the Holy *Quran* at the *ziarat* of the Prophet, and after praying seek guidance as to whether he would be pleased at his spending a year in this small room. Or would he be pleased if he went back home and spread his message among the people? After sleeping that night, he came to me early in the morning and informed me that what I had advised him to do was right and that the next day he would leave for his village to serve his people. And, God willing, when I returned safely, he would work with me. I also gave him some money. He left and we spent a few more days here, and then left for *Bait-ul-Muqaddas*, from the small port of Rabigh of the Hejaz, via Egypt. When our boat docked at the port of Suez and we disembarked, I also intended to visit the cities of Cairo and Alexandria. I approached an Egyptian officer and told him this. I also told him that we were his brothers in Islam, and that I hoped he would help us out in this. On mentioning the word 'Islam', he smiled and said, 'Today you are in need, so you are my Muslim brother. And if tomorrow, the British were to attack us, then where would this Islam and brotherhood be? You, the people of Hindustan, what do you know about what being a Muslim actually means? Your Islam is just the pursuit of money. You are such a nation that just for eight annas from the British, you have subjugated the whole world to the slavery of the British. And if we are the slaves of the British, this is also because of you. If it was in our power, we would not permit such despicable people to step on our soil.' On hearing this, I fell silent. We spent ten days here in quarantine, and after that, left for Palestine, *Bait-ul-Muqaddas* and Syria. In *Bait-ul-Muqaddas* my wife tripped and fell down the stairs at the mosque and was injured. After a few days, she died. 'Surely we are Allah's, and to Him shall we return.' We then buried her there.

In Palestine, the Jews have established well-planned settlements, planted citrus orchards and developed new cities, and continue to do so. But the Muslims are still steeped in ignorance and are patiently waiting for the coming of Imam Mahdi. They do not do anything for themselves, but wait for his advent to do everything on their behalf. They are such a lazy and useless lot that, let alone the Mahdi, the Prophet himself had come to them but they did not support him and so he failed in his mission. In *Bait-ul-Muqaddas* I had extensive exchanges of views with my fellow Muslim Arabs about this. When I would step out of the *Bait-ul-Muqaddas*, and would see the barren wasteland, I would ask and be told that it belonged to the Arabs. On land which was cultivated, there would be a small bungalow and a citrus orchard. When I would ask about this, I would be told that it belonged to a Jew. And similar was the case in the villages. The villages of the Jews were neatly laid out, clean and tidy. Plus, when I went out in the morning, the Jews, both men and women, would be busy in their work, and when I did the same in *Bait-ul-Muqaddas*, where I used to go to a restaurant in the morning, there would be no one there; and when I went there in the afternoon, then too there would be no one. But when I visited it in the evening, it would be crowded. Tables would be neatly set out, and the customers would be well and neatly clad. Some would be drinking tea, some coffee and some grape juice. And when I would visit the restaurant of an Arab, whether in the morning, afternoon, or evening, it would be crowded with customers lazily smoking their shishas. Their restaurants would not be as clean as those of the Jews. They would be busy playing some game, which I did not understand. One day I said to these Arab brothers, 'Which world are you living in?' That they should open their eyes a little and look around them. That whenever I travelled and saw uncultivated land and desert, it belonged to them; and wherever there was good cultivated land, a bungalow and a citrus orchard, it belonged to the Jews. I asked them to look at their lives and then the lives of the Jews. If they did not have exposure and knowledge, at least they had eyes to see with. One from amongst them replied that they were selling these barren lands to the Jews to rehabilitate them. And this, according to their faith, was the final century, that the Imam Mahdi would come, and everything would be theirs again. Initially I thought that the maulanas had kept only us Pukhtuns patiently waiting for the Imam sahib to come, but evidently, they had also made the poor Arabs wait for him. Now, sometimes I think that I should go to Palestine and ask the Arabs whether the lands now belong to them or to the Jews, as the fourteenth century of the *hijra* had concluded.

One day I met a young Arab outside the *Bait-ul-Muqaddas* mosque. I knew a little Arabic, and so picked up a conversation with him. I told him that *Bait-ul-Muqaddas* had developed substantially since the British occupation. They had built new roads and buildings in it. He looked at me as if to say something, but then thought the better of it. I asked him why he had kept quiet. He asked me whether I was an Indian. I asked him why he was asking. He told me that Indians were not good people and had nothing better to do, than to act as informers for the British. In this land of Palestine, people held the Hindustanis in great contempt. They were not to blame, because of the way the Hindustani army had treated them during the war. For this, may God give them their just retribution. The Hindustani army consisted mostly of Muslims. I replied that

I could at least tell him this much that I was not an informer. He asked me of what use would roads and buildings be to them; they and their land were on the road to poverty and destitution. This was because the Turks would spend money which they had generated in Palestine, in the country; while the British, like leeches, were busy sucking their blood. He said they plunder us and send the money to England. He then sighed deeply and said that God was now punishing them for their ungratefulness and what they had done to the Turks. He said that now they pine after the Turks, but the time has passed. He then asked God for forgiveness and prayed for relief from the claws of the oppressors and said that this was the condition of Syria as well.

Syria is divided into two parts. One part, which is now called Lebanon, has its capital at Beirut. This is a beautiful city on the shore of the Mediterranean Sea. Here, the Americans have established a big university for the teaching of science and the arts. In the other half, called Syria, there is a dearth of water. It is mostly mountainous, but its inhabitants are so industrious, that they have brought both the mountainous and the plain areas under cultivation and have mostly planted vineyards. Both the vineyards and the villages have been laid out in a very orderly manner. Its inhabitants are well off. In the areas which have a Muslim majority, its capital is Damascus. This too is a very beautiful city. Streams flow in it near the houses and in the streets. It has a lot of water and its land is very productive. But its inhabitants are not as industrious and development oriented. The villages here are also not as well laid out but are haphazardly located and the houses are built of mud. Syria is a Protectorate of France. Here I noticed a praise worthy attribute in its citizens: there is love and amity between the Christians and Muslims. They do not have the disunity and hatred which I found among the Muslims and Jews of Palestine. In my view, the French are devoid of the bad habit of creating disunity and hatred among their subjects in order to maintain their hold over them. The British, on the other hand, follow a policy of divide and rule.

In a hotel in Beirut, I talked to an Arab Muslim. He had come for a meeting of a committee constituted by the French, who were of the view that the imparting of mere education to the subjects was not enough; that industry and vocational training also had to be organized for their welfare. I was surprised that it was barely ten years since the French occupation, and they had concerns for the educational and vocational development of their subjects. Compared to this, in Hindustan, the British had been in our country for over two hundred years, and still the poor subjects were waiting for development of industry and vocations. From Syria, I went to Iraq and spent two days in Mosul. This is a small and beautiful town with a river. The consumption of wine and luxurious items has increased in its inhabitants. If the British were to occupy this place for long, these people would be totally ruined. From Mosul, I proceeded to Baghdad where I stayed for quite a few days. Baghdad is a lovely city, through the centre of which flows a large river. Here too, there were numerous pubs and wine shops. The wine shops were mostly owned by Hindustanis who had come here immediately after the British occupation. The British have also settled many Armenians here. From Baghdad, I went to Karbala and Najaf. Both these are greatly venerated towns. People from far away countries, particularly the Shias, come here to visit the tombs of Hazrat Ali and those of the other imams. These tombs are built in a very grand and lavish style which pleases the heart immensely. The Shias, unfortunate people till this day, wail loudly on coming here, and hit their heads against the railings on the tomb. On seeing them, one is reminded of the past. From Najaf, I went on to Kufa, a small town located on the banks of a river. The reason for its small size and under-development is explained by the people as the betrayal of Imam Hussain and his progeny by its inhabitants at the time, so God punished them in this fashion. If they had remained loyal and had been victorious, this fate would not have befallen the town and its inhabitants. It would have developed in the way that Baghdad, the capital city of Iraq, had done. The British have constructed many canals here, and those lands which are not irrigated by the canals are irrigated by pumps from the river. A young Arab was travelling with me by train. I told him that with the coming of the British, their land had seen tremendous development, which in turn has hugely benefitted them. He laughed at my observation and retorted that undoubtedly this was a very effective strategy – to divert the attention of the people, and that what I termed as 'development', was not real development for a country or its people, and nor had the British done this for their progress. This was meant to put them to sleep and make them oblivious to their present predicament. So that they are kept busy with all this and they can rule quietly over their country. But this was a web of slavery, which the British had spread for their subjugation. In Iraq, there are no Christians or Jews, but the British have embroiled the Sunnis and Shias in continuous strife. After spending a few days in Basra I finally returned safely to Karachi.

When the British established their control over Iraq, they encouraged two things: the consumption of liquor and womanising. In every town of Iraq there are numerous liquor shops and prostitute dens. There is music and debauchery; they have contributed significantly to the moral degradation of the people. Once I was roaming in the streets of Basra. When I arrived at a crossing, I saw a scaffold erected with a noose hanging. On inquiring I learnt that many Arab nationalists had been hanged here, and they had subjected the Arabs to many atrocities. In the newspapers of Hindustan, we would read about stories of the brutalities of the French against the Arabs, but there was never any mention of the brutalities of the British against the inhabitants of Hindustan. It appears that some newspapers of Hindustan do not have a conscience. They report only what the British ask them to. Here also there is a lot of hatred for the Hindustanis because in the garb of Muslim brotherhood, they have acted as spies against the Muslims, and have been instrumental in the hanging of many Arab nationalists. It is befitting that there is such hatred for the Hindustanis here. If the Iraqis were to regain even a little autonomy, the first thing they would do would be to extradite them from their country. When I arrived in Karachi, I found that there was a Pukhtun *thanedar* posted at the port. When he saw me on the ship, he embraced me and forced me to accompany him to his home. Nawabzada Amin Ullah Khan of Toru was also in Karachi at the time. He was a high-ranking officer in the administration of the railways. When he learnt of my arrival, he came and took me home with him where I spent a few days in great comfort in an atmosphere of love and affection. I then left Karachi for Uthmanzai, where I arrived safely.

The *Pukhtun*: Newspaper and Periodical

When I was in jail, I had deliberated at length over the condition of my people. I concluded that no nation can progress without the use of its mother tongue and there can be no knowledge or skill in them without this. I had, therefore, resolved that I would publish a periodical in Pukhto to educate the Pukhtuns and make them aware of events in the world and to turn their attention towards their own language. I would also ensure that the *Anjuman* plans to educate children in their own language. The fact is that, at that time, there was nothing in the Pukhto language, and nor was Pukhto in anyone's mind. The Pukhtuns, as a race, were so lacking in understanding and so innocent that knowledge of their language seemed demeaning to them. A nation that considers its language demeaning, dishonours and demeans itself and loses its mother tongue. And if it loses its mother tongue, its identity is lost with it. Immediately on my release, I put forth both these proposals to the *Anjuman* but due to financial difficulties, no concrete steps could be taken. I took the responsibility for the periodical on my own head and told Abdul Akbar Khan and Abdullah Shah to seek permission for the publication from the government. However, three years went by and they could not even apply for the permission for the magazine. I realized that without my personal intervention, the task would remain undone. So towards the end of 1927, I decided to do it myself, and soon after submitting the application to the government, got the permission. In 1928 I started publishing the monthly *Pukhtun* magazine from Uthmanzai bazaar. This was the first periodical in the Pukhto language published in the land of the Pukhtuns. The Pukhtuns are a generous people but will not spend on such things, and are not accustomed to spending on causes such as newspapers and periodicals. I spent a lot of money on it from my own pocket. This monthly magazine infused a new life, both in the men and women of the Pukhtuns, and it became immensely popular amongst them. Let alone our own land, the Pukhtuns everywhere – in Europe, America and Australia, learnt about it and subscribed to it and contribute to it financially. It created love for Pukhto in the hearts of the Pukhtuns, and it was also widely read in Afghanistan. Abdul Hadi Khan Dawee told me that when the *Pukhtun journal* would reach Kabul, they would read the articles on nationalism and it would create a greater closeness and love for Pukhto. And it had such an impact on King Amanullah Khan that he made a public announcement that the people should learn Pukhto and that, after three years, Pukhto would be both the official language of Afghanistan and a medium of instruction in schools and colleges. Abdul Hadi Khan also told me that they had arranged for a magazine to be published and named it *Pukhtun*. Amanullah Khan then asked him whether it was appropriate to have every magazine of the Pukhtuns named 'Pukhtun'. He then changed the name to *De Pukhtano Zhagh (Voice of the Pukhtuns)*. But, unfortunately, the British could not tolerate this and after only a few issues of this magazine were published, a revolution started in Afghanistan. Amanullah Khan was dethroned and Bacha Saqa became the ruler for a short time.

Our *Anjuman* arranged *mushairas* for the promotion of Pukhto and to bring about a change in the thinking of the poets. We fixed prizes for the best poem recited at these functions. Once a year, when the annual *jalsa* of the foundation of the *madrassah* was held, a *mushaira* would also be held at the same time. Because of this, a revolutionary change took place in the Pukhtun poets and their poems, which were replete with black tresses and moles of the beloved, gave way to poems of unity, brotherhood and national progress. There was a rekindled passion in the country and the people, and such fervour overtook both men and women that, on the day of the *jalsa*, it would be difficult to find a place. People from every corner of the province and every *tapa*, whether rich or poor, considered it their moral obligation to participate in the *jalsa* of the *Anjuman*. There were special arrangements for the segregation of women, and hundreds of women too would participate. But unfortunately, the people responsible for the *Anjuman* were unable to reform themselves; our internal rifts had widened to such an extent that we were unable to perform our duties effectively. If only our *Anjuman* had kept up our work of preaching and publishing, and continued with our tours, we would have progressed to a much greater extent. It was our misfortune and the misfortune of our people that the *Anjuman* was not free from its internal squabbles. It could have toured the countryside and awakened the unaware Pukhtuns and inculcated feelings of brotherhood in them. Finally, things came to such a state that Khadim sahib was successful in creating a rift between Abbas Khan and Abdul Akbar Khan. This caused even greater harm to the *Anjuman*. Then Khadim sahib set himself on the task of creating a rift between Abbas Khan and me. But fortunately, he was unable to succeed in his endeavour. One summer I went up to the Murree Hills for a vacation; the field was then left open to Khadim sahib and his intriguing mind. He created an impression in the minds of Abbas Khan and some others in the *Anjuman* that no tree can prosper and thrive in the shade of a large one, and whatever sacrifice and effort they might make in the cause, the credit for it would be given to me. When I returned from Murree and saw the attitude of some responsible members of the *Anjuman*, I was very distressed. There was propaganda against me everywhere. I consulted Haji Abdul Ghaffar Khan, and collected the people of the *Anjuman* through him, and appealed to them that what they were doing was not a good thing and that its result would be the destruction of our *Anjuman*, and that, for the sake of God, they should have pity on their nation that had been destroyed and that we should not destroy it further. That we should not make false accusations against each other and should also not indulge in backbiting; that whatever criticism they had, should be voiced face to face and openly. That if they had any complaints or suspicions against anyone or thought that he had done something wrong, they should not be backbiting, as this benefitted no one and was damaging to the cause. At this, Abdul Akbar Khan and *Mian* Abdullah Shah would smile, and address Khadim sahib and question him, 'Khadim sahib, how could we accuse anyone behind his back?' Anyway, all this talk happened in a joking manner. In the evening when we had our meal in the *hujra* of haji Abdul Ghaffar Khan, some of our members were about to leave with Abbas Khan for the night, so I too accompanied them. There I started the discussion and asked them why, despite being such intelligent men, they had pretended as if they knew nothing? Abbas Khan gave me a clear answer: that when a tree becomes large and shady, smaller saplings cannot prosper in its shade, until its branches are adequately pruned, and that they wanted my branches to be pruned somewhat. I laughingly told him that I feared he might be subjected to the cruel joke of exposing his children to the danger of a burning sun by the pruning of the shady tree for the sake of a sapling, which might not provide the required shade. I continued with my efforts hoping that they would be reformed. But they were not reformed. Finally, Abdul Akbar Khan succeeded in creating a rift between Abbas Khan and me in a *jalsa*. When I came back to the village, I concluded that the reform of the present *Anjuman* was difficult. I decided to resign from its membership. In the resignation letter, I mentioned that there would be no decrease in the quantum of my annual donation to the *Anjuman*. In fact, I would increase it and that I would, like the other members, be an ordinary member and would be ready to render any kind of service to it, but that from now onwards I should not be considered a member of its management committee, and nor would I participate in its meetings. Whatever efforts the government was able to undertake to ruin the *Anjuman*, it was already doing. But even a government as powerful as this one could not harm the *Anjuman*. In fact, it was on the path of progress by the day. But the British could not inflict even a small percentage of the damage that the *Anjuman* suffered at our own hands, because of our internal rifts. The *Anjuman* remained in name and slowly began to shut down in various places, and its annual *jalsa* ceased to be held. After my resignation, Abbas Khan also did not stay in the committee for many days. He resigned and discontinued his annual donation to the *Anjuman*. He forced his brother, Faiz Muhammad Khan, to stop his donation too, even though Faiz was extremely upset about all this and expressed his dissatisfaction to me. But he was not prepared to oppose his elder brother. Abbas Khan started a propaganda campaign against me and the *Anjuman* but was unable to meet with any success.

When the condition of the *Anjuman* went from bad to worse, only then did Khadim sahib realize the extent of the damage that he had inflicted. He began earnest efforts to try and placate me and, every day, he would sing a new nationalist tune. But this had no effect on me because the entire destruction of the *Anjuman* was his handiwork. When one professes one thing and does another, those exhortations do not have a positive impact on anyone. When he would pester me a lot, I would say to him bluntly that, 'Khadim sahib, you are responsible for all the destruction brought upon the *Anjuman*, and one day, you will be made to account for all this before God and the *Anjuman*.' One day he told me that I should become the engine of the *Anjuman*, gather my strength like the engine of a train, and pull all the bogeys of the *Anjuman* behind me. I replied that, 'Khadim sahib! The *Anjuman* can harness and pull only those bogeys behind it whose brakes were not applied! And those bogeys that have put their breaks on, they cannot be pulled by the engine.' Sometimes he would broach the issue of touring the countryside with me. But I had just one answer for him that, 'I cannot go on tour with you. But if the *Anjuman* orders me to do so, I would be ever ready to obey its order.' As the Pukhto adage goes, I 'drew a line' before Khadim sahib and only then did he somewhat realize what his mistake was and began to feel it.

Amanullah Khan

When commotion began in Afghanistan, it was not a revolution, but a tumult. Amanullah Khan fled to Kandahar. Bacha Saqa took possession of Kabul. The English language newspapers started a propaganda campaign against Afghanistan and expressed happiness over the takeover of Kabul by Bacha Saqa. I thought what development could we expect of the British in Sarhad when they could not even tolerate the progress of the Pukhtuns in Afghanistan? I immediately decided that it was important to make the free tribesmen understand this situation, and so began my tours. Village by village, from town to town and from one area to another, I held *jalsas*. By the grace of God, the Pukhtuns were awakened from their slumber, understood the danger they confronted, and realized their own backwardness, and prepared to assist Afghanistan. In some areas, some of the *maulanas* opposed this, but when they saw the mood of the tribes, they gave up their opposition. The tribes stifled the opposition of those who did not desist, for personal gain. We were assisted in our task by our nationalist poets, who ignited a fresh nationalistic fervour in the hearts of the people. In this regard, Torsam Khan of Dwasaro helped us immensely. He would compose poems and we would have them published in the *Pukhtun* magazine. One couplet from it, goes as follows:

Ma ba way da salray zamoong qaum kay khalal day,
Us day woleedo che da jheeray khawand ghal day!

I used to say this man was, for our people, a disgrace,
see now for yourself, how the bearded are all rogues!

This couplet became so popular that when people saw a bearded man, they would cry out the one with the beard is a rogue. In those days, no one with a beard could roam the streets of the Qissa Khwani bazaar without fear. Khan Mir Hilali accompanied me on all my tours. He wrote such poems and so vividly described the conditions in Afghanistan, that on hearing them, every Pukhtun understood the predicament they were in and I did not find it necessary to dwell on this aspect in my *jalsas*. In this, the students of our *madrassah* played a major role. Our *Anjuman* also prepared itself to offer every kind of financial and material assistance. The grief and suffering of the Pukhtuns of Afghanistan was felt by the Pukhtuns of Sarhad as their own, because we are brothers and one nation. I cannot describe the passion that arose in the Pukhtuns of Sarhad to help their brothers in Afghanistan. Whether rich or poor, educated or illiterate, whether woman or man, everyone empathized with the situation in Afghanistan. People were ready to help in any way they could to restore Amanullah Khan's government and would pray for the success of 'our King, Amanullah Khan'. There have been many kings in the history of the Pukhtuns, but the love and affection exhibited for Amanullah Khan has never been matched by any other king.

Amanullah Khan would claim that he was a revolutionary king of the Pukhtuns. This was true. He created a strange sort of revolution amongst the Pukhtuns. When I look at the Pukhtuns today, I am amazed at the speed at which the transformation amongst them has occurred in terms of brotherhood, nationalism, and political consciousness. A revolution is like a flood. When it comes, it sweeps away those who are asleep; and those who are awake benefit from it. In the revolution of Afghanistan, the Pukhtuns of Afghanistan were drowned and we, the Pukhtuns of lower Pukhtunkhwa, benefitted from it. This was because we were awake and aware. For the Pukhtuns of lower Pukhtunkhwa, organizing *jalsas* and prayers for their brothers in Afghanistan was not enough. They wanted to participate physically in the grief and difficulties of Afghanistan. They wanted to be with their brothers and share the travails of their brothers with them; to treat their injured brothers and to help the successors of those who had been killed, leaving behind wives and children. For this, we formed a committee and named it the Afghan *Hilal-e-Ahmar*. The task of this committee was to assist the Pukhtuns of Afghanistan, both medically and financially. Area by area, village by village, people arranged to collect donations. In a short while we organized a medical mission which, under the patronage of my older brother, Dr. Khan Sahib, decided to go to Afghanistan. In extending assistance to Afghanistan, no Pukhtun lagged behind; however, the people of Bannu, the family of the Kundis from Dera Ismail Khan, the Khans of Sudham, the Khans of Baezai, Qazi Ataullah Khan, Ali Asghar Khan, Ali Gul Khan and *Mian* Ahmad Shah sahib, are worthy of great praise in this regard. But how could the British be in favour of such an effort? How could they accept the fact that the Pukhtuns of Sarhad would go to help Afghanistan, as this would result in the establishment of our national consciousness and brotherhood. This is not what they wanted.

We were not given permission to travel to Afghanistan. I tried my best to convince the others that, even without their permission, it was necessary for us to leave for Afghanistan, and that we did not need the permission of the British or their passports. However, my view was not upheld by the committee. I also told the committee that until such time that Amanullah Khan was in Kabul, the British would never give us permission to go there. But the committee would respond that, if we were to go without permission, our medical supplies would be stopped. The first objection the British had was that we were going in order to assist Amanullah Khan, but the question was whether he had solicited our help. If we were to provide written proof of his approval, only then would they give us permission. *Mian* Jaffar Shah and I were tasked to go to Amanullah Khan and bring the letter of authority. But I pointed out to the committee that we were going to help our nation and our Pukhtun brothers. What had the permission from Amanullah Khan to do with this? We are going to help the Pukhtuns.

We first went to the lawyer, Tijarat Lala, in Peshawar, so that he could have the authority letter sent to us. However, when the letter did not arrive, we decided to go to Kandahar to get it directly from Amanullah Khan. A grand *jalsa* of the Pukhtuns was held in Shahibagh. I informed *Mian* Jaffar Shah of my intention and told him that these were all lame excuses of the British. They, to the extent possible, would make every effort to deprive our delegation of the authority letter to proceed to Afghanistan, and that they would realize this very soon. We went to Naukhar and spent the night there, where a big *jalsa* was held. The next morning, we got into the train at Naukhar station and travelled to Rawalpindi. Maulana Ishaq Hazarvi sahib[16] and many Muslims of the city had come to the Rawalpindi station to meet us. When our train arrived in Lahore, Maulana Zaffar Ali Khan and many leaders of the Muslims and Hindus had come to see us. They made us get off and took us to the city where they took out a big *jaloos,* although I was not in favour of this. The next day a large *jalsa* of the Hindus and Muslims was held in which speeches of solidarity and assistance with us were delivered and resolutions passed. The next day we left by the Karachi Mail train for Quetta. At the Sukkur railway station, Hazrat Maulana of Sindh and some Muslims from Sindh had come to meet us. We held lengthy discussions with them and changed trains for Quetta. Early next morning we reached Sibi. Our train was at the station and we were wondering where to get a cup of tea from, when Captain Sahibzada Muhammad Khurshid[17], Assistant Political Agent of Balochistan, accompanied by a khan of Pabbi, the superintendent of Police, came to our compartment. I suspected that they had come for us. They started chatting with us and then invited us to have a cup of tea. We thanked them, but said that we might miss the train. On the assurance that the train had a long stop at Sibi, we accompanied them to the bungalow of Captain Khurshid and had our tea. We were in a hurry, lest we missed our train. Little did we realize that the government was not prepared to allow us to proceed further. The government had sent Sahibzada sahib and the khan of Pabbi[18] to persuade us to return to Peshawar. But we did not agree to this, and despite a lot of persuasion, we were forcibly made to board another train. They handed us over to the police to escort us across the border of Balochistan. When the train reached Jacobabad, the police made us disembark. We proceeded to Jacobabad city and rented a small place. We informed Peshawar that the government had not allowed us to proceed to Quetta and had forced us to return from Sibi station, and that they were not allowing us to go to Kandahar. That we had resolved not to comply with this unjust decision of the government and would move in the direction of Kandahar again the next day. The next morning, we sent a telegram to the resident of Balochistan, informing him that we were not prepared to accept this unjust order of his, and that we were informing him that, tomorrow again, we would leave for Quetta. We caught the night train and when it arrived the next morning at Sibi station, what do we see but that armed police, along with an Englishman, were waiting for us. When the train came to a halt, the Englishman came to our compartment and forced us to get off. This time, Sahibzada sahib and the khan of Pabbi were not with them. We thought that they were taking us to the jail, but the Englishman took us to the waiting room and posted a double guard on us. He seemed to be a very decent Englishman. He indicated to me when he spoke, that he failed to comprehend the policy of this government. He said, 'On the one hand, it proclaims that we are impartial, and yet it tells you to go to Afghanistan and get permission from Amanullah Khan. On the other, they order me to ensure that I should not allow you to go. Moreover, it is prohibiting you and not allowing you to take your medical relief delegation, which is concerned only with medical assistance and relief, and nothing else.' In the early evening when the train returned from Quetta to Sibi, we were made to board it and then disembark at Jacobabad. We realized that the government was not prepared to allow us to proceed towards Kandahar on any condition. So, we did not consider any further travel between Sibi and Jacobabad as worthwhile and decided that we would go to Delhi instead and meet the Afghan consul general to see whether he could arrange for our letter of authority. And so, we went to Delhi and met with the consul general. He expressed great sympathy for us and sent a telegram to Amanullah Khan who had the authority letter sent to us. On that day, we found out in Delhi that the British had sent for the brother of the Hazrat of Shorbazar, who lived in Kathiawar, and that he was to be sent to Afghanistan with the *Powindahs*, who were his *mureeds*, to incite rebellion amongst them against Amanullah Khan. This was because the British had found out that some sympathy had been generated for Amanullah Khan amongst the masses, and it was feared that he might succeed in getting his throne back. We took leave of the consul general and left for Sarhad. When we arrived in Peshawar, we learnt from the trade minister of Afghanistan that a farman from Kandahar, signed and sealed by Amanullah Khan, had come for us. Despite this, the government resorted to tricks and made us waste our time. When I was convinced that the government would, on no account, give our delegation the required permission, I informed the members of our party that these excuses of the government were intended to make us stay back. That if they were to wait for the permission, they would have to do this indefinitely, and would not be able to help Afghanistan in any way. Moreover, did the government not have a consulate in Afghanistan? Then what was the requirement of passports for us? We were not going to Afghanistan on the responsibility of the British, we were going there on our own; then what need did we have for permission from the British? But most of my companions were of the view that, in that case, we would not be able to travel freely between here and Afghanistan, and difficulties would be created for us regarding the transfer of medical supplies, and nor would we be able to provide financial assistance to our Afghan brothers. I said to them that, in such circumstances, we would be just left waiting. We will not be able to help Afghanistan in any way. Moreover, until such time as Amanullah Khan remained in Afghanistan, we would not get the required permission.

It was under these circumstances that a few of my companions and I decided that we would leave for Afghanistan without the permission of the British. We held a *jalsa* in Peshawar and put before the people the fact that the British were not giving us permission; and that we did not consider it necessary to have their permission. Afghanistan was our brother country and we would take this responsibility upon ourselves to go to our brothers. That whoever wanted to accompany us and was prepared to come, could join us immediately. There were many people who responded to our call and were ready to join us. When the report of the proceedings of this *jalsa* reached the government, it immediately sent me a telegram asking for applications from those who wanted to go to Afghanistan for medical relief work, along with copies of their photographs, for them to issue authority letters for our travel. I understood their intention, but most members of the delegation were of the view that I unnecessarily suspected every move of the government because of my intense hatred for it. I kept quiet and abandoned my intention of travelling without the authority letter and we dispatched our applications for the passports.

Nadir Khan

For many days, rumours were afloat in the city that Nadir Khan, along with his brothers, had left France. I learnt that he had arrived in Peshawar and was staying with the Afghan trade counsellor. Dr. Khan Sahib and I went to call on him. I already knew him and Hashim Khan. We had a long meeting. Many people tried to persuade them to go to Kandahar, and Amanullah Khan had also sent emissaries to him, but Nadir Khan was not prepared to go to Kandahar. One day he and I happened to be alone in a room discussing the future of Afghanistan, when he told me that whatever he did, he did for the sake of Amanullah Khan. I told him that the people were saying that they were trying to install the son of Habibullah Khan, who happened to be his sister's son, as king. He told me, 'You will be alive, and I will also be alive. If ever I made him king or became king myself, you can come and blacken my face and say to me that – Nadir, you have not fulfilled your promise.' After a few days, Hashim Khan left for Jalalabad, and Nadir Khan and Shah Wali Khan left for Zazai. He forcefully took a promise from me to meet them the next day in Thall, where they would be, and that I should get there to see him. Next day, I went to Thall, but Nadir Khan had left by then. At the time of departure, I met Hakim Khan in the car. He was leaving for Zazai to meet Nadir Khan. I gave him a letter in which I wrote to Nadir Khan that he had not been able to fulfil his first promise, and that God alone knows what would become of his second promise. Except for me, all my other companions were of the view that the government would allow us to proceed to Afghanistan. But I thought otherwise, because I was convinced that they would not allow a king such as Amanullah Khan, who was a known well-wisher of the Pukhtuns, to remain on the throne of Afghanistan. But our wishful brothers were hopeful that permission would come in a day or two.

It was the time of harvest and, in order to collect donations for Afghanistan, we were touring the Baizai area. The people, full of sincerity, promised to donate all their *zakat* to us. The Pukhtuns were ready to help their brothers in Afghanistan in every way. Khushal Khan[19] and I left for Mardan by way of Barikao and Skhakot. When we arrived in Mardan, we learnt that Amanullah Khan had abandoned his resolve to fight and had come to Quetta. This was worrisome as well as sad. Khushal Khan left for his village, and I went to Qazi Attaullah's house, and collapsed on a bed. After a few days, when Amanullah Khan arrived in Bombay, I was persuaded by Dr. Khan Sahib and some friends to go to Bombay and call on Amanullah Khan to discuss the affairs of Afghanistan and seek guidance from him, and to find out that, if we were to extend any support to Afghanistan, whom should we assist. He also asked me to find out what his views were about Nadir Khan and his brothers. I, accordingly, went to Bombay. Abdul Hadi Khan Dawee was there with Amanullah Khan, and through his facilitation, I met him. I broached the subject of his return to Afghanistan, but he was totally disappointed with Afghanistan and had abandoned the thought of ever returning. He seemed fed up of the Pukhtuns. When I concluded my call, he talked to me in Pukhto. During the discussion, a mention was also made of Nadir Khan and his companions. I asked him whom we should give the donations to, which were collected in the name of Afghanistan. In response, he said to me, 'You can give this to Nadir Khan and help him.' We took leave of each other in great grief. In the hotel, he was accompanied by several other sardars. We met all of them as well. Abdul Hadi Khan accommodated me as a guest in the house of the Afghan consul in Bombay, and at lunch time I met and talked to several other sardars. They felt that Amanullah Khan would certainly return, because the generals who were busy trying to remove Bacha Saqa from the throne had no unity amongst them and could not come around to agreeing on a leader. They could all be persuaded to agree on Amanullah Khan. Among these generals was Nadir Khan who had sought the assistance of Zazai for the capture of Kabul. The other was Ghulam Nabi Khan who was descending on Kabul from the direction of Turkistan. I returned from Bombay and gave all this information to the *Anjuman-e-Hilal-Ahmar*. I put forth the proposal that all the money deposited with the *Anjuman*, and the supplies provided to us by the people for the medical mission, should be sent to Nadir Khan. But certain lawyers, led by Ibrahim Khan[20] of Cheena, opposed this. I think this was merely an excuse to get back their donations. Finally, it was decided that those who did not want their money to be sent to Nadir Khan, had the right to take their money back, although this was against the law of the *Hilal-e-Ahmar*. Almost all the lawyers who had given us any donations had them reimbursed. Despite this, we sent fifty thousand rupees, in cash, to Nadir Khan and all the assistance, in kind, that people had donated. We also arranged for further donations in the area. During these days, everyone was full of enthusiasm. Our boys at Islamia College, Peshawar, had collected a lot of donation for Afghanistan. It was the month of December and the colleges were closed for winter vacations. One of my friends from my school days, *Mian* Akbar Shah of Badrasho, thought that it was necessary to create an *Anjuman* of the Pukhtun youth. He broached the subject with me in the *hujra* of *Mian* Ahmad Shah that the youth of Sarhad want to get together and, if I were to make arrangements for the event, it would be a big favour to them. I told him that I was always ready to be at their service, but instead of Peshawar, if they were to choose Uthmanzai as a venue, it would suit me better. He agreed to my proposal and we gathered in Uthmanzai. I had also invited some members of my *Anjuman* to exchange views with them. Discussions started about the need to establish a Youth League in Sarhad. Some participants thought that, instead of a Youth League, the name of the *Anjuman* should be *De Subah-Sarhad de Zwanano Jirga (The Youth Jirga of the Sarhad)*. However, the president of our *Anjuman*, Abdul Akbar Khan, and its secretary, Khadim Muhammad Akbar, opposed this. They were of the view that there was already a viable organization of the Pukhtuns, and that there was no difference between the aims and objectives of the existing and the proposed organization. So, instead of setting up a new organization, the need was to develop the existing one. But the youth were very enthusiastic and did not agree to this. Our people are generally under the impression that progress can only be achieved with the setting up of a new organization.

It was October 1929, when I received a telegram from Nadir Khan about the capture of Kabul. A wave of happiness swept over the whole region. The nation's resolve was fortified, and processions emerged from both sides of the land. People danced in happiness; *gharabeen* and guns were also fired. All these processions collected at Uthmanzai and a big *jalsa* was held. In this *jalsa*, leaders delivered their speeches, and I, too, addressed the congregation. During the speech, I told the Pukhtun youth, 'Learn a lesson from the victory at Kabul. A large part of the success in Afghanistan is because of your efforts. There was no task in the world which could not be accomplished, but only if people are determined to do it. Napoleon used to say that there was no such word as "impossible" in his dictionary. You are asleep and were unaware about the world. I am making you aware.' With the capture of Kabul, Nadir Khan proclaimed himself the king. We were surprised at this because he had promised us that he would not become king. Let alone us, he also broke all the promises that he had made to his own people. In those days, I met Abdul Hadi Khan, who was leaving for Kabul. When he saw me, he laughed and said, 'The wretch did not even uphold one promise. If he desired kingship, he should at least have proclaimed a constitutional monarchy!' This disloyalty of Nadir Khan had a bad effect on our people. But what could be done? We left it to God to punish him, so that no one else should do this to his people. After the resolution of the conflict in Afghanistan, we had nothing else to do. I made *Mian* Ahmad Shah sahib agree, and so we decided to set off on a tour of our province. Abdul Akbar Khan, *Mian* Ahmad Shah and I set off on a tour of Kohat, Bannu and Dera Ismail Khan. The speeches they delivered were on the *Jirga*, or the Youth League, and I would discuss national issues with the people. In every place, our tour proved to be a great success.

10

Organized Political Activity

The All-India Congress *Jalsa* in Lahore

IN DECEMBER 1929, THE ANNUAL *JALSA* OF THE ALL-INDIA CONGRESS was scheduled in Lahore. Since Lahore was close to Sarhad, many people from the province went to see it. *Amir* Mumtaz Khan, the headmaster of our Azad School in Uthmanzai, and I resolved to attend it. We were not part of the Congress but were in the *Khilafat* movement, and went only as onlookers. The Congress *jalsa* had a very positive effect on the youth of Sarhad, particularly the fact that even the Hindu girls were associated with the struggle for freedom. We walked among the participants. The nationalistic fervour of the women volunteers was quite impressive. All my companions who had travelled from Sarhad gathered there. The Pukhtuns were greatly affected by the women. This had a tremendous impact on every one of them, and the spark of service to their land and people was kindled in their hearts.

Khudai Khidmatgari

When we returned from Lahore, we held a big *jalsa* in Uthmanzai. I addressed my people and told them that they were in deep slumber, and that not only the men, even the Hindu women had woken up and, along with their men, were struggling for the freedom of the country. They should wake up and get ready. They should see that the British were proclaiming that they had conquered Hindustan, that it now belonged to them and they will now rule over it. Its riches and wealth were now theirs to enjoy. The Hindus, on the other hand, are telling the British that their land has been forcibly occupied. Now that they had become aware of the situation and had united, they would recapture their land from them. It was their land and it would be soon ruled by them. I asked the people whether they were aware of these developments or not? 'I will make you aware,' I said. 'Be aware that the fight between the Hindus and the British is over this: the British proclaim that they will rule over Hindustan, and the Hindus are saying that they will rule here; while the Muslims are enjoying the slumber of blissful oblivion. So, my Pukhtun brothers, I ask you a question – what will you do? Will you remain sitting on the sidelines and praying for both parties? And will you spend your lives in slavery and "*Pathithob.*" (When we were boys, we played with walnuts. We would draw a big circle and place walnuts in the middle. There would be two players. The third player would collect the walnuts for others and was called the *pathi*. Whoever would win the walnuts, would give him two walnuts). So, oh Pukhtuns! I am asking you, do you prefer a life of "*patthitob (being a pathi)*" or do you consider yourselves the rightful owners of this land? Rise and prepare yourselves, and make your land your own!' The *jalsa* concluded with great enthusiasm and my speech had a tremendous impact on the Pukhtuns. At night, Abdul Akbar Khan, Sarfaraz Khan and Hijab Gul, accompanied by some other young men, came to our *hujra* to see me and discussed the formation of a political party. I explained things to them in detail, that this was not a matter of just fun and games; this was something very difficult to achieve. There were many obstacles and thorns in its way. The next evening, they came again. I told them that their minds were still obsessed by my speech. That they should study the history of the world, that whoever had decided to serve humanity, had to face pain and undergo hardships. That they should, for the third time, think seriously about this matter. On the third evening, they came back and told me that they had given the matter serious thought and consideration, and that they were prepared to undergo all kinds of hardships and sacrifice in the service of the nation. We then sat and thought about what this new party should be called. I was of the view that the Pukhtuns were unaware of the concept of service, and that we should give the new political party a name that would make the Pukhtuns aware of this concept and fire their imagination. Several names were put forth, but we did not like any of them. That night, the name of *Khudai Khidmatgar* (Servants of God) came to my mind and I proposed the name the next day when we met. They too liked it, and we finalized it with a prayer for its success.

We Pukhtuns consider 'God's work' and 'service' as that which is being undertaken for the sake of God, without any expectation of personal gain. Since God is not in need of our service, it is His creation (humanity) which stands in need of service.

In our area, the maulanas had prohibited the playing of dhols and *surnas*. An elder of the musicians (*demaan*) had told his juniors to hang their drums from the beam in the room. God was bound to bring back Islam one day. So, we told the musicians to bring out their dhols and their *surnas*. They were very happy and joined the *Khudai Khidmatgar*, and we left first on a tour of Hashtnagar and then of Doaba. When we would arrive near a village, we would start playing the dhols. And when the people heard its sound and that of the *surna*, they would be surprised because their use had been prohibited by the maulanas. Whoever heard them, whether men, women or children, would gather around and follow us. When we would reach the centre of the village, the beating of the dhol and the playing of the *surna* would stop. Most of the people of the village would have collected. Playing the music helped us a lot. I would deliver a brief speech that, 'Oh Pukhtun brothers! We are your brothers. We are your *Khudai Khidmatgar* and have come to serve you. Come! Let us build this destroyed home of ours. Just have a look at the world. If you do not have knowledge, you do have your eyes. The various people and nations of the world have reached up to the sky and we have been left behind on earth. They are human beings like the rest of us, but we have stretched out our hands to them, begging money from some and grain from others. God has gifted us with a heaven-like land. It is full of wealth and treasures, and look at our state in it! We do not even have enough maize to quell our hunger. Why have they developed, and we have been left behind? They have brotherhood, nationalism and unity amongst themselves. We are ridden with factionalism, envy, vengeance and hypocrisy. Today's world is one of nationhood. If you were to become a nation, you too would prosper both in this world and in the next.'

Our speeches had a great impact on the people and wherever we went, men, women, children, the young and the aged, would join us. The maulanas issued a fatwa that Bacha Khan is *Dujjal*. It was said of *Dujjal* that when he comes, he will be followed by women, men and the children. The maulanas would say to the people, 'Can't you see that men, women and children follow him when he comes?' Whichever young man wanted to join our party, he was required to take an oath. We would tell him that this was a very difficult path to tread. It was strewn with thorns, hardships, impediments and sacrifices. If he was ready to face these, only then should he become a *Khudai Khidmatgar*. Then we would tell him that God was not in need of our services. Service to God consists of service to humanity (His creation), for His pleasure. Then we would say to him that they would have to abandon factionalism and rifts, because it was due to these that our homes were destroyed. And if somebody were to be harsh with him, he should not seek revenge and retribution. He was to exercise patience. We would also tell him that he was to shun violence, because the Pukhtuns had been reduced to these traits by violence. The violence of the Pukhtun was against his brother. A *Khudai Khidmatgar* would serve his land and people for the sake of God only. He would have no other objective in mind. He will abandon customs and rituals and would do physical labour for two hours every day. When he would take this oath, only then would we write his name in the list of the *Khudai Khidmatgar*.

People hold strange views about non-violence. Lots of propaganda is voiced about it and misunderstanding is created in the minds of the people. Some say that if anyone slaps you on one cheek, turn the other cheek to him. Others would say that lie supine and allow your opponent to tread over you; they would say that you must lie down and allow yourself to be beaten, you will not move either hand or foot. Some would say that the Pukhtuns were a brave and a great nation and that Ghaffar Khan was making them weak and faint-hearted. In short, all sorts of things were said about it. In fact, non-violence is a power; it also has an army like that of violence. But the weapon of non-violence is preaching, and that of violence is the gun. Non-violence generates love amongst the people. It creates courage and determination. Violence generates hatred, fear and faint-heartedness. Some people are of the view that violence is necessary for defence. They give no thought to the fact that if you resort to violence, then you have abandoned the path of non-violence. The truth is that non-violence has its own defence. Non-violence does not have defeat, and in violence, defeat is involved. Just like there is a system of violence, similarly, non-violence has a complete system. Violence is easy, and its path is also easy. Non-violence is difficult, and treading its path is also very difficult. To slap someone in response to being slapped is very easy; but to bear a slap patiently, is a difficult proposition.

Tours

After Hashtnagar and Doaba, *Mian* Ahmad Shah and I left on a tour of Sawabai. We toured many villages and many people joined the movement. We started constituting *jirga* village by village. From there we left for Peshawar, Khalisa and Daudzai and toured the villages of these areas. We also toured Mardan and the Baizai countryside and went to Sudham and Rustam. Sahibzada Khurshid of Adina and Maulvi Shad Muhammad sahib of Torlandai came to me and then, with them, I toured the area from Amazo Garhai to Naranji. In this tour, Khurshid sahib's cycle proved to be of great help to us. We also toured on foot. Sahibzada sahib would mount his bicycle and would arrive at our destination ahead of us. By the time we got there, he would have already gathered the people of the village. When we would start our speech, Sahibzada sahib would leave for the next village on his bicycle. In this way, we would hold nine or ten *jalsa* a day. During these tours, we managed to do a lot of work and hold many *jalsa*. The main reason for this was that it was the month of Ramzan and there was no question of eating or drinking during the day. The time usually wasted in entertainment was profitably utilized. For Eid, we all went back to our villages. On the second day of Eid, a big fair was to be held in Charsadda, called the 'Nasro Mela'. The *Khudai Khidmatgar,* with their dhol and *surna*, went to this mela in a congregation. At the time, the uniform of the *Khudai Khidmatgar* was made of white, homespun cotton. This would get dirty very quickly, and when this happened during the tour, it would not look nice. In the mela, people from near and far had congregated. We held a big *jalsa* there where thousands of people participated. There was enthusiasm and passion in our people. I would repeat the same speech at every *jalsa*. Then we proceeded to Khalisa where a big *mela* is held in Akbarpura. Many people had gathered, to whom we explained the aims and objectives of our party. On the way, a *Khudai Khidmatgar* asked someone for directions. When the man saw the dhol and *surna* with him, he asked him to play, and only then would he show the way. The

Khudai Khidmatgar told him that he should ask the man in the back of the crowd, and if he tells him to play, he will do so. When I arrived on the scene the man got embarrassed and showed us the way. From Akbarpura we proceeded to Taru and then by train to Naukhar. We held a *jalsa* there in Sadar Bazar and explained the aims and objectives of the *Khudai Khidmatgar* movement to the people. For the night, we went across the river to Naukhar city. The arrangements for the evening meal had been made by Mazullah Khan. Gul Ahmad and Younas Khan had arranged for the *jalsa* to be held on the *shamilat* of Naukhar. The next day both the khans and the common people participated in the *jalsa* in large numbers. Sarbiland Khan, Sarfaraz Khan, Ameenullah Khan, Hazrat Badshah, *Mian* sahib along with his sons, Feroz Shah, Sarwar Shah and Abdul Diyan, participated and the *jalsa* was a big success. In Naukhar, a lot of enthusiasm was generated and Hazrat Shah Badshah made an announcement in the *jalsa* that he had donated two of his sons, Feroz Shah and Sarwar Shah, to Bacha Khan for service to the *Khudai Khidmatgar* movement.

In Naukhar, we constituted a *jirga*, where many people had joined the movement. Sarwar Shah was appointed the General of the *Khudai Khidmatgar*. I have already mentioned the fact that the uniform of the *Khudai Khidmatgar* was made from white homespun cotton. The *Khudai Khidmatgar* complained to me that this white uniform got dirty very quickly and that there was no arrangement to wash it either. So, it would be appropriate if we were to colour it. I allowed them to do so. By coincidence, they coloured it red. The *Khudai Khidmatgar* made red uniforms for themselves. Each *Khudai Khidmatgar* would make his own uniform himself. The colour red had a great effect on the hearts of the people, because it looked nice and the young men would look very handsome in it. All the *Khudai Khidmatgar* coloured their uniforms in the same colour. It was on account of this red uniform that the British again started their propaganda against them, that this was a movement of the Bolsheviks. At that time, we did not know that the Bolsheviks had a red uniform. This was just a coincidence. Until that time, I had neither read a book of Marx or of Lenin, or Gandhiji, nor had I heard of them. From Naukhar we came to Kheshko and held a *jalsa*. Many people joined our movement. Saif-ul-Mulook and Taj-ul-Malook were appointed the *mashers* of the *Surkh-Posh* (red shirts). Then we came to Nisatta. Here too a *jalsa* was held and many joined the movement. It was a manifestation of God's grace that such enthusiasm had overtaken the Pukhtuns that whichever village we visited and the people heard about it, they would come to us in no time. And after my speech when I made an appeal and asked whether there was anyone among them who would, for the sake of God, come forward and serve His creation, one would get up and say that his name be written, and after him another and then another would get up for their names to be listed. Thus, many people joined the fold of the *Khudai Khidmatgar* movement.

When the number of our *jirga* members and *Khudai Khidmatgar* increased, we formed an organization of them, and Sarfaraz Khan of Uthmanzai was appointed as the *Salar-e-Azam* of the uniformed *Khudai Khidmatgar*. On top of the *deodai* of their *mandai*, there was a *balakhana*. That became the office of the *Khudai Khidmatgar*. This was our central office. Second to Sarfaraz Khan was Rabnawaz Khan, who became the *Salar*. Ameen Jan Khan was appointed the *Salar-e-Azam*. Inzar Gul was the *Salar* of Peshawar district and Munir Khan the *Salar* of Mardan. Similarly, such appointments were made in Kohat, Bannu, Dera Ismail Khan, Hazara and Lal Sarang.

In those days, Kulli Khan[21], who was the assistant political officer of the Moomand, summoned the *mashers* and told them that it was recorded in history that the inhabitants of our area would be pushed out to Bhutan and they would leave their native land. If they did not support us and not join our movement, the government would give them these lands. There was a *Khudai Khidmatgar* from the Moomand area, who was from the village of Itakai near Takht-e-Bhai. He came and told me about this. At that time, we had several very capable Moomand tribesmen who had enrolled themselves in our movement. I told him to call for the influential Moomand elders of the area so that I could come and talk to them about brotherhood and kinsmanship, and make them understand the truth about what Kulli Khan had said to them. I told these Moomand brothers of mine that the tribal distribution of lands amongst the Pukhtuns had already taken place and every tribe has been apportioned its due share. Whatever Kulli Khan was now propagating was meant to create a rift amongst us. Our lands would neither be given to them by the British and nor could they do so. If they were to be given land, it would be us who would give it to them; that they should come and join forces with us for the liberation of our country. Moreover, when we liberate this country, then I promised them I would give each family twenty *jareeb* of land each. We Pukhtuns owned a lot of land. Each one of them can get a share in it. However, this does not mean that they should take over a piece or somebody's entire land holding. This is because our tribal division of lands had already taken place, and this would give rise to disunity and bloodshed in our homes. Regretfully, I must admit that these brothers of ours did not agree with me. When the government of Qayyum came, he opened this issue afresh, and when Bhutto took over, he gave a further boost to it, and in this way, inflicted great harm on us, and severely hampered our political and economic development.

The *Khudai Khidmatgar* movement had such an effect upon the young and the old, upon men and women that I was amazed and admired my people and how quickly they had responded to my call. The position of the children was such that when I visited a village, they would all come to me and stand in a line, and each one would want and expect that I should kiss them. I, too, loved them a lot and wanted to kiss each one of them. I am a very tall man and they were children, so when kissing them, I would have to bend down quite a lot. This would be very difficult for me and it would tire me out, but even then, I would manage to kiss all of them, and they would feel very happy about it. These children had, in their villages and hamlets, formed their own organizations. They would hold *jalsa* and *jaloos*, they would go to each other's villages and would take part in our *jalsa* and *jaloos*. Similarly, the girls had also made red uniforms for themselves and memorized nationalistic poems. They would recite them to the other women. The *Pukhtun* magazine would be read with great interest. The habit of reading newspapers was also inculcated by the *Khudai Khidmatgar* movement.

The police would always be surveilling us and would inform the government by the hour. When the government realized that the movement was spreading quickly among the people and they were getting more and more enthusiastic about it, and that the movement had become very popular and dear among the Pukhtuns, it became agitated and wondered what had come over the Pukhtuns. I, too, was amazed at this grace of God, that in such a short while it had generated such love, brotherhood, kinsmanship and life amongst the Pukhtuns, with such little effort on our part. The government started thinking about how it could put an end to this movement. When some of the khans of our area would go to call on our deputy commissioner, he would also discuss and wonder the reason why Ghaffar Khan would roam from village to village, and what was his purpose?' They would come and tell me all about what had transpired between them. I would tell them to go and inform the deputy commissioner that all I desired was the unity and progress of the Pukhtuns so that they could abandon their blood feuds, groupings and enmities and, instead of destruction, turn their attention towards rebuilding. One day Khushal Khan, from Barrikot in the Sudham area, called on me and informed that the governor sahib was asking what this was that I had started. I told him that my objective was not to confront the government. I wanted to bring about the social reform of the Pukhtuns, and to do away with their harmful customs, practices and factionalism. And if the Hindus and Sikhs were busy creating love and brotherhood and unity amongst themselves, then what sin is there if the Pukhtuns also undertake their own reform? Were they not also their subjects? So Khushal Khan informed me that they were of the view that once the Pukhtun becomes united and is reformed, what guarantee was there that he would not be used against them? I replied that he should go and inform the governor sahib that the guarantee of races was mutual trust and confidence. They should repose trust in us. The government then sent me a response, asking me what I was up to. I replied that I was only doing what was the responsibility of a good government. This was their work that I was doing for them, and explained things to them in detail. But how could they possibly be satisfied with what I said. So, from all this I reached the conclusion that the government did not have good intentions towards this movement of ours.

The *Jalsa* at Marghuz and the Tribal Compact

Once we set off on our tours, we would usually tour all the districts; and when we started from one end of the province, we would normally go to the other end. It was in those areas where we found worthwhile workers, that the movement would prosper. Our movement among the Yousafzai progressed extremely well, particularly in the Sawabai *tehsil,* where there was hardly a village in which we did not have a *jalsa* or did not have a committed *Khudai Khidmatgar.* Among the Yousafzai, our general, Munir Khan of Manerai and the *Salar* in Marghuz, who was Khalil-ur-Rehman, and the *Khudai Khidmatgar* of Marghuz village, were all very good people. They would work for the movement in their area on their own initiative. Our *Khudai Khidmatgar* had one praiseworthy quality: when anyone joined the movement, or became a member of the *jirga,* they would work tirelessly, day and night in their area and would never stay home. In March 1930, they came and met me, informing me that they had worked hard in their area and many people had joined the movement. So they wanted to collect all these people and hold a *jalsa* in Marghuz. This was the first *jalsa* of the *Khudai Khidmatgar* movement. *Mian* Ahmad Shah sahib and Abdul Ghafoor of our village, who was the older brother of Master Abdul Karim, would recite poems in a lovely voice. With them, a few other uniformed *Khudai Khidmatgar* went to Marghuz and participated in the *jalsa.* People from the entire area had gathered. *Mian* sahib delivered a speech and other people also delivered speeches and recited beautiful, nationalistic poems. When I looked around, I was amazed and wondered how this passion for nationalism had been created in our poets. The people would be so impassioned and motivated on hearing their poems, that I wondered how such a change had come over them. Muhammad Umer Khan of Manerai, in his speech, differentiated between the rulers and kings of the past and the present. He said that the rulers and kings of the past, when on tour, would feast at the expense of the people, give them awards and recognition; and the rulers of the present, when on tour, let alone awards and feasts, eat everything at the expense of the poor subjects. This speech went down very well. I was presiding over that *jalsa* and was the last to speak. I told the audience that I would not deliver a speech; I would only put forth a proposal for their consideration. I said to them that many speeches had been delivered, but they should always keep in mind that, in this world, people who generally remained quiet and were more concerned about action always attained their objectives. I told them that the Pukhtuns were overburdened with the weight of customs and rituals and that one of the objectives of our movement was also precisely this, to lessen this burden. But I was scared in case these *jalsa* became another burden on the Pukhtuns, so I put forward this proposal for their consideration, that in whichever village our *jalsa* was scheduled, the participants would neither eat food nor drink tea, and nor would anyone stay there for the night. They would all have to return to their villages, and if they could not get there in time, then, too, many people should not accommodate themselves in one village. In the village, if night overtook them, they would not be guests of any one *Khudai Khidmatgar*. Each of the *Khudai Khidmatgar* of the village would bring them their meals and they would eat together. No one would go to extra trouble by cooking special food. In addition, if it was tea time, no one was to have more than two cups of tea. This proposal was accepted unanimously and the *jalsa* came to a successful close. The elders of Marghuz came to me and invited me to lunch. I told them that this was putting them to unnecessary trouble. The residents of Marghuz are very good people; whether khans or the poor people, or the skilled workers, they were all enthused and united. They told me that it was not at all inconvenient for them. That all the people of the village had contributed towards the meal of the participants of the *jalsa* – some had brought *ghwari*, chicken and some flour. I told them that they were all in agreement on this, so they were not inconvenienced, but that there are other villages, which are not as united and if we were to hold *jalsa* there they would be put to a lot of trouble. And if they were to cook this meal, it would become the standard practice. The Pukhtuns are such a race that if one village does something, the other would do it for the sake of competition, upholding their honour. They accepted what I said. In the evening when the *jalsa* ended, our uncles in Marghuz (my grandmother was also from this village) told me that they had already cooked a meal for me and that I should spend the night with them. I asked them whether they were not present in the *jalsa*. I reminded them that, in the *jalsa*, this proposal was unanimously accepted that the village in which the *jalsa* was held, the guests would neither be fed, and nor would they spend the night there. And that this was unacceptable that one proclaims one thing and does another. I persuaded them with great difficulty and went to the adjoining village of Bamkhel and spent the night with Bacha sahib, who had made me promise him that when I visited the area, I would be his guest for the night.

A Huge *Jalsa* and *Mushaira* in Uthmanzai

The *jalsa* that we had held up to now were at the *tehsil* and district levels. Now we decided that we would hold a mammoth *jalsa* at the provincial level. This was because I now realized that the *Khudai Khidmatgar* movement had created a new enthusiasm amongst the Pukhtuns. We extended an invitation to all the Pukhtuns of the Frontier and fixed 21 and 22 April 1930 for this *jalsa* at Uthmanzai and arranged to have a grand *mushaira*. The theme of the *mushaira* was:

Jang de azadai la hamesha zalmi watalee dee!

For freedom's sake, the (Pukhtun) youth have always
to the battle gone!

The announcement of the *jalsa* alarmed the government and it became suspicious of our intent. Summons began to arrive for the khans of Uthmanzai. The government wanted that, for whatever reason, the *jalsa* should not be held so that they did not get a bad name, and that the khans and inhabitants of Uthmanzai should themselves oppose it and not give them an opportunity to hold it. But the government failed in this deception, because the khans of our village had already joined the *Khudai Khidmatgar* movement. Only Muhammad Umer Khan had not become a member; the rest of his family had all signed up. The government had also dismantled some of the bridges over the rivers but was not successful in its endeavour. Thousands of men and women participated in the *jalsa*. It was a great success, particularly the parade and march-past salute of the *Khudai Khidmatgar*, which had a tremendous impact on the people. The British had, from the start, intended not to allow us to do this work. But by the grace of God, we managed to work for about three months. When we returned from the meeting of the Congress in Lahore, we got down to work in January 1930, and in April, I was arrested by the British; but before that our message had reached the Pukhtuns. On 22 April, the guests of the *jalsa* had barely left when I told Arbab Juma Khan of Bartehkal as he was taking leave that he had many sons, so I would be grateful if he could spare one of them, Arbab Abdul Ghafoor, for the *Khudai Khidmatgar* movement. He replied that he would bequeath him to us, in the name of God. From Peshawar, Ali Gul Khan, Lal Bacha, and many other workers of the Congress party, had come to attend this *jalsa*. When they were leaving the *jalsa* they told me that, the next day, they were starting their campaign of civil disobedience and would begin to grind salt in Pabbi and that I should also come there as an observer. He added that they were not *Khudai Khidmatgar* but still had participated in our *jalsa* and that even if I was not a member of the Congress party, I should at least go and see the proceedings!

11

The Gujarat Jail and Alliance with the All-India Congress Party

Arrest in 1930

On 22 April, on their request, I left for Peshawar. When I reached the thana at Nahaqqi, the police was waiting for me. They stopped the lorry in which I was and told me that they had received orders for my arrest. I told them that I had no objection but wanted to see the arrest warrant. They did not have one but asked the driver to stop and stay where he was. The driver, poor man, had already brought the lorry to a stop. At this point, the policemen from Charsadda arrived in another lorry and showed me the arrest warrant. They arrested and took me back with them to Charsadda. They locked me up in a women's room in the Charsadda lock-up. I had borne the expense of the *jalsa* in Uthmanzai, while all the arrangements had been made by Haji Shahnawaz Khan. He had made excellent arrangements. In the *jalsa,* all that he did was to occasionally call for silence. He was also arrested, just for this. *Mian* Ahmad Shah was sitting in the room I was taken to. They then brought out Haji Shahzad Khan, Abdul Akbar Khan and Sarfaraz Khan. Soon the news of our arrest spread all over the area and thousands of people collected. By the grace of God, Dr. Khan Sahib, my older brother, also arrived. All these people were not *Khudai Khidmatgar.* Their intention was to kill Kulli Khan, who was the assistant commissioner of Charsadda. But when Dr. Khan Sahib found out about this, he told the people, 'Oh brothers! This movement of ours is based on the principle of non-violence. We have promised God that we will not resort to violence.' He tried his best with the crowd to prevent them from killing Kulli Khan and directed it to disperse and return to their villages. However, they kept sitting. If Dr. Khan Sahib had not been there, there would have been a lot of bloodshed. When the government realized that the crowd was not dispersing, it called for a cavalry regiment from Mardan and brought the soldiers to the gate of the lock-up and stationed a lorry there. Many policemen and cavalry troopers circled the lorry. We were made to sit in the lorry, and with some troopers in front and others at the back, we proceeded towards Mardan. Thousands of people had lined up waiting for us; we signalled to them not to resort to violence. When we arrived at Sarderai, thousands of *Khudai Khidmatgars* from the Sheikho *tapa,* under the command of General Fateh Muhammad, were standing on the road and had blocked it. From the lorry, I asked them not to resort to violence and that if they were annoyed at our arrest, they should move around in the countryside and promote the *Khudai Khidmatgar* movement. They let the lorry pass by and we arrived in Mardan. We spent the night in the Mardan jail. Early the next morning, we left Mardan. The people of Mardan, who had heard of our arrest, were standing on the road when we were brought out from the jail. We were driven to the Risalpur cantonment and were locked up in the police station. The Hindus and Muslims of Naukhar, and all those who had learnt of the arrest, came to Risalpur to meet us. The government itself, through its policies and actions, propagated the fact of our arrest on a large scale. After a while, Kulli Khan, the assistant commissioner of Charsadda, along with his staff, arrived and our case was brought before him. What case? It was a case brought by the government, and its decision was also that of the government. I knew that we were going to be jailed. No bail was demanded of me. But they exhorted my companions to leave the movement and provide bail and go back to their homes. But they refused and told him that, after all, what should they provide bail for, and asked what crime they had committed. They all refused to be let out on bail. So, we were all sentenced under Section 40 of the FCR to three years' rigorous imprisonment each. In the early evening, we were moved from here because the people had come to know of our arrest and had collected at the Naukhar railway station. The government moved us to Jehangira railway station to board the train for Gujarat.

Gujarat Jail

Early the next morning, we arrived in Gujarat, and from the railway station, we were taken to the jail office. The *darogha* sahib had not yet awakened from his sleep. We waited for his arrival in the office for quite a long time. When he came, he took charge of us from our escorting police. Our names were entered in the register. It was broad daylight when we entered the jail. Some other political prisoners had also arrived. When they heard about us, they waited for us at the jail gate. They embraced us and took us to the barrack and arranged some tea for us. This jail was meant for those political prisoners of Sarhad, Punjab and Delhi, who were given either 'A' or 'B' class. Every day, about ten political prisoners would be brought here and we would be busy with them all day. The next day, Ali Gul Khan, Lal Bacha, Lala Pelra Khan, along with ten or twelve *razakars* were transferred here from the Peshawar jail. Our number was increasing by the day. When our numbers increased, our political prisoners put forth the proposal that we should now make a committee from amongst ourselves, which should safeguard our rights and interests. A committee was thus consituted with everyone's consensus. Now the question was who would be the president. Everyone unanimously suggested that I should agree to be their president. But I was never enamoured by such things. On this occasion too I expressed my inability to accept the offer, and so someone else was appointed. The secretary was also chosen. Every demand of ours would be put forth by him to the authorities. This improved the working of our committee and was of benefit to us. One day the inspector general of prisons, Punjab, and the superintendent of our jail visited us. My cell was the first on their route. I was sitting inside at my weaving frame. They came and stood at the door of my cell. They did not enter it and I did not go up to the iron bars to greet them. The practice was that common criminals would go towards the bars of the cells; but I was a political prisoner and was not obliged to do so. When they reached Maulana Zafar Ali Khan's cell, he told the inspector general that he wanted to discuss a few things with him, on behalf of the political prisoners. But he replied harshly, that there were 20,000 prisoners in the jails of Punjab; that he was concerned about their welfare and did not have time for just a few political prisoners. The political prisoners learnt of this exchange, and when he finally came to see them, some were sitting, some were asleep and some had stretched out their legs before him. When he saw all this, he brought the inspection to an abrupt end and went to the office, and left the office in great anger and disdain.

The Qissa-Khwani Incident

My companions from Peshawar informed me that on the night of 23 April, when I was being arrested, they too were arrested in Peshawar city. Allah Baksh Burki, who was secretary of the Congress Committee, was in his office that night. The police had gone in search of him to his house. Since he was not there, he escaped arrest. The next morning, however, he was arrested from the office. Many people gathered when the news of his arrest went out. He was to be seated in the police car, but the people prevented this. The police took him on foot to the thana at Kabuli Gate, with the *jaloos* of people following him. When they were approaching the thana, a huge crowd had collected. The ensuing commotion increased so the army troops were called out. These were Hindustani troops from Garhwal in Nepal. They were ordered to fire, but they refused – they said that the crowd was unarmed, it was neither rioting nor fighting, then why should it be fired at? They withdrew them and called in the British army troops. Upon arrival, they relentlessly fired at the crowd and many people were killed and wounded.

In Gujarat Jail

The next day, all of us, the political prisoners from Sarhad, were sitting together when someone came and informed us that a complement of political prisoners was coming from Bannu. They were Sardar Ram Singh, *Hakeem* Abdur Rahim Sahib and Sevak Ram. We embraced them as they entered the jail. They apprised us of the province and told us that, despite the British brutality, political work was doing well. On hearing this I felt very happy because I was not at all concerned about my own self but about the movement of the Pukhtuns, as to whether it had been suppressed by the government. We too would receive letters from home, that the movement was at its peak and that the number of the *Khudai Khidmatgar* had increased from hundreds to thousands, and the more efforts the government made to suppress it, the more it spread.

The father of Mahmood Ali Qasuri sahib from Lahore, Maulana Abdul Qadir sahib, also came to be lodged in the Gujarat jail. He had no place, so I brought my friend, Sarfaraz Khan, to my cell and gave his cell to Maulana Qasuri sahib. Similarly, Maulana Kifayatullah of the *Jamiat-e-Ulama-e-Islam*, Hind, and Nazim Maulana Ahmad Saeed sahib were also in this jail. They would occasionally invite me for a meal. Nazim sahib used to cook delicious *dal* and *halwa*.

We were two types of political prisoners in this jail – 'A' and 'B' class. We were given the same food and enjoyed the same privileges, with just one difference. The 'A' class prisoners could sleep outside in the open, and the doors would not be closed behind them whereas the 'B' class prisoners used to sleep inside their cells and the doors would be locked. Another difference was that the 'A' class prisoners could ask for food and fruits for themselves from the market, while 'B' class prisoners could not. Here only Agha Lal Bacha, *Mian* Ahmad Shah, Abdul Akbar Khan and I were in 'A' class. The rest were all in 'B' class. After a few days, Agha Lal Bacha and Abdul Akbar Khan were transferred to 'B' class. We used to sleep out in the open while our other companions slept indoors. It was unbearably hot. Ali Gul Khan fell ill from the oppressive heat. It did not seem right to me that we should sleep out in the open, while Haji Shah Nawaz Khan, Sarfaraz Khan, Abdul Akbar Khan, Ram Singh, *Hakeem* Abdur Rahim and Ali Gul Khan should sleep indoors. We put the issue before our committee. They discussed it with the superintendent. We also sent several applications to the government, but no one took notice. The inspector general of prisons had also come. He had gone away very annoyed with us. He, too, did nothing for us and nor was the government prepared to do anything. Finally, when we were disappointed and realized that appeals and requests were of no use, we decided that some concrete action needed to be taken. Our superintendent was Raja Sahib; and he was in fact a Raja, and a very decent man. He advised us to write down our complaints and hand them over to him, so that he could dispatch them to the inspector general. We wrote out all our demands and gave them to him. It was sent to the inspector general with some favourable comments from him. Many days passed but no answer came. When we got tired of waiting, we decided to take some action. But our 'A' class companions from Punjab did not agree and said that agitation in jail was not desirable.

This stand of theirs was right, in principle, because they did not need to agitate. They were quite comfortable. Only the 'B' class prisoners were in severe discomfort. As the heat increased, Ali Gul Khan's condition worsened. He would perspire excessively. Finally, we decided that we would take a stand on the issue. And if anyone, of their own volition, joined our agitation, they would be welcome to do so, and if not, then too they were at liberty not to do so. We started our agitation and decided that we would refuse to be locked up that night, and if the jail authorities used force, we would hold each other's hands. The time for being locked in arrived. After all of us had our meal, we all gathered to be counted and sat close to each other on the lawn and held each other's hands. We told the jail officials that we were not going to agree to be locked in, and if they wanted to use force, they had the authority to do so. Most of the 'A' class prisoners did not take part in this agitation with us. Let alone the others, even the president and secretary of the *Khudai Khidmatgar*, Abdul Akbar Khan and *Mian* Ahmad Shah, did not take part and would stay far away from us. They told me that I had always advised them not to agitate in jail, and that now I myself had started this. I told him that I could not bear to see that I should be in comfort while my other companions should have to face discomfort and be in difficulty. Due to this, I was compelled to agitate. The jail staff immediately informed the superintendent sahib. He came to the office and discussions began. He asked how he was to blame for all this. That he was ready to do all he could for us and why were we then agitating against him? I replied that we had not taken this step against him, but against the government, and that he should not be upset at this. Finally, it was decided that today we should agree to be locked in, and tomorrow he would telegraphically seek an answer. We told him not to be annoyed with us, but that we had decided not to be locked in of our own volition but would offer no resistance on being forcibly locked up. That the jail wardens could pick up each one of us and take us to the barrack. He agreed to this. The next day, early in the morning, news came that they should be locked up in the enclosure meant for women and the gate shut behind them. Inside this enclosure, it was up to them whether they wanted to sleep in the open or inside. In short, we obtained all those privileges for the 'B' class prisoners which were available to the 'A' class.

British Brutality and Pukhtun Resolve

These were the events of the jail. I shall now tell you of the position outside. When we were arrested, the infantry and cavalry came to Uthmanzai. At first, they ransacked the office of the *Khudai Khidmatgar* and set it on fire. Before doing so, they caught hold of all the *Khudai Khidmatgars* present and threw them from the upper story onto the road. My son, Wali, who was then a young lad of thirteen or fourteen years, was present in the office at the time. An English infantry soldier tried to bayonet him, but a Hindustani officer held his hand up and prevented the blow and saved him. He then caught him by the arm and threw him down the stairs from the attic. The forces surrounded the village and arrested all the members of the *Khudai Khidmatgar*. The troops would patrol the streets and the lanes. They would enter each house and if they took a fancy to weapons or anything else, they would take it away. When all the *Khudai Khidmatgars* were arrested, the deputy commissioner stood up in the centre of the crowd gathered near our *madrassah* and, in a loud voice, asked, 'Is there anyone here of the red clothes?' In this crowd, Khan Muhammad Abbas Khan of our village was also present and called out to his servants upon hearing this taunt. His *hujra* was very near to the scene. They poured red colour into a cauldron and he coloured both his and his servants' clothes red and put them on. They returned to the scene dripping with red colour and stood before the deputy commissioner and proclaimed in an equally loud voice, 'Here are the red-clothed people!' The deputy commissioner arrested them, but this cry of theirs generated such enthusiasm for the honour of the Pukhtuns that no matter how hard they tried, the British could not get rid of these red clothes. Abbas Khan was not a member of the *Khudai Khidmatgar* and had resigned from the *Anjuman*. He was estranged from us, but nonetheless he retrieved the honour of the Pukhtuns.

The British laid siege to our village. They would not allow the people of the village to leave, nor those from outside to enter it. Although people were prevented from moving out (of the village) on the orders of the British, the cattle had to stray out into the hamlets and the Sholgara area in search of fodder. There were no arrangements for cattle fodder in the houses. Whenever the cattle would emerge from the houses to go to the fields, the cavalry would charge at them. When the cattle would try to swim across the river, it would be shot at and killed. Many poor tenants lost their cattle. Adjacent to the shrine of Khkaar Baba, there was a large open space. The residents of the village were all assembled there to be beaten and humiliated and would be directed to put their thumb-impressions on statements denying their association with the *Khudai Khidmatgar*. All the *Khudai Khidmatgars* had been arrested. But putting their thumb impressions on denial applications was considered a great shame for the Pukhtuns, so, they would not do so. They would then be made to carry boulders to the mound on which Khkaar Baba's shrine was located. They were told to build a huge headstone for the shrine. When this was completed, the British told the inhabitants that they had buried their Bacha under it. On this, one man put his thumb print on the document and the British official told him that he could go home if he wanted to. When he went home, his wife was washing clothes. She asked him how he had managed to come home. He told her that he had been released. She asked how they had let him go when they were not releasing the others. That, surely, he must have put down his thumb impression? She asked him to show her his thumb. It was covered in blue colour. She had a *sobalray* in her hand. She presented it to him with the words, 'Here! You dishonourable wretch! Take this and wash clothes with it! I am leaving for the battle!' The man was ashamed of himself, regretted his act and begged his wife for forgiveness, pleading with her not to do so, as he would go back. When he returned, the official asked him the reason. He informed him that his wife would not allow him to stay at home, and that now he was even prepared to be sent to jail. He promptly sat down with the people who had stayed behind. This siege lasted fifteen days. The British did their worst, but the common people did not put down their thumb impressions (on denial applications), because those who did put down their thumb prints, would become the laughing stock of the village and be humiliated.

The siege of Prang and Charsadda lasted for twenty-one days. There were many troops involved in this siege. The villages were encircled, and the troops would patrol the streets. Whoever emerged from their homes were beaten up. The Azan and Friday congregational prayers were also stopped. Any *Khudai Khidmatgar* would be caught and arrested; the common people were made to lie naked in the hot sands and their houses would be searched. But there was unity amongst the people. Those who had grain in their houses would distribute this among the poor. The inhabitants of the sparsely populated hamlets nearby would come to the village early in the morning; they would hoe and weed the crops and irrigate them and then go home for the night. The inhabitants of the Sholgara would help people store their crops. This siege proved to be unsuccessful. The brutalities were terrible. However, they had one advantage. The villages that were under siege and were burnt were along the roadside. So, when the common people witnessed this cruelty, their hearts were filled with hatred for the British and empathy for the *Khudai Khidmatgar*. This led to widespread propaganda in our favour.

On 27 May, there was a *jalsa* in Gujaro Garhai at which Captain Murphy, who was stationed in Mardan, arrived with the police. He carried a stick, like the one carried by the *Gujars* (to control their cattle with). He would mercilessly beat people. When he started beating the people and entered their fold, there were some students amongst them who were surprised at the fact that this Englishman was proceeding empty-handed and nobody was saying anything to him. The *Khudai Khidmatgar* were bound by non-violence, so these *taliban* picked up a small axe and started hitting him with it. Captain Murphy fell on the ground and a woman who was giving the participants of the *jalsa* water to drink, threw her pitcher on his head. He was killed. When the news of his death reached Mardan, the assistant commissioner of Mardan, Hay, called for the army and, although the people found out, they continued with the *jalsa*. At that very time, it became windy and started to rain and so, the *jalsa* dispersed before the troops arrived. If the army had attacked the *jalsa*, there would have been bloodshed. To take revenge for this Englishman, on 28 May, the troops entered Takkar. They laid siege to the village and fired randomly upon the people, also using machine guns during this onslaught. Many children, youth, men and women were martyred. They burnt down the house and the *hujra* of *Khudai Khidmatgar* Malik Hashim Khan. They also burnt down the *derai* of the father of *Salar* Shamroz Khan. When the people of the villages of Shergarh and Jalala found out, they came armed to help Takkar. So, the British stopped the siege and left for Mardan. After this, the troops went to Lundhkhwar, where they burnt down the house and *hujra* of *Khudai Khidmatgar* Ghulam

Mohammad Khan, and inflicted brutalities on the people of the village. Similarly, in Kohat too the British fired upon the people and the *Khudai Khidmatgar,* and many people were martyred. They would throw the *Khudai Khidmatgar* into cold water and dip them in and out of it. In the village of Speen Tangi Hatikhel of Bannu, there was a *jalsa* of the *Khudai Khidmatgar.* Qari Fazle Qadir was standing on the stage, reciting from the *Quran.* He was shot by an Englishman and was martyred. Many *Khudai Khidmatgar* were wounded and martyred. In Manai *tehsil* of Sawabai, the police went to the house of the maulana sahib and burnt it down. They set fire to his *Qutubkhana,* which had in it many religious books, copies of the *Quran* and Hadith and valuable books on jurisprudence. They were all burnt. They went to the house of maulana Abdul Hai Sahib in Rustam, and ransacked his books and belongings and arrested him. In those days, there was not a village in the entire province with *Khudai Khidmatgar* that the army did not enter; in which the offices of the *Khudai Khidmatgar,* their homes, their cattle, and their red clothes were not burnt; and in which the people were not subjected to brutalities.

These brutalities awakened the Pukhtuns. Thousands of youth, from Malakand (in the north), to Dera Ismail Khan (in the south) dyed their clothes red and stood shoulder to shoulder for the liberation of their land under the red flag. The *Khudai Khidmatgar* movement spread among the free tribes to the Moomand, to Bajawar, to the Afridis, Aurakzais, Wazirs, Mahsud and Bittanis. The tribesmen of Moomand and Bajawar, under the leadership of the Haji Sahib of Torangzai, occupied Klrappa. The conflict lasted for three months; night and day, they would be bombed. Habib Nur fired a pistol at the British assistant commissioner of Charsadda early one morning in the courts, but the bullet failed to go off. The assistant commissioner was saved; Habib Nur was arrested and hanged the next day in Peshawar. Qulli Khan, the assistant political officer of the Moomands, wanted to implicate the leaders of the *Khudai Khidmatgar* in this case; Habib Nur flatly refused and told Kulli Khan that he had come of his own volition for the assassination attempt, but had failed. Just imagine, these people call themselves Muslims and Pukhtuns, but are always ready to assist the British in the most despicable manner. How were we, the *Khudai Khidmatgar,* to blame? We were only fighting for their rights. Many

Afridis came down from their hills, invaded the city of Peshawar and fought the troops; they raided the *makhlri* godowns where grain was stored and set it on fire. Raids also started from Waziristan and destroyed many army troops. This was for the first time ever that the tribesmen from Bajawar (in the north), from the Moomands to the Wazir and Mahsud, all rose in unison in support of their Pukhtun brothers and refused peace initiatives until Bacha Khan and Gandhiji were released.

The Congress and Us

We were in the jail in Gujarat, when two of our companions, *Mian* Jaffar Shah Kakakhel and *Mian* Abdullah Shah of Qazikhel, Charsadda, came to see us. I was forbidden to have any visitors, but they met with my other companions. They informed us that the government had blocked all the exit points from the province. Nobody could leave the province and nobody from outside could come into the province. It had started terrorizing the people to eliminate our movement. That they had crossed the Indus and come, because all the ferries were occupied by the government forces. They had come to me for advice. Such brutalities were being committed on the Pukhtuns but the world was unaware of all this. When they met with companions, they came and informed me of all that had transpired. We were still a part of the *Khilafat* movement. There was no Muslim League in our province yet. We had remained with Punjab in the *Khilafat* movement and many of our erstwhile companions were in the Muslim League. We gave the visitors the advice that they should go to the leaders of the Muslim League in Hindustan and apprise them of the atrocities that they were being subjected to at the hands of the British. Also, to tell the world, that the *Khudai Khidmatgar* movement was one of social reform. We advised them to go to Lahore, Delhi and Simla and meet with the Muslims and inform them of our circumstances. However, when they returned after meeting the Muslim League leaders, they informed us that they were not prepared to assist us because they were a party that had been formed by the British, in opposition to the All-India Congress. Since our struggle was against the British, how then could they be expected to assist us? We instructed them to go and meet with the leaders of other political parties in Hindustan and tell them about their situation. They were able to meet leaders of most parties but, except for the Congress, no party was prepared to help us. The Congress leaders asked us about our struggle against the British. We informed them that it was over the liberation of the country. They again asked about the method of our struggle. We replied that it was 'non-violence'. They informed us that this struggle and strategy were also theirs. We, too, were slaves and so were they; the British were our enemies and so were they theirs. We wanted freedom, and so did they. If we were prepared to ally with them, they were ready to assist us. After this conversation, we advised them to return to the province and consult with the *jirga*. Whatever the *jirga* decided would be acceptable to us. The provincial *jirga* accepted the proposal that we should ally with the Congress. The provincial *jirga* allied with the Congress, and they immediately sent a delegation headed by Vithalbhai Patel to Sarhad to inquire into the allegations against the British and submit a report to the Central Legislative Assembly. However, the British stopped the members of the delegation at the Attock bridge. They based themselves in Pindi and started their investigations. Our Muslim brethren of Punjab complained that though we were a Muslim party, we allied ourselves with the Hindu Congress. I must first respond to this and say, that Congress is not a party of the Hindus; it is an all-Hindustan party and represents all the people of Hindustan. Jinnah sahib was also a member of this party. Furthermore, how did we come to join the Congress? If the Muslim League had come to our assistance as requested, what did we have to do with the Congress? The fact is that it was their attitude that compelled us to ally ourselves with the Congress. We Pukhtuns were being swept away by the floods. We approached them (saying that) that they were our Muslim brothers, (asking them) to extend a helping hand to us. But they did not extend a helping hand to us. Congress agreed to do so. I must proclaim to all the Muslims of the world to now do justice and decide whether they are to blame, or us. After a few days, Haji Abdul Ghaffar Khan, Ubaidullah Khan and Sultan Khan came to see us and gave us all the news of the land on political matters. They told us that the Pukhtuns were enthused to such an extent that could not be put into words. The more the British inflicted cruelty on the people, the more the courage and enthusiasm of the people increases. That we should not worry, this was a movement for the sake of God, and He would assist them from the Unseen. When we heard this, we were all very pleased. When we were leaving, I gave Ubaidullah Khan a message for the Pukhtuns: 'Oh Pukhtun brothers! Do not be afraid or disappointed. This is but a trial from God for us; be alive to this situation and prepare yourselves for service to God's creation.' This message had a very positive impact on the people when it was published in the newspapers. The government ordered the superintendent of the jail to stop all further meetings of mine, so that no one from outside could meet me.

Some prominent leaders of Punjab and Delhi were detained with us in jail. People would come to meet with them. They would publish our views in the newspapers. I shall forever remain grateful to these leaders for the help which they gave us when in jail. They had some differences amongst themselves, but they all maintained a good relationship with us. Here, whether they were Hindus, Sikhs or Muslims, they were like our own brothers, always at our beck and call. And the Hindus were evermore ready to serve us, more than the Muslims were. Here we had a Pukhtun jamadar who oversaw all the affairs inside the jail. He was a very good man who had a lot of empathy for us and was always ready to do work for us, even if it involved some danger. I would prohibit him from it and tell him that he was a government employee and should not do anything which would harm him later.

The Patel Committee Report

The Patel Committee completed its work and published its report. Immediately on its being published, the government confiscated it. However, this Report was taken by the Congress to Europe and America. When is was published, the government realized its mistake and sent a delegation to us in jail, requesting us to make up with it. The reforms of 1919 would be immediately implemented, and for the future, we were promised that whatever reforms were granted to Hindustan, they would also be extended to us in the Frontier. In fact, we would be given even better treatment. But the condition was that we should break our alliance with the Congress. We came back, collected all the political prisoners and consulted them over this issue. Some believed we should resort to 'diplomacy'. I told them that diplomacy was nothing more than hypocrisy, and I was not a hypocrite. So, we did not accept the proposal of the government. After a few days, *Mian* Ahmad Shah started thinking that the government had jailed us without any justification, that there was no legal proof against us, and we should submit a review petition. He had also spoken to Abdul Akbar Khan, Haji Shahnawaz Khan and Sarfaraz Khan about this and obtained their consent. *Mian* sahib did not consider that this was the FCR. In this, there were two things: whether to be jailed or set free on bail. So, he talked to me about the review petition. I did not agree with him on this because this was against our principles. But I did tell him that they could go for the review petition if they wanted to; I would not be party to it as this was against our principles. *Mian* sahib asked me why I considered it so and started to argue with me. I told him that he should observe the outside world and see for himself the games which the British played with our nation, and the atrocities to which it was subjected; and here I was comfortably sitting in jail, eating and drinking – and yet could not bear this detention. Every action that I took and every weakness that I displayed, had its effect on our people; and even a little weakness of mine caused a great loss to the people. For this reason, I was compelled not to agree. The other major reason was that this movement of ours was based on non-violence and non-cooperation. These words of mine influenced them and they also abandoned all thoughts of a review petition.

My Companions of the Gujarat Jail

Our nights and days in jail were being spent very comfortably because there were prisoners of all temperament. There were great scholars and prominent political leaders, with books to suit different temperaments. I had distributed all my time over various activities. I had devoted a major part to the study of religious books, and used to exchange views with great scholars. In all my life I had not devoted so much time to the pursuit of my studies as I did in this one year. The other beneficial thing here was that every second or third day, we would all get together and debate and speak on different topics. And sometimes some learned companions would deliver speeches on specific subjects and try to make us all understand their intricacies. Dr. Ansari sahib had set up a parliament of us, for us to learn about national and administrative issues. From time to time, sessions of this parliament would be held, and for our education and training according to the standard practices of Parliament, speeches would be delivered on national affairs. In short, this detention here taught me a great deal. I tried my best to have lessons of the *Quran* and *Bhagwad Geeta* started here, because in Hindustan, whether we are Muslims, Hindus, Sikhs, or Christians, we are not aware of each other's religions, and nor has anyone attempted to make us aware. In fact, selfish people have created religious prejudice and hatred amongst us. The faiths which God has sent to the world, are all His. These have not been sent to create prejudice and hatred, but to create love and affection. I was successful in this and the lessons started.

Pandit Jaggat Ram, who was a member of the party of the Mutiny and had been jailed for twenty years and had been repatriated during these days from the Andaman Islands, was a great nationalist, a good scholar and a very good man. He would give lessons from the *Bhagwad Geeta* and I would translate the *Quran*. Many people attended these classes, and when they got to the real meaning of this education, they would be amazed, and ponder over the education that God gave them and the erroneous path that they were currently on. The prejudice and hatred that was created in the name of religion was reformed to a great extent and we became aware of the principles of each other's faiths. I had a benefactor named Lala Sham Lal. A leading advocate, he would read out English books to me. I benefitted greatly from his company. Another was Raizada Hansraj who was from Jalandar. He was very kind to me. When people would visit him, he would share the food that they had brought, with us. Along with that, he would regularly bring many new books and share them with us. Every day, early in the morning, Haji Shahnawaz Khan would prepare tea and cook food, thus freeing us form this chore. He was a very resourceful person and would collect all kinds of news of happenings in the jail for us. Whatever happened in the jail, and if someone had a visitor, he would be aware of it and would have met the visitor himself first. The jail officials were fed up of this habit of his. They would try to prevent him from this, but he could not be prevented from visiting the main gate of the jail. He was a very tolerant and well-meaning person. However, *Mian* Ahmad Shah fell out with him over some very trivial matter. He quarrelled with Haji sahib and stopped drinking tea with us. *Mian* sahib was of a difficult and sensitive temperament, and the jail is also such a place that one becomes very irritable in it and is ready to quarrel over very trivial issues. He also quarrelled with me and Safaraz. In the jail, we could play games and in these too *Mian* sahib would sometimes get upset and quarrel. I would look inwardly at myself and would detect several weaknesses and defects. One shortcoming that I had was that of garrulity and wanting to debate everything; and the other was my short temper. I used to feel this greatly and often wondered how I would be able to get rid of them. I used to try but they had taken such a hold of me that it was impossible to rid myself of them. To reform myself, I resolved that one day in a week I would fast, but this abstention would not only be from food and drink, but from speech as well, and I would ponder over my own weaknesses to reform myself. So when I used to offer the morning prayer, I would shut the door of the cell and would remain seated till the evening in meditation, repeating the attributes of Allah. I would come out of the cell to eat after the evening Azan. This abstinence benefitted me.

After some time, the backache with which I was afflicted in the Dera Ghazi Khan jail recurred. Dr. Ansari sahib examined me and prescribed something for me, and imposed a restriction on the eating of meat. On account of the medicine and abstention from meat, I felt a little better. The designated civil surgeon of our jail, who was an Englishman, would have no work to do whenever he came. Everyone would go to Dr. Ansari sahib for consultations, because he was such an eminent and renowned physician. But the Englishman took it to heart and wrote to the inspector general of prisons, who ordered that, except for the designated doctor of the jail, treatment by anyone else was prohibited. I was also affected by this order. I gave the symptoms of my illness to the English civil surgeon. He told me that I could not use Dr. Ansari's prescription for my treatment, so I said to him that he should then give me a prescription. He prescribed some medicines for me, but they provided no relief and my ailment increased. The next day, I went and showed him Dr. Ansari's prescription, which had benefitted me. He changed the medicines, but even that was of no help. I again reminded him of Dr. Ansari's prescription, but he told me that I could not use this prescription. So, I told him that, as of today, I did not wish to be treated any further, that I would not take the medicines he had prescribed, nor those of Dr. Ansari's. He replied that, in that case, who would be responsible for my health? I told him that I would be responsible for my own health. On hearing this, he was infuriated and walked away. For two months, I could not leave my bed. I could not walk. It would also be difficult for me to answer the call of nature. I suffered a weight loss of 10 kilogram. I entrusted myself to God for protection. Gradually I improved, and after some time got up from bed; the pain in my back had decreased considerably.

Raja sahib was our superintendent. In jail, our Sikh brethren raised the issue that they ate meat killed by *jhatka*, and that they should be allowed to perform this. Raja sahib was a very compassionate man. He was a traditional Muslim of an age gone by. He was not prepared to agree to this proposal of the Sikhs. So, he told them that this was not possible, and for this reason, they could not be fed with this meat. They told him that they should be given chickens instead at their own cost and they would themselves perform *jhatka* on them. However, the government was not prepared to concede to this and directed him to do something to resolve the issue, so that *jhatka* was not resorted to, and the government also did not get a bad name. The superintendent *Syed* Agha Lal Shah summoned us to the office and prepared us to oppose the *jhatka* and inform the Sikhs that their proposal was being opposed by their own Muslim colleagues from Sarhad and so, for this reason, the government could not give them permission. The Sikhs put forward the proposal to me and I collected all our Muslim companions from Sarhad to discuss it. As the discussions started, Agha Lal Badshah and some other companions opposed the request from the outset. I told them that undoubtedly, *jhatka* was not permitted in Islam, but it was permitted for the Sikhs. The other thing I discussed was, whether they would eat the meat of the *jhatka* or would we have to eat it too. If they were to eat it, then of what concern was it to us, or what harm was it to us? And I asked Agha Lal Badshah that if someone were to prevent him from eating *halal* meat, would he be upset or happy about it? He replied that he would be upset at this. Similarly, in prohibiting *jhatka*, others would also be upset. So at least for us, the *Khudai Khidmatgar*, it was not right to offend others. We told our Sikh brethren that we had no objection to their eating meat of animals slaughtered by *jhatka*. So, Agha Sahib agreed with me and it was decided that, as far as we were concerned, our Sikh brothers should be allowed to do as they pleased. I told them that the government was refusing to give permission; it wanted to create a spectacle of this and wanted to create a rift between our Sikh brothers and us. This is exactly what happened. The next day orders came that the government could not give permission to anyone for *jhatka* in jail. When three months went by, Haji Shahnawaz remembered his business and every now and then would threaten us with seeking bail. I thought at first that he was joking; then I learnt that he really intended to leave. In those days, peace talks were going on between Mahatma Gandhi and Lord Irwin, the viceroy. I would comfort him saying that truce was around the corner but the news came that the talks had failed. News also came that Haji Sahib's younger brother had been arrested and was sentenced to three years' imprisonment. I would reassure him, but it had no effect. His paternal uncle, Muhammad Azam Khan, and Umara Khan, came and informed him that his mother was unwell and his brother, Akbar, had also been arrested and all his business had suffered badly; that he was not a *Khudai Khidmatgar*, so why then did he not seek bail? All this talk persuaded him to seek bail. His concerns had grown when his brother was jailed. The next day he received a letter that his mother's condition was very serious. This saddened him even more. His immediate family consisted of himself and his brother. He had no other siblings. There was no one left to look after his mother. They were two brothers, and both were now imprisoned. In short, without consulting me, he secretly sent a letter to the village to have bail posted for him. The next day what did we see, but that Mir sahib, his paternal nephew, brought his bail bond to the Gujarat jail and we learnt that Haji had signed his bail bond. Pandit Shanta Ram and I took him aside and tried our best to make him understand that this act of his was not in consonance with his position and standing, and it would be proper if he could wait a while longer, and to entrust the health and well-being of his mother to God. Haji gradually softened his attitude and came around. But when he left us, he was seen by Agha Lal Badshah and Ali Gul Khan who asked him whether he had deposited bail. He had then told them that he had wanted to do so but that I had persuaded him to wait a while, so he had decided to postpone the issue for the time being. They told him that since he was intent on leaving, what was the need for spending these extra days in jail? What they said influenced Haji sahib, and without telling me, he went to the office and signed the bail bond. When I learnt of this, I went and told him, 'Haji! You are bent on leaving. But remember that you will live to regret it, and then you will remember my words, but time would have gone by.' He lowered his gaze and did not reply. I left him, and he left for the village. I do not know with what consideration in mind Ali Gul Khan and *Syed* Lal Bacha had given him this advice, because in those days they did not get along with the *Khudai Khidmatgar* as they were allied with the Congress. When Haji sahib arrived in the village and saw the prevailing conditions and the enthusiasm of the people, and realized that his near and dear ones were very critical of what he had done, he wrote me a letter stating that he wanted to meet me. But I refused his request. When he got really fed up, his relatives advised him to recall his bail bond and go back to jail. He said to them that he had made such a grave mistake, imprisonment was not enough atonement for it. Finally, one day he picked up his gun and shot himself. When I got the news of Haji's death, I felt very sorry at not having allowed him to meet me. Haji Shahnawaz Khan[22] was a very useful person. Following his death, no one else dared to ask for bail. When news of Haji's death reached Gujarat jail, all our companions were extremely grieved as he was liked by everyone. All the political prisoners got together and prayed for the departed soul.

At the time that we were sent to Gujarat jail, the building of this jail had not yet been completed. When the building was completed, our barracks and cells were open and the government was now building partitions between them. No one objected to the back walls, but the front walls were disliked by everyone. One day *Mian* Ahmad Shah sahib told me that instead of the front wall, they should install iron grills. I told him that this would not be done by the government without an agitation, so if he wanted, we would begin an agitation. He agreed and I took the other political prisoners into confidence, who all agreed as they respected me a lot. When the superintendent sahib learnt of this development, he came and advised us to write an application to the government to this effect. We wrote an application, and everyone signed it. When the application was put before *Mian* Ahmad Shah, he refused to sign it. The man who brought the the application told me that *Mian* sahib had refused to sign it. I took it from him and went to *Mian* sahib who wrote a note on it to the effect that he was against agitation in jails and signed the note. I was very upset and I told him that this agitation had started because of him and that what we were doing was upon his advice. To this *Mian* sahib replied that he liked agitation but only if other people did it! I kept quiet at this and left *Mian* sahib's cell and tore the application to pieces and wrote another one and gave it to the superintendent. After a few days a reply came that, instead of walls, grills should be installed. When the number of political prisoners increased greatly, and I saw that some of them were angling for the job of the committee president, I resigned from the post. The political prisoners were upset and tried to persuade me to take the resignation back, but I refused on the basis that the presidentship was not my inalienable right, that others should also be given the opportunity to serve. Zafar Ali Khan became the next president. However, his period was very strange. Whenever anybody had a problem, the prisoners would say that he was their Sardar sahib. And when the problem was resolved, they would forget all about him. Sometimes their attitude towards him would be such that I would begin to pity the poor man. Many times I told him, guardedly, to resign, but he liked the chair and was not prepared to leave it. This was the reason that he lost the respect of his fellow prisoners. The presidentship was not such a big thing but it was a national duty. If it had the backing of the prisoners, it would last. But if it was against their wishes, it would harm us and become a source of dishonour. So, it was necessary that, instead of complying with one's own interest, one should respect the wishes of the nation.

Many Englishmen would come to inspect this jail. If they happened to exchange a few pleasantries with any of us, he would be elated and recall with great pride that he was known to the Englishman. When misfortune befalls a nation, one becomes a fool, even if one has a rational mind. If these Englishmen had treated us a little less harshly and arrogantly, we would never have turned against them. Minister Emerson had come out on a tour and was coming to this jail for inspection. The minister sahib came, and the prisoners tidied up their cells for him. He was also accompanied by other Englishmen. My cell was at the beginning of the inspection route. I was sitting beside my weaving frame when he arrived. I thought he would enter it, and I would like to greet him and talk to him, but he did not enter and remained standing at the door. The superintendent sahib told me that the minister was asking what it was that I wished to say. I replied that I wished to say nothing. He again told me that the minister wanted to speak to me. I replied that I did not wish to talk because if he had really meant to speak with me, he would have entered my cell. Only the ordinary criminals would talk to him from behind the grill and I was a political prisoner. The minister stood still for a moment and then walked on. The deputy commissioner of Gujarat also accompanied him. When he left, the deputy commissioner came to my cell. I rose to greet him. On this, he was surprised and asked me why I had neither stood up to greet the minister nor spoken to him. I told him that I was a *Khudai Khidmatgar* and considered hatred for God's creatures as a sin, and that the service of God is the service of his creation. That he too was an Englishman and here I was, talking to him. I was a political prisoner and needed to be treated as one. The minister had not come to me, and so I also did not go to him. With these words the misunderstanding was removed.

Raja sahib treated the political prisoners very well and the government did not want this. His own subordinates and the police sent adverse reports (i.e., diaries) to the government, that he treated political prisoners well and they were enjoying life in jail. For this reason, Raja sahib was transferred to Sialkot, and the superintendent at Sialkot, Rai sahib, replaced him. He was a strict disciplinarian. The other thing about him was that he considered the rules of the jail as the law of God. But the government failed in its intentions and, on account of our unity, he lost his nerve and could not have the rules of the jail implemented. On taking over, Rai sahib stopped the entry into the jail of all those items which the contractor used to get for us, stating that these was not permitted under jail rules. So, the contractor would sit at the main gate of the jail, and whoever wanted to buy something from him could go and get it. When we learnt of this development, we took the unanimous decision that no one would go to the gate. The superintendent sahib sent for us frequently, but when he realized that we were not complying, he rescinded his orders and allowed the contractor to come inside and bring the items with him. Rai sahib was thus compelled to revive all the concessions, which the Raja sahib had allowed us. It was during these days that Sarfaraz Khan's older brother, Sarbiland Khan, came to meet him. He was refused this meeting on the grounds that he did not know how to speak Urdu, and meetings which were held in Pukhto were not permitted because the superintendent did not understand it. When we learnt of this, we were shocked and saddened. We raised slogans of 'Inquilab Zindabad!' (Long Live the Revolution). The next day was a parade. We refused to take part in it. When Rai sahib saw this turn of events, he sent some men to Sarbiland Khan. They found him at the station. He came back and met with Sarfaraz Khan. When Rai sahib met with failure in his many initiatives and realized that he could not succeed as long as we stood united, he started sowing seeds of discord amongst us and cultivated relations with the Hindus. He convinced them that he was their Hindu brother and any harm that came to him was their loss. So, if they did not help him, this would be tantamount to harm for the entire Hindu community. This propaganda had the desired effect on some of the prisoners. When any problem arose, he would say to the Hindus that if they failed to assist him, harm would come to their Hindu brothers. Another weakness which I observed in the leadership of Punjab was that whenever they got together, they would be brothers, but when a little selfishness took over, a Muslim became a Muslim and a Hindu became a Hindu. When this attitude is rampant in the members of the Congress, then what can be said for the masses? This is the reason that the roots of the Congress were never strengthened in Punjab and the Hindus and Muslims never became brothers and it became difficult to be self-reliant and attain swaraj.

As comfortable as we were in the Gujarat jail, the 'C' class prisoners were very uncomfortable in the jails of Punjab. Replacing Raja sahib with Rai sahib is evidence of the ill will of the government towards us. Some of us thought that since our other brothers in Punjab or in Sarhad are in difficulties in other provinces, it is incumbent upon us to forgo our personal comforts. Some 'C' class prisoners from Punjab had sent us letters that we were not concerned for them at all; that we were enjoying ourselves in and outside the jails; that, this time, if we were freed, they would not allow us to sit on stage again. Some leaders were also concerned about this but were not ready to do anything about it. Gandhiji's son, Devadas Gandhi, who was with us in this jail, took a stand on this, and began to confer with us in the matter. One day he also talked to me about this problem. At first, a debate took place on the issue of whether to include those from Sarhad in this matter.

Some Punjabis thought that the government of Sarhad was a tyrannical government and their agitation would have no effect on them. So, it was necessary that they take up the struggle only for the political prisoners of Punjab. But finally it was decided that it was also necessary to include our tyrannized brethren from Sarhad in the agitation. He asked my views on the matter. I replied that I would like to consult with my other jail colleagues from Sarhad. We were eleven political prisoners from Sarhad in this jail. I discussed the question with them and told them that a decision had been taken in favour of the 'C' class prisoners, that we would refuse to avail all available concessions, until better treatment and good food was authorized for them. For this, a campaign would be launched in the newspapers of Hindustan. I told them that this was a rare opportunity for us prisoners from Sarhad. If we were to join this agitation with them, there would be good publicity for our prisoners as well all over Hindustan. The first to respond was Abdul Akbar Khan who said that he was not ready for this. Ali Gul Khan and Agha Lal Bacha seconded his views; only Sarfaraz Khan opted to say that if we were to forego our benefits and concessions, he would also give them up. When I realized that my companions were not prepared to forego their privileges, I put forward the proposal that this should be done only when everybody's consent was available. However, Ahmad Shah *Mian* sahib said that everything should be decided on the votes of the majority. I told him that decisions involving hardships cannot be taken by a majority vote, because only a few people are ready to take on hardship. Sardar Ram Singh told him that he should allow me and himself to face the consequences. Ali Gul Khan and Lal Bacha put forth the proposal that they would find out and if everybody was of the view that we should forego our privileges, we would do so as well. On this, there was consensus and Ali Gul Khan was appointed for the purpose. I understood what was going on, because until the very end, nothing came out of this letter writing, and while we waited patiently, we were released.

Similar incidents also occurred in the proceedings of our own committees. There, too, those who are morally weak and unable to bear hardships would always oppose a useful proposal and thereby harm the interests of the land and its people. It is important not to include such morally weak people on our committees. Devadas and his other companions forewent the privileges of their class and began to feed on the diet of the 'C' class prisoners. I used to feel ashamed of myself that my companions, who shared the same objectives as I did, lived one kind of life, while I enjoyed the comforts of a better class. But I was under the compulsion of the majority decision of my companions. Some leaders fell ill but could not, out of deference to Devadas, take a different position. Rai sahib was surprised at this development. The propaganda about the agitation began to appear in the press. Finally, Rai sahib addressed a letter to the government, asking it to allow him to transfer the leader of the agitation from this jail. The government gave him the permission and the first person to be transferred was Devadas followed by Dr. Saif-ud-Din Kitchlew. He also transferred one or two other prisoners. When the others saw this, their stance weakened and gradually, on the persuasion of the superintendent, reverted to their class. Initially people were very angry with them but gradually, their supporters increased. Only three persons remained in the agitation and the others reverted to their class and the agitation came to an end. Political prisoners should take every step on their own and not compel others to do so. When those who have been compelled find an opening, they usually flee from the scene.

Sometimes our political brothers start an agitation on petty matters and get themselves into a lot of trouble. When we were in jail, our beds used to be tied with chains as a precaution against their possible use as ladders to scale the walls and escape. So, our brothers started an agitation against this practice. I told them in vain that the beds were being chained and not us, but no one listened to what I had to say and we landed up in a big mess. I do not approve of agitation over trivial matters in jail and am of the view that we should not agitate in jail over petty issues. If there is a major political issue and one wants to agitate over it, then there is some point in this. The superintendent of our jail, Rai sahib, was a very odd man. Whenever he found that a prisoner was happy in this jail, he would have him transferred. If a prisoner would ask to be transferred, he would not do so. He would say to me that political prisoners were very comfortable in this jail and that I probably like it, but I would reply that I was not happy here. So, he would not get me transferred. But he had Ahmad Shah, *Hakeem* Abdul Rahim Sahib and Lal Bacha transferred, who were very happy with the conditions of this jail and did not want to be transferred. He also suggested the transfer of other prisoners but talks between the government and Gandhiji had started, and due to this, these people remained here.

When peace was concluded between Gandhiji and Lord Irwin, the 'A' class prisoners were released. I, too, was an 'A' class prisoner, but was not released. I questioned the superintendent on this, but he replied that he was under instructions that I was not to be released until Sir Fazl-e-Hussain and Sir Sahibzada Abdul Qaiyum had met me. I told him clearly that he should write to the government that the time for that had passed, and that I did not wish to meet them. That even if they came to meet me, I was not prepared to discuss anything with them because, earlier, when we were in trouble, they would not meet me and now, when calm was restored, they wanted to meet me. I requested him to tell them not to take the trouble of coming. The next day *Mian* Jaffar Shah and Abdullah Shah came and briefed us on political developments and said that the government did not want to release me. That people in government had spoken ill of me to Mahatma Gandhi, and that Mahatma Gandhi had sent them to talk to me. I was amazed to hear this. I thought that when one was a member of a political party or was allied to it, how could one not comply with its decisions and negate its principles? Moreover, I had heard that our governor sahib, Sir Stuart Pears, had informed the government that, in this province, two people could not be accommodated at the same time, that it would either be him or me.

Release

Gandhiji had been apprised by my companions about my stand and some had even gone to meet him. Mahatmaji called on Lord Irwin, the viceroy, and told him that I was a man of the Congress Party and why was I not being released? That by not doing so, he was violating the terms of the agreement. The viceroy replied that these Pukhtuns were deceiving him; Pukhtuns and non-violence was a contradiction in terms. That he should visit Sarhad and see for himself the violent nature of the Pukhtuns. Gandhiji told him that if he was not prepared to release Bacha Khan, then the pact between them stood abrogated. So, I was released. Abdul Akbar Khan and Sarfaraz Khan were released before me but had not yet returned to their villages and were staying in Gujarat city. When they learnt of my release, they came to greet me at the gate of the jail, and when I was exiting, thousands of Hindus, Muslims and Sikhs had gathered. They seated me in a car and led me through the streets of the city in a *jaloos* and then a big *jalsa* was held. I thanked them and delivered a brief speech because I had received many telegrams and phone calls from friends. A friend of ours from Jhelum arrived with a car and we left for Lahore. Although I had telephoned people in Lahore that I was coming, they forced me to go to Jhelum. But when we neared Jhelum and I saw the men and women who had assembled to welcome us, I thought to myself that if we had not decided to come here, these people would have been very disappointed. Our *jaloos* went through the entire city and we then came back to our friend's place and planned for the journey to Lahore. The train was scheduled to depart for Lahore at 1 a.m. in the morning. In short, we were not able to get even a little rest but went straight to the station.

My Reception in Lahore

Sarfaraz Khan left for the village while I and Abdul Akbar Khan took the night train to Lahore. Maulana Zafar Ali Khan, Pandit Santanam Singh, along with other companions, were waiting for us at the station. We left for Pandit Santanam's place. Agha Lal Bacha and Ali Gul Khan were already there. Ali Gul Khan had arrived from Peshawar to take back Agha Lal Bacha because he had been jailed for a year, and had been released before us. After a while, we received the news that women had picketed the women's section of the Lahore jail, and when Mrs. Subhadra Joshi was talking to me in a great flurry, her daughter arrived and told her to get up. Picketing had begun and all of us left for the jail in cars. When we arrived there, we saw a flag on a pole in front of the jail with women seated all around it, reciting nationalist poems. The issue was that they were not releasing Mrs. Asaf Ali and the other women said that they would not leave this place until she was released. With great efforts, we persuaded them to abandon their protest. On our return, we saw Mukaram Khan of the *Khudai Khidmatgar* movement from the village of Tarnab in the Sholgara area of Charsadda, along with some other companions, in the boys' jail. They had climbed on the roof of a barrack and were gesturing to us. We told them not to worry, that they would also be released in a few days. These were those boys of ours who had been jailed for picketing liquor outlets in Lahore.

The time set for the *jaloos* was 4 p.m. The workers and activists of Congress gathered at the set time. Arrangements had been made for me to ride in a car, but I said that I would go on foot, with the rest of the *jaloos*. Hindus, Sikhs and Muslims had collected at many spots on the route to welcome us. They would garland the members of the procession and *sipasnamas* were presented on behalf of the Hindus and Muslims. At one point, a Muslim also gave me a *kulla* and a *lungi* and he told me to tie a turban instead of wearing a cap on my head. There were many women with us in the *jaloos*. I got very tired but when I saw their love and enthusiasm, I refused to sit in the car. By the evening, the *jaloos* ended, and we arrived at the venue of the *jalsa*. It was packed with people. Thousands of men, women, Hindus, Sikhs and Muslims had collected. Since we were to leave for Peshawar by the night train, we requested the organizers of the *jalsa* to make the proceedings as brief as possible. In response to the *sipasnama*, I delivered a short speech and thanked the organizers. I said in my speech that we should not sit at home, oblivious to what was happening. That we should work as hard as possible because this was not a lasting truce, but an interregnum. And, on my part, I would try to prepare one hundred thousand *razakars* on the principles of non-violence for the forthcoming struggle. In pursuit of this objective when I later left on a tour of the Sudham area of Mardan district, they told me in a rhymed *sipasnama*, that the one hundred thousand *razakars* of which I spoke in my Lahore address, did not suit my status and political standing. From this, the kind of enthusiasm for the cause that had overtaken the Pukhtun youth was obvious. When the *jalsa* concluded, so many people flocked around me that the car I was in could not move forward. I requested them to make way for us or we would miss our train connection. They cleared the way, but because of the crowd, one of the doors of the car was damaged. However, we managed to get to the station on time and catch our train, and reached Rawalpindi station at the time of the morning azan, to be greeted by cries of 'Inquilab Zindabad'. I was awake, but my back was in pain and I could not get up. Finally, when I heard Sethi sahib's voice, I realized that the crowd had come for us. Sethi sahib was jailed in the Gujarat jail. I got up with great difficulty and got down from the train. When the people saw us, they were jubilant and insisted that we should leave with them. I managed to release myself and informed them that people would be expecting me in Peshawar and that I would come again. At sunrise, we arrived in Campbellpur. I was unable to get up when I found that a *Khudai Khidmatgar* had entered our compartment. I felt happy when I saw them and called out to him. He was jubilant at this and ran outside and informed others. On this, I saw that Zareen Khan of *Mian* Isa along with a few others came and embraced me. I found out that they too had been released from the jail in Dera Ismail Khan. When I saw them, I felt fine and the backache disappeared.

We all occupied the same compartment and had a long conversation. The train started off and arrived at Naukhar railway station. Uniformed *Khudai Khidmatgar* along with other people were waiting for us at the station. I did not consider it appropriate to leave the compartment. I feared that the train might leave so I stood at the door of the compartment and spoke a few words to the crowd. The train left and arrived in Peshawar shortly thereafter. Many people had come to the station. Cars were waiting outside the station for us. *Mian* Ahmad Shah, Abdul Akbar Khan and I occupied one car while Lal Bacha and Ali Gul Khan occupied the other car. Our *jaloos* went through all the major streets of the city, and after that, we left for the village because there too many people were waiting for us. When we arrived at the Nahaqqai police station, the place from which I was taken into custody, a gate erected there and Khan Abdul Ahad Khan of Daudzai, Takhtabad, was waiting there to welcome us. We exchanged greetings with the people and took our leave of them after I had delivered a short speech. Crowds had assembled at many places along the way. Finally, we arrived in Charsadda where thousands of people had collected. We did not consider it appropriate to get down from the car. Abdul Akbar Khan, *Mian* Ahmad Shah and I delivered speeches from the car and left for Uthmanzai. Thousands of people accompanied us. When we arrived at the Uthmanzai graveyard, we got down from the cars and proceeded to the graves of those who had been martyred by the British some days ago, in the *jalsa* at Uthmanzai. This incident occurred here when the *Khudai Khidmatgar* were holding a *jalsa*. The troops came to prevent it and surrounded it. They ordered the people not to do the *jalsa* and to disperse. But they refused to budge. So, they fired upon them and martyred two of them while the rest ran away. Our *jalsa* used to be well attended by the women as well. One of them was a young woman, who was, my niece, Dil Ara. She was the sister of *Salar-e-Azam*, Rab Nawaz Khan. She came out of the group of women and ran towards the *jalsa*. Amongst those who were fleeing was a man who called out to her and asked her what she was up to. Did she not see that people were being fired upon? She replied that, 'Oh you dishonourable ones! I am going to face them because you are running away!' On this taunt from the girl, the people returned and surrounded the troops. When the commander of the troops asked what it was that the people were demanding, Saadullah Khan told him they wanted to search them to reassure themselves that they would not carry away the dead with themselves. On this, the soldiers left the crowd and went away. I delivered a short speech in memory of the martyrs and told the gathering that the sapling of liberty prospered only with the blood of the martyrs; and the sapling that we had planted, it was to be hoped, would grow into a tree quite soon because our youth had watered it with their own blood. From here, the *jaloos* broke up and Abdul Akbar Khan and *Mian* Ahmad Shah returned to their villages. I, along with my well- wishers went to our *hujra*. The house was full of women and so I went to see them. Most of my friends took their leave of me but I could not rest because the visitors kept coming. When several people would collect, we would come out into the open and I would address them all in a short speech. Many women would also come. Our women were also very enthusiastic, and their political consciousness had developed. When we saw this enthusiasm of the people, we realized that the ground was ready, and it was now time to sow. It was necessary to take full advantage of this opportunity. This was because, it was my belief that this temporary truce with the government would not prove to be at all durable. So, we set to work among the Pukhtuns. We would not consider whether it was night or day, but toured the length and breadth of the province, village to village, and house to house. I made everyone understand the prevailing situation in the world and was reassured. God had blessed me with very good companions and associates who had all been well trained in jails, which are like training grounds for national political workers. Our *Sahib-e-Haq* Sahib of Tangi was a very sincere worker of the *Khudai Khidmatgar* movement. If anyone who would argue with him, he would ask him whether he had gone to jail for the sake of people and the land. When he would say 'no', he would say to him, 'You do not understand the meaning of the *Quran*. When I went to jail, only then did I understand the *Quran*.' Our method of work was that we would begin our tour of the province at one end and eventually get to the other end. We worked with the same dedication and sincerity all over the province and its districts. But our movement was successful in those places where we managed to enrol *Khudai Khidmatgar*.

12

The Gandhi–Irwin Pact

Our Tours and Experiences
Tours (Hashtnagar, Doaba, Katozai)

FOR A FEW DAYS, I WAS TAKEN UP COMPLETELY WITH VISITORS. BUT WHEN their numbers decreased, *Mian* Jaffar Shah, Abdullah Shah and I went on an extended tour of the province. We toured Sawabai and Naukhar by car and went for the night to *ziarat* Kaka Sahib. Thousands of people had assembled at places to welcome us. Brotherhood, nationalist feeling, love and affection had been generated in the Pukhtuns. The people were so enthused and charged that I find it difficult to express it in words. In the *jalsa* at Naukhar, the locals presented me a red *juba* and said that I should always remember that it was dyed red in their blood, and I should not forget the oppression that they were enduring. We were delayed so we arrived after the scheduled time. The *Khudai Khidmatgar*, poor souls, had come out some distance from the village to welcome us. We proceeded to the *hujra* of *Fakhr-e-Qaum Mian* Hameed Gul and went first to give condolences to his family. The next day we held a *jalsa* at the *Ziarat*. After we returned to the village I started on a tour of the villages of Hashtnagar and Doaba and brought the aims and objectives of the *Khudai Khidmatgar* movement and the *jirga* to the attention of the people. It was heartening to see women participate in the *jalsa*. But it was in the *jalsa* at Tangi that I really saw women's participation at its best and felt exhilarated. I have always believed that the development of people was possible only when its women stood shoulder to shoulder with their men, like the second wheel of a two-wheeled cart. I am grateful to God that our efforts bore fruit and our women have been awakened; and, if all goes well, our nation will now move forward and progress. From

Tangi we went to Abazai. To the north of Tangi lies a small village in which some very sincere *Khudai Khidmatgar* workers lived. These people were subjected to many atrocities at the hands of the land-owning family of the Kakakhel *mians* of Abazai during the time of the British. They would exhort them to abandon the movement, but met with no success in their evil designs. All the difficulties that these brave *Khudai Khidmatgars* faced at their hands, they bore with great patience and courage. From here, we crossed over to the Doaba tract. The people of Katozai had come out of their village to welcome and greet us. This was the *markaz* of Doaba as well. There was a large crowd gathered. We held a *jalsa* and highlighted the objectives of our movement. For the night, we went to the village of Matta and held a *jalsa* there as well. From Matta, early the next morning, accompanied by the *Khudai Khidmatgars*, we went to Sikhano Derai. On the way, learning of our visit, people came out to see us and join the *jaloos*. When we arrived at Shabqadar Derai our numbers had increased to be in the thousands. After the *jalsa* in Derai, we bade farewell to the people of upper Doaba and halted at Ambadher for the night. The people of this village were somewhat lazy and reluctant of joining the movement. I appealed to the women of the village and told them that this land belonged equally to the men and the women, and if the men were reluctant to join the movement, then they should gird up their loins and come forward and fulfil the promise that they (the women) had made to me:

Ke de Zalmo na poora na shwa,
Fakhr-e-Afghana, jeenakai ba dey gateena!

If the Pukhtun youth should falter, trust us, Fakhr-e-Afghan!
That we, the girls,
Shall, in your cause victorious be!

Before the *jalsa,* they proclaimed that they were ready for their work and that, under my leadership, they would serve the nation. After the *jalsa*, I, along with a few of the *Khudai Khidmatgars* went to Dolatpura where we offered our evening prayers and held discussions with the people. We returned to Ambadher for the night. The next day we went to Sukar and held a *jalsa* there, and then crossed the river to Tarnab. After another *jalsa* in Tarnab, we came to Uthmanzai for the night.

The Congress *Jalsa* in Karachi, 1931

Since it was time for the All-India Congress session scheduled in Karachi, I stopped further touring, and started preparing for travel to Karachi. I suggested that one nominee of each *Khudai Khidmatgar* *jirga* should accompany us, and their expense should be borne by the concerned *jirga*. Two benefits were to be gained from this. One, the *Khudai Khidmatgar* would gain a lot of experience from this journey. Secondly, it would be a source of positive publicity for us all over Hindustan. My proposal was accepted by the *jirga*. They were trained for a few days by General Azmat Khan, who was a very able and courageous general. When we arrived in Peshawar, the *Khudai Khidmatgar* had already organized several *jalsa* and *jaloos*, publicizing their aims and objectives. Forty-six *Khudai Khidmatgar* nominees, along with Haji Abdul Ghaffar Khan, Maqsood Jan, Abdullah Shah and I, left Peshawar by train for Karachi.

The Positive Impact of the *Khudai Khidmatgar* (*Surkh-Posh*/Red Shirts)

With Sarwar Shah appointed the commander of the *Khudai Khidmatgar*, and Maqsood Jan as the treasurer and manager, one early evening in March 1931, we boarded the train from Peshawar to Karachi. At every station, we would get off and move like a *jaloos* on the platform to beat of the dhol and music of the *surna*. This was an effort to publicize the movement. We arrived in Lahore the next morning and here we were to change trains. Many people had come to greet us. The *Khudai Khidmatgar*, to beat of the dhol and music of the *surna*, marched in a line. It was a sight to be seen. It had such a positive impact on people that one of my friends remarked: 'It is evident from today's demonstration that, as of today, the government of the British is no more; it is (now) the government of the *Khudai Khidmatgar*.' We then got into the train and it moved on, to the people's slogans of 'Inquilab Zindabad!' A few stations ahead a man and a woman asked me for permission to sit in the compartment of the *Khudai Khidmatgar*. I told them that there was no space for them there, and that they would be uncomfortable. But on their insistence and love, I allowed them to do so. Later, I learnt that the man was the father of Bhagat Singh, who had been hanged a few days ago in the Lahore jail[23] for terrorism, and that the woman was the senior teacher at a girls' school in the city of Julandhar. We did not deem it proper to play the dhol or *surna* before Bhagat Singh's father, but he compelled us to do so. He said that his son had given the ultimate sacrifice for the sake of the land and its people; that he should not be considered as dead and we should celebrate his life. The woman was a die-hard nationalist. She made the *Khudai Khidmatgar* memorize many nationalistic poems and wrote them out for them to memorize and would recite them along with them. At every stop, the *Khudai Khidmatgar* would get out and form two lines and march up and down the platform to the music of the dhol and *surna*. They would shout the slogans of 'Inquilab Zindabad!' and '*Fakhr-e-Afghan Zindabad!*' (Long Live Fakhr-e-Afghan). All the onlookers on the platform would move along with them. They would feel very happy on seeing them and this appeared to them as a very moving, though strange, spectacle.

The Schedule at Karachi

We arrived at the Karachi station to a tumultuous welcome. Abdul Khaliq Khaleeq sahib, along with some other Pukhtuns, was also amongst the people who had gathered to welcome us. Many Pukhtuns of Karachi had come but they were waiting outside the station. When we got down from the train and the *Khudai Khidmatgar* adjusted their uniforms, a few activists of the *Bharat Sabha* with Diwan Roshan Lal from Peshawar, who were also wearing red shirts, came and asked me to stop playing dhols to honour the martyrdom of Bhagat Singh. I asked whether they were more grieved about Bhagat Singh, or for his father; that his father had travelled with us from Lahore; that the *Khudai Khidmatgar*, out of deference to his grief, had stopped playing music, but on his insistence had played on as he said that Bhagat Singh had sacrificed his life for the freedom of the country and its people and that he was still alive. So, this was an occasion to be happy. That he was present at this station and that they should ask him, and if he said so, we would certainly stop playing the dhols.

Thousands of people were waiting for us outside the station. On behalf of the Pukhtuns, Khaleeq Sahib presented the welcome address. I also delivered a brief speech and thanked him. The

Pukhtuns wanted that we should accompany them on foot, in the form of a *jaloos,* to the *pandal* put up by the Congress. But someone informed us that Mahatma Gandhi had prohibited all kinds of *jaloos.* For this reason, we boarded the waiting buses and were unable to comply with their wish and expressed our regrets to them. But they were annoyed with us over this, nonetheless.

When we arrived at the *pandal,* we heard whistles calling the *razakars* to readiness. However, when they found out that we were the *Khudai Khidmatgar,* they calmed down. The fact was that when Gandhiji was scheduled to arrive, some red-shirt clad members of the Bharat *Sabha* had gone to the station with black flags. They had also spoken very harshly and insultingly to him. So, when we appeared in the *pandal,* and our uniforms being red, someone shouted out that, 'the *red shirts* have come and are attacking the Congress *pandal.*' The press in England and Hindustan misreported that the Red Shirts had taken black flags to welcome Gandhi and that they had revolted against the Congress. The newspapers in England published long articles on this and gloated over this development. But (as the Pukhto saying goes) 'a lie is short lived' and lasts only for as long as the truth does not appear on the scene. We were taken to a camp set up by the Congress where large tents had been pitched. There were a number of tents, but I felt that five would suffice for the *Khudai Khidmatgar.* We had barely settled down when some reporters arrived and started asking questions about our opposition to Gandhiji. I told them that all this was vicious and spurious propaganda and that we had no differences at all with either Congress or Gandhiji, and whatever has been published did not have an iota of truth in it. In the early evening, Pandit Madan Mohan Malaviya's son came to meet me and made me write a long statement in this regard and sent it to all the newspapers of Hindustan.

The women and men from Hindustan were anxious to meet me and the *Khudai Khidmatgar.* Thousands of visitors used to come to see us because the Pukhtuns were always projected as barbarians, and here we were, occupying the highest rung of humanity and nationalism with them. Pernicious propaganda had been carried out all over Hindustan about the Pukhtuns that they were a violent and bloodthirsty race. But now they were treading the path of non-violence, shoulder to shoulder with the Congress, and were facing the cruelty and oppression of the British, with their chests as shields.

They considered the Pukhtuns and the alliance with the Congress as a strange phenomenon. When they saw the *Khudai Khidmatgar* workers themselves, and witnessed what they practiced – their organization, sincerity and non-violence – they were reassured. Their minds were cleansed of all the propaganda that had been unleashed against the Pukhtuns. Many people would come to me and ask me all sorts of intriguing questions. I would make them understand as much as I could. I am extremely grateful to God that I was able to contradict and put to rest all the misrepresentations that had been deliberately created in their hearts and minds to a great extent. The other thing was that, for this Congress session, people had come from all over Hindustan. They all came to know the truth. When the *Khudai Khidmatgar* would go to the Congress langar for their meals, the rich and influential of Hindustan would be standing ready to serve them, and each one of them would make efforts to associate themselves with them. And wherever the *Khudai Khidmatgar* went, people would give them enormous respect. And when the Annual Session of the All-India Congress was about to start, Gandhiji sent Jawaharlal Nehru and Sardar Patel, the leading lights of the party, to the *Khudai Khidmatgar* for them to take part in the inaugural session, along with their musical instruments. Jawaharlal Nehru and his wife, Kamla Devi, along with their friends, came to see the parade and music. The fame of the *Khudai Khidmatgar* spread all over Hindustan and, on account of them, the Pukhtuns were projected in a very favourable light, and the stains of the reputation were wiped clean off their foreheads. It was because of them that people came to know the Pukhtuns and became fond of them.

In the Congress Session and in the *pandal*, the *Khudai Khidmatgar* had freedom of movement to go where they pleased. The Pukhtuns who were earlier shunned all over Hindustan and considered murderers and dacoits, now came to be highly regarded, and the Congress high command had such implicit faith and confidence in us that they entrusted the management and safety of their women on us. The fact was that this was a very difficult task to perform; it could neither be done by the police and nor by the *razakars* of the Congress. But the *Khudai Khidmatgars* carried out their obligations in such a responsible manner that the world stood amazed at the discipline in their ranks and their management capability. Even a high-ranking police official, who had been nominated for the management of the *jalsa*, took off his cap as a mark of respect to the *Khudai Khidmatgar* commander, Azmat Khan, and shook his hand and thanked him. Besides the *Khudai Khidmatgar*, his orders and directions would be complied with by the police. This, too, left a good impression on the Congress and all of Hindustan.

Karachi is home to many Pukhtuns who first came to the city in search of livelihood. They wanted to invite us, the *Khudai Khidmatgar*, to a meal and had also collected donations for this. A few of the leaders came to our camps along with Khaleeq Sahib and expressed their desire to me. I thanked them greatly for their love and sincerity, and told them that they were our brothers and we were at their service but did not agree to having a meal. The Pukhtun is so badly astray, that spending his money on feasts was not a desirable thing to do. When they shared that donation had been collected for the purpose, I suggested that instead of a cooked meal we should be given cash, which would come in handy to us. They agreed on this. The next day we went to meet them. Other inhabitants of Karachi had also come. They gave me a *sipasnama* and along with it a donation of two hundred and fifty rupees. I thanked them for their love and generosity and delivered a short speech in response to the *sipasnama*, and accepted the money with gratitude on behalf of the *Khudai Khidmatgar*.

In Karachi, the annual session of the *Jamiat-e-Ulema-e-Hind* was being held. Maulana Ahmad Saeed sahib, who was the Nazim, wrote to me. Maulana Ahmad Saeed sahib, the Nazim, Dr. Sahib and Maulana Kifayatullah had been imprisoned along with us in Gujarat jail, and we had developed a very good relation with them. He wanted the *Khudai Khidmatgars* to take part in their *jalsa* and assist them in its management. We gladly accepted their invitation and dispatched the *Khudai Khidmatgars* to assist and serve them. I also participated in their *jalsa*. They were very happy with the organization and service of the *Khudai Khidmatgars* and highly praised their services to me.

Tour of Hindustan

The Congress session ended and after the *jalsa*, we divided into two groups – one group comprised Haji Abdul Ghaffar, *Mian* Abdullah sahib and Saadullah Khan, along with *Khudai Khidmatgar* members who decided to return; and the other group was with me who wanted to tour Hindustan and carry out our own publicity. The first group left for the village while the second group for Bombay on the invitation of the Muslim members of the INC (Indian National Congress). Many Pukhtuns and people of Karachi had come to see us off when we boarded the steamer. After we had taken care of our baggage, we all stood in line and played our dhols and *surna* from the ship. At the wharf, the Pukhtuns began to dance the *shahdola* and created such a splendid scene that all the passengers on the ship, including the English, stood to watch this performance. One Englishman was so enthused that with a red flag in hand he jumped into the fray, but a police officer came and separated him. It was an exhilarating spectacle. We reached Bombay the next day, where thousands had gathered at the port for our reception, because a lot of publicity had been done on our behalf in the newspapers. However, our ship was not allowed to berth at the wharf where the people had gathered. They made us disembark at another wharf. But in no time the people collected there as well. They took out a big welcoming *jaloos* for us in the city. Our visit was highly publicized. We held *jalsas* in many places. The other thing was that our visit had some effect on the local Muslims as well. This alarmed and agitated the British. They began to falsely propagate that we had been specially commissioned by the Hindus to play the dhol and *surna* next to the mosques. The Muslims of Hindustan lacked the political consciousness that is evident in the Hindus. Political consciousness in people does not descend from the sky; and when politically conscious men are born, they create and generate political consciousness in their people. The Muslims are good people, but such people, unfortunately, have not yet been born among them. Just consider these leaders of the Hindus and Muslims: the Hindu leaders are nationalists, but those of the Muslims are Khan Bahadurs and Khan Sahibs! Whatever they seek is meant for themselves or for the British. There is no one who has the interest of the poor Muslims at heart and that is why they have lagged behind the Hindus.

We were presented a *sipasnama* on behalf of the Parsi community as well. The *jalsa* was attended by thousands of women and men. After thanking them profusely, I explained the need and reality of the *Khudai Khidmatgars* and shared that this movement was to free the oppressed from the cruelty of the oppressor, and everyone who is an oppressor – whether a Muslim or a Hindu or an Englishman – is ever ready to oppose them. God is not in need of anyone's service; the service of God is to serve his creation.

From Bombay, we came to Delhi. Here, too, thousands had come to receive us. Our arrangements were taken care of by the *Jamiat-e-Ulema-e-Hind*. We went there and rested. In the evening, they arranged for our *jaloos* to traverse the streets of the city. What can I say about the love and sincerity which the Muslims and Hindus displayed? Along the entire route, the crowds would shower our *jaloos* with flower petals, and from one place to another, we were presented with *sipasnamas*. When the *jaloos* ended in the evening, men and women had collected like ants at the place of the *jalsa*. After thanking them, I delivered a speech and said that I hoped that, by now, all the misgivings and doubts, which the detractors of the Pukhtuns had implanted in their minds, would have been removed. I also paid tributes to the courage and sacrifices the women of Delhi had displayed in the struggle for freedom, mentioning that when the women of a nation wake up and come forward for the sake of freedom, that nation could not remain subjugated for long. Such nations will attain their objectives in no time.

The *jalsa* concluded successfully, and we proceeded to the railway station and boarded the train. After a while, Gandhiji with some of his companions also boarded the same train for Amritsar. At every station, people would come to see him. The noise used to be so intense that we were not able to get any sleep, and nor could Gandhiji. A large crowd had gathered at the Saharanpur station. They had not been informed but had also decided for a *jalsa*. At midnight, men and women had gathered in thousands near the railway station, waiting for us. Gandhiji flatly refused to get down. After talking to him, some people came to me and begged, saying that in the dead of night thousands of men and women had gathered and that if I too did not get down from the train, they would be very disappointed. They also informed us that another train was scheduled to arrive after an hour. So, to satisfy them, I agreed and was moved by people waiting patiently for us. What a shock and a disappointment it would have been if they could not meet any of us. My meeting satisfied them to some extent. I spoke briefly, in what could be called a speech. I did not have the time, and so got back to the station. Shortly afterwards, another train arrived, and we resumed our journey. Raizada Hans Raj, who was from Jalandhar and had been detained with me in Gujarat jail, was a very good man. Whenever we met him, his wife would bring special and delicious meals for us. I had promised to get down with him, and we had every intention of disembarking at Jalandhar and visiting him and leaving for Amritsar by the next train. However, when our train arrived at Ludhiana, the news of our coming was already out. Women and men had come to the station and they tried to persuade us to get down and go with them. They forced us to return from Jalandhar to Ludhiana with them. We promised to do so and managed to put them off on this account. Despite our assurance a woman accompanied us all the way to Jalandhar. Lala Hans Raj and his wife and family, along with many others, had come to the station with the intention of travelling to Amritsar. Such a commotion was created at the station that I cannot describe it. Some *Khudai Khidmatgars* remained seated in the train and some got down with me, but they were unable to get their baggage down. We proceeded to Jalandhar and visited a girls' school. After delivering a brief speech, we left on our return journey to Ludhiana in a lorry with Lala Hans Raj. Many people had gathered outside the town. We wasted a lot of time in *jaloos* but held a mammoth *jalsa* here. But, unfortunately, we missed our train. The Muslims of Ludhiana arranged a lorry for the *Khudai Khidmatgar* and from here we left for Amritsar. We arrived in Amritsar in the evening. The people displayed a lot of affection for us in the bazaars, where they would surround our lorry. Finally, with great effort, we arrived at the place where Gandhiji had got down. We learnt that even Gandhiji had been put to a lot of inconvenience at the station and was unwell. I went to call on him. He had covered his head and face and was in considerable discomfort. I saw all my companions of Gujarat jail – Muslims, Hindus and Sikhs. The journey had also taken a toll on me and I felt unwell. For this reason, I considered it appropriate to take leave of our Sikh brethren and return to the village.

Return to the Village
I took leave of my brothers in Amritsar with some effort and told them I was unwell and could not do anything, and if they compelled

me to stay on, I was likely to get worse. They agreed and allowed me to leave.

Back in Uthmanzai I rested for a few days, and when I felt better, I decided on a tour of the province. I visited Kohat, Bannu and Dera Ismail Khan. Invitations had also been extended to me by the office bearers of the committees. I left on a tour of Tall and Hangu. On the tour, I was accompanied by the son of Qari sahib of Manlrgano Banda. He had a beautiful voice and would recite nationalist poems: 'We are not scared of your grindstones, oh rulers! Why do you frighten us?' This would have a positive effect on the people. On the way the Afridi inhabitants of Darra Adamakhel had learnt of our coming. They were sitting at different locations waiting for us and arranged for tea. Welcoming gunshots were heard. I tried my best to stop them from firing as I believed in non-violence but they were free people and could not be restrained. We got down at the place where they had collected and I delivered short speeches, informing them of the meaning of *Khudai Khidmatgari*. From here we first went to Tall and then returned to Hangu. And from there, after meeting our *Khudai Khidmatgar* brothers and attending the *jalsa*, we returned to Kohat city. The people of Kohat had organized a big exhibition but the festivities were disrupted by rain. After the *jaloos*, we held a *jalsa* where, in my speech, I invited the audience to constitute committees and join the movement. The next morning, we set off for Bannu and held *jalsa* on the way in Lachi, Ahmadi Banda and Banda Daud Shah, and Karak. We toured the area in and around Zarki. On the return journey, we stopped at Latambar and held a *jalsa* in the *hujra* of Muhammad Afzal Khan. In Kohat we had some excellent workers, one of whom was Abdul Ghaffar from Zarki, who had dedicated his life to national service. At the time of committing suicide, he had left a written note in my name, in which he wrote:

'In my capacity as a Khudai Khidmatgar, I had, in the presence of God, given you a pledge, that I would serve His creations to gain His pleasure. And no matter what difficulties and problems should arise, I would cope with them on principles of non-violence. But because, in the name of the Muslim League, the Government headed by Qayum Khan, apart from beating, jailing, and confiscating the property of the Khudai Khidmatgar, is also humiliating our women, my Pukhtun honour and pride could not tolerate this. It is only proper that I should

*have got hold of a gun and taken my revenge from these oppressors, but
since I had pledged that I would remain committed to non-violence, I
am taking my own life, and along with God, seek your forgiveness as
well, that I have not been able to remain steadfast to my pledge.'*

In this district, there were about one hundred thousand *Khudai
Khidmatgars*. Here the Khan of Latamber had planned for our
tea. We were still busy drinking tea when the *Khudai Khidmatgars*
from Bannu arrived and we left with them. The Bannu *Khudai
Khidmatgars* had also made an elaborate programme for our visit
and took out a mammoth *jaloos* through the streets of the town.
Thousands of people participated in this grand *jalsa*. *Salar* Yaqoob
Khan and Vishva Mitra had worked very hard arranging this. They
had united the Hindus and Muslims to participate. I delivered
a speech elaborating on the essential points of the *Khudai
Khidmatgar* movement. From here, we left the next morning for
Dera Ismail Khan. In Mirakhel Naurang, Israri and Lakki Marwat
we held *jalsas* along with one in Kakai, Shahbaz Khel and Paizo.
Since Lakki Marwat was on our route, we also held a *jalsa* there.
Near Dera Ismail Khan we saw the familiar attire of Pukhtuns from
upper Pukhtunkhwa, and we turned in to see them. We were still
engaged in conversation with them when a car approached us and
its occupants told us that the inhabitants of Dera city had come out
and were eagerly awaiting our arrival. When we neared the city, we
saw that thousands of people were waiting for us. On seeing our
car, they repeatedly raised the slogans *Inquilab* and *Fakhr-e-Afghan
Zindabad*. They had closed the bazaars, shops and the streets and
large ornamental gates had been erected in a few places. In my
view, many prominent leaders had come here in the past, but no
one had received such a rousing reception. They mounted me on a
horse and led it to the *jaloos*. Thousands of men and women were
standing on the roofs of the houses to witness the spectacle. The
British had tried to exert a lot of pressure on the Hindus not to
take out the *jaloos* and arrange my reception on such a grand scale
but failed completely. This *jaloos* was arranged almost entirely by
the Hindus. During these days in Dera Ismail Khan, there was
a lot of enthusiasm for the national movement. Around the city
also the movement was widespread. In Tank, Kulachi, Gul Imam,
Gomal Bazaar and Paniala people were joining the movement in
droves. In the city, in addition to the men, young boys and women

were also taking out *jaloos*. One day a women's *jaloos* was passing through the bazaar. When it reached the Dr. Jhanda Ram Chowk, the inspector general police of Sarhad, S. Mangar, gave orders for its dispersal. But the women refused to comply. Infuriated, the inspector general drew his revolver to shoot, when suddenly a young man from the *jaloos*, Sardar Bhagwan Singh, caught him by the hand and asked, 'Are you not ashamed of yourself to pull a gun on women?' The inspector general sahib's hand shook, and the revolver fell to the ground. Despondent, he returned to his bungalow. A policeman recovered his revolver and returned it to him. Revenge was taken for this act of courage from Bhagwan Singh in the communal riots of 1931, when he was arrested and charged for the murder of a *darogha* and subjected to prolonged periods of torture and inhuman treatment. He was only set free when they failed in establishing a case against him.

The government was not too happy with the Hindus, and this was the reason that after five months they incited the Muslim-Hindu riots and instigated them to fight against each other. The riots that ensued led to looting of wealth and property of the Hindus; houses and bazaars were set aflame; and many Hindus as well as Muslims were killed. Property worth hundreds of thousands of rupees was destroyed. A Khan Bahadur from Paniala[24] conferred with the deputy commissioner and the assistant commissioner, Sheikh Mahboob Ali Khan, to put two lorries at Sheikh Mahboob Ali's disposal and directed him to provide red clothes to his servants and make them understand that they wanted to create disturbances in the city. He said that when he would telephone him, he was to equip his servants, dressed in red, with pistols and guns and send them immediately to the city for loot and arson. He did as he was directed. It was the policy of the British deputy commissioner that, on the one hand, the Hindus would be beaten up and their wealth and properties looted and, on the other, the *Khudai Khidmatgars* would be blamed for it and they would publicize the event all over Hindustan, so that the Congress would begin to harbour suspicions about their intentions and detach themselves from them. At night, a grand *jalsa* was held and I delivered a brief speech and expressed my great pleasure at the unity between the Hindus and the Muslims, and sincerely hoped that they would be able to maintain this unity and strengthen it further and take a lead role in the struggle for freedom. The next day, we went to Kulachi where the Gandapur khans and Ramzan Khan all joined the movement. Here the *Khudai Khidmatgar* general was Kanwar Bhan Narang sahib. Later, he became a *salar*. A *jalsa* was held where people joined the folds of the *Khudai Khidmatgar* movement with great enthusiasm, and we even constituted a *jirga*. From Kulachi we proceeded to Tank, the place of some very powerful Pukhtuns. Many people took part in the *jalsa* and joined our movement. From here, via Bannu and Kohat, we reached back to Peshawar.

Tour of the Pukhtun Areas of Punjab

When the *Khudai Khidmatgar* movement was formed, the two adjoining districts of Campbellpur and Mianwali were very near to us. Most of the population was Pukhtun. Both these districts bordered the Sarhad province. Campbellpur was a part of Peshawar Division, and Mianwali that of Dera Ismail Khan Division. At the time that the movement began, these districts were separated from us and made part of the province of Punjab. As these districts are in our neighbourhood, we wanted to tour these as well, but the government did not allow us to go to Campellpur district. Even when we formed our own ministries, we were not allowed to go there. Once, at the time of our government, we wanted to go on a tour of the Campbellpur area and thought that now that national governments were in place, we would be allowed to tour. However, when we crossed the Attock bridge, the police was ready and waiting for us with drawn bayonets. With barricades on the road, they asked us to return as they would not allow us to proceed further. I told them that we would not turn back. When we realized that they would not let us go, we got off from the lorry and sat by the road side at the foot of the hill. After hours when they realized that we were not going to go back, they brought the lorry and made us sit in it and we left in the direction of Campbellpur. But instead of Campbellpur they took us to Khushal Garh. They took us across the Abaseend river and left us in Kohat. Similarly, whenever I or the *Khudai Khidmatgar* have made up our minds to tour these districts, we have not been permitted. We would also occasionally visit Mianwali, as well as the Chach area of Campbellpur. Once when we went to Isakhel, the nawab of Isakhel would not allow us to hold a *jalsa* there. He had armed his servants with big lathis and they would beat anyone who came for the *jalsa*. I decided that I would walk through the bazaar and, while doing so, I would deliver my speech. Despite this, whenever people would gather to listen to my speech, they would be beaten with the lathis. In short, let alone holding a *jalsa*, I was not even allowed to speak. But there was a Hindu who invited us and arranged lunch for us in his serai. He was sent for by Nawab sahib not to allow me to come and to expel me from the serai. But he refused to comply with Nawab sahib's orders and we spent the night as his guests. The next day being a Friday, we thought that many people would assemble for the afternoon congregational prayer. So, we decided to go as well and join the prayer, and if an opportunity presented itself, we would also address them. The mosque was surrounded by the lathi-wielding servants of Nawab sahib. And when we entered the mosque, we found to our surprise, that there was no one there for the prayer. It was completely empty. We learnt that the nawab's men were surrounding the mosque because they anticipated that we would come for the Friday prayer. His men had stood guard outside the mosque and had prevented anyone from entering it. When we realized that in this area nobody would allow us to do political work, we returned to Sarhad.

One of our *Khudai Khidmatgar* generals from Mardan, Shah Wali Khan, along with some other workers had once gone to Pindi Gheb *tehsil* of Campbellpur district. They were proceeding in a *jaloos* and he had a *Khudai Khidmatgar* flag in his hand while others were following him. When they approached the *hujra* of subedar Dost Muhammad Khan, he and his son, Ghulam Muhammad, obstructed their path and fired a shot at the general sahib. He was martyred. They then beat up the other *Khudai Khidmatgars* with lathis and pelted stones on the other participants of the *jaloos* and scattered it, and the *jalsa* also dispersed. Our Punjab brethren complained that I was working only for the Pukhtuns. I told them that our movement was for the service of God's creation (humanity) and that we have tried our best to be of service to everyone. That I have come on several occasions to Punjab, but no one has allowed me to work.

After this when the British declared that they were leaving Hindustan, I went to Mianwali once again and held a large *jalsa* at Daudkhel. The Pukhtuns of Mianwali are Niazis by tribe and are courageous Pukhtuns. They attended our *jalsa* in great numbers and with enthusiasm. I still remember my speech on the occasion, where I said, 'Today's world is one of nationalism. You understand, those nations imbued with the spirit of nationalism and brotherhood have been able to progress and ascend to the skies. We too are a nation, then why have we been left behind? We have lagged because we are not nationalist in outlook, and do not have love, unity and brotherhood. So, I have come to say to you that you are my people, but you have given up your mother tongue, the Pukhtunwali code, culture and brotherhood. You have even changed your dress and adopted the *lang*. And I tell you this also that when a bird separates itself from the flock, it loses its way. Now the time for a decision has come. This was my duty as a Pukhtun and as your kinsman, to come and ask you what course you want to take. Will you go along with us or with Punjab? We were separated by the British; now that the British are leaving, will you re-join us or remain with Punjab?' From amongst them a man got up and said, 'We are your brothers and are Pukhtuns, and will revert to the Pukhtun fold. We will teach our children how to speak Pukhto; not only the children but we ourselves will learn Pukhun as well. But you should promise us that at least once every six months you will visit us.' I made a promise to them and the *jalsa* dispersed. The country was liberated and gained independence. Pakistan was created but I have not, till now, been able to fulfil my promise of visiting them. This is because ever since Pakistan was created, let alone Mianwali, I have not even been permitted to work in my own province. On the contrary, for the time that I remained in Pakistan, I would either be in jail or confined to my house.

Our Mission and the Scheming of the British

When the British realized that this movement was spreading like wildfire amongst the Pukhtuns, fear overcame them and they started efforts to try and destroy it. First, they started a propaganda campaign against us in the English language newspapers of Punjab that this movement was against the Congress. This was intended to separate us from the Congress and deprive us of the party's and Gandhiji's support. But I, immediately after consultation with *Mian* Ahmad Shah and other companions, issued a statement that this government had started a baseless propaganda campaign against us; that we are friends of the Congress; that we have not parted ways, nor would we do so in future. The other thing was that the English language newspapers of Punjab, which were under the influence of the government, started the propaganda that I had been given 60,000 rupees in Bombay for the Afridis, although this was totally false. I had not solicited donations from anyone in Hindustan and nor had received any money. Nor have I resorted to ways that would create a schism and ill will between me and my Afridi brethren. But lies can never compete with the truth. One day, at the Lahore railway station, I saw the editor of the daily *Inquilab*. The editor was also known to me. But when money becomes the focal point of a nation's existence, it has no consideration for friendship. He came and embraced me, and I asked him since when he had become such friends with the Afridis and cultivated such cordial relations with them. That he did not assist them when the British cannons were shelling them. I also told him that was it possible for a Punjabi to have sympathy with the Afridis. They were part of my nation and I was their servant. Then how was it possible that he would sympathize with them more than I did. He replied that since we were in alliance with the Congress, and their policy was to oppose the Congress, they were against us and wrote against me. I told him that we would leave the Congress but that we had approached the Muslim League and it was not ready to assist us in any way. The truth was that they had compelled us to ally ourselves with the Congress. He lowered his gaze and walked away. Islam had come to the world to liberate its followers and to save the weak from the brutalities of the oppressors, but today the Muslims of Hindustan were in favour of slavery, they were the friends of oppression – and still professed to be Muslims!

The Sarhad Jirga in Place of the Congress Committee

We believed the name of the Sarhad Congress Committee should be changed to the 'Sarhad Jirga', because our people did not understand the former and we, the *Khudai Khidmatgars*, though allied with the Congress, were not an integral part of it. The other consideration was that the members of the Congress from Sarhad would oppose and not support us. That is why we demanded that the name of the 'Congress Committee' should be changed to '*jirga*'. All our provincial *Khudai Khidmatgars* and the members of the Congress in Sarhad gathered and collectively constituted a *jirga*. All the workers wanted that I should agree to become its president. But I was not prepared for this, and so, two other names were proposed for presidentship. The people of Peshawar city proposed the name of Ali Gul Khan and we (the people from the villages) proposed the name of *Mian* Ahmad Shah, who was elected by a majority vote. For the post of general secretary, I proposed the name of Pir Bakhsh, an advocate of Peshawar; he was unanimously elected, and we set to work. Our work increased by the day and the movement was making great strides. A national consciousness, a spirit and an awareness had been generated among our people and was increasing by the day. The government, always looking for ways to destroy the movement and put a stop to my tours of the villages, started a false propaganda campaign against me in the press, making false allegations about me to Gandhiji. But Mahatmaji did not get caught in their web of lies. When, at the time, I decided on a tour of Kohat district and got some *Khudai Khidmatgars* to join me, the Sarhad government wrote to the viceroy that Kohat district was the centre of recruitment for the army, and if I were to conduct the tour, they would lose their hold over this area. So it was necessary that I should be arrested. The viceroy informed Mahatma Gandhi that they were going to arrest me. Mahatmaji replied that if this were to be done, then the truce that had been established between them would be broken. When I began the tour of Kohat, the government sent four officers for me to end it. One was the deputy commissioner, the other a captain of the police, the magistrate of the area, and the fourth was an English officer of the Border Police, who spoke very good Pukhto. They were directed to tour the villages and persuade the people to not let me enter the villages or collect to hear my speeches. But all this effort failed to dent the enthusiasm of the people. Whichever village that we went to, this group would have preceded us. They would inform the people that I was on the way and not to allow me to enter. They asked the people to arrest us if we resisted. They also suggested that villagers/locals should not speak to me or attend the *jalsa*. In one village we were scheduled to hold a *jalsa*, they also arrived there. In my speech I was saying that we were *Khudai Khidmatgars* and, in the name of God, had prepared to act for the service of people and this nation. That this country and this nation was theirs too, and asked whether there was anyone amongst them who would join us in this service (*khidmat*). One man got up and said, 'Write my name down'; another got up and said 'Write my name down,' and yet another got up and said, 'Write my name down.' On this, the English Border Police officer approached me and asked what spell had I cast on these people? That the people used to be scared of even one policeman, in front of whom they would not even be able to recite the *kalima* (recitation from the *Quran*). And that now, in front of those policemen they had no fear and were proposing their names for *Khudai Khidmatgari*. I told him that I was not responsible for this, but they were. This was the natural outcome of their sustained oppression.

As we proceeded to Bannu, we held various *jalsa* in Lakki Marwat, Sarai Naurang and other villages. We constituted *jirga*. Many were enrolled in the movement. We toured all the villages in the vicinity of Bannu city. We held *jirga* in each village and explained to people the prevailing political situation. In Hatikhel, we organized a *jalsa* at the very spot where, in 1931, British troops had opened fire on a *jalsa* and had martyred and arrested many people. When we approached Hatikhel, a police officer served a notice to me under section 144 of the criminal procedure code, directing me not to go there. I refused to accept it. Then I thought the better of it and said to myself that if I went, the police would stop the *jalsa*. So, I sent my *Khudai Khidmatgar* companions to the jalsa and I myself proceeded to Latambar and went to sleep in the *hujra* of Khan Muhammad Afzal Khan. In the evening, Muhammad Afzal Khan along with my *Khudai Khidmatgar* companions returned from the *jalsa*, and told me how successful the it had been and how the people had cursed and shamed the government for not allowing me to attend. We returned to Kohat and toured the places which we were unable to cover earlier. We constituted *jirga* and enrolled many as *Khudai Khidmatgars*.

Visit to Bardoli on the Invitation of Gandhiji

When we arrived in Kohat city, we learnt that Gandhiji had invited me to visit him in Bardoli. Since the only part of Kohat district I had not toured was Hangu, I decided that on completing my tour, I would go to Bardoli. We toured Hangu and constituted *jirga* in several places. However, another messenger came informing me that Gandhiji wanted I should leave all my work and get to Bardoli right away. Our work was almost complete and so the next day, I went to Peshawar and from there left for Bardoli. When I arrived in Bhopal, the ADC of Nawab sahib, Shoaib Qureshi sahib, who had been our companion from the days of the *Khilafat* and was the son-in-law of Maulana Muhammad Ali Johar and was also a benefactor, was waiting for me. After exchanging the greetings, he informed me that Nawab sahib desired that I should break my journey, have a little rest and, in the evening, he would be his special guest at a banquet. I told him that Gandhiji would be waiting for me in Bardoli, and that my gratitude may kindly be conveyed to Nawab sahib and that I would visit him on my return journey. But he was insistent, and so I got down from the train and accompanied him. When I arrived at the guest house, maulana Shaukat Ali was also present there. The next morning, Nawab sahib told me that he would take me to call on the viceroy and that whatever I had to demand of him would be given to me, and that I should not go to Bardoli. But I did not agree to this proposal. They pressured me a great deal, but I was adamant in my refusal to accept. I took leave of them the next day and left for Bardoli. Sardar Patel and Devadas (Gandhiji's son) had come to the station to receive me. Near the station was the *ashram* of Bardoli. I met with Gandhiji. In the early evening, I accompanied Gandhiji on his stroll. A Muslim inspector of the CID followed us, but when we noticed him, he felt embarrased and left.

Gandhiji would discuss the political affairs of Sarhad with me once a day, for a short while. But he had not yet disclosed to me that he had summoned me on the complaint of the provincial government. One day a Muslim *lambardar* named Patel came to invite me and told Gandhiji that, if he permitted, he wanted me to be his guest at a meal. He gladly gave him permission and, at the time of taking leave, told him to feed me a lot of meat; that here they had almost killed me by feeding me *dal* continuously. The *lambardar* took me home, which was beautiful and very well kept. He was a very loving person. I will never forget his sincerity and love.

Tour with Devadas

Devadas Gandhi, on the advice of Gandhiji, took me on a tour of Bardoli and showed me all the *ashrams*. I greatly admired the simplicity of life in these *ashrams*. It affected me to such an extent that I began to visualize the construction of such *ashrams* for the training of the *Khudai Khidmatgars*. The people of Bardoli had given many sacrifices in the struggle for independence, and for this, the properties of many people which had been auctioned were in the possession of others. Here the relationship between the Muslims and Hindus was also very good, and despite the efforts of the government, the Muslims had not bid for the auctioned lands of the Hindus, and even the few holdings that they had purchased had been returned to the original owners. In all my speeches I always said that the country belonged jointly to both Hindus and Muslims and requested them to remain united for its liberation. And if someone does not have the courage to take part in the struggle for freedom, he can at least not take part in the auction of the land holdings of the freedom fighters. And if anyone has bought them, then it was only appropriate for them to surrender them to the original owners. I exhorted the Muslims to wake up because if they continued to slumber, the wave of revolution which was in the offing would drown them. Because a revolution was like a flood, drowning nations that are asleep; and those that are awake, it makes them prosper. They should wake up and organize themselves and benefit from the revolution.

After a few days Jawaharlal Nehru also arrived at the ashram in Bardoli. All of us, including Gandhiji, left for Bombay. From Bombay, Gandhiji, Devadas and I went to Gujarat. Here Gandhiji laid the foundation of a new *ashram*. Nearby was an Arabic *madrassah* of the Muslims. When they learnt of my arrival, they came to see me, and Devadas and I accompanied them to see the *madrassah*. Here, there were many Pukhtun students. I felt very pleased at seeing them and talked with them at length. The *madrassah* was well laid-out. The teachers and students were amicable and talked to me affectionately. On the demand of the students, I delivered a brief speech. I was very happy to meet them because I expected many things from them. I told them that if they were to study history of the world, they would come to know that nations gained their freedom through the sacrifices of their students. They also compelled Devadas to speak, and he also delivered a brief speech. From here we travelled to Madras and toured the surrounding areas. I had spent many days away from home and wanted to go back, but Gandhiji would not let me go and nor would he tell me the reason for having me summoned. He would talk to me about the political affairs of Sarhad, and then would be in correspondence with the government. One day, I read in the newspapers that a misunderstanding had arisen amongst *Mian* Ahmad Shah, Abdul Akbar Khan, Ali Gul Khan and Pir Bakhsh, and that they had split into factions and the *jirga* had split into two parties. This was very upsetting because I am extremely averse to groupings and factions, and it is my conviction that any nation which is disunited and breaks up into factions cannot attain its objectives. And today, when we find ourselves as slaves, the cause for this is the disunity in our ranks. I expressed my intent to Gandhiji that, since these developments had taken place because of my absence, it was imperative for me to return. It was only after this that Gandhiji revealed to me all that had transpired with the Viceroy Lord Willingdon. I told him that all this was a pack of lies, and he should write to the viceroy that this was all false propaganda against me, and if he was not convinced then we would also go to see him personally; and that he should summon the people who had sent him all these false stories so that the truth could be ascertained. Gandhiji agreed with this proposal of mine. He undertook to write to the viceroy to become the judge. He also included in his letter to the viceroy that Lord Irwin had impressed upon him the importance of visiting Sarhad and seeing the current state affairs for himself, and so, he too would visit Sarhad. The viceroy replied that there was no need for us to visit him, and nor did he consider it appropriate and wise for him (Gandhiji) to visit the region at this juncture. Gandhiji understood that I was in the right, and that the British did not want me to go and get down to my work. He then asked Devadas to take me to Ahmedabad and show me the *ashram* and introduce me to people there. Devadas and I left for Ahmedabad. Khurshid Behan met us at the railway station, and the three of us went to the *ashram*.

The *ashram* in Ahmedabad is very beautiful. It is situated in an unusual spot on the bank of river Sabarmati. I was taken around the *ashram*. The women and men gathered and exhibited great love and affection for me. In the evening, when I was finished with my prayer, they all came to me and questioned me about Sarhad and its people. I was surprised when I heard some of their questions because their information and views were based on falsehood and propaganda to defame us. It was the desire of Khurshid Behan that I should accompany her to a Pukhtun pir, who was next to Ahmedabad and had many followers. She thought that if he were to join the movement, we would be able to accomplish many things through his auspices. I told her that though I had no objection to this, this kind of work was not for the likes of pirs. That I had, in my time, sought help from many such people. Devadas also endorsed my contention and so she refrained from pursuing it any further. After much discussion and debate with Khurshid Behan, she expressed the desire to accompany me to Sarhad. And when we left again to join Gandhiji, she too came along with us and told Gandhiji that, if he allowed her, she would go to Sarhad for *khidmat*. He allowed her but wanted her to give this matter great thought and consideration.

Ahmedabad was ruled by Muslims rulers for six hundred years. We visited many historic buildings. The city also has many industries producing cloth. We visited them as well. There is a large national college of the Hindus here, called Vidyapith, which I went to see. The people at Vidyapith invited me and I spent a night there. This is a beautiful campus with a magnificent building. This college has produced many staunch nationalists and nurtured them. They have rendered great sacrifices for the freedom of India. At the time when I went to see the Vidyapith College, I saw a boy who was working on a carding implement. On asking, I found out that he was Gandhiji's grandson. There were no students in the college at the time of my visit; they had all spread out all over Gujarat and were touring the villages. From this, I realized that this was truly a national college which had generated a national spirit in its students, and the education that was being imparted to them was real education.

There are many Pukhtuns in Ahmedabad. I also met them and explained the *Khudai Khidmatgar* movement. On my last day in Ahmedabad a big *jalsa* of the Hindus and Muslims was held in which thousands of men and women took part. I thanked them for their love and affection in coming to attend this *jalsa* in such large numbers and told them that we had created a new brotherhood, which was called the '*Khudai Khidmatgari*'. I shared with them that God was not in need of service. The service of God was the service of His creation (of humanity). Whether Hindus or Muslims, we were no different from each other and were all God's creation. After this *jalsa* when we returned to Gandhiji, he had received a response from Lord Willingdon, the viceroy. On seeing me he smiled and said that I was telling the absolute truth and the government was telling lies. The truth is that the government is afraid of the *Khudai Khidmatgar* movement and does not wish it well. I understood, and reality dawned on me. The viceroy was of the view that we should not visit him and had written (to Gandhiji) that there was no need for him to go to Sarhad. Gandhiji told me to return and get down to work. The truth was that the government, through its false propaganda, wanted to create a rift between us and Gandhiji, had me arrested, and suppress our movement. But when the government understood that Gandhiji was siding with us, we were freed from its claws. It realized that if we were to be arrested, the truce concluded with the Congress would be violated. Many of our workers had been detained under section 144 of the criminal procedure code. They meant to arrest me, but failed. I stayed with Gandhiji for a month and when he was reassured, he allowed me to take leave. Devadas accompanied me up to Ahmedabad. At the time of my departure, Gandhiji's secretary, Mahadev Desai sahib, came and handed me over a long letter, which the assistant commissioner of Charsadda had written to him. This was that same Englishman who had been fired at by Habib Nur in an unsuccessful assassination attempt, for which he had been hanged. A mention of the play staged by the *Khudai Khidmatgar* at Babara was also made in it. He instructed me to send a reply for this to Gandhiji. I put the letter in my pocket and boarded the train. I spent one night in Ajmer, one in Jaipur and one in Delhi, and then returned home to my village.

The Play Staged in Babara and our Weak Companions

The more the government ill-treated us, the more aware we became and rose up in self-defence. And the more our movement prospered and the number of the *Khudai Khidmatgars* increased, the more the government would increase the intensity of its repression. Some children of Charsadda and Babara, just to amuse themselves, staged a play, but the government was looking for an excuse. I was on tour. The deputy commissioner summoned our secretary, Abdul Akbar Khan, and our companions Abdullah Shah and *Mian Ahmad Shah*, and intimidated them to such an extent, that Abdul Akbar Khan disassociated himself from the organizers of the play. He did not have the courage to tell the deputy commissioner that this was only for the amusement of the children. Such plays have been enacted by boys before, but governments do not give them much importance. When the government realized our weakness, immediately the next day troops and cannons were called out in Charsadda and the boys who had staged the play were arrested. Troops were also let loose in the streets of Prang, Babara and Charsadda. The other thing was that, in a *jalsa* held in the Jamia Masjid of Charsadda, *Mian* Ahmad Shah ridiculed these boys. As a result, the government arrested them and sentenced one of them to one year and the other two to two-and-a-half years' imprisonment each over such a trivial matter. When I returned from my tour, I went to Prang, Babara and Charsadda, gathered the people and delivered a speech, advocating patience and reassuring them, and criticized this policy of the government, telling them that the play was meant for the amusement of the boys but the government took it so seriously. The grief and disappointment which had overcome the people was dispelled, and they were reassured by what I said. The deputy commissioner had panicked and frightened our companions to such an extent that they became highly critical of me, saying that I toured all day delivering irresponsible speeches. That so many people had become *Khudai Khidmatgars*, it was now difficult to control them. For this reason, they were tendering their resignations from the movement. Because they were our old associates, I did not want them to part ways, and so we decided to confer with Qazi sahib Attaullah Khan and Sameen Jan Khan in Mardan. We spent a night with Qazi sahib. We broached the subject at night. I had strange companions. Instead of complementing me on the tireless work, they also said that I should stop participating in *jalsa* and stay quietly at home. I told them not to compel me to leave the work, and that I would work in accordance with their wishes. That they should give me a written speech and I would deliver that to the people in the *jalsa* instead. But they would not even agree to this and told me that if I continued with the *jalsa*, they would tender their resignations. Qazi sahib, Sameen Jan Khan and their companions were siding with them. I told them that the truce between Gandhiji and Lord Irwin was temporary, and the Round Table Conference would not succeed, and when this failed, then the first thing the government was bound to do is to have me arrested, and whether we deliver speeches or not, we would still not be secure. So, God has given us this time. It was necessary to take advantage of this and occupy ourselves night and day and go to our people. And if they were of the view that I should not mention in my speeches that 'We have broken one horn of the British; Rise, oh! Pukhtuns, and let us get rid of the other one as well!', then they should tell me – if I was not to say this, then what was I meant to say? They told me to say that we had extended a hand of friendship to the government. I asked them if the Pukhtuns would understand this at all, and the enthusiasm which I wished to generate in them, whether I would be able to do so. Reluctantly, I was compelled to agree with what they said, so that they would not leave me, although I did not consider this to be appropriate. It was also strange, because two of our *jalsa* had been scheduled and announcements had been made: one in Sudham and the other in Speena Warai, in the Khalil area. I was told not to go there. *Mian* Abdullah Shah and Jafar Shah said that they were going to resign because they feared that the government was going to arrest them. We tried to reassure them, but they did not agree. It was suggested that if they resigned, they should not publicise this in the press because the government would take undue advantage of this. But they did not agree to this either. They wanted to show to the government that they were sick and tired of this movement. Our other companions implored them that such news could not be kept hidden from the government. But even then, they announced it in the newspapers. It was late in the night and although we went to bed after this discussion, I was very restless and could not get a wink of sleep. For one, there was no one willing to serve them; and if one or two came forward to do so, no one gave them an opportunity. In the morning, when Qazi sahib and I went for our walk, I said, 'Fine! Now that you are compelling me to act in such a disgraceful manner, on the Day of Judgement, when things are being accounted for, I will grab you by the collar and you will be responsible for this. And the harm that this decision of yours will inflict upon the people and the nation will be on your head.' Not too happy with this development, Qazi sahib responded, 'What can I do? I do not consider this course of action appropriate. But if we do not agree to it, they will desert us and leave us high and dry.' When we were having tea, Qazi sahib discussed the scheduled *jalsa* in Sudham and Spina Warai with them and made them allow me to attend these *jalsa*, on the condition that they should accompany me, and that I would deliver only the kind of speeches that they wanted me to. So *Mian* Ahmad Shah accompanied me to one *jalsa* and Abdul Akbar Khan to the other. In the *jalsa* of Sudham the *sipasnama* given to me by the people also contained the statement that my declaration in an earlier speech in Lahore of raising one hundred thousand *Khudai Khidmatgars* did not suit the status and standing of the Pukhtuns, and that they were prepared to raise more. Because of the efforts of Qazi sahib, all the khans and people of this area were ready to join us in our efforts. When the *jalsa* at Spina Warai started, many women had also come to attend it. An aeroplane came and dove down over them and many of them left, but when I called out to them, taunting them, they all came back. The pilot flew his aeroplane many times over their heads. When the women refused to be frightened, he flew off, disappointed. When the *jalsa* ended, I returned to the village with *Mian* sahib. The other *jalsa* were not held and there were no more *jalsa* and I was not permitted by my companions to leave the village. When I stopped going to the people, they came to me in Uthmanzai. My work continued and was proceeding well. *Mian* sahib, who was the secretary of the *Loya Jirga*, called a session at Uthmanzai for the transaction of some important matters. When this was done, Pir Shahenshah and Sardar Ram Singh asked me to resume touring. I replied that I had no objection to doing so, but that the president, Abdul Akbar Khan, and Abdullah Shah sahib, had put an embargo on my doing so. If they desired that I should resume touring, they should obtain their permission. They compelled *Mian* sahib and I got the permission and left on tour with them. I toured Kohat and Bannu village by village and spent many days there. Many *jirga* were formed and many *Khudai Khidmatgars* were enrolled. When I returned, I found that *Syed* Fazl-e-Latif had decided to hold a big *jalsa* in Harichand and had extended invitations to all the Moomand and Ranizai (tribes). A large crowd had congregated for the *jalsa*. In my speech I said,

'Oh, Pukhtun brothers! We all belong to the same nation and are the progeny of the same ancestor. Our example is that of a tree with numerous branches but the same trunk, and if anyone cuts one of its branches, harm comes to the shade of that tree; and if the trunk of that tree dries up, then all its branches dry up. These days the British are busy slowly cutting off these branches. You should wake up. For if these branches are finished, then your children will be exposed to the heat of the sun, and the protection over their heads will be no more. And if the trunk were to dry up, then all the branches will also dry up, not one will remain. I am reminding you that the enemy is busy annihilating you and is making efforts to ensure that the bark dries up. If you allow it to dry up, you will be destroyed. Rise! Put your own house in order, set aside your differences, and become one nation, so that you are a success both in this world and in the next.'

After the *jalsa* I left with *Syed* Latif Bacha for Badragga and then Ranizai. When I returned from there, another *jalsa* was organized at Lundkhwar. Many women participated in this *jalsa* and pledged:

Ka de zalmo na poora ne shwa,
Fakhr-e-Afghana, jeenakai ba day gateena!

If the Pukhtun youth should falter,
Trust us, Fakhr-e-Afghan! That we, the girls,
Shall in your cause victorious be!

From here I left for a tour of the Baezai tract. With Ghulam Muhammad Khan I toured the Baezai and Shamozai tracts. I was very pleased with the performance of the Baezai workers because they had put in a lot of effort in their area. The greatest thing that pleased me was that wherever *jirga* was held, women with spinning wheels would be seated on the roofs of houses and in the orchards, and before the start of the proceedings, they would be busy spinning. The other significant aspect of this tour was that Ghulam Muhammad Khan and Zareen Khan looked after my comfort. They had worked a lot among the womenfolk. In Lundkhwar, a women's *jalsa* was held in which thousands participated. They gave me a *sipasnama* and also delivered speeches. I felt very happy about the participation of women because without its women, no nation can prosper. This is because the nurturing of our children is completely in their hands, and of the two wheels of our cart, one is a woman and the other a man. So, you figure it out for yourselves, that if one wheel is punctured, how can the cart move forward?

From here, Ghulam Muhammad Khan and I went for a day to the Yousafzai where a grand *jalsa* was held. Thousands of people and *Khudai Khidmatgars* had gathered. I had rarely seen such a big *jalsa* elsewhere. I delivered a speech, that the *Khudai Khidmatgar* called themselves *Khudai Khidmatgar*, but that God was not in need of service (*khidmat*). Service to God is service to His creations (to humanity); and that His creations were not only the Muslims, but all His creations – whether Hindu, Sikh or Christian. It was incumbent upon us to eliminate oppression from the world and to save the oppressed from the clutches of the oppressors. We would always oppose that nation and government which oppresses humanity, even if the oppressor is our Muslim brother. The other thing is that our service will always be selfless and for the sake of God alone. No matter how much we are oppressed, we shall not seek to take revenge, in fact, we shall be patient and try to reform the oppressors. When the *jalsa* ended, we went for the night to Sudham. Here, our companions *Amir* Muhammad Khan, Mehrdil Khan and Shakirullah Jan Bacha, and their associates, had done some excellent work. Here, too, a large *jalsa* was held. The women of this area had also been motivated with the passion of freedom. After the tour of this area, a large *jalsa* was held in Saleem Khan Derai, where all the Moomand inhabitants of the area had collected. I explained the aims and objectives of our movement to them: that this movement of ours was one of brotherhood, and we are trying to create a brotherhood among all the Pukhtuns, to drive away anger, petty kinsman rivalries and enmities from their hearts, so that all this could make for unity, sympathy, love and amity, and all Pukhtuns are welded into one nation.

'Oh brothers!' I said, 'If you make yourselves into one nation, then no enemy can subjugate you, and exploit the wealth of your land which God has blessed you with. But because of your disunity, others are enjoying the spoils of your land. You will be able to attain success both in this world and the next. And this is such a potentially rich land that not one of you will remain poor, you will all be khans.'

It was a very successful *jalsa* and the people understood the aims and objectives of the movement, and it dispersed to the deafening slogans of 'Inquilab Zindabad!' and '*Fakhr-e-Afghan Zindabad*!' We proceeded onto Manga Dargai and met with people there.

Our movement here was progressing very well and we held many meetings. Due to all this touring and public speaking, my voice had become hoarse and hurt my throat. I fell sick and tried to take some rest, but rest was not part of my fate. If I did not move out to meet people, they would come to the village to meet me. I could not rest. I would do my best to make them understand but failed. This was a demonstration of their love for me and would take offence if I would not talk to them.

The Excessive Brutalities and Oppression of the British

The government of Sarhad did not care for the success of temporary truce brought about by the Gandhi–Irwin Pact[25]. Every day it would bring in a new order or law against us. First, the *Khudai Khidmatgars* were forbidden to enter the cantonment areas; then they were stopped from using the main roads. Then orders were issued proscribing the holding of *jalsa* for four miles on either side of the main roads, and wearing the uniform in public was also banned. In addition to all this, movement from area to area and the assembly of four or more people was prohibited by orders issued under Section 144 of the criminal procedure code. The police was authorized to arrest without a warrant from a magistrate. Police *raj* (rule) was imposed in the Frontier Province. One day, I was on my way to offer condolences on the death of a son of Khan Bahadur *Mian* Musharraf Shah sahib. I was accompanied by four *Khudai Khidmatgars* clad in uniforms. When I approached the Jrando Adda near Mardan, on seeing us a police sentry ran and shut the main gate of the road and refused to allow our car to proceed further. There being no other way, we got out of the car and told him that this was the main road and there was no other access road and requested him to open the gate. He retorted that he did not know anything of main roads; that his orders were not to allow anyone in red to travel on this road. If anyone were to object, he was to shoot them. He pointed his rifle at us and dared us to move on. Those who recognized me pleaded with him to open the gate. But he was under orders from his officer and could not open the gate. We returned and took the road along the canal bank and came out near the Police Lines and informed the *thanedar* of what had transpired. He suggested it would be best for us to meet with their sahib, i.e. officer. I replied that this was his sahib's own order and what could possibly come out of the meeting? That they should consider that if this was the treatment given to me, what must be the treatment given to the common *Khudai Khidmatgars?*

In the villages, the policemen would beat innocent people; they would ride through the villages mounted on horses and violate purdah of the women. But we on our part stuck fast to the truce and refrained from doing anything for which we could be blamed. All these adversities we bore with great patience. Finally, things came to such a pass that, instead of the usual physical beating, the *Khudai Khidmatgars* would be killed in cold blood. The practice was that at night the offices of the *Khudai Khidmatgar* movement would be raided by the border police, and whoever was on duty would be arrested. Whatever he had on him would be stolen and he would be shot. Similarly, a subedar of Urmar village, who was a *Khudai Khidmatgar*, was also killed. The poor man kept shouting out to them that it was him, the subedar, but he was martyred. The inhabitants of the village overpowered and disarmed the police, but our movement had influenced and brought about such a transformation in the Pukhtuns, that they did not subject them to any violence. They only reported the matter, and when the assistant commissioner came, they returned the confiscated weapons. The British were infuriated at the fact that violence was not resorted to. The British would compel the people to resort to violence so that they could have an excuse to really take their own out on them and destroy them in the process. The *Khudai Khidmatgars* were non-violent; they had entrusted their lives to God and were of the belief that, one day, their sacrifices would bear fruit and freedom would dawn. The British tried to instigate us to violence, for which they had an answer, but they had no answer to non-violence. The British would often say that, 'The non-violent Pathan is more dangerous than the violent.'

When we returned from the annual session of the Congress in Karachi, the governor of our province expressed the desire to meet with me and sent messages through several people. But when I saw the oppression and brutality of the British, my heart could not come to terms to meet him. I saw no prospect of any good for the nation emerging from it, because on the one hand, our Ranizai detainees were not set free, and on the other, due to a play staged by the children (in Babara), they had arrested them and subjected the *Khudai Khidmatgars* to a reign of terror. For these reasons, I rejected the offer. However, despite this the government was insistent that I should meet them. So, one day my older brother, Dr. Khan Sahib, came and told me that since the government was so keen on it, I should meet them. But I asked him why the governor would not like to meet with the president and the secretary of our party, because they were the people in authority and I had no responsibility. And if they wanted to meet me, I would do so on the condition that they were prepared, in all sincerity, to solve the problems to which our party had been subjected. But the governor did not agree to this and informed me that, in politics, there was no sincerity. So, I sent back the message that if there was no sincerity in politics, I would not like to meet him because my politics was based on sincerity. And thus the meeting could not be held.

After a few days, *Mian* Ahmad Shah went to see the Deputy Inspector General Police of the province, Mr. Lawther, who was the head of the CID. They both went to call on the governor, where he raised the issue of my refusal to meet him. On this, *Mian* sahib came to me and insisted that I should do so. I told him that I had no objection to meeting him but that I could not see any benefit in this; that the discussion which he had with the governor was not reassuring, nor was the response of the British about their troops in Prang; that they (the British) had the power and the authority, and (hence) their response was blocking of the road, considering the policeman who blocked the road was one of our own Khattak tribe. However, my rejection offended *Mian* sahib and he called the *jirga* into session and put forth this issue for consideration. The *jirga*, by an overwhelming majority, decided there was no need to hold this meeting. This offended him even further. With much pleading by Qazi sahib and Ali Asghar Khan, *Mian* sahib was persuaded to agree with the majority decision. When I asked why Ghulam Muhammad Khan and Firdos Khan had raised their voice in favour of the meeting, they laughingly replied that they had done so out of fear, that if I did not meet with the governor, they would be arrested, and a fight would start.

When the workers of a party take decisions based on fear, it harms the nation and the party. The government did not allow this matter to rest here. The government informed the viceroy about it and started a false propaganda campaign against me (stating) that I hated the British and I had personal enmity with them, which is why I refused to meet them. The viceroy also complained to Gandhiji along these lines. Gandhiji wrote to me to meet with the governor and said that he appreciated the reasons for which I did not want to meet him. Finally, I was compelled to place the matter before the executive committee of the *jirga* and, with its permission, met with the governor in the Government House in Nathiagali.

I informed the governor about the oppression of *Khudai Khidmatgars* and the prisoners of Ranizai, but despite these talks, there was no perceptible change in the policy of the government. In fact, the measures taken to curb the movement became even harsher. The truth is that all these meetings are not intended for the welfare of the people and the nation. Their main purpose is how to deceive and misguide one; how to make him forget his aim and succeed in winning his cooperation. In all the meetings that I have had with the authorities, I have not been able to see anything else but inducements in them. The government, on the pretext of people not paying land revenue tax, began to implement a series of harsh policy measures. Not that the *Khudai Khidmatgars* had refused to pay land revenue, but the price of grain had become so cheap that the landowners were fed up and were unable to pay the land revenue. The arrears of land revenue had not only piled up against the *Khudai Khidmatgars* more than them, the arrears were outstanding against the 'government maliks' and the khans. But no action was taken against them. Only the unfortunate *Khudai Khidmatgar* were harassed. Their cattle was auctioned and they were imprisoned, and a propaganda was carried out against them that they were refusing to pay the land tax and also persuading others not to do so. This was totally false. The people had no money to pay land revenue with, and nor did the *Khudai Khidmatgars*. The *Khudai Khidmatgars* would say to the government that it should treat them as it did everybody else; that they were also their 'subjects'. When some people found out that the government was pleased with the *Khudai Khidmatgars* being harassed, they instituted false cases against them. In Doaba area, the *Khudai Khidmatgars* were subjected to great injustice at the hands of Jabbar Khan and Malik Almir. In Abazai, Aftab Gul *Mian*, Yahya Gul *Mian* and their kinsmen and relatives locked the *Khudai Khidmatgars* into rooms and set their haystacks on fire to asphyxiate them. These Kakakhel *mians* had such love and affection for the British and were so loyal to them, that whenever they would hear of the arrival of the *Khudai Khidmatgars*, they would pick up their guns and would be prepared to kill them. I cannot describe the cruelties that Abdullah Jan *Mian* and his son inflicted on the common people on the pretext of recovery of land revenue. He had confined people to rooms and tried to asphyxiate them with smoke from the haystacks. And Fazal-ur-Rehman Khan of Shabqadar also humiliated the women. In our villages in Hashtnagar, the police *thanedar* would go on tour asking people whether there were any *Khudai Khidmatgar* here. If there were, they would be beaten and humiliated in public. Once, a few children from Shakoor village, in Malakand Agency, were on their way to visit me. When the police found out, it first tried to intimidate them, but when this did not have any effect, they beat them mercilessly and broke their heads. One of these children with a broken head was sent to Gandhiji, who was then in Simla, by my brother Dr. Khan Sahib. He told Gandhiji the whole story. The truth is that the British had gone totally mad in those days and did not differentiate between the innocent and the guilty. Gandhiji informed the viceroy of all this through a letter, informing him that he wanted to go to Sarhad to investigate this. But the viceroy refused to give him permission. The British were responsible for all the atrocities to which the Pukhtuns were subjected. They did not want Pukhtuns to organize themselves, develop unity and political consciousness in their ranks.

Devadas Gandhi's Tour of the North-West Frontier Province

Mahatma Gandhi wrote again to the viceroy that if the government did not allow him to visit the Frontier, then it should permit either Jawaharlal Nehru or Sardar Patel to do so and conduct an inquiry into the situation in the region. But the government refused this option as well. Gandhiji then wrote to the viceroy asking for permission for his son, Devadas. This was refused as well. Finally, when Gandhiji got frustrated with the government, he wrote to the viceroy and declared his intention of visiting the Frontier, irrespective of whether permission was granted or not. It was only after this that Devadas was allowed on the condition that there would be no *jalsa* or *jaloos*. Devadas came but we did not organize a welcoming *jaloos* for him. When he arrived, he informed us of Gandhiji's wishes. When we were about to leave Peshawar for Uthmanzai, we told Devadas that, from Peshawar to Uthmanzai, all along the road at ten yards, we intended to post *Khudai Khidmatgars* for his protection. But he advised against this. The next day when we arrived in Tehkal, we learnt that Arbab Abdul Ghafoor Khan and Ashiq Shah Bacha of Bahadur Killi and many innocent *Khudai Khidmatgars* in Tarkha had been arrested by the government. Also, that the father of Arbab Abdul Ghafoor, Arbab Juma Khan, had arranged a meal for Devadas. All our workers from the Khalil and Moomand tracts were present and informed Devadas about all the cruelty that the government had inflicted on us. The next day, we left for Uthmanzai. When we were leaving Peshawar, we had no car. So we sat in a lorry. When we crossed Shahibagh, the car of Zarin Khan of Torangzai approached us. Two good looking *Khudai Khidmatgars*, immaculately attired in their uniforms, were seated in it with a red flag flying on the car. We got down from the lorry and sat in the car with red flag. Devadas, Khurshid Behan and I occupied the rear seat and sped away. A notorious dacoit, who was known as Qazi Mafroor, was stationed by Kulli Khan, the assistant political officer of the Moomand area, in the jungle of bull-rushes on the bank of the Sardariab river. When our car approached, and the dacoit saw the two *Khudai Khidmatgars* sitting in the front, he thought that this must be the general's car, and so he retreated into the bull-rushes. The dacoits did not know that we were travelling by car, because we had left the bus stand in a lorry. But the lorry, which was following us was intercepted and fired at. This was the lorry in which we were travelling initially. Some passengers were wounded while all the others were deprived of their valuables. When the lorry reached Charsadda, we were informed of the mishap. The driver of our car also informed us that he had seen a man rise from the rushes. In all probability, they must have thought that this car seemed to be that of the general because it also had a flag and he believed that some soldiers were sitting in it. They had also been informed in advance by Kulli Khan that Bacha Khan and his companions had left in the lorry. That is why they did not pay any attention to the car and fired at the lorry. We went to the hospital in Charsadda to meet the wounded. When the people heard about these dacoits and what they had done, they came out in search of them along with the *Khudai Khidmatgars* from Agra and the surrounding villages but could not find them. When they (the dacoits) reached Tirah, our Afridi brethren had already learnt of the incident. They caught them and took back the valuables they had looted and killed the leader, Qazi Mafroor. They also took from them the money that Kulli Khan had given to them for committing the crime. They sent the money and the valuables to us which we promptly returned to the owners. This included a pistol too.

Our Afridi brethren were of the view that if these guests of the Pukhtuns, Devadas and Khurshid Behan, had been killed by them, the Pukhtuns would have been put to shame across Hindustan. This was the reason that the Afridis killed the dacoits; otherwise, the tribesmen do not kill those who take refuge with them. The British were prepared to give the Afridis a lot of money as ransom for the safe return of these outlaws, but they refused to oblige.

I am grateful to God that this plan of the government failed. If Gandhiji's son or Khurshid Behan, who was the granddaughter of Dadabhai Naoroji (a well-known Parsi member of the Congress), who was a founder of the Congress Party, had been killed here in the Frontier, the British would have got an opportunity to carry out a propaganda campaign against the Pukhtuns. They would have disgraced the Pukhtuns all over the world and made both the Hindus and the Parsis highly critical of them. And the good impression about the Pukhtuns which had been created by the *Khudai Khidmatgars* in Hindustan and on the Congress Party would have been sullied. This would also have led to parting of ways with the Congress, leaving the *Khudai Khidmatgars* alone to face the brutalities of the British, and would have left the Pukhtuns shamefaced before the world. But our *Khudai Khidmatgars* are selflessly serving God by serving humanity. He too has, on every occasion, helped us and saved us from the mischievous schemes of our enemies.

From Uthmanzai we left for Doaba because on the pretext of recovery of land revenue, the people of this area had also been subjected to cruelties. In Shabqadar a woman and her young daughter were subjected to such cruelty that we all wept when we heard about them. She informed us that even now she was not being allowed to come to us. That Khan Bahadar Kulli Khan had also pleaded with her that whatever she demanded would be done, but only if she did not testify before us. From Shabqadar, we then proceeded to Gonda where we recorded the evidence from the people. From here, we returned to Uthmanzai. On the return journey, I showed Devadas the dirty lock-up in the jail meant for those who had been brought in for non-payment of land revenue. Many khans were sitting here who were arrested. The next morning we went to the Malakand Agency, because here also the British had committed many brutalities. In Skhakot, in the *hujra* of Rahat Khan, we met many people of Ranizai who had collected and recorded all the atrocities inflicted upon them. Devadas wanted to visit Malakand and Chakdarra. We left but the police at Dargai locked the gate on the road to us. We telephoned the political agent of Malakand, telling him that we wanted to travel only up to Chakdarra on the road, but permission was not granted. So, we returned. At Dargai, a large crowd had collected. I told them that, 'Oh Pukhtun brothers! Give this matter some thought, that the land belongs to us but authority over it lies in foreign hands. We are not even allowed to roam about in it!' The next morning, we left for Mardan and Sawabai. From Mardan, I left for Nathiagali for my meeting with the governor of the Frontier, while Abdul Akbar Khan and *Mian* Ahmad Shah stayed behind with Devadas Gandhi who was taken all over the province. I recounted tales of the brutalities of the British to the governor, Mr. Pears. He laughed and said that he had summoned Olaf Caroe, the deputy commissioner of Peshawar. That he had a small head but was hot-headed, and he would put some ice on it to cool his brain down. Even after this meeting there was no difference in the tough attitude of the British. The governor also told me that they had decided to send me to the Round Table Conference, as a representative of the Frontier. I informed him that we had already taken a decision in this regard, which was that there would only be one representative of the *Khudai Khidmatgars* and the Congress and that would be Mahatma Gandhi. The governor was somewhat taken by surprise on hearing this but did not say anything. The meeting ended and while bidding me farewell, the governor said that he hoped that I would keep my *Khudai Khidmatgars* under control. I replied that I could keep the *Khudai Khidmatgars* in control but that he, too, should control his people.

I took leave and came to Changla Gali to spend the night with Dr. Khan Sahib, who was there for the summer. The next day, I met my daughter Mehr Taj in Murree. She was studying at the Jesus and

Mary Convent at the time. I also met Sheikh Taimur sahib who was later the principal of the Islamia College, Peshawar, and was very kind to me. For the night, I came to Peshawar and the next morning left for Uthmanzai. The next day, Devadas and his companions also returned from the tour of the province and we decided to leave for Bombay. The president of the *Khudai Khidmatgar*, Abdul Akbar Khan, and the secretary, *Mian* Ahmad Shah, impressed upon me to try and substitute the Congress Committee, with the provincial *jirga* of the *Khudai Khidmatgars* and that, instead of two organizations, there should only be one. That evening, we were the guests of *Mian* Ahmad Shah. Muhammad Zaman *Mian* sahib persuaded *Mian* Ahmad Shah to accompany us to Bombay. Devadas and I were very pleased at his accompanying us, and so we left for Bombay the next day. On the way, Devadas and *Mian* sahib put in order their papers regarding the Inquiry.

13

The Round Table Conference

A MEETING OF THE ALL-INDIA CONGRESS COMMITTEE WAS BEING HELD in Bombay for which members from all over India had come. When we arrived at the Bombay railway station, *Mian* Ahmad Shah came to me looking very grim. He told me that Devadas had asked him to stay where the Congress delegates were accommodated and that this amounted to his being rejected by them. *Amir* Muhammad Khan of Hoti informed him that he had been told the same thing but that he had told Devadas that he would stay wherever *Fakhr-e-Afghan* sahib was to stay. But *Mian* sahib said that he had been told not to stay with them and could not go with them. I tried to reason with *Mian* sahib but to no avail. One of my Muslim companions had come to the railway station and had brought a car and I managed to convince *Mian* sahib to travel with them but *Mian* sahib was greatly offended. The next day, we went to call on *Mian* sahib but his mood was still off. A Pukhtun benefactor from Galyara village told me that *Mian* sahib was so very upset that he was planning to leave for his village. When Devadas heard of these developments, he told him that he had asked him to do so for his own benefit, because, here, he would be inconvenienced by having to sleep on the floor with dal chapati for a diet, whereas the arrangements for the guests of the Congress Party were much better. Even this failed to satisfy *Mian* sahib. I also pleaded with him not to go back, so that we could decide on our pending issue of the provincial *jirga* with the Congress high command. Plus, the other group of the Congress from Peshawar was also here, which is why his presence was extremely essential. The next day, by the time we realized, *Mian* sahib had left for the village. Our proposal was placed before the Congress Working Committee, and for us, the name of *Da Subah Sarhad Loya Jirga* (*the grand jirga of the Sarhad*) was approved and I was authorized to structure it as I pleased.

Differences between the Members of the *Jirga*

A brother of ours from Peshawar city, Sardar Abdur Rab Nishtar, raised an objection that the *Khudai Khidmatgar* were not really bound by the principles of the Congress, on the contrary, that we were raising slogans sectarian in nature. For example, he said that we raised the cry of '*Nara-e-Takbeer, Allah-u-Akbar!*' Gandhiji asked him the meaning of *Allah-u-Akbar*. Nishtar sahib answered with 'God is great!', to which Gandhiji said, 'What, was God ever small?' So, he failed in his attempt. After this we left for the Frontier. On arrival, I set to work and left on a tour of Mardan and Sawabai. Although *Mian* sahib was annoyed with Devadas, he ended up harming his own people. He became my opponent and tried to establish another party when we reached the village. He also convened a meeting of the Frontier *Loya Jirga*, to motivate it against accepting the decision taken in the Congress Working Committee at Bombay. I was informed of this, and so I arrived on the day of this *jirga*. *Mian* sahib placed a proposal against the decision in Bombay and delivered a speech in this regard. It was supported by Abdul Akbar Khan and Ghulam Muhammad Khan of Lundkhwar. I then apprised the members about the reason for this decision. The members agreed with me and the Bombay decision was confirmed. When I went on tour to Sawabai, I was very pleased because the *Khudai Khidmatgar* here had worked very diligently in every village. Each village now had its own *jirga* and the *Khudai Khidmatgar* had enrolled themselves in great numbers in the movement. Our movement was at its best either in Charsadda *tehsil* or in Sawabai *tehsil*. The *Khudai Khidmatgar* of Sawabai told me a very interesting story. They asked me whether I knew that they had a very old relationship with Haji sahib of Torangzai. They told me that when I first came to the area and the *Khudai Khidmatgar* movement started, they had gone to call on Haji sahib in Ghaziabad in the Moomand territory. There they broached the subject of the *Khudai Khidmatgar* with the eldest son of Haji sahib, Fazl-e-Akbar Bacha Gul. He had warned them against joining the movement, saying that it was not a good movement. They were surprised to hear this. They then asked Haji sahib privately because he was their

pir. They informed him that Bacha Khan had started the movement
in their area and that they, along with many others, had joined the
movement. They asked him to tell them whether the movement
was good or not. Haji sahib asked them whether the movement was
for or against the British. They told him that it was against them.
He then told them that this was a jihad; that he had not been able
to effectively oppose the British. That he had escaped from their
clutches and sought refuge in these black hills, and that Bacha Khan
had put his chest out as a shield to the difficulties of imprisonment.
They told me that he advised them to join the movement and
strengthen his (Bacha Khan's) hands. They informed Haji sahib
of Torangzai that his eldest son had told them not to be part of
the *Khudai Khidmatgar*. He sent for him and advised him not
to speak in this way, or else he would disinherit him! The *Khudai
Khidmatgar* of Sawabai said that they were pleased that Haji sahib
stood firmly with me.

When the provincial *jirga* decided in my favour, *Mian* Ahmad
Shah resigned from the post of president, which was accepted, and
the members left for their villages. I was feeling somewhat unwell
from the strain of the tours. I went to Peshawar so that Dr. Khan
Sahib could treat me and to get some rest. But Ramzan Khan of Dera
Ismail Khan came and asked me to accompany him to Dera where
there had been a lot of destruction. The government had instigated
the Hindus and Muslims into fighting each other and many people
had been killed, and a lot of property and infrastructure had been
burnt down.

My Visit to Simla

When I arrived in Peshawar, I received a telegram from Mahatma
Gandhi urging me to leave for Simla immediately. Ramzan Khan
and I decided that, on return from Simla, I would go straight to
Dera Ismail Khan. When Ramzan Khan told me about the killing
of the Hindus and the destruction of their properties, I understood
that the British had avenged themselves for the enthusiastic
welcome they had given me on my first tour of Dera when the *jaloos*
walked through the entire town, which had been beautified for the
occasion. The deputy commissioner had specifically instructed them
not to attend my *jalsa* or *jaloos* and, if they did, there would be
destruction. But they did not agree. I was very upset to hear about

this unfortunate event and wondered how long the British would shame our Muslim brothers all over the world by involving them in such heinous activities.

I left for Simla by train with two *Khudai Khidmatgar* volunteers. When our train reached Lahore, Sardar Sardool Singh Kolishar, along with some other companions and friends, had come to the station. The Sikhs were holding a big conference in the city and they had come to attend it. The venue of the *jalsa* was close to the station so they made me go with them. In the *jalsa* I met with all my Gujarat jail inmates. It was raining and so I delivered a brief speech and told my Sikh brothers that, in 1857, it was due to them in Punjab and us in Sarhad that Hindustan became a slave. Now, it was our collective duty to rise and liberate Hindustan. The friction and divisions which the British had created between us were very dangerous for the liberation of Hindustan; that we should selflessly serve the cause of the nation and of the land. When the *jalsa* concluded, Raizada Hansraj sahib forced us to accompany him to Jalandhar. From Jalandhar we left by train and finished the last leg of the journey by road. Jawaharlal Nehru had come to receive us at the bus station in Simla. We accompanied him to Mahatmaji's residence but he had left for a meeting with the viceroy. Once he returned, Mahatmaji briefed us about his meeting. He told Jawaharlal and me that the government was not prepared for an inquiry into the affairs of the United Provinces and the Frontier. Now, it was up to both of us to decide on a future course of action. We both replied that whatever he considered appropriate, we would support it. It was decided that Mahatma Gandhi should attend the Round Table Conference. Previously, it had been decided that if the government refused to investigate the atrocities committed in these two provinces, Gandhiji should not attend the Round Table Conference. However, we arrived at this conclusion after great consideration that the Round Table Conference was concerned with the freedom of the entire Hindustan and the refusal of the government to conduct an inquiry into the brutalities committed in two provinces was not enough reason for Gandhiji to not attend the conference. Cars arrived and the luggage was loaded. When Gandhiji spoke with Emerson, the Home Secretary, over the phone, he found that apart from the inquiry into the affairs of the two provinces, the government had backed down from other decisions that had already been agreed upon with Mahatma Gandhi.

Mahatmaji offloaded his baggage and asked the cars to leave and decided against attending the Round Table Conference. When the cars were about to leave, Jawaharlal told Gandhiji that arrangements needed to be made because they only had one day before the scheduled date of departure. The drivers of the cars needed to be told to remain ready for tomorrow. Mahatmaji was very peeved on hearing this and retorted that there was no need for arrangements. He said that, 'If the Government wants that I participate in this Conference, then it should take care of the arrangements for me to get to the port on time.' I told Gandhiji that he should remain firm in his stand and speak firmly to the government, and that he would see it would agree to all his demands because this was a strange government. Gandhiji laughed and said that he was now prepared to become a *Khudai Khidmatgar*. It happened as I had predicted. The next day the government agreed to all his demands and decided on a special car to take Gandhiji (to the port), and made reservations via telegram through the Bombay mail, directing the ship not to sail witout him on board. At the time of departure, Gandhiji said that though he had no hope of any outcome.of the Conference, he was going only to please Lord Irwin; that there was no hope for success of the Conference and that we should continue with our work. He added that Howell, the Foreign Secretary and Emerson, the Home Secretary, had written to him that they did not want to meet him but wanted to meet them (the *Khudai Khidmatgar*). I told him that I had no desire to meet the Englishmen but would meet if he so desired. At the time of his departure, I said to him, 'Gandhiji, the Frontier is poor and oppressed. Please don't forget it!' On hearing this he laughed and said, 'How can I forget my Sarhad brothers!' Both my *Khudai Khidmatgar* companions went ahead of Gandhiji and me, and we followed. There was such commotion that I was left far behind in the crowd, while the two *Khudai Khidmatgar* companions accompanied him to the station. Just before boarding the train Gandhiji pulled the two *Khudai Khidmatgars* close to him and said that if they had not been there, he would not have been able to make it to the station.

Our Engagements in Simla
When the police officials and the people observed the *Khudai Khidmatgar* on this occasion, they were impressed by our behaviour

and the way we managed things and praised us. The *Khudai Khidmatgar* established their good reputation in Simla, and when we walked through the bazaars, let alone others, the English and their ladies would run after us and point us out as 'the red-shirts.'

The next day, the son of Khan Bahadur from Punjab, who was a student in Islamia College, Peshawar, invited me for a cup of tea. I told him that his father was an employee of the government and that he might come to grief. But he did not agree, so I accepted his invitation. The father of this student lived in the Cecils Hotel. We were invited to tea there. I, along with other two *Khudai Khidmatgars*, went to the hotel. Many Englishmen were sitting, drinking tea. When they saw us, they were surprised. The host had arranged a special place for us to have our tea. He had also invited Sir Feroz Khan Noon, who was a minister in Punjab at the time, and two contractors from Punjab. Sir Feroz Khan Noon arrived shortly after we sat down, and when he saw me, he raised a hue and cry saying, 'Khan Sahib! What a calamity that you have teamed up with the Congress! Now they will not give us our due share.' I suggested that we sit down and talk. When he calmed down a little, I said, 'Malik sahib, what else could we have done? We have been sent to the Congress by you. If you had helped us, what need was there for us to ally ourselves with the Congress? We had first come to you at Lahore and told the Muslim League that, as Muslim brothers, our movement was common and a movement of reform. We are not against the government of the British. We want to reform our own people. But the British have let loose a reign of terror on us, and the world was unaware of our plight. We expected the Muslim League to bring our position to notice of the world, and ask the British what sin the Pukhtuns had committed that they were being subjected to such brutalities. We also went to Delhi and Simla to meet with the leaders of Muslim League, but you did not extend a helping hand. In these circumstances, what else could we do? We were compelled. The flood was drowning us, and the Congress gave us a helping hand. So, we allied ourselves with them. And even now,' I told him, 'if the Muslims of Punjab extend a hand of friendship, we would not bother to seek the friendship of the remaining Muslims of Hindustan. If you are willing to do this, we are prepared to part ways with the Congress.' The Working Committee of the Congress was in session and I suggested that I would resign from it. In response, Sir Feroz Khan Noon said, 'We will consider and then give you a reply.' His reply, of course, never came. After sixteen years, I met him in the province of Bihar where communal riots had broken out on a large scale and said to him, 'Malik sahib, I am still waiting for an answer from you!' He laughed and lowering his eyes in shame, went away.

When our discussions and tea ended, our host invited us to lunch in Simla the next day. When we arrived for lunch, English men and English women were sitting there while arrangements for us were made in a separate place. We were accompanied by representatives of the *Civil and Military Gazette* of Lahore, and *The Statesman* of Calcutta. The editor of the English daily started a conversation with me saying that, now that a truce had been established, there was no need for the *Khudai Khidmatgar* and that I should immediately dissolve this movement. I told him that I agreed but on one condition, that the British should leave this country and give it freedom. This movement would then automatically come to an end. On hearing this, he lost his temper and all of us seated around the table laughed at him. Most guests took their leave after lunch. Only Khan Bahadur sahib, his son and the journalists from Calcutta remained. Khan Bahadur sahib asked me about the *Khudai Khidmatgar*. I recounted the history of the movement to him. He then informed me that he had received many false reports about this movement of ours, but now he realized that this was very a good movement and its purpose was to be of service to humanity. Finally, he told me that he, too, was a *Khudai Khidmatgar* and would like to be photographed with my two companions. He then brought an English photographer and took a photograph with us.

Meeting with the Foreign and Home Secretaries

Early evening, a letter arrived from Mr. Howell, the Foreign Secretary, to see him the next day at ten in the morning. The letter also informed that a rickshaw would be sent for me. I thanked him for the offer but informed him that I was a *Khudai Khidmatgar* and did not take rides in rickshaws pulled by men, and that I would walk to his office.

The next day, exactly at 10:00 a.m., I arrived at his bungalow. He came out and took me into his office. After a while, Mr. Wylie, the Assistant Foreign Secretary, also arrived. He was well-known to me. He had been the deputy commissioner of Peshawar and had also been a settlement officer. I told them all that needed to be said. He said that the relations between the Pukhtuns and them were always very cordial and asked what had happened to drive a wedge between them and us? I looked at Mr. Howell and told him to put this question to Mr. Wylie, as he was well aware of what had happened and who was responsible for it all. A discussion took place between me and Mr. Howell about the movement. Mr. Howell indicated the possibility of extremely pleasant 'prospects' for me, but I told him that I could live on two paisas: one for a roti, and one for a fried eggplant. That God had gifted me with everything and whatever I was demanding was for the benefit of my people. In reality, and just like Mr. Howell had said, the relationship between the Pukhtuns and the British was always good. Amongst the British, it was people like Mr. Griffiths, Jamieson, Major Cole and Caroe who came and ruined this relationship. At this point a telephone call came from Mr. Emerson, the Home Secretary, who wanted me to meet him on the way back from here at his bungalow. Mr. Howell was a gentleman and spoke to me very politely. He had spent his entire career with the Pukhtuns in the Frontier. When our meeting ended, Mr. Wylie said he would escort me to the office of the home secretary. Mr. Howell himself walked with me to his office, he neither got into a rickshaw nor mounted a horse. His horse was brought behind us by the stable boy. The home secretary's orderly was waiting for me. The foreign secretary and I took leave of each other, and the orderly guided me to the home secretary's office. The home secretary was a strange man. He first told me that I had delivered a speech at Meerut saying the British had white faces but black hearts. That if he published the contents of my speech in the newspapers in London, nothing would be given to the province and all the British would turn against me. I told him that I had explained the reasons for this statement in my speech, and that I would be happy if my speech were to be published. Not only should this part of my speech be published, but all of it should be published so that the people of England get to know the truth. He said, 'You are trying to put pressure on the government by saying that if it does not give us our rights, we will resort to various kinds of actions against it. Has the British government become so weak that it would be afraid of your pressure tactics?' I told him that this was not any kind of pressure; that I was a *Khudai Khidmatgar* and that whatever my people desired, I informed the government accordingly. *Akhtar pat maylre ne dae* (Eid is not a secret paramour). If the government did not accede to our demands, then we would resolve the matter as we considered appropriate. The man softened a bit and said that they were ready to give us our rights. Finally, he told me that the *Khudai Khidmatgar* were not really bound by non-violence; they always resort to violence. I told him to cite some examples. At this he called in his secretary and directed him to produce the file. He did so, but no evidence of violence could be identified. He told me that when the leaders were arrested in Sarband, the people accompanied them up to the thana raising the slogans of '*Inqilab Zindabad*!' I told him that I had today, for the first time, learned from him that sloganeering was violence. When innocent leaders are arrested and taken to the thana, people accompany them shouting slogans. The meeting came to an end and I took leave of the home secretary. How different Emerson and Howell were from each other. The truth is that Emerson had served in Punjab, and Howell had served in the Frontier with Pukhtuns. When I was going back to my hotel, the editor and reporters of *The Statesman* of Calcutta, together with my host of the tea and lunch, were waiting for me. They forced me to accompany them to Cecils Hotel. When we were seated in the editor's room, they told me that I should call on the viceroy the next day. Khan Bahadur sahib also came in and supported this proposal. I told them that I had wanted to meet Lady Willingdon, but that she was sick. So for this reason, I was not prepared to see only the viceroy and would meet both on some other occasion. I had no desire to meet the viceroy because I had no business to discuss with him. But they insisted and so I agreed that if he were to write an invite to me, I would meet him. They informed me that he would not do this. So, I told them that I, too, had never requested anyone for a meeting. They told me that even Mahatmaji wrote to the viceroy for a meeting. I told them that **that** must be his principle, and that **this** was mine. When I had no business to transact with him, what was the need for a meeting? In Simla I was staying with my friend Rai Bahadur sahib. They telephoned him and put forth another proposal. But I rejected that as well. The next day they talked to Rai Bahadur sahib over telephone and won him over to their side. In short, he told me not to write a letter to the viceroy for a meeting and that this should be done by my secretary. Since I had no work with the viceroy, all this talk about seeking a meeting with him seemed counter-productive to me. But all these companions forced me and had a letter written to the viceroy. It was signed by Taj Muhammad, as my secretary. They telephoned the viceroy's secretary and said that they were sending a letter seeking an appointment with the viceroy, which should immediately be shown to him. He felt pleased and I informed Rai Bahadur sahib that they were forcing me to do something that was against my conscience. I added that whenever someone has compelled me to act against my conscience, its outcome has not been favourable. By the early evening a response came to the letter that the viceroy was not feeling well, and the meeting could not take place the next day. His secretary wrote a personal letter to me and expressed his sincere regrets over telephone, saying that the viceroy was not annoyed with me and that I should not misunderstand the response. The truth was that the viceroy had taken offence that I had not written personally to him. The contents of my meeting with Mr. Howell and Mr. Emerson had also been conveyed to him. I can, in hindsight, say that this was entirely my fault. I should not have entered into such conversations and arguments with these people. In such meetings, we should not speak too much. And if we are to confer or discuss anything, this should be with like-minded companions, who think like us. There is no need to convey our innermost feelings and thoughts to everyone.

I felt better after resting for a week in Simla. I met with many Hindus and Muslims and made efforts to remove all those misgivings and suspicions which the British had created in their hearts about the communal riots in Dera Ismail Khan. I told them the facts about the *Khudai Khidmatgar* movement and assured them that the organization had been founded with the purpose of service to humanity, for the freedom and development of the land. We also held a large *jalsa* in Simla in which I elaborated on the aims and objectives of our movement. On Friday, I offered prayers in the Jamia Masjid in Simla after which, I also delivered a short speech on the purpose for which Islam had been revealed, and the conditions of the Muslims of the time, and of today. Today they were living under slavery, and apparently liking it, although there was no slavery in Islam. I also met the consul general of Afghanistan. In short, during this brief sojourn, I promoted the cause of the *Khudai Khidmatgar* movement far beyond my hopes and expectations.

From Simla, I went to Ambala on the invitation of Lala Doonichand, an old friend from jail. In Ambala also we held a *jalsa* at night, after which I met with several Hindus and Muslims. The unfortunate Muslims, because of lack of leadership, have been deprived of every modicum of political consciousness. They have no political party, and nor do they work for any other political party.

From Ambala I travelled to Lahore to Pandit Santanam's home, also a friend from jail. We called a conference of representatives of the free press and rebutted all the malicious and tendentious news ascribed to me after my interview with the editor of the *Civil and Military Gazette* in Simla. He had reported in his paper that Bacha Khan was parting ways with the Congress. When this news reached Nawab Sir Sahibzada Abdul Qaiyum sahib, he sent a special messenger to me in Lahore, to warn me to beware and not to disassociate myself from the Congress, because if I did, the British would not concede any reforms for the Frontier Province. One of my friends from Lahore told me that whenever I came to Lahore, I always stayed with the Hindus and not with the Muslims. I told him that I had many Muslim friends in Lahore. Which one had ever extended an invitation to me that I have not obliged? I am a Pukhtun. The Pukhtuns, even in their own homes, do not sit down to a meal without an invitation.

14

Working in my Own Province

Tour of Dera Ismail Khan

WHEN I REACHED DERA ISMAIL KHAN, I FOUND THAT RAMZAN KHAN had been arrested by the government. The destruction in the city and the animosity and hatred between the Hindus and Muslims was very upsetting. I sent for some Muslim and Hindu elders from Kohat and Bannu to visit the city and try bring about reconciliation between the two communities. We conferred and met the Hindus and Muslims separately. On the one hand, the situation was very bad and, on the other, the government was interfering in it. It sent its men after the Hindus and the Muslims and would not let us resolve the issue. The poor Hindus would agree but the wealthy and influential amongst them would not let them arrive at a resolution. The Muslims played into the hands of the lawyers and would not agree to a truce, because they felt that their legal practice would be affected. In Dera, those residents who did not have a good relationship with the government were particularly affected. This was all the handiwork of the government. Sheikh Mahboob Ali Khan was the assistant commissioner in Dera; he had earlier destroyed Kabul for the British in the reign of Amanullah Khan and was now doing the same in Dera Ismail Khan.

Along with my companions, I went to Paniala and met with that Khan Bahadur and those so-called Red Shirts who had started the riots in Dera. The Khan Bahadur told me that Sheikh Mahboob Ali Khan, the assistant commissioner, had sent him two lorries to transport these men (the so-called Red Shirts) and that they were the collaborators of the government, and whatever they were instructed to do, they did. I told him that this may be the government but that this was his own nation, and no one committed such atrocities against one's own nation. His son, Ghulam Sarwar Khan, who had returned from Aligarh University, met with great affection. I requested him to make his father understand, that if tomorrow a national government was formed, what answer would he have to give to it? We took our leave and returned to Dera.

Through the good offices of Khan Bahadur Abdur Rahim Khan Kundi, Colonel Knowle, who was the deputy commissioner of Dera Ismail Khan, invited me for talks. But I did not consider it appropriate to visit him at his bungalow and informed Abdur Rahim Khan that if it was possible to meet him at his place, I would have no objection. The deputy commissioner also agreed. But Mr. Edmonds, who was the inspector general of police of our province and had come on tour to Dera, dissuaded the deputy commissioner from meeting me. But he himself had a meeting with me in the house of the Nawab of Dera. Though the inspector general was a good man, he was not good at deliberations. During the course of the discussion, he told me that he could arrest me any time for the speech I had delivered against the government with regard to the staging of the play at Babara, because a responsible companion of mine had put the blame on the organizers, whereas I had criticized and put the blame on the government. I told him to be the judge and decide whether the reaction of the government was not a joke blown out of all proportions; and whether making a mountain out of a molehill of a play put up by children was befitting for a mighty government of a nation such as theirs. He then asked me if I did not like the government, why did I not emigrate to some other land? On this I asked him whether this land was ours or his. He replied that it was ours. I told him that there was no reason why I should leave my land and settle in another. Would it not be a better proposition if they were to leave it to us, I asked? We dispersed after tea.

It was Ramzan Khan, who I went to meet in jail, described the riots in detail. I was busy negotiating a truce between the Hindus and Muslims, but to no avail. The opinion of the wealthy Hindus was that they had been put in a predicament at the hands of the *Khudai Khidmatgar*. They told me that because of this movement the authority and standing of the government that once existed was no more. The government was weakened and could no longer ensure peace and order, and they had been looted and destroyed consequently. They wanted a strong government. I laughed when

I heard this. I replied that it was fine by me, the government is not to blame. I asked him about the scale of loss he had sustained, and how many *Khudai Khidmatgar* were in the city. He said that he had personally suffered no loss and nor were there any *Khudai Khidmatgar* in this city. I told him that those who had suffered losses had given to me, in writing, that the riots were the outcome of the machinations of the government.

Return to Uthmanzai: The Problem of Ahmad Shah

During this period, I received a letter asking me to return at once to Uthmanzai because circumstances were such that it needed consultations. I did not go but continued in my efforts to bring about a truce between the Hindus and Muslims. But, instead of nearing a truce, we were moving further away from it. At this point, General Azmat Khan arrived with a letter requesting me to leave for Uthmanzai immediately. At night, when I asked Azmat Khan if everything was alright he told me that *Mian* Ahmad Shah had begun to oppose us. Our work in the city was in disarray. So, early the next morning we all left for Uthmanzai. When we arrived, *Mian* Ahmad Shah, in opposition to me, was busy in efforts to create his own faction within the *Khudai Khidmatgar*. He was also sowing disaffection amongst the members of the *jirga* and had started to correspond with them. I felt hurt, because I did not anticipate such a reaction from an educated person like *Mian* Ahmad Shah; that he would, on such petty provocation, try to create such disaffection and animosity among our people. I was further grieved by the fact that the government was extremely pleased at this turn of events and had instructed its officers to give all support to *Mian* Ahmad Shah, and oppose Abdul Ghaffar Khan. *Mian* Jafar Shah and Abdullah Shah wanted that I, along with some companions, should join them in their village and discuss matters face to face. I agreed and, the next day, Ahmad Shah, Abdullah Shah, Taj Muhammad Khan, Haji Abdul Ghaffar Khan, Abdul Akbar Khan and I, went to *Mian* Jaffar Shah sahib's village. After dinner, we started the discussion. Ahmad Shah and companions were talking randomly, without saying what was gnawing at his heart or was unable to do so. The night wore on, so I told him to come to the point. He still avoided doing so and, finally, said that the decision of the *Loya Jirga* was unacceptable to him, and that a *jalsa* should be held and this issue should be placed before it for a final decision. I responded that this was fine by us; but if the *jalsa* were to decide that we should not disassociate ourselves from the Congress, would he be prepared to accept that decision? He answered that he would then resign. I told him that he had already resigned; and that if he was not ready to accept the verdict of a *jalsa*, then what was the need to convene it? He then said that he had no faith in the Hindus and feared that they may deceive us and we would not be able to do anything about it. So, I should let them form another political party so that tomorrow, if need be, we are free to make our future plans independently. I replied that I was not a hypocrite and that I could not permit him to do so because I did not consider this beneficial for our nation. As for the Hindus deceiving us, there was no truth in this thinking that our alliance with the Congress was tantamount to our being tied to them, with no room to manoeuvre, despite what the Hindus did. Infact, I promised him that the day Congress deceived us, I would disassociate from it. He would then lead, and we would follow him, and whatever he ordered would be done. He should at least wait until then. After all, wht did he think of me. I did what I thought was best for my country. Abdullah Shah and Jafar Shah endorsed what I said and said that the Round Table Conference was in progress in London, that it was a time of 'gain or loss' for us, and that we should wait for its outcome and set aside our differences. They then mentioned a particular government official and told Ahmad Shah that they had been informed by the official to tell Ahmad Shah to let this matter rest, as the government was feeling extremely satisfied with this situation, and had sent orders to them to assist Ahmad Shah against Abdul Ghaffar Khan. We made *Mian* Sahib agree to abandon his opposition to me, and let events unfold and wait for the result.

We all felt happy at *Mian* sahib's reconciliation and went to sleep. The next morning, after prayers, Abdullah Shah, Abdul Akbar Khan, Haji Abdul Ghaffar Khan, Taj Muhammad Khan and I went to see *Mian* Jaffar Shah's orchard. However, after a while I was informed that *Mian* Ahmad Shah did not stand by his decision of the night before. He had now taken a different stand and had been able to get Abdul Akbar Khan on his side. At this juncture, a messenger came and informed us that breakfast was ready. When we sat down to breakfast, *Mian* Ahmad Shah again went over the same ground. I told him that we had already come to decisions on these matters the night before. Finally, Ahmad Shah *Mian* sahib revealed what was in his heart. He told me that he could not bear to see that everyone should agree with what one man said. I reminded him that everywhere in the world people followed one leader and that this was of benefit to the nation, for everyone to be united behind one man. This helped in achieving national objectives. But one should carefully consider whether what that man does is in his own interest or in the interest of the nation; whether he was doing it on his own, or in consultation with his colleagues. Leaders reach a certain position on the basis of their service to the nation and not on the basis of opposition; that he should put in more efforts than I do in the service of the nation and then it would listen to him more than to me; that when he was enjoying himself in London, I was undergoing hardship in jail. One positive outcome came out of these discussions that everyone became aware of the real intentions and objectives of *Mian* sahib. Abdullah Shah and Jaffar Shah exhibited a non-partisan approach. Abdul Akbar Khan stated that he would not take part in politics but promised that he would assist Haji Abdul Ghaffar Khan and Taj Muhammad Khan in the affairs of the school. We all left for our respective villages but Abdul Akbar Khan and *Mian* Abdullah Shah forced us to accompany them to Qazikhel. We realized that Abdul Akbar Khan was a weak person and we feared lest *Mian* sahib should deceive him. Abdullah Shah, who was a cousin of Ahmad Shah, did not wish him well. Abdullah Shah was a huge manipulator and was an expert in creating situations, and he was behind the staging of this drama.

We went to Ahmad Shah's village as guests of Akbar Jan, who was Abdullah Shah's brother. After lunch, Haji Abdul Ghaffar Khan approached me and said that Abdul Akbar Khan's attitude and views had completely changed. I asked him to make him understand, but he replied that this had been to no avail. On my return to the village I learnt that *Mian* Ahmad Shah and Abdul Akbar Khan had published a long article describing how we had melted like sugar in water and had lost our independent identity. This article carried the signatures of Ahmad Shah, Abdullah Shah and Abdul Akbar Khan. We collected some of our members and, on their advice, published a suitably worded response. After this, I left again with a few *Khudai Khidmatgars* on a tour of Dera Ismail Khan.

The Tour of Dera Ismail Khan

It was during this tour of the region that we learnt that the governor of our province, Sir Stuart Pears, had fallen down a hillside and died and that Sir Ralph Griffith, a former military officer, was appointed in his place. We knew Griffith's views and thinking, as he had a long career in our province. When he was the political resident for Waziristan, he had expressed his views on our movement to one of our *Khudai Khidmatgar* and said that if a little blood were to be shed, it would be good. On being appointed governor, he wrote to Simla that he wanted to arrest Abdul Ghaffar Khan and that this was a most opportune moment and it should be seized; that division had cropped up amongst us. But Simla did not agree with him, responding that the Round Table Conference was in session and the central government feared that Mahatma Gandhi might take a stand against the government in his (Ghaffar Khan's) favour. They wrote to him that these differences would automatically destroy our movement and there would be no need for any interference by them. They were looking at these developments from the perspective of the rest of Hindustan and little realized that the Pukhtuns were a different people. They were now alive and had not been politically conscious in the past, but had now been made aware of things.

We pressed on with our work and our tours because I could see that the government was intent on arresting us soon. We toured from village to village and made the people understand the situation and pressed the point that our struggle was based on non-violence. We would not take revenge from anyone, as we were *Khudai Khidmatgar* and God would take our revenge from the evil doers. We were on tour in Sabtano and having concluded our last *jalsa* at midnight had just returned, when Ubaidullah Khan of Umarzai, who was an SP in the police, came with a letter from the governor. The governor wanted to discuss my speeches, delivered in Dera Ismail Khan, and wanted me to return to Peshawar. I wrote to him that I did not make speeches that were against the law and if he had received any information to the contrary, this must be the fault of his secret police. Also, that I could not return at this juncture because I had informed people about my entire programme, and could not leave midway, but after concluding the scheduled tour of Dera Ismail Khan, would come to Peshawar. And if he still considered it necessary, I could then meet with him. The government did its best to make sure I do not tour certain areas of the district, and for this, sent Khan Bahadur Abdur Rahim Khan to me. But our local companions did not consider this appropriate and so we toured all the concerned areas. We then went to Bannu, where our General, Azmat Khan, had arrived before us to start the preliminary work. We conducted a village to village tour of Bannu district. When we left the village of Kakki for the Marwat area, we came across Saadullah Khan, Khurshid Behan and the brother-in-law of Jawaharlal. They told us that Jawaharlal had instructed them to immediately constitute the *Loya Jirga* of Sarhad and begin work according to the usual procedure. Agreeing with this instruction I asked them to send out invitations to people for the *jalsa*. We fixed a date for the meeting of the *jirga*, after which they left for Peshawar and I left Bannu for a tour of Kohat District. This was also conducted in a very orderly fashion. Here, we had thousands of *Khudai Khidmatgars*. We held the *jalsa* and toured from village to village and from *tapa* to *tapa*. Just as we had started our tours for the unity of the Pukhtuns, so had *Mian* Ahmad Shah commenced his, for their disunity. But one of his activities was in addition to ours. He would print posters against us and had initiated an adverse propaganda campaign in the press. The editors of the Punjab newspapers were his friends because their objective was to ruin the Pukhtuns. Our Generals, Inzar Gul and Abdul Malik *Ustaz* of Charsadda effectively countered this opposition of *Mian* Ahmad Shah and they failed in their mission. When we concluded our tour of Kohat and went for the night to Pir Shaheen sahib's house, some of our sincere companions from Hangu, who were concerned about *Mian* sahib's propaganda, came here for clarification and asked me what I had done by merging the separate party of the Pukhtuns with the Congress Party; that I used to lecture them that our party and movement was of the Pukhtuns. I told them that the movement was, as previously, a movement of the Pukhtuns and that we had only concluded an alliance with the Congress Party because they, too, wanted Hindustan to be liberated from the British, and that this decision to ally ourselves was taken by the *Loya Jirga*. That we were, at the time, in Gujarat jail when Abdullah Shah and Jafar Shah arrived and informed us that the British had started to treat the *Khudai Khidmatgar* very cruelly and wished to decimate the movement and sought advice as to what they should do. As I was not permitted to have visitors, Akbar Khan and Ahmad Shah met with them and we collectively advised that they should go and first see the leaders of the Muslim League. They returned to inform us that the Muslim League was not prepared to help us out, and that the Congress was of the view that since we wanted Hindustan to be liberated and had adopted the principle of non-violence as they had, they would be prepared to help us. We suggested that they should place the matter before the *Loya Jirga* for consideration. The *jirga's* verdict was that we should ally ourselves with the Congress. The put in the press the conditions we faced and a delegation of Congress leaders was sent to conduct an inquiry into these. This is the blessing of our alliance, that I am walking around as a free man and holding *jalsa* with you, otherwise I should have been jailed long before now. The fact that they were now busy in advancing the mission of the movement was also a blessing of the Congress, otherwise the British would never have allowed them to do so. They were re-assured by what I said and left for their village.

On our return to Peshawar we learnt that the British had taken a freight company to task, i.e., of the *ghalreebaanaan* associated with our movement. This was difficult work which could not be performed by the locals. These were all outsiders, mostly our Moomand brothers, who were all enrolled as *Khudai Khidmatgar.* The Government instituted cases against them and pressurized them to leave our movement or leave the land. Some of them had cases filed against them that they were not inhabitants of the country, and that they were being expelled under the relevant provisions of the law. These people were a strong, sturdy and hard-working lot and were true-blooded Pukhtuns. Their ancestors had migrated from Afghanistan and were living in the settled districts. They were told to go back to their country. The truth is that these poor people were residents of this land from the time of their grandfathers. We organized a large *jalsa* in Peshawar's salt trade market against the injustice of the British. This was attended by thousands of men and women. Our protest had a positive impact on the government's policy, in as much as it withdrew the criminal cases against these Moomand and relaxed its policy in this respect.

This continuous touring and lack of rest took a toll on my health. I left for the Murree Hills for a few days of rest. Qazi Attaullah and Ghulam Muhammad Khan were already there.

The *Loya Jirga* of Sarhad

The Congress had authorized me to reconstitute the Sarhad *Loya Jirga* as I pleased, but I collected all the members of the *jirga* in Peshawar and tried to ensure that no difference of opinion should arise in getting together with the Congress *Jirga*. However, our brothers from Peshawar did not agree to this. I told the delegates from Kohat and Bannu that I did not wish to arbitrarily appoint a president and that they should nominate one with consensus. They chose Pir Shaheen Shah and so he was appointed as president; Saadullah Khan was chosen unanimously as the secretary. We decided that the central office should be in Uthmanzai, because it was the first centre of both the movement and the *jirga*. The *jirga* of the province was thus constituted, and its office bearers elected, and the Congress high command was informed. A country and people are indeed very unfortunate when some people are born who are themselves not ready to serve the nation and oppose those who are prepared to do so. Such people, when they go to jail for a while, consider themselves to have become leaders and begin efforts to advance themselves. They are consumed by their desires; and if some, for the sake of God, come forward to serve the nation, they begin to oppose them. But no one can stop those who selflessly serve the cause of the nation. Opposition is generated by personal rivalries. As with *Mian* sahib, we also pleaded with our brothers from Peshawar that there was nothing to gain from the offices except the service of the nation; and that they should join hands to do it collectively. But they too were consumed by their desires, and started a campaign against the movement and the *Khudai Khidmatgar* and paid no heed to the fact that, by doing so, they were only harming the interests of the nation and strengthening the chains of slavery.

The 1931 session of the Congress Working Committee was scheduled in Delhi. I travelled with Ghulam Muhammad Khan of Lundkhwar to attend the session. I put forth a proposal in the working committee that up to now our detainees from Malakand Agency had not been released as a result of the Gandhi–Irwin Pact; and that the government had informed them that the agency was not included in the Pact. We requested the working committee to recommend to the central government to release our detainees. We were told to wait for the return of Gandhiji from the Round Table Conference.

The Tour of Hazara

Ghulam Muhammad and I returned to our villages on the conclusion of the Working Committee meeting. I called for almost twenty-five *Khudai Khidmatgars,* one from every *tapa,* to accompany me with great show and fanfare all over the district of Hazara as I had not toured this region at all. In this tour, a pupil of Satti Jan, Bachagai, a young lad who was blessed with a melodious voice, also accompanied us. He would sing soul-inspiring nationalist songs. *'Angreza za, khpl watan ta, ker-rayga* (Oh! Englishman, go back to your land, run away!').' I sent a capable and young *Khudai Khidmatgar* secretly to the Chach area to find out about the situation there and also to confer with the people, in confidence, about the prospects of my tour to the area because the government did not permit the *Khudai Khidmatgar* to enter Chach and would turn them out very harshly. So I wanted to go there without warning, so that by the time that the government got wind of it, I should already be there. Early morning, we left Peshawar by train. We had sent prior notice to *Hakeem* Abdus Salam sahib. When our train arrived at the Shahderai railway station, *Hakeem* sahib was there to welcome us. We changed trains for the journey ahead. Many people had come to welcome us when the train reached Haripur. Since our programme was to go to Paklai, I did not get off the train and stood in the door of my compartment and thanked the assembled people for the welcome and promised that we would visit them on our return. A little way down the track, we saw a car in which some Red-Shirts were sitting and driving it alongside the train. When I saw them, I felt very happy and thanked God that here too the *Khudai Khidmatgar* had a presence. Like the deputy commissioner of Kohat, when the deputy commissioner of Hazara, Hopkinson, learnt of my arrival, he lost his cool and did not know how to react. After a great effort, he convinced Ghulam Rabbani Khan[26], an advocate, that he would have his brother, who was a suspended sub-divisional officer of the public works department, reinstated in service if he would agree to oppose me in Hazara. From the Havelian railway station we visited and introduced our movement in all the villages which were close to the road. At Abbottabad, mid-way through the bazaar, large crowds had assembled on hearing of our arrival. As we were approaching Mansehra, Abdul Qayyum Khan Swati, an advocate, who was my companion from the days of the *Khilafat* and had been in jail with me, was waiting for me along with some other prominent elders near the village of Sufaido. From him we learnt that Ghulam Rabbani, on the instigation of the government, along with some others, was waiting for us with black flags. We slowed down as we had never experienced such a spectacle before in our province. Some people even tried to stop our vehicles. However, I saw a very peculiar man, who had a black flag in one hand, and with the other was saluting us. Later, we learnt that these people had been tricked, had been brought without being briefed, and given the black flags.

Finally, we arrived in Paklai. The people of Baffa had come two miles out of their village to welcome us. In Baffa we were staying on the banks of the river in a beautiful place. When these people learnt of the black flag episode, they were very upset. The residents of Hazara are ethnically Pukhtun but they have given up their mother tongue. The inhabitants of many villages, because of the black flag episode, developed great sympathy for us and joined our movement. The Baffa *jirga* and the *Khudai Khidmatgar* had organized a large *jalsa*, which was also attended by people from the surrounding villages. My heart had also received a shock because of the black flag incident but one should not be saddened by such things in political life. Since it was my first experience and I had never in my own province been confronted with such a situation, it had such a depressing effect on me. This can be considered a weakness on my part. I delivered a powerful speech in the *jalsa* and told the participants that they had forgotten their mother tongue, Pukhto, and that is why they no longer lived by the Pukhtun code of life. Some inhabitants of Paklai also delivered speeches and our *jalsa* concluded on a very successful and confident note. Haji Faqira Khan also arrived from Peshawar. He is an excellent activist of our movement and works tirelessly in his district of Hazara. We prepared a programme to tour Hazara in consultation with Haji Faqira Khan and some other workers. We held *jirga* at several places in the Paklai area. The Paklai area is the only belt in Hazara which retains the original mother tongue of Pukhto and our movement is very popular here. When we arranged for a *jalsa* at Shinkiari, the government sent some of its men to create disorder in it. By the grace of God, they did not pluck up enough courage to carry out their designs. In Hazara, the government was trying to create hurdles in our way. But the people had now become aware and

Ghulam Rabbani's black flags had helped us greatly by creating awareness and understanding among the masses. We held our final *jalsa* in Dhodial. The inhabitants of this area are full of Pukhtun pride and honour. They at first did not think of holding a *jalsa*, and nor did they intend to join our movement, but they were driven to this by the black flag episode of just this one man, Ghulam Rabbani. The efforts that the government would make against us turned out to be beneficial for us and harmful for them because all our efforts were directed towards the people's welfare. From here, we returned to Mansehra. Thousands had collected to welcome us and our *jaloos* paraded the streets and bazaars of the city. When we approached the house of Ghulam Rabbani, the place resonated with slogans of 'Inquilab Zindabad' by the participants of the *jaloos*. Some people even tried throwing stones at his house but I stopped them. I can say with confidence that if the government had not arranged for the black-flag episode, this *jaloos* would probably not have been as big.

From Mansehra, we proceeded to Sufaida and declared our intent to hold a *jalsa*. All the khans of Sufaida were very kind to me; but Abdul Qayyum Khan and Ghulam Rasul Khan were my friends from jail. We rested well at night. The next morning, I held discussions with some elders of the area and all doubts and misgivings created by the false propaganda of the government were set to rest. Just as we were preparing to leave for the *jalsa*, a police inspector from Mansehra brought a letter from the deputy commissioner. He told me that the deputy commissioner, accompanied by the superintendent of police, had also arrived in Mansehra. The letter advised me not to debate the objectives and methods of the movement with Ghulam Rabbani in the *jalsa*, and asked who would be responsible if violence erupted. The official confided in me that all this mischief had been planned by the deputy commissioner. I told him to remain silent as he was an employee of the government. I wrote back to the deputy commissioner that in this matter, there was no place for public debate; and that I had come here to promote the *Khudai Khidmatgar* movement, and my job was to publicize the movement, whether to accept or reject it was up to the people. As for violence, I told him our philosophy was that of non-violence. Even if violence was resorted to against us, we would not retaliate. In these circumstances, however, if violence did break out, he would solely be responsible for it. By the time we arrived in Mansehra, vast numbers of people had joined us on the way while thousands had collected at the *jalsa* venue. I also saw some other people near the venue. On inquiry, I learnt that these were people supporting the government. They had been lured into opposing us by prospects of a free meal and other inducements. They were to hold a rival *jalsa*. Ghulam Rabbani was busy delivering a speech but I did not understand what the speech was about.

In my speech, I dwelt on the aims and objectives of the *Khudai Khidmatgar* movement and made the people understand that God was not in need of our service – service to Him meant service to His creation. This land was given to us by God, just as He had given other nations their countries. The purpose was that they and their children should live on the land. The land was ours, but authority over it had been usurped by others. This was the reason why our children were hungry and thirsty while our rulers were enjoying themselves. Slavery was a curse of God and it was incumbent upon us to strive and free ourselves of this curse. This was only possible if we were to cultivate nationalism, brotherhood, unity, love and affection in ourselves. Today's world was one dominated by nationalism and they could very well see that those who were united, were successful; and those nations beset with internal rivalries, factionalism and disunity, were unsuccessful. The *jalsa* concluded on a successful note. Nobody can stop every act undertaken for the sake of God. The government failed to achieve any success in its deceptions and machinations. Next to the venue of the *jalsa* was the house of one of our benefactors where we rested. Many well known people of the area had come to attend the *jalsa*. I held discussions with them. On the suggestion of Haji Faqira Khan and *Hakeem* Abdus Salam, we decided that I should take a group photograph with the *Khudai Khidmatgar* at Paklai, who had been subjected to hardships and cruelty by the government, and who had spent periods in jail and been caned. One of the khans amongst them, Ali Gohar Khan, told me that his father, out of fear of the government, was an inveterate opponent of the movement and that he had been expelled from his home, because he had joined the movement. He added that he did not care for this and was making every effort to awaken his oppressed people. I learnt from another maulana sahib that when they were being flogged, he told the superintendent that he was an *alim* and so he should not be stripped naked. As a result, he was given thirty stripes while his other companions were given fifteen stripes each.

Another characteristic of the *Khudai Khidmatgar* of Paklai had a great effect upon me. When I was leaving, I told Ali Gohar Khan and a few other leaders that if they agreed I would like to take them with me to Peshawar for an excursion. Though they wanted to, they had a lot of work in their district, which they could not afford to neglect.

We left Paklai and Mansehra. *Hakeem* Abdus Salam sahib of Haripur was our companion. He had accepted the invitation of Niamatullah Khan to stay with him for the night. His house and *hujra* were located some distance from his village. We spent a restful night. *Hakeem* sahib had reserved a lorry for our trip next morning, but it never arrived and we decided to walk. In every village that we passed, we would stop and talk about our movement. This travel by foot proved beneficial because we were able to address and sensitize many people on the way. When we approached Nawa Shehr, many Hindus and Muslims were waiting for us, shouting slogans of 'Inquilab Zindabad' and took our *jaloos* through the streets of the town. We were tired and were taken to a place to rest. For the night, we went to another place. Early the next morning we met with people who had come to see us. Here we learnt that the government had pressurized both the Hindus and Muslims to boycott us but had failed. The next day, when we went to the *jalsa*, thousands of Hindus and Muslims had collected and it turned out to be very successful. I made the people aware of the purpose of the *Khudai Khidmatgar* movement and told them that whoever God had granted a country to live in, authority over it was with them. It was only us, unfortunate people, who owned a land with authority in the hands of foreign rulers, who enjoyed its benefits. It was incumbent on us to collectively strive to liberate our land. We would prosper and so would our children. When I finished my speech, a certain qazi from Peshawar, who was an inspector in the police, approached me and asked where I would be going next. When I told him that I was going to Abbottabad, he informed me that section 144 had been imposed there and that he had been sent by the superintendent of police to prevent an assembly of more than four persons, which was prohibited under the order. I told him that then we would go in fours, but that I did not think that the superintendent of police would stand by the order because, by doing so, we would get great publicity. When we started leaving in groups of four, the qazi sahib realized what I had said and took my message to the superintendent of police. Soon he returned and informed me that the superintendent had allowed us to proceed collectively. The inhabitants of Kakul and the villages in the vicinity had come to invite me to accompany them to their villages, but our programme for Abbottabad had been finalized, so I promised them that I would visit them when I came next. Our *Khudai Khidmatgar* were playing their music on the way. When we approached the limits of Abbottabad, an inspector on the roadside stopped our lorry and ordered us not to play the music. When I asked him if he had any written orders, he did not have any. I told him that without a written order, we would not stop playing our music. He even threatened to take me to the deputy commissioner. We had no objection to wherever he would take us, but we said that he would have to come with us in the lorry, because if he did not, then people would collect around us and this would be a violation of the order which had been imposed under section 144. But he disregarded what I said and walked ahead of our lorry and we directed the driver to drive slowly behind him and continued to play our music. Whoever heard the drums and the pipes joined the procession. When we arrived at the Police Lines, a crowd had gathered. The police, along with their officers, were standing by. We were told that the musicians were wanted by the deputy commissioner. I asked them about the offence they had committed; and if they were to be taken in despite being innocent, we would accompany them. A lot of time passed during this commotion; the music was playing, and people were gathering. At this point, inspector Bahadur Khan approached me and pleaded that we should stop playing the music. I directed that the music should stop. It was a spectacle to see. Students from school, clerks from their offices, and the locals from the city gathered around us. If the government had not meddled with us, we would not have got so much publicity and such a large crowd would not have known anything about us. After a great deal of discussion, we were allowed, and we proceeded to the Islamia High School in the city to rest. The next day being a Friday, we announced that a sermon would be delivered at the Jamia Masjid and that all the Hindus and the Muslims should collect and come there to hear it. We rested for a while and then we exchanged views with the people of Abbottabad about the movement. I told them that we were one people. We, too, should make efforts for our liberty and progress; and if we were to indefinitely remain slaves in this impoverished condition, we would be ruined. Our real mission was to generate love and affection, a nationalist outlook and unity of action in the people. Many Hindus and Muslims would come just to see us, and everyone could do so. Gurkhas, other soldiers, and women and children also came to see us. We talked to them about the importance of love and affection and made them aware of the mission of our movement; that we would selflessly, and for the sake of God, work for their welfare. The government had imposed section 144 in order to prevent a *jalsa* here, so that the people should not find out about our movement. When the government learnt that the next day was a Friday and people from the surrounding villages were also coming in for the Friday prayer, the deputy commissioner called for the imam of the Jamia Masjid and requested the committee members that no matter how, I should be prevented from addressing the congregation. We spent a comfortable night. When we were having breakfast, the imam sahib, accompanied by the committee members, came and spoke privately with me. I told them to inform the deputy commissioner that we could not agree to this proposal, because a mosque belonged to all the Muslims, and one Muslim could not prevent another from entering it, that this was our faith and we did not have the strength to prevent a Muslim from giving a sermon in the mosque. He, however, had both the authority and power, and why did he not prevent them? Then I told him that the deputy commissioner had no other purpose in this; he knew full well that the mosque belonged to every Muslim but he was only trying to make us Muslims fight amongst ourselves and create disunity in our ranks. Why should we Muslims, at the instigation of our enemies, create rifts amongst ourselves? My talk had a very good effect on them and they left to meet the deputy commissioner. When the deputy commissioner understood that his move had backfired, he refrained from doing anything further. So many Hindus and Muslims gathered in the mosque that it was difficult to find a place in it. After the prayer, I rose and went to the pulpit and recited four verses of the Holy *Quran* and translated them for the people: God, the Almighty, has proclaimed to seek His assistance in unity and patience; and that He says that whoever was to give his life in the way of God, he is not dead, but is alive. But we are not aware of it; and God has proclaimed that He is on the side of the patient; that He puts those who believe in Him, to trials and tribulations of loss of life, wealth, children, crops; and whenever they experience hardships in His path, they proclaim that they belong to God and would, for sure, return to Him. Such people are entitled to His mercy, and they are on the right path. In another place, He proclaims that, amongst us, there should always be a group of those who leave their own work and deter people from evil and make efforts to guide them on the right path. 'Oh brothers,' I said, 'we have, for the sake of God, dedicated our lives to the service and well-being of God's creatures. If you, too, want to serve humankind and want to please God, join us in our *"Khudai Khidmatgari"* so that this world becomes a paradise for us and we are entitled to paradise in the hereafter.'

The *jalsa* concluded on a very successful note. We were preparing to leave when the son of one of the khans of our village, who was a sub-inspector here, came and told me that inspector Bahadur Khan had sent him to me to direct me that, at the time of our departure, we should not play our music. I told him that I did not understand what objection he had to our playing the flute. He should be informed that if he had a personal objection to our playing music, then I would have it stopped. And if it was not personally objectionable to him, then what did he have to do with our music? In our country, our native officers do not realize their duty and nor do they perform it effectively; and they always carry out the wishes of their English officers, which are not part of their official duties.

The lorry was ready; we boarded it and left for Haripur. On the way, people had gathered at the Havelian railway station where I delivered a short speech. People were also waiting for us in Sarai Saleh, but had dispersed as we were late. The inhabitants of Haripur had come out some distance to welcome us. We arrived late in the evening and they raised slogans of 'Inquilab Zindabad' and 'Fakhr-e-Afghan Zindabad,' and our *jaloos* paraded through the streets of the city. We then had our dinner and retired for the night. I had sent the Bakshali Gujarat Shahzada sahib to Chach ahead of us to find out about prevailing conditions there and to report back to us. He returned to Haripur and told me that the people of Chach were very enthusiastic and eagerly awaiting our arrival and that it was essential that I should go. I fixed a date with him and repeatedly told him that word of this should not get out because the government would then put obstacles in our way. The next day we went to the house of our hosts where a maulvi sahib tried to reach out to me. He was being stopped by the *Khudai Khidmatgar,* but I asked them to let him be and I made him sit next to me. When lunch time came, some people tried to remove him, but he, by force, participated in the lunch. My companion, Muhammad Akbar Qureshi, told me that, last night, a few people carrying black flags had come and were standing by the roadside, but when they saw the crowds collect, they got flustered and could not speak. I told him that the crowd was so large that I was not able to notice the black flags. When we arrived at the venue of the *jalsa,* the police was standing there with batons. When I got up to speak, I saw the maulana speaking loudly and gesticulating, and some people were standing around him. The people said that these persons had been collected by the government. They are the khans and the maliks and were holding a *jalsa* in opposition to us.

First we had decided that we would go for the night to Kalabat to hold a *jalsa* there the next morning. In the *jalsa,* I announced this. Kalabat is this side of the Abaseend river and Sawabai is on the other side. The inhabitants of Yousafzai and the Khan of Sawabai, Muhammad Zaman Khan, were well-known to me. I had seen him once in the *hujra* of Sahibzada Fazl-e-Rehman[27] of Kotha. He had extended a very firm invitation to Qazi Ataullah Khan and me to visit him. I did not know that, upon the instigation of the government, he would not allow me to go to his village. When we neared Kalabat, we saw Muhammad Zaman Khan's uncle with his retainers, armed with lathis in their hands, standing by the roadside, waiting to stop us from entering. This was so even though arrangements for our *jalsa* at Kalabat had been made by one of their cousins, Mehdi Zaman Khan, who had invited us. The driver of our lorry, being a fearless man, refused to stop when I asked him to as I wanted to speak to the khan. He said to me that I did not know these people; these are Hazarawal Pukhtuns, and he increased the speed. The khan stood in the way of the lorry. The lathi-bearers encircled us. The driver drove straight into them; they broke ranks and our lorry got across. They ran after us but could not catch up, and we got to the village. In Hazara, section 144 had been clamped down, so the next day, we collected the people in the mosque. Outside the mosque, the assistant commissioner, along with the khans of the village and the police, was present and listening to my speech. I said in my speech that, 'Oh Pukhtun inhabitants of Hazara! The Yousafzai occupy both banks of the Abaseend river. Just have a look at the other side and compare the situation there and the one prevailing here. I have toured the entire province and everywhere the government has instigated the people against us, but we have never been confronted with black flags. We have experienced this phenomenon only in Hazara. Nor has anyone picked up the lathi against us to prevent us from visiting their village; nor have they organized *jalsa* in opposition to us. We have experienced all of this in Hazara only. They are also Pukhtun and so are you. Let us determine the cause of this. Whatever little thought I have given the matter, the reason appears to be that you have given up the use of your mother tongue, Pukhto. Not only have you abandoned Pukhto as a language, but you have also given up Pukhto as a code of conduct. Oh, Pukhtuns of Hazara! Remember what I am about to say. Those who have abandoned their language, are lost people. And those who look down upon their own language, have lost their status and standing.' At departure, the driver of our lorry was beaten up by the police and told not to come for us the next day. When we came to the bus stand, the lorry was not there. *Tum-tums* were standing around, but the police had also prohibited them from taking us. There was one owner of a *tum-tum* who declared that he did not care about the police and was willing to take us. We loaded our luggage on his *tum-tum* and walked along with him. The entire route was through the hills. The scenery was fascinating. We addressed the people of all the villages along the way. *Hakeem* sahib and our colonel sahib of Haripur, Muhammad Hussain Khan, had gone ahead of us to decide. But after the experience at Kalabat, we concluded that we must send our local companions ahead to clear the way and decide before we went. One of the young khans of the area had made arrangements for us. His village was located on the bank of the Abaseend river. It had a small landholding but very productive. We went for the *jalsa* for which the inhabitants of the area had gathered. The people from across the Abaseend had also come. The people of this area understand Pukhto and the Pukhto poems affected them greatly. We also spent the night as the guests of that young khan. The police had pressurized him not to entertain us, but he paid no attention to this. The next day, the khan of the adjoining village invited us. When we went there, the khan told us that an advocate of Ismaila, *Mian* Ali Haider Shah[28], who was the extra-assistant commissioner of Haripur, and Bahadur Khan of Pirpai, who was the inspector there, had put a lot of pressure on him not to invite us, but he had replied that we were his guests and that he would invite them too, because they were the rulers and we were his guests. The khan laughed and told me that these two were from Peshawar and called themselves 'Pukhtuns'! All the obstacles and hurdles that had been created for us in Haripur were the result of these two government officers. This was not the only problem we faced. The village that we had informed of our arrival to hold *jalsa* was twelve or thirteen miles away. To get there, we had reserved a lorry. When the time for departure came, we learnt that Ali Haider Shah and Bahadur Khan had impounded the lorry in the thana. The driver vociferously told them that he had promised to make the lorry available for the trip and had also taken the fare from us. But these brothers of ours from Peshawar told him to forget about us and to take them because when the government needed a lorry, how could he use it for others? No one else in the entire province had ever played with us the games that Ali Haider Shah and Bahadur Khan played with us in Hazara. Khushdil Khan, the deputy superintendent of police was the other officer who was even worse than these two.

When we came to know all this, *Hakeem* sahib Abdul Salam was very concerned. He proceeded to the bus stand in search of a vehicle and we left on foot after him. We had covered six miles when *hakeem* sahib arrived with two cars and we managed to fit in with great difficulty. We were physically fit and would usually conduct our tours on foot; but then we had plenty of time. Here, we were concerned about those people who were awaiting us and feared that while waiting for us, they might, in their disappointment, disperse. In this travel by foot we benefitted to the extent that we were able to address the people of all the villages situated along the way. When we neared the venue of the *jalsa*, the poor participants were waiting for us. This village, like the previous one, was situated on the bank of the Abaseend river and was located near the thana. The *jalsa* concluded with great success and I made the people aware of the mission of the *Khudai Khidmatgar* movement. The Mashwani tribe had come down from their hills to attend the *jalsa*. They promised to join the movement. Wherever we went, Ali Haider Shah and Bahadur Khan would follow us. We remained in this village for the night. All the men of the village collected in the evening and *hakeem* sahib and I delivered speeches. I got promises from them that they would, in future, wear local, home-spun clothes.

The president of our movement, along with a few *Khudai Khidmatgars,* had come from the village of Zarobai, across the Abaseend river. They told us that when we were free from touring Hazara, we should visit their village as well. We had not shared the date of our departure. No one knew in which direction we would head after the tour of Hazara. The police from Sarhad and Punjab had also come. They were also trying to find out. I asked *hakeem* sahib to arrange five *tum-tums* for us. Even then, we did not disclose where we would be going. When we left for the railway station, we asked the *Khudai Khidmatgar* from Zarobai to leave and promised them that, on completing our tour of Chach, we would come to Sawabai and visit their village. I disclosed my programme at this juncture, when a *thanedar* from Chach overheard me and left us in a hurry and forcibly occupied one of our *tum-tums* and reached Chach before us. I made *Hakeem* Abdus Salam sahib and the workers from Hazara take their leave, after thanking them profusely. Only the colonel sahib of the *Khudai Khidmatgar* of Haripur accompanied us to Chach. The road was not paved and covered with sand. The countryside was a waste land interspersed by dry stream beds. The horses were labouring, and we would usually get off and walk along. In many places, the people had come out on to the road to see us. We talked to them. I would be amazed at the affection and sincerity of the common people, and would thank God that he had showered His blessings on the Pukhtuns and instilled in their hearts feelings of brotherhood and a national spirit. When we approached Chach, thousands of people, with flags in hand, were waiting for us outside the village. We got down from our *tum-tums* and, together, we crossed the border into Punjab. The khans, maliks and the police were standing by the roadside. They had rifles, swords and black flags in their hands. The road was rough, surrounded by a sandy wasteland, and many people. When we approached the crowd, the *Khudai Khidmatgar* and the rest of the crowd stopped. The Khan of Toru, Abdul Rahim Khan, came towards me and said that the police had blocked the road and that there was an Englishman with them as well; that they are not allowing us to move onward. I asked him whether they had a written order with them and why were we being prevented from moving ahead. He answered that they had no written order. The police had fixed bayonets on their rifles and were pointing them towards us. I directed them that if they did not have formal orders then we should move on without being scared. The Englishman was the superintendent of police of the district and was a very short-tempered and evil person. On a previous occasion, too, when our *Khudai Khidmatgar* had come to Chach, he had ordered their drums to be pierced and had taken away their flags and had prevented them from entering Chach. He had given the police instructions to open fire, but when our crowd approached, it got so overwhelmed by the sheer numbers that it did not open fire. In this crowd, the Englishman was also pushed back. When he realized that the police would not open fire, he himself got hold of a rifle, but Amin Jan Khan bared his chest before him and dared him to shoot. He, too, was overwhelmed and asked Amin Jan Khan where Abdul Ghaffar Khan was. Amin Jan Khan, realizing that he would not open fire, pointed me out to him. He came towards me and with great difficulty told me that he had orders with him. I raised my hand and the *Khudai Khidmatgar* came to a halt. I told the Englishman that it was a big folly on his part not to have shown the orders to me. We were ready to obey the orders of the government. If the firing had taken place and people had died, then who would have been responsible for it? He admitted his folly. The order directed that we were not allowed to hold a *jalsa* or *jaloos* here. I reassured him that the order was acceptable to us. We were near the border with Sarhad province and so I asked him whether we could hold the *jalsa* there. He told me that certainly we could do that as the restriction was applicable only to Punjab. The crowd, along with us, crossed over to Sarhad side of the border and we held a large *jalsa* there, for which the inhabitants of all the villages of Chach had come. I explained the purpose of my visit and explained the mission of our movement. I told them that they, too, were Pukhtuns like us. We were the children of a common ancestor; that we desired that they should also enter the fold of this new *Khudai Khidmatgar* brotherhood with us. There would be one *jirga* for all of us which would take decisions on all national issues, and through this we would be continuously made aware of each other's problems and difficulties. We would also then become a nation like the other nations of the world and we and our children would prosper.

After the *jalsa* concluded we were left alone in the ground. We were preparing to leave when the extra assistant commissioner from Ismailia, Haider Shah, and the inspector from Pirpai, took me aside and told me that they wanted to discuss a few brotherly affairs. I had seen the extent of their 'brotherhood' and feelings for me during my tour of Hazara. These slave brothers of ours are a strange lot. When they are in need, they become our brothers, and when they side with the British, they are prepared to take all kinds of measures against us at their behest. I asked them what it was that they wanted to discuss with me. Haider Shah said that I was fully aware that the government had imposed section 144 on me in that area and I could not hold any *jalsa* or deliver speeches. So, it would be better for us if they were to make lorries available to us and we accompanied them to Haripur and, from there, proceeded to Peshawar. I had seen them sitting with the English superintendent of police and talking to him. He had given them the necessary instructions that we should be made to leave the area. I told him that we were not prepared to return, and nor did we wish to tour the area any further. That we had been invited by the Khan of Ghurghushti and that we would stay the night and take the road back to Peshawar the next day. I divided my *Khudai Khidmatgar* into groups of four and left for Ghurghushti with *Salar* Abdur Rahim Khan of Sudham and arrived at the *hujra* of the khan. After the evening prayer, I met with people from different villages who had collected at the *hujra*. We all sat down for the evening meal. It somehow slipped my tongue that the English superintendent of police was a good man. On this, our *Khudai Khidmatgar* colonel from Haripur remarked, 'He was not at all a good man, he became a good man later. At first, when he approached us, I had a flag in my hand and he attacked my flag and snatched the flag from me. When I pulled the flag and freed it from him, he then attacked me, creating a commotion. Moreover, he had ordered the policemen to open fire, but the policemen lost their nerve. They were already familiar with the *Khudai Khtimatgar*.

This superintendent had been harsh with the *Khudai Khidmatgar* on the first occasion and had snatched flags from them and had also pierced their drums and only then returned them. He had thought that, on this occasion too he would succeed, but this time God disgraced him and he became so powerless that it is difficult to put into words. What to talk of this, the more important thing was that the authority with which the people viewed the government, vanished overnight.'

The night was spent in great comfort and laughter. The next morning the *Khudai Khidmatgar* were at breakfast and the colonel of the *Khudai Khidmatgar,* Muhammad Hussain Khan, was standing guard when I heard his voice. On enquiring, I got to know that a few officers had come but were not allowed to enter as I was having my tea. I asked to let them in. When they entered, I laughed and said, 'What other Nadir Shahi orders have you brought?' One of the officers laughed and said 'My name is Nadir!' I invited him to a cup of tea. When I finished my tea, he handed me over another, directing me, under section 144, to immediately leave the area. I told him that I accepted the orders and would leave immediately after lunch. However, after we had our lunch we learnt that the police had instructed the drivers of the *tum-tums* and the lorries not to allow us to use their services. We could not even hire a *tum-tum* for our baggage. I then formed groups of four of the *Khudai Khidmatgar,* we picked up our own baggage and left. By afternoon, we came to a village by the roadside. We stopped for the afternoon prayer but when the locals found out about our presence, the mosque filled up. After the prayer we made the people aware of the tyranny of the government and the mission of the *Khudai Khidmatgar* movement. We made them understand that this government prevented us Pukhtuns from any kind of progress or advancement or unity.

Return from Hazara

At this point again, the same officers arrived on the scene and told me that I had violated the orders under section 144. I asked whether this was violated even by offering collective prayers. They could not say anything to this and so they showed me another section of the law and ordered us to get out of Punjab state and if we did not, we would be dealt with under the law. I wrote to the deputy commissioner that they had deprived us of the use of the lorries and *tum-tums*, and that we had no other means of transport, and nor did we have aircraft to enable us to comply with this order; that we had no objection to leaving the state if they could arrange for us to do so. After this, the officers placed tree trunks on the road at different points, to block our movement. We found out that the deputy commissioner, along with the superintendent of police, maliks and khans, were awaiting our arrival further ahead by the roadside. So, I went ahead of the *Khudai Khidmatgar* and when we got closer to them and they became visible, the inhabitants of the surrounding area collected here and started following us. We stopped them from doing so, saying that orders under section 144 were in force, but they could not be controlled. The magistrate and the superintendent of police came and informed me that they had been able to persuade the deputy commissioner to have arrangements made to provide transport for us. The deputy commissioner also came to see us. During our conversation, the *Khudai Khidmatgar* were mentioned. The deputy commissioner told me that, 'Your ideology is not one of non-violence. This is merely a façade. Now that you have no power, you are not resorting to violence but when you have power, you will then resort to violence.' I told him that our movement was based on the truth and we are not hypocrites. The *Khudai Khidmatgar* got into the lorry and, when I was about to get into the car, the deputy commissioner asked me not to return to that area. I told him that Chach was inhabited by our Pukhtun brethren and if the part that they lived in is separated from Punjab, I would not return! As we were leaving the superintendent of police made me sit with him in his car and made the *Khudai Khidmatgar* board the lorry. The *thanedar* was also sitting with me in the car. He asked me how much salary I paid to the *Khudai Khidmatgar*. I laughed at his question and responded that, unlike them, everyone was not a donkey for hire. That each one of these people was a landowner in his own right and spent his own money in this work. He wanted to know what they got out of it to which I replied that their reward was to see their nation liberated from slavery. The Pukhtuns abhor slavery and they are not prepared for a life of subjugation.

We reached the Attock dak bungalow, which is in a very scenic spot. We were sitting in the veranda, looking onto the Abaseend river.

He (the deputy commissioner) told me that the Pukhtuns were a different people from the rest. I told him that he had not seen the true Pukhtuns and that if he were ever to come to Peshawar, we would show him the real Pukhtuns. When we got to Khairabad, we got down from our transport, and the Englishman very affectionately took leave of us. He also embraced our young *Khudai Khidmatgar*, Bachagai, and I thanked him profusely for the kind gesture. We were waiting for our next lorry in the bazaar of Khairabad when the people found out and many collected around us. We boarded a lorry for Naukhar and reached there in the evening. We would have arrived earlier but, on the way, a soldier saw us and, with gun in hand, ran towards us. He ordered the driver to stop and, pointing his rifle at us, warned us not to move or else he would shoot. I told him that we were helpless and had no answer to his rifle. If it was not allowed that the *Khudai Khidmatgar* move together, then he should tell us so that we could get off. At this point his subedar arrived on the scene. He also said that he had no specific orders with him and that he would go and consult his English officer. The officer also arrived. He took one look at us and went back. He told them that this was a matter for the police. Finally, when the police arrived and allowed us to proceed, I said to them that we could not understand why we had been stopped. The police officer laughed and said that the brains of the government had been affected!

In Naukhar, I dispersed all the *Khudai Khidmatgars*. At this point, an Englishman arrived and asked the *Khudai Khidmagar* to meet me. After meeting him, we left for Peshawar. On our way, one of the tyres of the lorry got punctured and it was late in the evening when we reached. The *Khudai Khidmatgar* stayed in the office of the movement, while I and Bachagai went to the bungalow of Dr. Khan Sahib. I had previously also received an anonymous letter in which I was informed that the government had decided to have me, my brother, and all my family arrested and removed from the country, and confine us to a small island. But I gave no credence to such rumours, because those who serve the people in the cause of Allah should be prepared to face such eventualities. Now, once again, my companions warned me that the government of Sarhad had written to the central government that, when I was arrested, I needed to be transported to a country which was far away. That first, when we were confined in Gujarat jail, I conducted the political affairs of Sarhad from there, and that this time around, I needed to be sent to such a place from where I did not get any news about the people of Sarhad. I was further informed that Sarhad government was trying to have me arrested soon. I told them that those who kept elephants had large enough gates for them to enter through and that they should not worry about all this. There was nothing of worry about when God was there. The government would look after its own affairs and we would tend to our own.

I was worried whether the government would allow me to tour Sarhad or not. However, I had conducted a successful tour of Hazara, from house to house, and one area to the next. Now, I was not concerned whether the government would detain me or not. It could do so whenever it wanted to.

The Haji Sahib of Torangzai and the *Khudai Khidmatgar*

At the instigation of Bacha Gul, a propaganda campaign had started against us. I could not believe it. I thought that since he was haji sahib's son, and his father was our well-wisher, how could he carry out propaganda against us? So, on 14 June 1942, during the Second World War, I secretly sent my son, Wali, to the Moomand area so that the government would not find out. Wali went and met with Bacha Gul and had many discussions with him. The Haji Sahib of Torangzai had died at the time and Bacha Gul was in full command. When Wali returned, I was scheduled to visit Sawabai the next day. On the way, in the bazar of Hoti, I came face to face with Maulana Gul Bacha. He took me aside and informed me that all the propaganda against me was being carried out by Kulli Khan, but in the name of Bacha Gul. That the next day, he was to go to the Moomand area to take a decision on this matter with Bacha Gul and would say to him that God had created me for their benefit and not to carry out propaganda against me and if he were to do so, he should then find another person to replace me.

I went for a few days to Uthmanzai to check on my personal affairs. I was worried about the possibility of being arrested and felt that it was not proper to waste time by sitting idle at home. I had finished touring the entire province. But I had received news of the *jirga* of the Khalil and the Moomand, that there were some people there who, on account of their limited understanding of events, were deceiving the people; and that they were engaged in certain activities without the permission of the *markaz* that were inappropriate. In the *jirga* and the *Khudai Khidmatgar,* there were also some people who, in the garb of religion, were sowing disunity in the ranks of the *Khudai Khidmatgar.* Also, due to the arrest of Arbab Abdul Ghafoor and Ashiq Shah Bacha, a streak of violence had emerged in the *Khudai Khidmatgar.* So, I told myself that I should go to this area. When I arrived in Uthmanzai, I found out that my paternal nephew, Abdullah Khan, who had gone on a hunger strike in the judicial lock up in Peshawar for failing to pay land tax, had been released by the government and taken to the bungalow of the Peshawar deputy commissioner in a car. I went back to Peshawar to meet him.

Tour of the Khalil and Moomand Area

I started on a tour of the Khalil and Moomand areas. Since section 144 was in force, we held a big *jalsa* in a mosque in Tehkal at night. The next day, we left on a tour of the villages. We had to travel by night from village to village, making people aware of the mission of the *Khudai Khidmatgar* movement. Once again, I obtained solemn pledges from the people in the mosques that they would on no account resort to violence but show patience even in the most adverse of circumstances, because God is on the side of those who are patient in adversity, and those who had God on their side would ultimately be victorious. We held *jalsa* in the Moomand villages of Tapa Papaoke, Bahadur Killi, Badaber, Sheikhan, Shahabkhel and Mattani. These were held in the mosques. Here, again, I took solemn pledges of non-violence from the *Khudai Khidmatgar.* The last *jalsa* we held was in Landai and I explained to the people that although they raised slogans about my 'kingship' this movement is not for a kingship or for me to become a king. That if they ever made me king, they should know that there is no concept of 'kingship' in Islam and, secondly, that they would be ruined in the process, at my expense. So, they should understand and make neither me, nor anyone else, their king. We do not want to create kings and we are not in need of them. We would have one leader, selected through the people's will and through consultation and he would be one who serves the nation. He would make no distinction between the khans and the poor, the maulanas and the *mians.* He would be one who is pious and honest and a well-wisher of the nation and the land, and one who had served the nation well and undergone many hardships for it and who was endowed with leadership qualities. The government which we form would be subordinate to the wishes of the party and the party would not be subordinate to it. Kingship is an evil system in which the country and its people suffer greatly. And if today a king is just and wise, tomorrow his son would succeed him; and who can then foresee that he, too, would be wise and just? When do kings ever want progress for their people? He would always worry that if the people become aware, they will remove him and, so, he would put obstacles in their path to progress. This land belongs to all us Pukhtuns and we will not make a khan of one man. It will be our effort to make a khan out of everyone. We would form such a government which is egalitarian, and everyone will benefit from it equally. Whether we eat only baked bread or we have cooked curry with it, we would have it jointly. There should be peace, justice and our nation should have one *jirga* which should select one man as our president.

Our *jalsa* used to be attended by women as well. The *jirga* of the Khalil and Moomand and the *Khudai Khidmatgar* were extremely well organized. In every village there is an office where someone keeps watch day and night. Every office has a clock which sounds the hour of the day. All this is under the able guidance of Arbab Abdul Ghafoor and *Syed* Ashiq Shah Bacha.

Manlrngano Banda, Urmar and Khaalisa

I was informed that Qari had decided on a big *jalsa* in his village, Manlrngano Banda, and had written to me that they were holding a training camp for the *Khudai Khidmatgar* of their area. My going there was essential. I accepted their invitation and proceeded early in the morning from Uthmanzai to the village of Satti Jan, because Bachagai told me that he would like me to go via his village. We had our breakfast with Satti Jan. The president and *salar* of Prang also arrived and then we all left for Nisata. When the people of Nisata learned of our arrival, many of them collected to meet me. I delivered a brief speech and told them that we must build our own house; we must put enmities and disunity behind us as these were our enemies and were destroying our homes. From Nisata we went to the river bank where a boat had been arranged and was ready. The president and *salar* sahib went back, and we crossed the river safely. The *Khudai Khidmatgar* had assembled in many places. They had brought a horse for me, but I went by foot. We arrived at Qari sahib's village where he had made excellent arrangements. He had decorated the office and its surroundings. People were sitting in the office. We exchanged views and after lunch left for the *jalsa*, which was at some distance from the village. Thousands of men and women had assembled. Speeches were delivered and poems were recited. In my speech, I first expressed sympathy with the sons of Qari sahib who had been arrested by the government. I shared with the audience that soon we were going to be put to the test by a lot of hardships, which will be imposed on us. If they bore all this with patience and equanimity then, hopefully, we would come out successful. I also told them that we, the *Khudai Khidmatgar*, served them in the way of God because they belonged to our nation. We were there for their benefit. That if there were some people in this land who could not undergo hardship for our benefit, let them not do so, but they should not obstruct our efforts. If they did not wish to assist us, that did not matter, but they should avoid becoming friends with the enemies of the land and its people. I then went to the womenfolk and told them that this country belonged as much to them as to their menfolk. That, in Islam, unlike what they believed, men were not greater than women. This is not in Islam. Greatness, in Islam, is determined by our actions. If a woman is pious and good, she is great. Similarly, so is a man. And if a woman is impious and involved in doing of evil, she is considered inferior in the eyes of God; as is a man. In this world, women are equal partners with men. Man and woman are the two wheels of a cart. If one gets punctured, the cart cannot move forward. The *jalsa* concluded successfully.

The *Khudai Khidmatgar* president of Urmar with many other *Khudai Khidmatgars* had come. They forced me to accompany them to Urmar. When we arrived at their office, I went to the family of our martyred subedar and condoled with his sons. His children came to me and I offered *fateha* and comforted them. I told them that death was a reality and no one could escape it. That their father had died in such a manner that God held it as 'life,' but we do not understand this. I said to them that until this world existed, his name would forever be remembered. At night, we held a *jalsa* in the mosque as here too meetings were prohibited. The next day we visited a village in the centre of Urmar where there was disunity in the ranks of our *Khudai Khidmatgar*. I made them understand the meaning of the mission and objective of the *Khudai Khidmatgar* and told them that they had not really understood the meaning of this movement and had forgotten that we had given a solemn pledge to God that we will put aside our petty rivalries, kinship enmities and disunity. That I was here to remind them that those who could not bring themselves to give up their enmities, kinship rivalries and disunity, should not join the ranks of the *Khudai Khidmatgar*, and that when they abandoned these things, they could become *Khudai Khidmatgar*. I asked them that if, as *Khudai Khidmatgar*, they could not give up these things then what is the point of this brotherhood? These things have destroyed us. The speech seemed to have had a positive effect on them. From here we left for a third village in Urmar. Urmar is divided into three parts. There also we held a *jalsa* in the mosque. To frighten us, the government had dispatched a contingent of the border police at the time of our *jalsa*. The people, however, were totally oblivious of their presence and so they left. From here I wanted to go to Kachauri, but I felt unwell. Also, it was two miles from the road and one had to walk to it. For the night we then went to *Mian* Gujjar and spent a comfortable night in Babu Fazal Ilah's *hujra*. At night, we held a *jalsa* in a mosque, and when the people learnt of my presence, many women and men came to attend, showing us great love and affection. The next morning, we went to Hazarkhanai. I was highly impressed by the local *Khudai Khidmatgar jirga* and their organization. We undertook a tour of the area by walking from village to village and made the people aware of the concept of non-violence, and stressed the virtue of patience in adversity. My tour of this area concluded.

Meeting with the Governor

I was not feeling well because I did not get continuous rest, either during the day or the night. Bachagai was a student of Sakhi Jan and would recite his poems. He, too, fell ill and so I asked him to return to his village. I went to Peshawar and stayed with Dr. Khan Sahib. He informed me about meeting with the governor and reminded me that when I was on tour in Dera Ismail Khan, he had sent him a letter about my meeting with him. Our former governor had been killed in an accident and, in his place, Sir Ralph

Griffith had been appointed and a meeting was fixed for 3 p.m. in the afternoon. The governor came to the door to welcome me and made me sit next to him. After the usual greetings were exchanged, the first question he asked me was how was it that he had spent most of his service career in Peshawar but had never met me. I told him that generally people who had their own personal business to transact came to meet the governor. Then we started talking about the *Khudai Khidmatgar*. He told me that they had a very cordial relationship with the Pukhtuns, but because of the heated and hard-hitting speeches of some people, that relationship had been vitiated. I replied that relationships were never spoilt by speeches, and that he would know about the kind of treatment that Jameson had given the Pukhtuns. On hearing this, the governor sahib lowered his gaze. Jameson was a superintendent of police who, in 1931, during the picketing of liquor shops, had the police hang pitchers filled with water from the testicles of the *Khudai Khidmatgars* in Charsadda, and brought a castration implement with which many *Khudai Khidmatgars* were castrated. He would continuously say that he would remove all traces of Pukhtuns from the land. He would strip the *Khudai Khidmatgars* naked and beat them until they were unconscious. He would then throw them, one by one, into a specially prepared ditch of urine and human excreta. This is considered by us Pukhtuns as worse than death. I told him that they should keep in mind that we *Khudai Khidmatgars* were also their subjects; that they should, at least, give us the same treatment which they gave to their other subjects. He reassured me that all subjects were being treated equally and that they did not arrest innocent people. I replied that I would not argue this point with him, but asserted that they were arresting most *Khudai Khidmatgar* without their having violated any law, and false cases were instituted against them. He retorted that they were surely guilty of something. I asked him what the khans of Sudham had done that they had been arrested and were being detained in the judicial lock up in Mardan. What speeches had Shah Pasand Khan and Allah Dad delivered? What was the offence committed by Sher Bahadur Khan and his other unfortunate companions? Finally, he started talking about a free Sarhad. I told him that they were spending crores of rupees on the political agent. What did they gain from it? He replied that they had protected the area administered by the political agents from the depredations of 'these tribesmen'. When I asked about the extent of the success they had achieved, the governor said that they were at it for the last thirty years but had not yet succeeded in their efforts. I told him to give us five years and only twenty per cent of the money that they would spend, and then to compare our results with theirs. If the path that we adopted was beneficial, then they should continue with it. He asked me about our strategy and I replied that we would spend the money on the education, health and welfare of the people, and would gain their confidence and reassure them that we had nothing but their welfare at heart. The Pukhtuns were such a people who, instead of the use of force, were persuaded more by kindness. When the governor sahib could not think of an appropriate response to this, he said that there was a great danger to this country from Russia and Afghanistan, and for this reason, they could not abandon their present policy, and nor could they reduce the forces deployed there. I told him to not even mention poor Afghanistan, because as he very well knew, they could not even maintain themselves, let alone mount an attack on us. Moreover, the other fact was that whichever king was not to their liking in Afghanistan, he could not rule the land. This leaves Russia, and if they feared that it was a threat to them, then it was necessary that they should give us authority over this country, because in the whole of Hindustan today, they did not have forces equivalent to the number of our *Khudai Khidmatgars*. I said that when you hand over authority to us and then, if the Russians want to invade our country, we will counter them. He noted many points I raised and told me that he was scheduled to leave for Delhi the next day and would bring the main points discussed in our meeting to the notice of the viceroy. He hoped that he and I would hold such discussions in future as well. I replied that just as he had despatched the police to get me this time, he should do so in future as well and my meeting with him could then be held. He said to me, 'You are a curious fellow. Just look outside and see how many people have come to meet me. I don't meet them. And here I am telling you to come and meet me and you don't come.' I told him that the people waiting outside had come in pursuit of their own personal interests, while I had no personal interest to pursue. The meeting ended and I returned to Dr. Khan Sahib's bungalow and arranged to travel to Naukhar the next day.

Jalsa in Naukhar *Tehsil*

On 12 December, early in the morning, I left for Naukhar *tehsil* in the company of my Moomand *Khudai Khidmatgar.* We went to the office of the *Khudai Khidmatgar.* The president, along with other *Khudai Khidmatgars,* was waiting for us. After a while, we left on a tour of the villages located on the banks of the river Kabul. On the way, I saw our general from Shahbaz Garhai in Mardan *tehsil,* whom the police was taking to jail in a lorry. He had been sentenced to two and a half years' rigorous imprisonment. We held a *jalsa* in the rain at Kandaro. After that the president and the workers of Naukhar left us and we crossed the river with the general sahib of Akora and held a *jalsa* in Pir Sabak. We went to Zara Maina for the night. The people had assembled and were waiting for us. We held a *jalsa* there at night and left early the next morning before prayers and held *jalsa* in the rest of the villages on the banks of the river. For the night we went to Khairabad. My health was no better than before. My throat was affected and I could barely speak. On account of prolonged fatigue, I got even worse. I would try my best to get some rest after each tour, but the people would not allow me to do so. We held a *jalsa* here at night. On 12 December, in the territory of the Khattaks, we decided for a big *jalsa* to be held on the river bank. Thousands of *Khudai Khidmatgars* from Sawabai had come to attend that *jalsa.* The people of Chach had also crossed over on goat skin rafts. After a little rest, I went for the *jalsa.* The poets recited their nationalist poems, which had a good effect on the audience. Finally, I delivered my speech and said that this was a struggle of patience, that we would not take revenge for being beaten up or cursed; we would be patient and entrust ourselves to God. We were *Khudai Khidmatgar* and God would avenge us on our enemies. I asked the participants to remove selfishness from their hearts and disunity from their ranks, because we had been ruined because of them. I also told them that I did not understand why we Pukhtuns stood in such awe of the British. We were human beings like them. Like them, we belonged to one nation. I encouraged them to generate a fear of God in their hearts, and not a fear of the British. I appealed to all of them that in whichever village a *jalsa* was scheduled, no arrangements were to be made for tea or food, and they were not to stay overnight there. I also said to the people of the village that they should not provide tea or food for anyone; that we were poor and could not provide tea to people. I said to them that they were unable to fast even for a day, for the sake of God, and that even if someone had cooked food for them, they should not eat it. If this was to happen once, then no one would take the trouble to provide food for them in future.

Jalsa in Sawabai *Tehsil*

I then left with Firdos Khan for his village, Manerai. On the way, an old man accosted me and said, 'Bacha Khan, I have only learned today from you that the Englishman is also a human being like me.' I spent the night on the way in comfort with Firdos Khan. The next day I attended the funeral prayer of a *Khudai Khidmatgar*. From this place, we left for Baja, because the khans of Baja, despite their innocence, had been arrested. Here we held a *jalsa* in a mosque and then proceeded to Kalabat. The government had succeeded in creating a rift amongst the people. Selfish people were doing mischief amongst them. I addressed them on this topic too, for them to consider the matter in depth. This had a positive impact. At the time of departure, the son of the khan of Kalabat told me to reassure myself as they were now aware of reality and no one could make them quarrel among themselves. From here, we went to Zarobai where we also held a *jalsa* in a mosque. Thousands of people collected and a very successful *jalsa* was held. I realized that the people were now politically conscious. From here, we went to Marghuz where we held a *jalsa* at night. The members of the *Khudai Khidmatgar jirga* and the *Khudai Khidmatgar*, in general, are very understanding, sincere and far-sighted. They told stories of all the hardship they had borne for the cause. They informed me that, for no rhyme or reason, the English superintendent of police had them beaten and asked the inhabitants of Kalabat to register criminal cases against them. But they refused to do so. Their general is a very competent and knowledgeable man, and it is on account of his efforts that the *Khudai Khidmatgar* of Marghuz are so passionate about their cause. The next day the president of a village to the west of Marghuz convinced us and so we went there for breakfast. People collected when they found out about our arrival. I also delivered a short speech about brotherhood and national unity and then, from here, proceeded to Kotha and then on to the adjoining village of Topi, because many workers from here had been arrested by the government. In Topi, picketing was taking place. We went to have a look and I asked them the reason. They replied that people here were selling foreign manufactured items when they should be selling items made in our own country. I then asked them what benefit there was for them in the locally manufactured things, and what harm was there in the imported ones. They answered that if goods made in the country are sold, the money would remain in the country and if goods made in another country were sold, then the money would be repatriated to the country of origin. I was very happy to hear this because this exchange took place with the *Khudai Khidmatgar* of a small village, who were uneducated. Here, too, the police had inflicted a lot of cruelty on the *Khudai Khidmatgar*. I realized that our people were now aware of things. I then delivered a speech in a mosque and told the people that the *Khudai Khidmatgar* would win the day for them. They were going to win their land back that their fathers and grandfathers had not been able to save from the British. No matter how ill-treated we were by the British, we do not blame them for it, because they were a foreign race and concerned about what would become of them if the Pukhtuns were to gain their freedom from them. The complaint that we had was from their servants. They belonged to our race, and this land belonged to all of us. If it were liberated, the entire nation would benefit. When the *jalsa* ended, the maulana sahib of Maiani told me that I must go with them as the inhabitants of Maiani also wanted to hold a *jalsa*. I told the maulana sahib that I was unwell and would come to their village when I was a little better. He agreed to this and we returned to Sawabai. In Sawabai, thousands of men and women had collected, and *Salar* Sahib Munir Khan, Najo Bhai and Firdos Khan had made excellent arrangements. I delivered a speech. The *Khudai Khidmatgar* gathered around me and demanded that I should stay with them for the night. I said that they could see that I was unwell and that, even in this condition, I was busy working day and night because, sooner or later, the government was bent on arresting us, to deprive us of the opportunity of serving the people. That it was just waiting for the Round Table Conference to conclude before acting. So, I was conducting as many tours as possible to make them understand the significance of unfolding events.

From here we went to Tulandai for the night, where we spent the night in comfort and got the required rest. Here I found out that *Mian* Ahmad Shah and his group were publishing pamphlets against me and distributing them to the public every month, and that a maulana sahib here was carrying out extremely vitriolic propaganda for him. I told them that we were working for the sake of God, in the service of the people. If the people were to help us, they would be able to gain their freedom; and if they were to oppose us, they will be destroyed. Without the active participation of the people, we would not be able to attain our objective. Only those who worked for their own benefit were worried. Those who worked for the sake of God were never worried or fearful. *Mian* Ahmad Shah criticized me in the press and through pamphlets, but I never published a response, because this would only end in mutual bickering and recrimination. I was busy in my work and did not bother to waste my time on all this.

Undoubtedly, falsehood generates misunderstanding among the people for some time, but when the truth comes forward, falsehood cannot hold its ground. The next day, when we went to offer *fateha* for an old friend and well-wisher, I came across an old maulana and my critic there. I told him that if, in politics, differences of opinion had arisen between us, this was not something bad, as the Prophet, may the peace and blessings of Allah be upon him, has proclaimed that a difference of opinion is a blessing for the Ummah, and that if it had become a curse for us, this was because of our personal rivalries. We should not give up on our former amicable relationship, and that when I come to their village, they should at least meet with me. After the *fateha*, we left for the mosque. I also made the maulana accompany me. The people had gathered. I asked the maulana whether he would like to say a few words but he refused. I addressed the people and told them that they should understand where their benefit lay and that I did not understand why some people opposed us. We were merely the servants of the people and underwent hardships to gain benefit for the nation. They too, like us, should oppose the British, because they had subjugated us. They had occupied the land of our forefathers. God had given this land to us and our children, but on account of the disunity in our ranks and our selfish attitudes, they were enjoying themselves on our land at our expense. People are saying that our *jirga* is no longer our own, and that we have, like sugar, been dissolved in the Congress, and the *Khudai Khidmatgar* had become their *razakars*. This is false and without foundation. Our *jirga* is our own and our *Khudai Khidmatgar* continue to be *Khudai Khidmatgar*. The truth is that we have allied ourselves with the Congress. The decision to do so was not taken by me alone but by the *Loya Jirga*, in consultation with *Mian* sahib and Abdul Akbar Khan. That they should recall that the British subjected them to brutalities, oppression and imprisonment when we were not allied with the Congress. When their *jirga* decided and we allied ourselves with the Congress, we were released because of their efforts – and so here I was delivering a speech in their *jalsa*. Had it not been for their efforts, we would still be languishing in jail. At this point, because of our unity, we had broken one horn of the British, and if we continued to be united, the other horn would soon be broken, and we would be released from their cruelty and oppression. We had joined ranks with the Congress for the sole reason of liberating our land. They should understand these matters.

People were waiting for my arrival in Kalu Khan. At this point, the maulana sahib told me that he also wanted to have a word with the people. I told him that I had already requested him to make a speech and he did not and that I could not wait any longer because many people were eagerly awaiting my arrival in Kalu Khan. On my taking leave, all the people at the *jalsa* also left and the maulana sahib was unable to deliver his speech.

When we arrived in Kalu Khan, the people had already collected at the venue. I said to them that they must be under the impression that I had come to share my grief on the arrest of Kamdar Khan. No! I had not come to express my grief. On the contrary, I had come to congratulate them, as they had such a brave and honourable khan, who had gone to jail for them and for the entire nation; and that I was congratulating his mother and his relatives, for this sacrifice by her son. I said, 'Oh my brothers, whatever you are being subjected to, you must be patient. For no one has ever profited from cruelty. The cup of oppression has been drained to the dregs! The more the British subject us to oppression and cruelty, the quicker would they ruin themselves and we would be rid of them.'

We then proceeded to Adina. There too I encouraged the *Khudai Khidmatgar* to be patient and then went to Ismailia. Here, the people were very enthusiastic at my coming, because the British had again started to oppress them. I strongly encouraged them to be patient and non-violent, and then arrived in Shahbaz Garhai in the evening. Here, our general sahib had been detained. Here too there was great enthusiasm in the people. I reassured them and congratulated the *Khudai Khidmatgar* on the arrest of the general sahib. We asked sahibzada sahib of Gujarat Bakshali to get a tonga ready for us but I did not disclose my departure to anyone. The place that we were to go to was a small village and the many policemen who followed us around would have been a big burden on its relatively few inhabitants. When anyone would ask sahibzada sahib (about our plans), he would say that we were scheduled to go to Gujarat Bakhshali. There was a small village by the roadside. When we sighted the police car, we rode into the village. The police did not find out and continued to proceed in the direction of Gujarat Bakhshali. When the people of the village heard of our arrival, the men and women, happy at my coming, came to see us. I told the gathered *Khudai Khidmatgar* that they should bring for us whatever food was ready with anyone; and if they did not have anything, then it was all right, as we would spend the night hungry, but that on no account should they go to the trouble of cooking specially for us. After food, we rested for a while as we had been without rest the entire day and were very tired. But the people had collected in the mosque and demanded that Bacha Khan should say a few words to them. After the prayer, I expressed my gratitude for their love and then spoke a few words about the *Khudai Khidmatgar* movement and stressed the point that they should bear all difficulties with patience.

The next day we went to Hoti. When we arrived at the Kalpanrai, what do we see but that the police had arrived and was waiting for us, seated on the bed of the stream. They told me that they had searched for me all night and had finally sat here. The rest of the police from Mardan had also been searching for me all night but could not locate me. The inspector handed over to me orders under section 144. In those, I had been banned from visiting the Malakand Agency. I had informed Ghulam Muhammad Khan of Lundkhwar to go there for a reconnaissance. He had gone and been arrested for violating orders under section 144. They had banned me because they thought that, once I learnt of Ghulam Muhammad Khan's arrest, I would certainly attempt to go and visit him, and the government did now allow us to visit the political agencies or the tribesman. We had done our best to visit the Tribal Areas and encourage the tribesmen to join us in the wearing of our red uniforms. Let alone the present government, even when the provincial government of the *Khudai Khidmatgar* was formed, then also we were not permitted to visit our tribal brothers across the administrative border. The truth was that even though the provincial government was set up in our name, the real authority over the Tribal Areas continued to be vested in the British governor of the province.

From Hoti we proceeded to Toru. One of our very old and brave *Khudai Khidmatgar* workers, Abdur Rahim Khan, had died. He had been my companion during the tour. And when we were leaving for Chach and the police attempted to block our way with fixed bayonets, he had asked me what to do and I had directed that they should advance. He was the first to do so. His death harmed our cause greatly. Since we were on tour, we could not attend the funeral. I reassured his mother and relatives, and went to his grave prayed for him. I then delivered a short speech in the mosque and told the people not to grieve at the death of Abdur Rahim Khan. God will certainly grant him forgiveness and create many people in his stead for service to Islam. Our next stop was Mayar. The president of Mayar was a very useful and sincere person. Many people had collected there. We stayed there for a while and I spoke a few words to the people.

From this place we returned to Mardan. Here, I learnt that the khans of Sudham had been released. I was really feeling unwell and I wanted to rest in Qazi sahib's place, but the people did not give me a chance to do so. I said to Qazi sahib that, in the evening, I would come to his place and told the people that I was taking leave of them. But they would not let me go. When I left for the bus stand, the people bade me farewell. The police was following us. We just could not shake them off. We were offering our prayers when the people learnt of our presence and the *Khudai Khidmatgar* quickly put on their uniforms and, within a short time, the people of the village collected. I thanked them for the love they had shown and then took leave of them and went to Qazi sahib's house. A khan from Sudham was already there. I congratulated him on his release. He informed me that my going to Sudham was essential because the government had spread hateful propaganda amongst the poor people to try and create misunderstanding amongst them. So I could make them aware of the true facts and remove the misunderstandings created in their minds. I told him that I was 'punctured' from the fatigue of the tours and wanted to rest for a few days and only then go to Sudham, by 20 December.

We left early next morning for the bus station. We hired a tonga and reached Dargai from where we walked to Gulabad. The people were full of enthusiasm. I spoke about the virtues of patience and non-violence. From Gulabad, I came to my own hamlet, Muhammad Narai, for the night. I intended to rest here for a few days but received news from Uthmanzai that on 20 December the *Loya Jirga* had scheduled a session in Uthmanzai. On reading the letter, I left for Uthmanzai after spending a night here. When we arrived in Uthmanzai the next day, we saw about twenty-five *Khudai Khidmatgar* officers from Naukhar arrive in a lorry. They told me that they had differences of opinion about who their general should be, and that I should decide on this. I replied that the *Khudai Khidmatgar* never quarrelled over appointments. No quarrels were involved in public service. Quarrels are generated by personal interest. They realized what I said and were all quite ashamed of themselves. Then I asked them to approach *Salar* Azam in with the matter and let him decide. They replied that he had gone to Maira. So I told them to go there.

The Session of the *Loya Jirga*

It was lunch time when *Salar* sahib arrived and came to our *hujra*. As I was unwell, I took leave of him to get some rest. The decision about their general was taken amicably and to their satisfaction. They left early the next morning. The members of the Sarhad *Loya Jirga* arrived and Hakim Abdus Salam first proposed that a deputation be constituted to reconcile *Mian* Ahmad Shah and Abdul Akbar Khan, so that they could re-join the *jirga*. I seconded the proposal but reminded everybody that we had not removed them. They had parted ways with us on their own account; and if they wanted to return, the *jirga* would have no objection. Shad Muhammad Khan of Doaba opposed the proposal on the ground that they had rebelled and were working against the *jirga*.

The other proposal was to seek financial assistance from the Congress. I strongly opposed this. I reminded the members that, up to now, we had not taken a penny from the Congress and yet people were criticizing us; and if they took financial assistance, the government and those people opposing us, would carry out vicious propaganda against us. I also told them that Jawaharlal had got upset with me over this issue in the session of the Congress Working Committee held at the house of Dr. Ansari. He told me that they used to give four or five hundred rupees a month to the former Congress committee in Peshawar; that our party now was much larger, and they could give us much more assistance. I asked him whether the country belonged solely to them, or also to us. That if it belongs to them and to us, then why should we accept their help? He got annoyed with me over this and told Dr. Ansari that I was very arrogant. So this proposal, too, was not approved. Then Sardar Ram Singh, one of our *Khudai Khidmatgar,* put forth a proposal that the speech which the prime minister of Britain had delivered about the rights of our province was not satisfactory and was, therefore, unacceptable to us. But Samin Jan Khan, a lawyer, opposed it and put forth the proposal that we should accept the proposed reforms. Qazi sahib and Ali Asghar Khan were of the view that we should accept what was offered and strive to get more. I said to the *Loya Jirga* that, in accepting these reforms, what progress would our province and people make? The British were not so devoid of understanding that they would confer rights on us from which we would benefit. So, I said that I would not oppose them in the proposal; that if anyone of them saw our collective benefit in it, then they should accept it. But this proposal was shot down by Shad Muhammad Khan of Doaba, who said that we had demanded total freedom and how could we now accept only those reforms which the rest of Hindustan had rejected? There did not appear to be any sense in this. The proposal of Samin Jan Khan was rejected and that of Sardar Ram Singh accepted. All other items on the agenda were also decided upon and the session came to an end. A few members of the *jirga* stayed for the night while others left.

On 22 December, a big *darbar* was scheduled in Peshawar where proposals were made about the reforms. Dr. Khan Sahib and I were also invited. Dr. Khan Sahib, Qazi Attaullah and I discussed whether we should attend or not. I was unwell. However, it was decided that, in these circumstances, when the government was busy oppressing the *Khudai Khidmatgar,* we should not attend.

My health deteriorated further, and I was inflicted with high fever and Dr. Khan Sahib took me with him to Peshawar for treatment. He put me up in his house and began treating me and prevented people from calling on me and seeing me. My care was rest.

15

In Hazaribagh Jail:
Mass Arrests Outside

UNEXPECTEDLY A TELEGRAM FROM SARDAR PATEL ARRIVED ABOUT THE visit of Gandhiji. I was unwell but reaching there was also essential. So, I decided that on the morning of 25 December, I would leave for Bombay by the Frontier Mail. Qazi Attaullah Khan, Samin Jan Khan and the general from Akora Khattak got ready to accompany me. It was decided that we would leave from Peshawar, Qazi sahib would join me at Naukhar, and the general would accompany us from Akora Khattak. But little does a man know what is in store for him. Fate laughs at our calculation and arrangements. On 24 December, I completed all my papers and arranged with a tonga driver to pick me up. I told Dr. Khan Sahib to come early in the morning on 25 December. He, accompanied by his English wife, was leaving for the village. At this point, Arbab Abdul Ghafoor's father, Arbab Juma Khan, came to inquire about my health. In the evening, Dr. Khan Sahib returned alone from the village, leaving his wife behind.

Our Arrest

After a while, one of our well-wishers came and informed us that he had learnt that later in the evening, we were to be arrested. Dr. Khan Sahib refused to believe this. He was of the view that if any such plan had been made, this would have been kept secret. I collected my papers and handed them over to my servant, Hanif Ullah, and instructed him to hand them over to Mrs. Khan Sahib. At this moment, Dr. Khan Sahib cried out to me that the police had arrived and had surrounded our bungalow. An Englishman came and told me that I was being arrested. I said it was fine and that I would thank him and his government for arresting me, because I was ill, and no one was allowing me to rest. Now, at least, I would get some rest. He was followed by an Englishwoman for whom I opened the door of the bungalow, seating her comfortably in a chair.

The government had no information about Mrs. Khan Sahib's coming here. The Englishwoman had been sent specifically to keep her company and to be with her at night. After a while another Englishman came and arrested us, on 24 December. We were brought out of the bungalow and seated in separate cars. Many policemen had been brought for our arrest. Perhaps they thought that we might physically resist them. Dr. Khan Sahib had come out in his pyjamas. I told him to change into regular clothes as it was not known where they intended to take us. When we crossed Peshawar, I thought we were being taken to Haripur jail. Soon we arrived at the Attock bridge but that was closed. The Englishman who was accompanying me got down from the car and called out to the sentry on duty to telephone a certain sahib, and to tell him to have the gate opened. We were made to get down after the bridge. There was a room here in the police post. I was feeling very unwell and could hardly walk. The Englishman had a bed brought out for me and I lay down on it. A bed was brought out for Dr. Khan Sahib as well. After a while, Qazi sahib arrived. After him, Sadullah Khan, my nephew, also arrived. Qazi sahib lay down with me and Sadullah Khan lay down with Dr. sahib and we had a comfortable sleep. Early the next morning, accompanied by the two Englishmen, we were taken to the Attock railway station where many policemen were waiting for us. A special train had been arranged for us. We were made to enter this train and a guard was posted in my cabin, armed with a rifle with a bayonet. The train chugged out of the station. You would recall that when I last met with the governor, he noted down what I was saying and had informed me that he would discuss the points I raised with the viceroy. The result of this was that, when the Round Table Conference failed, I was the first to be arrested in Hindustan, thereby demonstrating that I was considered the most dangerous political leader. The governor had taken notes for this specific purpose. The night that I was arrested, another five hundred elders of the *Khudai Khidmatgar* had also been picked up and jailed.

Mass Arrests and Violence

After my arrest, mass arrests of the *Khudai Khidmatgar* from all over the province started. When the number of those arrested reached the thousands, the government stopped their arrests. Then the police spread out all over the villages and systematically began to beat the *Khudai Khidmatgar* with lathis. They would immerse them in freezing water and their homes were looted. The *Khudai Khidmatgar* began the picketing of the *tehsil* headquarters in Charsadda. Batches of twenty *Khudai Khidmatgar* would come to the *tehsil* each day, picket there, and be subjected to a beating by the police. Despite this, the people willingly courted arrest.

Compared to the other jails, the jail at Haripur was overflowing with *Khudai Khidmatgar* prisoners. In this jail alone the number exceeded thirteen thousand. They were subjected to great cruelty so that they would be compelled to ask for pardon. In the coldest part of winter, they were issued just one blanket each, and that too infested with lice. The barrack floors were of bare cement, which they were forced to wash with cold water. They had just one pair of ill-fitting clothes, which they had to wash and dry. It would rain, so they were forced to hang them on the railings to dry, meanwhile wrapping themselves up in their blankets. The night would be spent sitting up because of the extreme cold. Every second or third day they were given a chapati to eat, which was only a mouthful. By the time one realized, it would be finished. Against this injustice and tyranny, an old Hindu *Khudai Khidmatgar* observed silence and undertook a fast unto death. Six months later he died, and his children carried his dead body from the jail to his native Bannu. Against this cruel treatment, Hayat Gul Kaka, a *Khudai Khidmatgar* from Uthmanzai, observed a fast for forty days. He broke it only on the assurance of the superintendent, Saranjam Khan, that he would accept all his demands. When Saranjam Khan became the superintendent, he reassured the prisoners and put a stop to the inhuman treatment meted out to them. Because of this, the prisoners called off their strike and began to work again. The British did not like his attitude of clemency with the prisoners. Saranjam Khan was transferred as a result and replaced by an Englishman, Smith, from the province of Bihar. At first, he was also hostile to the *Khudai Khidmatgar*, but they reciprocated this hostility with their usual bravery. The wearing of rough uniforms made from sacks, putting them into fetters, beating them with sticks and other punishments were meted out to them. For three long years, the *Khudai Khidmatgar* were subjected to torture, but Smith was not successful. It was after this, that his attitude and behaviour towards the *Khudai Khidmatgar* changed.

Abdullah Jan and his father from Kattozai were brought before Kulli Khan, who was the assistant commissioner of Charsadda. He tried to intimidate Abdullah Jan. The court was teeming with people and the police was present in great numbers. Addressing Abdullah Jan, Kulli Khan told him that he had recited a poem against the British to the effect that, 'I love the revolution and, for it, shall sacrifice my life!' Abdullah Jan retorted that even now he recites this with great pride, and in a loud voice proclaimed, 'I shall love the revolution though my head be on the gallows!' Tales such as these of the bravery and spirit of our youth abound. They were undaunted and could not be intimidated by anyone or anything. This story is but one example of this.

In Hazaribagh Jail

The government had nominated a Sardarkhel inspector of police to deal with us on our journey. A contingent of the police of each province through which our train passed would be present for our guidance and safety. The inspector from the Punjab police was with us and had the responsibility to shut the windows of our compartment whenever we opened them. Finally, I told him that, 'Inspector sahib, we are not women, that each time we open a window for some fresh air, you come and shut it, so that nobody can see us.' The Sardarkhel inspector was a close acquaintance of both Dr. Khan Sahib and Qazi sahib, and often used to say that Dr. Khan Sahib had saved his life. Qazi sahib was very fond of reading the newspaper. He would ask the Sardarkhel inspector for a newspaper, but he, out of fear of the government, would not give it to him. It is a principle of mine that, whenever arrested, I never ask the police accompanying me for anything. When our train would stop at stations for refuelling with coal and to get water, our windows and doors used to be shut and if we wanted to get down, the inspector from Punjab would not allow us. When our train reached the United Provinces, an English officer and sergeant came to take charge of us. After doing so, the Englishman came to my compartment and opened its door. He asked me to get down and to take a stroll on the platform to stretch my legs. Just compare the behaviour and attitude of this English officer and the Muslim officers of Punjab. We were at war with the British and were trying to take the government away from them, and here was our Muslim brother from Punjab, for whom we were trying to get the government. It was the day of Christmas. The English officer, with great love and affection, brought some alcohol and offered it to me. I regretted and told him that I did not drink. He was surprised to hear this. I will never forget his tolerance and affection. When we arrived in Allahabad, Dr. Khan Sahib was separated from us and sent to Nainital jail. Then they made Sadullah Khan get down and he was sent to Banaras jail. When we entered the province of Bihar, Qazi Attaullah was made to get off and was sent to Gaya jail and I was dispatched to Hazaribagh jail. This jail was located some forty miles from the railway station. When I was made to sit in the car, I had two Englishmen with me. One was a deputy commissioner and the other was the superintendent of police. The Sardarkhel inspector also accompanied us. When I sat down, I was given an English newspaper, which the Sardarkhel inspector refused to give to his friends and benefactors. When I entered the jail and was taken to my barrack, the officer of the jail, who was a Hindu, asked me who the police officer accompanying me was. I asked why he was asking me about him. He said that he seemed to him to be a very vile person. He told me that he was a dangerous man and that I should be cautious of him. I was locked up alone in a barrack. Other than the superintendent and the jailer, no other person could see me. The path in front of my barrack, used by the inmates of the jail to come and go, was barricaded. I was extremely worried about the welfare of the *Khudai Khidmatgar* in the Frontier.

I fall sick when I am alone. Here I was all alone. I could neither sleep properly and nor did I have an appetite. One night I dreamt that there was a big river, beside which was a large dome. I was sitting inside the dome when it flooded, shaking to its foundations. I got very frightened and feared that it might collapse on me. But, after a while, the flood subsided, and the dome remained intact. When I woke up, I was so relieved that it was all a dream. Most of my fears regarding the fate of the *Khudai Khidmatgar* were reduced, because I interpreted the flood in the dream as one which came over our movement but passed safely without drowning it. Then I thought that if I were to sit idle all day, my health would be badly affected. Some occupation and work was needed to spend the time. I asked the superintendent to give me a pick and a hoe so that I could work on the land in front of my barrack and develop it to plant vegetables. He assigned two prisoners to assist me in the task. I made the land cultivable and planted vegetables and flowers. I benefitted in two ways from this endeavour: one, I found work which occupied my time, and secondly, I had companions to talk to.

I was a state prisoner. The deputy commissioner would come and visit me on the first of every month. Fond of vegetables and flowers, he would occasionally bring me seeds. He was a very humane and good man. Six months passed and he himself noticed that my health was getting worse. Without my asking him, he wrote to the government of the Frontier that I needed companionship, and that my friends in Gaya jail should be transferred here. Qazi Attaullah Khan was there, who was in even greater difficulty than I was. I would at least be able to get some sleep in bits and pieces but he, poor man, could not sleep at all. Due to his being lonely, he did not sleep properly for an entire year. Of all the jails in Hindustan, the one in Gaya was the hottest. Qazi sahib and I were in the same province i.e., Bihar, while Dr. Khan Sahib and Sadullah Khan were in another province i.e., the United Provinces. But Sir Ralph Griffith, the governor of the Frontier, was against us and did not want to put us together, and so, instead of Qazi sahib, he had Dr. Khan Sahib transferred to Hazaribagh. After a year, Qazi sahib was sent to where Sadullah Khan was.

Adjacent to my barrack was the one in which women political workers, including the sister of Dr. Rajendra Prasad, were detained. One day the deputy superintendent of the jail came and told me that he was in an extreme difficulty. The women political prisoners were insisting that he should allow them to meet Rajendra Prasad, otherwise they would begin to agitate. This he could not do. He wanted me to intervene on his behalf and dissuade them from agitating. I sent them a message and relieved him of this worry.

When Dr. Khan Sahib came and saw that I was confined to my barrack, he informed me that, in Nainital jail, he would walk in the open with Jawaharlal. So he decided to ask the superintendent of the jail for permission to do so. The superintendent from Punjab, was with Dr. Khan Sahib during the First World War but was a coward, and hence, refused. But Dr. Khan Sahib was adamant and finally we could walk outside our barrack. Babu Rajendra Prasad and other prominent leaders of Bihar, including Acharya Kripalani, were detained here. They neither knew of my presence, and nor was I aware of theirs.

One day, when we were strolling outside, by coincidence we came across one of their associates. He was surprised to see us and asked since when were we here. I told him that I was here for the past eight months, while Dr. Khan Sahib had joined me a few days ago. He informed us that several political prisoners were here from Bihar. Thereafter, we would occasionally visit them. The people of Bihar are very good people. The deputy superintendent of the jail, who was a good man and a class fellow of Dr. Rajendra Prasad, showed great sympathy for the nationalists. One day we suggested to him that, before the release of each political prisoner, he should arrange for him to meet us, so that we could entertain him as a guest. Though the inhabitants of Bihar are good people, they are afflicted by acute caste barriers. In living together with us their rigid attitudes in this regard were somewhat reformed. One day, while entertaining a political prisoner, we had tea accompanied by sizzling pakoras and fried brinjal. I would give him the tea in a cup and hand out the pakoras to him. Dr. Khan Sahib would hand out the fried brinjal to him and he would eat the pakoras and brinjal with his tea. When the tea finished, he laughed and told us that they were so caste-ridden that one day a Muslim postman came and handed his letter over to him, and when he did so, he himself held on to one edge of the envelope, while the postman held onto the other (so as not to touch him). At this point, he was standing next to me. He poured some water over me and exclaimed, 'You have been defiled!'

I had a lot of love for the leaders of Bihar. I can never forget their love for me. The Biharis, both men and women, are a brave lot. They have offered many sacrifices for the freedom of the country. I will now tell you the story of a woman, who was imprisoned with us.

A Brave Woman

One day the deputy superintendent came and was in a jovial mood and told me the story of a woman who was detained in the jail. That day, her husband, who was a lawyer, had come to visit her along with their five children. He begged her that she should keep the younger two in jail with her and that the older three children would stay with him. But the wife asked him to look after them all. Although she was prepared to look after all of them, but as he had not listened to her, he should look after all of them. The deputy superintendent said that he asked the woman why she refused to keep the children. She replied that when the Congress made the call for agitation, she had asked her husband to join as it was for a national cause. But he had replied that he would do so after a couple of pending cases in court. After a few days, when she repeatedly asked him whether the cases had concluded, he would reply that a few still remained. When she realized that he was making excuess and was not ready to go to jail, she had come herself for the picketing and was consequently arrested and left the children with him. A nation whose womenfolk display such bravery and consciousness of national goal, is bound to achieve its objective. And this is the reason that the British were compelled to leave our land.

After Dr. Khan Sahib's arrival, we were transferred to another barrack. There was plenty of land lying arid next to this barrack. I asked the deputy superintendent to help me develop this land. He gave me two prisoners for this and I got down to work. There was an *arat* installed on the land. I made this functional and cultivated sugarcane and different kinds of vegetables. The papayas of Bihar are famous for their sweetness. I prepared a large piece of land and planted them on it. The deputy commissioner would come on his monthly visit. He took a lot of interest in my work and would occasionally provide me with good radish and turnip seeds, and would tell me that agriculture was his hobby. This jail was located on the edge of a jungle. We would, from time to time, hear the roaring of lions. At night, many snakes would enter the jail. They were so poisonous that if one was bitten and not injected immediately, he would be dead in two hours. I was used to taking a stroll after the evening meal. The superintendent would discourage me from this. But I replied that if I did not walk I would neither be able to sleep nor digest my food. So, we then bought a gas lamp which would be lit and carried by a servant behind me when I was taking my walk. When the monsoon broke, the snakes would multiply and be found wriggling, wherever there was a body of water or puddle. These snakes were small but lethal. I used to wake up early in the morning. One day when I woke up and was putting on my shoes, one shoe overturned, and I saw a small krait slide out of it. God saved me from its bite. We had a servant here who would entertain and engage Dr. Khan Sahib in interesting conversations. There were several prisoners here from the nearby jungle. The servants would tell Dr. Khan Sahib that they, both men and women, would clasp each other's hands and dance together. One day we asked him the reason for his imprisonment. He replied, 'I killed a man! When the criminal proceedings against me started, my relatives hired a lawyer for me. The lawyer told me what to say. However, I told him that this was lies and that I did not lie. Lawyers have made the people accustomed to lying. The truth is that ever since these lawyers have been created in this country, lies and false cases have increased manifold. But I did not lie and told the truth, and, on account of telling the truth, I was saved from the gallows.'

The government did not give me an allowance for my children although it did so for those of Dr. Khan Sahib and Qazi sahib. The other game they played with me was to instigate my tenants to deprive me of my land holding, which was quite substantial. Due to lack of money, my son, Ghani, was forced to abandon his studies in America and come home.

My papaya orchard had begun to bear fruit and we had eaten one or two papayas when orders came for our release. We had planted many papayas that had now ripened. Although this was against the rules of the jail, I had got special permission to do so from the inspector general. When we were leaving, both the jail staff and the inmates of the jail were sorry to see us leave. They said to us that when we leave, they would uproot all the papaya trees. Their fruit was exceedingly sweet. Initially the cultivation of papayas inside the jail premises was permissible. The permission was withdrawn only when some prisoners had uprooted the trees, placed their trunks against the wall and escaped.

Until the time that Dr. Khan Sahib was transferred to the jail, the arrangements for my food were extremely bad. There was a vast difference between our cuisine and that of the Biharis, and I did not know how to cook. When Dr. Khan Sahib came, things improved. Because he was a good cook, he taught our helper. Every Sunday I used to fast. I also used to observe silence. I did so because I was in the bad habit of talking too much and losing my temper. For my *paishmanay*, Dr. Khan Sahib would cook for me himself. At this time when Gandhiji had gone on a hunger strike, I too had followed suit. I recall that this was for eight continuous days.

Dr. Khan Sahib told me that when they were in the jail at Nainital, Jawaharlal had said that the Congress Party wanted to financially assist the *Khudai Khidmatgar*. He said that he had agreed to this proposal. I told him that, in doing so, he had committed a grave blunder and that we were not prepared to accept assistance from the Congress. We, too, were struggling for the freedom of our land just as the Congress was. So, I did not consider their assistance as appropriate and my refusal earlier had annoyed Jawaharlal. Why should we seek assistance from them? We, the *Khudai Khidmatgar*, numbered about two hundred and fifty thousand in all. What would be the scale of the assistance that the Congress intended? The other point was that any assistance they might provide would not be enough for them all. This would, therefore, sow disunity in their ranks. So, when Kripalani was being released, I told him that we did not want any financial assistance from the Congress. That Jawaharlal had mentioned this to Dr. Khan Sahib and he had agreed to this. I told Kripalani that he should tell all the leaders that Abdul Ghaffar says that the *Khudai Khidmatgar* will not take any assistance from the Congress.

When our cook learnt of our release, he broke into tears. I asked him whether he was upset about our release. He replied that he was not. On the contrary, he was happy, but was concerned about his own fate. The jail authorities were also upset at our release and I, too, was extremely upset at having to leave my papaya trees.

16

Proscribed from Visiting the Frontier and Punjab

Proscribed from Visiting the Frontier Province

AFTER THREE YEARS OF DETENTION, WE WERE RELEASED FROM Hazaribagh jail in 1934 and went to Patna as guests of the woman whose husband had refused to court arrest, while she had done so and had been detained along with us. In Bihar, we had many political companions detained with us and had an excellent relationship with them. When they learnt of our release and we arrived in Patna, Rajendra Prasad and all the other leaders came to see us. They organized a large *jaloos* for us and held an equally large *jalsa*. After the *jalsa*, the government served a notice prohibiting us from visiting the Punjab or Frontier Provinces. Gandhiji and Pandit Jamnalal Bajaj had sent an invitation to us, that since we had been banned from visiting Punjab and Frontier, we should proceed to Wardha.

The All-India Congress Working Committee Session

The All-India Congress Committee session was scheduled in Bombay. The Congress reception committee decided that I should become the president of the party. I received a telegram from Rajendra Prasad that though he had been elected as president, he was leaving the post in my favour. I sent a telegram to him saying that I was an ordinary soldier in the *Khudai Khidmatgar* movement and that I was not prepared to serve as the president of the Congress. I would, however, serve the party as an ordinary member. The *pandal* of this session was erected in my name, with the gate beautifully decorated, and dedicated to me. Abdul Khaliq

Khaleeq sahib and other Pukhtun brothers who had come to see me also participated in the session. Spending a few days in Wardha we travelled to Calcutta. In a grand reception, the Calcutta Corporation gave us a warm welcome.

When I was leaving for Calcutta, I had consulted Gandhiji. I could not visit the Frontier or Punjab, and nor could I sit idle because I was a *Khudai Khidmatgar* and had to serve the people. Now the only places remaining in Hindustan were Bengal and Sindh, where the Muslims were in a majority. I asked him what his choice of province was where I should work. It was decided that work needed to be done in Bengal. In my speeches delivered in the Muslim areas, I spoke about the fact that I had come to serve them and that I wanted to work in the villages, because, for one, the majority lived in the villages, and those who were unaware and afflicted by hardships also lived there. Secondly, newspapers and radios were available in the towns, while they were not available in the villages. Since I had come to bring about awareness among them, I would visit the villages.

In Calcutta, the Muslims had an *Anjuman* whose President was Suhrawardy sahib.[29] Other prominent leaders like him were also members of the *Anjuman*. I was invited by the *Anjuman*, where, in accordance with the customs of the people, arrangements for a musical session had also been made. When the time for music and songs came, I expressed a desire that this was enough and that we should now also discuss some matters of public importance. When I expressed the desire to visit the Muslim dominated areas of the city and the Muslim villages, so that I could start work there, I requested these leaders to provide me with someone who could translate what I said into Bengali. They made the excuse that these areas were malaria inflicted and that going there was a health hazard. In other words, let alone travelling and rendering services, they were also trying to prevent me from visiting these areas, because they feared that this would have an adverse impact on their leadership.

I was disappointed and frustrated with the attitude of the Muslim leaders and informed Dr. Praful Chandra Ghosh, member of the Congress working committee, requesting him to accompany me to the villages, because the villagers understood only Bengali, which I did not know. He readily agreed to assist me in whatever capacity I needed. But he warned me that the people of Bengal were lifeless, and asked what I intended to do here. He and I left on a tour of the villages. Whichever village we would go to, I would begin to work according to my methodology. We would go to the people, we would speak to them and I would tell them that Hindustan was a very rich country. Every household had its milk, lots of *ghee* and rice. But what had come over it now that it was facing shortages of these commodities, and our children were naked, hungry and miserable? They, poor souls, would listen to me attentively and give a lot of thought to what I said. Towards the end I would remind them that until such time that this country was not freed from foreign domination, and the authority for managing its affairs had not been entrusted to them, they and their children would not develop and prosper. This country had been gifted to us by God, but because of our lack of understanding, selfishness and disunity in our ranks, authority over it had been snatched from our hands by the British, and they were enjoying our legitimate wealth. We toured the area for a few days and then selected a central place to hold a *jalsa*. In our first *jalsa*, fifty people came. A few days later, when we held a second *jalsa* two hundred people came to attend it. Thus, the consecutive *jalsas* attracted more and more people. At this point, I said to Praful Babu, 'You said that these people are lifeless, but you can see now for yourself that these people are not lifeless, they are very much alive and responsive. They are not lifeless. But, unfortunately, these poor people have no one who cares for them or sympathizes with them and who will awaken them.' Since the Congress session was starting we went to Bombay to participate in it. During my stay in Calcutta, Ghani and Wali were both with me.

In the session of the All-India Congress Committee in Bombay, a few representatives of the Christian organizations came to meet me and extended an invitation for me to meet with their organization. They questioned me about the *Khudai Khidmatgar* movement. I told them the entire history of the movement; that when people enrolled themselves in the movement, they take a pledge before God to serve humanity. The service of God lay in the service of His creation. I also recounted to them all the incidents and the inhuman treatment that we had gone through.

Till then, I did not know that telling the truth also amounted to an offence under British law. The Congress session ended and we returned to Wardha. I conferred with Gandhiji and arranged to return to Bengal. I decided that, until such time that I could return to my own province, I would work in Bengal. When the government learnt of this, it said that the Hindus of Bengal were wide awake, and if the Muslims too were woken up, things would not bode well. So, the police came and arrested me for the speech I had delivered to the Christians and took me to Bombay. When I got down at the station, many women and men had assembled to meet me. I was taken to the jail and criminal proceedings were initiated against me. Gandhiji sent me a message that this was not the time to be in jail, that it was a time to put in maximum efforts for the fulfilment of our mission; that I should not go to jail but should tender an apology. I sent a reply to him that I knew very well that the government would not spare me, so why should I seek a pardon? But he was adamant and instructed me to simply say that I regretted what I had said. I was quite convinced that the government would not set me free, but I agreed to do as Gandhiji had instructed. However, despite that, I was sentenced to two years rigorous imprisonment.

At the Sabarmati Jail

I was kept for a few days in the Bombay jail and then transferred to the Sabarmati jail in Ahmedabad. This jail had an English superintendent. He was an extremely short-tempered man who considered the rules of the jail as those of God. I was detained all alone in a barrack. Even the ward *lambardar* was not allowed to enter it. He would bolt both the doors and would sit outside himself. There was a lot of difference between our food and the food eaten here. I was in 'B' class. But there was no difference between the 'B' class of this province and the 'C' class of our province. There was no bed for the 'B' class prisoners to sleep on, and they would sleep on the floor. There was nobody to talk to. There were many monkeys here. To pass time I would play with them. Because of the bad food, I fell ill and came down with influenza. Despite this serious ailment, no one took me to the hospital, and nor was I provided with a bed in the ward. I was on the bare cement floor. The mat that I had been provided with was so short that when I stretched my legs, they would land on the cement floor. Plus, the blanket given to me was so small, that when I covered my head with it, my feet would be exposed; and when I covered my feet, my head would be uncovered. All this vengeful treatment had two reasons. One was that when Mr. Emerson had come on an inspection from the Gujarat jail, he was then a minister of the Punjab government. I was sitting at my weaving frame, he did not enter my cell and I did not, like the other ordinary criminals, go to the steel railing to greet him. He had been offended by this. Now he was the home secretary of the central government. The other reason was that when I was in Simla, in connection with a meeting of the Congress working committee, I was told to meet with the viceroy. I had no business to transact with him, and meeting with him without a fixed agenda seemed to be like wasting his time. So, I said that I had no work with him and so why should I meet him? If the viceroy had work with me, then it was up to him to take the initiative and I would certainly comply. I spoke the plain truth in equally plain words, but it was taken amiss and considered as an insult to the viceroy.

While I was in prison, Safia Somjee came to meet me. At the time, she was the commander of the women *razakar* of the Congress for Hindustan. She later married Sadullah Khan (Dr. Khan Sahib's son). Gandhiji too came to meet me in Sabarmati jail. When he saw me and learnt of the treatment I was given, he was very upset. With his effort, after a while I was given 'A' class (in prison). Before Gandhiji, Sardar Patel had also come to meet me. Gandhiji, according to his usual practice, joked with me during the meeting and made me laugh a lot. There were restrictions imposed on meeting with me to the effect that, except for relatives, I could not meet anyone else. I had no relatives in Ahmedabad. Off and on, Sadullah Khan's wife, Safia, would come to see me. At first, she was also put to a lot of inconvenience in getting permission. She got permission after a prolonged effort, even though she had said that she was the wife of my nephew and was a relative.

The prisoners in this jail were treated very badly. I was always kept confined to my own barrack and was not even allowed to walk outside. No one could come near me. One day I happened to be returning from a meeting, which used to be held in the superintendent's office above my ward, when, on coming out of his office, I saw a group of five prisoners standing there. They were being searched. They were naked, except for a small loin-cloth that barely covered them from the front and the back. A string was tied around their waists. I was shocked to see them as I had not seen anything like it in any other jail. From the line-up, a prisoner would be produced one at a time, his loin-cloth would be removed, leaving the poor prisoner stark naked. He would then be made to sit on his haunches and then get up in rapid succession several times. I commented on what a vile and demeaning procedure this was. I was told that some prisoners shoved things up their anus and brought them into the jail. This was the reason they were made to sit and get up so that these items could fall out from the pressure of doing so.

I was given an 'A' class cell, but there was a vast difference between the food of the Gujaratis and the Pukhtuns. There was no cook here who knew how to cook our food. During this period, the inspector general of prisons came on a tour. When he came to me, I told him of my difficulty and requested him that he should transfer the cook who cooked for me in the Bombay jail. The other request I made was to be transferred from here to some other jail because the climate of this place did not suit me. The inspector general sahib was a good man who had served in the Frontier Province. He told me that he would arrange for me to be transferred to Punjab and to have a Pukhtun cook from the Frontier to serve me. I told him, but in vain, that Punjab was not prepared to have me, that I was proscribed from Punjab and that I did not want a Pukhtun cook. He should give me my own cook from Bombay. His intentions were good. He thought that if I got transferred to Punjab, I would be nearer to home, and the Pukhtun would serve me according to my wishes. But he was unaware of the reality. He tried but the Punjab government refused to accept me; and from Peshawar the government sent a prisoner who did not have the faintest idea of how to cook, and, to beat it all, was also a patient of tuberculosis. Once again, I was transferred to the district jail at Bareilly. There was a central jail there as well which also had political prisoners. If I had been taken there, I would have been more comfortable. But they were bent on torturing me, and this is how the time of my imprisonment was spent there.

Bareilly Jail

I was confined alone in the district jail at Bareilly in a small barrack all by myself. The rest of the jail building was on a mound while my barrack was down below. I would descend to my barrack from the jail through a staircase. I generally fall sick when left alone for long, so I requested the superintendent to assign me some land, which I would rehabilitate and grow vegetables on. My request was granted and I got down to work. Dr. Khan Sahib, like me, was also banned from visiting the Punjab and Frontier Provinces. But when the election to the sole seat of the Frontier in the Central Legislative Assembly of India was announced, the *jirga* of the Frontier nominated him as its nominee to contest the election. Though Dr. Khan Sahib was not allowed to go to the Frontier for his election campaign, even then he won the election by a very wide margin. And when he was elected as a member of the central assembly, he could go to the province.

Sadullah Khan and his wife also came to visit me in the Bareilly jail. He told me that the governor had informed him that, for my comfort, he had sent a cook from the Frontier. I laughed at this and asked him to express my gratitude to the governor for sending such a great chef to serve me. I told them that he was suffering from tuberculosis and had been intentionally sent to infect me as well. And he was not a cook either! And that I had him transferred after a great deal of effort. Ghani and Wali had also come to this jail to meet me. When Dr. Khan Sahib was elected member of the central assembly, the government of the Frontier Province allowed him to visit the province. He, along with his wife, came to meet me. His daughter, Maryam, and my daughter, Mehr Taj, were also with him. Before the meeting, Dr. Khan Sahib had also quarrelled with the jail authorities. They had informed him that, in jail, not more than three persons could meet with a prisoner, and they happened to be four. Permission to meet me would be accorded by the Frontier government. This had been given to them through a letter. The next time, Qazi Attaullah Khan and Samin Jan Khan came. Samin Jan was contesting elections from the Naukhar constituency to the provincial sssembly, and the *Khudai Khidmatgar* of the constituency were opposed to him because, while in Haripur, he had indulged in irresponsible talk. He wanted that I should write to Qari sahib and Saiful Malooq of Kheshgi not to oppose him. I told him that I was a prisoner. This was up to those who were not in jail. But I was compelled by them, and so wrote the letters. On account of my intervention, they gave up their opposition to him, and he was elected as a member. But when he was not selected at the time of the formation of the government, he got annoyed with us, and the same Samin Jan, for whom I wrote letters of recommendation because of Qazi sahib, and on the basis of which he was returned to the assembly, turned against Qazi sahib and started opposing him. Just as the *Khudai Khidmatgar* movement is a selfless movement, based on service in God's way, whenever a true *Khudai Khidmatgar* has been returned to the assembly, he has proved himself worthy and of benefit to his people. But whenever he has been returned based on selfish motives and his personal relationship, he has usually not been elected, and anyone who **has** managed to get elected, has never been of any help to them. Rather, instead of benefit, he has harmed the party. Barrister Abdul Ghafoor Khan was never a *Khudai Khidmatgar* and nor did he have any national service to his credit. But because of his friendship with Dr. Khan Sahib, he was nominated as a candidate of the party. He was also expecting to be made a minister, but then, how many can be appointed as ministers? There were just four ministers to be appointed, and there were many who were in line. Dr. Khan Sahib's bungalow had become the centre of party factionalism and, in the end, these selfish people turned out to be unfaithful to the party. Similarly, Ghulam Ghaus and Jehangir Khan Kundi failed to even get elected.

I used to work on my assigned plot of land in jail. There was a barrack adjacent to it on from which I could hear crying and wailing all the time. One day, I asked the prisoners working with me as to what was happening. They were scared that if Shahji were to find out, then who would come to their assistance? They told me that Shahji sahib beat the prisoners to extract money from them. He also confined them to cells. And if this did not give the required results, then they were stripped naked and made to sit opposite each other. Each one was provided with a pair of tweezers and made to pluck each other's pubic hair. The prisoners were absolutely fed up and at their wits end at the hands of this Shahji sahib. At last, Mr. Palmer, the inspector general of Prisons, retired and went on pension. Mr. Salamatullah Khan was appointed in his place. Mr. Palmer was a very corrupt man, and the jailers would provide him a share of the money extracted from the prisoners, and there was no one to hold him accountable. Colonel Salamatullah Khan was a good person. When he came to Bareilly for the first time, he paid a surprise visit to the jail. It used to be his practice that he would not give prior information of his visits, so the jail staff continuously stood in fear of him. When he came to the gate of the jail and saw that the prisoners were outside, busy cleaning, his suspicions were aroused, and he immediately called for their tickets. It was early morning, and no one expected that the inspector general sahib could ever arrive so early. Shahji had brought out many prisoners for cleaning in order to earn himself a good name. But he was caught in his own machinations and was suspended. The prisoners were very relieved and expressed great joy. The *darogha* of the jail was also very corrupt and had a bad character as well. Next to mine was the barrack of the women. He used to visit it often. From the experience that I have of jail, the women prisoners are always subjected to immoral practices at the hands of the jail staff.

During winter, one could manage in this jail, but the summers were very difficult. For one, my barrack was in a depression. It was narrow and surrounded by high walls. My barrack was small and full of iron fences, on top of which pieces of burnt clay were lying. It had small apertures at intervals. The sun would shine through them. The minister of jails of the United Provinces was Maharaj Singh. A sympathetic and good man, he would come to the jail and talked a great deal with me. He wrote and recommended that I should be transferred to a jail located in a cooler climate. In April and May, it is extremely hot in the United Provinces and in June, the monsoon breaks. When this happens, the weather becomes pleasant.

In the Jail at Almora

The government made me spend the hottest months of April and May at Bareilly and when it was June and the monsoon broke, I was transferred to the Almora jail. I protested to the jail authorities that during monsson people generally came down from the hills to the plains, and here I was, being sent to the hills. But this was the government's order. The government was not interested in my well-being but was only carrying out its own propaganda that they treated their political prisoners well.When I arrived at the jail in Almora, the officials there were also surprised, that the government had played a fine joke on me. Almora used to be in the grip of rains in the monsoons, at times for eight to nine days continuously. It was raining, and I would be alone in my barrack. Because of the rain and gales I was usually sick. When I was in the jail at Bareilly, the inspector general Salamatullah Khan came to see me. As already mentioned, he was a very good person. He asked me whether I had any complaint to make. I replied that my cook who has been sent out from the Frontier did not know how to cook and was also suffering from tuberculosis and that I should be freed of him. So, he was transferred and sent back to the Frontier. There was no person at the Almora jail who could cook for me and, to add to my woes, I was also not feeling well and could not eat anything. Still, I needed someone to cook for me. The superintendent was a good man who had a lot of sympathy for me. He tried to arrange for a good cook for me from elsewhere. He asked me when he was about to write to the government, and I tried to stop him from doing so, but he wrote nonetheless. The government transferred a prisoner from the Bareilly jail on the plea that he was my former cook. He was not my cook at all. On the contrary, he was my sweeper. The next day when the superintendent sahib came, I told him that although he might not believe what I said, but that what I had predicted had happened. The government of the British is blind and oblivious to the needs of those in whose hearts there is love for their motherland and its people. After some time, the inspector general sahib came to Almora on tour. He met me and said to me that it rained very frequently here, and my health was also failing and that if I wanted to, he would transfer me to the Bareilly central jail because there were other political prisoners there as well. But I had a short time to go before my release, so I spent it in this jail and was set free in the month of August 1936.

Release from Jail

On being released, the superintendent handed me a notice from the government in which it was laid down that I could not visit either the Frontier or Punjab provinces. In my view, the major reason for this was that, in those days, the elections to the provincial assembly of our province were scheduled. They didn't want to take any chance as my arrival in my province could influence the voters and lead the *Khudai Khidmatgar* to return with a majority. Similarly, when in 1932, Dr. Khan Sahib and I were released from the Hazaribagh jail, he and I were both banned from visiting Punjab and the Frontier because, at that time, elections to the central assembly had been scheduled. Even though I was not allowed to enter my own province, our *Khudai Khidmatgars* won nineteen of the forty seats contested, because we had put in a lot of effort in the province and had made the electorate aware of the importance of their vote, and political consciousness had been generated in them.

Visiting Wardha

When I came to the gate of the (Almora) jail, I saw many Congressmen gathered outside who had learnt of my release. I had intended to go to Wardha, but the people of Almora would not let me, and so I spent a night with them. They had arranged for a huge *jalsa* at night at which I delivered a short speech and left for Wardha the next morning. Our trains were to be changed at the station and many people had come to meet me there. I got down from my compartment for them. I intended to spend the time available between the two trains at the railway station, but they forced me to accompany them to the city. After having lunch, I returned and boarded another train. When I arrived at Wardha station, Jamnalal Bajaj, Mahadev Desai and many others had come to welcome me. I learnt that Mahatmaji was not in Wardha but was living at Sevagram, which was about four miles away. The next morning, after spending the night at Wardha I went to Sevagram. At Sevagram, there was a room where Gandhiji was sitting with a few people. He was very pleased to see me and came out to greet me. He made me sit beside him and started asking questions.

Seth Jamnalalji's son had accompanied me to Sevagram. He said that, while in Wardha, Bacha Khan should stay where he and Dr. Khan Sahib had stayed in 1934. Gandhiji also wanted this but I wanted to stay in Sevagram. However, I later realized that I may cause others discomfort because there was only one room and there were six people living in it, including Gandhiji's wife and a few other women. Gandhiji read my mind and said to me that if I was not going to be uncomfortable, they would not be inconvenienced at all by my presence, that there was another room available for the women. I would certainly not be inconvenienced, and I was happy being with Gandhiji. My needs were very limited. Next to Gandhiji's mat, on the floor, another one was spread out for me. We were many people in this room, but I was not uncomfortable, because our purpose was the same, and we had the same ideology, and because of it we were one. The Pukhtuns have a saying that 'if the heart is large, the space is never too small.'

Meeting with My Children

Learning of my release, my children Ghani, Wali and Mehr Taj came to see me. Two years of Mehr Taj's education had been lost. It was a boon, however, that Mehr Taj and Maryam, Dr. Khan Sahib's daughter, who were of the same age and were very fond of each other, came with him for these two years. After meeting me, Wali returned to the village, while Ghani and Mehr Taj stayed behind with me. Here, only boiled food was served at meals, which Wali did not like, but Ghani and Mehr Taj did not seem to mind. I was concerned about getting admission for Mehr Taj in a good Muslim school, but I could not find one to my satisfaction. A lot of time was wasted in this effort. Finally, due to my frustration, and with the help of Professor Mujeeb sahib, I got her admitted to a school in Lucknow. Ghani also left for Gola Logan Nath and got a job in a sugar mill there. Ali was the only one who remained. He was studying at Colonel Brown's Cambridge School at Dehradun. When his vacations started, he also came to me in Wardha. This was a school run on the lines of an English public school. He knew English but not Urdu. I did not consider this to be in his interest. I decided to get him admitted in a school in which, together with English, Urdu was also taught. In consultation with Gandhiji, I admitted him to a Cambridge School in Panchgani. This is a hill station near Poona and has an excellent climate.

Elections and the Working Committee of the Congress

In those days, elections to the assemblies were about to be held, so the Congress Working Committee convened to firm up a strategy. The question was, what kind of people would we give tickets to, to contest from the platform of the Congress party? I believed that we should give tickets only to those faithful Congress workers who were tried and tested and had rendered financial and personal sacrifices for the nation. Most members were of the same view and it was decided that prospective candidates who signed the Congress ticket and had enough financial resources, would be preferred to award tickets to. In this way, the Congress would win many seats. However, such people have also harmed the Congress party substantially, particularly at the time when the Congress decided to quit governments. From the first session of the Committee, in which I participated, I realized that members had differences of opinion. On one side, there was Jawaharlal, and on the other was Sardar Patel, along with C. Rajagopalachari.

I discussed this with Gandhiji as well, who was unhappy at the developments of these differences. Because I was not involved in these groupings, I had a good relationship with both groups. I tried my best to reduce the differences between them. I was successful in this effort to a large extent. The Congress had scheduled a *jalsa* in Bombay. Since I had been jailed in Bombay, the people were eager that I should participate in it. Gandhiji was not in favour of this and opposed my going to Bombay. He feared that I would again deliver a speech and the government would again find an excuse to detain me. When Jawaharlal found out about this, he was very upset and went to Gandhiji and took permission from him, taking the responsibility upon himself, and took me along with him to Bombay.

My Stay in Bombay

I was warmly welcomed in Bombay. The Christian Association of Bombay, where I had given a speech for which I was jailed, gave me several welcome addresses along with other parties. In the drafting and passing of the resolutions in the working committee, the large differences of opinion that once existed were no longer there on account of my efforts. After the *jalsa*, I spent a few days with Safia and Sadullah Khan, and then proceeded to Sevagram. All kinds of people would come to Sevagram to meet with Gandhiji and not just politicians. Life at Sevagram was very simple and regular. Gandhiji did not like the fact that the number of people were increasing here, so finally, he made them take their leave. The number of both women and men had grown. There were only two rooms for them to live in. There were no inhibitions between men and women. Generally, the boys and girls would sleep together in the veranda. I, however, was not in favour of this practice. Those boys and girls were admittedly virtuous and pure; but I was against putting them to the test. I, therefore, decided that the boys and girls should occupy separate verandas. Gandhiji also accepted this proposal.

In 1937, the elections of the Congress approached, and the name of C. Rajagopalachari was proposed and selected for the post of president. However, after some days, on account of an incident in Madras, he withdrew his candidature, but this was only an excuse on his part. The truth was that he wanted to contest for a seat in the Madras assembly. If he had become the president of the Congress, he would automatically have been debarred from doing so. Therefore, Jawaharlal decided to contest for the post. After a few days, a session of the Working Committee was held in Sevagram. Sardar Patel proposed that Jawaharlal should not contest elections for this office for a second time. Jawaharlal suggested that if I, Bacha Khan, were to contest, he would withdraw in my favour and if 'Bacha Khan does not stand, then I will stand.' I was not prepared to offer myself as a candidate. When he became the president of the Congress for the second time, he issued a statement to the press from which some people drew the conclusion that he achieved his success because of socialism, and that this was the victory of socialism. Some members of the Congress Committee debated this issue, and decided that, in answer to this, they should issue a rejoinder to the press. Babu Rajendra Prasad and Sardar Patel prepared a statement and signed it. It was brought to me by Mahadev Desai for signature, but I did not view the statement as the press did, so I refused to sign it. I told Gandhiji that it would be best to send a telegram to Jawaharlal, asking him what he meant by his press statement. I told him that as far as I could make out, this was not the meaning of his statement. The telegram was dispatched, and an answer came back promptly: that our interpretation of his statement was not correct. Gandhiji had a lot of love for Jawaharlal, who himself regarded Gandhiji as a father. But some people were trying to create misunderstanding between them. Till the time that I was there, I would make efforts to dispel these. I would also do the same for the other members of the working committee because I considered disunity a hurdle in the way of our mission. In whichever party or group disunity emerges, then, instead of succeeding, it fails in its mission.

The Congress Session at Faizpur

Faizpur was selected as the venue for the annual session of the All-India Congress Committee in 1936. Faizpur is a village in the province of Bombay. I would always remind Gandhiji that the nation lives in the villages and he agreed with me. For this reason, they (the Congress members), like us, began to involve the villages in the struggle, because the masses live there; and a movement which reached the masses ultimately achieves success. This was the reason why we sought the assistance of the Pukhtuns, young and old, from village to village. It is my belief that the inhabitants of the towns are educated because there are newspapers, and there are also many facilities for education and training. The villages are deprived of these facilities and so there is no political consciousness.

Congress Nagar had been put up on a grand scale. There were separate places for the members of the working committee to stay in and the place for me was bigger than the others. I thought, and this was the thinking of the members of the working committee as well, that delegates from the Frontier would be coming in large numbers and would have to be put up with me. But, unfortunately, no one came to attend this meeting from the Frontier. Mehr Taj, Maryam and Lalee had accompanied me, but they were not staying with me. They were with Safia in the camp meant for the girls. Safia was the commander of the women *razakars* of Bombay province and had come with her for service in the camp. Mehr Taj and Maryam had also enrolled themselves in the *razakar* and would be working all day. In those days, M.N. Roy (the communist) had been released from captivity and had come to attend this session. Many laudatory articles about him had appeared in the newspapers. Those people who had gone to Tashkent would also sing his praises. But when I saw him from close and engaged him in discussions, he did not appear to me to be worthy of the praise showered on him. He would talk to the members of the working committee as well. He would try to get himself into the good books of Mahatma Gandhi and would fawn on him. He also delivered a speech in the Congress *pandal,* but it carried no weight and was not well articulated. This was because when a speaker has one thing in his heart and voices another, the speech falls flat and has no effect on the audience. I was under the impression that whatever he did was for the purpose of becoming a member of the working committee, and when he realized that this was not possible, he gradually began to oppose the policies of the Congress. Matters came to such a pass that there was no stauncher opponent of the Congress than him, and he would also criticize Mahatma Gandhi.

At the Faizpur Congress session, whenever I found the time, I would visit the surrounding villages. The conditions of these villages were very bad. They were overwhelmed by poverty and ignorance. The conditions in the Muslim villages were even worse. The main reason for this was that there were a few people amongst the Hindus who would ask about them and would make them aware of the conditions in both this world and the next. But the unfortunate Muslims had no such people to turn to. They just awaited the grace and kindness of God to assist them. The extent to which I have toured the villages of the country, I have observed that the enthusiasm of the Muslims is no less than that of the Hindus. The other thing is that the Muslims are above the distinctions of the caste system and issues of untouchability, while the social structure of the Hindus is based on it. To the extent that I have experienced, the Hindus are more backward socially than the Muslims. The extent to which the Muslims can develop and improve their conditions quickly, the Hindus cannot do so. This is because nations cannot prosper merely on claims and speeches. Only those nations prosper where pious and selfless people present themselves for the service of their people. May God, by His grace, cause such persons to be born amongst the Muslims.

Misunderstandings about the Pukhtuns

When I would be in Hindustan, I would do my best to clear the misunderstandings about the Pukhtuns. N.C. Kelkar, who was a very learned and prominent leader of the Hindus, told me that in the Frontier and the Tribal Areas, the lives and honour of the Hindus were unsafe. When I asked him if he had ever been to the Frontier, he replied in the negative. I told him that these misunderstandings were the result of the vicious propaganda of the enemies of the country. The lives, property and honour of the Hindus were safer there than in Hindustan. The tribesmen were willing to sacrifice their lives for the sake of their Hindu clients. In British Hindustan, both here and there, the government was resorting to such policies to divide the Hindus and Muslims and make them enemies of each other. This would not sink into the mind of Kelkar, that such fair Englishmen could resort to such unfair tactics. So, I asked him who had engineered the Hindu-Muslim riots in Multan in 1922. At whose instigation were Muslims and Hindus slaughtered in Kanpur? And yesterday, whose hand was behind the Hindu-Muslim riots in Bombay? In Lahore, what was the genesis of the Shaheedganj riots? In Kohat and Dera Ismail Khan who was behind these Hindu-Muslim riots on such a large scale? Why were Hindus and Muslims all over Hindustan at each other's throats? After a great deal of thought, he replied that we should write books and bring out periodicals in this regard. I told him that we have limited means. In fact, they should visit these areas, observe the conditions in these places themselves and then publicize them. That they were aware of the conditions and developments in America and Europe but did not bother to acquaint themselves with even one part of their own country. They did not make inquiries themselves, nor did they visit these areas, but believed what others had to say.

The best place to tackle the misconceptions and misunderstandings generated about the Pukhtuns was Sevagram, because this was visited by people from every country, and of every ideology and thinking. I would have an ideal opportunity to engage them and counter all this. Moreover, I could tour different parts of Hindustan and, besides holding the usual *jalsa*, would also interact with the Hindus and Muslims of these areas. I made the members of the Congress Party agree to pass a resolution about the Tribal Areas in this session. Some responsible members of Congress were convinced that this was essential for the freedom and peace of Hindustan, that they should develop a cordial relationship with the people of the Frontier. But they were unaware of the many impediments and hurdles strewn in their way. This was because the British never wanted to see the development of a cordial relationship between the inhabitants of the Frontier and the Tribal Areas. The British were not providing us an opportunity to develop a fraternal rapport with our tribal brothers. How then could they provide such an opportunity to the people of Hindustan?

Sevagram used to be visited by many European men and women, like Father Ellwin, Father C.F. Andrews and Rosemary. Compared to the women, the men exhibited greater sympathy. Sometimes they would ask me about the Tribal Areas and the *Khudai Khidmatgar*. One day, a few Englishmen came on a visit of Sevagram. They had the Bishop of Kanpur accompanying them. The Englishmen would ask me questions about the Tribal Areas and I would give them answers. During this exchange, the padri sahib (Priest) said that he had been posted in the Khyber Agency and was aware of the Afridis. They were not good people at all because they stared the British in the face. I smiled at this and asked why they stared at them haughtily. He replied that this was because they held all Englishmen in contempt. I replied that these views of his were not based on fact. The truth was that they looked upon the British with contempt, because when they looked at them, they considered them to be those who with canons, machine guns, and bombs, destroy their homes and villages and kill their women, men and children. When I said this, the other Englishmen laughed and the padri was greatly embarrassed.

Ministries

The elections to the assemblies in the country were held and, in most of the provinces, the Congress representatives were able to win the seats. The success of our candidates in the Frontier Province took the British and their supporters by surprise. They saw that the pillars of their strength had crumbled. Nawab Sir Muhammad Akbar Khan Hoti, the biggest of them in the province, was defeated at the hands of *Amir* Muhammad Khan Hoti. Nawab Sir Sahibzada Abdul Qaiyum was defeated by a *Khudai Khidmatgar*, Abdul Aziz Khan of Zaida. Arbab Sher Ali Khan was defeated by Arbab Abdul Ghafoor Khan of Tehkal. The nawab of Teri was defeated by *Salar* Aslam Khan of Ahmadi Banda in Kohat. Khan Bahadur Kulli Khan fell at the hands of the *Khudai Khidmatgar* General, Sahib Gul. In this way the loyalist khan bahadurs, rai bahadurs, khan sahibs, and rai sahiban were felled by the *Khudai Khidmatgar.*

The elections under the Government of India Act, 1935, proved to the world in general, and to the British in particular, that the Congress party was indeed the representative organization of the masses of Hindustan. The proof of this lay in the fact that, of the then eleven provinces of India, the Congress obtained a majority in eight. In the remaining three Muslim-majority provinces, local parties gained a majority. In the Frontier Province, which is a Muslim-majority province, 93 per cent of the popular vote also went to the Congress.

Four days later, a convention was held in New Delhi in which the successful candidates of all the assemblies came together and debated the question of what steps they should now take. To accept and form governments or not? Many workers of the Frontier came to attend this convention. After a long time, I got the opportunity of meeting them. Heated debates were held in the working committee for a few days. Jawaharlal was strongly opposed to the formation of ministries and most of the members of the working committee supported him. I, too, was at first opposed to the formation of ministries, but then changed my opinion, because even those members of the working committee who were in favour of forming ministries said that they were in favour not because they wanted the reforms of the British to succeed, but so that they could ensure their failure from within. The advantage of forming the ministries was that, by doing so, we would strengthen the Congress party. If we failed to do so, we would immediately leave the government. The other point stressed by those who opposed the formation of ministries was one related to the special powers conferred on the provincial governors under the Government of India Act of 1935. The decision was not to form ministries until the governors gave assurance to the members that they would not interfere with the ministries. After many days of discussion, the working committee approved the proposal favouring the formation of ministries. In the convention, many speeches were delivered, both against and in favour of this proposal, but the majority endorsed the proposal of the working committee. After the approval, the president obtained an oath of loyalty from all the members, after which they all dispersed. I stayed behind in Delhi and then returned to Wardha.

Our Stay at Wardha and Sevagram

Ghani and Mehr Taj stayed with me for the duration of my stay at Wardha. Lalee (Ali Khan) did not like his new school, so he was admitted to the school in Wardha. The headmaster of the school, Naekom, was a good man and an ardent nationalist who voluntarily worked for a very meagre salary. His wife was the holder of two master's degrees and, like the husband, was an ardent nationalist. She also worked for a pittance in the girls' school. Both husband and wife had a good relationship with me. Sevagram, where I was staying, was four miles from Wardha. It was difficult for Lalee to travel daily between Sevagram and Wardha, so he stayed with the headmaster and his wife. When Mehr Taj would come on holiday, she would stay with me in Sevagram. Wali was in Wardha and would visit me in Sevagram every other day. Lalee would also come here whenever he had a holiday. One day, Ghani came early in the morning to Sevagram. It was Gandhiji's birthday. When we sat down to lunch, Ghani told Gandhiji that today was his birthday and he had come early for it, to enjoy the many delicious dishes that would have been cooked, but he saw that it is the same old boiled and tasteless pumpkin, which he always eats, that has been served. Gandhiji told Ghani to come to Wardha every day early in the morning. Ghani laughed and said that he could not travel every day for so long just for the sake of boiled pumpkin. If it had been pulao and fried chicken instead, he would be prepared to do so. This was all said in jest and was taken as such. The next day Gandhiji said to me that these were youngsters and should not be forced into anything, and he thought that we should arrange for the meals of their choice to be cooked for them. I told him that Ghani was only joking and would never agree to this proposal. Gandhiji did his best with him but could not make him agree. Similarly, he had worked on Mehr Taj, but she also had declined. I was very happy to see that they displayed so much upbringing and culture, and that they cared for the sentiments and feelings of others.

In the village of Sehgaon, which was close to Sevagram, Gandhiji had appointed a salaried person for its cleanliness and sanitation. I did not agree with him because I was of the view that the people of the village should be taught to regard the cleanliness of their villages as their own personal obligation and to do it themselves. The other thing was that Hindustan had hundreds of thousands of villages for which crores of rupees would be required if they were to be kept clean by paid workers. It once so happened that a salaried sanitary worker of Sehgaon demanded an increase in his salary. His salary was increased at one stage but this time they did not increase it. So, he left work and left the village. A message arrived that the sanitary worker had left work. So Gandhiji said that we should go there and do the cleaning work ourselves. We took along all the paraphernalia and left.

In those days, an eminent engineer from Switzerland had come to Bihar in connection with the rehabilitation work of the earthquake-affected villages and was now on a visit here. Lalee was also on holiday. I told him to get ready to come with us. When I told him we were going to clean a village he began to cry and protested that he was not ready to clean people's faeces. So, we left him behind. When we arrived in the village, we paired up. The engineer was a very good person and was as tall as I was. He and I paired up. Gandhiji did not have a partner, so we paired up our own sanitary worker with him. We started with the cleaning but we realized that the people of the village were not pleased with what we were doing; the places which we would clean would immediately be dirtied again by the men, women and children, as soon as we moved on. The engineer informed us that he felt these people had no feelings of gratitude for the work we were doing. It appeared as if they were protesting us. He and I really felt this – that a person of Gandhiji's stature should go to a village for a cleanliness campaign and the villagers should express their displeasure in this fashion. I was very saddened by this. When we returned, a friend reassured me that we should be grateful to providence that we had not been stoned by them and could clean the area. Meera behan and Kanu were with us. Kanu was Gandhiji's grandson, and Meera behan was the daughter of a British admiral, who had placed her services at the disposal of Gandhiji, for the service of the teeming millions of the poor of Hindustan. They, too, had gone for cleanliness work to a village near Wardha; but the people of the village would not permit them to do so. When they did not listen to them and kept on cleaning, the villagers stoned them. An even stranger incident that occurred was that, when we returned and our sanitary worker at Sevagram found out that we had gone to his village for sanitation work, he left work. According to their faith and belief we had become untouchables, had become impure and to serve the impure was a sin for them.

We had dug a very fine well at Sevagram for our drinking water. This well had very sweet water. The villagers also filled their pitchers from it. However, after this incident, they stopped doing so. Close to us was another well, the water of which was not drinkable. They would rather get water from this well. Those people who worked for us here were at the bottom rung of the Hindu caste system, which was called the *Achhut* caste (untouchables) and the other Hindus do not allow them to get close to them. In some places, even if their shadow falls on them, they are polluted by it.

The Ministries of the Congress

The Congress party returned to the assemblies in most provinces of Hindustan. In the Frontier, despite great opposition of the government and all its shenanigans, out of forty members, nineteen *Khudai Khidmatgar* won their seats. The government had fully exploited all its influence and connections against them and, to oppose them, had combined all the khans, maliks and lawyers. Their lifelong enmities were patched up. Still, I can say with confidence that the *Khudai Khidmatgar* would have returned as the majority party had they not made some mistakes and if they had avoided factionalism and selfishness from their ranks and had nominated some men of principles as their candidates. Despite this, they had a solid block of votes in the assembly. Compared to them there was no other group or party. Even then, the government started its dishonesty and, in violation of democratic practices, Sir George Cunningham, the governor, invited Sir Sahibzada Abdul Qaiyum to form the government. He consequently managed to form a government. To begin with, he did not even have a party of his own to back him. He had been defeated in his own constituency by Abdul Aziz Khan. So, he went to Hazara and was elected in a bye-election from a constituency vacated for him by Raja Sikandar Zaman. He was a British loyalist and all the loyalists sided with him out of necessity. But even then, this government could not last for more than six months and, despite the efforts of the government, a vote of no-confidence was passed against it and the *Khudai Khidmatgars* formed their own government. The Congress had initially declined from forming ministries in those provinces in which they had a clear majority, because Gandhiji had put forth a demand to the government. This was that the governors should not interfere unnecessarily in the work of the ministries. The Government of India Act 1935 had reserved all powers for the governors and they could, under the law, interfere in both major and minor decisions of the ministers. The government did not accept this demand because the dispensation under this Act was no more than a sham. The British were not prepared to hand over power and authority to the Indians. At first, the Congress declined to form ministries, so the government formed ministries of its own people. These, however, could not last because they did not have majorities to back them in the assemblies. But after a while, mutterings began amongst certain members of the Congress against this, and C. Rajagopalachari was not prepared to accept the prospect of not forming the ministries. We were then in Peetal, which is a village on the seashore. Gandhiji summoned Rajagopalachari to Gujarat. Sardar Patel was also there. Gandhiji held discussions with them over two days and nights but failed in making them change their views. They insisted that they should form ministries unconditionally and they also believed that, during the period that we had stayed away from the ministries, the interests of the people and the country had been harmed. Rajagopalachari left and we were all upset with Rajaji's attitude. But, fortunately, the government accepted Gandhiji's condition of non-interference by the governors in the day-to-day functioning of the administration. Except for Sindh, Bengal and Punjab, Congress ministries were formed in all the remaining provinces of Hindustan.

These were days when we were staying some distance from the village of Sehgaon. Weather-wise this was a good place but during the monsoon season it was difficult to walk around. The road was also a dirt track and the inhabitants also had plenty of cattle. Usually it was very muddy all around us, with both cattle and humans finding it difficult to walk in the mud. On the other hand, lots of stones were available in the mounds and the fields, with which we could have easily paved the roads. But, on account of disunity and lack of organization, this task did not take place. Gandhiji started the work, and in a year's time we paved one of the roads. There were many mosquitoes here, but malaria was not rampant. Once Gandhiji had a serious attack of malaria. He would also not have medicine for it. When he lost consciousness, we called for the civil surgeon to examine him. He proposed that he would take him to the hospital; but let alone be taken to the hospital, he would not even have medicine. All of us persuaded him and finally made him agree to be shifted because we were extremely worried. His illness had greatly flustered us all. We all accompanied him to the hospital. Within a few days, his health improved. One day a man came to the hospital. He had two or three snakes with him. He placed his basket in front of him and lifted its lid. There were many kinds of snakes in it. He started taking them closer and closer to Gandhiji, but I did not allow him to do so. Snakes cannot be trusted. The man desired that, to gain grace, he would put the snakes around Gandhiji's neck. Gandhiji laughed, but I did not allow him to do so. The man said that he had charmed the snakes and will be responsible for any harm caused. I replied that if harm occurred, of what worth would his responsibility be? It would be much better if he did not do what he intended to. So, I prevented him from it. In another place in Sevagram, another one of our companions fell ill. He had continuous fever. After a few days, Meera behan also fell ill with a persistent fever. She said to me that it looked like she had been afflicted with the same fever. We were worried for her, because the British normally die of this kind of fever but we did not tell her this. I looked after both very well, but I would be particularly worried about her and would tend to Meera behan more assiduously. In those days, a friend of Mahatama Gandhiji's had built a place of worship in Banaras, to which followers of all faiths could come and worship God as they pleased. To inaugurate this, Mahatmaji and I went to Banaras. Mehr Taj was also with me. Many men and women had been invited for the inauguration from all parts of Hindustan. In this place of worship, people of all faiths recited from their Holy Books, and offered prayers in accordance with their own rituals. In my view, after the advent of the British, this was the first occasion that religious leaders of all faiths had come together in one venue with such love and affection and were praying together.

Banaras, Delhi, Gujarat and Kathiawar

From Banaras we went to Delhi, and then to Kathiawar in Gujarat. In Kathiawar, I went to Gandhiji's house and met with his relatives. They all had a lot of love and affection for Gandhiji. After spending a night there we travelled to Ahmedabad, where a very big college for Hindus is located. We went and stayed at Vidyapith. Vidyapith is a national college, because when its alumni complete their education, they proceed to the villages and serve the cause of their nation there. The people of the Ahmedabad municipality gave us a welcome address. They are very good people who love Mahatmaji greatly and were no less than anyone else in the struggle for liberation. After a few days, we returned to Sevagram. The more I toured Hindustan, the more I would see that in every province, from the point of view of political, economic and educational advancement – in fact, from every point of view – the Muslims lagged far behind the Hindus. The more I thought about these matters, the more I would reach the conclusion that it was not only Gandhiji, not only Jawaharlal, not only Malaviya, not only Patel, not only Rajendra Prasad, not only Subhash, not only Rajagopalachari, in fact, there were hundreds of people like them who were physicians, engineers and other professionals, who had established colleges and were busy serving the interests of their nation. Many such people located in the villages, were not allowed to work by vested interests who put hurdles in their way. But, despite this, they were doing their best to promote the well-being of the villages with great patience and courage. No power can remove them from the task of serving their people. The distinguishing characteristics of these people were that they led very simple lives and could manage with very little. One day in Wardha, a *jalsa* of the workers of the surrounding villages was held. The workers had all gathered there. I too went to see the newly established *ashram* in Noba, and took part in that convention of the workers. They were very poor and weak. I took great pity on them. I told Jajoji, who was the president of this organization, and Naino Baji, who was its secretary, that they were the asset of the nation, and some arrangements must be made to feed them; that they are physically weak and could not be expected to serve their people and country. Jajoji said that he agreed with me and that now I needed to move the proposal in the *jalsa*. When I moved the proposal that their salaries should be increased, one person from amongst them got up and said that our country was very poor. To begin with, there was no employment to be found, and even when some work was there, the wage for a man was only three annas, and for the women, ten paisas, and they, despite this, received a four anna daily remuneration. That their employers ate no better than them. There was no need to increase the salaries because these people will then say that they cannot even find dry, barley bread, while their servants enjoy rich food.

The other point was that the rich traders among the Hindus assist the liberation movement to the tune of thousands and lakhs of rupees. Compared to this are the Muslims. You should observe for yourselves as to who is there amongst them to serve the nation! Their educated, rich traders, and lawyers who, let alone donating rupees, do not even think of the prosperity or the freedom of their country. This is the reason why Muslims are facing a decline. This is the reason that in Hindustan, the Hindus are on an ascent, and the Muslims are on a decline. I experienced among the Muslims of Hindustan, that those who are the well-wishers of the British are the leaders of the Muslims. In these conditions, how can they prosper?

Concern about the Conditions of the Muslims of Hindustan

I have travelled all over Hindustan and found that the Muslims have enthusiasm, but they have no one to empathize with them and care for them. Dr. Zakir Hussain sahib would sometimes visit Sevagram. I had a good rapport with him. He was the principal of Jamia Millia in Delhi. I recounted my impressions of touring Hindustan and the effect that they had on me, and told him that until a true servant of the Muslims was born amongst them, they would never be able to make progress. Among the Muslims, it was essential to work patiently, and, like the Hindus, it was necessary for them to create sincere workers to work for their progress and to construct several *marakiz*, for this work. I have reached the conclusion that nations do not achieve progress merely through ritualistic prayer. It is essentially work which does so. And nor is it only through *jalsa* and *jaloos* that they can be awakened. So, I resolved to work for the Muslims and to establish centres of reform for them; and until I was permitted to return to my own province, I would serve them. But I was worried that if ever I was not allowed to return to my own province, then who would serve them? I would eventually not remain here, as I owed greater responsibility to my own people. So, if he, Dr. Zakir Hussain, agreed and considered it appropriate to work for the Muslims, then he should help me out in this and identify some people to assist me. So that when I left, they should be there to take over, and the sapling which we plant, they should be able to nurture it and not allow it to dry up. The other main issue is one of money. The Muslims give a lot of ritual charity but are not prepared to donate towards the development of humanity. That was the reason that, amongst them, a movement for development would have minimal chances of success.

I had thought that this work should begin from the province of Sindh because of the large Muslim population, mainly backward in every respect. Our other companion was of the view that it should begin from Bengal. The professor sahib from Saharanpur expressed the view that if we were to start from there, it would progress very quickly and would then spread as quickly to the rest of Hindustan, because the Muslims of the United Provinces, when compared to those of the other provinces, were more development oriented and knowledgeable. The other thing was that there were many religious *madrassahs* in Saharanpur in which there were many *taliban* from

Sindh and Bengal, and people from every province could be found there. This was the educational capital of the Muslims of Hindustan and, if the proposed *markaz* was built here, then these *taliban* could be expected to work in Bengal, Sindh and other provinces. We all agreed on Saharanpur as the venue of the centre and decided to begin work from there and were patiently waiting for a few men to be identified as assistants.

I waited for a few days in Sevagram. When no answer came, I accompanied Jawaharlal to the United Provinces. I had promised Babu Rajendra Prasad that I would go with him to Bihar and conduct tours. I was in Allahabad when Professor Abdul Bari sahib arrived and he and I both proceeded to Patna and put up at the Sadaqat *ashram*. This *ashram* was on the banks of the Ganges river and was beautiful. It was built by a Muslim barrister from Bihar, named Mazhar-ul-Haq. He had also sided with the Muslims against the British in the affair of the Kanpur mosque. It is a pity that after his death, there was no one in the Muslim community to maintain the *ashram,* and for this reason, it was left to the Congress to inherit. These days it was the office of the working committee of the Congress party in the province of Bihar.

We were making a programme of tours of the province, when news of the Punjab Mail train accident came, and immediately the workers of the Congress arrived there for assistance. Many people had been killed in the accident and it was difficult to identify the bodies, whether they were Muslims or Hindus. Those that were considered Hindus were being cremated, and those who were thought to be Muslims were being buried. Besides numerous corpses, many were also injured and were brought to the big hospital in Patna. May God not show such scenes of despair and pain to anyone. It was a scene of horror. After a few days, we finalised the programme of our tour and spent quite a few days touring the province of Bihar. The grave of Sher Shah Suri is in the province of Bihar. When we held a *jalsa* there, we went to offer a prayer at his mausoleum. His grave is a simple structure. Surrounded by water, the dome is beautiful. I prayed for the soul of Sher Shah in all sincerity, because he was a very successful politician of the Pukhtuns; was an intrepid Pukhtun warrior who had defeated the Mughals and had regained the government from them and re-established their rule over Hindustan. The Grand Trunk Road from Calcutta to Peshawar was built by him. To maintain his hold over Bihar, he gave many *jagir* to the Pukhtuns. We also saw the progeny and the *jagirs* of those families. One or two of them even invited us to a meal but they no longer display the splendour of their forefathers. They had forgotten their ancestral language. What a pity that the Pukhtuns suffer from such a major weakness, as to easily abandon their mother tongue. There are many Pukhtuns in the United Provinces as well, suffering the same fate. Dr. Zakir Hussain sahib is a Pukhtun of the Afridi tribe. When the mother tongue is abandoned, one becomes alien to one's own kith and kin. The Pukhtuns owned extensive land holdings in the province of Bihar, but on account of profligacy had been reduced to poverty.

After the tour of Bihar, I returned to Sevagram. For a long time, the members of the Congress party were after me and wanted me to visit Sindh and work with the Muslims of that area. I also was of the same view because the Muslims of Sindh have really lagged and are oppressed, and we *Khudai Khidmatgar* are friends of the oppressed. From Sevagram I left for Sindh. I wanted to spend some time there. Reaching there, I made a comprehensive programme of my tours and started off from Hyderabad. The Muslim Leaguers had made a programme to disrupt my tour, but the chief minister of Sindh, who was a very good man and a staunch nationalist, got wind of this and directed the Muslim League, that Abdul Ghaffar Khan has come here to serve the people and that everyone should support him. That if they could not help him, then it is shameful to create mischief. He told them that he had learnt of their mischievous intentions and if, during my tour, they created any mischief, he would then take them to task. Because of this, the Muslim League stayed away, and I conducted my tour satisfactorily. In those days, the chief minister of Sindh was Khan Bahadur Allah Bakhsh Soomro. He had a lot of affection for me. We held *jalsa* in Hyderabad and interacted with many Muslims and Hindus. From here, we went to Karachi where we spent many days and did a lot of work. From Karachi, we went to Sukkur and from there to Balochistan because we thought that it was far more important to work in Balochistan.

Tour of Balochistan

For quite some time now, our brothers from Balochistan wanted me to visit and work there. I had tried to visit the region a few times, but the government would not allow me. In those days Abdul Samad Khan Achakzai, who was a true servant and leader of the Pukhtuns of Balochistan, was pressing me to go there. On the way, I met with Allah Bakhsh Soomro and we discussed the political situation in Hindustan at length. He was not in favour of the idea of Pakistan because he was forever complaining against the Punjabis and was not ready to join them. He was ready for the prospect that if Sindh, Balochistan, the Frontier and Kashmir were to get together, this would be a very good thing. Later, Allah Bakhsh Soomro, on account of political opposition, had the Muslim Leaguer, Ayub Khuhro, killed.

On the way to Quetta, when our train entered the limits of Balochistan, I had a lurking fear of being detained and made to return, because in the past I had been made to return many times. At every station when I would see a police officer, I would imagine that they had brought orders for my externment. However, I arrived safely in Quetta. I am of the view that the government, which had allowed Jinnah sahib, who was a Muslim Leaguer, to enter Balochistan, had allowed me to do so as well because I was associated with the Congress.

Abdul Samad Khan Achakzai had come to the railway station to receive me along with many other Hindus and Muslims. I spent a few days in Quetta and then proceeded on a tour of Fort Sandeman, Qilla Abdullah, Hindu Bagh, Gulistan, Chaman, Loralai and other places in Balochistan. It was a very successful tour and I felt even happier to observe that the Pukhtuns and the Baloch had been awakened politically from their slumber. In my *jalsa* and *jaloos,* I discussed with them the brotherhood of the Pukhtuns and the Baloch, and in this, most Pukhtuns and Baloch agreed with me. Some Pukhtuns complained about the attitude of the Pukhtuns of Peshawar. Later I learnt that the reason for this was the conduct of Pukhtun government officials from the Frontier Province i.e., officials from the Peshawar valley who were employees of the British in Balochistan. The officers had not dealt justly with their brethren; in fact, they had adopted a pharaonic attitude towards them and had created an aversion in their hearts for all Pukhtuns of the Frontier. I reassured them and made them understand not to hold all Pukhtuns from the Frontier accountable for the sins of a few officers. May God not allow other Pukhtuns to become so dishonourable, like these few. The government was not ours but was in the hands of the British. Moreover, most of these officers belonged to those families of the khans, *mians* and the maulanas who, to please the British, had meted out such harsh treatment to them, or were still doing so. They did not extend such treatment to them only, but were doing so to us, in our own province as well. This was a very strange thing indeed, that here these Pukhtun officers had teamed up with those Punjabi officers who, together with them, were looting the Baloch and Pukhtuns of Balochistan. After the tour of Balochistan, we came to Jacobabad. Here, Dr. Jeet Ram, who was the president of the local Congress, and Muhammad Khoso joined us. A big *jalsa* of Hindus and Muslims was held in Jacobabad. In this *jalsa* it was the intention of the civil and police officers to do some mischief. However, on the intervention of the chief minister of Sindh, Allah Bakhsh Soomro, no disruption occurred. We conducted a tour of all those areas of British Balochistan in which the majority is of the Pukhtuns. Abdul Samad Khan Achakzai and I were of the view that we should also visit the area of the Baloch. Dr. Jeet Ram and Muhammad Amin Khoso were also of the same view. When the time for the *jalsa* came, I intended to hold it in the mosque, which was located at the entrance of the bazaar. My other companions were of the view that it should be held in the open space, which was located at some distance from the bazaar. So, arrangements for the *jalsa* were made. When the proceedings started, a sardar of the Baloch arrived on the scene, walked by the venue of the *jalsa*, and stared at it. A little while later a group of Baloch armed with axes intermingled with the crowd and started attacking people. When they would strike a person, they would call out 'Ali, Ali' (Hazrat Ali). They were merciless. Except for the head, they did not strike any other part of the body. In no time at all the ground was empty. Dr. Jeet Ram and Muhammad Amin Khoso were seated on chairs on either side of me. When all the people had fled and I was left alone, they surrounded me and made every effort to ensure that I, too, should run away, but I stood my ground. That day I had shaved my head and was sitting bareheaded. I understood well that they would aim at my head, but I refused to flee. I wanted to see what they would do. On my right hand was Amin Khoso who had been struck on the head, had become unconscious and fallen from his chair; on my left hand was Dr. Jeet Ram. He had also been struck on the head and, on becoming unconscious, had fallen in the mud on the ground. They started circling me, hoping that I, like the others, would also run away. When they realized that I was not about to do so, and that they had accomplished their assigned task, they fled. I got up and when I looked around, I saw blood spurting from the heads of Dr. Jeet Ram and Muhammad Amin Khoso. There was no one else. It was a strange scene. It appeared as if they had been given specific instructions regarding Dr. Jeet Ram and Muhammad Amin Khoso, and different instructions had been issued about me. Later, it came to light that the Baloch sardar was a great friend of theirs and he was obliged to them in many ways. We sent a man in a car for the civil surgeon. We picked them both up and laid them out on beds at the place we were staying in. Their condition was deteriorating. Abdul Samad Khan and our other friends were also wounded but not as fatally. We learnt from the locals that they knew of the incident and had reported it in the *tehsil* as well, but the officials did not wish to intervene. The truth of the matter was that the whole affair was arranged on the instigation of the government. Not only here, but all over Balochistan, the government had tried to disrupt our *jalsa*, but the Pukhtuns still had some semblance of 'Pukhto' and honour left in them to respect and protect their guests. In the early evening the political agent of the area, who was an army captain and a Hindu and who had planned the whole incident, came to me with his assistant to make inquiries. He told me that if we wanted to institute criminal proceedings against those involved, he would arrange for the complaint to be registered. The assistant was from Peshawar area and was a resident of Dhobian village in Sawabai *tehsil*. I told him that we, *Khudai Khidmatgar*, never took revenge from anyone; we were friends of the oppressed and our revenge was always taken by God. When they were talking to me, despite the strength and authority of the government, they looked ashamed and pale-faced. By the time the civil surgeon arrived the wounded were in bad shape, especially Mohammad Amin Khoso. Upon arrival, the doctor tried to put a stop to their bleeding and informed us that their condition was serious and that nothing could be done for them here. That it would be best to get them to the Jacobabad hospital. We put them into cars and arrived in Jacobabad in the late evening. The civil surgeon was a very good man and, upon our arrival, made excellent arrangements for their treatment. Early the next morning I visited the hospital. The civil surgeon had arrived before us and gave me the good news that now there was greater hope of their survival. When they were completely out of danger and their condition improved, I left Jacobabad for Hyderabad. Our train arrived at the Hyderabad railway station early in the morning when it was still dark. Professor Malkani, along with other Congress workers, had come to the station. I was taken by surprise and was very happy, because Khan Bahadur Allah Bakhsh, the chief minister, was also present there. I was amazed because our people in authority never go to welcome people like us. And I was happy because he had such love and affection for the servants of the common people. Our people in authority lack this attribute. In Hyderabad, the members of the Sindh working committee had gathered, and after the people's *jalsa*, I held discussions with them. After a great deal of discussion, they informed me of two significant developments and told me that whenever I got to Wardha, I should provide this information to Gandhiji and other members of the Congress working committee. One development was that the *Khaksar* movement amongst the Muslims was gathering strength day by day. That if the *Khudai Khidmatgar* movement were to be initiated amongst the Muslims of this province, it would be a good development because this was a national movement which generated feelings of brotherhood and amity amongst the Hindus and the Muslims, while the *Khaksar* movement generated feelings of parochialism in the Muslims. I told them that such work could only be initiated by people like them.

When somebody's heart is filled with sympathy and love for his nation and land, only then would other people be prepared to listen to what he was saying, no matter what nationality or religion he belongs to. In addition, they said that they could do nothing for the people and nor were they allowed to do so by the Congress leaders of the province, G. Ram Das and Daulat Ram, who could not accomplish anything for them in their assembly. Nor could they visit the villages to educate and make people aware. I asked them why this was so. They said that, for the working of the Congress, most donations and subscriptions are given by the affluent people to Ram Das. That the influential people do not want to have any laws passed in the assembly for the benefit of the public. Nor do they want the members of the Congress to visit the villagers and the labour class, to awaken and make them aware, because this would not be in the interest of the rich. For this reason, they could not do anything for the people. Moreover, even if **we** did so, and they joined us, these deprived people would not be able to give us donations. It would be best that I put this problem of theirs before the working committee members of the Congress party.

Soon my visit to the region was over and I travelled back to Wardha. When I reached there, Ram Das was also present. I recounted the whole affair in his presence to all the members of the working committee. Rafi Ahmad Kidwai sahib, who was the vice-president of the Congress at the time, told me, 'Oh Bacha Khan! Why are you Pukhtuns after us and creating difficulties for the government?' I asked in what respect had we created problems for the government and had unjustifiably bothered them. He then told me that Inayatullah Khan Mashriqui had been arrested by them and he had asked for pardon. That they released him and then, from the Frontier, Pukhtun *Khaksars* came to him, pulled out their revolvers, and threatened to kill him on the pretext that he had disgraced them when he had asked for pardon. He denied the allegation of asking for pardon and said that this was all fabricated and took an oath on the Holy *Quran* in front of them, that he was not about to leave the *Khaksar* movement. He then, out of fear of these people, started his movement afresh, so we arrested him. He again asked for pardon. His followers got fed up with him and his movement declined. The success of every movement is dependent on its leader. If he is clever and brave, the followers are also brave and understanding. If the leader is weak and shortsighted, then the followers are also weak and devoid of vision.

17

The First Government of
the *Khudai Khidmatgar*

I RETURNED TO MY OWN PROVINCE AFTER SEVEN LONG YEARS. I HAD BEEN
arrested in 1931 and returned in 1937. Our people had been
subjected to great cruelty and oppression, but their enthusiasm had
not died. From their faces, I could tell that their hearts were filled
with passion. When I was away, the red shirts were also not to be
seen. The government had banned them. When I came back, the
red shirts returned. When the *Khudai Khidmatgars* heard that I
had returned to my province, they disregarded all prohibition. They
all wore their red apparel, but the government did not bother them.
All restrictions imposed on the *Khudai Khidmatgars* were lifted.

In my absence, whatever excesses the government could
perpetrate on the people in general, and the *Khudai Khidmatgars*
in particular, it did. It had employed every tactic to destroy the
Khudai Khidmatgar movement but had failed. In fact, the *Khudai
Khidmatgar* movement had spread further and there was greater
understanding and political awareness amongst the people. After
a few days, I accompanied the members of the provincial assembly
to Abbottabad. There a session of the assembly members had been
convened. Many inhabitants of Hazara had gathered to see me.
After the welcome, a *jalsa* was held in which I thanked the people.
I was a guest of the people of Hazara. Ghani and Wali were also
with me. Separate arrangements had been made for our stay. In
those days, there was a difference of opinion between the Muslim
League and the opposition. The government of Sir Sahibzada
Abdul Qaiyum did not want their ministries to be dissolved; while
the *Khudai Khidmatgars* were striving to dissolve it. Sahibzada

sahib had collected prominent maulanas and *mians* around himself. They would hold *jalsa* every day and would fabricate stories and deliver speeches against me. The truth was that I was neither a member of the assembly and nor was I the leader of the party. A prominent maulana of Hazara, Muhammad Ishaq Mansehrvi, who also happened to be a companion of mine during the *Khilafat* movement and had done a lot of work in Hazara, so much so that the people would carry him on their shoulders in a *jopaan* and the British had confined him to the limits of Rawalpindi district, in his speech informed the people that I, Abdul Ghaffar Khan, had gone to Rawalpindi one day and he was with me, and that I did not even offer a single prayer during the whole day. And when during the *jalsa* at night, the Hindus and the Muslims placed the *Geeta* and the *Quran* before me, I did not devote much attention to the *Quran* and held the *Geeta* in my right hand and the *Quran* in my left hand. All this was a fabrication on the part of Maulana Ishaq sahib. No doubt, I had gone to Pindi for the *jalsa*, but the maulana had come only for a short while and had, at the time, told me that he would not participate in the *jalsa* of the people. But since this *jalsa* had been organized for me, and I was a *mujahid* of Islam, he would attend it. No one offered me any copies of the *Quran* or *Geeta* in this *jalsa*. In fact, during my whole life, nobody had offered me a copy of the *Quran* or *Geeta*. In a nation in which such people are the pillars of religion, how can that religion survive on such pillars? In those days, the British wanted to organize an opposition party against the *Khudai Khidmatgars*. So, through the auspices of Sahibzada sahib, the Muslim League was formed overnight and its *jalsa* started. Shortly before this, Jinnah sahib had visited the Frontier Province with a view to the making of the Muslim League but had failed in his efforts and had gone back very disappointed. This was because, at the time, this was not the policy of the British and they did not want the formation of any kind of political parties in the province. In these *jalsas* also, Maulana Ishaq delivered speeches against the Congress and in favour of the Muslim League. In one of the *jalsas,* a man told him, 'Maulana sahib, when your nephew, Pir Kamran, had contested the election on the ticket of the *Khudai Khidmatgars,* you had campaigned on his behalf, and had told us that the *Khudai Khidmatgar* movement was a very good and nationalist movement. What has happened today and what is the proof that the *Khudai Khidmatgars* have become a bad and a Hindu party?' Similarly, there were many other maulanas who had been in jail with us and had come out successful from this trial but failed in resisting the lure of money. One of our nationalist workers, maulvi Shakirullah sahib, a member of the *Khudai Khidmatgar,* and a candidate for elections from Naukhar, *Mian* Jaffar Shah, began to oppose us and became a friend of Khan Bahadur Taj Muhammad Khan. After a few days, we were guests of Khan Bahadur Saadullah Khan of Umarzai. He was a minister in the cabinet of sahibzada sahib, who had also been invited to the lunch. When sahibzada sahib arrived, he sat with me. After the usual greetings he said to me that, formerly, the eyes of Hindustan would be fixed on the North-West, and whatever the people of these parts would say, they would do so accordingly. But, unfortunately, the eyes of the inhabitants of the North-West were now turned towards Hindustan, and whatever they say, is implemented. I said to him that, 'Sahibzada Sahib, you are not fully aware of the situation and that is why you are speaking in this vein. The position is still the same. It has not changed. Still those people were looking to us; even now, whatever the people of the North-West say, they do so accordingly.' When the *Civil and Military Gazette* published the wrong news that Bacha Khan was disassociating himself from the Congress, this very same Sahibzada Abdul Qaiyum, sent a special messenger to me to Lahore, who carried a letter for me. I had come from Simla to Lahore at the time and met with the messenger there. He had said to me that sahibzada sahib had asked him to tell me that, 'Bacha Khan, for the sake of God, do not disassociate from the Congress. And if you dissociate from the Congress then the British would not concede any political reforms for our province.' After many discussions, I started discussing the affairs of the province with him. I told him that the rights that the government had conferred on us, I admit, are incomplete and, on account of this, we could not achieve for our people the things which our hearts so earnestly desired. But, even then, these rights still contained in them some basics for the Pukhtuns and that if we were to work together, we would replace the British by the Pukhtuns as the owners and rulers of the land. So, I asked him whether, in opposition to the British, he could become the ruler of the land now. He responded, 'I am neither a ruler and nor can I become a ruler, because I am not prepared to oppose the British.' I said to him, 'That is fine. I prefer the Pukhtuns to become the rulers of their land in place of the British.' He replied that, undoubtedly, his heart also desired just that. I told him that this could only be possible if he gave someone else the opportunity to wield political power. He replied that he was ready for this. So, I advised him that it would be in his interest if he were to tender his resignation from membership of the assembly, because I did not relish the prospect of a vote of no-confidence being passed against his government. He promised to do so. But what I have learnt since then was that Sir George Cunningham, the governor, did not let him do so and this unfortunate event came to pass which I had tried to prevent. With the passage of the vote of no-confidence against him, the leader of the *Khudai Khidmatgars,* Dr. Khan Sahib, was asked by Sir George to form the government, which he did.

The Government of the *Khudai Khidmatgars*

For consultations regarding the formation of the government, Maulana Abul Kalam Azad and Babu Rajendra Prasad came to Abbottabad. Members of the *Khudai Khidmatgar* party who wanted to become ministers started campaigning among the *Khudai Khidmatgar* members. Their leader was Samin Jan Khan Advocate. He was very keen to become a minister in opposition to Qazi Ataullah. Many party members were with him. The main reason for this was that Qazi Ataullah did not canvas and had not contacted anyone for the purpose, to the extent that he made no mention of this even to me, even in passing. After consultations with the *Khudai Khidmatgar,* I, Dr. Khan Sahib, Maulana Abul Kalam Azad and Babu Rajendra Prasad got together and thought over the emerging scenario. I was of the view that ours was a very small province and that we should not have a cabinet exceeding three members, or at the most four. During this process, Samin Jan also came to me and told me that he was agreeable if he and Qazi sahib were to be made parliamentary secretaries, however, not him alone but with Qazi sahib in tandem. This is the same Samin Jan Khan for whose sake Qazi sahib had come to see me in the jail at Bareilly and compelled me to write a letter to the *Khudai Khidmatgar* leadership of Naukhar, advising them not to oppose him. He had become a member of the assembly. When Samin Jan Khan realized that a ministership did not depend upon the votes of the members, but the pleasure of the chief minister, and that I was also against the concept of the parliamentary secretary, because our province is small and could not sustain a large cabinet, and nor was there much work in the province for us to do, we decided that Dr. Khan Sahib should be assisted by three ministers: one Hindu and two Muslims. Since the members from Hazara had joined us and voted against Sahibzada Abdul Qaiyum, we had promised to take one minister from them. This left one ministry. So, Dr. Khan Sahib took Qazi Ataullah, and, from Hazara, he chose Muhammad Abbas Khan. Amongst the Hindus, I wanted Lala Banju Ram from Dera Ismail Khan to be chosen because he was an old worker of the Congress party who had also spent many years in jail and was a man of principles. However, Maulana Abul Kalam Azad and his companions thought that Rai Bahadur Ishar Das was the most capable and influential man amongst the Hindus and should be the third minister. However, as most of us were in favour of Lala Banju Ram, he was made minister. The truth is that the Congress pursued Rai Bahadur while we preferred the *Khidmatgar*. When our government was formed, we thought that, as much as we were able to, we should assist the people. We passed two resolutions in the assembly. One reduced the land revenue and the other related to the reservation of some money for a drinking water supply scheme for the Marwat area. And we intended to do so each year until the supply of water to this area became adequate. In Karak *tehsil* of Kohat district, the situation was so acute that the women had to fetch drinking water from places as far away as twenty miles or even more. The effort of the government was to ensure the availability of drinking water in every area; and when the government resigned after two years, it had reduced the distance of availability to about eight miles, and water supply had been extended to most villages. The problem of drinking water would have been completely resolved, but the factionalism of the Pukhtuns did not allow this to happen. This is because each village would demand that water should be supplied to it first. For this, we constituted a committee whose membership I accepted, because this was for the welfare of the people. But, regretfully, on account of differences of opinion between the *Khudai Khidmatgars*, we could not benefit the people the way we wanted to. This work remained incomplete. The Congress considered it as important for its ministries that the advocate general of the province should not be appointed at the behest of the provincial governor. That, in fact, this authority should be with their ministers and that the governor should appoint whom they select. In the province of Bihar, a major difference of opinion had arisen between the governor and the cabinet, which almost led to the resignation of the cabinet. In those days, Sir Sultan Ahmad was the advocate general of Bihar. He was a well-wisher of the government. And so, the governor did not want him to be removed from office. The cabinet, on the other hand, wanted to appoint someone loyal to the party in his place. On this, a quarrel took place between the governor and the cabinet ministers. And when the governor realized that the cabinet was prepared to resign over the issue, he accepted their nominee, and Sir Sultan Ahmad was removed and the Congress nominee appointed. Similarly, I, too, was of the view that the nominee of our cabinet should be appointed as the advocate general. In those days, Sardar Raja Singh was the advocate general. Dr. Khan Sahib raised the issue with the governor, but he was not prepared to remove him. The result was that we, i.e., Dr. Khan Sahib and I, were deprived of the inheritance of a few of our hamlets. If there had been an advocate general of our choice in office, then action would have been taken in accordance with the recently legislated law on the subject. The inhabitants of our province would not have been harmed and our inherited hamlets would not have been taken away from us.

Hawa Galli was a beautiful location and because of my poor health I rested here for a few days. From here, accompanied by Faqira Khan, I left on a tour of Agror. In 1930, when we formed the *Khudai Khidmatgars,* the movement was in tune with the temperament of the Pukhtuns and spread amongst them very rapidly. But the British did not give us an opportunity and arrested us after just three and a half months, and excesses were committed against the nation and the *Khudai Khidmatgars.* But the crueller the treatment meted out to us, the more rapidly the movement spread. The British were not able to suppress our movement and when our temporary truce between Gandhiji and the Viceroy Lord Irwin, came into effect, even then the British did not allow us to work. They would oppose us by imposing section 144 from place to place. In Hazara, particularly, they created many difficulties for us and we were unable to work to our satisfaction. The other limiting and discouraging factor was that the faction led by *Mian* Ahmad Shah had parted ways with us. They too had spread a lot of adverse propaganda against us. But they failed in their nefarious designs. Now that we had returned to our province after seven years and the government of the *Khudai Khidmatgars* was also formed, we started afresh to re-organize them. In Hazara also we got an opportunity to work to our hearts' content, and so I began my tour of the area.

Our Ministers and the British

When our first government was constituted, the bureaucracy, whether the Englishmen or the locals, was in a panic and fearful. Corruption and oppression came to an end but, unfortunately, this did not last long. The officers came to know our ministers, mingled with them, became familiar with their temperaments and established social relationships with them, and then followed their own policies and ways. Let alone corruption, the government and the *Khudai Khidmatgar* movement were harmed. If my proposal had been acted on, the damage would have been minimal. My proposal was that the ministers should not develop social relationships with the British and mingle with them, beyond what their work required, because it has been my experience that nations in slavery are weak and not able to stand up to the rulers. There is a magnetism in the rulers which attracts slave nations. This was the reason why I used to make it a point to avoid the British. They used to spread propaganda against me and say that I had an aversion for them in my heart. I am a *Khudai Khidmatgar* and the service of God is service to humankind. Are not the British the creation of God? Moreover, this is not to say that, in this trial, only our ministers had failed. If anyone of us were put to this test he, too, would not have been able to cope with it. Only those persons can save themselves who can keep away from such temptations. I considered the social contacts of Dr. Khan Sahib as very dangerous politically, because society has a great impact on him. When he had returned from England, he was anglicized to a great extent. The British seemed to him as pure and truthful and his own people seemed dishonest. I admit that the British are pure and truthful but only for their own nation. And for other nations, and particularly in politics, they are not like that.

In those days, Jawaharlal came on a tour of the Frontier Province. When Pandit Jawaharlal Nehru came to our province for the first time, we took out a large *jaloos* for him all over Peshawar city. Thousands of *Khudai Khidmatgars* stood for him at all vantage points of the route and then a large *jalsa* was held at Shahibagh in his honour. Many government employees and the general public had turned out for it. Nationalist poems were recited. Although Jawaharlal did not understand Pukhto, he was greatly impressed by the poems and the atmosphere of this event. When this poem was recited: 'our red apparel has been worn out, by the servants of the khans!' many people cried. When we were proceeding towards Tehkal, a Sikh, who was a commander of the *Khudai Khidmatgars*, clad in his red uniform and crying out the *Nara-e-Takbeer* preceded us. I told Jawaharlal to observe that he was a Sikh, but here so much unity and nationalism had been generated by the *Khudai Khidmatgar* movement, that he had no qualms about calling out the *Nara-e-Takbeer*. Dr. Khan Sahib complained to Nehru about me, that I was preventing them from cultivating social relationships with the British. Jawaharlal discussed this at length with me, that this attitude of mine was less than cultured. I told him that I agreed that this was not good, but that there was more harm to this than good. So, of what use would that cultured outlook be to us, which was harmful for our country and our people? But he compelled me that it was not proper for me to interfere in such matters. So, I kept quiet. Whenever I would go to Peshawar, I would observe that either Dr. Khan Sahib would be the guest of the British, or some of them would be his guests. His social relationship with the officers became so intense that, let alone official work, they even started interfering in the affairs of our homes. So then Dr. Khan Sahib changed his attitude and reverted to his old stance with regards to his own people and the British, which had been altered through a great deal of effort by him. The fact was that Dr. Khan Sahib was of the view that the government, in general, and the governor sahib were prepared to extend every type of cooperation to his government. But the reality was far removed from this. They would, on the face of it, be very patronizing towards Dr. Khan Sahib to demonstrate their loyalty. However, behind his back they would, both personally and through other people, carry out propaganda against the *Khudai Khidmatgars* and the ministers, and make efforts to harm our movement in several ways. The officer in charge of every government department would impress upon his subordinates that promotions in their careers were dependent upon his evaluation. Similarly, they would incite the khans and *arbabs* against our government and plant it in their minds that now they no longer enjoyed the influence that they formally wielded. And that whatever little was left of it, even that the *Khudai Khidmatgars* were taking away from them. That if they wanted to regain their old status and identity then they would need to assist and strengthen the hands of the government and weaken the *Khudai Khidmatgar* movement. This could only be brought about when all the khans, *arbabs* and maliks got together and got united and, in opposition to the *Khudai Khidmatgars*, made one single political party and then collectively worked for the success of that party all over the land and brought the people over to their side. They would also say this to the maulanas and the *mians*. Mr. Tollinton, who was the assistant commissioner of Charsadda, started this campaign against the *Khudai Khidmatgar*. He summoned Khan Bahadur Saadaullah Khan of Umerzai, consulted him, and took into confidence the khans, maulanas and lawyers of Hashtnagar and Doaba, and established the Muslim League as a political party. Similarly, all over the province, the khans, maulanas and the lawyers, through the auspices of the government, established the Muslim League and started propaganda against us. Before this, there was no Muslim League in our province. Mr. Muhammad Ali Jinnah sahib had come specially to create this party, but had failed. The strange thing was that our government would appoint those officers who would work for the Muslim League. These officers would be great sycophants and the personality of Dr. Khan Sahib was such that he could not resist flattery. If the *Khudai Khidmatgars* would even broach the subject of someone being a flatterer, he would not believe him, and his own *Khudai Khidmatgars* would appear as liars to him. And those officers whom they would themselves have appointed, Dr. Khan Sahib would consider them as loyal, but they would continuously work against the *Khudai Khidmatgars*. Once, Haji Muhammad Aslam Khan of Bannu, told me that Khan Bahadur Dilawar Khan, assistant commissioner, was trying to form the Muslim League in opposition to us. Haji sahib was a very truthful person and a great friend of ours and was also a very sincere *Khudai Khidmatgar*. He informed me that he had told Dr. Khan Sahib that Dilawar Khan was involved in this work and that he should be transferred out. But Dr. Khan Sahib did not believe him and thought that he might be deceiving him. Haji sahib was very upset at this. I somewhat reassured him asking how many officers we would have to transfer. If Dilawar Khan was transferred and someone came in his place, did he think that he would not then be involved in the same work? I decided to broach the topic with Dr. Khan Sahib. He was certain that Dilawar Khan was not doing all this and the Haji sahib was exaggerating things. To ascertain the truth, I visited Bannu myself and spent a few days. I inquired from impartial, non-partisan people and found that, for membership in the Muslim League, Dilawar Khan was even pressurizing Muhammad Nawaz Khan. Muhammad Nawaz Khan was the khan of Gul Imam and was a lawyer in Bannu. He had a good relationship with me and was very sympathetic to our cause. His brother, Muhammad Zafar Khan, was one of our responsible *Khudai Khidmatgars*. Their entire family was foremost in the service of working for our party and he was not a liar and crafty person, like all the other lawyers were. I decided to find out the truth about Dilawar Khan from him in such a way that he would not realize what I was up to. I went to his place, sat with him and began discussing matters with him. Towards the end, I asked him whether he too had been invited to join the Muslim League. He confirmed this. But as soon as he uttered this, he regretted what he had said, and told me that I had lured him into it. I returned to Peshawar and informed Dr. Khan Sahib about what I had found out. The truth was that the *Khudai Khidmatgars* were also to blame in all this. There were many such *Khudai Khidmatgars* who would transmit false information to the government and, for this reason, Dr. Khan Sahib was firmly of the belief that they were all liars. Amongst the *Khudai Khidmatgar*, there were many truthful people, but there was also a sprinkling of those who lied. Because of them, even those who were truthful were not free of suspicion. When our government was formed, new people came to us, and we enrolled them in the party. These people had joined not for the sake of service, but for power and money and to give the *Khudai Khidmatgars* a bad name. This was a big mistake on our part, to have these people join our party. It was essential that when our party attained power, we should not have enrolled these onlookers, these self-serving and temporary people into our party. Moreover, if they were to be enrolled, it should have been ascertained that they were not joining the party for their own, selfish objectives but for the service of the people. It was Dr. Khan Sahib's belief that the governor of our province, Sir George Cunningham, was a very fair person and considered him a friend and helper. I did not share his view. I conceded that Cunningham was a very competent officer and a good man. But even a very good Englishman could not be good for us, because our and their national interests did not coincide.

Gandhiji's Tour

Now, in the Frontier, we had our own government. Since there was no prohibition on his coming, Gandhiji also visited us in 1938. The welcome which was given to him has a historical significance. The aspect which impressed him the most was the order and discipline of the *Khudai Khidmatgars* in uniform, and the way they silently controlled such large crowds in the *jalsa* and *jaloos*. He also observed the sincerity and love they exhibited while doing so. He also saw the love and enthusiasm which the common people had in cooperating with the *Khudai Khidmatgars*. A leader as well-travelled as Gandhiji and one who had seen the world, was compelled to observe that, 'I have in my entire life not seen such well-organized and disciplined *jalsa*!' This generated the hope in Gandhiji that these brave and proud Pukhtuns would not only attain the objectives of their lives, but would also get freedom for Hindustan, and through this would also make the world aware of the power of non-violence. Gandhiji would smile and say that all last night he had not slept in the train, because at every station in Punjab, crowds would gather. They would be pushing, shoving and shouting. Gandhiji would stuff his ears with cotton wool due to this. I recall that story of Jawaharlal Nehru. When he was coming on a tour of Punjab for the first time, he said that, at all the railways stations, the crowds would be yelling and shouting and not allowing them to get a wink of sleep. Nehru recalled this in his own inimitable manner 'It was every man's effort to get his mouth as near to my ear as possible and to shout, Inquilab Zindabad *(Long Live the Revolution)*,'as if *Inquilab* could be brought about by shouting in Jawaharlal's ear. But when the train came to a halt at one railway station, and as he was preparing himself again for the yelling and shouting and put his head out of the window, what did he see but that from one end of the platform to the other, the *Khudai Khidmatgar* stood, clad in their red apparel. There was no pushing, shoving or yelling. An elder came up to him and stated in a matter of fact way that they had come for his welcome. He got down and they, collectively, offered their *salams* to the sound of dhols and *surnas*. Jawaharlal said that he was so impressed that he got goosebumps and then, turning his face towards *Mian* Iftikhar-ud-Din, who was the president of the Punjab Congress party at the time, said, 'There was no need for anyone to tell us that we had entered the land of the civilized and gentle Pathans!'

When Gandhiji embarked on his tour of the Frontier Province, the first *jalsa* was organized at Charsadda. Fida Abdul Malik was the president and Inzar Gul was the *Salar*. The excellent work these two did in the province, which drew equally good people to the movement, was never done earlier nor can it be replicated in the future. When Gandhiji arrived at the venue of the *jalsa*, people in their thousands were seated there. On his coming, not one person moved from where he was sitting. Gandhiji's car drove up to the stage and we got down there. The people were sitting in silence, listening to the speeches. Gandhiji was extremely impressed with this *jalsa*, and when he got up to speak, he said that he had travelled all over the world, had attended many, but he had never seen such a well-disciplined crowd. Then, he left just as he had come. The car was driven up to the stage, he sat in it, and when he had left, the *jalsa* dispersed. Neither at the time of arrival nor at the time of departure did anyone leave his place. The leadership of our party was not on account of being a khan. This was based on service to the people. Our general in Uthmanzai was a tanner. His name was Ziarat Gul. Many khans, *arbabs*, maliks, maulanas and *mians* functioned as their subordinates. Their orders would be obeyed like salaried servants; and not only theirs but everyone who was in authority, no matter who he was by caste or profession. There was a wonderful brotherhood and love amongst the *Khudai Khidmatgars* and every task they were assigned was accomplished with great love and care. After Peshawar, Gandhiji proceeded to Kohat. When we arrived at Dara Adamkhel, many Afridis had gathered to welcome him. There were some Hindus amongst them as well. These were those who lived in the Tribal Areas and had shops there. I told Gandhiji to ask them whether, in these free Tribal Areas, their lives, properties and honour were safe or not, and whether they were ever subjected to dacoities. To Gandhiji's question, they replied that everything belonging to them was safe, and if anyone were to commit excesses against them, they would be opposed and taken to task by their patron tribes. I told him that, 'Gandhiji, all these dacoities are just political in nature. They are carried out under the government of the British and are there to terrorize you.'

Wali was our driver and took us around. From Kohat, we went on to Bannu and then onwards to Dera Ismail Khan. From there, we returned to Peshawar and then went to Mardan. From Mardan we went to Hazara, from where Gandhiji left for Hindustan. Gandhiji left feeling very satisfied with the discipline and non-violence of the *Khudai Khidmatgars*. Gandhiji had such love and affection for the people of the Frontier that he told me, that if I wanted, he would stay six months in Sevagram and six months here. Sardar Patel was unhappy over Gandhiji's tour of the Frontier and always had differences of opinion with him over the issue. He did not want Gandhiji to visit the Frontier again. Patel was always trying that the Muslims should not join the Congress Party. There was just one member of the Congress who was a Muslim, but he considered him a Hindu. So, he had warned him to beware and not allow the Muslims to join the Congress.

The lawyers and barristers of the Frontier had, through Sardar Abdur Rab Nishtar, presented a welcome address to Gandhiji in the bungalow of Dr. Khan Sahib. They had written in it that they were proud of the fact that he, too, belonged to their profession. Gandhiji gave him a very interesting answer, to the effect that he was not of their profession. That since he began serving God's people, he had left this profession. That they, too, should consider leaving their profession and devote themselves to the service of the country.

It was shortly after the formation of our government when I received an invitation to an 'at home' at the government house, from the governor. Like the other guests, Dr. Khan Sahib had also been invited. In those days, a session of the working committee of the Congress had been convened at Calcutta. I was supposed to attend this and so discussed with Dr. Khan Sahib whether we should attend the 'at home' or not. I told him that Congress ministers were not allowed to attend any kind of social functions arranged by the government. He replied that it would be better if I were to ask Gandhiji and then inform him. If he agreed, then the telegram should say only 'yes,' and if he did not agree, then I should just write 'no'. When I arrived in Calcutta and asked Gandhiji, he said that they did not participate in such functions, so I sent a telegram to Dr. Khan Sahib, saying 'no'. When the telegram reached him, he informed the governor accordingly. The governor did not keep this to himself but, at the party, carried out a lot of propaganda against Dr. Khan Sahib. He told Malik Khuda Baksh, in the presence of some other guests, that Dr. Khan Sahib wanted to attend the party but received instructions from above not to do so. When I returned and learnt of this development, I told Dr. Khan Sahib that this man was no friend of his and that this talk was not one of friendship. In fact, it was far from decent. However, Dr. Khan Sahib's temperament was such that he would remember such matters for a few days only, and then forget all about it.

In Calcutta, Subhash Chandra Bose and his brother, Surat Chandra Bose, had made excellent arrangements for the working committee's session and had thought of the comfort of every member. He accommodated Gandhiji in his own home. I was accommodated at the house of a big *taluqdar* and the same was the position of the other members. He looked after Gandhiji very well. I was seated beside Gandhiji when Subhash babu also came. He had not yet recovered fully from his ailment so Gandhiji told him that he could not be expected to effectively handle the affairs of the president of Congress. He did not agree with this and said that he could do so; that he was much better now and could cope with the work involved. I realized that all the efforts that he had put in to organizing this session was because he wanted the members to vote in favour of the proposal nominating him for the post. In those days, Lalee had not yet taken his entrance exam and was at Wardha. When Jamnalalji Bajaj was coming for the session, he brought Lalee with him. He was very fond of Lalee and allowed him to spend only one night with me. On the conclusion of the session, he left with Gandhiji for Wardha and I returned to my province.

The Ministers and the *Khudai Khidmatgar*

We had agreed to form the government so that we could strengthen our party and weaken the hold of the British. So, we put a stop to all the monetary awards from the government because, in this way the recipients received the money from the public treasury but served only the British masters. Similarly, we put an end to the institution of the honourary magistrates because they were the party of the British. The other measure that we put in place was to end the *chowkidari* of the maliks, which was a means of subjecting the poor to excesses at their hands. We also intended to do away with the *lambardari* system in the villages, because the *lambardars* were also a strong party favouring the British. We wanted to appoint a *naib-tehsildar* in every *tehsil* for the collection of land revenue. We were, however, unsuccessful in this because certain members of the assembly from our party were themselves *lambardars*. This was the outcome of our wrong selection of candidates for the assembly and, in future, we should draw a lesson from this. The other issue was that in Kohat, in the *jagir* of Teri nawab, there were two oppressive taxes collected from the poor, which were *bua* and *tirni*. A resolution was passed in the assembly to do away with these.

Now let me tell you of another strange matter. One day Qazi sahib and I were taking a stroll in the evening in Abbottabad. We saw that ahead of us there were some girls being followed by boys. I did not like this. I asked Qazi sahib whether the ministers had enough powers to stop this because these were our children. Their honour was our honour, and their dishonour was our dishonour. Qazi sahib informed us that they did not, under the law, enjoy such powers. I asked him of what use was this government when we could not protect the honour of our daughters, sisters and mothers.

There were some improvements in the education system of the province as well. Finally, schools were established, of which a significant number were for girls. But we could not promote the cause of education to the extent that we wanted to, because only a small amount could be allocated for it in the annual budget of the province, the major portion of which went as salaries of the staff. We, however, managed to make some saving in this. Instead of an Englishman, we appointed a native as director of education and abolished the position of inspector. There was more possibility for greater savings, but the reform involved was beyond our remit. In the matter of education, the excesses which the British have committed against us have not been committed anywhere else in Hindustan. For the children of the Pukhtuns, minimal arrangements were made even for this low quality of education; and for the education of girls, no attention was paid at all. The other injustice done to the Pukhtuns was not to arrange for primary education in their mother tongue, but in an alien language. The Pukhtuns would make efforts to establish *madrassahs* for the education of their children, but the government, instead of assisting them, put hurdles in their way and tried to shut them down. Our government also took the step of declaring Pukhto as a compulsory subject in the *madrassahs*. On the other hand, our people had spent all their lives under the British and had never experienced their rights and nor were they aware of their rights. We had earned two annas as income, and the people wanted an expenditure of a rupee. And let alone this, there was also no distinction between legal and illegal. Every man was under the impression that there was loot to be had and that others had benefitted, whereas he was left behind. Let alone the people, the position of the *Khudai Khidmatgars* was the same. They would continuously be sitting in the bungalows of the ministers. The *tehsils* and thanas were never free of them, and whatever anyone demanded, if it was given, then it was fine; and if it was not possible, then they would criticize the government. When I would observe these activities of the *Khudai Khidmatgars,* I would be amazed and would ask myself whether these were the same people who had vowed before God that they would, for His sake, serve their nation and country without any self-interest. But what was unfortunate was that whenever there was a vacancy or an employment opportunity in the government, more than a hundred *Khudai Khidmatgars* would apply for it. But the job would only be one and could be given to one applicant only. He, too, would be a *Khudai Khidmatgar*. The remaining *Khudai Khidmatgars* would be disappointed and criticize their government and movement wherever and whenever they got the chance. Not only would they criticize, they would also abuse and bad-mouth the government.

The days when an examination for vacant posts would be held, there would be a strange spectacle. There would be applicants in the hundreds, and with each one, generals, colonels and presidents of the *Khudai Khidmatgars* would turn up to intercede. The strange thing would be that they would also come to promote the sons of those whose fathers would have, as government employees, subjected them to all kinds of atrocities and who were also friends of the British in the existing government. I would consider this conduct of the *Khudai Khidmatgars* as most shameful and uncalled for. Whether the applicants benefitted or not, these people did, as they would have free rides in cars and free tea and meals. The other major fault in all this was that all applicants could not be employed, so they and their relatives would taunt the *Khudai Khidmatgar*, that they underwent all the trials, tribulations and imprisonment, while all the benefits accrued to others.

Our government also committed the grave blunder that it repealed the brutal law which we had opposed all our lives, and under the provisions of which the British had jailed me all my life. Our government had repealed this law, but it was reinforced later by the British, through our government. Let alone conferring with the *Khudai Khidmatgar*, the government did not even consult me before doing so. The party should also have been consulted, and if it did not agree, then the ministers had no right to re-enact this black law. For one, the authority of the British increased with this law, because the people flocked to them in the hope of being appointed as members of the *jirga* and, secondly, many of our people were jailed under this Frontier Crimes Regulation, and then we could not do anything about it because we had, through our own government, re-enacted it. And I had been jailed all my life by the British under this law! On the other hand, all government officers, on the instigation and backing of the British government, started a vicious propaganda campaign against us. They did not bother about and nor did they respect our government. Many times, in front of me, they would talk to people against the *Khudai Khidmatgars*. Similarly, I was once on tour in the Koi Daman area of the Moomand with Ashiq Shah Bacha and the *thanedar* of the area, who was on tour with us, would speak against us to the people. He would tell the people that, 'Bacha Khan does not slaughter a cow.' To the extent that, in a big *jalsa*, some people, on the prompting of a *thanedar*, raised a ruckus and asked me during my speech whether I had slaughtered cows. I told them that I was not a butcher and that Islam was not about the slaughtering of cows. This reached the ears of Dr. Khan Sahib and other ministers. At first, Dr. Khan Sahib did not believe Ashiq Shah Bacha and when he did, even then he could not take any action against that *thanedar*. Let alone this, in our own village there was a gambling den. Dr. Khan Sahib had come personally on three occasions to have it shut down, but it was not shut down, because this was the job of the police and the police did not support him as it had a share in its earnings. Dr. Khan Sahib had once himself caught an official taking a bribe. A case was instituted against him but, finally the magistrate exonerated him. The truth was that government officers were not scared of the ministers because they could not be punished by them. Whichever officer our government was not satisfied with, and whom it had decided to punish, the governor and senior British officers would immediately transfer him to the agencies of the centrally administered Tribal Areas and, in this way, would manage to save him. The result was that government officers would flagrantly disobey the orders of the ministers and would not cooperate with them in any manner. Moreover, Dr. Khan Sahib thought that the government officers were cooperating with their government. A case was made out against the superintendent of police, Khushdil Khan, for stealing trees and foolproof evidence was collected against him. The governor came and told Dr. Khan Sahib that he would have the man transferred from his post, but that he should withdraw from the prosecution of the case instituted against him. Dr. Khan Sahib had been informed by his companions that this man was an evil person who had committed many atrocities against the *Khudai Khidmatgars,* and had also humiliated and jailed them, although they were innocent. But Dr. Khan Sahib was a strange man. Moreover, he had him transferred on the intervention of the governor. This was most harmful to us and our party; and this was the reason that the government officials did not cooperate with us, and whatever the British directed them to do, they would do. It was the belief of these government employees that authority did not lie with the government but with the British. Similarly, the members of the assembly and the district boards also forgot that they had been elected through the votes of the people, and that all that they did should be for the people who had elected them. The strange thing was that, in the district boards and in other places, whoever they elected as chairman, if he would work honestly and sincerely and would live by their principles and not accede to unfair demands, they would try to unseat them. It was a matter of great regret that they would not give their votes to their *Khudai Khidmatgar* brothers, who have spent years in jail with them, but to others who were unknown to them and from whom they could expect undue favours. The khan of Jhagra was one such person, who had fed them well. The other thing about him was that he was a strong man of the

British and willing to do anything at their behest. He was not from among the *Khudai Khidmatgar,* but they all became his friends and they helped him to succeed, instead of one of their own. Even the ministers would not bother to consult with anyone. They had been put into such a frenzy by the *Khudai Khidmatgar,* that they did not even confer amongst themselves, and nor did they follow any principles in their decision-making.

The viceroy came on a visit to the region and he was given a warm welcome. Dr. Khan Sahib participated in the banquet in his honour. I received a telegram from the Congress high command, asking what we had done. Similarly, within our members of the provincial assembly there was factionalism, and even in the district boards there was grouping. The *Khudai Khidmatgar* also suffered from this, let alone the others. *Mian* Jaffar Shah and Arbab Abdul Rehman of Gulli Garhai had also created a rift between Dr. Khan Sahib and Qazi Ataullah. Dr. Khan Sahib and Qazi Ataullah were two of our most prominent and responsible *Khudai Khidmatgar* and, before joining the cabinet, had a lot of love and affection for each other. When we would go out on tour, the British would carry out propaganda against us. They would tell the maulanas that we were bolsheviks, abandoning religion and them. They would tell the khans and maliks that we were taking away everything from them and giving it to the poor. Why was it that the maulanas did not sit down with us to ascertain the truth, but rather believed what they were told by the British? The khans and maliks would come and ask us questions about these matters. I was on a tour of the Doaba area when some khans and maliks came and shared that they had heard that we were going to take away their properties and give them to the poor. I said to them that God has blessed us with a land, which was replete with wealth and bounties. If we were to gain our freedom, and this land became our own, and we united and developed it, no one would remain poor anymore. We would all become khans. We had no intention of taking over their property and land. On the contrary, we wanted to improve the quality of their lives as well and feed the hungry. If the poor were well fed, what possible objection could they have to this? That if they happened to visit the land of the British, let alone others, (they would see that) their labourers also owned houses and cars. So, I asked them whether they owned a car, whether they owned a house. I said that if our movement were to succeed, the condition of the maulana would improve and so would that of the khans and the maliks. All that we are doing is not for ourselves, it is for the people and the country.

When we initiated our cleanliness campaign and went to the villages, we would have brooms in our hands. We would sweep the mosques, *hujras* and the streets. The agents of the British would then tell the khans, maliks and the maulanas that the actual meaning of this campaign was that death should sweep them all away, leaving their land and properties to be inherited by us. But because of our effort, brotherhood, kinsmanship, nationalism and political consciousness had been created in the people. So, the more propaganda that was carried out against us, the more would the sympathy of the people be aroused in our favour. This was because they saw that we were only serving them and were engaged in a tussle with the British for their rights and, in the process, were undergoing hardships, difficulties and terms in jail. The people would say that we were the ones who suffered prison terms but demanded rights for them. This was the reason for the sympathy that the people had for us. The people knew that the reforms of 1919 were unacceptable to Hindustan. The inhabitants of Hindustan felt that they were inadequate. But the nawabs, khans, *sahibzadas, syeds* and spiritual leaders of the Frontier demanded these reforms. However, the British would not concede them. They told them that the Pukhtuns were not aware of the principles of governance; that they were uncivilized people. They understood well that these reforms had been won for them by the *Khudai Khidmatgars*. The masses also knew that their vote had power, because governments were formed by their votes and the vote had been gained for them by the *Khudai Khidmatgars*.

The truth is that our movement was greatly harmed by our gaining political authority. These selfish people were waiting for an opportunity to get power. When power was attained, they entered our ranks. They had not come to serve, they had come to exercise power and for the sake of attaining power, they created factions amongst us. Power is not something evil. All our striving is also for the sake of political power. However, power is not only just to get a government, but to serve the people. It was the principle of us, the *Khudai Khidmatgar*, that whenever we would appoint someone for work, we would all get together. I would inform them of the task at hand and that we needed someone for it, and that they should select someone who could do it. They would identify someone and let me know. Thus, nobody would be disappointed. There would be no complaints and no opposition. In Turlandai, we were to select the president of the *Khudai Khidmatgar.* Afridi Khan was elected as the president. He came to me and said that he was a *Khudai Khidmatgar* and would serve whether he was or was not the president. That their maulvi sahib was anxious for the post, so would I not agree that it should be given to him? I told him that if this is what he wanted, then this is also what I want: that he should observe what is happening in these political parties today. There are quarrels in them, there is opposition, factionalism and divisiveness. All for the sake of political power.

I have always told this nation that until such time as it produces, selfless, honest persons who are devoted to the service of the people, neither this land nor the people can throw off the yoke of foreign domination.

Then there is the vote. I am not against the institution of voting. The manner in which we decide our tribal and family matters, is this not voting? And is it not democracy? And have we not got the right to vote after numerous sacrifices? But I am of the considered view that we must educate our people about the meaning of their votes; and also make them understand that votes must only be cast in favour of those who deserve them. One should not sell one's vote or cast it in favour of a relative merely because of his relationship to one. I believe those who sell their votes, should be deprived of their right to vote. On account of the selfish people having entered their ranks, even the *Khudai Khidmatgar* have become selfish.

The British knew that ours was the political party based on principles, and whatever we proclaimed, we did. We had told the people that whoever won the election, would get to enjoy its fruit. The British were also aware of the fact that we were not in the mould of the other political leaders who, whatever promises they extended to the masses at the time of the elections, did not even fulfil one of them. So, when we formed the government, they became fearful of the outcome and began to intrigue against us. One day, Qazi sahib came to me and told me that Dr. Khan Sahib had come to an agreement with Governor Cunningham that there would be a competitive examination to fill job vacancies, and only those who were capable would be recruited, and if this were not done, administration would weaken. For the resolution of such issues, we had constituted a committee to which we would put these up. I was also a member of this committee. I instructed Qazi sahib to convene a meeting of the committee. When the meeting started, I asked Dr. Khan Sahib whether he had taken a decision with the governor. Dr. Khan Sahib replied that if there were to be no competitive examination, then competent candidates would not get a chance to compete and the quality of the administration would deteriorate. I told him that I had known people in the government of the British who were government employees but did not even know how to sign their name. Moreover, whenever someone came for government service, the first thing they would be asked was whether they had done any service to government or not. Only those would be taken who had rendered personal services to the government. So, it was necessary for us as well, that before recruiting anyone we should reassure ourselves whether he or his father had any service to the nation to his credit. These *Khudai Khidmatgar* were mostly very poor people. They cannot even educate their own children in their villages. And the rich, let alone here, they can afford to educate their children in Europe and America. So, this means that the sacrifices are rendered by the poor and the benefits are reaped by the children of the khans who have been the allies of the British during our struggle for freedom. I agree with the merits of competition, but on the condition that the children of the poor get the same education as the rich provide for their children. I told them that if they did not agree with this, then it would be better for them to resign from the government. Dr. Khan Sahib replied that he was resigning from this committee.

In short, I reached the conclusion that we should leave the government at the earliest opportunity because, instead of benefiting, it was proving to be harmful to us. Differences among our members of the provincial assembly were increasing by the day. Some would be complaining against Dr. Khan Sahib and some against Qazi sahib. This would not be based on any principle, but based on personal interest. Things reached such an unfortunate pass that members of the Congress committee of Hazara met with some opposition members in the dak bungalow of Attock, located in the province of Punjab, to discuss measures to overthrow the government. But only God knows why a decision was not arrived at. Some people thought that Khan Bahadur Saadullah Khan[30] and Aurangzeb Khan disagreed on who would be the chief minister. The president of the All-India Congress Committee, Maulana Abul Kalam Azad, himself came to the Frontier Province but was unable to resolve this issue. This was because issues of personal interest can never be resolved to the satisfaction of everyone. Some members of the assembly forced me to interfere in this matter. They were also of the view that it would be in our interest to resign from the government. I was, from the very beginning, of this view but did not wish to interfere in the work of the ministers because they were ultimately responsible. I convened the *Loya Jirga* of the *Khudai Khidmatgar* and placed this issue of resigning from the government before it. All the members were of the view that the government was not cooperating with us, so it was necessary for us to resign and that this was not benefitting our movement but was proving harmful to it. The meeting concluded, and I constituted a committee of three people from amongst them and instructed the members of the provincial assembly to assemble the next day and to give their views to the committee individually. The next day when the committee started its work, except for *Amir* Muhammad Khan Hoti, all the members opted in favour of the continuation of the government. I was amazed at this and came outside and, addressing all the members, asked how was it that yesterday they were all against the continuation of the government, and today they were all in its favour. Dr. Khan Sahib said that if he were permitted, he would reveal the secret. I allowed him to do so. He said that they were all the view that the government should continue but should do only that which they recommended. But we did not agree to this. So, to pressurize us they had raised the issue of resignation from the government. We dispersed, but my opinion about resignation of the government was firmed up even further, and I put forward this proposal to the Congress high command on several occasions, to allow us to resign from the government of the Frontier Province. But they did not allow us to do so and would tell us that they would decide to resign from all the ministries simultaneously. But thanks be to God, the Second World War began in Europe in 1939.

Resignation of the Ministries

When the Second World War started in Europe, Britain declared war on Germany. At the same time, it also declared war against Germany on behalf of Hindustan. The Congress raised an objection to this and stated that, from the last elections, it was evident that it was the representative of the people of Hindustan. So, it was necessary to have obtained the opinion of the people of Hindustan before announcing war on its behalf. The other demand that they put forth was that if the declaration of Britain and its allies was correct, that they had entered the war for the sake of peace, tranquillity and freedom, then Congress would pose the question of whether Hindustan was included in this or not. The Congress further added that we were, without a doubt, waging a struggle for these very principles, and were extending this assurance to the government of the United Kingdom, that Hindustan would also stand shoulder to shoulder with them in this war, and would not shrink from any sacrifice, but on the express condition that the government of Britain declares that, on winning the war, it would grant total independence to Hindustan.

Because the government of Britain refused to issue this declaration, to protest this, all the provincial Congress ministries collectively and simultaneously resigned and, thank god, we were spared the humiliation. After the break-up of our government, I went on a tour of the province. The stagnation which had set in on account of the government was gradually overcome by our efforts, tours, *jalsa*, *jaloos* and speeches. The war had started in Europe. It was necessary for the Congress to take the people into confidence about the war and about its policy towards it. The Congress working committee convened its session at Wardha for this purpose. Pandit Jawaharlal Nehru had gone to China. He was, via telegram, asked to return and did so by air. In the working committee, it was decided that they would re-assemble the following month to take a final decision in the matter.

After this, the British constituted Muslim League ministries in the provinces, but a Muslim League government was not formed in our province. Governor Cunningham used to say that he was not prepared to form a Muslim League government here; and that if he were to make a government, it would be led by Dr. Khan Sahib. Our people were happy with this, that he was not making a Muslim League government, but I did not agree with this. I did not like what the governor was saying because I was of the view that if a Muslim League government were to be formed, the people would realize the difference between this government and that of the *Khudai Khidmatgar*. But the same governor, who was not in favour of a Muslim League government, finally formed one. On its formation, the nationalists were very upset, but I was happy. The people were surprised at this. I would tell them that our people were very strange and asked whether they did not see that we had won two annas and they were asking for a rupee. We did not have a rupee and so they were annoyed with us. We had won a two anna coin, which we would offer them; but the Muslim League would not even offer them this. And this is exactly what happened.

18

The Nuts and Bolts of the *Khudai Khidmatgar* (End of 1942)

IN DECEMBER 1942, THE CONGRESS WORKING COMMITTEE PASSED THE civil disobedience resolution and decided that this civil disobedience should be resorted to only by members of the All-India Congress Committee, but also by the central assembly members and the provincial assembly members. Detailed operating procedures in this regard were also distributed. In Peshawar, we gathered at the office of the *Khudai Khidmatgar*. We would call each member individually, repeat all the circulated instructions and take a pledge from each to follow them. Barrister Abdul Qayyum was a member of the central legislative assembly. When Dr. Khan Sahib contested elections for the provincial assembly, he resigned from his seat and, in his place, had Barrister Abdul Qayyum Khan of Peshawar city elected as a member. I did not have much trust in him. Not only him, I also did not have much confidence in all the members of the assemblies that they would follow the instructions in letter and spirit, so I did not permit him to be nominated. But Dr. Khan Sahib intervened on his behalf and so I had to give permission. It was also said that these members might get arrested. I thought that it would be good if they are arrested but if not, they should not sit at home but go from village to village, talking about the civil disobedience. But, unfortunately, not many people complied with these instructions. Mostly, people went to the villages for a day or two and then quietly sat at home. Let alone not complying with the instructions, the lawyers amongst them started their legal practices and the first to do so was Barrister Qayyum. The position of the lawyers from Hazara was such that the *Khudai Khidmatgar* would picket the courts and shut them down. The *Khudai Khidmatgar* would get arrested and, in these very courts, the Satyagrahi lawyers would take on people's cases. But the strangest thing was that these lawyers neither absented themselves from the courts, nor did they resign from the movement. I personally had these barristers and lawyers assemble at one place and informed them that their actions were against the principles of the *Khudai Khidmatgar*, and that they were, by their conduct, defaming both themselves and their party; that they should leave either the courts or the party. They were not prepared to do either because there was money to be made at the courts, and in the party there was honour and respect. Some of our *Khudai Khidmatgar* companions did excellent work. They toured amongst their people from village to village, made them understand, but the government would not arrest them. At last, they got tired and left the work. There were very few such dedicated workers in our party. Our educated cadres did not concern themselves with the welfare of the people or the nation, and nor did they exhibit any sympathy or interest in this. On the contrary, for the fulfilment of personal interest, they would oppose the movement. In September 1941, in village Sherpao of Hashtnagar, we had established a camp on the other side of the road to the east. This had crops all around it and deep ravines. Major Cole was the assistant commissioner of Charsadda. He was a bitter opponent of our movement. In fact, every Englishman is an opponent of our movement and considers us their enemy and are all the time considering how to harm our movement. But even then, they do what they must in an appropriate manner. But Major Cole was different.When he heard about our camp, he called for two Kakakhel brothers, *Mian* Abdul Qayuum and *Mian* Abdul *Hakeem*, and instructed them to kill me in the camp at night. He further informed them that if they killed me, he would not only honour them greatly, but would also give them a handsome monetary reward. He also told them that they would not be arrested for the crime, and nor would criminal proceedings be initiated against them. Both the brothers were notorious dacoits. But my time was not up. They came three nights in a row to the camp to commit the murder. But the security of the *Khudai Khidmatgar* in the camp was so strong that they did not get the opportunity. It was by coincidence that Zaidullah Khan of Umerzai killed both the brothers in broad daylight, and he became an outlaw for it, and thus saved God's innocent creatures from their cruel ways. Let alone this, the same Major Cole created a big problem for us in our own family. He incited our paternal cousins against us and told them that if they killed Dr. Khan Sahib and me, he would transfer all our inherited lands in their names. He also promised that no one would so much as question them about this. We had a paternal aunt whose husband and children had all died. My father was her husband's only legal heir, but he was a very kind-hearted man and so he left the property to her to enjoy during her lifetime. This was spread over four villages and she enjoyed the usufruct of the land for twenty-five years. When she died, we were entitled to inherit this property, but Major Cole did not hand it over to us. Raja Singh, the advocate general, who had been imprisoned with me in Mianwali jail, was a very noble person and a committed nationalist. He had been jailed in connection with the affair of Gurubagh. He told the governor, Sir George Cunningham, that this was a wrong decision. This was the same governor who was a benefactor and friend of Dr. Khan Sahib and promised that he would cooperate with us in every possible manner. Dr. Khan Sahib had great trust in him and believed that he was a very honest governor. When Raja Singh informed him that a wrong decision had been taken in this case, the governor replied that he should let this be and not interfere in these matters. Major Cole summoned Sultan Khan, who was also my maternal nephew, to the *tehsil* and told them that he had apportioned the property in their names but that they had not yet dealt with Dr. Khan Sahib and me, and consequently, he was thinking of taking it away from them. So, on the instigation of Cole, they attacked Dr. Khan Sahib's son, Abeedullah Khan. Inspite of hundreds of shots fired at him, he was saved by the grace of God. The police of the Khanmahi Police Station also arrived at the venue of the attempted murder and witnessed everything. However, when Abeedullah Khan went to the thana to lodge the FIR, they refused to accept it. Dr. Khan Sahib went to Iskandar Mirza,[31] the deputy commissioner, Peshawar, who was a great friend of his and informed him about what had happened. He said that this was a problem for the police to resolve. The intention of the assailants was to attack Dr. Khan Sahib and me, but both of us were in Hindustan at that time. To make matters worse, the daughter of that paternal aunt of ours, whose mother's inheritance was passed on to her, died.

According to Shariat, I would inherit half of the property, which the government had deprived me of till now.

After the camp at Hashtnagar, our next camp was organized in September 1941 in Hazara. We would, for the training and education of the *Khudai Khidmatgar,* organize such camps and hold *jalsa* with them. Our *jalsa* was held in Abbottabad. Speeches were being delivered. I was also was sitting on the stage when Khanmir Hilali sahib started his speech. When he took the name of Jinnah sahib, I immediately tugged at the helm of his shirt and sat him down, and getting up addressed the *jalsa,* 'Oh *Khudai Khidmatgar* brothers! We are *Khudai Khidmatgar.* God is not in need of anyone's service. Our work is to serve God's people. Our work is not to object to what others do and find fault in it. We should not complain against other people and find fault with their leaders; our work is to lay our programme before the people. We are demanding rights for you and this cannot be done by us alone but if you join forces with us. The land belongs to you and to us. The nation belongs to all of us and this work is for all of us to do.' Whichever *jalsa* I attended and if anyone in it were to mention the name of any party or its leader deprecatingly, I would make him sit down and would try to make him understand that he was a *Khudai Khidmatgar* and had no right to criticize any other party or its leader. If he had anything to say to the people, it should be about his own party. The truth was that these were our principles.

In this camp, it was decided that we would organize a big camp in Uthmanzai for the representatives of the *Khudai Khidmatgar* from the entire province. This was held in November 1941, in which the *Khudai Khidmatgar* from every part of the province and members of the *Loya Jirga* took part. There were 360 *Khudai Khidmatgar* and 150 members of the *Khudai Khidmatgar jirga*. In addition to these, there was Sheikh Abdullah, Bakhshi Ghulam Muhammad and Afzal Baig, along with their companions from Kashmir. Similarly, from Balochistan there was Abdul Samad Khan Achakzai with his companions. In this way, we continued with the organization of the camps all over the province, in which the training of the *Khudai Khidmatgar* was imparted in a very satisfactory manner. Our contact with the masses was strengthened through the various *jalsa* as we identified many potential workers and leaders who served the nation and the movement well.

In 1941, Japan also entered the Second World War. It attacked Philippines, and when it arrived at the border of Burma, Congress deemed it proper to reconsider its decision for the third time. For this, a meeting of the working committee was scheduled at Bardoli. This was a very crucial session and it continued for ten days. A difference of opinion on principle arose between the members. This was whether to adopt the path of non-violence, or not. The Congress had all along adopted the policy of non-violence, but in these days, it was the opinion of most members that if the British were to give us our rights, then we would be prepared to assist them in any manner, and would also, in the process, sacrifice the lifelong principle of non-violence. But Gandhiji was not prepared for this, and nor was I in agreement with them on this. Gandhiji and I were on one side, and the rest were all against us. When the proposal was put to vote, it passed. Gandhiji and I resigned from the working committee because of this and it was decided that, as soon as possible, another meeting of the All-India Congress Working Committee should be convened at Wardha, and this decision should be placed before it. I was in Wardha when I received a letter from Hyderabad, from Ghani and his father- and mother-in-law, informing me and congratulating that Ghani had had a daughter. So, I then proceeded to Hyderabad in the Deccan, where Roshan's older sister had come to receive me and I went with her to their home. Roshan's father showed me the main monuments of Hyderabad. Outside the city, they had a beautiful home. I wanted to stay a few more days with them and they also did not want to let me go. But I came back to the village and restarted my political work.

The meeting of the working committee concluded and we all returned to our respective places. When the All-India Congress Committee session approached, I went to Bombay and stayed for the *jalsa*. On account of the poor diet of the jails, my teeth had got infected, and I had them extracted and dentures put in. I had informed Sadullah Khan, an engineer in the Bombay Corporation, of my arrival. He came to the station to receive me and took me home. Safia, his wife, was a committed nationalist and would always take great care of me. In those days, Younas Jan was also in Bombay and was staying with me. He had a good rapport with Jinnah sahib and used to tell me many stories about him. He used to say that Jinnah sahib would confide in him that he was surrounded by selfish and dishonest people, and if a person like me were to join his party, then he would be able to accomplish many things. Every morning when he would leave the house, I would caution him against mentioning my name to Jinnah sahib. I thought that he would certainly talk to him about me and feared, in case, without consulting me, he might commit himself to him on my account and I considered the Muslim League a party formed by the British. But Younas Jan did not act on my advice and, finally, mentioned me to him. Jinnah sahib told him to extend an invitation to me for tea on his behalf. That evening, however, I was scheduled to go to a Congress *jalsa*, and so I expressed my gratitude to him over the telephone but conveyed my regrets. I then left for Wardha.

For the session of the Congress working committee, delegates had come from all the provinces of Hindustan, because this was a very important session. The resolution which the working committee had passed in Bardoli was placed before it and debated at length. I too thought that I should put my views before the members, but the president of the session, Maulana Abdul Kalam Azad, did not give me permission, and so the resolution was ratified by a majority vote. After it was passed, I resigned from the Congress. Maulana sahib requested me not to talk about this with the newspaper reporters as it was now up to him to have it suitably published in the newspapers. However, the agreement would be that I should appoint a person from my province in my place, and if the workers of my province needed my views, I would not hesitate to offer my views. The Congress withdrew from its decision of individual Satyagraha. No matter how much it tried to please the British, but in their hearts, there was no compassion for us and not even one of our demands was accepted.

The Congress session concluded, and I left for Peshawar. I convened a meeting of the provincial *jirga* and unanimously had Dr. Khan Sahib elected as the representative of the Congress on the working committee. I reassured the members of the *jirga*, entrusting them with work, I assumed responsibility for the work of the *Khudai Khidmatgar*. Despite this, Maulana Abdul Kalam Azad did not publicize my resignation from the Congress but made it public after some time. In those days, the Japanese were advancing with great speed on all war fronts. They inflicted many reverses on the Americans and the British. The war reached the borders of

Hindustan. They occupied Burma and were advancing with speed. I began to fear that if they continued to advance at this pace, it was quite possible that they would soon occupy a portion of Hindustan, which could generate disturbance all over. I was convinced that when the British thought that they were in danger at the hands of the Japanese in Hindustan, they would then surely try to create disturbances in the country. News had also reached us that the British, through their agents, had organized three kinds of groups in the Tribal Areas. To the extent that a meeting of one of the groups of Moomands had been convened at Shabqadar, through Khan Bahadur Kulli Khan, to which the governor of the province, Sir George Cunningham, had gone personally. We felt that the British would try to make the Pukhtuns fall out amongst themselves. So, we thought that we should send our own people to these areas to make them understand that we Pukhtuns are the progeny of the same ancestor, but that it was the British who had kept them apart from us. You may recall that when, in 1930, the British made life hell for the *Khudai Khidmatgar,* our Pukhtun brothers from the Moomand, the land of the Afridis and till Waziristan, stood together in opposition to the British. On account of this, the British concentrated all their attention on the Tribal Areas, to ensure the effective separation of the tribes from the rest of the Pukhtuns. But no amount of efforts to ruin the relationship between us and our tribal brothers, through deception and lies, were successful. When I initiated the *Khudai Khidmatgar* movement, many a times, I tried to go to our brothers in the Tribal Area, as this was a movement of the Pukhtuns. But the British did not allow me to do so, as they did not wish to see the development of brotherhood between us. The tribal issue was an issue of us Pukhtuns. In my view, it was a matter of life and death. I started a tour of my own province, so that I could confer with my own people over this matter and prepare the *Khudai Khidmatgar* to go into the Tribal Areas, to contact their Pukhtun brothers and make them aware of the present situation, and to generate in them feelings of brotherhood and unity.

In those days, the British had sent Sir Stafford Cripps, a cabinet minister, with a view to mending fences between Hindustan and the British. I was in Kohat at the time, when Dr. Khan Sahib telephoned and informed me that he had been summoned to attend the working committee meeting of the Congress in Simla.

I agreed with him and told him to attend because we all felt that if the British were to peacefully give us our rights, there could be no better development for us than this. Dr. Khan Sahib went to Simla for the meeting. At the time, the British were facing a very difficult situation. The Japanese were advancing like a flood and everyone thought that an agreement would be reached with the British, and they would give us our rights. But the British could not be brought around to the idea of leaving Hindustan. On the failure of these negotiations, the people of Hindustan were very disappointed and were convinced that the British would not give us our rights. They also began to suspect that the British would rather leave Hindustan to the Japanese, than to us. People also started saying that nothing could be achieved through non-violence and that, to liberate our country, we should resort to violence. This led to violence in many parts of Hindustan.

The Europeans and the Americans are very strange. Before the War they, and their newspapers, were full of praise for Gandhiji; and considered non-violence a very good strategy for peace and development of the world. But when the war started, the British and Americans needed assistance and started on a campaign of violence. So, when the Congress or Gandhiji would mention non-violence, they would frown upon it; and they used to bring out lengthy articles against Gandhiji in the newspapers. When I would read these articles, I would laugh at these people, and they would seem to me like my own people: selfish and without principles.

Dispatch of Delegations of the *Khudai Khidmatgar* to the Tribal Areas

I concluded my tour of the entire province. Many big *jalsas* were held and all the *Khudai Khidmatgars* were consulted. All agreed with me that at this critical time, it was required that they should go to their tribal brothers and make them aware of the unfolding political situation. I started on a tour of the province again and, for this work, many young people in every district offered their services to me. When I returned from the tour, I dispatched Shad Muhammad Khan *Megay* to the Malakand Agency, where there were many *Khudai Khidmatgar*. In 1930, when the movement was initiated in the other districts, it had also started in the Malakand Agency. The Pukhtun brothers of this agency played a major role.

Shad Muhammad worked for some time there, but when the political agent learnt of this, he was arrested, and sentenced to three years' rigorous imprisonment.

The British were not prepared, on any account, to allow us to work in the Tribal Areas. But we had also resolved that at this critical time, we would work with our tribal brothers, come what may, because this was a matter of life and death for us. We resolved to work irrespective of whether we were allowed by the British or not, and to try to bring about awareness and unity in the Pukhtuns. Sir George Cunningham, the governor of our province was a very soft-hearted, gentle, intelligent and clever person. I wrote him a letter on the following lines:

'Today the world is witnessing the onslaught of a powerful revolution. We are afraid lest it creates trouble for us in our homeland, and we destroy each other. So, to establish peace we consider it necessary to dispatch delegations of our *Khudai Khidmatgar* to the Tribal Areas, to make the tribesmen aware of emerging political currents. We assure you that we will not work against your government there. We have been overtaken by our own troubles, and are concerned, about ourselves, and will talk to them about our brotherhood, empathy and nationhood. We hope that you will, as expeditiously as possible, grant us your permission, to carry out this task.'

A few days went by, but no answer came to my letter. I then wrote to him again and said, 'Whether you like it or not, we cannot wait any longer for your permission; and if we do not receive a reply by a particular date, we will be compelled to send our delegations to the different areas. We have fixed 5 August 1942 as the date for sending our delegations.' I sent this letter through Younas Jan to the governor, who was in Nathiagali. When Younas Jan arrived in Nathiagali, he found out that the governor had summoned all the political agents and deputy commissioners to Government House and was conferring with them on the issue. Younas also told me that the decision was not to stop us from working in the *Settled Areas* of the province, but that in the autonomous Tribal Areas, they would do their best, through the political agents, to disrupt our work to the extent possible and ensure that we did not succeed in our mission. Younas Jan brought me a reply to my letter. In that, the governor had given us permission of sorts. The next day we sent a delegation, led by Kamdar Khan, via Malakand to Bajawar. When the delegation arrived in the Malakand Agency, the political agent had summoned the khans and maliks of Malakand and Swat Ranezai and had them block the route of our delegation and would not allow them to proceed any further. The British had created a big problem for us and wanted us to fight amongst ourselves. They told Kamdar Khan, the leader of the delegation, to turn back as they would not allow them passage. He told them that turning back was not an option for them; that they would either go forward or die; and if Bacha Khan were to direct them, only then would they return. Although the intention of these khans and maliks towards us was bad, and they had been sent by the political agent for mischief, but when they saw the enthusiasm of their own people, they could not muster enough courage to block their way. Then a *jirga* of these very khans and maliks came to see me in the *markaz* and pleaded with me that the political agent was taunting them and asked me to direct the delegation to return. I tried to make them understand that I had dispatched the delegation for the welfare of the Pukhtuns. Finally, it was decided that, in Malakand, the work in the agency would be carried out by the local *Khudai Khidmatgar,* and the British would not prevent them from doing so, and that this delegation would travel via Kot and Agra to Bajawar Agency. I gave them a letter addressed to the leader of the delegation; that they should travel via the Uthmankhel route instead of Kot and Agra to Bajawar. The inhabitants of the village of Kot were Kakakhel *mians* who, to please the political agent, beat up members of our delegation. They were pelted with stones and their shirts were torn off their backs. In Bajawar, too, the British had sent spies before the arrival of the delegation and bribed the locals and told them that the delegation consisted of Hindus who had been sent by them to subjugate the Muslims. A matter of great regret is that Bacha Gul sahib, the elder son of the haji sahib of Torangzai, had also spread such propaganda amongst the people. In one place, boys had been instigated to kill the members of the delegation but were stopped from doing so by their elders who asked them to wait until we came and were interrogated by them. When the delegation reached the village, and was seated in the *hujra*, Abdul Malik Sahib got up and told them that:

'Oh, our Pukhtun brothers! Bacha Khan has sent us to you to inform you that the world has been overtaken by the flood of wars, and that if you are not made aware of this and take precautions, then you will be drowned by it. Bacha Khan has further directed us to inform you, his brothers, to put aside your factionalism and rivalries; establish truces, patch up enmities, so that we are able to assist each other and protect ourselves from the advancing flood. Bacha Khan has also said that you should also spin your own yarn and make your own cloth, lest the mills shut down because of the war and you are left naked, without cloth; and to store grain in your homes so that you do not have to face the possibility of hunger.'

We sent another delegation, under the leadership of Fazl-e-Rahim Saqi sahib, to Bacha Gul sahib on 19 August 1942. First it met with Bacha Gul sahib and told him that I had said that, in the past, we maintained a very good relationship with them, and asked what had now led him to issue Fatwas of *Kufr* (declarations of infidelity) against us in the newspapers. That the political agent of Sikho Derai, Kulli Khan, goes to every khan and tells him that Bacha Gul sahib had issued Fatwas of *Kufr* against Bacha Khan; that it is our firm belief that the British themselves are doing this. Bacha Gul sahib told Saqi sahib a long and convoluted tale and admitted that he had done so, so that this would be printed in the newspapers and people would stop following Bacha Khan. The British had also consulted with the government of Afghanistan, that if they lost the war to the Japanese, the entire Frontier Province would be left to them. They were to unleash all the Pukhtuns, in the name of Islam, against the Japanese. And if they managed to defeat them, then they could form their own government over it. Bacha Gul stated that he was paving the way for this development. Saqi sahib replied to him that there were other organizations also in the Frontier and asked why they did not take steps against the *Khudai Khidmatgar.* He laughed and said that Bacha Khan was a big obstacle lying in their way and all the other organizations could be dealt with, with only one blow of the fist. But Saqi sahib found out that whatever Bacha Gul sahib was up to was at the behest of the Afghan *Sadr-e-Azam,* Muhammad Hashim Khan. The delegation then travelled over the entire Moomand territory from village to village and made everyone aware of my message of brotherhood and unity. Our Moomand brothers everywhere raised their hands in prayer for peace and brotherhood. The elders and maliks of the Moomands had all turned against Bacha Gul because, in Afghanistan, he had ignored merit and standing and enabled his sycophants to obtain *lungis*. This delegation returned after fifty days and came to see me in the *markaz* and gave me a detailed report on the outcome of their tour. I had also sent a delegation to our Afridi brothers in Tirah but, for some reason, it returned without accomplishing anything. So, I told Saqi sahib of Wardaga that I wanted him to proceed to Tirah with two other *Khudai Khidmatgar*, to convey my message of brotherhood and unity to the Afridis; that if the scourge of this war should come to our land, then we would be able to help each other in such times of difficulty. And if, by the grace of God, we were able to win freedom for our land from the British, we would then be able to form a democratic government of all the Pukhtuns. Saqi sahib, accompanied by Faqir Muhammad Khan of Razar and Abdul Majid Khan of village Pawaki in Peshawar *tehsil*, then left on 21 October 1942 for Tirah. The political agent of Khyber had tried to prevent them by deploying over two thousand *khasadars* at different places on all the routes leading to Tirah. But they successfully evaded them and managed to reach Tirah. They organized tribal *jirga* in the eight main tribes of the Afridis and in fourteen clans (*khels*) of the Orakzai tribe. They toured the whole of Tirah. The local tribesmen gave them brotherly treatment. Before the departure of this delegation, Khushal Khan Malikdinkhel had come to me and told me to send the delegation to his *hujra* and that he would assist them. I told him that we had no money and that we were working in God's cause. He, however, insisted and stated that he was also working for God. So, I instructed the members of the delegation to go to his *hujra*. From my own pocket, I gave some money to Saqi sahib for their expenses and for the *jirga*. When they went there, they set to work. The *jirga* was also held and they started to tour different parts of Tirah. Sheikh Mehboob Ali Khan[32] was the political agent. Since the government was not in favour of our work, he was set after them. In those days, Ashiq Shah Bacha, without my permission, followed them to Tirah. I do not know why he said that Khushal Khan Malikdinkhel had begun to suspect that the delegation had a lot of money with them, and that Hindustan was ready to help them in every possible way. Then Ashiq Shah Bacha returned and Khushal Khan demanded money from Saqi sahib. Saqi sahib informed him that they did not have any money; that they carried stale bread in their shirts and went for the *jalsa*, and that if they wanted to sell themselves and their country to someone, then they should discuss it with them directly. Khushal Khan gave them an abrupt answer, asking them to leave his *hujra*, as he was not in need of paupers. So, Afzal Khan Zakhakhel took the delegation members home and worked with them for two and a half years, all over Tirah, as service in the name of God. During this period, they lived with the Sahibzada family of Barwan.

In Tirah, there were only two spiritual elders who were not under British influence. One was the maulana sahib of Sokanni Angoori, and the other was Sahibzada Abdur Razaq of Barwan. The son of Mahmud Akhundzada, Muhammad Saeed, told them bluntly that all their work and the running of their langar was with the assistance of the British. A similar answer was given to them by the religious elder of Ghantazay. To the Wazir tribesmen I sent a one-man delegation of Mirza Taj Muhammad *Khamosh*. He arrived in Waziristan and met the Faqeer sahib of Ippi and conveyed my message of goodwill and brotherhood. He did not, however, conduct any tours of the tribes, because the Faqeer sahib had told him that there was no need for him to do so here as this tribe had already been organized against the British, and that it acted in accordance with whatever he directed them to do. So, he returned. In another delegation, I sent Abdul Haqeem, Satti Jan and Abdur Rehman, General of the Bhittani tribe, to the Mehsuds. But they were both arrested by the government. Satti Jan was sent back and Abdur Rehman of Tank was jailed for two years, for accompanying a resident of Hashtnagar, Charsadda, to the Mehsud territory. I sent one delegation consisting of the *Khudai Khidmatgar* of Tal and Hangu to Kurram Agency, who stayed in a mosque. The political agent of Kurram sent his maliks and elders after them. They told them that it would be in their interest if they were to go back from here and not tour the area. They asked them why. After all, they were all Pukhtuns from the same area; that they had come to their territory and they had gone to theirs. The maliks told them that they were under the compulsion of the political agent and could not allow them to visit their area. After a great deal of discussion, they tied the hands and feet of the members of the delegation and put them in a truck to take them to Tal and Hangu. They, in time, came and informed me of what had transpired.

On account of these delegations to the Tribal Areas, and their exchanges and discussions with the tribesmen, a transformation came about in their attitudes. Feelings of brotherhood and amity were generated amongst the Pukhtuns. The leader of our delegation to Bajawar was Kamdar Khan. The delegation also consisted of President Muhammad Israr, Fida Abdul Malik and Nazim Sarfaraz Khan. When Kamdar Khan returned, his other companions stayed behind and lived with *Mian* Sahib Abdul *Hakeem* of Chingai. To educate the children, a *madrassah* was also opened. This, too, had a very good effect on the inhabitants of Bajawar. One of our *Khudai Khidmatgar* was travelling from Bajawar to Peshawar when he was robbed, in the territory of the Moomand. The inhabitants of Bajawar were very offended by this and organized a reprisal party. Not only was the money recovered from the thieves, but they also tendered an apology.

The government in Afghanistan and the British, between them, did their utmost to ensure that our delegations to the Tribal Areas failed in their mission. I had realized that, for the success of every mission, a *markaz* was essential and, for this purpose, I surveyed many locations which, for one reason or another, I rejected as unsuitable. Along the riverbank, there was a wasteland to the west of the Sardaryab bridge, and between the villages of Koodo and Sardaryab. A mile upward to the south was a green patch of land and there was a jungle all around it. It was lonely and secluded. We liked this as a sight for the *markaz* and the Pukhtuns of Agra and Koodo donated this land as *waqf* for it.

In August 1946, after holding the camp in Charsadda, each one of us cut as many branches of the willow trees from Munir Khan's orchard as we could and walked towards Sardaryab. The arrangements for their plantation had been made by Muhammad Israr Khan, the president. We went and put up the pillars and mounted the beams and rafters, and on top of them, spread the branches and reeds, and took up residence there. Night and day, I would be accompanied by nine or ten *Khudai Khidmatgars*. Whatever work they had, they would come here to me for it and whatever work I had with them, I would inform them through the *Khudai Khidmatgars*. The land here was uncultivated. Every morning, after breakfast, we would take our baskets and set to work, to till and plant vegetables. All the work involved in the building of the *markaz* was done by the *Khudai Khidmatgars* themselves. Right from arranging for the bricks, transporting to the construction. I, too, would work along with them and would fetch bricks from the masons. From every *tapa*, ten or fifteen *Khudai Khidmatgar* would come every day, in turns, with food. They would work for a week and would then be replaced by the next batch. We intended to construct a school and a hospital as well, and many people had expressed the desire that they would build houses for themselves here; so much so that we had decided on dedicating land for a graveyard for ourselves here as well. When Barrister Qayyum became the chief minister, he decided on dismantling the *markaz* and auctioning the land. The khans of Agra told him not to dismantle it, as it was, even otherwise, their ancestral property; that they would buy it in the auction and convert it either into a hospital or a *madrassah*. Qayyum insisted on dismantling it and demolishing this symbol of the *Khudai Khidmatgar* movement; because if this remained and when they would happen to pass by it, they would proclaim that this used to be their *markaz*. No one was prepared to take part in the auction. Finally, Noor Muhammad, a Moomand settler from the village of distributary number six, (Shakh Number 6), bought it and dynamited it down to its foundations.

The Quit India Movement

When the Cripps Mission failed, the people of Hindustan were extremely disappointed and began to think that, without a resolute opposition, the British would not concede anything to them. In those days, the session of the (Congress) working committee had been scheduled in Bombay. At this time, the Congress passed the Quit India Resolution and Mahatma Gandhi and all the members of the working committee were arrested. Immediately on their arrest, across the length and breadth of Hindustan, a resolute struggle began against the British, because the key workers of the Congress had all been arrested. There was no prominent worker or leader left in the field, and the masses, too, had reached a stage of acute disappointment. So, instead of non-violence, they adopted the path of violence. The British met violence with violence, which they also wanted, as they did not know how to cope with non-violent protests. And for violence they were so well-equipped and prepared that they controlled this movement quickly. They meted out such cruel and harsh treatment to the people that no nation on earth, from the most barbarous ever, would have done. Let alone the men, the women were also subjected to such treatment, that I am ashamed even to write it down. During this time, incidents also occurred and, in addition to the police and the army, the British fired machine-guns from planes and dropped bombs on villages. In the Frontier Province, our *Jirga* and *Khudai Khidmatgar* also gathered to deliberate over the matter and decide how to respond to the challenge. The Congress had, in each province, appointed a 'dictator'[33] to organize the opposition to the British. I was thus appointed as 'dictator' for my own province. In this meeting, Haji Faqira Khan asked me that since I had been appointed as the 'dictator' of the province, why am I summoning them to a meeting that I should just give the orders and they would obey them. I told him that though this was correct, I was not temperamentally suited to be a 'dictator' and that I would do everything in consultation with my companions. The product of many minds, I told him, is always better than that of one. In the meeting, Haji Faqira Khan of Hazara said that we should resort to the cutting of telegraph wires and demolish bridges. I reminded him that though this amounted to violence, I would allow him to do so. But all I wanted to say was that anyone who cut a wire or demolished a bridge, would have to go right away to the thana and file a report that he was responsible for doing so, because he did not want a government of the British. The benefit of this would be that the common people of the villages would not be subjected to violence at the hands of the police. Whatever punishment there would be, would have to be borne by the perpetrators, and if they were not prepared to do so, then the residents of the villages would be subjected to a lot of violence, and whatever sympathy they had for us, would be converted into hatred. Therefore, this proposal was dropped. Another proposal was put forth by me. This was that we should first send a delegation to every court and native officer, to inform him or her that the Quit India resolution had been passed by the Congress, and that they should resign from their jobs. This resolution was passed. The other proposal was that we would assault the courts of British officers and force them to abandon their chairs and tell the people to resolve their disputes locally, in their homes; that they should not go to the British for this, as the British were the enemies of our people and our country and were ruling over us through their servants. When our delegations did not yield any significant results, we then started to assault the courts.

Assaulting the Courts

The *Khudai Khidmatgar* conducted assaults on the courts in Peshawar, Mardan, Kohat and Bannu. Initially, nobody would arrest them but beat them mercilessly. This would be done by the police, which would be accompanied by the ruffians of the khans and the *arbabs,* armed with lathis. Some Moomand tribesmen had also been called for to help the government and to beat the *Khudai Khidmatgar*. The situation was somewhat same in Mardan, the only difference being the absence of the ruffians of the khans. Most *Khudai Khidmatgar* would be wounded, some with broken heads, arms or legs. Some would die during the beating. When the *Khudai Khidmatgar* assaulted the office of the deputy commissioner Peshawar, the Deputy Commissioner Iskandar Mirza, along with other lathi-yielding men, came out holding a lathi himself, and started beating the *Khudai Khidmatgar*. Even the British had not picked up the lathi against us. But this Muslim brother of ours did so. The *Khudai Khidmatgar* would break the cordon of the police and additional police and attack the courts. Said Akbar, a *Khudai Khidmatgar*, received a blow from Iskandar Mirza on the heart and was martyred on the spot. The British never resorted to beating themselves. The chief commander of these attacks was Shakirullah Jan Bacha of Gujjaro Garhai, who had organized these assaults with such consummate skill and courage that even the British, who were opposed to him, admitted this achievement of his.

The (*Khudai Khidmatgar*) commander of the Mardan assault was *Salar* Munir Khan, and then Abdul Aziz Khan. He, too, had carried out these assaults with exemplary courage. The strength and scale of the assaults was either in Peshawar or in Mardan. In Mardan, before every court, the police and additional police would be standing guard, ready with lathis. The *Khudai Khidmatgar* would arrive. They would shout '*Allah-u-Akbar*' and '*Fakhr-e-Afghan Zindabad*' and would break the police cordon and enter the courts, while these policemen would charge with their lathis. Their limbs would be broken and then they would be pushed into lorries, driven some distance, and thrown out. I would go on tour to keep myself abreast of these developments, and the government did not prevent me from doing so. Finally, the government policy changed and the *Khudai Khidmatgar* who did these attacks, in addition to being beaten, were also arrested. The government also began to analyze how it could neutralize my efforts. I was on the way to Mardan for work, when I saw the police waiting for me. I was arrested and told that I was not allowed to enter Mardan. I was taken back to Peshawar, and confined there. The next time, I left for Kohat and near Spina Thana, the police was waiting for us. The police made us get down from the lorry and forced us to spend the whole day in Spina Thana. In the evening, we were brought back to Peshawar and released. I did not consider this method of the government as appropriate and organized a *jalsa* at Chowk Yadgar in Peshawar city. In this *jalsa*, I put forth three things to the people. One was that the strategy adopted by the government towards me, was no more than a joke and that it should not crack these jokes at my expense. The government should either have me arrested, or it should let me be. The other thing was that if, by God's grace, we were successful and won our freedom, then they should remember what I was about to say – that this land belonged to the nation and to us Pukhtuns. Whether maize or wheat, we will all eat it jointly. It would not be that some would go hungry, while others would be eating pulao. Our third task was that we would ensure that the poor were fed first. Only then would we consider the rights of those who were well fed. The fourth thing was that neither would we make anyone a khan or a *bacha*. We will not make one person all-powerful, for this would lead to deprivation for many people, while a few others would be enjoying life at the people's expense. In our government, power would vest in the people and in their *jirga*. In this *jalsa*, I also made an announcement that on 27 October I would leave for Mardan with a group of *Khudai Khidmatgars*.

Accordingly, on the decided date we collected at the Charsadda stop and I, along with fifty *Khudai Khidmatgars*, left on foot for Mardan. On the way, at several places, the people had come out on the road to welcome us. We spent the night with the *Khudai Khidmatgar* of Gulabad, Manga-Dargai. The next morning, we left for Mardan. When we were on the move, a group of *Khudai Khidmatgar* from Sawabai, under *Salar* Munir Khan, joined our group. After the prayer, we set off again. I was in the middle of the group and had spread my companions out around me. Sardar Khan of Prang had wound his *saadar* around his waist, in a symbolic gesture of readiness, and was leading the group. He would, from time to time, cry out, 'Oh Pukhtun brothers! Beware! The Pukhtuns are engaged in a battle against the British, for their rights. You are our brothers. Do not, for the sake of the British, oppose us. Fight for your own and the honour of your nation.' When we arrived near Mirwais Ghundai, there were many people accompanying us. I asked Wali, Master Karim, *Salar* Munir Khan and some other people to leave us, so that all of them would not be arrested at the same time. Wali had a camera with him. He said he was taking photographs, but I stopped him from doing so. I told my companions to work among the masses. When we arrived at Mirwais Ghundai, we saw an Englishman standing there with a lathi. The police with him had similar lathis. The Englishman came towards us and made the policemen surround us. The speech of Sardar Khan had had some effect on the people. They did not beat us, but when the Englishman raised his lathi and ordered them to beat us, they did so mercilessly. Some had their legs broken, others their arms. Two of my ribs were also fractured. I was bundled off in a car and taken to the Police Lines, where they threw me into a small room. This had a cement floor. During this commotion my clothes were all torn. I was lying on the floor. When my body cooled off, I was aching all over. After a while, the same Englishman entered my room with the same lathi in hand. I was in pain and he was trying to bully me. When I answered him, he lost his temper and ordered that I should be handcuffed. From there they put me into a lorry and took me to the Naukhar cantonment. A car was waiting there for me in which two Englishmen were seated. Khushdil Khan, who was a very cruel police officer, accompanied me in the car. To impress the two Englishmen, he spoke to me very insultingly. I was in pain but managed to say to him that Pukhtuns never spoke in this manner; that he had achieved his purpose in as much as the Englishmen had heard what he had said, and that he would be promoted for it. And this is what happened! I was taken to Haripur jail and was confined to a cell. Though there was a hospital and some doctors; but they were not for me. Prisoners are not considered God's creation. My whole body was aching, and I spent the night in great pain. The next morning the doctor examined me. The superintendent informed the government that I was better. They put an announcement in the newspapers that I was all right. There was a Hindu doctor at the hospital. He said to the doctor in charge that he would be responsible for the outcome of my health. That he would have to take the blame, and that it was his responsibility to inform the government of the facts. Accordingly, the doctor wrote to the government that the first report was incorrect and that I was not well. The government dispatched a civil surgeon who examined me and then he took me to the military hospital in Abbottabad. An X-ray was taken, which showed that I had two broken ribs. The civil surgeon himself tied up my ribcage and put a plaster around my chest. With the tying up, I was slightly relieved.

When we started our campaign of civil disobedience against the British, they started working against the government of Afghanistan through the maulanas. The strange thing was that the British had a fatwa of *kufr* drafted against me, both Bacha Gul and the maulana *of* Manki signed it, and the maulanas of both groups supported it. It was an odd thing that, in religious matters, the followers of the maulanas of Hadda and of Manki have never agreed. They were bitter opponents of each other and branded each other as Kafirs. But in the case of the fatwa against me, they agreed, because this had been imposed on me by the British. The other thing they said was that Afghanistan is also a Pukhtun nation and that the people of the Frontier should join it. They publicized this in the newspapers. Many *jalsa* would be held in which speeches were delivered to the effect that this part of the country should unite with Afghanistan, but the British did not say anything to them. The third thing they said was that they had called Haji Muhammad Amin to Peshawar. He had emigrated from our area and had become a pir in Hadda. This was done by the British, through Bacha Gul, and in cooperation with the Afghan government. Here he tried to draw the political attention of the Pukhtuns away from the British, so he decided to picket the 'streets of the prostitutes. At the time, the *Khudai Khidmatgar* were mounting assaults on the British courts, and all their attention and efforts were directed towards the liberation of their land from the British. At this juncture, Haji Muhammad Amin Khan arrived on the scene, the maulanas allied themselves with him and Arbab Abdul Ghafoor of Tehkal also came out in support of them and diverted the attention of the public away from the British. This is the same Muhammad Amin who, in the Masjid-e-Nabavi, in the presence of the spirit of the Prophet, may the peace and the blessings of Allah be upon him, had promised me that he would ally himself with us and serve the people. When they would go for picketing, the prostitutes would emerge and tell the people that, on the one hand the *Khudai Khidmatgar* were picketing the courts, while (actually) they had come to picket their private parts! The picketers would lower their eyes. But after two or three days, Iskandar Mirza had the prostitutes removed so that he could claim credit for this. No matter how much Bacha Gul and his associates opposed us in the border areas and in the country, their efforts bore no fruit, as people's sympathies were with us. The proposal accepted was that the need of the hour was to hold many *jalsa* against the British all over the province and, in them, make announcements that we were now free. And after that, delegations were to be constituted to go to all the local employees of the government in the thanas, courts, *tehsils* and districts, and appeal to them to leave the service of the British and come out in support of the struggle of their people. I am writing this with great regret, that despite a great deal of effort by these delegations, only one person resigned from service, and he was Yahya Jan, the headmaster of the Peshawar Islamia High School. Amongst the employees, there were many *Khudai Khidmatgar* who had been recruited at the time of our government and whose fathers were also *Khudai Khidmatgar.* Not one amongst them resigned. And the strangest thing of all was that, of all the government servants, those employees whom we had recruited would be crueller to the *Khudai Khidmatgar* and sometimes they would also fire upon them. The reason for all this was that they wanted to be in the service of the British, had been recruited due to the efforts of the *Khudai Khidmatgar* and wanted to prove their loyalty to the British, so that the British would not suspect them.

In 1942, by the time I was brought back to Haripur jail from the Abbottabad hospital, the arrests of our *Khudai Khidmatgars* had started. They would shout slogans not only on the way, but also in Haripur jail, when confined to their barracks. It was our principle not to violate jail rules, while in jail. The superintendent wrote to the inspector general, that the jail was resounding with their slogans. The inspector general who was an ex-army officer, came to the jail. He spoke to me and said that it was all right if they shouted slogans of *Allah-u-Akbar* and *Fakhr-e-Afghan Zindabad*, but that they should not shout the slogan of '*Bartania Barbad* (*Destruction on Britain*)'. I spoke to the *Khudai Khidmatgar* and told them that raising slogans in jail was inappropriate. I asked them about the many concessions that the jail staff had given them. They were free to have tea, they were given milk, they could cook their own food and they were not searched. All this was because I too was present there. So, if they did not refrain from sloganeering and were bent on continuing to do so, I would be transferred from amongst them and all these concessions would be withdrawn. If even then they wished to continue with their agitation, they should then listen carefully to me, and not abandon this. They were not to shout slogans all at the same time; but do so in batches of ten, in each barrack. If one batch was sent to solitary confinement in their cells, then the next batch should take up the slogans, so that the movement did not die. But I told them that I must remind them that if they were to establish peace with the jail staff now, it would be with honour. If I were to be transferred to another jail and they were to be put through hardships, and then they were to plead for peace, that would amount to dishonouring themselves. However, the sloganeering didn't stop. Two days later the jamadar came for me and informed me that the superintendent had called me to his office. When I arrived, the police were waiting for me. The papers of my transfer were completed, and I was taken to the Abbottabad jail and confined to a small room. This little room was isolated and separate from the main jail. There was no one there to talk to.

When I was transferred from Haripur, the jail staff started to treat the political prisoners very harshly. They shouted slogans for a few days but finally gave up and regretted not having taken my advice. Their elders informed the jail officials that they wanted to make peace with them. They agreed, and the shouting of slogans came to an end. If they had listened to me, I would not have been transferred to Abbottabad, and they, too, would not have undergone so much hardship, and nor would they have been obliged to accept peace with lowered eyes. I was provided with an aged prisoner as my servant in the jail in Abbottabad, who would cook for me. One day I asked him what all the noise was, made by the prisoners in the barracks below my room after about midnight, as it woke me up. I asked him to tell them that if they wished to recite from the *Quran*, they should please do so to themselves, so that I did not wake up. He told me that there was noise because this was Abbottabad and, when it snows, the prisoners feel very cold. They have been supplied with only two old blankets each. The *darogha* of this jail, Umer Baig, was a Muslim and was nicknamed the 'penny-thief'. When he came to me the next morning, I told him that the prisoners did not have blankets and should be provided with them. He told me that there were no blankets available in the store. He was very regular in prayer. When he was transferred, he was replaced by a Hindu *darogha*. On his taking over, when the prisoners complained, he issued two new blankets to each one of them. When I learnt of this, I asked him whether he had requisitioned the blankets. He replied, 'No, these were lying in the store.'

The deputy commissioner of Abbottabad was a Sikh, a very good man. When he came to the jail on a visit, he told me that Sir George Cunningham used to say that he would not appoint anyone other than Dr. Khan Sahib as the chief minister of the province. But after some time, he had appointed Aurangzeb Khan from the Muslim League as the chief minister. One day this deputy commissioner came to the jail. He was looking very crest-fallen and told me that the governor used to say that, other than Dr. Khan Sahib, they would not appoint anyone else as the chief minister. This was his way of expressing his sympathy for me. I replied that I was happy that the governor had given the government to the Muslim League and appointed Aurangzeb Khan in place of Dr. Khan Sahib. He was surprised and asked me the reason. I told him that I was happy that the nation had seen the performance of our government and now they should experience the government of the Muslim League and judge the difference between the two for themselves. The other thing was that this government enjoyed fewer powers and our people had never been in power, and nor did they know anything about government. There was not a thing that we could do, as it was not in our power, whereas the people demanded that things should be done for them. No matter how much we tell them that we cannot do so, as it was not within our power, they do not believe us and get annoyed with us. Not only annoyed, but they also begin to oppose us. The second thing is that we have just two annas in hand and they demand a rupee. So where can we provide the rupee from? They have experienced our government and now they will experience that of the Muslim League and get to know the reality. And it happened exactly like this. If we had not resigned from government, it would have been difficult to win the next election. The Muslim League would have won it. The people saw that we had just two annas in the rupee, but we gave these to them, and that whatever was in our power to do, we did for them. But the Muslim League would not even let them come close to themselves and would not do anything for them. One day, Colonel Smith, who was the inspector general of jails, came on tour to Abbottabad and came to where I was lodged. When he went out, he told the superintendent that he had put Bacha Khan in a room meant for pigeons. The superintendent gave Colonel Smith a very respectful answer, that these were the orders of the provincial government, and what could he do in the matter? Colonel Smith immediately telephoned the governor from the jail and asked him whether anyone dealt with a brave adversary as he had done with Bacha Khan, that I had been confined to a small room all by myself. The governor felt ashamed at what he had done and repealed his orders. He directed that I should be given a better place and good companions. When Smith sahib came again and asked me who I wanted as companions and that I should choose them myself. So, I chose Sherdil Khan and Wali, and he had them transferred to Abbottabad. When they came, they informed me that *Salar* Inzar Gul was in Dera Ismail Khan jail and was very sick. So, I told the superintendent to give us our own people for cooking. I was again asked to recommend names. I told him I wanted Inzar Gul, who was in the Dera jail. When Inzar Gul came, he was so ill that he could hardly walk and could not climb the stairs leading to the room where we were. But the doctors treated him, and we made the doctor prescribe a good diet for him. He started to improve by the day. My small room could hardly accommodate two beds, and there was no other place available on the floor to sleep on. So *Salar* sahib occupied the space below my bed, and Sherdil Khan occupied the space below Wali's bed. After a few days, orders came, and the room near me in the hospital was allotted to Wali and the others. I remained in my room and the other three were shifted to that other room.

We were in jail when we learnt that there was famine in Bengal and many people had died of hunger. Whatever rations the government gave us we would consume half and save the other half for the people of the calamity-affected region. When we had saved a substantial quantity, we asked the government to send it to Bengal. But the government neither sent it, nor returned it to us. In those days, Wali's eye was infected. He had just this one eye. He had lost sight in the other one, when infected by measles. We were very worried. The superintendent called for the eye specialist from the Army Hospital, but to no effect. We told the superintendent to inform the government about this. Wali wanted to go to Bombay to consult his own doctor. Sir George released him unconditionally and gave him permission to have himself treated in Bombay. When he was leaving, I told him that he had been released for treatment, and until his jail term was over, he should not take part in any kind of activity against the government.

Many of our companions were released, and some remained in Haripur. I was transferred back from Abbottabad to Haripur. The jail officials told those who were in Haripur that they were not to come to the office in a group but select one representative on their behalf, when they had any work. So, they elected one person, with consensus, for this purpose. Since he was their nominee, it was necessary that the jail officials should respect him and when he would visit the *darogha's* office, he would make him sit with him on a chair. If he were to visit the doctor in connection with their work, he, too, would make him sit next to him on a chair. But his companions would hurl abuses at him when they would see this. One would remark that he had got a chair to sit on with both the superintendent and the doctor; another would say that he went and got a cloth for dusting in their name but used it for himself. This was the state of the leadership of our *Khudai Khidmatgar.* When I got to the jail, most of the prisoners of 'C' class were accommodated in several barracks, and the prisoners of one barrack were not allowed into any other barrack. I told the jail authorities that every Sunday the political prisoners should be allowed to get together. They allowed us to do so. We would get together every Sunday and deliberate over national affairs and the affairs of our movement. So, we would get the required experience. We had one general who was a very good man, whom they had selected as their leader. But they would constantly be criticizing him. So, one day I summoned him and told him to tender his resignation. He went and gave them a resignation. On Sunday, when we collected, they asked me to become their leader and if I wouldn't agree to this, then I should appoint one from amongst them.I gave them no answer and diverted the discussion to some other topic. The next Sunday, when we reassembled, they again wanted me to appoint a leader for them. So, I got up, and looked each one of them up and down. When I did so, I told them that I could not find anyone amongst them who was shameless, degraded and dishonourable enough to be appointed as their leader; that they were a strange lot and called themselves *Khudai Khidmatgar* and spent terms in jail; that when they appoint someone as their leader, then they should not curse him. This was very unfortunate. They kept quiet and did not broach the issue of leadership with me again. When we were in Haripur jail, a prisoner came up to me and said, 'Oh Bacha Khan! These *Khudai Khidmatgar* brought me to this jail and assured me that, within three months, I would be free. I have spent six months and am asking them to release me and they are not doing so.' I told him I would get him released and that he should proceed straight away to the office. I have always forbidden the *Khudai Khidmatgar* from doing this I told them, 'Do not force anyone to go to jail or induce them through deceit, pleading or subterfuge. You think that if many people go to jail, we would be able to pressurize the government. By taking the weak to jail, you are giving yourself a bad name and defaming your movement. I do acknowledge that if many people go to jail, the government is over-awed, but only if they are strong and follow our principles.'

I had kept chickens in jail and I would feed them myself. They were so used to me that some would perch themselves on my shoulders, while others would climb into my lap. One day I had kneaded the dough rather hard. I was feeding them. Some were perched on my arms, others were in my lap and some sat on my head. Colonel Smith was on a tour to the jail. When he came to me, he saw this spectacle. So, he turned back all the jail officials who were accompanying him and approached me from behind. I was unaware of him, but he was standing behind me. He saw what I was doing. He asked me what I was doing. I told him that there was a lesson for them in what I was doing. 'See, it is well known that we keep these chickens to slaughter and to eat. But when I treat them with love and feed them well, they perch on my shoulders, arms, and some sit on my lap. You should take a lesson from them. See, they are animals but when shown love, they do not get off my lap. And man is the most superior of God's creations. If he is loved, why would he then not become a friend?'

Colonel Smith was a brave man and was fond of those who were brave. He confessed that he had lost the battle against us. Later he developed a liking for the *Khudai Khidmatgar* and treated them well and with respect. I had such a strong influence on him and he had so much respect for me that, in 1947, when we were holding a *jalsa* at Sikhoderai, I saw Colonel Smith leading his son[34] by the hand, onto the stage. After exchanging greetings, he requested me to pass my hand over the head of his son (to bless him). I brought him close to me and asked Colonel Smith why he had come to me in the *jalsa*; that he was a government servant, and if Pakistan were created, he would be forced to leave his job. He laughed and said that the day Pakistan came into being, he would not be here. He also hated the Muslim League and had them beaten up in Peshawar jail because Barrister Qayyum had tried to intimidate him by saying that if they (the Muslim League) came to power, what would they (the British) do? This was indeed true. The day that Pakistan came into being, on one side the Pakistan flags were being hoisted and guns were being fired and, on the other, Colonel Smith with his family was on the Khyber Mail, en-route to England.

In 1945, some of our members thought that if we formed the government in our province, in addition to everything else, political prisoners who were in jail for over three years, would be released. Amongst our assembly members, some were very keen to form the government. They were not prepared for a civil disobedience movement. They could not carry out raids. They were busy in their own professions, whereas the *Khudai Khidmatgar* were getting killed, jailed and wounded during the assaults on the courts. So, the people did not look kindly upon them, because they were neither willing to work themselves, and nor would they permit others to do so. They also allowed my son, Lalee, to participate in the raids. When they started their efforts to form the government, *Saki* sahib and the camp commander, *Salar* Sher Ali Khan in the Yakatoot camp, began to oppose them and convinced Dr. Khan Sahib to join them as well. They summoned all their assembly members from across the province to the camp at Yakatoot, to get their cooperation in the formation of the government. But when they would arrive, *Saki* sahib would brief them, and this meeting also bore no fruit. Finally, when *Saki* sahib proceeded to Tirah, the field lay open to them. They made Dr. Khan Sahib agree and sent a delegation to Gandhiji to tell him that conditions in the Frontier Province were different from the rest of Hindustan. That we would benefit from the formation of our government, and we would be able to release our political prisoners. Gandhiji asked them to discuss the issue with Bacha Khan. So, they sent a delegation to me in Haripur jail, which recounted the whole episode to me. I informed them that I was not in favour of forming a government, which did not have full powers. Such a government, instead of benefitting, would prove harmful to the people and the movement. As for the question of the release of the political prisoners, they should not worry about us. We were not fed up being in jail. They went back, and I learnt a few days later that they had formed the government. Some political prisoners were released, and some remained in jail. When the time for my release came, I insisted that until all political prisoners were released, I would not go out. They came to me again and said that the government had imposed the most stringent sections of the law on the other political prisoners. That they were trying and that, likely, they would be released in a few days, but that I should come out. So, I was released. Also I was not well those days. When I am alone in jail, I usually fall sick. Gandhiji was in Bombay at the time.

Journey to Bombay

Once out of jail, Gandhiji wrote to me to come to Bombay. Whenever I went there, or to Sevagram, I would spend a night in Delhi with Gandhiji's son, Devadas. His wife was the daughter of C. Rajagopalachari. They would look after me well. I would usually travel third-class by train and would get very tired. Here I could rest.

The next morning, I left for Bombay. Gandhiji was staying at Birla's house. I also went and stayed there. One day he started a discussion on non-violence. I told him, 'Gandhiji, you have been preaching non-violence in Hindustan for a long time now, whereas I am a newcomer to it and have only recently started preaching the concept to the Pukhtuns. I do not have the means and workers to assist me, like you have. In the year 1946, you can see how much violence was committed in Hindustan during our opposition. But in the Frontier, despite the cruelty and provocation of the British, the Pukhtuns did not resort to as much violence. This is even though Hindustan does not have the wherewithal for such violence, which the Pukhtuns have access to.' In response, Gandhiji said that non-violence is not for the faint-hearted. This is for the brave, and the Pukhtuns are braver than the inhabitants of Hindustan. That is the reason why they did not resort to violence.

One day I was sitting with Gandhiji when a man came, who was wearing clothes worth two annas. He put his hand into his pocket, took out a wad of notes, and put it before Gandhiji. He asked him how much it was. He was told that it was seventy thousand rupees. Gandhiji said to him, 'Make it into one hundred thousand.' He left and returned the next day with one hundred thousand rupees. Similarly, Gandhiji told his secretary, Desai, to tell the inhabitants of Bombay to raise ten lakh (one million) rupees for him, as a donation for the Harijans. There were three people sitting with him. They told Desai not to make any appeal for donations. One informed him that he would donate two hundred and fifty thousand, the other said that he would donate the same amount and the third told him that he would do the same. They said that they needed a fourth person and the amount that they needed would be complete. Similarly, when Gandhiji started the campaign for liberation, he asked the masses for a *crore* of rupees as donations. The nation donated more than this. And when he would ask for one person for national service, one hundred would be prepared to place themselves at his disposal. And whatever task he would identify for the uplift of the nation, thousands of people would place themselves under his command.

But whatever we managed to do in the Frontier, we did simply by preaching and with empty hands. This was because no one has assisted us financially. And yet some people would blame us, that we had not done any development work but had misappropriated the people's money.

The Harijan colony was in Delhi and Sevagram was in Wardha. When the *prarthana* would begin, I would, before everybody else, recite from the Holy *Quran* and would translate its meaning for the people. After me, a Japanese follower of Buddhism, would explain his religious hymns, and then the *prarthana* would begin. Gandhiji's heart was filled with the same respect for all religions and he considered all faiths as the truth. I also have the same belief. I have studied the Holy *Quran* and the *Geeta* in depth. When I was imprisoned in Dera Ghazi Khan jail with the Sikhs, I had heard the major portion of the Guru Granth Sahib from them. I was eager to study Buddhism because we were its followers before the advent of Islam. But, unfortunately, I could not get hold of any book. During my days in the Mission High School in Peshawar, I had, studied the Bible. I had gone through the Torah in jail. I was also eager to study the books of Zardasht (Zoroaster), the Prophet of the Parsi faith, because he had been sent to us by God. He was born in Balkh. God proclaims in the *Quran* that to each nation He has sent a guide from amongst themselves. But, unfortunately, till date I have not located any literature on Zoroastrianism. Khurshid behan and other Parsi friends had promised to find some books on it for me to read, but no one did so. My faith is affection and love and the service of humankind. Religion has always brought a message of love and brotherhood to the world. Those people whose hearts are devoid of love for their fellow human beings and those whose hearts are filled with hatred, anger and partisanship, are very far from the teachings of these faiths.

At the time of the elections, the Muslim League had dispatched Major Khurshid from Punjab to the Frontier. He had been dismissed from the army for misconduct. He was sent on a mission to create internal strife and violence amongst the Pukhtuns. He would deliver speeches, inciting violence. He would say that there were only a few *Khudai Khidmatgar* leaders who had any influence over their followers. That they needed to be assassinated and that people should be identified who would, for ten or twenty thousand rupees, murder these leaders, because without the elimination of these leaders, their road would be blocked. This man had come to Sarhad to make the Pukhtuns fight within their homes, and if they were able to assassinate the leaders of the *Khudai Khidmatgar*, the people would try to take revenge by killing the leaders of the Muslim League, since the sympathy of the nation was with the *Khudai Khidmatgar*. So, in this way, a civil war would break out amongst the Pukhtuns and they would be destroyed. Major Khurshid wanted not only to destroy us but, in the process, destroy the Pukhtun nation.

Zalmai Pukhtun (Young Pukhtun)

When we came to know of the actual intentions of Major Khurshid, our people organized a new party under the leadership of Ghani for the protection of the *Khudai Khidmatgar*. Called *Zalmai Pukhtun* (Young Pukhtun), young men, who did not believe in the commonly understood concept of non-violence, joined this organization. They joined it with the belief that, although the *Khudai Khidmatgar* were committed to non-violence and they themselves believed in non-violence, violent designs were being drawn up against them. It was announced that this organization was meant for the sole purpose of ensuring the safety of the *Khudai Khidmatgar*. In opposition to this, the Muslim League formed the *Ghazi Pukhtun* (Pukhtun Holy Warrior) organization. But the Pukhtuns, as a nation, were overwhelmingly for the *Zalmai Pukhtun*; and the khans who were in the Muslim League, and were the bootlickers of the British, reached the conclusion that the nation was for the *Zalmai Pukhtun*. So, if a fight between the *Zalmai Pukhtun* and the *Ghazi Pukhtun* were to take place, not one Muslim Leaguer would be left alive. For this reason, Major Khurshid was unsuccessful in his mission. I, too, tried to ensure this by preaching patience to the *Khudai Khidmatgar*, so that civil war did not break out amongst the Pukhtuns, and their ill-wishers failed in their objectives. The volunteers of the *Ghazi Pukhtun* would visit our camps and hurl insults and abuses at us, because they knew that the *Khudai Khidmatgar* were non-violent and would not retaliate physically against them. But the khans living around our *markaz* warned them, that if they came here again, they would not go away alive. Thus, they saved us from this curse of God. The leader of the *Ghazi Pukhtun* was the son of Khan Bahadur Umar Khan of our village, Uthmanzai.

19

The Elections – Cabinet Mission – Interim Government

Election

THE ELECTIONS WERE IN THE OFFING, SO I DECIDED THAT I WOULD NOT personally take part in them because victory in the election is essentially to form a government. We had a government but its condition was such that its subordinates were carrying out propaganda against it, and the ministers were helpless onlookers.

In Calcutta, a joint session was scheduled of the Congress working committee and its parliamentary board. I went to attend this session, specially organized for the elections. While in the session, I explained the position prevailing in the Frontier Province and shared that elections were meant to form ministries; that we should win the election and form the government. We had a government, but the British and their associates were carrying out a propaganda campaign against us, and we lacked the power even to question them about what they were doing. So, I informed them that I would not take part in the forthcoming elections. The parliamentary board was, however, of the view that, no matter what it took, I must be persuaded to take part in it. But it was unable to convince me. When the session concluded, I told Gandhiji that he had heard what I had to say and my decision not to take part in the election was final. He also agreed with my decision.

I left for the village. Since I was against taking part in the elections, I opted to do some political work, as I could not sit idle at home. I started touring the province. The government had started opposing us vigorously. I found out that it had closed down Islamia College, Peshawar, and was also closing all the other colleges and schools in the province and was sending their students to villages and town to canvass for the Muslim League. I also found out that British women were also touring the province and were telling the womenfolk of the khans and maliks that they had come to their home to ask them for their *lupatay*, that their *lupatay* were their votes, and that they were to vote for them. To spread their propaganda, the daughters of Begum Shah Nawaz and other girls had come to the Frontier Province. From Punjab the Muslim League boys studying at Aligarh Muslim University, the students of Islamia College, Calcutta and from other places in Hindustan, and many leaders and workers had come to the Frontier Province. In addition to these, the government and the Muslim League mobilized the pirs of both Punjab and the Frontier. They were told that this was not the time to sit idle, but to come out into the field. They had convinced the Pir sahib of Manki, Amin-ul-Hasnat, to contest the elections in opposition to us. I knew him well and had also gone to condole with him on the demise of his father. The Pir sahib sent a messenger informing that he was coming to call on me. I told the messenger that he should not take the trouble that I would call on him instead. I went to meet him at the bungalow given to him by the government in the Peshawar cantonment. He took out a paper from his pocket and said that it had been given to him by Jinnah sahib, and that if Pakistan came into being, Islamic Shariat would be enforced in it. I told him that he could lick the paper. He was surprised and asked me why. I asked him whether there was a role for Jinnah sahib in the enforcement of Islamic Shariat. I asked him how he would be able to enforce it. I further told him that he, perhaps, was familiar with the injunctions of Islam. So, he should figure out for himself that if, tomorrow, the Islamic Shariat was to be enforced here, what would be the condition of these Muslim League leaders. When I saw the enthusiasm, interest and efforts of the British and their women in opposing us, I changed my mind. There was only a month to go for the election and so I started my work. The 1946 election was the last election of a united Hindustan. This election was given a direction by the Muslim League, sharing with the masses that it was over the issue of Hindustan and Pakistan; whether they wanted a united Hindustan or Pakistan. Whether they wished to side with *Kufr* with Islam. This was an election over the *mandir* and the masjid; over whether they would vote for the mosque or the temple.

Our party did not give tickets to *Mian* Jafar Shah and Arbab Abdur Rehman of Gulloo Garhai, because they were creating rifts between Dr. Khan Sahib and Qazi Attaullah, and they would also complain, and tried to incite Dr. Khan Sahib against me. They would tell him that, this time, I had decided to make Qazi Attaullah the chief minister, instead of him. All this was a pack of lies as Dr. Khan Sahib was our choice for the chief minister. All we had to say was that Dr. Khan Sahib should not be in-charge of the portfolio of Law and Order and should allot this to Qazi sahib, because Dr. Khan Sahib could be easily duped by government officers, but not Qazi sahib. But Dr. Khan Sahib declared that if Jafar Shah and Arbab Abdur Rehman were not given party tickets then he, too, would not contest the elections. We were compelled by Dr. Khan Sahib and supported them. Jafar Shah and Arbab Abdur Rehman were *Khudai Khidmatgar* only in name and when Pakistan came into being and the government of Qayyum Khan was established then, before everyone, Arbab invited Qayyum to his *hujra*. He instructed Jafar Shah as well, and they both declared their membership of the Muslim League. They both told him that they would also try to persuade other *Khudai Khidmatgar* to join the Muslim League.

The Pukhtuns were not as emotional as the Muslims of the rest of Hindustan. We had worked a lot with them. They had become politically aware. We had toured from village to village and house to house, all over the province. We had made them understand things, and they had, as a result, become politically aware and were well acquainted with the tenets of Islam and could no longer be duped by anyone in the name of Islam. Here, the *Khudai Khidmatgar* had put in a lot of effort. In Hindustan, the Muslims were poor and not made aware of Islam by anyone. They were not politically aware either. These attributes are not generated in a nation on their own. They are only brought about when people are born amongst them who are passionately fond of their people and their country and are prepared to work for them.

In Hindustan, till now, there were no such leaders among the Muslims and that is why they are duped in the name of Islam and selfish people take advantage of this. The other thing is that the leader of the Muslims of Hindustan was always the man who was a favourite of the British. He would either be a knight, khan bahadur or nawab. In this one month, the *Khudai Khidmatgar* campaigned tirelessly night and day and even though the British and the Muslim Leaguers had done their utmost, the Muslim League was defeated in the election, and the *Khudai Khidmatgar* won elections with a huge majority. In a house of fifty there were thirty-one *Khudai Khidmatgar*, two seats were won by Jamiat-ul-Ulema-e-Hind, and the remaining eleven were won by the Muslim League.

Of the six districts in the North-West Frontier Province, we won the districts of Kohat, Bannu, Dera Ismail Khan, Mardan and Peshawar. In Hazara, too, the inhabitants are Pukhtun, but have abandoned their mother tongue. We were successful in areas with Pukhto-speaking population, while the Muslim League was able to get more seats in Hindko-speaking areas. The effort that the government employees had put into opposing us was not even put in by the Muslim League. We considered this act of the government illegal, so we conferred and decided that we would not form the government. We also resolved that we would not form the government till such time that legal action had been initiated against all those government employees who had, in contravention of the instructions and rules of government, campaigned against us and till they had been punished under the relevant laws. Dr. Khan Sahib did not agree with this decision of ours. Sadullah informed Sardar Patel of this decision. When Sardar Patel came to know, he dispatched Maulana Abdul Kalam Azad to the Frontier to resolve the issue. We had a session in Peshawar.

I told the maulana sahib explicitly that if we did not have the power to act against those government employees who had taken this step against us, then we were not ready to accept the government. Maulana sahib returned to Delhi, and there, obtained a letter from the viceroy and then returned to Peshawar. In the letter, the viceroy had conceded to our demand in an ambiguous and vague manner. So, we formed the government, but on the condition that the powers of the government would vest in the central committee of the *Khudai Khidmatgar*. It was my view that two *Khudai Khidmatgar* from every district should be co-opted onto the committee, but on the condition that these members would not socialize with government employees, nor would they have a relationship with members of the Cabinet and nor would they make job recommendations to accommodate anyone. They would concern themselves with making a programme for the government to implement and the government would not depart from this approved programme. For this purpose, I toured the entire province and identified members from the movement to be part of the committee. The committee was constituted, but, unfortunately, it could not carry out its objectives. This was because its members could not put their own selfish interests aside. Even our decision to take legal action against those government employees who had worked against us in the election, which we had made a condition before our forming the government, was left unimplemented.

Members of the Constituent Assembly

Now we were confronted with the issue of membership of the constituent assembly. In that connection it was decided that the number of seats which fell to the share of each province would be filled through the votes of the members of the respective provincial assemblies. Our share was three members. We elected Maulana Abul Kalam Azad and me. The Muslim League had influenced the thinking of the Muslims of Hindustan to such an extent and there was no Muslim like the Maulana, who was a great Muslim scholar, and was also a politician who had undergone hardships in the liberation struggle. But nobody elected him from Hindustan. We had him elected from the Frontier Province. For the third seat the Muslim League nominated Sardar Bahadur Khan from Hazara. This was both the central legislative assembly and the constituent assembly. The Muslim League boycotted this. I pleaded with the Muslim members of the Muslim League to come and join us in the task; and that we would inform the Hindus that if they wanted to establish a 'socialist democracy', we would join them in this. There was a lot of benefit for the Muslims in this, because the Muslims are the poorer community in Hindustan, and the Hindus are much better off. There was a provision in the constitution that when the central government was constituted, each province would have the right to secede from the federation by a majority vote of the provincial assembly. If we, at any time, came to the conclusion that we could not have the federation, then we could each, in the Muslim majority provinces of NWFP, Sindh, Punjab and Bengal, through resolutions in the assembly, secede and form a separate country of our own. If the Muslim League had accepted that proposal, then neither Punjab, nor Bengal, would have been partitioned at independence. But the Muslims of the Muslim League were so shortsighted that, whoever was not in the Muslim League, would not even be considered a Muslim.

The Cripps Mission

When the Second World War started, the political leaders of the United States declared that, until the political problem of Hindustan was resolved, it would not be able to ally itself with the British in the war. So, they started to exert pressure on the British government to give freedom to Hindustan. President Roosevelt repeatedly stressed this with Mr. Winston Churchill, the British prime minister. So, the British also felt that they should consider this proposal of the Americans. For this, the Cripps mission was sent to Hindustan. But this mission was a failure. The British position in the war was deteriorating by the day. So, the Americans again turned towards them. Lord Wavell went to London and conferred with the secretary of state for India, to call a round table conference to resolve the political problems of Hindustan. Mr. Jinnah stated that only the Muslim League would nominate the representatives of the Muslims to this conference, and those of the Hindus should be nominated by the Congress Party. Maulana Azad, who was the president of the Congress at the time, did not agree to this. He used to say that the Congress would take part in the conference based on Hindustani nationalism. Because of this major difference, this conference also failed. It was quite amazing that the British government stood firmly by its stand, that the Congress should recognize the Muslim League as the sole political party representing the Muslims. Because the truth was that, when the elections were held in Hindustan in 1937, the Congress had an undisputed majority in nine out of the eleven provinces of Hindustan. The remaining three were Muslim dominated and were with the local parties. The Muslim League had no victory in those elections. In Sindh, it was the government of Allah Bakhsh Soomro, who was a nationalist, and was supported by the Congress members. In Punjab, it was the government of the Unionist Party, in which the Hindus and Sikhs were partners with the Muslims. Similarly, the government in Bengal was that of Maulana Fazlul Haq, who was running his government with the assistance of non-Muslims. However, despite all this, the British insisted that the Congress should acknowledge the League as the sole party representing the Muslims. They went to the extent that the Simla conference failed and ended, due to this single issue. It is an interesting fact that if we were to take present-day Pakistan, and place before us the results of the 1937 elections, the reality of the British and the Muslim League would become clear. In those elections, there was not a single member of the Muslim League who was successful from Sindh and the Frontier Province. And in Punjab, there was only one member. In other words, in all these three provinces, of the 155 seats, the Muslim League had won just one.

The Simla Conference and Cabinet Mission

Soon after the Simla conference failed, elections were held in Britain and the Labour Party assumed power and announced that, whatever was decided before, regarding Hindustan, would be put into practice.

From the past events, one thing had become apparent that they were sincere in what they had started. However, after the failure of the Cripps mission, Churchill's cabinet had decided that, until the successful conclusion of the war, the issue of Hindustan should be shelved.

When we realized that the British were compelled to give freedom to Hindustan, I told Gandhiji that this time around he should consider forming the government himself, because he had seen that when a powerless government is nominally in control, the ministers do not listen to anyone. Now, full powers would be given and so it was more necessary that he should be fully in control. And that if he were not to take control himself, and were to put his son Devadas there, I reminded him that power was such a thing that it would also change his attitude. Then, even he (Devadas) would not accept your guidance. It would be more appropriate if he were, like Lenin, to assume power himself. If Gandhiji had listened to my advice and taken control of the government himself, and it had completed its tenure and, after that, if he had not wished to continue, then, like Mao, he could have left it.

I do not know the reasons why he did not agree with what I said. If he had taken charge of government, Hindustan would not have experienced destruction on the scale it did. Soon after the assumption of power by the Labour Party, it sent a Cabinet mission to Hindustan.

On 8 February 1946, Lord Pethick Lawrence, Secretary of State for India, announced in Parliament that the British government was sending a cabinet mission to Hindustan to hold talks with the representatives of the country about granting independence to Hindustan.

That delegation came to Hindustan in the winter of 1945–46. This mission comprised Lord Pethick Lawrence, Secretary of State of India; President of the Board of Trade, Sir Stafford Cripps, and the First Lord of the Admiralty, A.V. Alexander. According to the cabinet mission plan, only three subjects were to be allocated to the central government i.e defence, foreign affairs, and communications. But this mission, in its plan, put forth a new proposal, which divided Hindustan into three Zones i.e. A, B, and C. This was because it was the thinking of the members of the mission that this would create confidence in the minds of the minority community. In Zone B were included the provinces of the Punjab, Sindh, NWFP and British Balochistan. These were the areas where the Muslims were in a majority. In Zone C were included the provinces of Bengal and Assam. In this Zone, the Muslims only had a slight majority. And in Zone A, all the other provinces of Hindustan were included. According to this, the Muslim-dominated areas enjoyed almost complete autonomy. In this respect, the Muslim majority in Zones B and C was certain and they had been given the right to assume all powers in their hands. As for the rights of the central government, it had control of only three subjects: defence, foreign affairs and communications. In this plan, it was included that any province which did not wish to stay in any particular zone could, through a majority resolution in its provincial assembly, opt out of the zone. The cabinet mission plan was accepted by both Congress and the Muslim League. In the beginning, Jinnah sahib was in opposition to this scheme. But when the mission explained in clear terms that it would neither accept the division of the country and nor did it advocate a free state, then Jinnah sahib accepted the proposals of the cabinet mission plan. On the last day, Jinnah accepted that the provision which the mission had made in the plan for the protection of the rights of the Muslim majority could not be a more just or fair decision, than this. He could not make the mission agree to the inclusion of more conditions. He told the council that the plan, which the cabinet mission had proposed, was the most that could be done for protecting the rights of the Muslim minority. For this reason, he advised the Muslim League to agree to the scheme and the council unanimously supported it.

The acceptance of this plan by the Muslim League and the Congress was an important and bright event in the history of Hindustan. From this, it was apparent that the difficult issue of the freedom of Hindustan was resolved through talks and conciliation, and not through violence and war.

At the time, the government of Britain was compelled to consider giving Hindustan its freedom. It dispatched a few responsible members of its cabinet to Hindustan, who arrived on the 23rd of March that year.

This mission started discussions with the All-India Muslim League and the Congress. For these consultations, they summoned representative delegations of four members each from both parties. These consultations started from 2 May 1946, in Simla. The Congress was represented by the following:

- Maulana Abul Kalam Azad, President
- Jawaharlal Nehru
- Sardar Patel
- And I, Abdul Ghaffar Khan

The Muslim League was represented by:

- Muhammad Ali Jinnah, President
- Liaquat Ali Khan
- The Raja Sahib of Mahmudabad
- Sardar Abdur Rab Nishtar

The Government of the Labour Party in Britain was represented by the following ministers:

- Lord Pethick Lawrence, Secretary of State for India
- Sir Stafford Cripps
- A.V. Alexander
- Lord Wavell, the Viceroy of India

Talks between these representatives began. In the first session, whatever was discussed, we four representatives of Congress went and conveyed the major points to Mahatma Gandhi. He told us that,

'The English are very clever and crafty. They will get you involved in talks and will deceive you. Before everything else, you should ask them whether they are prepared to leave Hindustan or not. Also ask them whether they are prepared to withdraw the British troops from our country or not.' The next day, when we went to resume our talks, Jawaharlal Nehru put these questions to them. In response, Lord Wavell said, 'To whom should we leave it? Neither the Congress nor the Muslim League are making peace. Then whom should we leave the land to?' In reply to this, Jawaharlal said, 'If you are not leaving it to us, then leave it to the Muslim League. But you should get out.'

This statement had a positive effect on Jinnah sahib and he assured them that they would come to a mutual agreement. After a meeting between Nehru and Jinnah, a decision was taken to the following effect: that a delegation be constituted consisting of one delegate each, from the Congress and the Muslim League. Its chairman would be someone who would be nominated with the consent of both parties. Those points, which were agreed to by the Congress and the Muslim League, would be accepted; and those over which there were differences of opinion and were complicated in nature, would be put up to the delegation for resolution. Lord Pethick Lawrence informed the delegates that we would have to constitute the three-member delegation within three days and send the names to them. We went and informed Gandhiji about this development. When, after three days, we were proceeding to the meeting, Gandhiji told us that whatever the Muslim League demanded, we should concede to them, but that things should not go wrong. When we came and took our seats, Lord Pethick Lawrence asked Jinnah sahib how they had resolved the issue. Jinnah sahib asked him as to which issue? When I heard this from Jinnah sahib, I cautioned him not to disrupt the talks, and further informed him that when we were coming to the talks today, Gandhiji directed us that, whatever the Muslim League were to demand, we should concede. So (I said), whatever they (the Muslim League) wanted, he will grant you; and that I would be the guarantor of this. Nishtar sahib went and stood behind Jinnah sahib. He stood there for a long while but Jinnah sahib did not pay any attention to him. So, he went and took his seat, and the talks failed. Pethick Lawrence said to him, 'Oh Jinnah sahib! You had promised!' But he did not answer and the mission failed, and we dispersed.

The Presidentship of the Congress

Till this time, Maulana Abul Kalam Azad had continuously remained the president of the Congress from 1939 onwards, because during the World War and the ongoing struggle in the country, it was not possible to elect a new president. When the War ended, the issue of a new president of the Congress arose. At the time, the general view was that Abul Kalam Azad should remain the president, because it was during his tenure that talks between the British Government and the leaders of Hindustan had taken place. Plus, it was during his presidentship that the Simla Conference had been held. The commonly held opinion was that it would be better if the question of the freedom of Hindustan was also concluded with him as the president, because there were differences of opinion among the leaders of the party as to who should replace him. Sardar Patel and his associates were trying that he (Patel) should become the president.

Maulana Abul Kalam Azad knew of all these developments. Considering this, he decided to tender his resignation from the post and not to contest it for another term. But he was of the view that, after him, such a person should take over who, in the difficult times ahead, should be able to run the affairs of the party according to the way of thinking of the Maulana sahib. For this, he considered Jawaharlal Nehru as the most appropriate person, and he expressed his views about Nehru in a statement to the press. Gandhiji was also in agreement with Sardar Patel becoming the president, but after this press statement of Maulana sahib's, he did not say anything further and Jawaharlal Nehru became the president.

Jawaharlal's Statement

After the acceptance of the cabinet mission plan, a very positive political atmosphere was created in Hindustan. However, following this, Jawaharlal Nehru, in a press conference in Bombay, gave such a statement, that it vitiated the short-lived friendly atmosphere.

On 10 January 1946, a question was put to Nehru in the press conference, that when the All-India Congress accepted the proposal, whether that meant that they had accepted the plan in its totality. In answer to this, he stated that, 'When the Congress sits in the constituent assembly, it will not consider itself as bound by these agreements and, at the time, it will decide in accordance with the prevailing situation, with complete freedom.' After this clarification, the press reporters asked whether this meant that amendments could be carried out in the cabinet mission plan. In response, Nehru declared that the Congress had only agreed to participate in the constituent assembly and it considered itself as entitled to make amendments in the cabinet mission plan.

The view of Maulana Abul Kalam Azad was that this was a very unfortunate development. He says in his book: 'I feel there is a need to record in detail, that the statement of Jawaharlal Nehru was wrong. It was erroneous to assert that the Congress could carry out whatever amendments it wanted to in the cabinet mission plan. The truth was that we had accepted that, at the centre, there would be a federal government and it would only have three portfolios with it. All other portfolios would be with the provinces and would be in their power. We had all accepted that the provinces would be divided into three groups: A, B, and C. In these provinces, the Congress had no power or right to bring about any amendments without the consent of the other parties.'

Reaction to the Statement of Jawaharlal Nehru

Nehru's statement did not go down well with Mr. Jinnah. This statement was such that it could not but have a bad effect on everyone. Mr. Jinnah took the stand that Jawaharlal Nehru's statement was a clear indication of the mentality of the Congress party. His reason was that if the Congress could so quickly change its opinion, while the British are still here, and power had not been transferred to the Congress, then in what commitments could the minorities repose their trust and confidence, after the departure of the British? That the Congress would not alter its stance and the attitude of the Congress would undergo a change, like what was manifested in Jawaharlal Nehru's statement. Immediately after this, Mr. Jinnah issued a press statement stating that, 'Everything has changed with this statement of the President of the Congress, and the need for considering everything afresh has arisen.'

Jinnah sahib directed Liaquat Ali Khan to call a meeting of the Muslim League council, and also issued a statement to the press that the Muslim League council, in its meeting in Delhi, had accorded its approval to the cabinet mission plan, because it had been assured that the Congress had endorsed it; and that this plan would form the basis of the constitution that was to be drafted for Hindustan. Now that the Congress president has given a statement that the Congress, through its majority in the constituent assembly, can bring about amendments in this plan, this means that the minorities would be at the mercy of the majority. In this statement, Jinnah sahib further added that the meaning of Jawaharlal's statement is that the Congress has rejected the cabinet mission plan. For this reason, it was now incumbent on the viceroy to invite the Muslim League to form the government at the centre, since the Muslim League has endorsed the plan.

The Interim Government

Thus, in September 1946, the Interim Government was formed. Jinnah sahib, at first refused but then, later, on 15 October 1946, after holding talks with Lord Wavell, agreed to the formation of the Interim Government and joined it. Lord Wavell wanted the Interim Government to be formed without any further delay. In those days, I was unwell so Gandhiji said that until I recovered, and they heard my views, they would not join the government. Lord Wavell telephoned Dr. Khan Sahib, the chief minister of the Frontier, telling him that he was dispatching his personal aircraft and to send Bacha Khan to Delhi in it. I was ill. I told him I would not travel by air, so I left for Delhi by train.

In Delhi, a debate was taking place in the Congress over two issues. One was that Jawaharlal Nehru was of the view that he would not take Sardar Abdur Rab Nishtar into his Cabinet because he had not been able to win his seat in his province; that he was not an elected representative of the people. This objection of Jawaharlal's had logic behind it. What right does a person have who, in his home province, cannot win his seat, to represent all of Hindustan in a democratic government?

The Congress had also raised this question before the viceroy, that in such circumstances, if Bacha Khan were to demand, then Sardar Abdur Rab Nishtar could be included in the Interim Cabinet, otherwise not. In addition, the Congress was of the view that it had given the right to the Muslim League to make nominations against the number of ministries given to the Muslims, and so the Congress had the right to nominate Hindus against ministries. It was, therefore, of the view that it was not prepared to accommodate any Muslims against the share of the Congress. I told them that we had no objection whatsoever to Sardar Abdur Rab Nishtar becoming a minister. I thought that he was a Pukhtun, and that if he is not accommodated, this would not provide an opportunity to another Pukhtun to become a minister. I said to myself that at least he was a Pukhtun and that he and I would not play such games with each other, which he later played. Jawaharlal Nehru complained to me about him, that he was taken into the Cabinet at my instance, and that he was not a good person at all. I also said that the Muslims had given many sacrifices in the Congress cause, and it would be appropriate if the Congress were to make the sacrifice of one seat for them. This would have a positive effect on the Muslims. The Congress accepted both my demands. Lord Wavell was of the view that the home portfolio should be given to the Muslim League. But Sardar Patel was adamant that he would not give this up for anyone else. So, Jinnah sahib said that he should be given some other important portfolio. The Congress offered him the finance portfolio. Sardar Patel considered this a blessing and fully supported it. The Congress said to Lord Wavell that the League should get the finance ministry. Lord Wavell also told Jinnah sahib to take finance. He informed him that he would convey his answer to him after two days. Ghulam Muhammad, who later became the governor-general of Pakistan, Muhammad Ali Chaudhary, and other Muslims who were working in the ministry of finance, came to the Muslim League leaders and expressed great joy, and told them that this was a critical ministry, and they congratulated them on this development, and also told Liaquat Ali Khan not to worry at all; that they would render them great assistance in the discharge of their functions. On this reassurance, Jinnah sahib agreed to accept the portfolio, and Liaquat Ali Khan became the finance minister.

Finally, the Congress formed the Interim Government, and the British, to bring a bad name to it, bombed Waziristan. When I learnt of this, I went and told Jawaharlal that he was the prime minister and that this was in the remit of his office; that he did not know anything about it and nor had anyone brought it to his notice. This would create a lot of misunderstandings in the minds of the tribesmen about their government. The other thing was that the government incurred expenditure amounting to crores of rupees in connection with the administration of the Tribal Areas. The money that goes into the pockets of the tribal maliks and the political agents is frivolously spent on trivial matters, at the discretion of the political agents and that this expense does not serve the tribesmen. And now that these powers had come into his hands, it was his duty to personally acquaint himself with the tribesmen of the agencies. These poor and oppressed tribesmen were good people living in a mountainous region. If treated kindly, with some means of livelihood created for them, the troubles, which they created from time to time, would cease. I made Jawaharlal agree to this, and he promised that he would tour the Tribal Areas and meet the people. He also said that whatever he could possibly do, he would do, for these people.

But when Jawaharlal decided to visit the Frontier, Governor Sir Olaf Caroe[35] went to Delhi and called on Jawaharlal and advised him not to visit the Frontier. When he refused to agree with him, he informed the viceroy to advise Pandit Nehru. The viceroy too advised Jawaharlal to change his travel plans. But Jawaharlal went ahead as planned. When Olaf Caroe returned from Delhi to Peshawar, he summoned all the political agents and directed them to make arrangements to oppose the tour. In addition to the political agents, he also prompted the Muslim League to create mischief.

When Jawaharlal arrived in Peshawar by air and was on his way to the chief minister, Dr. Khan Sahib's, bungalow, he was met by the booing of the Muslim Leaguers in the cantonment, although political activities were prohibited in the limits of the cantonment area, and nobody could take out a *jaloos*, and nor was anyone allowed to raise slogans. Just pause and think for a while. Dr. Khan Sahib was the chief minister of the province, and Jawaharlal was the prime minister of Hindustan and had come on an official tour! This was all Caroe's mischief and whatever the officers, the police and the Muslim League did, was at his behest and with his backing. All the impediments that were put in our path were created by Governor Caroe.

Jawaharlal and the Tribal Areas
We started our first tour from Waziristan and when we were about to leave on tour, Caroe pressurized Jawaharlal not to take me with him. He told him that since Dr. Khan Sahib was with him; what need was there for me? Jawaharlal, however, did not agree and

asked me to come along. The political agents of Waziristan were both Englishmen. They opposed us in a civilized manner. We first went to Miranshah, where a representative *jirga* of tribesmen had been collected and the tribesmen were sitting on the ground. For the political agent and us, there were chairs. I sat on the ground with the *jirga* members. When Jawaharlal started his speech, they all rose and proclaimed that they did not accept the government of the Hindus. These tribal brethren of ours are a strange lot. Jawaharlal had come for their welfare and informed them of this in his speech as well. From here, we then proceeded to Razmak where the same game was played out, but it was so intense that one malik, Jahangir Khan, withdrew his hand when Dr. Khan Sahib extended his for a handshake, and told him that he was a friend of the Hindus, and that he would not shake hands with him. When we were leaving Razmak, our accompanying security contingent consisted of Hindu soldiers. They told Jawaharlal to address them. He obliged, after which they shouted slogans of Jawaharlal, Gandhiji and Bacha Khan Zindabad. Since arrangements for our tour in Waziristan were in the hands of the army, and they were Hindus, we experienced no disturbance here.

When we returned to Miranshah, the two political agents and the Resident for Waziristan were present. Jawaharlal asked them about the welfare schemes they had utilized the crores of rupees on, which were spent on the tribesmen annually. They had no answer, as they had done nothing for the people. So, I interjected and said that they had done a lot for the Pukhtuns. The English officers were pleased with my remark, but when I followed this up with the fact that this money had inculcated bad habits and the love of money in them, that when offered money they would do anything, irrespective of good or bad, the British officers were crest-fallen.

From Miranshah we went to Wana. This was the headquarter town of South Waziristan. Dewan Shiv Saranlal was the political agent here. We were given a huge reception and the tribesmen had brought the traditional two sheep, to welcome us. People listened to Jawaharlal's speech in pin-drop silence.

Torkham

From Wana, we returned to Peshawar, and the next morning we started our tour of Torkham, in the Khyber Agency. The political agent of Khyber was a Muslim. His name was Sahibzada Khurshid. When we arrived in Jamrud, we saw Afridis sitting at a short distance from the road and when they saw us approaching, they menacingly waved the shoes they were holding in their hands, at us. We continued straight to Torkham. This was the boundary between Afghanistan and Hindustan. While we were having tea here, a young Afridi came up and told the political agent that we were their guests and should not be treated like this. When we started on the return journey and approached Landikotal, the political *tehsildar* came running up to the political agent and told him that the Shinwaris had gathered. When we arrived there, we were pelted with stones. The political agent was leading us. He got out of his vehicle and told the accompanying *Khasadars* to open fire on the tribesmen. The assembled crowd dispersed after a few shots were fired. The glass window-panes of our car were shattered by the stones, but we were saved. Sahibzada sahib was a decent man and would, for our safety, always be ahead of us.

Malakand Agency

The next day, we left for Malakand Agency. Sheikh Mahboob Ali Khan, the Muslim political agent here, was from the village of Sheikhan, west of Peshawar cantonment. He did not have a good reputation. When we were leaving on the tour of Khyber, the arrangements were made by the local police. I told Dr. Khan Sahib that these arrangements should be made by the army, as in Waziristan. And if he could not provide the army then we would plan through the *Khudai Khidmatgar* ourselves, because the political agent could not be trusted. We found out that Sheikh Mahboob Ali had come and met with Governor Caroe. This man was a very loyal agent of the British and had no conscience. He was a very mean and vicious person who was responsible for the destruction of the Pukhtun nation. In the service of the British high commissioner to Afghanistan, Humphry, he was largely responsible for the overthrow of Amanullah Khan, the ruler of Afghanistan; and he had had him replaced by Bacha Saqao. The riots against the Hindus in Dera Ismail Khan had also been instigated by him, while was the assistant commissioner there at the time. But Dr. Khan Sahib was a strange man. When we got down from the plane in Risalpur, only the police was there for our protection. I was very upset and decided to not accompany them on the tour at all. But I could not leave Jawaharlal alone. We left Risalpur in a car. When we reached Skhakot, Rahat Khan and his companions were waiting to receive us. A little while later, Sheikh Mahboob Ali Khan also arrived. After a while, we took leave of them. The Sheikh had conspired against us and had planned for our 'reception', but we arrived before the time that he had fixed for mischief to be done. We were sitting in his bungalow having tea when we heard people's cries. At night, he flattered Dr. Khan Sahib. A great sycophant, he was also trying to be particularly amiable to us. Adjacent to his bungalow were two rooms; it seemed as if they were meant for guests. Jawaharlal and I went to sleep in these rooms and Dr. Khan Sahib was accommodated by him in his own bungalow. He had not arranged for a *jirga* to meet with us. Rahat Khan, our *Khudai Khidmatgar* colleague from Skhakot, arrived, so we told him to inform the people of the area to come and see us in the morning. When the Sheikh learnt of this, he had his car damaged and prevented him from reaching out to our associates; and even those who received the message and came, were not allowed to meet with us. Early the next morning, Rahat Khan informed us that Sheikh Mahboob Ali had summoned many people and warned us to be safe. We had two lorries which transported the police, and in each lorry, along with the police, there was one Englishman. We found out that they had gone from here to Dargai for the night. When Rahat Khan informed me about all this, I spoke to Dr. Khan Sahib and informed him that the Sheikh had prepared this plan of mischief. The sheikh was standing right in front of us and was listening to our conversation. He came to Dr. Khan Sahib and asked him whether he could ever stoop to be such a bastard? He also asked him whether he was not a Pukhtun? And further added that Dr. Khan Sahib was like a father to him, so why would he be disloyal to his own father and not ensure his safety? Dr. Khan Sahib had one major weakness – he was easily swayed by sycophants. I told him that until our guard arrived, we would not leave. Our police guard and the sheikh were complicit in the plot, and that is why they did not spend the night here, and had not come to Malakand, till then. But the sheikh said to Dr. Khan Sahib 'Come, let us go!' Despite my strong opposition Dr. Khan Sahib decided that we should leave. Our car followed Sheikh Mehboob's car. When we arrived at the gate of the Fort, a few Englishmen emerged from it. They were waiting for us. We got out of the car and entered the Fort with the Englishmen. The Sheikh sahib left, leaving us alone. After some time, we came out from the fort. A little further down the road, there was a lorry parked on the road blocking it and many people were standing on the hill-top, and started pelting us with stones, to shouts of '*murdabad* (down with)'. Dr. Khan Sahib was sitting in the front seat and Jawaharlal and I were sitting in the rear seat. A stone hit me on the head and I suffered a black-out for a moment and fell on Jawaharlal, and he fell on me. Sheikh Mehboob's man, who was with us in the car had a revolver strapped around his waist. Dr. Khan Sahib saw it and drew it out from the holster and, taking his arm out of the window, said to the crowd to get away, otherwise he would fire at them. He said the same to the lorry driver. The lorry also moved away. All this happened next to the fort, which was right next to the road. This was the prime minister of Hindustan, but neither the Englishmen, nor the government officials came to help us.

When we descended from the top of the Malakand pass, we came face to face with the police guards and the two Englishmen. When we got to the bottom of the pass, it was all rocks and boulders. I told the Englishmen, 'Fine guards you are, can you not see the condition we are in? I had thought that Mahboob Ali would also have arranged for people to protect us; and you are charged with the responsibility of our safety. Whatever has happened, has happened. Now, kindly put one lorry ahead of us, and the other behind our car. And if you see a crowd by the roadside, the lorry in front should stop and the police should get down and ask the people to move away. And if they refuse to do so, the police should charge at them with lathis. If they do not disperse with the lathi-charge, then the police in the lorry at the rear should resort to aerial firing.' We started our journey again. When we arrived in Dargai, a crowd had gathered there to receive us. Sheikh Mahboob Ali was also standing with them. Once again, we were pelted with stones. A man threw a stone at Jawaharlal's head, but I managed to deflect it with my arm. My arm was fractured but I saved Jawaharlal. There was another man who had a pot full of faeces which he flung at us. I and Jawaharlal were saved but Dr. Khan Sahib was covered in the mess, from head to toe. Sheikh Mahboob Ali, the political agent, was standing by and advised us not to travel on the main road and that when we came across a dirt road, we should take it, as it led straight to Charsadda. That there was a large crowd waiting for us further on, which had blocked the road and he feared that violence on a large scale may take place. I was against this and was of the view that we should continue travelling on the main road, but our security guards refused to do so. So, we took the *kacha* (unpaved) road and reached Peshawar.

Sardaryab

The next day we were scheduled to visit the central *markaz* of the *Khudai Khidmatgar* movement in Sardaryab. I told Dr. Khan Sahib that we would neither take his police nor the army with us for security, and that we had no need of his arrangements; that we would rely on our own people. For our travel from Peshawar we arranged for our *Khudai Khidmatgars* in uniform to line both sides of the road to Sardaryab; and so, both sides of the road were secured. Our ideology was one of non- violence, but when the people learnt of our Malakand experience, they came to assist and protect the *Khudai Khidmatgar,* with their weapons, and stood in great numbers on both sides of the road, shoulder to shoulder, with them. Caroe had ordered Manki sahib that, where the road leading to Mathra met the metalled Charsadda road, he should prepare the sheikhs of the Mullagori tribe to attack our cars at that junction. But when they saw the strength of the *Khudai Khidmatgar*, they could not muster enough courage to carry out their orders. Those sheikhs live with the Khalil along the boundary of the Khyber agency.

Near the *markaz* at Sardaryab, the Muslim Leaguers of Gulbela had gathered in large numbers, but they also stood back from attacking us. The Pukhtuns of Hashtnagar, along with their many followers, came armed to the *markaz* to assist us. When the Muslim Leaguers saw their numbers and their strength, they ran away. In the morning when we were preparing for the journey, I came out of the room, and what do I see, but that several Englishmen gathered on the lawns of the chief minister's residence, and army soldiers standing on the road. I asked the officers not to bother, that today we had made our own arrangements, and it would be best if they left and took their troops along and did not follow us.

We left for the *markaz*. Besides the *Khudai Khidmatgar*, there was a huge crowd collected to protect us that I am unable to describe it. We arrived at the *markaz* safely. There was a large crowd milling in the *markaz*. The *jalsa* started with nationalistic poems being recited, and Jawaharlal delivered a very impressive speech. He said that he was very happy at the fact that, in the land of the Pukhtuns, a few drops of his blood had been shed, and that he hoped that this government, full of deceit and cruelty, would very soon come to an end. After Jawaharlal's speech, I also said a few words to my Pukhtun brethren, and told them that it was a well-acknowledged fact the world over that the Pukhtuns were a very hospitable people, but on the instigation of Governor Caroe, those traditions have not been maintained. Here they had treated their honourable guest in such a vile manner, that they would have to hide their faces in shame from the world. All this, Caroe had done through the Pukhtun, Sheikh Mahboob Ali Khan. The only sin of Jawaharlal was that he had proclaimed that he was setting out on a tour of the Pukhtun tribesmen for their welfare and Caroe had asked him not to do so, and not to interfere in their administration of the Tribal Areas. He, however, told him that he would go; that he was responsible for these areas; that they were under his government. He had come to the Frontier Province and the Tribal Areas for the welfare and development of the Pukhtuns. The next morning Pandit Jawaharlal Nehru took leave of us and left for Delhi.

Maulana Abul Kalam Azad sahib has written in his book: 'In the Pukhtuns, hospitality is a big quality; but that they lacked this attribute and were thrifty. For this the Pukhtuns were tired of them.' He goes on to say that once our associates were his guests (and) 'When I brought out biscuits with tea, they were very pleased and asked me what they were called. That they had seen them in Dr. Khan Sahib's bungalow, but he had not offered them any.' Maulana sahib had not bothered to ascertain the truth of the matter but has recorded it. It is not part of our culture that one should eat something and not offer it to others. We are such that whatever we eat ourselves, we also offer to our guests and our servants, and sit down to eat together. In our *markaz*, too, the practice was that when we would sit down to our meals, and had cooked for ten guests, even if twenty additional guests came, we would sit down together and share the food amongst ourselves. We continue to do so even today.

I am surprised that Maulana sahib should be recounting this tale because Dr. Khan Sahib was so hospitable that he had taken hospitality to a fault. I fail to understand who had gone to Calcutta to meet him. Similarly, he also writes that, at the time of the elections, the Congress had given us a lot of money but that we spent very little of it, and so, many candidates, for want of expense, were defeated. We, the *Khudai Khidmatgar* have never taken even a paisa from the Congress. In fact, Jawaharlal got annoyed with me over this very issue and had complained to Dr. Ansari Sahib that I was very proud. When I was leaving for the meeting of the Congress working committee, all the members would buy a second-class ticket. I never did so. However, if our parliamentary board had received any money from them, I do not know anything about that. Every paisa has been spent for the purpose intended, and all the candidates that they nominated, were all elected, and with large majorities too. So how does this question then arise? The surprising thing is that Maulana sahib raised the objection that we, in the Frontier, did not spend all the money that we received on the election process. Common sense would say that if, in the Frontier, the *Khudai Khidmatgar* won all the seats that they contested and were in an absolute majority, and did not spend much on the elections, this amounted to a major political success for them. Maulana sahib had chosen even to criticize this.

The Presentation of the Budget

We were confronted with a major difficulty when Liaquat Ali Khan presented the budget for the new financial year. It was an avowed policy of the Congress to reduce economic disparity and gradually replace the existing capitalist system by a socialistic one. This was also stated in the election manifesto of the Congress party. Jawaharlal had issued many statements referring to the excessive profits which different classes of capitalists had made during the War. It was well-known to the common people that a major portion of the profits made had been concealed and no income tax had been paid. That meant that the government had been deprived of a substantial amount of income. We believed, to recover this amount, the government should institute very strict measures because this revenue was due but had not been paid. Liaquat Ali Khan prepared such a budget which, prima facie, was in accordance with the declared policy of the Congress, but its actual objective was to give it a bad name. This was because the demands of the Congress were presented in an un-implementable form. The taxation proposals were so formulated as to make the moneyed classes profligate, and to harm industry and commerce. Along with this, he had also proposed that a commission be appointed to inquire into all unpaid taxes and decide for their collection. We all wanted that, in the distribution of wealth, there should be greater equality and those who had not paid taxes be held accountable. So, for these reasons we were not, in principle, opposed to the budget of Liaquat Ali Khan. In the meeting of the cabinet, Liaquat Ali Khan said that his proposals were based on the public statements of the responsible leaders of Congress. He acknowledged that if Jawaharlal had not made his public statements then his mind would not have been mobilized in this direction. About the budget the practice is that the finance minister formulates it in accordance with the wishes of all his cabinet ministers. But in this case, Nawabzada Liaquat Ali Khan presented only a summary of it to the cabinet members and did not take them into confidence about its details.

In so far as the budget related to routine matters, the cabinet endorsed his proposals, and so he obtained the required stamp of approval from it. He then made the budget in such a manner that it not only amounted to extremism, but it was intended to harm the national interest as well. We understood that this budget, on the face of it, was in accordance with Congress policy and politics. The Congress had all along declared that we would oppose a capitalistic system and would give the poor their due share of the national wealth; so, for this reason we could not object to this budget, in principle.

The Mountbatten Mission

Lord Mountbatten was appointed as the governor-general of Hindustan after the removal of Lord Wavell. Before coming to Hindustan, the Labour Government had thoroughly briefed him on all their problems and their desires. Mr. Atlee had given him instructions that before 30 June 1948, it would be necessary to transfer complete power to Hindustan.

Lord Mountabatten arrived in Delhi on 22 March 1947 and on 24 March took the oath of office as viceroy and governor-general. In his short speech at the occasion he stressed that, within a few months, ways would be found to resolve all problems. At that time, the differences between the Congress and the League had reached such an impasse that they could not be resolved without the efforts of a third party. After the Calcutta riots in 1947, communal riots had started in Bihar and Noakhali, and then later, violence broke out in Bombay. Till that time Punjab was peaceful, but there, too, signs of disquiet and trouble were beginning to emerge. Malik Khizr Hayat Khan had resigned as the chief minister of Punjab on 2 March. In the protests of 4 March, thirteen people were killed, and many were wounded. These criminal riots spread to other parts of the province as well. In Amritsar, Rawalpindi and Taxila, these disturbances took a heavy toll. On the one hand, communal emotions were on the increase and, on the other, the law and order machinery of the government was weakening. In the central government, because of the non-cooperation between the members of the League and the Congress, conditions were deteriorating even further. The members of the central government took up adversarial positions against each other. The government seemed as if it was in a state of stupor. The League had the finance ministry, which is considered the foundation of the government. It must be remembered that Sardar Patel was solely responsible for this predicament in which the government found itself, because he was concerned about retaining the home ministry and had given the finance ministry to the League. The finance ministry had many capable Muslim officers at the helm of affairs who were cooperating with Liaquat Ali Khan in every possible manner.

The British were successful in their old game. They were successful in creating such conditions in the land which the Congress and League could not resolve by themselves; and so, finally, they had to turn back to them to find a way out of this impasse. And Mountbatten gradually put forth his plan of partitioning Hindustan before the Congress, and created the impression that, in the present circumstances, there was no other solution to the problem but Partition.

Mountbatten was a very intelligent and far sighted man. He would find out what his Hindustani companions were feeling in their hearts. When he realized that Sardar Patel was prepared to accept his plan of partition of Hindustan, then, to bring him on board, he used the full potential of the power of his personality, charm and deceit. In his discussions, he would compare Sardar Patel to a walnut; his exterior was hard, but when broken, the interior emerged soft. After the conquest of Sardar Patel, he turned his attention to Jawaharlal. Initially, Jawaharlal would not entertain any thought of partition and his reaction would be very strong. But Mountbatten pursued him until, gradually, the strength of his opposition to the idea broke down. When it gradually became clear that Jawaharlal had also come around to the views of Sardar Patel about the partition of Hindustan, I was very saddened. This was because we considered this not so much as the partitioning of Hindustan, as that of the Muslims. I was, from the beginning, of the view, and I still believe, that the Cabinet Mission plan was the best solution for the Muslims in every respect. It would have ensured the unity of Hindustan and also provided each community the opportunity for a free and respectable existence. Even if you consider the benefits in this for the Muslims, one could not hope for a better solution. In provinces with Muslim majority, they would get full provincial autonomy in internal affairs. If we consider the provinces of a federal Hindustan, and give Balochistan a provincial status, then, in the federal government, they would have assumed an equal status with the Hindus.

Maulana Azad says that, 'I have thought over all these matters at great length. I wondered why Gandhiji had so very quickly changed his opinion. I think that this was the outcome of the influence of Sardar Patel. Patel would openly declare that there was no solution to the problem other than partitioning Hindustan. From experience, it has been established that it is not possible to work jointly with the Muslim League.'

It was necessary that Sardar Patel should have given importance to another matter as well; that Lord Louis Mountbatten said that the Congress had agreed to the weakening of the central government only for the purpose of pleasing the Muslim League; and for this reason, the provinces were given full provincial autonomy. But in a country with such vast differences between the people in terms of language, faith and culture, the weakness of the central government strengthens the viewpoint of the enemy. If one is set free from the League, then arrangements can be put in place for a strong central government, and such a law can be legislated which would prove beneficial for the retention of the unity of Hindustan. Mountbatten advised that in the North-West and in the North-East, a few small pieces of Hindustan should be given to the Muslim League; then from the rest of Hindustan, a strong state can be created. This reasoning had a great effect on Sardar Patel, who believed that combining with the Muslim League would jeaopardize the unity and stability of Hindustan. In my view it was not only Sardar Patel, but also Jawaharlal who believed in this reasoning. This reasoning, when recapitulated by Sardar Patel and Mountbatten, also led to the weakening of Gandhiji's opposition to the idea of partition. When Mountbatten saw that people were strongly opposed to the Cabinet Mission plan, he prepared an alternate plan for Partition, as he had wanted. Whenever the issue of partition came to the forefront, the issue of Bengal and Punjab assumed great importance. Mountbatten said that since Partition was based on the principle of Hindu and Muslim majority areas and since, in certain parts of Punjab and Bengal, Muslims were in a majority, for this reason, both these provinces also needed to be partitioned. But he advised the Congress leaders not to raise this question, yet. He assured them that, at an appropriate time, he himself would raise this question. At this time, Mountbatten had worked out the details of his Partition plan, and so he decided to go to London for talks with the leaders of the government of Britain. I met with Mountbatten on 14 May in Simla. I discussed matters with him for a while. Then I appealed to him not to bury the Cabinet Mission plan; that we should resort to patience because there was still hope for the success of this plan. If we agreed to partition in a hurry, then Hindustan would be harmed greatly. I also told him that he should also keep in mind all the possible consequences of partition. Before Partition the Muslims and Hindus had attacked each other in Calcutta, Noakhali, Bihar, Bombay and Punjab. If, in such circumstances the country is partitioned, streams of blood would flow and the British alone would bear the responsibility for this. But Mountbatten immediately assured me that he would not allow anyone to riot and would prevent blood from being spilt. Once Partition is accepted in principle, then he would issue orders to prevent any communal riots from taking place. But then the whole world came to know that, after the announcement of the Partition plan, communal riots took place in many parts of the country and rivers of blood flowed freely, and innocent women and children were slaughtered, and no worthwhile measures or action was taken to prevent the civil war between the Muslims and the Hindus.

Direct Action and Equality

In Punjab, fighting between the Hindus and Muslims had begun. When news of it used to be reported in the press, the hatred between the two communities would become even more intense. In 1946, when the riots which had started between the Hindus and Muslims spread to Calcutta and Direct Action Day was observed by the Muslim League, it was like adding fuel to the fire. In the city of Calcutta only a few Hindus were killed at the instance of the Muslim League, but the Hindus avenged themselves for this in Bihar. The Muslims are not well-organized, and the Hindus are. They did not slaughter or loot as many people in Calcutta as they did in Bihar. They killed and looted and committed arson on a large scale. I had personally gone to Bihar to help the Muslims. We would occasionally tell Suhrawardy sahib that the destruction which took place in Bihar was all because of the Direct Action call of the Muslim League, and that he was responsible for it. He said that he had a written communication in his possession and that when the time for investigating the truth came, he would reveal its contents. In Calcutta, many people from Bihar were killed. On the pretext of getting even, a lot of brutality was committed against the Hindus at Noakhali. The policy of the British to divide and rule was successful. The British were very happy at this handiwork of the Muslim League, because due to these stupidities committed by Hindustan, the British civil servants wanted to prove and show to the British Labour Party that the people of Hindustan were ready, like savages, to drink each other's blood and eager to eat and flay each other's flesh; and that they were unaware of the consciousness to live with each other like human beings. And for this reason, it was still necessary for the British to rule over them, and that they should not be given a government of their own. And if this did not happen, they would destroy each other.

In Bihar

The Muslim League was the creation of the British. For this reason, they took undue advantage of the conditions in Surat. To disturb the peace and order there, the British and the Muslim League were in agreement.

With all this destruction, the passions of the Muslim League had not cooled down. It was conspiring in stoking the fires of communalism and was benefitting politically at the hands of the afflicted, who were being instructed to migrate to Bengal. I was immersed in worry for these tyrannized and oppressed people and wondered how I would be able to rehabilitate them in their own homes. But they had been so misguided by the Muslim League that they did not like what I said to them. So, I decided to meet the Muslim League leaders who were accommodated in the palatial residence of barrister Muhammad Younus. Whenever I would visit them, I would find them busy eating and drinking, and they would tell me that they would not hold discussions with me. When Nazimuddin told them that it was necessary for them to talk to me, they agreed. I requested them that the people had been harmed enough, and should be left to themselves now, and that they should not wreak more havoc on them. Was the destruction that was brought upon them not enough that they were now being persuaded to migrate to Bengal? If they did settle there, I would have no objection to this. But if this was intended only to make their political objectives evident and take advantage of them for this purpose, then this was wrong. But these Muslim Leaguers had no mercy in their hearts. I also met with my old benefactor, Feroze Khan Noon here, after sixteen years. I asked him that he had promised that they would confer on what we had said, and would give us a reply, but that he had failed to do so up to now. He was a very honourable man. He lowered his gaze and gave me no answer. The fact is that in Simla he had complained that we had associated ourselves with the Congress. I had said to him that we had come to you (the Muslim League), but you had not assisted us, and we were confronted with a big problem, and so we then approached the Congress. That even if now, Punjab were to ally itself with us, I would have resigned from the Congress. He had then told me that they would confer amongst themselves and then give me an answer.

Most of the Muslim residents of Patna had fled their homes and were living in camps, leaving their valuables buried in their homes. They wanted someone to go with them and assist them in retrieving these valuables. But the Muslim League could not, out of fear, leave the city. When they were disappointed with the Muslim League, they asked me if I would accompany them. I told them that I had come to Bihar to be of service to them and, wherever they wished, I would go with them. So, I would transport some of them each day to their homes, in my own car, to retrieve their buried valuables. The Hindus would glare at them but say nothing, out of respect for me. I went to them in their camps and told them that the monsoon was about to break and that they should come so that I could resettle them, but they paid no heed to my advice, because the Muslim League had promised to take them to Bengal. But when they experienced the sufferings and difficulties on their way to Bengal, they approached me. I went to the government of Bihar and since all the ministers had remained confined with me in the Hazaribagh jail, they quickly arranged for them to be rehabilitated. When I informed Gandhiji of this development, he cut short his Noakhali tour and came to Bihar to help resettle the Muslim residents. With his arrival the momentum of our work also increased. When we saw Gandhiji, our strength, courage and resolve were renewed. Like him, we also toured the affected areas and, let alone the men, the women also knew that we had come out to serve them and were no longer afraid. This had a very positive effect on the people, because here in Patna the position was that the Muslim League leaders, out of fear, could not even move about in the city. A nation that has strong and brave leaders becomes strong and brave, and a nation that has cowardly leaders, becomes cowardly. I was also told something by Pyarelal; that Sardar Patel was opposed to my touring Bihar, but that Gandhiji had told him that this did not concern him and was uncalled for.

Mridula behan [Mridula Sarabhai] was also accompanying Gandhiji and, at the time, was also his secretary. She, too, had a lot of sympathy for the Muslims. She would take them to Gandhiji and they would recount to him all the difficulties and troubles they were confronted with. The elders of the Congress did not like this and they were making efforts that she should leave Gandhiji. She came to me and told me what was happening and said that they wanted to separate her from us. I reassured her and asked her not to worry, as nobody would succeed in separating her from Gandhiji. I went and informed Gandhiji and she stayed on.

I was in Bihar to help rehabilitate the uprooted Biharis and was staying on for this purpose. But when the riots started in Punjab, I got worried. Gandhiji informed me that he would look after the rehabilitation work and that I should return to the Frontier. In the Frontier Province, because of the *Khudai Khidmatgar* movement, the relationship between the Muslims, Hindus, and Sikhs was amiable. In fact, they were all like brothers. This movement was a movement for service to God's creation and humanity. This movement had created such feelings of love, brotherhood and unity in the Muslims, Hindus and Sikhs, that there was no example like it, in the past. This movement was village–based. Its centre was also in the village, because most of the nation lives in the villages. The difference between this and other movements was that the other movements originated in the cities and spread out into the villages, but this movement originated in the villages and then spread to the cities. History has shown that movements originating in the cities have come to an end at the hands of the rulers, but village-based movements cannot be ended easily, like our *Khudai Khidmatgar* movement which, despite all the troubles and oppression that it was subjected to by the government, has remained unaffected and is intact.

To cope with the riots which took place in Bihar, Muslim League *razakar* from our province went to Bihar. They had not gone to do service; they had gone to increase the hatred between Hindus and Muslims. When they were returning from Bihar, they brought many human bones back with them, which they carried from village to village in the Frontier and carried out a virulent propaganda campaign against us. By doing this, they intended to light the fires of hatred among the Muslims, Hindus and Sikhs. But they were not able to do so and met with failure, because here, on account of the *Khudai Khidmatgar* movement, the roots of enmity had been removed.

When Lord Mountbatten announced the Partition plan and that a referendum would be held in the Frontier, this had a very bad effect on our province and riots started here as well. The Muslim Leaguers began slaughtering innocent people in the bazaars, streets and lanes of Peshawar city. The bazaars of Peshawar city were shut down. The Hindus and Sikhs remained locked up in their homes. Even in their homes, their lives, honour and wealth were not safe.

When we realized that the government officers were not willing to extend any kind of assistance to us, but were in fact doing their best to give our government a bad name; that although we were in government and the officers were not prepared to listen to us, we decided and ordered Amin Jan, *Salar-e-Azam*, to send ten thousand uniformed *Khudai Khidmatgar* to Peshawar. As soon as these orders were received, ten thousand *Khudai Khidmatgars* arrived in Peshawar and, immediately on arrival, they allowed the Hindus and Sikhs to come out of their houses. They opened their shops and restarted their businesses. The *Khudai Khidmatgar* were posted as guards at their shops to prevent the Muslims Leaguers from doing any mischief. The lives, honour and properties of the Hindus and Sikhs were thus secured. Similarly, in the entire province, wherever there were *Khudai Khidmatgar*, the lives, honour and properties of the Hindus and Sikhs were secured. Amongst them there were also some Anglophile Hindus who would dance to the tune of the British and the Muslim Leaguers. They demanded that the government of the *Khudai Khidmatgar* should be removed and governor's rule be proclaimed in the province. They understood little as to who was behind this entire game. All this had been manipulated by the governor himself. But then a deal was made between Lord Louis Mountbatten and the Congress leaders to the effect that he would arrange to have Bengal and Punjab divided and that the Congress should agree to hold a referendum in the Frontier Province. Following this, on 3 June 1947 the announcement of the Partition was made, and it was also announced that in the Frontier Province the people would be asked whether they wanted to join Hindustan or Pakistan. Just look at the injustice and cruelty of the British: Punjab was being partitioned, Bengal was being partitioned, and there the opinion of the population was not being solicited through a referendum, and here, in our province, no one bothered to put the question to a popularly elected provincial assembly. The truth of the matter is that in our province an election had been held a few months ago over the issue of Hindustan and Pakistan and the people had expressed their will. What was the need to do so again? If the leaders of the Congress had not been unfaithful to us and had not agreed to the partition of Hindustan, then in the Frontier Province the Hindus, Muslims and Sikhs would not have suffered so much in terms of loss of life, property and honour.

At this time, many Muslim Leaguers were arrested by the government and were thrown into prison. They were not used to being in jail. Their incarceration was neither imprisonment nor jails. For them it was like going to a restaurant. It was a strange game. At night, they would go home; during the day, they would roam in the bazaars. They would meet with friends and relatives. The reason for all this was that the governor was not cooperating with our government and was bitterly opposed to us.

When they were released from jail and came to Delhi, I was also there. There, I met with them and told Samin Jan Khan, 'Oh young man! This Pakistan that you are making, at least give some thought to the question of how the Pukhtuns will fare in this land. The majority is that of Punjab and so the authority will also be of Punjab.' He replied that they were bent on making it now, but if they found that it was not in their interest then they would undo it! It is a great pity that Samin Jan Khan is no longer around otherwise I would have asked him to come and see the position of the Pukhtuns in Pakistan today.

The Partition Declaration

Lord Mountbatten returned to Delhi on 30 May 1947, and on 3 June, based on the approval of the British government, announced the plan for the partition of Hindustan. With the announcement of this plan all hopes of Hindustan remaining united were dashed. In approving the plan of Partition so quickly, the British government kept their own, rather than the interests of Hindustan, uppermost in their minds, because the British government would have influence over such a government in which the power was in the hands of the Muslim League.

The Session of the Working Committee

On 3 June 1947, a meeting of the Congress working committee was held. Sardar Patel and Rajagopalachari were, from the start, in favour of the partition of Hindustan and against the Cabinet Mission plan. But when, in the meeting, Gandhiji also opted for partition, we were all left surprised. The other question was that of the referendum in the Frontier. This question, too, was included in Lord Mountbatten's Partition plan. This question was hotly debated at length and reasons were put forward. Here Sardar Patel and Rajagopalachari also put great pressure on the working committee members, and finally it agreed to this as well. And thus, both the partition of Hindustan and the holding of a referendum in the Frontier Province were endorsed by the working committee.

I was amazed at this, and said to myself that if they had already decided these matters, then why were they holding discussions and meetings with me on them?

At this time, I put forth an appeal to the working committee and told them that we had always sided with the Congress and extended a helping hand to them, and now the Congress was abandoning us and not helping us. This would have a very adverse effect on the Frontier Province. If the Congress were to leave the *Khudai Khidmatgar* to the wolves, this would be tantamount to a betrayal of the province. Gandhiji took this appeal to heart and said that he would speak with Mountbatten on this issue. The next day on 11 June, Gandhiji and I went to meet Mountbatten and discussed the matter with him. He considered the presence of Jinnah sahib as essential for this. When Jinnah sahib, Gandhiji and I got together on this, Jinnah sahib said that, 'He is my Muslim brother and I will talk to him in private.' So, I told Gandhiji that since he preferred this, then if he permitted, I would talk to him alone. He agreed. Jinnah sahib told me that he would grant us provincial autonomy, but no action was taken on this. I did not know until then that all decisions between Mountbatten, the Congress and the Muslim League had already been taken. It was only when I read Maulana Azad's book, *India Wins Freedom*, that I found out the truth. So, I asked myself how could action have been taken on it because these matters had already been decided, and Lord Mountbatten had already bargained away our province, so how could he have accepted Gandhiji's demand and how could Jinnah sahib have accepted mine? Yes, the possibility was there that, if before these decisions were taken Gandhiji had broached this issue with Mountbatten, its acceptance would have been possible.

On this matter, Maulana sahib has recorded in his book that:

'To discuss these matters a meeting of the Congress working committee was called on 3 June 1947. Before everything else, the future of the Frontier was discussed. The Mountbatten Plan had placed the Frontier in a very tight spot. Abdul Ghaffar Khan and his party had always supported the Congress and had opposed the League. The Muslim League considered them as their arch enemies. In the presence of the bitter opposition of the Muslim League, they had managed to form a Congress government in the province, and this government was even now in power. Because of Partition, the

Congress, and the *Khudai Khidmatgar,* were both confronted with the same problem and difficulty. In reality, the meaning of Partition was that they and their party, the *Khudai Khidmatgar,* would be left at the mercy of the Muslim League. We realized and understood full well the effect that this decision regarding Partition would have on Abdul Ghaffar Khan. It appeared as if at this time they had taken leave of their senses; but not a word came from his lips. Then they appealed to the working committee and reminded them that they had always sided with the Congress, and if the Congress were now to leave them to fend for themselves, this would have a very adverse effect on the Frontier Province. Their enemies would make fun of them, and their friends would remark that until the Congress stood in need of them, they supported the *Khudai Khidmatgar;* but when the need for reconciliation with the Muslim League arose, then they did not even bother to consult them and their leaders, and no longer opposed the partitioning of Hindustan. Khan Abdul Ghaffar repeated this a number of times, that if the Congress were to throw the *Khudai Khidmatgar* to the wolves, this would be tantamount to the betrayal of the Frontier Province.'

After that meeting of the working committee, we returned to our province. We told the government that since the Congress had agreed to the partition of Hindustan, in these circumstances, there was no need for a referendum to be held in the province; because this would create an atmosphere of feuding and kinship-rivalry among the people. Since the viceroy did not concede to our demand, we again called a meeting of our provincial *jirga* and placed these political developments and differences of opinion before it. The *jirga* decided that if the government was determined on holding a referendum here, then it was necessary that the Pukhtuns should be given their right of full self-determination and, in addition to the option of Hindustan and Pakistan, they should have the option to vote for an independent and free State of Pukhtunistan.

But when the British refused to concede to this demand and did not include the option for an independent Pukhtunistan in the referendum, the *jirga* decided that since the Congress had accepted the partition of Hindustan, there was no need to hold a referendum here. And if the government was determined on holding a referendum, we would boycott it.

The Intrigue of the Congress and Mountbatten

The truth was that this momentous event took place and it was planned to take place, because arrangements had been made for it, a long time ago. When Mountbatten had, before the announcement of the Partition plan, come on a tour of the Frontier Province, section 144 had been imposed in the province and the holding of *jalsa* was prohibited. The governor of the Province Sir Olaf Caroe was a bitter opponent of ours and was a great supporter of the Muslim League. To pressurize Mountbatten, he had, through his political agents, assembled, through the maliks, a large crowed of tribesmen who provided a big spectacle for Lord Mountbatten. At the time of Lord Mountbatten's departure, he told him, 'These Pukhtuns need to be taught such a lesson, that even their children would remember. Because in Hindustan there were ten crore Muslims who did not oppose us, and these people allied themselves with Congress in opposing us.' Lord Mountbatten took all this to heart and flew back to Delhi. In Delhi, Sardar Patel was demanding the division of Hindustan; and he (Mountbatten) wanted to punish the Pukhtuns and hand them over to the Muslim League. They both agreed that Congress wanted Bengal and Punjab should be divided and Mountbatten wanted a referendum should be held in the Frontier. Lord Mountbatten accepted their demand and agreed to their division of Punjab and Bengal; but as a quid pro quo for this, said that they should accept the holding of a referendum in the Frontier. So, Congress accepted this demand and Mountbatten had Punjab and Bengal partitioned. They both bargained at our expense. We, the *Khudai Khidmatgar,* had tried our best to bridge the differences between the Muslims and Hindus; and no matter where I was in Hindustan, I tried my utmost to attain this objective to create affection and unity between the Muslims and Hindus; and to remove hatred and enmity from them. I managed to achieve this to a great extent. But, after Partition, you see for yourself the conditions we are confronted with. Whatever we had managed to achieve, it has all been allowed to be swept away by the flood. In Pakistan, what brutality the Hindus and Sikhs had to bear; and in Hindustan what are the Muslims going through? Such a lot of hatred and enmity has been generated, that all hopes of reconciliation have been dashed, giving birth to many problems.

The Infidelity of the Congress

The Congress had been waging the struggle for the liberation of Hindustan for the past sixty years, but the British, let alone total independence, had not even granted them limited freedom. But when the Pukhtuns joined them in this struggle and gave sacrifices in Qissa Khwani, Takar, Uthmanzai, Kohat, Hathikhel, and Mirwais; and in similar fashion our tribal brothers allied themselves with the Pukhtuns and waged a jihad for the liberation of Hindustan, and bared their chests as shields to the guns and tanks of the British and stood firm like a mountain before their onslaughts, only then were the British compelled to agree to the independence of Hindustan. We had allied with the Congress in the struggle for freedom on the condition that we would jointly liberate the country and free ourselves of the yoke of slavery. But when the time came, all the promises made to us were discarded, and nobody asked us about our future. Instead, the referendum about opting to join Pakistan or Hindustan was forced down our throats; and we were treated as pawns and bargained away in this deal. The sacrifices were given by us, our blood was shed, our properties and wealth were ruined-and the benefits went to others. The leaders of the Congress would consult me on all issues and would not do anything without having first consulted me. But on this all-important matter, let alone consulting with me, I was not even informed. I am annoyed over the fact that even the Congress working committee showed no sympathy or extended any help to us. They tied us by the feet and hands and handed us over to the Muslim League. We had defeated the Muslim League in the elections, then what was the need for another election? If someone wanted to contest the referendum with us, then they should have, on our demand, done so on the issue of Pakistan or Pukhtunistan. This referendum was over Hindustan and Pakistan, and we, on account of the betrayal by the Congress, were not opting for Hindustan. That is why we did not wish to participate in this referendum and decided to boycott it.

The British used to tell us to leave our association with the Congress, so that when they would give anything to Hindustan, they would give us more than that. But we did not abandon the Congress, they abandoned us. The more unfortunate thing is, what have we done to them, and what have they done to us? I have no complaint against Sardar Patel and Rajagopalachari. I have a complaint against

Jawaharlal and Gandhiji; that they too agreed with them in this matter. The Congress leaders said that the conditions were such that there was no other way, other than Partition. But who created these conditions? They themselves are responsible for them. If they had not partitioned Hindustan, then Hindustan and the Hindus would not have experienced such bloodshed. Whatever happened, has happened, and, in the words of Maulana Azad, 'Whatever I have seen was no more than a dream.' But I am of the view that this was a grand intrigue; this was disloyalty; this was a betrayal to which we were subjected.

In our land, there are certain people who, on the instigation of our ill-wishers, ask what have the *Khudai Khidmatgar* done? And they also ask what has non-violence been able to accomplish? And if a few of our people, who in their simplicity are taken up by what these few selfish people say, I must remind them that the *Khudai Khidmatgar* had two objectives; one, to liberate the country and the other to spread love, brotherhood, nationalism and unity among the Pukhtuns.

Just have a look at this – awareness has been created, and the country also has been liberated. Then consider that all this has been achieved through non-violence. There has been no violence. Also consider that the *Khudai Khidmatgar* have created in the people, in the hearts of the Muslims, the Sikhs and the Hindus, such love and affection for each other, and awakened such brotherhood in the minds of the people, that up to now, those Hindus and Sikhs, who had been forcibly driven out of the Frontier Province, still refer to themselves as *Khudai Khidmatgar*. Whenever I have visited Hindustan, I have felt the same love and affection in the hearts of the Hindus and Sikhs. When, at the time of Partition, violence and riots broke out in Hindustan, the *Khudai Khidmatgar*, for the protection of the lives and properties of the Sikhs and Hindus, had to face a lot of troubles and difficulties. And wherever the *Khudai Khidmatgar* were, they had managed to save them from harm's way, and had saved their lives and property. On the other hand, see what the Congress did; it created so much hatred in the hearts of the Hindus and Muslims of Hindustan, and see how much violence they resorted to. But the fact is that non-violence was their policy and it was our ideology and still is. We had been liberated and the British were about to leave our land, but on the instigation of Lord

Mountbatten and Sardar Patel, we became the slaves of slaves. I am not saddened by this fact so much, because if the Pukhtuns, in fact, become Pukhtuns, then nobody can in fact enslave them. But I am saddened that the movement of the *Khudai Khidmatgar,* which had been created with such effort, difficulty and trials, has been destroyed and its tried and tested structure has almost been demolished.

De zlra pe bagh may gallai wushwa,
Boya chay biya sparlay rashee wuspalree Guloona!

The hail has struck my heart's garden,
Denuded it of flowers;
Ah! If only spring would come,
and make the blossoms bloom again!

Abdul Ghaffar
13 July 1981

20

Dear Readers

THIS WAS THE STRUGGLE OF MY LIFE. I HAVE WRITTEN THIS BOOK AT A time when I am separated from those companions who were with me during those momentous events of my life, and who knew a great deal about them. I repeatedly tried that they should assist me in this effort, but I have not been successful in this. In this connection, there were many manuscripts which my companions and I had written, but these have all either been destroyed or, if they exist with someone, I have not been able to access them. I have now grown old and my memory is not what it was. Many names and incidents have escaped it, and that is why I am conscious of the fact that this book may have several shortcomings. I am also aware, that when you read this book, then at some places, some details, some recollection of events, some personalities worth a mention, and some names, would be recalled by you. Kindly take out time and make a note of these in the appropriate places, and then convey them quickly to me, because I wish to bring out a second edition so that all the deficiencies are made up, you are satisfied, my duty is adequately discharged, and history is faithfully recorded.

Remembrance

I had no desire to write my autobiography, because I prefer practical work and action over speaking and writing. But Ajmal Khattak, Fazlur-Rahim Saqi, Abdullah Khidmatgar Bakhtani, Sadeequllah Rikhteen and Faqir Muhammad Baizai have repeatedly requested me that this is an important task, and that I should write it. So, based on their memories that were with me, and on my own, I have written this autobiography.

During the time of writing, composing and publishing it, these people I have mentioned helped me a great deal. I am very grateful to them and pray that they should, in future, be of assistance to their people and their land.

Abdul Ghaffar
13 July 1981

Epilogue
Bacha Khan's Life after Partition (1947) till his Death, 20 January 1988

IT COULD BE SAID THAT, WITH THE CREATION OF PAKISTAN AND HIS pledging of allegiance on 23 February 1948 to the new state in the first meeting of the constituent assembly of Pakistan, which was attended by Abdul Ghaffar Khan in the presence of Muhammad Ali Jinnah, Bacha Khan would have attenuated the animosity of his sworn opponent and erstwhile companion in the *Khudai Khidmatgar* movement, Barrister Abdul Qayyum Khan. Qayyum Khan of the Muslim League had been entrusted the reins of government in the North-West Frontier Province, as chief minister. This had come about because of the dismissal of the *Khudai Khidmatgar* government, led by Dr. Khan Sahib, in April 1948. But, unfortunately, this was not to be. Bacha Khan, and his two older sons, Ghani and Wali, and the other prominent leaders of the movement continued to be hounded from pillar to post by Qayyum Khan. They were imprisoned under Section 40 of the Frontier Crimes Regulation, 1901, and harassed in every other manner. On 12 August 1948, an unarmed, peaceful assembly of men, women and children of the *Khudai Khidmatgar* was mowed down by the police and the Frontier Constabulary at Babara, Charsadda, at the instigation of Qayyum Khan, and the direct orders of Gul Muhammad Chajjar, the assistant commissioner of Charsadda. By some accounts, more than 600 followers of Bacha Khan were massacred. This all but broke the back of the movement and decimated its dedicated cadres.

Such was the animosity of the chief minister with his erstwhile leader, that the desire of Muhammad Ali Jinnah to mend fences with him and ask him to assume the leadership of a programme of economic development to ameliorate the lot of the rural poor, was thwarted by Qayyum Khan who painted a dismal picture of the imminence of Pukhtunistan, if Bacha Khan were to be politically accommodated in any way. Initial overtures made to Bacha Khan by Mr. Jinnah in Karachi, soon after the oath-taking ceremony, could not be followed up by the proposed meeting with him at the *Khudai Khidmatgar* headquarters in Sardaryab, due to the role played by Qayyum Khan, who warned Jinnah that Bacha Khan was plotting his assassination. He was consequently arrested in 1948 and remained under detention until 1954. He was released in 1954 and then, on account of opposition to the One Unit, was imprisoned again and remained so until 1957. He was released for a short while in 1957 only to be detained again in 1958.

It was not before the removal of Qayyum Khan from the political scene of the Frontier in 1954, that Abdul Ghaffar Khan could come to his home province by the government of Sardar Abdur Rashid, the chief minister. This came about in a session of the constituent assembly of Pakistan in Murree when, in reply to a question by Jogindarnath Mandal, a Hindu member from East Pakistan, the central government asserted that it had no objection to his release, but that he was being detained by the provincial government. On this, Sardar Abdur Rashid rose in his seat and proclaimed, in unequivocal terms that he had absolutely no objection to his being released. Bacha Khan was received triumphantly at the Attock Bridge and brought to Peshawar in a historic procession which took many hours to arrive at its destination. His sons and other *Khudai Khidmatgar* were also released under the orders of the chief minister. But even so, the historic opportunity of reconciliation and the possibility of a turn in the political development of the province, in accordance with the desire of the Quaid-e-Azam, was irretrievably lost.

The *Khudai Khidmatgar* continued to be hounded until 1955, when the provinces of Sindh, NWFP, and Balochistan, were abolished and merged into one province (One Unit) of West Pakistan. Under this arrangement both East and West Pakistan attained parity in representation in the Central Assembly. The western wing of the country now got one instead of four provincial assemblies. In 1955, Dr. Khan Sahib was inducted into the recently formed Republican Party and appointed as chief minister, West Pakistan. The pressure on the *Khudai Khidmatgar* eased, therefore. However, in 1958, while in office, Dr. Khan Sahib was assassinated by a disgruntled *patwari* and the repression was renewed as the *Khudai Khidmatgar* mounted a strong opposition to the One Unit and pressed for the restoration of the former provinces.

In September 1956 Bacha Khan was arrested from his home in Shahibagh and brought to trial in the West Pakistan High Court in Lahore before Justice Shabbir Ahmad. In January 1957, he was sentenced to rigorous imprisonment and a fine. He was set free in 1957. Along with Maulana Bhashani, G.M. *Syed* and *Mian* Iftikharuddin, he formed the National Awami Party in July the same year. In 1957, General Iskander Mirza, the minister of defence, manipulated his election as the President of Pakistan. Between 1955 and 1958 there was a rapid succession of governments at the centre until President Iskander Mirza, with the support of General Ayub Khan, C-n-C of the Pakistan army, imposed martial law in the country and abrogated the constitution of 1956. After a few days of dyarchy, Iskander Mirza was eased out as president and sent to the United Kingdom on forced retirement with his second wife Naheed. General Ayub Khan became both the president and chief martial law administrator. He promulgated a new constitution in 1962, which was a presidential form of government, based on indirect election, by an electoral college of basic democrats. This was a system under which both wings of Pakistan came to be organized into an equal number of union councils consisting of groups of villages which elected representatives to the union councils, based on universal adult franchise. The union councilors thrown up by this election formed an electoral college for the election of the president and members of the national and provincial assemblies. Political parties were banned, and many leaders disqualified from contesting elections under the Elective Bodies (Disqualification) Order. Most of the leaders were imprisoned. The *Khudai Khidmatgar* were bitterly opposed to this system of government and started a vigorous agitation against it. In 1965 elections under the Constitution of 1962 were held. Miss Fatima Jinnah was the joint candidate of the combined opposition parties, which Wali Khan played a prominent role in organizing and promoting. The opposition lost the election but the campaign infuriated Ayub Khan to no end.

In 1962, Bacha Khan was declared Amnesty International's Prisoner of the Year. In 1964, he was allowed to proceed to the United Kingdom for treatment, where he was advised to go to the United States. He, however, voluntarily went into self-exile in Afghanistan. From here he went on a short visit, in 1967, to India where he was received by Indira Gandhi, the prime minister. A contribution of 8,700,000 rupees was made by the common people of India to his work. On return he constituted an educational trust with the money.

From Afghanistan, he returned to the Frontier in December 1972, to a massive popular response, following the setting up of the National Awami Party Government in the Province. In 1984, he visited India again and participated in the centennial celebrations of the All-India National Congress. In 1985, he was awarded the Jawaharlal Nehru Award for International Understanding. Later, in 1987, he was awarded the Bharat Ratna, India's highest civil award. In 1984 he was also nominated for the Nobel Peace Prize.

In 1969, the Pakistan National Alliance forced Ayub Khan to resign. He now handed over power to Agha Muhammad Yahya Khan, the commander-in-chief of the army who immediately imposed martial law and abrogated the constitution of 1962. He dissolved the One Unit, and integrated the princely states of Dir, Swat, Chitral and Bahawalpur and set a date for country-wide elections based on universal adult franchise. In 1971, Zulfiqar Ali Bhutto and his People's Party came to power in the Western wing of the country, while the province of East Pakistan seceded and formed a separate country, Bangladesh, under the leadership of Mujib-ur-Rahman and his Awami League. After the election, the Jamiat-e-Ulama-e-Islam, led by Maulana Mufti Mahmood, in association with the National Awami Party of Abdul Wali Khan, which was the successor political party of the *Khudai Khidmatgar,* assumed power in the North-West Frontier Province. In 1973 this Government resigned in sympathy with Balochistan, where the government was dismissed by Prime Minister Zulfiqar Ali Bhutto. Bacha Khan and his associates went back into the all-too familiar mode of opposition to the government and his detention for sustained periods, in government rest houses, resumed. On 23 March 1973, the notorious Federal Security Force attacked an opposition rally of the Awami National Party, led by Abdul Wali

Khan, in Liaqat Bagh, Rawalpindi, killing dozens of workers. Wali Khan narrowly escaped as the bullet meant for him killed a party worker standing next to him. Ajmal Khattak, a prominent leader of the party, and some others, fled to Kabul where they remained until 1986.

In 1975, a cache of arms was unearthed in Quetta and it was alleged by the government that this was provided by the Embassy of Iraq and was meant for the creation of a greater Balochistan and Pukhtunistan. The National Awami Party was banned on 10 February 1975, and the Hyderabad Tribunal (1975–79) tried the leaders of the defunct party for treason and acting against the ideology of Pakistan. On 2 April 1975, a case was registered against Bacha Khan and he was detained and sent to Khanpur Rest House but was set free in August 1976. A case of treason was brought against Abdul Wali Khan and some other party leaders and they were imprisoned in Hyderabad jail. Riots broke out on a large scale in Lahore and the army was called in. However, the brigadier commanding the local brigade refused to comply with the order to resort to firing. When Bhutto and his Peoples Party won the elections for the second time in 1977, the opposition cried foul and alleged massive rigging. A combined opposition soon took shape around Nawabzada Nasrullah Khan in the shape of the Pakistan National Alliance. The Awami National Party was in the forefront of this alliance.

Negotiations were held between the government of Zulfiqar Ali Bhutto and the Pakistan National Alliance on how to resolve the political crisis. Substantial head way was made, and a major decision seemed to have been taken when, in July 1977, General Muhammad Zia-ul-Haq clamped martial law on the nation and Wali Khan and his associates were set free, in a rare gesture of good will by him.

Between 1978 and 1982 Bacha Khan remained in Kabul and visited India several times. On 28 April 1982, he returned to Pakistan.

Nawab Muhammad Raza Khan Qasuri's son, Ahmad Raza Khan Qasuri, who was a member of the National Assembly, frequently embarrassed Bhutto in the assembly by asking awkward questions which infuriated him. He directed Masood Mahmood, the Director-General of the infamous Federal Security Force, to do away with Ahmad Raza Khan. A trap was consequently laid for him but, unfortunately, his father was killed in the encounter. A murder case was registered against Bhutto by Ahmad Raza Khan and he was convicted by the Lahore High Court. This was upheld by the Supreme Court and Bhutto was hanged in Rawalpindi jail on 4 April 1979.

Bacha Khan continued to struggle for the rights of his people. Touring the Frontier in his vehicle, accompanied by a lone companion besides the driver, he was single-handedly successful in galvanizing public opinion against the construction of the Kalabagh Dam, resulting in a decision by the government that this could only be constructed following a consensus of all the provinces. Kalabagh is a narrow gorge through which the waters of the Abaseend and the Kabul river flow, below their confluence at Attock. A hydro-electric dam had been planned here. However, it was feared that, in addition to the bridges on the Indus river at Attock and Khushal Garh, the towns of Nowshera, Akora Khattak and Shaidu, and the Grand Trunk road from Attock to Nowshera, would also be submerged. Kalabagh remains a bone of contention in Pakistan, till today.

Bacha Khan fell seriously ill in May 1987 and was taken to New Delhi. While in hospital there, he suffered a stroke, and went into coma. He was flown back to Peshawar in August and was taken to the Lady Reading Hospital, Peshawar. He remained in coma from August 1987 till his death on 20 January 1988, at the ripe old age of 98 years. Rajiv Gandhi, then prime minister of India, flew to Peshawar to attend his funeral prayers. He was buried in Jalalabad, Afghanistan, where warring factions declared a truce for his funeral and hundreds of Pakistanis crossed the Torkham border, to pray for their great leader.

Ghani Khan, his eldest son, referred to him as 'The first Pathan I knew, and the greatest I have known!' In the words of William Shakespeare, while referring to Brutus in his play *Julius Caesar*, he pays the following compliment to Brutus:

> His life was gentle, and the elements so mixed in him,
> That nature might stand up and say to all the world,
> 'This was a man!'

Bacha Khan's Achievements – An Assessment

After more than sixty-five years of relentless struggle it can well be asked what the achievements of Bacha Khan and his determined *Khudai Khidmatgar* have been and what, if any, has been their legacy for the Pukhtuns.

The achievements of Bacha Khan and his party can be categorized under three main headings: as a social reformer, as a promoter of education, and, finally, as a political leader. His role as a social reformer was concerned with bringing about a transformation in the social stratification of Pukhtun society which, over the centuries, had developed a structure no less rigid than the caste system of the Hindus of the subcontinent. The social stratification system was anchored in the division of Pukhtun society into the agrarian land-owning class and the various other classes meant to serve the needs of an essentially agrarian society. As the Pukhtun tribes emigrated south from Afghanistan about six hundred years ago, into what is now Khyber Pakhtunkhwa, they came to hold the tracts of land they presently have, through a great tribal distribution. Within each tribe the land was further distributed fairly based on the numerical strength of each clan. Soon, status came to be conferred based on land owned. In addition to the main land-owning class of Pukhtuns, some land was owned by the spiritual aristocracy such as the *miangan, sahibzadgan, piran, syedan, akhunzadgan* and *qazian.*

Bacha Khan instilled a measure of dignity and pride in the *kasabgers* (agriculture related working classes) by allowing them to join the *Khudai Khidmatgar* and by giving them leadership roles based on merit. In fact, the most dedicated cadres of the *Khudai Khidmatgar* consisted of people from this caste. The highly reprehensible practice of the *kasabgars* having to sit on their haunches when interacting with the khans in the *hujras,* while the latter sat comfortably on beds, was done away with. It was largely owing to the efforts of Bacha Khan that caste distinctions were attenuated, if not totally removed, and the levelling process of society was consciously started in a new interpretation of the concept of Pukhtun and 'Pukhto'.

Bacha Khan's struggle of social transformation of the Pukhtuns also included the emancipation and empowerment of women in all fields. He insisted that women should be given the rights which Islam has conferred on them and hence believed passionately in their right to inheritance of property. He also worked hard to bring them into the field of politics by associating them with his *Khudai*

Khidmatgar movement. His *jalsa* were attended by women and they were also involved in his campaign of spinning cotton-yarn on the *sarkha*, or spinning wheel, for the making of local *khaamta*. They served as the backbone of the movement by ensuring that their men did not abjure their oath of loyalty to the movement. He wrote a pamphlet in Pukhto, 'The Empowerment of Women in Islam'. This pamphlet dealt with the status of women in Islam and the usual question regarding the testimony of women. In this context, he has discussed all the nine verses of the Holy *Quran*, instead of just the one verse selectively quoted in this matter, which equates the testimony of two women with that of one man. He was supportive of the education of girls and had his own daughter, Mehr Taj, educated in the best of institutions available.

As a promoter of education, Bacha Khan was conscious of the need for educating the Pukhtuns since his adolescent years. However, he could only give concrete shape to this after he formed the *Anjuman-e-Islah-ul-Afaghina*. Under its auspices, the first thing that he did was to establish the Azad School in his native village, Uthmanzai. After this successful experiment, he went on to establish other schools on its pattern, as voluntary welfare institutions, not only in Charsadda but also in the other districts of the Frontier Province to which his *Khudai Khidmatgar* movement spread. The government of the day actively discouraged this activity and put hurdles in his way for recruiting teachers. He was not able to make much headway in this field, because of the impediments for which the government was responsible, and then due to the closure of the schools already established. In subsequent years, when the *Khudai Khidmatgar* party formed governments in the province, he gave priority to education in budget allocations of the province. Passionately fond of education as he was, it was his singular misfortune that the circumstances of his life denied him the opportunity to take his own education to its logical conclusion. What turn his life would have taken had he done so, though interesting, is a matter of pure conjecture and speculation. His innate political tendencies, however, were so powerful that it can be safely assumed that the course of his life would not have been much different. He, however, would have been much better equipped intellectually to cope with the many problems he encountered along the way.

What then were his achievements in the political field? He was both a success and a failure. He was a success in as much as his *Khudai Khidmatgar* party attained political power twice in the Frontier Province, before Partition. He was a failure, in as much as he and the *Khudai Khidmatgar* had set out to free India from the yoke of British subjugation as one integrated entity, which did not happen. Though he and the *Khudai Khidmatgar*, in alliance with the Congress Party, freed India from British rule, they were only partially successful in attaining their goal. Success came about only with the Partition of India. This saddened him a great deal. He can, however, not be blamed for this, as it was essentially Mahatma Gandhi, Jawaharlal Nehru and Vallabhbhai Patel of the Congress Party, who, despite Bacha Khan's strong and consistent opposition, agreed to Lord Mountbatten's plan of partition. The communal riots which followed Independence were a negation of his passionately held principle of non-violence, which caused him unimaginable grief.

He was as fond of his mother tongue, Pukhto, as he was of anything in his life and chose it as the medium of expression in his writings. He firmly believed that it is only with the development of the mother tongue that people can prosper, and it is this which gives one pride in one's origins and identity. To promote it he founded the *Pukhtun* magazine. This became the mouth-piece of the *Khudai Khidmatgar* movement and contained both prose and poetry, principally from the pen of his eldest son, Abdul Ghani Khan, under the pen name of *lewanay falsafi*, or the 'mad philosopher.' He, in time, became one of the most acknowledged poets of Pukhto and established new trends and genres in Pukhto poetry.

Another achievement of Bacha Khan was to persuade Amanullah Khan, the ruler of Afghanistan, to declare Pukhto as the national language of Afghanistan, over Dari, at the time. The holding of national *mushairas*, or poetry recitation sessions, in which the *tarha misra*, or opening verse, was indicated to the poets, was another significant contribution of his. They were required to compose their poems around this. The *tarha misra* was indicative of nationalist and patriotic themes. These *mushairas* gave a much-needed fillip to Pukhto and encouraged several budding poets. Pride in racial origin, culture and language is one of his enduring legacies to the Pukhtuns.

As to his legacy for the Pukhtuns in the field of politics, this was most definitely the inculcation of political consciousness in the common Pukhtun woman and man. His other more palpable success has been the enduring existence of his political party, the *Khudai Khidmatgar* which, under successive changes of name as the National Awami Party and the Awami National Party, under his leadership and then of his son, Abdul Wali Khan, his daughter-in-law, Begum Naseem Wali Khan, and his grandson, Asfandyar Wali Khan, has endured and attained political power, as a partner, in both federal and provincial governments, a number of times. To this day it continues to be a major political force with many political achievements to its credit, not the least of which is the re-naming of the province as Khyber-Pakhtunkhwa.

Love for humanity, irrespective of caste, creed or colour, religious tolerance and appreciation of a pluralistic society, peace and peaceful co-existence, and a non-violent approach to resolve conflicts and problems, was the philosophy of Bacha Khan. This, he religiously pursued throughout his long and meaningful life. The present chaotic times need another man cast in the mould of Bacha Khan, and willing to take up the challenge, to bring peace to this troubled region on both sides of the Durand Line.

His enduring legacy for the Pukhtuns can be summed up most effectively by these verses from an anonymous Pukhtun bard:

De Pukhtano de mulk bay takhta, bay qalanga Bacha;
De har Pukhtun de zlra pe takht nasta Malanga Bacha;
Qam ta pesay lakka Laila pesay Majnun razee –
Har kalla rasha!

Oh, King of the Pukhtuns, but, without a throne, or tribute paid;
Upon the throne of every Pukhtun's heart, Is seated King of all Pukhtuns –
The Prince of mendicants and saints! Your people love you like Majnun, Laila, ever welcome in our hearths and homes!

Notes

1. Her name was Shama. She was married to Attaullah Khan of Uthmanzai and was the mother of Sultan Muhammad Khan (1900–1975), who was the biggest landowner of his village and also a *lambardar*. He was survived by three sons – Aslam Khan, Bahadur Khan and Jehangir Khan.

2. Khurshid Bibi was married to Burhan Khan of Razar village and was the mother of Jehanzeb Niaz (1927–2015), who was jailed for some time along with Ghani Khan and other *Khudai Khidmatgars* and was the youngest member of the group, which has been immortalized in Ghani Khan's famous poem on his companions in jail.

3. Qazi Attaullah (1895–1962) was a trusted and intimate lieutenant of Bacha Khan. He was a prominent member of the *Khudai Khidmatgar,* and later of the All-India Congress Party. He belonged to Landi Arbab, village on the outskirts of Peshawar. He was educated at the Mission High School, Peshawar, and struck up an association with Bacha Khan there. This friendship resulted in his joining the *Anjuman-e-Islahh-ul-Afaghina,* and later the *Khudai Khidmatgar* movement.

4. Gandhara Civilization existed in the now northern Pakistan and Afghanistan from first millinieum BCE to the beginning of second millinieum CE. The extent of the region included the Peshawar valley, the hills of Swat, Dir, Buner and Bajaur.

5. The ruins of this ancient city are located on the outskirts of the modern city of Charsadda, in the Khyber Pakhtunkhwa province of Pakistan. Pushkalavati was the capital of the ancient Gandhara kingdom before the sixth century BCE, when it became an Achaemenid regional capital, and it remained an important city until the second century CE.

6. Babur defeated Ibrahim Lodi in the First Battle of Panipat in 1526, and thus began the Mughal reign.

7. The Hotak dynasty was established in 1709 by Mirwais Hotak after leading a successful revolution against their declining Persian Safavid overlords in the region of Loy Kandahar ('Greater Kandahar') in what is now southern Afghanistan. It lasted until 1738 when the founder of the Afsharid dynasty, Nader Shah Afshar, defeated Hussain Hotak during the long siege of Kandahar and started the reestablishment of Iranian suzerainty over all regions lost decades before against the Iranian arch-rival, the Ottoman Empire, and the Russian Empire. At its peak, the Hotak dynasty ruled briefly over an area which is now Afghanistan, Iran, western Pakistan, and some parts of Tajikistan and Turkmenistan.

8. A grand tribal council that serves a legislative function.

9. Ahmad Shah (1722–1772) belonged to the Durrani tribe (also known as the Abdalis). He is considered to be the founder of the modern state of Afghanistan. At its peak, the Durrani Empire encompassed all of Afghanistan, most of Pakistan, parts of northern India (including Kashmir), northeastern Iran and eastern Turkmenistan.

10. The Battle of Nowshera was fought in March 1823 between the forces of Pashtun tribesmen with support from Muhammad Azem Khan Barakzai, the Durrani governor, against the army of Maharaja Ranjit Singh. This battle was a decisive victory for the Sikhs and led to their occupation of the Peshawar valley.

11. He was a Muslim revolutionary leader from Rai Bareli. In 1826, he provided an Islamic challenge to an expanding Sikh empire when he arrived in Peshawar with a few hundred disciples, to establish an Islamic state among Pashtun tribes in the area with the support of his network. During the last years of his life, his supporters designated him *Amir al-Mu'minin* ('Commander of the Believers'), and Shaheed ('martyr') after his death in the Battle of Balakot in 1831.

12. Rowlatt Act (February 1919). Passed by the Imperial Legislative Council of British India, the Act allowed certain political cases to be tried without juries and permitted internment of suspects without trial. All non-official Indian members of the Council (i.e., those who were not officials in the colonial government) voted against it. The Act faced strong opposition, triggering a massive non-cooperation movement, spearheaded by the Congress party. In April 1919, protests against the arrest of two prominent leaders

under the Act in Punjab, resulted in the Jallianwala Bagh massacre, in Amritsar. The government of India repealed the Rowlatt Act in March 1922.

13. Literally meaning 'Migration'.

14. Khan Bahadur Dilawar Khan, an alumnus of the Mission School in Peshawar, was a Pukhtun from the village of Jhanda, Sawabai. He was the son of Qadir Khan of Jhanda, the leading khan of the village, and was recruited into the provincial civil service on the basis of the services of his father to the British Raj. He joined as an extra-assistant commissioner and rose to the rank of the home secretary of the government of the North-West Frontier Province. This was no mean achievement. He was posted to Bannu as a magistrate and, on the basis of the good work that he did in controlling the *Khilafat* movement and weaning away the maulanas from it and also persuading the *lambardars* of the Revenue Department to take back their resignations from performing government duties, he was posted as the first Hindustani assistant commissioner to Charsadda Sub Division by the then deputy commissioner, Ralph Griffith. He retired from government service and settled down on his land in Charbagh. He had four daughters and two sons, Abdul Hameed Khan and Abdur Rahim Khan.

15. Haji Sir Abdullah Haroon was a wealthy businessman and philanthropist from Karachi. He belonged to the Memon trading community of Karachi and was a shipping magnate. He was a supporter of Muslim causes and greatly assisted the Sindh *madrassah* at Karachi, a reputable school which has the honour of being the *alma mater* of Muhammad Ali Jinnah. On Mr. Jinnah's suggestion, he founded the daily *Dawn*, an English language newspaper from Karachi. He was a staunch member of the Pakistan Muslim League. He used to support Islamic scholars and sent them for education to the Al-Azhar University in Cairo. Sir Abdullah Haroon had three sons, who have all passed away. His grandson, Hussain Haroon, remained Pakistan's permanent representative to the United Nations for a number of years.

16. Maulana Ishaq Hazarvi was from Mansehra in the then Hazara district. He later became the *khateeb* of Hazara and was quite an influential figure in the religious politics of the district.

17. Sahibzada Khurshid (1900–1950) was the son of Sahibzada Khalil-ur- Rahman and the great-grandson of Hazrat Saeed *Amir* of

village Kotha in the Utman sub-tribe of the Mandanir–Yousafzais of Mardan. He was amongst the first fourteen students of Islamia College, Peshawar and joined it in 1914. After passing his F.A Examination at the Punjab University, he was selected for the army and sent to the academy at Sandhurst, in the UK, through the patronage of Sir George Roos-Keppel, the then chief commissioner of the North-West Frontier Province. On being commissioned into the British Indian Army, he joined a battalion of the Punjab Regiment. On becoming a captain, he was seconded to the Indian Political Service, again through the good offices of Sir George Roos-Keppel who happened to be a friend and collaborator of his uncle, Sir Sahibzada Abdul Qaiyum, the founder of the Islamia College. At the time when he is mentioned in the autobiography of Abdul Ghaffar Khan, he was posted as the assistant political agent of Sibbi in Balochistan. On Independence, as Lieutenant Colonel Khurshid, he was appointed in 1948 as the political resident in the North-West Frontier Province and successfully negotiated the allegiance of the States of Dir, Swat, and Chitral and the independent tribes of the Centrally Administered Tribal Areas, to Pakistan. The same year he was appointed by the prime minister, Liaqat Ali Khan, as the first Pakistani agent to the governor general of Balochistan. In 1949, he was appointed by Liaqat Ali Khan as the first Pakistani governor of the North-West Frontier Province on the resignation of Sir George Cunningham, who, on completion of his tenure, had gone home to England, but had been recalled by Liaqat Ali Khan and requested to shoulder the responsibility of the office of governor N.W.F.P. Sahibzada Khurshid, who died of cardiac arrest in January 1950 in the Government House, Peshawar, after being in office only for a few months. He was survived by his son, Sahibzada Muhammad Salim, and five daughters, three of whom have since died.

18. Khan of Pabbi. The reference is to Said Hassan. He was a deputy superintendent of Police, posted at Sibi, Balochistan.

19. Khushal Khan was a very prominent landowner and progressive agriculturist of the Babukhel clan of the Sudham area who belonged to the village of Barikab.

20. Muhammad Ibrahim Khan was a prominent lawyer of Peshawar who belonged to village Cheena in the present district of Charsadda. He was the first directly appointed district and sessions judge in 1933.

In 1946, he was appointed as additional judicial commissioner and, in 1947, took over from Sir James Almond as the judicial commissioner, a post he held with distinction until superannuation in 1955. He was also awarded the insignia of Sitara-e-Pakistan in recognition of his distinguished service.

21. Khan Bahadur Kulli Khan was from the small hamlet of Zarki in the Khattak area of Karak, which was then part of Kohat district. Now it is a district on its own. He was assistant political officer, Moomand, and assistant commissioner Charsadda at the time. He later rose to be a political agent. He was an astute 'political officer' par excellence and very skilled in the handling of the tribes. He had two wives – the first a Khattak lady from his ancestral area from whom he had a son, Aslam Khattak, and a second, a lady from Bannu who bore him two sons, Yousaf Khattak and Habibullah Khan, and three daughters. Aslam Khattak was educated abroad in England and, after stints of service in the jail and education departments as director public instructions, he held ambassadorial appointments at very critical times in Baghdad and Kabul. He entered politics and was returned a number of times from his native constituency of Karak both to the provincial and the national assembly. He was also appointed governor of the Frontier Province in the time of Zulfiqar Ali Bhutto of the People's Party. He served as a federal minister for quite some time and died at the ripe old age of over ninety years. His half-brother, Yousaf Khattak, joined the Muslim League and was one of its prominent leaders in the Frontier Province. Habibullah Khan joined the Indian Army before Independence as an officer in the 9 Baloch Regiment and after Independence rose to the rank of Lt. General and held the post of Chief of Staff of the Pakistan Army at retirement. On retirement, he entered the world of business and established an industrial empire from scratch. He had three sons – Raza Kulli, Ali Kulli and Ahmad Kulli. Raza, on being educated abroad in England, returned to share the burden of management of his father's industrial units. Ali joined his father's battalion and, like his father before him, rose to the rank of a Lt. General before retirement. Ahmad Kulli joined the Pakistan Air Force but retired early on in his career.

22. Haji Shahnawaz Khan had three sons all committed to Bacha Khan and his *Khudai Khidmatgar* movement. The eldest was Dost Muhammad Khan followed by Pir Muhammad Khan and Suhbat

Khan. All three were present at the Babara massacre where, by some accounts, more than six hundred peaceful participants of the protest rally were butchered.

23. Bhagat Singh was hanged on 23 March 1931.

24. This was Khan Bahadur Mehraban Khan of Paniala.

25. The Gandhi–Irwin Pact was a political agreement signed by Mahatma Gandhi and the then viceroy of India, Lord Irwin, on 5 March 1931 before the Second Round Table Conference in London. Before this, the viceroy, Lord Irwin, announced in October 1929, a vague offer of 'dominion status' for India in an unspecified future and a Round Table Conference to discuss a future constitution. During the Second Round Table Conference which was held in 1931, the two Mahatmas – as Sarojini Naidu described Gandhi and Irwin – had eight meetings that totaled 32 hours. Gandhi was impressed by Irwin's sincerity. The terms of the Gandhi–Irwin Pact fell manifestly short of those Gandhi prescribed as the minimum for a truce. Below are the proposed conditions:

(a) Discontinuation of the civil disobedience movement by the Indian National Congress

(b) Participation by the Indian National Congress in the Round Table Conference

(c) Withdrawal of all ordinances issued by the British Government imposing curbs on the activities of the Indian National Congress

(d) Withdrawal of all prosecutions relating to several types of offenses except those involving violence

(e) Release of prisoners arrested for participating in the civil disobedience movement

(f) Removal of the tax on salt, which allowed the Indians to produce, trade, and sell salt legally and for their own private use

Many British officials in India and in England were outraged by the idea of a pact with a party whose avowed purpose was the destruction of the British Raj. Winston Churchill publicly expressed his disgust '...at the nauseating and humiliating spectacle of this one-time Inner Temple lawyer, now seditious fakir, striding half-naked up the steps of the viceroy's palace, there to negotiate and parley on equal terms with the representative of the King Emperor.'

In reply, the British Government agreed to:
(i) Withdraw all ordinances and end prosecutions
(ii) Release all political prisoners, except those guilty of violence
(iii) Permit peaceful picketing of liquor and foreign cloth shops
(iv) Restore confiscated properties of the satyagrahis
(v) Permit free collection or manufacture of salt by persons near the coast
(vi) Lift the ban on the Congress

The viceroy, Lord Irwin was, at this time, directing the sternest repression Indian nationalism had known, but did not relish the role. The British civil service and the commercial community favoured even harsher measures. But Premier Ramsay MacDonald and Secretary of State for India, William Benn, were eager for peace, if they could secure it without weakening the position of the Labour government. They wanted to make a success of the Round Table Conference and knew that this body, without the presence of Gandhi and the Congress, could not carry much weight. In January 1931, at the closing session of the Round Table Conference, Ramsay MacDonald went so far as to express the hope that the Congress would be represented at the next session. The viceroy took the hint and promptly ordered the unconditional release of Gandhi and all members of the Congress working committee. To this gesture Gandhi responded by agreeing to meet the viceroy.

Gandhi's motives in concluding a pact with the viceroy can be best understood in terms of his technique. The Satyagraha movements were commonly described as 'struggles', 'rebellions' and 'wars without violence'. Owing, however, to the common connotation of these words, they seemed to lay a disproportionate emphasis on the negative aspect of the movements, namely opposition and conflict. The object of Satyagraha was, however, not to achieve the physical elimination or moral breakdown of an adversary – but, through suffering at his hands, to initiate a psychological process that could make it possible for minds and hearts to meet. In such a struggle, a compromise with an opponent was neither heresynortrea son, but a natural and necessary step. If it turned out that the compromise was premature and the adversary was unrepentant, nothing prevented the Satyagrahi from returning to non-violent battle.

26. Ghulam Rabbani Khan was a member of the provincial legislative assembly of the Frontier Province, from Hazara, as a part of Nawab Sir Sahibzada Abdul Qaiyum's United Muslims Nationalist Organization.

27. It was reported to me by Akram Khan Lala Yarakhel, of the village, that when Abdul Ghaffar Khan visited the village for the first time, in connection with the *Khudai Khidmatgar* movement in 1921, Sahibzad a Fazl-e-Rahman, a grandson of Hazrat Saeed Ameer of village Kotha, and a retired extra assistant commissioner of village Kotha, made arrangements for him to meet with a representative group of village elders. Being a retired employee of the government, he did not wish to be present himself, but selected representatives from each section of the village to meet him. The function was arranged on the top of the mound in the village on which the Sahibzada family graveyard is located. The names of some of those who took part in the event are below. Most of these elders were known to me personally during the last part of their lives. Their names, along with their tribal sub-sections, areas follows:

Kabir Khan, Ghulamkhel; Ali Khan, Ghulamkhel; Khawaja Muhammad, Ismailkhel; Mahmud Khan, Nazim, Samakhel; Juma Khan, President *Khudai Khidmatgar*, Mitakhel; Sher Ali Khan, Barakhel; Inayat Khan, Ghulamkhel; Azad Khan, Tahirkheli; Mazullah Khan, Khwajikhel; Rahmat, Majar *Khudai Khidmatgar*; Mir Aslam, Maliar; Khan Bahadur, Ismailkhel; Maulvi Isa Khan, Panjpao, Secretary *Khudai Khidmatgar*; Rasul Khan, Samakhel. The names of the others who participated have been forgotten.

28. *Mian* Ali Haider Shah was an alumnus of the Mission School, Peshawar, and was a senior contemporary of Abdul Ghaffar Khan. On completing his education, he joined the provincial civil service and served in different capacities in the Frontier Province. After Independence, he served as the secretary of the provincial assembly until he was superannuated from that post.

29. Hussain Shaheed Suhrawardy later was one of the prime ministers of Pakistan for a short period before the advent to power of General Muhammad Ayub Khan.

30. Khan Bahadur Saadullah Khan was the *Masher* Khan of village Umerzai and was the chief of the *Batikhel* clan of the Umerzai

sub-section of the *Muhammadzai* tribe. He was an employee of the British government and retired from the post of a deputy commissioner. On retirement, he became an associate of Nawab Sir Sahibzada Abdul Qaiyumas chief minister of the province.

31. Iskander Mirza hailed from Patnain the province of Bihar. He joined the Indian Army and then transferred as a captain to the Indian political service. He served most of his career in the Frontier and served as deputy commissioner both in Mardan and Peshawar districts. On Independence, he served as the secretary, ministry of defence and was responsible for the imposition of martial law after the anti Qadiani riots in Lahore. Through political manipulation he rose to be the first president of Pakistan and, on the instigation of General Muhammad Ayub Khan, the commander-in-chief, played into his hands for the imposition of martial law all over the country in 1958. After a short while, General Ayub eased him out and sent him on pension to the United Kingdom where he lived in obscurity with his second wife, Naheed Iskander Mirza, until his death.

32. Nawab Sheikh Mehboob Ali Khan was a scion of the Sheikh family of village Sheikhan on the outskirts of the Peshawar cantonment. He was a member of the prestigious Indian Political Service and had served the provincial government well in a number of field postings. He was physically a man of enormous proportions weighing well over twenty stones. He was a rich man by the standards of the time and matched his wealth with his hospitality, with the fame of his table at Shai Khan, at which both the well-to-do and the relatively poor, were equally welcome. In 1947, when there was an acute scarcity of grain, he shared whatever he had with those of his village who did not have any. He was an outstanding 'political officer' who had both a hand in the formulation of policy and its implementation. He had an incisive intellect and could be relied upon to find a solution to the most complex of 'political problems' and issues. He played a very prominent part in the removal of Amanullah Khan from the throne of Afghanistan.

Despite his weight and his far from handsome face, he had a certain charm about him which was irresistible to the English ladies of the time, of which he did not fail to take full advantage, to further his career. When he died in the winter of 1948, the Pakistan flags flew at half-mast on all government buildings for three days across the Frontier and all the government officers wore black arm-bands. He had one daughter, Sylvia, who later married Sheikh sahib's nephew, Mazhar Ali Khan, but sadly died in childbirth.

33. A post given the ultimate authority by Congress High Command, to take decisions.

34. His name was Shelley Smith and he was educated at the Bishop Cotton School, Simla, where he was affectionately known to his school mates as 'smellypoo!'

35. Sir Olaf Caroe, after service in the Frontier and in Delhi, was appointed as the last British governor of the North-West Frontier Province(1946–47). In 1958, he published a comprehensive and definitive history of the Pukhtuns, *The Pathans*. He also co-authored a book with Sir Evelyn Howell of translations into English verse of some well-known poems of the famous Pukhtun warrior and poet, Khushal Khan Khattak.

Notes sourced from experience and Wikipedia.

Glossary

Achhut: Untouchable.

Ainda: A traditional, tribal Pukhtun game, played by young men. It is essentially a young man's game, consisting of two teams and two home-bases, at either end of a ground. From one team, a youth goes out some forty yards and is followed by a couple from the opposite side, whose aim it is to catch him and throw him down, before he reaches home-base. (Source: Social & Religious Life in Bannu Excerpts from Gazetteer of the Bannu District, 1887. http://www.khyber. org/publications/031-035/sociallifebannu.shtml#Villages%20&%20 Houses%20of%20the%20People.

Al Hilal: The crescent.

Alim: A scholar recognized as an expert in Islamic law and theology.

Allah-u-Akbar: A phrase meaning 'God is most great', used by Muslims in prayers and as a general declaration of faith or thanksgiving.

Amir: Leader.

Amlook: Dried persimmon.

Angai: A traditional village guessing game commonly played in the evenings by young girls and boys. Two teams of 5 to 8 players each first appoint their pairs, on the opposite side. The captain of each team then mixes up the order of the players and arranges them in a row, seated behind a wall or a sheet, so that the teams are not visible to each other. The objective is for these partners to be paired off, without seeing each other. The captain of team A starts the game by calling out to the captain of team B, saying 'Angai, angai, who is your partner?' The captain of team B names the player in team A whose pair is first in line on his own team. If he/she guesses this wrong, team B's pair in team A has to give his pair a piggy-back ride. The game ends when all pairs are guessed. The winning team is the one that gets the most, right guesses and makes the most pairs. (Source: Ayub Khan, Pakistan & Behroz Khan Wahdat, USA).

Anjuman-e-Islah-ul-Afaghina: Association for the Reform of the Afghans.

Ansar/s: The inhabitants of Medina who took Prophet Muhammad and his followers (the Muhajareen) into their homes when they emigrated from Mecca (the hijra).

Arat: Persian wheel, to pull water from a well.

Atarn: One of the oldest of traditional Pukhtun, community dances. According to some, it dates back to Zoroastrian times i.e., around 2000 BCE. Others date it back to King Yama's celebration of Nauwroz and warriors dancing and circling around a fire. It is usually performed to the beat of a double-headed barrel drum, with a large number of dancers moving slowly in a large circle at first, and then speeding up as the beat quickens. There are many different regional variations of Atarn. It is the national dance of Afghanistan and the Pukhtun areas of Pakistan. In the past, it was performed both by men and women together.

Auliya: A saint.

Ayat: A verse of the Holy *Quran*.

Azan: The Muslim call to ritual prayer made by a muezzin from the minaret of a mosque.

Baba: An elder or father or saint.

Babu: A respectful title or form of address for a man, especially an educated one.

Bacha: King (Pukhto); Badhshah in Urdu.

Bahadur: An honorific title, originally given to officers in British India.

Bait-ul-mal: The national treasury.

Bait-ul-Muqaddas: The sacred house i.e., Jerusalem.

Balakhana: Attic.

Balghamai: Amall tea cups without handles used for green tea.

Banda: A hamlet.

Bangian: Addicts.

Bangreewatae: A village game played by young girls, similar to pick-up-sticks but played with broken bangles or *bangree*. Broken bangles and one whole bangle are thrown into a pile with players then trying to remove the whole bangle without disturbing the others. The one who removes the whole bangle without doing so, wins.

Bani Umayya: The 'children of Umayya'. The Umayyad dynasty, the ruling family of the Muslim caliphate, ruled between 661 and 750 and later ruled Islamic Spain. The Umayya were a prominent clan of the

Quraysh tribe of Mecca. [The Prophet Mohammad (PBUH) belonged to the Bani Hashim clan of the Quraysh.] Mawyia, one of its governors, established the Umayyad Caliphate in Syria in 661, which marked the beginning of the Umayyad dynasty, the first hereditary dynasty in the history of Islam.

Baniya: Member of the caste that is involved in trade and commerce in the Hindu caste system.

Banreechegh/s: Traditional version of a merry-go-round. Made with a central wooden pole with a rotating plate at the top to which long ropes are attached, which are held by children, who then run around, swinging from it.

Batyaraan: Cooks.

Bazaar: A market.

Bhagwad Geeta/Geeta: 700-verse Hindu scripture part of the epic, *Mahabharata*. It has been presented as a dialogue between Kshatriya prince, Arjuna, and his charioteer, Krishna, on the importance of doing one's duty and faith in God.

Bhat: Minstrel.

Bolshevik: Follower of Lenin in the Russian revolution of 1917.

Bua: A tax imposed on house owners by the Nawab of Teri in Kohat. The Nawab was one of the beneficiaries of the British politics of patronage. The British allowed him to impose this tax, in return for his allegiance. (Source: Ethnicity, Islam and Nationalism. Muslim Politics in the North-West Frontier Province (Khyber Pakhtunkhwa) . 1937–1947. Sayed Wiqar Ali Shah. National Institute of Historical and Cultural Research. Centre of Excellence, Quaid-i-Azam University, Islamabad, 2015).

Brahman: A member of the highest Hindu caste, originally that of the priesthood.

Bulbuls: Nightingales.

Butawa: Livestock feed.

Butt: Open, clay oven.

Chapal/Chapalay/Chapalray: Sandals.

Chapati: A flat round bread cooked on a griddle.

Char darwesh: Reference to the moral of the story from *The Tale of the Four Dervishes* by Amir Khusro (Ghasseh-e Chahar Dervish – Persian), written in the thirteenth century.

Charbaita: A genre of Pukhto poetry.

Chatak: One-sixteenth part of a *seer*.

Cheelam: Hookah or Sheesha.

Cheendro: A team game played by girls, like hopscotch. A rectangular diagram with 6–8 squares is made on the floor. A round striker is used by the players and moved from square to square by hopping on one foot and moving the striker with one foot. Players avoid getting the striker on the lines of the diagram. The objective is to get the striker from one end of the diagram to the other.

Chehla: Seclusion or a retreat.

Chowkidari: Gatekeeping.

Churchurai: Sparkles (firecrackers).

Churian: Sweepers.

Daffedar/s: Equivalent rank to sergeant in British Indian army.

Dal: Lentils.

Darai: Floor-spread made from cotton yarn.

Dargah: The tomb or shrine of a Muslim saint.

Darogha: The deputy jailer.

Darwais or Darwayan: An accountant or *munshi*.

Dastarkhwan: The sheet spread out on the floor on which food is laid out and guests sit around it for meals.

Demaan: Cast of musicians.

Deodai: Entrance of a home.

Dervish: A member of a Muslim (specifically Sufi) religious order who has taken vows of poverty and austerity. Dervishes first appeared in the twelfth century; they were noted for their wild or ecstatic rituals and were known as dancing, whirling, or howling dervishes according to the practice of their order.

Desi-Sardar: Viceroy commissioned officer.

Dhol: Drum.

Dolai: Palanquin. Here, used to carry the bride. A small structure covered in elaborately decorated cloth, perched on two wooden sticks, carried by men.

Dujjal: Anti-Christ.

Dunkacha: Raised platform, also used to pray on.

Eidgah: Open enclosure commonly used for Eid prayers.

Faqir/s: A person/s who has devoted his life to the preaching of the teachings of a religious saint.

Farman: Royal decree.

Fateha: Funeral prayer.

Fatwa/s: Declaration/s issued by a maulana or learned man on a religious issue.

Gaitkai: A traditional village game of the Pukhtuns, similar to hopscotch. (Source: Behroz Khan Wahdat, USA). Or a game played with small stones or 'gitkai' with which one stone is used to target others lying on the ground. Stones now have been replaced with marbles. (Source: Abaseen Yousafzai, Pakistan).

Galrain: Traditional, small manufacturing units to produce *gur* or jaggery. The process involves taking the juice out of sugarcane through a press, putting the juice in a huge flat-bottomed pan and boiling it for hours. The cooked jaggery is then put into large moulds, to cool and is then manually made into small, round pieces.

Ganrai: Traditional, small manufacturing units to produce *gur* or jaggery. The process involves taking the juice out of sugarcane through a press, putting the juice in a huge flat-bottomed pan called a *pur* and boiling it. The cooked jaggery is then cooled and manually shaped to form rough balls. Often dried fruit (walnuts, almonds, etc) are mixed into this, before eating.

Gazaaray: Tobacco snuff (same as *naswar*).

Gharbeenoona/Gharbeen (singular): A blunderbuss or shotgun.

Ghatay wrujay: Fat-grained rice, eaten with clarified, melted butter.

Ghaza: Jihad or holy war.

Ghazi: Holy warrior.

Ghilman: Handsome youth promised to the faithful in heaven, as companions.

Ghwaree/ghee: Clarified butter, to cook in.

Goot: A special drink of milk and dried fruit served at engagements and weddings. The word 'goot' literally means 'a sip.'

Gud: Lame.

Gujar: Pastoral, agricultureal ethnic group in the region.

Gur or gura: Jaggery, made out of sugarcane molasses.

Guru Granth Sahib/Granth Sahib: The principal sacred scripture of Sikhism. Originally compiled under the direction of Arjan Dev

(1563–1606), the fifth Sikh guru, it contains hymns and religious poetry as well as the teachings of the first five gurus.

Hadith: Sayings of the Holy Prophet.

Hafiz: One who has memorized the whole of the Holy *Quran*.

Haji: A Muslim who has been to Mecca as a pilgrim.

Hajj: The greater Muslim pilgrimage to Mecca, which takes place in the last month of the year and which all Muslims are expected to make at least once during their lifetime if they can afford to do so. It is one of the Five Pillars of Islam.

Hakeem/s: Practitioner/s of herbal medicine.

Halwa: Sweet or dessert.

Hanafi: Follower of the school of jurisprudence of Imam Abu Hanifa.

Haram: That which is forbidden in the religion of Islam.

Har-pashakaal: The most trying months on account of their heat and humidity, corresponding to mid-June to mid-August.

Hashish: Hash, drug made from cannabis resin.

Hassanian: Reference to the Prophet's grandsons.

Hijrat: Flight, exodus or emigration.

Hilal-e-Ahmar: Red-Crescent.

Hindu: A follower of Hinduism.

Hoors: Beautiful virgins who will be companions of the faithful in heaven.

Hujra: The meeting house for men, in which bachelors also sleep at night

Imam Mahdi: Muslims believe that Imam Mahdi will appear at the end of times to rid the world of evil and injustice.

Inquilab: A revolution or uprising (often used as a political slogan).

Jagir: Land granted by the ruler or state under the *jagirdari* system. A pre-British practice and practised by the British in India. Included powers to govern and collect taxes, by the appointed feudal *jagirdar* (lessee).

Jaloos: Procession.

Jalsa: Public meeting.

Jamadar: An Indian officer in a sepoy regiment; a minor official or junior officer.

Jamat: Assembly, group, congregation.

Janaza: The funeral prayer of a Muslim.

Jareeb: Measure of land equivalent to half an acre.

Jeelab: The act of seeing someone off; farewell.

Jhatka: Slaughter of an animal by cutting the neck clean, to prevent bleeding; practiced in Sikh religion.

Jihad: Religious war.

Jirga: A group of elders of a family, clan or tribe, which takes decisions on matters of importance.

Jirga-Nasheen: Head of a *jirga*.

Jopaan: A small cot on which, seated, a religious luminary would be carried by his disciples.

Juba: Robe.

Kabaddi: A sport of Indian origin played by teams of seven on a circular sand court. The players attempt to tag or capture opponents, repeating the word 'kabaddi' to show that they are doing so.

Kafir: In Islam, a non-believer; denier of the truth.

Kalukhani: Glazed earthenware dishes traditionally used on special occasions.

Kameez: Shirt.

Kandwaan: Large, earthen storage containers.

Kaptan: Captain.

Kasabgar/s: The cadre of labourers equipped with different skills and employees on a seasonal payment system of grain by the land-owners from the performance of agriculture-related tasks.

Katlama/s: Sweet, fried bread.

Kebab: A dish of pieces of meat, fish, or vegetables roasted or grilled on a skewer or spit.

Keer: Rice Pudding.

Khaamta: Home-spun cotton, woven by the *Khudai Khidmatgar* as a sign of self-reliance and the boycott of British-made factory cloth. Women and men in the movement wore clothes of local *khaamta* and the *Khudai Khidmatgar* workers dyed these red.

Khairat: Charity.

Khaksar: A movement for independence started by Allama Mashriqi in Lahore, Punjab, in 1931.

Khalifa: The successor of the *Amir*.

Khan: Title given to rulers and officials in central Asia, Afghanistan, and certain other Muslim countries.

Khanate: Fiefdom.

Khasadar: Local militia of tribesmen set up by the British in the Tribal Areas.

Khidmat: Service.

Khilafat movement: A pan-Islamist movement during British Rule wherein all Muslims of India aligned themselves with the nationalist cause of independence.

Khilwat: Seclusion or a retreat

Khilwatkhana: Place of seclusion or retreat.

Khudai Khidmatgar/Khidmatgari: Servants of God/the act of service in God's name.

Khumaan: Large, earthen storage pots.

Komedan: Commandant.

Kotwali: The police station of a district headquarter town.

Kufr: Disbelief in the truth i.e., teachings of Islam; one who disbelieves is a Kafir.

Kulcha/s: A small, round Indian bread made from flour, milk, and butter, typically stuffed with meat or vegetables.

Kulla: The cap on which the turban is tied.

Kuza: An earthen-ware receptacle of water with a long hand and a spout which is used for ablution in the mosques before offering prayers

Lakhkar: Force of volunteers.

Lalee: Bacha Khan's nickname for his son Abdul Ali Khan. The word means 'dear' or 'beloved'.

Lambardar: This has two connotations; when used in jail terminology, it refers to the prisoner who has spent a substantial portion of his sentence and has been given some authority over his fellow prisoners for enforcement of jail rules. When used in the context of the land revenue administration, it means the headman or malik of the village who is responsible for the collection of the land revenue dues of the government in return for a small monetary compensation.

Lance-Naik: Rank below Naik, in British Indian army.

Landi Mari: A traditional village game played by boys in two teams of five to six boys each. Players of team A sit on the shoulders of the players of team B. Each pair of players has a circle drawn around them and can only move within these. The team B players try to drop the team A players off their shoulders. One player from team B has a *landi* or a stick made up from a rolled-up sheet and whacks the team

A players who drop to the ground. Once all players of team A have been dropped to the ground, the game continues with team B players now getting on the shoulders of team A players. (Source: Behroz Khan Wahdat, USA).

Lang: Loin-cloth, as compared (here) to the *partoog/shalwar* worn by Pukhtuns.

Langar: The cook-house or kitchen of a dargah (residence of a saint or pir) in which communal meals are provided, made of rations donated by followers.

Langarkhana: Place of cook-house or kitchen of a dargah (residence of a saint or pir) in which communal meals are provided, made of rations donated by followers.

Lathi/Lathis: Sticks.

Loota: Clod of earth.

Lungi: The cloth which is wound round the *kulla* (cap) as a turban. A *lungi*-holder is one who has a turban of honour. The awarding of the title of *lungi* was introduced by the British colonialists in the Tribal Areas. Lungi holders were and are an important link between tribes and the administration.

Lupatay: Veils worn by women.

Madhay: Traditional wedding songs in praise of the groom's family

Madrassah: A learning institution of the Muslims based on the *Quran* and located in the mosques; during the British rule, this term were applied to the primary schools built by the government.

Mahtabai: A type of firecracker ie like a little missile tied to a cane stick and planted in the ground. When lit, it takes off, exploding in the sky in multiple patterns. (Source: Usman Qazi, Balochistan).

Maira: Sparsely populated area.

Makhlri: An area then on the outskirts of Peshawar city where the British had an ammunition dump.

Maktab/s: School/s.

Malik: The chief of a village or community.

Malikana: Tribute (cash or kind) originally paid to tribal leaders of Maliks.

Mandai: Market place for trade of agricultural commodities.

Mandao: Foyer.

Marakiz: Plural of Markaz.

Markaz: Centre of learning or training.

Mashaloona: Flaming torches.

Masher/s: Elders.

Maulana: Muslim prayer leader.

Maulvi: A Muslim doctor of the law.

Mawajib: The assurance allowance paid by the government to the free Tribesmen.

Mecca: A city in western Saudi Arabia, an oasis town in the Red Sea region of Hejaz, east of Jiddah, considered by Muslims to be the holiest city of Islam.

Meesray: Stanzas.

Milad: A religious function during which prayers referring to the birth of Prophet Mohammad (PBUH) are recited.

Mimbar: The pulpit in the mosque from which the imam addressed the congregation and lead the prayer.

Mohtamim: Manager of a *madrassah*.

Motammar: A reference to the *Motammar-e-Alam-al-Islami* i.e. the World Muslim Congress, founded at a meeting of eminent Muslim leaders in Mecca in 1926.

Muallim: Arabic for the person who helps a haji to perform Hajj, on the annual pilgrimage to Mecca and Madina.

Muazzamah: Exalted or respected.

Muhajareen: Those who seek refuge away from their homes with someone.

Muharram: The first month of the Islamic calendar. Muslims observe and respect Muharram as the month in which Hussein, the grandson of Prophet Muhammad and son of Hazrat Ali, was martyred in the Battle of Karbala.

Mujahid: One who fights in jihad or holy war.

Mujahideen: Those who wage the religious war or jihad in Islam.

Munawarrah: Enlightened, applied to Madina.

Munj: A tough grass used to make ropes.

Munshi: Accountant.

Mureed: Disciple.

Mushaira: A meeting in which poets gather to recite their poems.

Mutawalli: Caretaker of the shrine of a Muslim saint.

Naib-*tehsildar*: A deputy or an assistant to a revenue district officer.

Naik/s: Equivalent rank of corporal in British Indian army. Lance-Naik is a rank below Naik.

Naindra: The money usually given by the guests of the waleema to the host and meant for the defraying of the costs of the wedding.

Nakeer and Munkeer: The two angels who record the good and bad deeds of a Muslim during his life time.

Nara-e-Takbeer: Slogan of God is Great.

Naswar: Snuff.

Naukhar: Nowshera (Urdu).

Nawab: A Muslim nobleman or person of high status.

Nawabi: Fiefdom.

Nawar: Strips of cotton of woven yarn used for stringing beds.

Nazrana: Tribute (cash or kind) paid to persons in authority by ordinary people.

Nikah: The marriage contract in Islam.

Ordandai (fire sticks): Sticks lit up with fire at the end, used in celebrations.

Padri: Priest in a Christian mission.

Paisa: Unit of money; there were four paisas to an anna and sixteen annas to a rupee.

Paishmanay: Pre-dawn meal/breakfast in *Ramadan.*

Pakai: Hand-operated fan.

Pan: Betel-leaf wrapped up to contain betel nut, aniseed, etc., commonly eaten in India and parts of Pakistan as a digestive.

Pandal: Marquee.

Pandis or Pandyan: Labourers.

Panlra: Slipper with a pointed toe.

Parachas: A family name, common in the Punjab in Pakistan. Commonly engaged in trade, at the time.

Partoog: Local, baggy trousers; *shalwar* in Urdu.

Patakhay: Firecrackers.

Patpatonay: Hide and seek.

Patta kunjaka (hidden shell): A traditional village game of the Pukhtuns. Players sit in a circle, facing inward, with one player moving outside the circle and placing a shell – *kunjaka* – (or any other, small object) secretly behind one of the players. That player is then either taken out of the game or h/she gets up and strikes another player with the object, following which the player who has been struck then places the object behind one of the remaining players. The objective is to avoid the 'kunjaka' and to be the last surviving player. (Source: Behroz Khan Wahdat, USA).

Patwari: The lowest ranking officer in the land revenue administration. He was responsible for the maintenance of the land record pertaining to land owners and tenants of a patwar-circle, including mortgage and redemption of land.

Pharaoh: A ruler in ancient Egypt.

Pikoray/pakora: Batter-fried snack.

Pir: A saint.

Poh-mah: The two months of a calendar year in which the cold is at its severest. They correspond to the months of 15 December to 15 January and 15 January to 15 February.

Pooch: A guessing game where one player hides a marble or another object in one hand and another player has to guess which hand this is in. (Source: Behroz Khan Wahdat, USA).

Pooja-path: The act of worship.

Powindahs: Pashtun nomads.

Prarthana: Hindi for prayer.

Pukhtunwali or Pashtunwali: Pukhtun tribal code of life; consists of defending honour with courage (*toora* meaning sword), exchange or reciprocity (*badal*), hospitality (*melmestia*), providing sanctuary or refuge to those in need (*nanawatai*).

Pulao: A choice dish of rice of the Pukhtuns eaten on festive and special occasions.

Purdah: Veil; practice of veiling by women.

Puzakai: Floor mat woven from reed.

Qadiani: Followers of the nineteenth century Mirza Ghulam Ahmad of Qadian who are held as heretics by orthodox Muslims.

Qalang: Tax or imposition.

Qazi: A Muslim judge who interprets and administers the religious law of Islam.

Qruth: Drained and dried yogurt or sour milk.

Quid pro quo: A favour of advantage granted in return for something.

Quran: The Islamic sacred book, believed to be the word of God as dictated to Muhammad by the archangel Gabriel and written down in

Arabic. The *Quran* consists of 114 units of varying lengths, known as suras; the first sura is said as part of the ritual prayer. These touch upon all aspects of human existence, including matters of doctrine, social organization, and legislation.

Qutubkhana: Library.

Rabab: String instrument originating in central Afghanistan.

Raj: Rule.

Ramzan/Ramadan: The ninth month of the Muslim year, during which strict fasting is observed from dawn to sunset.

Razakar: Volunteer.

Risaldar: Mid-level rank in cavalry and armoured units of the Indian Army.

Rojay: The Muslim lunar month of fasting from sunrise to sunset; Ramadan.

Roti: A flat round bread cooked on a griddle.

Saadar: Large piece of cloth used for several purposes by both men and women i.e., as a shawl, as a spread, etc.

Sahib: Respectful address to Europeans in India; English women where often addressed as 'Memsahib'. Used as a title of 'Sir' in British India.

Sahib-e-Haq: The chief maulana.

Salar-e-Azam: Commander-in-chief of the *Khudai Khidmatgar* volunteers.

Salami: Tradition of giving a bridegroom money when he visits his in-law's home after the wedding.

Samsara: Monitor lizard.

Sang-e-paras: A mythical stone that is believed to turn certain metals into gold upon contact.

Sardar: The chieftain of a tribe. In the Indian army, it was used as a term of respect for the Indian officers commissioned by the viceroy.

Sarkha: Spinning wheel.

Satyagraha: A policy of passive political resistance.

Satyagrahi: A person who practises the policy of satyagraha.

Sayid: A Muslim claiming descent from Muhammad, especially through Hussain, the prophet's younger grandson.

Seer: Measure of weight equivalent to 1.2 kilograms.

Serai: Hotel; inn.

Shahdola: A folk dance of Pukhtun youth in which the dancers move in circles, jumping to the drum beat and clapping their hands.

Shaheed: Martyr.

Shakkar: Brown sugar.

Shalwar: A pair of light, loose trousers.

Shamilat: Land held in common by the village community.

Shariat: The religious and social code of the Muslims.

Sharif: A name, a descendant of the Prophet Muhammad through his daughter Fatima, one of noble ancestry or political preeminence in predominantly Islamic countries. (Source Merriam-Webster Dictionary).

Shatai: A corn cob.

Shawqadar/Shaban-al-muazzam: The month in which Prophet Mohammad was born.

Sheera: Wheat bread soaked in meat gravy.

Sheikh: Follower of a saint.

Shisha: A hookah.

Sholgara: Waterlogged land. A place in Charsada.

Shrangae: A traditional village game of the Pukhtuns.

Shukrana: Tributes (in cash or kind) paid to religious authorities.

Shurta: Arab term for police.

Siparah: Section of the Holy *Quran*.

Sipasnama: Address of welcome.

Skhat: Funeral alms (often in kind) distributed to the maulanas after the funeral.

Sobalray: A heavy piece of wood used for washing clothes by beating them.

Spalanee: Commonly known in the West by the Persian name *Esphand*, *Aspand* or *Espand*. Herb seeds dropped over hot coals of which the smoke is believed to ward off the evil-eye.

Sunnat: The practice of the Holy Prophet of Islam.

Surkh-Posh: Red-shirts i.e., the *Khudai Khidmatgars* who wore red uniform.

Surna: Flute.

Swaraj: Self-rule.

Syed: A respectful Muslim form of address.

Talib: Student. Plural is Taliban.

Taliban: Students.

Taluqdar: A landowner or one belonging to the ruling class, a native officer who collected revenue for the government.

Tambal: Duff (musical instrument).

Tang-takor: Music or the sounds of musical instruments.

Tapa: Clan; also, a word for a genre of Pukhto song (couplet).

Taraveeh: Additional prayers performed by Sunni Muslims at night in the month of *Rojay/Ramadan*.

Tarboor/s: Cousin i.e. father's brother's son. The word also has the connotation of an enemy, due to agnatic rivalries (between paternal cousins) being common in Pukhtun society. Tarboorwali refers to enmity between paternal cousins.

Tarboorwali: Enmities among tarboors.

Tarha misra: Opening verse of a poem.

Tathee: A traditional village game of the Pukhtuns.

Tehsil: A division of the land revenue administration.

Tehsildar: Revenue officer in charge of the administration of a *tehsil*.

Thana: The station house or police station.

Thanedar: Station House Officer (SHO) of the police.

Thekedar: Contractor.

Tirni: A tax imposed on cattle-grazers who owned more than two goats. Imposed by the Nawab of Tirni in Kohat, one of the beneficiaries of the British politics of patronage. The British allowed him to impose this tax, in return for his allegiance. (Source: Ethnicity, Islam and Nationalism. Muslim Politics in the North-West Frontier Province (Khyber Pakhtunkhwa) 1937–1947. Sayed Wiqar Ali Shah. National Institute of Historical and Cultural Research. Centre of Excellence, Quaid-i-Azam University, Islamabad, 2015).

Tonga / Tum-tum: Horse-drawn carriage.

Torah: The book of Prophet Musa or Moses. Islam believes in the revelation of four books from Allah, through four Prophets ie the *Torah* revealed to Prophet Musa, the *Zaboor* (Psalms) revealed to Prophet Dawud (David), the *Injil* (the Gospel) revealed to Prophet Isa (Jesus) and the last one being the Quran revealed to Prophet Mohammad.

Totkay: A firecracker that explodes when struck on the ground. (Source: Usman Qazi, Balochistan).

Ulema: body of Muslim scholars who are recognized as having specialist knowledge of Islamic sacred law and theology; a member of an ulema

Ummah: The whole community of Muslims bound together by ties of religion.

Ustaz: Teacher.

Uwama: Means 'the seventh' refers to the visit of the bride's relatives to the bridegroom's house, which takes place seven days after the groom visits his in-law's home, following the wedding.

Vakeel: A lawyer or solicitor.

Wesh: 'Distribution', a Pukhtun tribal system of land distribution and rotation whereby land is allocated to clans for a fixed tenure of a number of years.

Wahabi: A follower of Abdul Wahab of Nejd who preached return to the practices of pristine Islam.

Waleema: The feast held the day after the wedding.

Walwar: Bride price; money paid for the bride to the bride's family by the bridegroom.

Waqf: A charitable endowment under Islamic law, typically involves donating a building, plot of land or other assets for Muslim religious or charitable purposes (Source: Wikipedia).

Yakkas: Boats

Zaboor: The book of Dawud or David.

Zakat: Annual payment made by Muslims, amounting to two-and-a-half percent of all earnings, and used for charitable and religious purposes. One of the five pillars of Islam.

Zamindar: Landowner.

Zango: Literal meaning is 'swing'. In this case a cable-car or pulley used to cross the river.

Ziarat: The tomb of the Prophet, or any other spiritual person.

Zindabad: Used to express approval or encouragement.

People who Made
this Book Possible

1	Abdullah Khan	Pakistan
2	Adam Khan	Pakistan
3	Adeeba Zaheen	Pakistan
4	Afrasiab Khattak	Pakistan
5	Amanullah Khan	Pakistan
6	Amena Kakakhel	Pakistan
7	Amina Humayun Khan	Pakistan
8	Anwar Ali Shah	Qatar
9	Asfandyar Wali Khan	Pakistan
10	Ashraf Jehangir Qazi	Pakistan
11	Ayesha Humayun Khan	Pakistan
12	Ayesha Tetlay	Pakistan
13	Azizullah Khan	Pakistan
14	Azra Nafees Yousafzai	Pakistan
15	Barrister Nafees Zeb	Pakistan
16	Bilqees Khan	Pakistan
17	Brig. Kamal Zeb	Pakistan
18	Dr Farhat Khurshid	Pakistan
19	Dr Riffat Hussain. M.D	USA
20	Dr Sharif Khan M.D	USA
21	Dr. Taimur Zeb M.D	USA
22	Dr. Waheed Sahibzada	Pakistan
23	Dureshahwar Sahibzada	Pakistan
24	Durand Maiwandi	Afghanistan
25	Farooq Azam	Pakistan
26	Fazal Ali Saadi	Pakistan
27	Foqia Sadiq Khan	Pakistan

28	Gauhar Saadullah	Pakistan
29	General Nadir Zeb	Pakistan
30	Gulandama Khan	Pakistan
31	Gulmina Bilal	Pakistan
32	Himayatullah Khan	Pakistan
33	Imtiaz Ahmad Sahibzada	Pakistan
34	Irfan Afridi	Pakistan
35	Ismat Shahjahan	Pakistan
36	Izhar Ali Hunzai	Pakistan
37	Jalila Ahmad Ali	Pakistan
38	JananMosazai	Afghanistan
39	Javed Iqbal	Pakistan
40	Khaleel Tetlay	Pakistan
41	Khalid Mohtadullah	Pakistan
42	Kishwar Saadullah	Pakistan
43	Layma Tabibi	Afghanistan
44	Lubna Farooq	Pakistan
45	M. Zia Jan	Pakistan
46	Mahvash Mohtadullah	Pakistan
47	Maliha Khan	Pakistan
48	Maryam Tetlay	Pakistan
49	Mehr Shah	Pakistan
50	Mian Ershad Zaheen	Pakistan
51	Mirwais Alizai	Afghanistan
52	Mishka Zaman	Pakistan
53	Mohammad Saleem Jan	Pakistan
54	Mona Naseer	Pakistan
55	Muhammad Zeeshan	Pakistan
56	Munawar Humayun Khan	Pakistan
57	Muzaffar Uddin	Pakistan
58	Muznah Iqbal	Pakistan
59	Nasir Ali Khan	Pakistan
60	Nasreen Wali Khan	Pakistan
61	Nayar Saadullah	Pakistan
62	Nilofar Afridi Qazi	Pakistan

63	Palwasha Hassan	Afghanistan
64	Parveen Wali Khan	Pakistan
65	Rashid Khan	Qatar
66	Rweeda Himayat	Pakistan
67	Samar Minallah Khan	Pakistan
68	Sami Sadat	Afghanistan
69	Sanga Mosazai	Afghanistan
70	Sarfaraz Hussain	Pakistan
71	Sayed Wiqar Ali Shah (Dr)	Pakistan
72	Shafqat Kakakhel	Pakistan
73	Shahla Sahibzada	Pakistan
74	Shahnaz Ali Khan	Pakistan
75	Shahrazad Shah	Pakistan
76	Shamyll Zeb	Pakistan
77	Zahra Khan	Pakistan
78	Zakia Wardak	Afghanistan
79	Zarak Khan	Pakistan
80	Zarghona Azizullah Khan	Pakistan
81	Zarina Tariq	Pakistan
82	Zarmina Ahsin	Pakistan
83	Zeb Tetlay	Pakistan
84	Zeenath Khalid	Pakistan
85	Zubair Yaqub	Pakistan
86	Zulfiqar Ahmad	Pakistan
87	Zulfiqar Ali Khan, late grandson of Bacha Khan	Pakistan

Index

Khan, Maulana Akhtar Ali, 187
Khan, Mehdi Zaman, 338
Khan, Mehrdil, 300
Khan, Mir Afzal, 22
Khan, Mir Qadir, 104
Khan, Muhammad Abbas, 120, 204, 248, 411
Khan, Muhammad Afzal, 282, 290
Khan, Muhammad Akbar (Nawab Sir), 391
Khan, Muhammad Akbar, 60, 201
Khan, Muhammad Akram, 120
Khan, Muhammad Amin, 209, 451
Khan, Muhammad Aslam, 415
Khan, Muhammad Azam, 259
Khan, Muhammad Din, 5
Khan, Muhammad Hashim, 442
Khan, Muhammad Hussain, 339, 344
Khan, Muhammad Israr, 445
Khan, Muhammad Nawaz, 203, 416
Khan, Muhammad Raza, 507
Khan, Muhammad Umer, 91, 92, 240
Khan, Muhammad Yahya, 506
Khan, Muhammad Zafar, 416
Khan, Muhammad Zareen, 120
Khan, Munir, 235, 238, 356, 445, 448–450
Khan, Murtaza, 93
Khan, Nadir, 115, 116, 143, 224–228
Khan, Nawabzada Amin Ullah, 214
Khan, Nawabzada Liaquat Ali, 485
Khan, Nawabzada Nasrullah, 507
Khan, Nazim Sarfaraz, 445
Khan, Niamatullah, 334
Khan, Purdil, 16
Khan, Qalandar, 98
Khan, Qayyum, 122, 282, 330, 332, 432, 465, 503, 504
Khan, Qazi Attaullah (Qazi Sahib), 2, 92, 98, 108, 119, 120, 199, 205, 221, 296–298, 303, 328,

338, 360, 362, 364, 365, 367, 368, 369, 372, 380, 381, 410, 411, 421, 425, 427, 428, 465
Khan, Qulli, 251
Khan, Rabnawaz, 235
Khan, Rab Nawaz (*Salar-e-Azam*), 270
Khan, Rahat, 308, 480
Khan, Ramzan, 120, 128, 285, 312, 321, 322
Khan, Raza (Nawab Muhammad), 507
Khan, Redi, 105
Khan, Saadat (of Torangzai), 201
Khan, Saadullah, 84, 100, 104, 270, 279, 327, 329, , 365, 368, 369, 378, 380, 386, 409, 436
Khan, Said Akbar, 96, 107, 108, 448
Khan, Saifullah, 3
Khan, Salamatullah, 381, 382
Khan, *Salar* Abdur Rahim, 343
Khan, *Salar* Aslam, 391
Khan, *Salar* Munir, 356, 448–450
Khan, *Salar* Shamroz, 250
Khan, *Salar* Sher Ali, 458
Khan, *Salar* Yaqoob 283
Khan, Samin Jan, 16, 21, 120, 296, 362, 364, 380, 410, 494
Khan, Saranjam, 366
Khan, Sarbiland, 118, 234, 262, 263
Khan, Sardar Bahadur, 467
Khan, Sarfaraz (Salar-e-Azam), 230, 234, 235, 242, 246, 255, 263, 264, 266, 267, 270, 445, 492
Khan, Shad Muhammad, 120, 361, 362, 439
Khan, Shah Pasand, 120, 352
Khan, Shah Wali, 225, 286, 505–507, 512
Khan, Shahbaz, 22
Khan, Shahnawaz, Haji, 242
Khan, Shahzad, 242
Khan, Shamroz, 32, 36, 41, 98, 250